W9-BDS-376

Cases on Collaboration in Virtual Learning Environments:
Processes and Interactions

Donna Russell
University of Missouri at Kansas City, USA

INFORMATION SCIENCE REFERENCE

Hershey · New York

Director of Editorial Content:	Kristin Klinger
Senior Managing Editor:	Jamie Snavely
Assistant Managing Editor:	Michael Brehm
Publishing Assistant:	Sean Woznicki
Typesetters:	Michael Brehm, Michael Killian
Cover Design:	Lisa Tosheff
Printed at:	Yurchak Printing Inc.

Published in the United States of America by
Information Science Reference (an imprint of IGI Global)
701 E. Chocolate Avenue
Hershey PA 17033
Tel: 717-533-8845
Fax: 717-533-8661
E-mail: cust@igi-global.com
Web site: http://www.igi-global.com/reference

Library of Congress Cataloging-in-Publication Data

Cases on collaboration in virtual learning environments : processes and interactions / Donna Russell, editor.
        p. cm.
    Includes bibliographical references and index.
    Summary: "Using a case study analysis, this book provides a unifying perspective for discussing the viability of collaborative virtual spaces as training programs for insurance brokers, forums to support at-risk university students, simulations of historical places, means to aid autistic children learn social skills, repositories for digital libraries, collaborative spaces designing new university programs and emergency response training"--Provided by publisher.
    ISBN 978-1-60566-878-9 (hardcover) -- ISBN 978-1-60566-879-6 (ebook) 1. Computer-assisted instruction--Case studies. 2. Shared virtual environments--Case studies. 3. Group work in education--Case studies. I. Russell, Donna, 1955-
    LB1028.5.C373 2010
    371.33"4--dc22
                                    2009021597

British Cataloguing in Publication Data
A Cataloguing in Publication record for this book is available from the British Library.

All work contributed to this book is new, previously-unpublished material. The views expressed in this book are those of the authors, but not necessarily of the publisher.

Table of Contents

Detailed Table of Contents

Chapter 1
The Making of the University Life Café: Harnessing Interactive Technologies
and Virtual Community for an Anti-Suicide Website for College Students 1
Shalin Hai-Jew, Kansas State University, USA
***Appendix by** Brent A. Anders, Kansas State University, USA*

The University Life Café is a new website that promotes mental wellness among university students, faculty, and staff, with a particular focus on suicide prevention. This publicly available site uses the power of social networking at its core to provide a sense of virtual community to members of the Kansas State University (K-State) community in particular, and to other college students in general. It delivers information on resiliency and protective issues against suicide through podcasts, audio files, images, text, and other types of contents. Users of the site who are K-State members may also access professionally created heuristics dealing with various aspects of mental health. This also strives to de-stigmatize communications about suicide, depression, and substance abuse and to encourage help-seeking behaviors. This site was co-developed with contributions from students, faculty, and staff, and partnerships from across the campus. This site is one part of a comprehensive, campus-wide plan, which engages students and faculty/staff, while respecting the race, ethnicity, cultural background, sexual orientation, and belief system of people on the K-State community. This chapter addresses the planning and strategies used in the building of this site.

Chapter 2
3D Design and Collaboration in Massively Multi-User Virtual Environments (MUVEs)................... 27
Steven Warburton, King's College London, UK
Margarita Pérez García, MENON Network EEIG, Belgium

This chapter describes an exploratory study in the use of the virtual world Second Life as an innovative space for situating collaborative activity in the field of art and design. The authors identify eight key affordances of Second Life for learning and teaching and elaborate the educational approach based on group orientated design briefs, carried out over a three-week period by the students. The results of the study reveal both the negative and positive aspects of using Second Life as an educational space. These range from access difficulties and the steep learning curve in becoming familiar with the technology, to the expansive social and creative freedoms that the world allows. The conclusions draw together an analysis of the emerging themes and present a set of ten good practices for developing and running successful collaborative activities inside virtual worlds.

Rebecca Gould, Kansas State University, USA
Elizabeth Unger, Kansas State University, USA

This chapter describes how the introduction of a learning environment can stimulate creativity and innovation in learning and extend that innovation to students at a distance. The learning environment consists of a room, technology, and an Internet assisted set of tools. This music learning environment is one of a series of learning environments created to enhance learning especially in the humanities. Capable of enhancing the instruction in music both for distance learning and for traditional students, this was accomplished at a midwestern comprehensive research university. The learning environment created through a strong collaborative partnership between faculty and professional staff provided an enhancement to music theory instruction. It has served as a stimulus to innovation in music performance, band director's instruction at a distance, instruction of music teacher students at a distance and also in the dance program. The result to date is a learning environment that has encouraged learning, collaboration and outreach to the international world of music. It is being shared with another institution of higher education to enhance their music programs.

Yongho Kim, Korea National University of Education, Republic of Korea

The case study is a chronicle of Korean elementary students' efforts to gain autonomous control of a foreign language, English, from the top down, that is, through use of English in communication (as opposed to mere exposure to English through study or through the passive absorption of comprehensible input). This communicative use of English is realized through materials pertinent to their overall development and not just to their language development. The materials include a surrogate self or avatar within a virtual learning environment which can, in principle, though not in this study, connect them with children all over the world. The question for this study is how the use of an avatar in a virtual learning environment brings about not only the learning of vocabulary and grammar (similar to the piecemeal learning that happens in any classroom) but also interacts with and even activates the child's overall psychological development the way that play awakens developmental functions on the playground.

This chapter describes the Center for the Advancement of Distance Education (CADE). CADE is a self-supporting unit within the School of Public Health at the University of Illinois at Chicago. CADE partners or contracts with university, government, non-profit and for-profit organizations to provide innovative technological solutions to meet a variety of educational, training, research and administrative needs. These collaborations include the creation of interactive online training modules, the design and development of websites, simulations, games and virtual worlds, mobile phone applications, multimedia production and Webcasting, course registration and learning management system construction, Web-based programming and database connectivity, and online data gathering and analysis. By expanding into new and emerging technological fields, CADE has managed to sustain continued growth in personnel, annual revenue, client base, and number of simultaneous projects.

Chapter 6

In the scientific field, argumentative practices can, under certain conditions, help students to elaborate scientific concepts from everyday representations. However, setting up activities that enable learning in a classroom is not an easy matter. A technological environment may be useful in order to sustain argumentation and to "keep track" of the discursive processes. This chapter presents a pedagogical case in science in which the learners take part in an argumentative debate mediated by a technological environment, called Digalo. The chapter focuses on a socio-cultural perspective, thus assigning a central role to social interactions, symbolic and material mediation in development and learning processes. The author describes a case in biology tested in two educational contexts, and discusses its psycho-pedagogical assumptions. From a qualitative analysis of the data, it appears that cognitive and argumentative processes are interconnected. This means that by articulating and making reference to the others' arguments, learners also develop a new understanding of the scientific content. The challenges for educational issues and the lessons that may be drawn from an analysis of this case are then discussed.

Chapter 7

This case describes the International Health Challenge, aimed at increasing physical activity and improving dietary habits via education, training and interaction in the virtual world of Second Life. Second Life (SL) is a dynamic, immersive, 3D, and global, virtual world, making it ideal for reaching residents of industrialized communities at risk for obesity. Participants selected a country of affiliation (Canada, Mexico, U.S., Switzerland, or unaffiliated), completed pre- and post-test online surveys, and were encouraged to monitor physical activity (PA) and dietary habits, learn health information and participate in virtual PA and fruit and vegetable sampling daily for 28 days. All materials were offered in English, French and Spanish. Virtual worlds hold promise for increasing access to interactive learning opportunities.

The smell of formaldehyde was in the air as students tenaciously poked with dissection probes at the frogs pinned to their dissection trays. The familiar comments of "Gross!" "I don't want to cut him," and "Hey, Mrs. M, what do I do now?" punctuated the air. It was the start of the annual climax of the seventh-grade biology curriculum, dissecting a frog. The teacher, already dealing with notes from parents objecting to their sons/daughters participating and the logistics of helping 30 students simultaneously, could not help but think that there had to be an alternative way of presenting the experience to the students. This case study was born from that familiar, frustrating scene, which occurs annually throughout school systems everywhere. The teacher in the scenario above was one of three from the Biology department at a middle school in northeastern Illinois. Her team came to the authors with the problem of finding an alternative means of instructional delivery that would yield substantially the same cognitive knowledge development in the students, help address the declining frog population, address the issue of science anxiety among students at the middle school level, and accommodate the learning modalities of the students.

Achieving student persistence and retention at the University of Houston has often been a challenge for the university. This case concerns using Second Life to develop a digital community of students from a single academic department to enhance student persistence toward graduation. It was postulated that the development of a digital community could strengthen the social cohesion of the students and thereby promote academic persistence. Students joined Second Life voluntarily or as part of their course requirements and then were invited to participate in various social and educational activities led by their classmates. The amount of time spent in Second Life was tracked and will be compared to academic performance.

Chapter 10

James Laffey, University of Missouri at Columbia, USA
Matthew Schmidt, University of Missouri at Columbia, USA
Janine Stichter, University of Missouri at Columbia, USA
Carla Schmidt, University of Missouri at Columbia, USA
Danielle Oprean, University of Missouri at Columbia, USA
Melissa Herzog, University of Missouri at Columbia, USA
Ryan Babiuch, University of Missouri at Columbia, USA

This chapter describes the iSocial project. The purpose of the iSocial project is to support the development and practice of social competence for individuals with Autism Spectrum Disorders (ASD) through a social-skills curriculum and online social interaction delivered via a 3D Virtual Learning Environment (3D-VLE). This chapter describes the background and rationale for developing iSocial, gives an overview of the system, and reports some of the results from a field test of a partial system implementation. The field test provides lessons about the initial system design and recognition of challenges to be faced. The key challenges include (1) finding best approaches for adapting effective teaching approaches to a 3D-VLE, (2) supporting online social interaction for a target population challenged to be social, and (3) amplifying the engagement of youth in support of achieving desired learning outcomes

Chapter 11

Shalin Hai-Jew, Kansas State University, USA

Digital libraries and repositories aren't often thought of as virtual learning environments. However, in function and designs, they are. A wide range of digital artifacts are archived on both private and public open-source digital libraries and repositories. There are digital collections of texts, maps, photos, sound files, geospatial resources, video, and 3D objects. There are repositories for particular fields of study as well as multi-discipline ones. These may be structured as ontologies or taxonomies in particular knowledge (or cross-discipline) domains. Recently, designers of digital libraries and repositories have been focusing more testing and design on making such spaces usable for collaborative learning and building networks of communities. This chapter will explore how to maximize collaborative learning and work in digital libraries and repositories by applying pedagogical strategies.

Chapter 12

Joan E. Aitken, Park University, USA

The purpose of this chapter is to provide a case study of the problem solving processes of a faculty who developed a new graduate program in communication studies. Students could take all courses online, all onground, or use a combination of the two delivery formats. For the totally online program, a key desire was to help students and faculty achieve a sense of a collaborative community. Students needed to get to know each other and feel a part of the whole program, even though course delivery for some students was totally online. Further, the faculty sought to motivate students to engage in a challenging program of research and application.

Chapter 13

This case is a narrative of the design, review, revision and implementation of an online training program for insurance brokers. The goal of the online training program is to develop advanced problem-solving knowledge and skills including communication abilities in trainees. The case is narrated from the perspective of the training manager with the reviewer's comments included during the review cycle of implementation. The evaluative review is completed using cultural historical activity theory to identify contradictions in the training process. The purpose of the case is to identify the development of advanced knowledge and skills resulting from the online training program. The results of implementing an online training program include 1) reduction in turnover, 2) cost savings and 3) training benefits for the regional branch offices and the trainees.

As a growing number of faculty use SL as a teaching platform, outside of anecdotal articles and the legal literature, no research exists on the many legal and ethical issues that affect course development. Ethical issues include abuse ("griefing") nudity and lewd behavior, and false/misleading identities. Legal issues include creation and use of copyrighted and trademarked items, faculty intellectual property rights in objects and course content, and criminal behavior. Following the experiences of the instructor and 5 students, their 12-week journey is documented through interviews, journals, weekly course activities, SL class dialogs, and in-world assignments. Additionally, 5 faculty and staff experts who teach or train in SL at this university were interviewed and consulted, as well. This study provides insight for designing courses that foster exploration of rich learning opportunities outside a traditional classroom-both real and virtual.

Chapter 15

This chapter describes the process of collaboration by occupational therapy (OT) and speech language pathology (SLP) students and faculty as they worked together to plan and implement an interdisciplinary open house event within the virtual environment of Second Life®. Key topics include applications of project-based learning for interdisciplinary team building, student and faculty roles and specific steps in planning, management, and production of the event, and analysis of challenges and supports in project implementation. Specific challenges to collaborative work are discussed, including difficulties inherent in teams composed of students at different levels, skill sets, and disciplines. The discussion of project-based learning, description of planning, management, and production processes, together with qualitative analysis of challenges and supports provides insights and "lessons learned" with application to future project development in virtual worlds.

Chapter 16

This chapter explores the question: Does online discussion produce critical thinking? It presents a selective review of the literature concerned with critical thinking and/or interaction during online discussion. It presents an experimental study of the effects of instructional media and instructional methods on critical thinking. The study tests the influence on critical thinking of online vs. face-to-face discussion, individual vs. group consensus in summarizing discussion, and discussion of examples of concepts vs. discussion of more abstract analysis. The purpose for reviewing the literature and carrying out the study is to increase awareness of variables that may influence the quality of discussion.

This chapter describes the e@Leader gaming platform. Whether online edutainment gaming can enhance intelligence, student learning, or scholastic performance remains hotly debated in education research circles. In response to this academic issue, and in order to address a number of educational policy questions asked of the authors by several government organizations, the authors have developed the online e@Leader edutainment gaming platform as a solution. Their e@Leader program is the first comprehensive 'learning by gaming' system to also be designed according to the findings of advanced machine learning and cognitive developmental neuroscience research. In 2008, the first empirical evidence was generated with its use, and together with its built-in assessment system, integrated into the school curriculum. Beyond this existence proof of concept, and practical program application for educational use, results of beta-testing with the e@Leader system across primary schools in two countries support the claim for tutored online educational gaming in enhancing intelligence, active student learning, and scholastic performances in English and math.

Chapter 18

Online learning is growing by leaps and bounds throughout North America. Christensen, Horn, and Johnson note that student enrolment in online classes has risen from forty-five thousand in 2000 to about one million by 2008 (2008, p. 98). Further, their extrapolations indicate that by 2019, fully fifty percent of U.S. secondary school classes will be online. Even if these predictions fall short, online education is positioning itself to be a potent factor in North American education. One of the more popular and successful ways to conduct online learning is via the blended or hybrid class model (Palloff & Pratt, 2001). Such classes feature both live-class interactions in a traditional classroom, and online interactions through some form of online learning environment. However appearances are deceiving: such classes cannot be run in the manner of a traditional class, even though they may take place, at least partially, in a traditional classroom setting. Due to the asynchronous nature of online learning environments, traditional means of control of the learning process quickly reveal themselves as unworkable, and the teacher has to adjust to news ways of working. As Palloff and Pratt note, "Teaching in the cyberspace classroom requires that we move beyond traditional models of pedagogy into new practices that are more facilitative" (2001, p. 20). This chapter explores how one teacher in a gr. 5/6 hybrid class manages the learning process in a through a combination of knowledge-building pedagogy (Scardamalia & Bereiter, 2003b) and protocological control, a way of controlling networks (Galloway & Thacker, 2007).

Chapter 19

This chapter describes the training course for school managers for the use of information and communication technology (ICT) that was developed at Sao Paulo Pontifical Catholic University, (PUC-SP), Brazil. This was a blended course, using face-to-face and online activities, providing school managers with the experience of using ICT to share experiences, and to learn about effective ways of using ICT for school management. Even though the school managers had no previous experience with technology they succeed in changing their working reality and understanding the use of ICT to interact, exchange documents and organize their ideas. This experience has produced two other important results. One is the interaction that enables the formation of collaborative networks and partnership among school managers. Social and cultural practices were considered for analysis concerning the subjects that contributed to the creation of the ICT culture in the school. The authors have considered this network and the building of this community as the seed of a community of practice (CoP), as proposed by Wenger (1998a). Second, it was possible to see a close relationship between Wenger's theory and Freire's (2003) educational approach, which showed that social transformations are constructed on the basis of participants' will and in the presence of leadership in a historic moment.

Foreword

I am very pleased to write a few words for this collection of cases on collaboration in virtual learning environments. I have been involved in the research and implementation of virtual learning environments for about one and a half decades. My introduction to virtual worlds started with the seminal work of Ashok Patel in the early 90s on conceptual network based intelligent tutoring that became the basis of virtual learning modules developed under Byzantium project. Research progressed since then from standalone applications to Web-based modules for individualized learning where a large number of learners could access the modules from any parts of the world. On one hand, products for classroom management started to appear, and on the other, research progressed through incorporation of adaptive features based on content and user exploration phenomena, cognitive profiling, introduction of mobile technologies, and consideration of real-time and real-life context. Researchers started to recognize the power of collaboration and learning communities, and the whole research stream of computer supported collaborative learning emerged. Recent years have also seen a lot of interest in 3-dimensional immersive environments that take collaboration to newer heights.

Most of this progress can be attributed to the exponential advancements in technology in recent years. These rapid developments have provided ample opportunities for virtual learning environments to be inclusive, multimedia-rich, and take advantage of both asynchronous and synchronous approaches, that we take for granted in hi-fidelity face-to-face environments. However, this has fuelled, once again, the possibility of technology driving the innovation, and pedagogy struggling to catch up with that. Lack of benchmarks means it is not easy to assess whether we are moving in the right direction.

This is where this edited collection comes at the right time, with the right focus on the use of virtual learning environments. The book contains a right balance between the research innovations and their practical use, and should serve as the solid grounding not only for the creation of benchmarks for further development but also to reflect on what shifts need to be made in pedagogy so as to foster effective collaboration in virtual learning environments and exploit the innovations to their fullest. The first step is to look at the experiences of early adopters and identify best practice examples. This collection is a valuable step in that direction.

It is pleasing to see that the book provides a rich variety of cases from different walks of life, ranging from an anti-suicide website and obesity prevention to music programs and interdisciplinary collaboration, using various types of virtual environments, including 3D words, multiuser environments, commonly used environments such as Second Life, and specialized custom-developed platforms such as e@leader. There is an excellent balance between the discussions on designing such environments to foster collaboration and analysis of how effectively collaboration is being supported in existing environments. Thus, this collection will provide food for thought to both researchers and practitioners, who are either using the virtual learning environments already or are looking for solutions that align with their community of learners.

Virtual learning environments are being used in all sorts of educational scenarios: formal, informal and non-formal learning ranging from classroom-based instructor-led education to just-in-time, interest-focused and community-driven situations that some could argue as not directly falling under the umbrella of education as we know it. The book offers a refreshing combination of cases from these different areas, hence providing a level playing field for comparison and for synthesis of common issues within this diversity.

A notable feature of these cases is the focus on societal issues that matter, rather than getting swayed away into the discussions on how good the technology is, while still keeping at the cutting edge of technological innovations, something that I must give credit to Donna Russell, who's editing skills made it possible.

While writing this short piece of my thoughts, I am privy to Donna' overview that precedes the chapters in this book. I wholeheartedly agree with her that while the chapters in this book individually provide stories within the context of their specialized disciplines, the book captures a holistic and evaluative perspective for designers, educators and researchers who are concerned with the wider applicability of these environments and are looking for directions for future of this area of research. This excellent combination of high quality and thought-provoking cases should serve as stepping stone for others who are ready to start their journey with collaborative virtual learning environments.

Kinshuk
Professor, Athabasca University, Canada

Kinshuk *is Professor and Director of School of Computing and Information Systems at Athabasca University, Canada. He also holds iCORE/Xerox/Markin Industrial Research Chair in Adaptivity and Personalization in Informatics. Before moving to Canada in August 2006, Kinshuk worked at German National Research Centre for Information Technology as Postdoctoral Fellow, and at Massey University, New Zealand as Associate Professor of Information Systems and Director of Advanced Learning Technology Research Centre. He has been involved in large-scale research projects for adaptive and mobile virtual learning environments and by early 2009, he has published over 260 research papers in international refereed journals, conferences and book chapters. He is the Founding Chair of IEEE Technical Committee on Learning Technology and Editor of the SSCI indexed Journal of Educational Technology & Society (ISSN 1436-4522).*

Preface

OVERVIEW

This book is a collection of case studies of collaborative virtual learning environments focusing on the nature of human interactions in virtual spaces and defining the types and qualities of learning processes in these spaces. Cases in the book discuss training and education in virtual worlds using case study evaluative research methods as a comprehensive methodology for understanding the development of advanced learning processes in collaborative virtual learning environments (CVLE). Using a case study analysis as a basis for this collection provides a unifying perspective for discussing the viability of collaborative virtual spaces as training programs for insurance brokers, forums to support at-risk university students, simulations of historical places, means to aid autistic children learning social skills, repositories for digital libraries, collaborative spaces for designing new university programs and emergency response training. As a result this book provides multiple cases of collaborative virtual learning environments in varied fields as a resource for designing, implementing or evaluating these emerging learning environments.

Collaborative Virtual Learning Environments

Collaborative virtual learning environments are both two dimensional (2D) and three dimensional (3D) virtual spaces that include multiple interactive aspects including collaborative dialogic forums such as chat rooms, discussion boards, live audio, information dissemination and presentation in multiple media including sound, video and animated graphics, and hyperlinks in the environment that link the learners throughout the learning experience. An excellent list of some of the relevant characteristics of a collaborative virtual learning environment is:

- A virtual learning environment is an intended information space.
- A virtual learning environment is a social space.
- The virtual space is represented through text only to 3D immersive worlds.
- Students are active and co-construct the virtual space.
- Virtual learning environments can also enrich classroom activities.
- Virtual learning environments integrate varied technologies and pedagogical approaches.
- Most virtual environments overlap with physical environments (Dillenbourg, Schneider, Synteta, 2002, p. 3).

3D collaborative virtual learning environments can be highly engaging to learners as they respond to interactions in the virtual worlds. These immersive virtual worlds are simulated environments designed using 3D graphics where the learners can interact via virtual characters, avatars, by taking on roles and responding to simulations. Immersive virtual worlds are designed around an interactive theme. These worlds can simulate real world events or fantasy worlds. Avatars can communicate using text, voice and gesture. Avatars can walk, fly, dance, run, gesture and change appearances. Interacting in these worlds through an avatar provides the learner with the potential to experience telepresence, a higher level of involvement in the virtual space. Instructional design theories, specifically problem-based learning (PBL) design principles, based on constructivist principles of learning can provide a basis for the design of these immersive virtual learning environments. Virtual problem-based learning environments engage learners in simulated problem spaces designed to encourage the interactions needed to develop advanced cognitive processes. Immersive virtual PBL environments designed based on constructivist theories of learning can potentially develop advanced cognitive processes as a result of the interactions in virtual worlds.

Problem-Based Learning Design

A problem-based learning environment is designed using social cognition processes including situated theories of learning (Cole & Engestrom, 1993; Lave & Wenger, 1991) and distributed cognition theories (Pea, 1993; Resnick, 1987; Salomon, 1993) where learners engage in socially mediated interactions and consider themselves active members of their community of learners within the context of solving the problem, a phenomena Lave and Wenger (1991) call legitimate peripheral participation (LPP) (Lave & Wenger, 1991). According to sociocultural learning theory students create meaning as a result of social interactions by attempting to resolve dissonance in an attempt to understand a problem (Vygotsky, 1978; Bruner, 1990). Research of collaborative online learning environments has shown that learners can develop higher levels of awareness and knowledge as a result of their dialog and interactions in online environments (Russell, 2005). When learners have the opportunity to articulate what they have learned and reflect on the knowledge they acquired in that process, they understand more and are better able to use that knowledge to solve problems (Russell, 2008).

Cognitive processes required to problem-solve include an active search for information, an immersion in task, a motivation to solve the problem, goal setting and the necessity to use divergent, analytical and evaluative thinking (Tan, O. 2003). In a problem-based learning environment the learner sees information as something functional and him or herself in control of using the information in pursuit of a particular goal (Bereiter, 2001). Problem-based learning is intentional learning where learners establish goals (Jonassen, 1999). Problem-based learning environments include authentic tasks that are intentional, active, and collaborative engaging learners in the purposeful application of knowledge and skills to solve a problem (Jonassen, Peck, & Wilson, 1999). The design of a 3D immersive virtual problem-based learning environment means considering the constraints of moving these problem-based learning processes and interactions into a virtual space. Considerations in designing an immersive virtual problem-based learning environment should include the potential to develop telepresence in these virtual worlds and the use of pedagogical agents to scaffold the development of advanced learning processes.

Telepresence

One critical aspect in a PBL environment is the high level of engagement by learners in solving problems that they perceive as meaningful (Jonassen, 2000). A design consideration then is whether learners in an immersive virtual world can feel a high enough level of engagement. The level of presence in virtual learning environments is telepresence. Telepresence is the sense that a person using certain technologies has that he or she is present in a location other than their real world location. Dr. Hayles described telepresence as "extending embodied awareness in highly specific, local and material ways that would be impossible without electronic prosthesis" (Hayles, 1999, p. 291). McLuhan writing about the then new media of television described electric consciousness as "putting our physical bodies inside our extended nervous systems, by means of electronic media, we set up a dynamic by which all previous technologies that are extensions of our bodies will be translated into information systems" (McLuhan, 1964, p. 57). In the book *Natural Born Cyborgs*, Andy Clark describes the ability of the human brain to respond to immersive environments as extremely opportunistic. He further states that "we should not underestimate the capacity of human brains in general—young human brains in particular—to simultaneously alter and grow so they can better exploit the problem-solving opportunities our technologies provide" (Clark, 2003, p. 45).

In a sociological phenomenology study of online games the researchers found that the online interactions of the players were considered by them to be real engagements occurring in real forms of community (Chee, F., Vieta, M., and Smith, R. 2006). In a study of the dialogic interactions in a multi-user real-time virtual world, the virtual interactions were found to have strong emotional connotations to the participants because the dialogs are intentional and included social effect and significance similar to real world dialogs (Wolfendale, J. 2007). In an ethnomethodological study of social identity in collaborative virtual environments the researchers found that, when enough context is established to develop a minimal amount of trust, users will recognise each other in the future and progress through all the phases of identity production in social conventions including greetings, acknowledging and leaving rituals, establishing groups, social positioning and expression of intimacy and social sanctions (Kauppinen, K., Kivimaki, A., Era, T., Robinson, M., 1998). Studies have shown that high levels of telepresence are possible in immersive virtual learning environments if these virtual environments provide a presence in the environment, interactivity in the environment and social forums for collaboration (Clark, 2004).

Pedagogical Agents

The design of an immersive virtual problem-based learning environment should include high levels of interactivity to increase motivation, engagement and goal-setting responses in the learners. The incorporation of artificial intelligence robots, AI bots, as pedagogical agents can increase student levels of telepresence and engagement levels. When you correlate the language processing and reasoning control of AI bots with an avatar's personification in the virtual world, a pedagogical agent becomes a powerful personification of knowledge response and representation. A study by Lester, Stone and Stelling found that pedagogical agents can be productive interactive aspects in a constructivist learning environment if the pedagogical agents are animated, include vocal behaviors and respond to a series of problem-solving tasks (Lester, J., Stone, B. Stelling, G. 1998). In a later study they found that pedagogical agents could serve multiple purposes in virtual learning environments including modeling complex tasks, tutoring learners and as an instructional guide (Johnson, L., Rickel, J., & Lester, J. 2000). These types of learner's interactions with a pedagogical agent are similar to the development of cognitive apprenticeship as defined by Anderson (Anderson, 1998). Additionally providing ongoing mentoring capabilities in virtual worlds scaffolds learners to higher levels of mastery in their zone of proximal development (Vygotsky, 1978).

Pedagogical agents are connected to an ontological knowledge base of information in the virtual PBL environment with the resulting ability to change and update knowledge representation and their responses to the learner. The learner's levels of engagement and motivation, both necessary to the development of advanced learning processes, can be sustained by ongoing interactions with pedagogical agents. Pedagogical agents can be guides, mentors, experts and provide assessment feedback in an immersive virtual problem-based learning environment.

Virtual Problem-Based Learning Design Template

The design of an immersive virtual problem-based learning environment should include the same design characteristics as a real-world problem-based learning environments including an interactive problem space for exploration, developmentally phased learning activities for the reinforcement of advanced cognitive processes, formative and summative assessments, and collaborative forums. Figure 1 is a virtual problem-based learning design template that can be used as a guide to design multiple virtual PBL environments. The model includes three phases that develop advanced problem-solving abilities including critical decision-making, inquiry, evaluative and collaborative processes. The template uses Bereiter's Scheme of Knowledge to assess formative and summative learning processes and knowledge response (Bereiter, 2001). The design template includes guides for group work, development of artifacts, use of pedagogical agents, and inquiry processes. Gaiaworld, an immersive problem-based learning virtual world, designed based on the template is described below and an instructor's guide for implementing Gaiaworld is included in Appendix A.

The virtual problem-based learning design template can be used to design virtual worlds that guide a learner through the development of problem-based learning processes in three phases. Each phase includes interactions with pedagogical agents in differing roles based on the level of user response. An example of an immersive virtual PBL environment is Gaiaworld. Below is the curriculum overview for Gaiaworld.

GAIAWORLD: IMMERSIVE VIRTUAL PBL ENVIRONMENT

World Characteristics

Gaiaworld is an island in the Teen Grid in Second Life. It is designed using the virtual PBL design template. It is a role-playing simulation designed to develop advanced cognitive processes and knowledge. Evaluation standards are included in the instructor's guide as well as a rubric for assessing performance standards. It is designed for fourth grade through high school. The learning goal is to develop the students' awareness and knowledge of global climate change by engaging them in a virtual simulation of an environment that has undergone drastic environmental damage. The students will interact with the virtual environment, each other and the inhabitants of Gaiaworld to develop a plan of action to save the environment. Their problem is how to restore the environmental damage caused by volcanic eruptions. The world is a jungle island. It should be built to include multiple volcanoes. One will eventually explode. It should include multiple species that are unique and endangered. The humans are hunters and gathers that have recently started farming and other diversified forms of labor. They have cut large sections of the forest causing erosion. They are living in wooden dwellings. The humans are having problems with limited access to good water and with population growth that makes feeding everyone difficult. They have a barter system of trade with other villages. The flora and fauna should include marker species such as coral that are used by scientists to study environmental damage.

Geoscientists (Students)

Students will study a world that has suffered a devastating natural disaster-a volcano explodes. As geologists, the students must go into the world before, during and after the disaster in a series of fact-finding missions. Their missions are:

Figure 1. Virtual PBL design template

Virtual Design	Problem Space (Banathy, 1996; Lawson, 1990) *Simulation designed as an interactive virtual environment that relates to a real world problem space.*
Pedagogical Agent used as Guide to aid learners as they explore the problem space. **Output:** Virtual artifact including a rationale for relevancy of the problem.	**Phase 1:** Why is the problem important? **Inquiry Processes:** Working in pairs, learners gather and analyze information in the virtual simulation to determine nature of the problem and to define the scope of the problem. (Barab & Duffy, 2000; Petroski, 1996). **Output used as input:** Knowledge that a diverse community needs impact the complexity of the problem. (Bereiter, 2001).
Pedagogical Agent used as a Resource Mentor to answer questions and find resources. **Output:** Virtual artifact including a conceptual understanding of an area of expertise and its application to solve the problem	**Phase 2:** How can we use our expertise to better understand the problem and develop a feasible solution? **Inquiry Processes:** Working groups, learners gather and analyze information about an area of expertise (Brown, Collins & Duguid, 1989) and how that area relates to the problem, (Bruer, 1993, Shulman, 1992) learners examine areas of expertise in simulated environments, determine the interdependence of the areas of expertise. **Output used as input:** Knowledge that a problem can look different and be understood differently from multiple perspectives.
Pedagogical Agent used as Survey Buddy to assess new knowledge and final projects. **Output:** Virtual artifact including a representation of the group's solution and conclusion about its short-term and long-term feasibility.	**Phase 3:** How can we use the knowledge and skills from Phase 1 and Phase 2 to develop a feasible solution? **Inquiry Processes:** Working in jigsaw groups (Aronson, Blaney, Stephan, Sikes & Snapp, 1978), learners develop a solution to the problem and assess the feasibility of that solution from the perspectives of the experts within the group and the needs of the community. **Outcome:** Knowledge has properties of use and value; is something that can be used and responded to.

Figure 2. Virtual Jungle Island in Second Life

1.	identify major ecological factors and report on pre-eruption conditions including human conditions
2.	short-term damage assessment immediately following the eruption with suggestions for minimizing damage
3.	long-term damage assessment with a report on changes and suggestions for controlling further loss.

Students will gather information on the environments before and after the environmental damage through 1) tests run on the virtual environment, 2) AI guides who respond to their questions and 3) research done using kiosks in the virtual environment. They will work in groups in the virtual world. Students will use a field book for taking notes in the world. They identify the major problems of the environment by testing the environment and interacting with AI guides and each other. The guides will give them clues to finding further information.

Real World Classrooms

In the real world classroom the facilitators implement a correlating study of climate change and environmental damage that includes developing a community project on a related issue such as reducing the carbon footprint in their community, recycling, improving water quality and reducing energy consumption. Before and after their virtual experiences teachers introduce and then conclude the learning activity by focusing on using the student's new knowledge to develop their community-based project. Some of the potential real world problems possible for anchoring this virtual PBL environment include:

- **Hydrology Problem:** The central region water reservoir is running out of water. How can the water reserve be protected from depletion?
- **Geology Problem:** Our region has a major earthquake fault. How can our community prepare for a potential earthquake?
- **Water Problem:** Our community has experienced continued growth and construction. The region has also suffered a drought over the past several years. How can the community maintain and protect their waterways from erosion and pollution caused by construction?
- **Air Problem:** The EPA has established an air pollution goal for our community. What are actions that the city can take to improve the quality of the air in our community?

Virtual Interactions

Instructors, pedagogical agents and collaborative work groups are all forms of interactions in the virtual world. Pedagogical agents will be used to interact with the students in each phase. During phase 1 the pedagogical agent will be a village elder who will be a guide AI bot. This guide's role is to help students inquire into the problem space, learn about the environment and the expert issues that need to be understood to solve the problem. During phase 2 the pedagogical agent will be a villager. There will be multiple villagers each with a different role and perspective. They will be the experts on the sub issues in the problem such as a fisherman who understands water issues, a farmer who responds to land use issues, and a traveler bot who has seen multiple scenarios for a wider perspective on the result of the phase 2 environmental changes. During phase 3 the pedagogical agent will be a village ruler designed to receive the students' plan of action for improving the environment and provide an assessment tool to the instructor.

Fieldbooks

Each time the student geoscientists visit the Gaiaworld they will add to their fieldbooks by taking notes and creating artifacts. All of the fieldbooks will be available through a learning management system designed for this unit. As a result of completion of activities, the students will move through levels of scholarship. In each level they will get additional capabilities in the virtual environment including the ability to design artifacts in the environment, new clothing or capabilities for their avatars and the ability to move into and present in the associated museum and scientist conference building. As a result, in further iterations they can function in the social dynamic of the humans living in Gaiaworld.

- **Phase 1 Virtual Activities:** During phase 1 students do an intensive study of the environment pre explosion. Students enter the world with a scientist's field book. They have a set of questions to answer and observations to record. They interact with the village elder (pedagogical guide) to understand the current (pre-explosion) state of the environment. To understand the terminology of the geoscientist they use a library kiosk. When they have finished they meet with their classroom facilitator. This first assessment is a survey. If they have completed their field notes they can post it on the learning management system web site for everyone to share their ideas.
- **Phase 2 Virtual Activities:** Once the volcano has erupted the students go in to explore a second time. The devastation includes a large percentage of the forests, loss of several animals, farmland and dwellings. They talk with a village farmer, traveler or fisherman. The pedagogical agents respond to student questions and focus them on developing a plan of action to help the environment recover. What are the expert issues that need to be understood to solve the problem? Who should be involved? What should be done? How does each aspect of the human and natural environment work together to recover? Again the students go to kiosks to get information on vocabulary and background information. Also the students write up a field note report that assesses the damage by comparing it to the previous field trip. They post their finished report in the learning management system for review and comments.
- **Phase 3 Virtual Activities:** Finally the students go into the world to implement their plan of action. They are able to create objects in the environment depending upon their level of development based on the completion of previous projects in the virtual world. . The final mission also includes talking to the village ruler. The village ruler is a pedagogical agent who is a form of assessment. He asks them for a report of the status of the village and how to develop a plan to aid in redevelopment and conservation. The village ruler will be a pedagogical agent who has preset questions and responses for survey assessments. The pedagogical agent also serves as a form of assessment of the student's plan of action to save the village. The students make suggestions for ongoing recovery and long-term recovery.

They post their final report in their bulletin board for others to comment on. They also create a storyboard of all their field observations. They can create an object in the simulation, a machinama video, a Powerpoint, or a website showing their ideas and their progressions. This scenario includes another island, Geoscientist Island, for the students to meet, present and display their findings. Everyone will visit an outside auditorium on another island to see all the presentations and discuss their findings. New objects and projects will be displayed in a museum on the Geoscientist Island. All of these phases will include a formative assessment by talking with a facilitator or designer's avatar. Each phase's fieldbooks will be assessed using a rubric designed for the artifact. The presentations are their final assessments and will be assessed using a rubric designed for this process.

The teachers' instructional design guide is included as an appendix A to this chapter. The instructional guide is a series of guided questions, possible activities and assessment guides for the teachers to use to develop their curriculum for this unit. The instructional guide includes a rubric based on Bereiter's Scheme of Knowledge for the end of phase 1. The instructional guide was designed using the virtual PBL design template. This example of an immersive virtual PBL environment includes the constructivist sociocultural learning theories and models that provide the foundation for the design of a problem-based learning environment.

Using a problem-based learning model based on constructivists theories of learning as a guide, educators can design virtual worlds that engage the learners in problem-solving, decision-making and critical thinking by involving them in simulations of real world events, explorations of worlds not otherwise possible. This includes the potential to design simulations of emergency rooms in virtual hospitals to train medical students, the design of virtual classroom simulations to train future teachers, the design of simulations of training programs for emergency response personnel to develop the necessary critical decision-making and evaluative problem solving processes as well as advanced knowledge needed in these professions. Understanding the potential of collaborative virtual learning environments to be productive learning environments in the development of knowledge workers in the knowledge age is the purpose of this book.

ORGANIZATION OF THE BOOK

This book includes case studies of varied collaborative virtual learning environments with insights into design, development and implementation of these emerging learning environments. There are nineteen chapters in this collection. Each is a unique contribution to the dialog on the characteristics and implications of the varied virtual learning environments.

Chapter 1 reviews the University Life Café, a new website that promotes mental wellness among university students, faculty and staff, with a particular focus on suicide prevention. This publicly available site uses the power of social networking at its core to provide a sense of virtual community to its members. It delivers information on resiliency and protective issues against suicide through podcasts, audio files, images, text, and other types of contents. Users of the site may also access professionally created heuristics dealing with various aspects of mental health. This also strives to de-stigmatize communications about suicide, depression, and substance abuse and to encourage help-seeking behaviors. This site was co-developed with contributions from students, faculty, and staff; it involved partnerships from across campus. This site is one part of a comprehensive, campus-wide plan, which engages students and faculty/staff, while respecting the race, ethnicity, cultural background, sexual orientation, and belief system of every member of our campus community.

Chapter 2 reviews the OpenHabitat project, a study exploring the experiences of art and design students and tutors engaged in collaborative learning and teaching activities within the multi-user virtual environment (MUVE) Second Life OpenHabitat represents a 15-month JISC funded project and collaborative partnership between three UK based institutions: University of Oxford, Leeds Metropolitan University and King's College London. The project focuses on the extraction of good practices and meaningful design approaches for collaborative and dialogic teaching activities in 3D virtual spaces.

Chapter 3 reviews the introduction of a collaborative virtual learning environment into a music program at a Midwestern comprehensive research university that can stimulate creativity and innovation in learning and extend that innovation to students at a distance. The learning environment consists of a room, technology, and an Internet assisted set of tools. This music learning environment is one of a series of learning environments created to enhance learning especially in the humanities.

Chapter 4 is a chronicle of Korean elementary students' efforts to gain autonomous control of a foreign language, English, from the top down, that is, through use of English in communication (as opposed to mere exposure to English through study or through the passive absorption of comprehensible input). This communicative use of English is realized through materials pertinent to their overall development and not just to their language development. The materials include a surrogate self or avatar within a virtual learning environment which can, in principle, though not in this study, connect them with children all over the world.

Chapter 5 reviews the Center for the Advancement of Distance Education (CADE), a self-supporting unit within the School of Public Health at the University of Illinois at Chicago. The center's services range from online continuing education and professional training to multimedia Web-casting and research data management, analysis and presentation. The case is a quarantine scenario designed for emergency training. "The Canyon Crossroads" was designed as a key transit point between two quarantine areas and two uninfected areas with a state border to divide the crossroads leaving quarantine zones in each jurisdiction. The local hospital was located in one of the quarantine zones and it is an official holding and treatment location for infected victims.

Chapter 6 presents a pedagogical case in science in which the learners take part in an argumentative debate mediated by a technological environment, called Digalo. The chapter focuses on a socio-cultural perspective, thus assigning a central role to social interactions, symbolic and material mediation in development and learning processes. The author describes a case in biology tested in two educational contexts, and discusses its psycho-pedagogical assumptions. From a qualitative analysis of the data, it appears that cognitive and argumentative processes are interconnected. This means that by articulating and making reference to the others' arguments, learners also develop a new understanding of the scientific content. The challenges for educational issues and the lessons that may be drawn from an analysis of this case are then discussed.

Chapter 7 reviews the International Health Challenge in Second Life with the goal of extending the real life mission, goals and activities of the Texas Obesity Research Center (TORC) of the University of Houston (UH) into Second Life (SL). This case investigates the utility of applying the ecologic model of health to virtual environmental settings to reduce the public health burden of obesity, with the case example of the International Health Challenge.

Chapter 8 reviews the case of the design and implementation of a virtual learning environment in a biology department at a middle school in northeastern Illinois with the problem of finding an alternative means of instructional delivery that would yield substantially the same cognitive knowledge development in the students, help address the declining frog population, address the issue of science anxiety among students at the middle school level, and accommodate the learning modalities of the students.

Chapter 9 reviews the use of Second Life to develop a digital community of students from a single academic department to enhance student persistence toward graduation. Achieving student persistence and retention at the University of Houston has often been a challenge for the university. It was postulated that the development of a digital community could strengthen the social cohesion of the students and thereby promote academic persistence. Students joined Second Life voluntarily or as part of their course requirements and then were invited to participate in various social and educational activities led by their classmates.

Chapter 10 reviews the iSocial project is to support the development and practice of social competence for individuals with Autism Spectrum Disorders (ASD) through a social-skills curriculum and online social interaction delivered via a 3D virtual learning environment (3D-VLE). This chapter describes the background and rationale for developing iSocial, gives an overview of the system, and reports some of the results from a field test of a partial system implementation.

Chapter 11 reviews how to maximize collaborative learning and work in digital libraries and reposi- tories by applying pedagogical strategies as designers of digital libraries and repositories become more focused on making such spaces usable for collaborative learning and building networks of communi- ties. This chapter will explore how to maximize collaborative learning and work in digital libraries and repositories by applying pedagogical strategies.

Chapter 12 provides a case study of the problem solving processes of a faculty who developed a new graduate program in communication studies. Students could take all courses online, all on ground, or use a combination of the two delivery formats. For the totally online program, a key desire was to help students and faculty achieve a sense of a collaborative community. Students needed to get to know each other and feel a part of the whole program, even though course delivery for some students was totally online. Further, the faculty sought to motivate students to engage in a challenging program of research and application.

Chapter 13 is a narrative of the design, implementation, review, and redesign of an online training program for insurance brokers. The goal of the online training program is to develop advanced problem- solving knowledge and skills including communication abilities in trainees. The case is narrated from the perspective of the training manager with the reviewer's comments included during the review cycle of implementation. The evaluative review uses cultural historical activity theory to identify contradic- tions in the training process.

Chapter 14 reviews the case of an instructor and students and their educational experiences in a graduate course in virtual learning and Second Life (SL) and will provide ethical and legal guidelines for teaching and learning at the university level and for others who teach in SL. As this generation grapples with the intersection of "real" reality, virtual reality, and increasingly three-dimensional technologies, little has been written about the legal and ethical issues, affecting teaching and learning in virtual worlds and no research has been done on them. This case study is of an instructor and students and their educational experiences in a graduate course in virtual learning and Second Life can provide some guidance on these issues and provide ethical and legal guidelines for teaching and learning at the university level and for others who teach in Second Life.

Chapter 15 reviews the use of online discussion to help participants reach a more critically informed understanding about the topic or topics under consideration, to enhance participants' self-awareness and their capacity for self-critique, to foster an appreciation among participants for the diversity of opinion that invariably emerges when viewpoints are exchanged openly and honestly, and to act as a catalyst to helping people take informed action in the world.

Chapter 16 explores the question: Does online discussion produce critical thinking? It presents a selective review of the literature concerned with critical thinking and/or interaction during online discus- sion. It presents an experimental study of the effects of instructional media and instructional methods on critical thinking. The study tests the influence on critical thinking of online vs. face-to-face discussion, individual vs. group consensus in summarizing discussion, and discussion of examples of concepts vs. discussion of more abstract analysis. The purpose for reviewing the literature and carrying out the study is to increase awareness of variables that may influence the quality of discussion.

Chapter 17 reviews whether online edutainment gaming can enhance intelligence, student learning, or scholastic performance remains hotly debated in education research circles. In response to this academic issue, and in order to address a number of educational policy questions asked of the authors by several government organizations, the authors developed the online *e@Leader* edutainment gaming platform as a solution. Their *e@Leader* program is the first comprehensive 'learning by gaming' system to also be designed according to the findings of advanced machine learning and cognitive developmental neu- roscience research. In 2008, the first empirical evidence was generated with its use, and together with its built-in assessment system, integrated into the school curriculum. Beyond this existence proof of concept, and practical program application for educational use, results of beta-testing with the *e@Leader* system across primary schools in two countries support the claim for tutored online educational gaming in enhancing intelligence, active student learning, and scholastic performances in English and math.

Chapter 18 reviews the concept of knowledge-building as an approach that is effective in online learning, and the concept of protocological control as a means of controlling the communications networks that evolve during the learning process. Teachers using online learning environments have found that traditional classroom control techniques do not work when applied online. Instead, other approaches need to be used. This chapter introduces data from a study involving students in a gr. 5/6 hybrid (online and face-to-face) class are used to illustrate how the teacher controls the learning process when the students all work independently of each other. The use of social network analysis as a tool for visualizing the communications networks that form is demonstrated.

Chapter 19 describes the training course for school managers for the use of information and communication technology (ICT) that was developed at Sao Paulo Pontifical Catholic University, **Brazil**. This was a blended course, using face-to-face and online activities, providing school managers with the experience of using ICT to share experiences, and to learn about effective ways of using ICT for school management. Social and cultural practices were considered for analysis concerning the subjects that contributed to the creation of the ICT culture in the school

CONCLUSION

This book anticipates the potentiality of collaborative virtual learning environments by addressing their inherent complexities using case analyses of varied learning environments. Consequently the book provides holistic descriptive and evaluative responses to identify the processes and interactions occurring in these environments. As a result this book provides support for designers, educators, and researchers as they respond to the potential of these learning environments. Using the integrative processes of case study analyses provides new insights into collaborative virtual learning environments and the interactive aspects that impact learning. This case study collection develops new insights and provides productive discussions on the potential of these highly engaging virtual environments.

REFERENCES

Anderson. C. (2001). Situative versus cognitive perspectives: Form versus substance. *Educational Researcher, 26*(1), 18-21.

Aronson, E., Blaney, N., Stephan, C., Sikes, J., & Snapp, M. (1978). *The jigsaw classroom.* Beverly Hills, CA: Sage Publications.

Banathy, B. H. (1996). *Designing social systems in a changing world.* New York: Plenum Press.

Barab, S. A., Hay, K. E., & Yamagata-Lynch, L. C. (2001). Constructing networks of activity: An in-situ research methodology. *The Journal of the Learning Sciences, 10*(1&2), 63-112.

Bereiter, C. (2001). *Education and mind in the knowledge age.* Mahwah, NJ: Lawrence Erlbaum Assoc.

Brown, J. S., Collins, A., & Duguid, P. (1989). Situated cognition and the culture of learning. *Educational Researcher, 18*(1), 32-42.

Bruner, J. (1990). *Acts of meaning.* Cambridge, MA: Harvard University Press.

Bruer, J. (1993). *Schools for thought.* Cambridge, MA: The MIT Press.

Chee, F., Vieta, M., & Smith, R. (2006). Online gaming and the interactional self: Identity interplay in situated practice. In J. P. Williams, S. Q. Hendricks, & W. K. Winkler (Eds.), *Gaming as culture: Essays on reality, identity, and experience in fantasy games* (pp. 154-174). Jefferson, NC: McFarland Publishing.

Clark, A. (2003). *Natural born cyborgs: Minds, technologies and the furture of human intelligence.* Oxford, UK: Oxford University Press.

Cole, M., & Engeström, Y. (1993). A cultural-historical approach to distributed cognition. In G. Salomon (Ed.), *Distributed cognition: Psychological and educational considerations.* Cambridge, UK: Cambridge University Press.

Dillenbourg, P., Scheider, D., & Synteta, P. (2002). Virtual learning environments. In A. Dimitracopoulou (Ed.), Proceedings of the 3rd Hellenic Conference Information & Communication Technologies in Education (pp. 3-18). Greece: Kastaniotis Editions.

Hayles, K. (1999). *How we became post-human.* Chicago: University of Chicago Press.

Johnson, L., Rickel, J., & Lester, J. (2000). Animated pedagogical agents: Face-to-face interaction in interactive learning environments. *International Journal of Artificial Intelligence in Education,* (11), 47-78.

Johnson, W., Rickel, J., & Lester, J. (2000). Animated pedagogical agents: Face-to-face interaction in interactive learning environments. *International Journal of Artificial Intelligence in Education, 1,* 47-78.

Jonassen, D. (2000). Toward a design theory of problem solving. *Educational Technology: Research and Development, 48,* 63-85.

Jonassen, D., Peck K., & Wilson, B. (1999). *Learning with technology: A constructivist perspective.* Upper Saddle River, NJ: Merrill-Prentice Hall.

Kauppinen, K., Kivimaki, A., Era, T., & Robinson, M. (1998). *Producing identity in collaborative virtual environments.* Paper presented at the Virtual Reality Software and Technology Conference 2008. Retrieved March 25, 2009, from http://www.vrst.org/vrst1998/

Lave, J., & Wenger, E. (1991). *Situated learning: Legitimate peripheral participation.* Cambridge, UK: Cambridge University Press.

Lawson, B. R. (1984). Cognitive studies in architectural design. In N. Cross (Ed.), *Developments in design methodology* (pp. 209-220). New York: Wiley.

Lester, J., Stone, B., & Stelling, G. (1998). Lifelike pedagogical agents for mixed-initiative problem solving in constructivist learning environments. *User Modeling and User-Adapted Interaction, 9*(1-2), 1-44. Retrieved March 26, 2009, from http://www.springerlink.com/content/nn964n8167u0526n/

McLuhan, M. (1964). *Understanding media: The extensions of man.* New York: McGraw Hill.

Pea, R. (1993). Practices of distributed intelligence and designs for education. In G. Salomon (Ed.), *Distributed cognitions: Psychological and educational considerations* (pp. 47-87). Cambridge, UK: Cambridge University Press.

Resnick, L. (1987). Learning in school and out. *Educational Researcher, 16*(1), 13-20.

Russell, D. (2005). Implementing an innovation cluster in educational settings in order develop constructivist-based learning environments. *Educational Technology and Society, 8*(2).

Russell, D. (2008). Group collaboration in an online problem-based university course. In O.-S. Tan (Ed.), *In creativity and problem-based learning* (pp. 173-192). Australia: Cengage Learning.

Salomon, G. (1993). No distribution without individuals' cognition: A dynamic interactional view. In G. Salomon (Ed.), *Distributed cognitions: Psychological and educational considerations*. New York: Cambridge University Press.

Shulman, L. (1992). Toward a pedagogy of cases. In J. H. Shulman (Ed.), *Case methods in teacher education*. New York: Teachers College Press.

Tan, O. (2003). *Problem-based learning innovation: Using problems to power learning in the 21st century.* Singapore: Thomson Learning.

Vygotsky, L. (1978). *Mind in society: The development of higher psychological processes.* Cambridge, MA: Harvard University Press.

Wolfendale, J. (2007). My avatar, my self: Virtual harm and attachment. *Ethics and Information Technology, * (9), 111-119.

APPENDIX A

Instructional Design Template for Gaiaworld

The purpose of this instructional design template is to guide the teacher through the development of a problem-based unit based on constructivist learning principles. This unit will be supplemented by the information learned in the virtual Gaiaworld described above. The facilitator chooses a real-world problem and then uses the virtual created reports to identify areas of expertise and sources of information in the real world unit.

What is the nature of the Real World problem students will as they do the Gaiaworld unit?

- **Hydrology Problem:** The central region water reservoir is running out of water. How can the water reserve be protected from depletion?
- **Geology Problem:** Our region has a major earthquake fault. How can Our community prepare for a potential earthquake?
- **Water Problem:** Our community has a experienced continued growth and construction. The region has also suffered a drought over the past 5 years. How can the city maintain and protect their waterways from erosion and pollution caused by construction?
- **Air Problem:** The EPA has established an air pollution goal for our community. What are actions that the city can take to improve the quality of the air in our community?

Meaningfulness for Students
Why do you think students will find the problem in this unit meaningful?

Unit Overview (continued)

Relevant Missouri Show-Me Knowledge Standards
Although several of the Missouri Show-Me Knowledge Standards could relate to the content in this unit, which knowledge standards will you integrate into the activities and projects of this unit?

Communication Arts

4   writing formally (such as reports, narratives, essays) and informally (such as outlines, notes)

6   participating in formal and informal presentations and discussions of issues and ideas

Mathematics

3   data analysis, probability and statistics

Science

7   processes of scientific inquiry (such as formulating and testing hypotheses)

8   impact of science, technology and human activity on resources and the environment

Social Studies

6   relationships of the individual and groups to institutions and cultural traditions

7   processes of scientific inquiry (such as formulating and testing hypotheses)

Others

Unit Overview (continued)

Goals and Objectives

Based on the Missouri Show-Me Performance Standards, what are the goals of the unit and what objectives will help students meet those goals throughout the three phases of the unit?

❶ Working as a researcher exploring geoscience issues in our region, the student will gather, organize, analyze, and apply information ideas:

Objectives: conduct research to answer questions and evaluate information and ideas use technological tools and other resources to locate, select, and organize information organize data, information and ideas into useful forms (including charts, graphs, outlines) for analysis or presentation

❷ While analyzing potential problems and solutions, the student will communicate effectively within and beyond the classroom.

Objectives: plan and make written, oral and visual presentations for a variety of purposes and audiences exchange information, questions and ideas while recognizing the perspectives of others use technological tools to exchange information and ideas

❸ Using the tools of inquiry to develop a plan of action, the student will recognize and solve problems.

Objectives: identify problems and define their scope and elements examine problems and propose solutions from multiple perspectives assess costs, benefits and other consequences of proposed solutions

❹ While considering the interdependence of human and environmental needs, the student will use critical thinking to defend decisions.

Objectives: explain reasoning and identify information used to support decisions reason inductively from facts and deductively from general premises

❺ As a scientist working with other scientists, the student will be a responsible group member and demonstrate positive leadership skills.

Objectives: develop, monitor, and revise plans of action to meet deadlines and accomplish goals work with others to complete tasks that require a coordinated effort

Expert Contacts

What experts in fields related to this unit will contribute to the design, development, and implementation of this unit with students?

❶ Geologist;
❷ Civic officials
❸ Economists
❹
❺

Unit Overview (continued)

Pre-Assessment
What knowledge and skills do you think are important for students to have in order to complete the projects in this unit successfully?

How will you identify students' prior knowledge and misconceptions about the problem?

Phase 1.

Critical Question
What is the critical question that students will respond to throughout Phase 1 of the unit?

Why is the **GAIAWORLD** problem important?

Objectives
Considering the goals of this unit, what are the objectives for students during this phase of the unit? You might consider the performance and knowledge skills required for students to complete the project in Phase 1 with little or no teacher support.

❶ use technological tools and other resources to locate, select, and organize information
❷ make oral and visual presentations for a variety of purposes and audiences
❸ identify problems and define their scope and elements
❹ explain reasoning and identify information used to support decisions
❺ work with others to complete tasks that require a coordinated effort

Problem-Solving Model
What part of the model for design problem solving best illustrates the problem solving that will occur in the work groups during Phase 1?

In Phase 1, students are not only gathering information to determine the relationship between the living and non-living aspects of Gaiaworld.

How does the problem solving process in this phase of the unit relate to the way experts in related fields solve problems?

Phase 1 Project Criteria
What project will students work collaboratively to complete during Phase 1 that relates to the critical question of this phase of the unit?

After gathering relevant, accurate, and clear facts and statistics about the **GAIAWORLD** issue in their community, the group will determine why the **GAIAWORLD** problem is important to their community. Their knowledge and ideas for the future of **GAIAWORLD** will be shared with other groups in the class with other groups of students from our partner schools.

What criteria will you expect students to complete when they work on the project collaboratively? Consider the objectives you identified for students' learning during Phase 1.

❶ locate relevant, accurate, and clear facts from different sources that help your group explain why **GAIAWORLD** is important to your community

❷ talk in your group about whether or not your group thinks **GAIAWORLD**, as it is today, can meet the needs of people in your community

❸ talk in your group about what your group thinks **GAIAWORLD** should do to better meet the needs of people in your community

❹ develop a plan for how to convince students from other communities why **GAIAWORLD** needs improvement in order to better meet the needs of people in your community

❺ present the plan to other workgroups in your classroom and improve your presentation before sharing it with students from other communities

---

Formative and Summative Assessment
How will you assess students' learning in regards to the objectives at the end of Phase 1?

see Phase 1 Group Scoring Guide for assessment of group products based on Bereiter's Scheme of Knowledge (levels 1-3)

Facilitating Activities
What activities do you think are important in Phase 1 to help your students meet the objectives of this phase of the unit and to successfully complete the project?

❶

❷

Initial Inquiry Questions
What kind of questions do you anticipate students posing at the beginning of Phase 1 that will guide them in answering the critical question in this phase of the unit?

Important Implementation Dates
What aspects of the activities in Phase 1 need to be scheduled or arranged ahead of time?

❶

❷

Resources and Tools
What resources and/or tools within your classroom, in your building, or in your community are necessary to help students during Phase 1?

❶

❷

Phase 2.

Critical Question
What is the critical question that students will respond to throughout Phase 2 of the unit?

How can we use our expertise in an area related to **GAIAWORLD** to better understand the problem and develop a feasible solution?

Objectives
Considering the goals of this unit, what are the objectives for students during this phase of the unit? You might consider the performance and knowledge skills required for students to complete the project in Phase 2 with little or no teacher support.

❶ conduct research to answer questions and evaluate information and ideas
❷ exchange information, questions and ideas while recognizing the perspectives of others
❸ examine problems and proposed solutions from multiple perspectives
❹ reason inductively from facts and deductively from general premises
❺ develop, monitor, and revise plans of action to meet deadlines and accomplish goals

Problem-Solving Model

What part of the model for design problem solving best illustrates the problem solving that will occur in the work groups during Phase 2?

In Phase 2, students will acquire expertise in an area related to **GAIAWORLD**, including problem solving strategies and conceptual knowledge. This will help them know where change could be effected in the system and help the revise their original vision for **GAIAWORLD**.

How does the problem solving process in this phase of the unit relate to the way experts in related fields solve problems?

Experts draw upon their prior experiences and knowledge and relate these to the unique characteristics of a current design problem.

Phase 2 Project Criteria

What project will students work collaboratively to complete during Phase 2 that relates to the critical question of this phase of the unit?

After gathering and analyzing relevant, accurate, and clear facts and statistics about an area related to **GAIAWORLD**, the group will determine how the area of expertise applies to development of a feasible solution to the **GAIAWORLD** problem that impacts multiple communities in Missouri.

What criteria will you expect students to complete when they work on the project collaboratively? Consider the objectives you identified for students' learning during Phase 2.

❶ locate relevant, accurate, and clear facts from different sources that help you understand your expert area related to **GAIAWORLD**

❷ talk in your expert area group about how your expert area affects the way we will solve the **GAIAWORLD** problem and how it affects each of your communities

❸ develop a plan for how to accurately communicate the following to students in your group: (1) the main ideas about the expert area and (2) how you think your expert area will help us solve the **GAIAWORLD** problem better

❹ develop your plan for communicating to students in your group

❺ talk in your group about how the areas of expertise are related and how the expert areas will help you solve the **GAIAWORLD** problem better

---

Formative and Summative Assessment

How will you assess students' learning in regards to the objectives at the end of Phase 2?

see Phase 2 Group Scoring Guide for assessment of group products based on Bereiter's Scheme of Knowledge (levels 3-5)

Facilitating Activities
What activities do you think are important in Phase 2 to help your students meet the objectives of this phase of the unit and to successfully complete the project?

❶   case study analyses of similar projects

❷

Areas of Expertise
*What areas of expertise are important to the **GAIAWORLD** problem that students will investigate in their groups?*

❶   ecology   ❻   human environment
❷   socioeconomics   ❼
❸   design   ❽
❹   public affairs   ❾
❺   natural environment (e.g., wetlands, habitat, species)❿

Important Implementation Dates
What aspects of the activities in Phase 2 need to be scheduled or arranged ahead of time?

❶

❷

Resources and Tools
What resources and/or tools within your classroom, in your building, or in your community are necessary to help students during Phase 2?

❶

❷

Phase 3.

Critical Question
What is the critical question that students will respond to throughout Phase 3 of the unit?

How can we use the knowledge and skills from Phase 1 and Phase 2 to develop a feasible solution to the **GAIAWORLD** problem?

Objectives
Considering the goals of this unit, what are the objectives for students during this phase of the unit? You might consider the performance and knowledge skills required for students to complete the project in Phase 3 with little or no teacher support.

❶ organize data, information and ideas into useful forms (including charts, graphs, outlines) for analysis or presentation
❷ use technological tools to exchange information and ideas
❸ assess costs, benefits and other consequences of proposed solutions
❹ explain reasoning and identify information used to support decisions
❺ work with others to complete tasks that require a coordinated effort

Problem-Solving Model
In Phase 3, students will work in their local group to propose a solution to the **GAIAWORLD** *problem that incorporates a plan of action for their community and multiple communities. They will apply the expert areas and assess their solution to determine feasibility.*

How does the problem solving process in this phase of the unit relate to the way experts in related fields solve problems?

Phase 3 Project Criteria
What project will students work collaboratively to complete during Phase 3 that relates to the critical question of this phase of the unit?

After gathering relevant, accurate, and clear facts and statistics about **GAIAWORLD** in their community, the group will determine why the **GAIAWORLD** problem is important to their community. Their knowledge and ideas for the future of **GAIAWORLD** will be shared with other groups in the class with other groups of students from our partner schools.

What criteria will you expect students to complete when they work on the project collaboratively? Consider the objectives you identified for students' learning during Phase 3.

❶ write a description of the problem, including facts and statistics, of the current condition of **GAIAWORLD** as well as a prediction for its future
❷ develop a hypothesis, or a statement describing how your group thinks the local organizations should develop **GAIAWORLD** to better meet the needs of people in Missouri
❸ outline a procedure, or a logically-defined plan of action, about how your group's idea would be implemented
❹ talk in your group about how to "test the feasibility" of your solution and plan; determine whether your solution could feasibly be implemented locally.
❺ using the results of your feasibility test, predict the success of your solution and plan and identify short-term and long-term problems that might occur because of your solution and plan of action

---

Formative and Summative Assessment

How will you assess students' learning in regards to the objectives at the end of Phase 3?

see Phase 3 Group Scoring Guide for assessment of group products based on Bereiter's Scheme of Knowledge (levels 4-6)

Facilitating Activities

What activities do you think are important in Phase 3 to help your students meet the objectives of this phase of the unit and to successfully complete the project?

❶

❷

Solution Generation

*How will you motivate students to develop solutions to the **GAIAWORLD** problem that incorporates state and local community needs from Phase 1 and the different areas of expertise from Phase 2?*

Important Implementation Dates

What aspects of the activities in Phase 3 need to be scheduled or arranged ahead of time?

❶

❷

Resources and Tools

What resources and/or tools within your classroom, in your building, or in your community are necessary to help students during Phase 3?

❶

❷

Phase I. Group Artifact Scoring Guide

	Learning	Accomplishing	Excelling	Exceptional
gathering information	Working with the teacher, the students found and used at least two resources.	With some teacher help, the students found and used at least two resources and identified if the information gathered was relevant.	The students found and used information from different types of resources, determined if the information was relevant, and explained if the information was reliable.	The students independently found and used information from different types of resources, judged the relevancy of information, and verified the reliability of information by cross-referencing.
using facts and statistics	The students and teacher worked together to identify and use facts and statistics to support their ideas.	With some teacher assistance, the students determined facts and statistics to support their ideas and could explain how some facts and statistics were connected.	The students could combine information, make connections between information, and identify relevant prior knowledge to support their ideas.	The students independently combined information, made connections between facts and statistics, recognized contradictions, and integrated prior knowledge.
working on a team	With teacher help, the students listened to one others' ideas and shared in the responsibility for completing work.	With encouragement, the students listened to one others' ideas, tried to compromise with each group members, and shared in the responsibility of completing work.	The students listened to one others' ideas, encouraged all group members to compromise, and actively shared in the responsibility for completing work.	The student listened to others' ideas, motivated all group members to compromise, and proposed a plan for sharing responsibility for completing work.
setting up the problem	With teacher support, the students identified and/or explained constraints in the **GAIAWORLD** system and stated a vision for the future of interstate.	As they described a vision for the future of **GAIAWORLD**, the students identified and explained constraints in the **GAIAWORLD** system including some that are related to the students' community.	As they described a specific vision for the future of **GAIAWORLD** in their community, the students identified and explained constraints in the **GAIAWORLD** system that are directly related to the students' community.	As they described a specific vision for the future of **GAIAWORLD** in their community, the students identified, explained, and prioritized constraints in the **GAIAWORLD** system that are directly related to the students' community, including constraints that are not apparent or are external to the **GAIAWORLD** system.

Acknowledgment

I would like to firstly acknowledgement my gratitude to the authors of the chapters in this book. I appreciate their diligence in preparing their chapters and all the supporting documents for publication in this book. I would also like to thank the Editorial Advisory Board. All the members of the Editorial Advisory Board are my colleagues at the University of Missouri-Kansas City's School of Education including faculty from the Curriculum and Instructional Design, Counseling and Educational Psychology and the Urban Leadership & Policy Studies in Education departments. Their expert reviews of the chapters were critical for the successful completion of the book. I would thank Dr. Kinshuk for writing a foreword for the book. His expertise in this area is greatly appreciated. Finally I would like to thank my husband, children, mother, brothers and sisters for all of their past and current support of my attempts to fulfill a promise I made to my father.

Donna Russell
University of Missouri at Kansas City, USA

Chapter 1
The Making of the University Life Café:
Harnessing Interactive Technologies and Virtual Community for an Anti-Suicide Website for College Students

Shalin Hai-Jew
Kansas State University, USA

***With an Appendix by* Brent A. Anders**
Kansas State University, USA

EXECUTIVE SUMMARY

The building of an interactive, user-driven website for college students to promote mental health and wellness (and to combat suicide) has revealed important strategies in the construction of such a socio-technical virtual learning environment. This project used a number of strategies to create allure to the site and to provide learning opportunities—through educational modules, virtual community mores of care for others, user interactivity, the support for student voices, and the use of artificial intelligence to enhance the security measures. Virtual learning environments that involve life-critical issues require an understanding of the domain field, potential site users, and thought-out strategies.

BACKGROUND: THE PROJECT

Suicide is the second highest leading cause of death for college students ("Suicide Statistics," 2009). K-State currently has around 18,500 undergraduate students, with about 300 non-resident aliens (overseas students who are in the US on student visas). There were also approximately 4,800 graduate students in 2007, and about 800 of these are international students. For a campus the size of K-State, this often means several suicides annually on average (Newton, 2009).

The campus Counseling Services support students who may be feeling emotionally frail, but there are many who don't use these services for many reasons. In that spirit, K-State endeavored to use the Web to support their students in building up

DOI: 10.4018/978-1-60566-878-9.ch001

protective factors against suicide through a federal grant from the Substance Abuse & Mental Health Services Administration (SAMHSA).

Research suggests that many students are entering colleges with serious psychological issues.

Given the increasing number of students entering college with serious psychological problems, campus suicide may currently be more prevalent. In a 2007 survey by the American College Health Association, which included more than 70,000 students at 107 institutions, 9.8% reported seriously considering suicide at least once during the past school year and 1.5% reported making at least one suicide attempt (Haas, et al., 2008, p. 15).

Suicidal thoughts among college students are prevalent, with more than half of 26,000 students across 70 colleges and universities repeating such thoughts in a recent American Psychological Association (APA) study (Willenz, 2008).

The implications of suicide may be far-reaching on a campus, which suggests the importance of a coordinated university effort: "Because student suicide completion can significantly affect a campus and student-body climate, there must be a coordination of campus services designed to attend to the diverse needs of suicide survivors" (Paladino & Minton, 2008, p. 645).

SETTING THE STAGE

The University Life Café is a new website that promotes mental wellness among university students, faculty, and staff, with a particular focus on suicide prevention. This publicly available site uses the power of social networking at its core to provide a sense of virtual community to members of the K-State community in particular. It delivers information on resiliency and protective issues against suicide through podcasts, audio files, images, text, and other types of contents. Users of the site who are K-State members may also access professionally created heuristics dealing with various aspects of mental health.

This site also strives to de-stigmatize communications about suicide, depression, and substance abuse and to encourage help-seeking behaviors. This site was co-developed with contributions from students, faculty, and staff; it involved partnerships from across campus. This site is one part of a comprehensive, campus-wide plan, which engages "students and faculty/staff, while respecting the race, ethnicity, cultural background, sexual orientation, and belief system of every member of our campus community," according to the grant. The site is not intended to be used in isolation.

For a university, reaching out to students to create awareness of suicide risk factors and the need to build protective factors is not just about risk management, it also involves promoting mental wellness for improved learning quality, learning retention, and the creation of a virtual community to promote socialization. Campuses are often seen broadly as protected environments, and this particular university (for example) has a firearms ban.

There are challenges with stress, student isolation, depression, and other life issues that may be partially mitigated through a website as a social connective tissue and that speaks through media contents that students enjoy (and that they may create and share) such as music, artworks, poetry, short stories, essays, and an evolving blog. This site may also serve as a bridge to professional counseling services by de-stigmatizing access to counseling services.

The Stakeholders

The primary stakeholders to this site are mostly K-State students, faculty, and staff. Secondary stakeholders are the larger public that may need the information and interactivity. Within K-State students, there are a range of diverse learners, such as international and military veterans. Nationwide, there are about 10 million full-time students in four-year colleges and universities, and for this

2

population suicide is the second leading cause of death.

In the suicide prevention situation, individuals served may be those who are in emotional distress and considering self-harm or suicide. The intermediary role between a possibly suicidal person and professional counseling services is also an important one: these may include concerned family, friends, and acquaintances. These may be faculty and staff. Here, telemedicine may provide support to these third-party observers "Internet-based ICTs enable such telemedicine delivery systems and provide a unique opportunity to reach intermediaries via the world wide web (sic)" (Wang, Phillips-Wren, & Forgionne, 2005, p. 398).

LITERATURE ON SUICIDOLOGY

The work on the University Life Café site aligned with the research findings in the field of suicidology, the study of the causes and prevention of suicide, so as not to send a mixed message or negative learning. Those working to develop the site are governed by the principle, *primum non nocere,* meaning "first, do no harm".

Globally

Suicide has been identified as an international public health issue, with the World Health Organization (WHO) reporting suicide as the cause of up to half of all violent deaths annually and leading to "one million fatalities worldwide each year, and has billions of dollars in economic costs" (WHO, 2004). By 2020, this number is estimated to rise to 1.5 million (Wang, Phillips-Wren, & Forgionne, 2005).

In the U.S.

Nationally, suicide is an important public health issue, which has drawn the attention of many who aim to create improved social conditions to stem the incidence of suicide. The American Association of Suicidology (2002) asserted that:

11.0 of every 100,000 Americans committed suicide and that suicide is the eleventh leading cause of death in the USA (AAS, 2004). Suicide is preventable (WHO, 2004), and one means of delivering healthcare for this persistent public health crisis is electronic (iTelehealth, 2004). In 1999, the US Surgeon General introduced a blueprint for addressing suicide—Awareness, Intervention, and Methodology (AIM) with the goal of increasing public awareness of suicide and its risk factors (Wang, Phillips-Wren, & Forgionne, 2005).

Risks in Young People

Suicide is a fairly large risk in the years leading up to university. "Every two hours and 15 minutes in the United States, a person who is under the age of 25 years old completes a suicide. As a result of the fact that suicide is one of the leading causes of death for young people between the ages of 15 and the age of 19, it's hard to imagine a high school teacher who hasn't been touched by this epidemic" (Fisher, 2006, p. 9).

Researchers cite a jump in suicide risk among American youth. "Suicide among youth in the United States has quadrupled during the past 50 years. As many as one in 10 students is seriously contemplating suicide at a given time, and each year 2 percent of girls and 1 percent of boys make suicide attempts" (Bostic, Rustuccia, & Schlozman, 2001, p. 81).

Others have observed a dramatic rise in youth suicides.

Suicide rates among today's youth have risen dramatically since the 1950s (King, 2001). Currently, suicide is the third leading cause of death for children ages 10-19 and the only cause of death to increase for 10- to 14-year-olds in recent years (Hamilton, et al., 2007). Suicide accounted for 7.2% and 12.4% of all deaths for younger and older adolescents, respectively, in 2004 (Hamilton, et al., 2007).Given these alarming statistics, school personnel have an obligation to do what they can to prevent suicides (as cited in Gibbons & Studer, 2008, p. 272).

Homicide Link in Youth?

One researcher has asked if there is a connection between suicidal ideation and homicidal behaviors. The profiles of young student shooters have offered some insights. "Nor can much comfort be taken from these profiles. Only 5% of the shooters were considered to be "delusionally psychotic." The largest group, according to the American Association of Suicidology (AAS), 'appears to be comprised of emotionally troubled and conflicted youngsters who are alienated, angry, and depressed. They feel unfairly treated by others, lonely, and isolated (even though they may have some friends).' 'Most horrific school violence that we've seen stems from suicidal behavior,' Ohlinger says flatly" (Levinsky, 2001, p. 51).

On Campuses

Among young people who make up a large part of the traditional college student demographic, suicide is a concern. "Suicide currently ranks as the third-leading cause of death among 15-to-24 year-olds, exceeded only by injuries and homicides. In 1997, the year with the most current mortality statistics, the suicide rate among this age group was 11.4 per 100,000. The suicide rate for adolescents more than tripled since the 1950s, while rates for the overall population remained virtually unchanged. A typical US high school classroom includes one boy and two girls who attempted suicide in the past year. The US Department of Health and Human Services designated the reduction of adolescent suicides to less than 8.2

per 100,000 and the reduction of injuries related to suicide attempts by 15% as goals to be achieved by the year 2000" (King, 2001, p. 132).

On college campuses, suicidal ideations (mentally conceptualizing suicide) are relatively common.

Even with the rates of completed suicide among college students, related phenomena such as suicidal ideation and attempts have been found to be common among this population. The US government recently estimated that for every completed suicide among youth, there are 100 – 200 attempts…Empirically supported factors contributed to suicidal ideation and behavior include, but are not limited to, low self-esteem, student stress, depression, loneliness, hopelessness, academic problems, relationship and family issues, financial concerns, and adjustment to college" (Paladino & Minton, 2008, p. 643).

However, that information needs to be balanced against other findings that "suicide ideation, attempts, and completed suicides are not always linked" (Gillman, Kim, Alder, & Durrant, 2006, p. 17).

Others observe, by contrast, that there hasn't been a dramatic change to the statistics of student suicide. The National Survey of Counseling Center Directors reports 1,404 student suicides over a 14-year period and adjusted suicide rate of 6.5, half the rate of the general US population (12.6 for all races) during this period when matched for gender and age. Counseling centers appear effective in treating suicidal students, for although the suicide rate for students who were currently or previously clients at campus counseling centers is three times the rate of other students, student clients have 18 times the risk of suicide compared to students in general. Identifying and referring students at elevated risk for suicide could further reduce the crude and relative rate of student suicide. However, even programs that do this only moderately well may require substantial increases in counseling staff (Schwartz, 2006a, p. 341).

Fallout from Campus Related Suicides

The effects of suicide resonate beyond the circle of those left behind by a person who has committed suicide. "The influence and residual affects (sic) of suicide are further amplified as the issue reaches across communities such as college or university campuses. College and university staff must improve their response to suicidal ideation with comprehensive assessment and intervention" (Paladino & Minton, 2008, p. 643). The repercussions of a student suicide have effects throughout the entire school (George, 2002).

The emotions of those at the school may be raised. "When a suicide actually does take place, it affects the entire school, with the school community collectively experiencing and amplifying all of the emotions that individual survivors feel, such as guilt, anger, anxiety, and denial. When a suicide occurs, schools must have a plan in place to address individual students' emotions and concerns, while at the same time preventing the possibility of additional suicides" (George, 2002, p. 13). The suicide "contagion" threat and "suicide clusters" risk require a balanced response by school authorities and an attentiveness to the "signals" put out by the students—for a lifesaving effort.

Avoiding Suicide Contagion

Mass media may play a role in "aggravating imitative suicide and suicide contagion," so schools have to take a measured approach in engaging radio, television, and other broadcast media (Schwartz, 2006b, p. 361):

The present consensus is that it is neither feasible nor wise to attempt to conceal student suicide from the media. This in part reflects the minimal impact that contagion contributes to the overall suicide rate. It also reflects the promise that media can actively avoid such outcomes by taking care not to sensationalize or romanticize

death by suicide and by highlighting the role of mental illness, a family history of suicide, and other risk factors (Schwartz, 2006b, p. 361).

Memorials of students who had died of suicide may involve negative learning or falsely glorifying suicide. "Memorials to the victim are rarely helpful because they suggest that the student is best remembered for a self-destructive act and also risk glorifying or validating suicide to other distressed students" (Bostic, Rustuccia, & Schlozman, 2001, p. 82). How these are handled by a university or college is critical.

ASSESSING SUICIDE RISKS

Assessing suicide risks may be difficult for non-professionals and professionals, who may be aware of at-risk symptoms and at-risk signs.

At-Risk Symptoms

At-risk symptoms are expressions of negative emotions, such as hopelessness, despair, or self-destructiveness. These involve suicidal comments that may "represent an effort by the student to communicate distress to others" (Bostic, Rustuccia, & Schlozman, 2001, p. 81). Suicidality is "a strong predictor of completed suicide and thus a useful focus for suicide prevention" (Russell & Marks, 2006, p. 19).

At-Risk Signs

At-risk signs involve behaviors—such as a decline in hygiene, a disinterest in school or work, emotional withdrawal, or other factors. "The American Association of Suicidology…says about 80% of people who attempt or complete suicide showed advance warning signs" (Fisher, 2006, p. 10). "Behavioral warning signs include being depressed, a change in appetite and/or weight, change in behavior, change in school performance, helplessness and/or hopelessness, loss of energy, loss of interest in once-pleasurable activities, giving away cherished possessions, morbid ideation, substance abuse, and being withdrawn or isolated" (King, 2001, p. 56).

Researchers have identified possible warning signs of adolescent suicide:

Some of the possible warning signs of adolescent suicide are: a decline in school performance; increased absenteeism; death or suicide themes dominating written, artistic, or creative work; loss of interest in previously pleasurable activities and withdrawal from friends; giving away prized possessions; sudden change in weight or personal hygiene; sudden and striking personality changes and changes in mood; depression; direct (e.g., "I wish I were dead") and indirect statements (e.g., "Nobody cares if I live or die") (George, 2002, p. 13).

An actual failed suicide attempt is a very critical sign of risk to that individual. "Warning signs of parasuicide or failed suicide indicate final acts of desperate at the most emotionally intense level" (Helsel, 2001, p. 93).

Stressors

Factors that may be stress-inducing in people's lives include recent disappointments; breakups of central relationships, and challenges with serious illness or the belief of being seriously ill (King, 2001, p. 56). Those in emotionally abusive relationships may be at increased risks. "Our analysis suggests that those involved in an emotionally abusive relationship in the previous 12 months were more likely to consider suicide than were those who were not in this type of relationship" (Gillman, Kim, Alder, & Durrant, 2006, p. 21). Interpersonal conflict may stress people. "The most common precipitant to a student suicide is an interpersonal conflict or loss, usually with parents or a romantic relationship" (Bostic, Rustuccia, & Schlozman, 2001, p. 81).

The Difficulties of Assessing Risk

Assessing suicide risk is difficult for the professionals in the counseling field. Some completed suicides are not preceded by warning signs or symptoms. People may give verbal indicators of a person feeling overwhelmed with life or not wanting to continue. "In addition to verbal markers of suicidal ideation, there are often behavioral signs: giving away valued possessions, putting personal or business affairs in order as though preparing for a long journey, dropping classes, experiencing declining grades, crying in class, exhibiting drastic and unusual changes in behavior, and obtaining the means to commit suicide (e.g, buying a gun, stockpiling pills)" (Paladino & Minton, 2008, p. 644).

A majority of those who commit suicide have expressed their distressing thoughts to a mental health worker recently before their completed suicides.

Fully 75% of all people who commit suicide have complained of suicidal thoughts to a mental health worker within 1 month of their death. Yet in many of these cases the seriousness of the problem is not recognized. Such detection problems fall into the class of diagnostic problems that Ledly and Lusted (YEAR) referred to in their classical paper. Since then several empirical studies have further substantiated both the problems and potential of computer aided diagnostic systems (Gustafson, Greist, Stauss, Erdman, & Laughren, 1977).

Some researchers are trying to improve the assessment of suicide risks without having to know a person's past history of suicide attempts (Gustafson, Greist, Stauss, Erdman, & Laughren, 1977). There are endeavors to surface suicide risk assessments even in the typical situation of incomplete data and informational asymmetries.

There are some assessments created to consider symptoms in a more regulated way, such as through a tool named BASIC-ID, which addresses "the modalities of behavior, affective responses, sensations, imagery, cognition, interpersonal relationships, and drug or biological influences" (Paladino & Minton, 2008, p. 648). A Suicide Resiliency Inventory examines the "demographic differences in protective and risk factors related to young adult suicide," to strive to understand not only who is at risk, but why (Rutter & Estrada, 2006).

Demographic Factors

Demographic factors may be considered in terms of assessing risk. Young people 15 to 24 are at higher risk. Males are three to five times more likely to die by suicide than females. GBLT (gay, bisexual, lesbian, or transgender) individuals are at increased risks of suicidal behaviors. Those who've suffered traumas, acute stress disorders and adjustment disorders may experience higher risk factors as well. People with psychiatric disorders, a family history of suicide or depression, and aggressiveness or impulsivity may be at increased risk of suicide. Unexpected sudden personal losses may lead to suicide risks. Access to lethal means like firearms or medications may increase the risk ("Risk and Protective Factors," 2008).

Lifestyle Factors

Another study had additional findings of descriptors of those who tended to have heightened risk of suicide. "Those students who seriously considered suicide more likely lived off campus, indicated they were emotionally abused, were in only fair health, experienced being assaulted, experienced unwanted sexual touching, or were not heterosexual. Students who were employed were significantly less likely to consider suicide" (Gillman, Kim, Alder, & Durrant, 2006, p. 17). Gillman, Kim, Alder and Durrant suggest that commuter schools have higher risks of more suicidal ideation.

BUILDING PROTECTIVE FACTORS

Protective factors not only include a strong social circle of safe, healthy friends and family, but also access to professional care in the community. The community itself should provide plenty of awareness and individual support. There should be ready help-seeking. There should be restricted access to lethal methods of suicide. Having cultural and religious beliefs that discourage suicide would also provide a layer of safety against suicide. The skills of problem-solving, conflict management, lifestyle management, and stress management may also be highly helpful.

External and Internal Protective Factors

Protective factors involve both external and internal ones. Religious affiliation serves as an important protective factor. "Catholic religious affiliation appeared to serve as a significant protective factor. These young adults appeared to have more internal and external protective factors accompanied by lower levels of hopelessness. These data appear to support the suggested protective qualities of religious involvement in a faith such as Catholicism that deems suicide to be sinful (Siegrist, 1996). Scores for participants in their junior year of college represented a complex pattern" (Rutter & Estrada, Winter 2006, p. 95).

Internal protective factors involve self concept and resiliency, which help people overcome adversity. "The ability to hold a sense of self and of personal power (self-concept) and understand one's ability to overcome a current challenge by recalling past personal victories (resiliency) are essential protective elements" (Harter et al., 1996; Osman et al., 1998, as cited in Rutter & Estrada, 2006, p. 91).

A campus may create a sense of protection, too, by instituting suicide prevention education for students, faculty and staff; they may put in place a peer assistance program. They may create a sense of school connectedness and an emotionally supportive environment to lower suicide rates (King, 2001). The literature describes a student-run support call center for young people through a trauma hotline that involves anonymity and privacy protections (Levinsky, 2001).

Proper Handling of Suicidal Signs and Symptoms

Those who may be intermediaries between students and professional counselors need clear training and messages about how to intervene. It is important to be able to address the possible suicide issue directly. While school staff may be reticent to bring up suicide in fears of precipitating an attempt, the opposite is apparently true (Bostic, Rustuccia, & Schlozman, 2001). Sensitive ways to ask if a student is feeling suicidal are suggested in the literature: "For example, after acknowledging the student's pain and hopelessness, one might say, "I'm wondering, have you had thoughts of harming yourself?" or "Have you had thoughts of ending your life?" Depending on the level of rapport with the student, a more direct approach (e.g., "Are you thinking about killing yourself?") may also be appropriate. A simple follow-up prompt (e.g., "Tell me about those thoughts you've been having") often is effective in eliciting additional information regarding the nature of the suicidal ideation. In cases in which the concerned person is building rapport, a reflective question (e.g., "What would you feel comfortable sharing regarding these thoughts you've been having?") may also be helpful" (Paladino & Minton, 2008, p. 644). Calling a student's bluff is "particularly unhelpful, replacing an effort to understand the student's pain with a challenge that could have a tragic outcome" (Bostic, Rustuccia, & Schlozman, 2001, p. 82).

CREATING A VIRTUAL WORK TEAM

The work team collaborated around a work site on the Axio™ Learning/Course Management System (L/CMS), which is also known as K-State Online. This site was used to communicate meeting dates. The survey part of the site collected information from potential users for the design team. Also, raw photos, meeting notes and meeting videos, memos, draft downloadables, and draft modules were all uploaded here for participant commentary and critiques. Resources like digital images were uploaded here for easy distribution.

THE USE OF CONNECTIVE TECHNOLOGIES

The Internet and WWW have been employed for the delivery of telemedicine and educational and preventative information to combat the incidences of suicide. According to the research, this approach of using the Net for providing psychological help has been around since the mid-1990s (Barak, 2007, p. 972).

Various sites have sprung up including those providing "psychological advice, support groups, testing and assessment, and counseling and therapy" even in the face of legal and ethical challenges. The use of the Internet with its "accessibility, anonymity, and unidentifiability"

Moreover, because of the accessibility, anonymity, and unidentifiability" makes it possible to reach many who would otherwise not be reached (Barak, 2007, p. 972). Internet-based technologies have shifted healthcare delivery trends. Some "store-and-forward" telemedicine" supports educational or prevention initiatives that enable users to make better informed decisions about their lifestyles and personal healthcare. These systems generally carry personalised, proactive, and intelligent features, empowering users with greater control over healthcare knowledge" (as cited in Wang, Phillips-Wren, & Forgionne, 2005, p. 399).

An interactive website named SAHAR (http://www.sahar.org.il) out of Israel applies psychological principles and emotional support to provide an anonymous, confidential environment to provide emotional support. The site was designed to "attract people in a crisis situation and offer them a listening ear, mental support, and warmth, provided by anonymous, skilled helpers." SAHAR also channels the different users for "free and open online support groups" as chatrooms and live forums for youngsters, adults, enlisted soldiers and "the fourth offering creative support…intended for those users who prefer to express their emotions through poetry, stories, and painting" (Barak, 2007, p. 975).

The interactivity on SAHAR would be both synchronous and asynchronous.

The website is accessed more than 10,000 times a month, or 350 times a day, a considerable number relative to Israel's small population. Approximately 1000 personal contacts with SAHAR itself take place, each month, of which at least a third of the distressed users are clearly suicidal. The forums receive over 200 new messages a day. SAHAR on numerous occasions has participated in rescue operations of individuals who threatened to commit suicide or were actually in the process of trying. In many other cases, a supportive conversation or a referral to appropriate help resources prevented hasty decisions by highly distressed, desperate people contemplating suicide. Feedback by users also indicates the success of SAHAR as a unique psychological application on the Internet (Barak, 2007, p. 971).

Collective Intelligence in a Culture of Caring

While this site was in development, there came a report that a Florida teen streamed his own suicide online (Friedman, Nov. 21, 2008, n.p.),

but several weeks later, police apparently were notified in time and foiled a potential suicide of a young 12-year-old in her grandmother's home (Police foil teen's suspected Web suicide," Dec. 2, 2008, n.p.). The risks of "bent souls" to do harm to others may be an issue of concern (Joy, 2000, as cited in Kurzweil, Mar. 2001, p. 89). The site needs to offer catharsis of some darker human impulses, not reinforcement. While this site taps into collective intelligence, it became clear that a culture of caring must be established and supported. There must be a constant awareness of site user needs, through the support of artificial intelligence (AI) to support them.

ADDRESSING LEGAL CONCERNS

The potential volatility and sensitivity of this issue makes the building of the site, its technological systems, its contents, and the site policies especially sensitive. There currently is no legal framework for the provision of healthcare information on the Internet (HON, 2004). "Legal issues involve confidentiality, security and liability. These aspects are among the most critical problems of telemedicine over the internet, especially when related to an extremely personal and emotionally charged subject such as suicide" (Wang, Phillips-Wren, & Forgionne, 2005, p. 408).

Three main areas of legal concern involve site user confidentiality, the security of user identities, and the avoidance of institutional liability. These issues have to be balanced against the ethical and legal impetus to provide protections and supports for learners.

Confidentiality

Users do have privacy rights—the "right to request restriction, right to review and copy personal information, right to request amendment of personal information, right to request receipt of communications in a confidential manner, right to receive an accounting of disclosures and right to a printed copy of the privacy policy page," according to some who have created and maintained a telemedicine site (Wang, Phillips-Wren, & Forgionne, 2005, p. 409).

Privacy is seen as existing in four human states—all of which relate to how they interact with others: solitude (total isolation from others), intimacy (a small group isolating themselves from others), anonymity (being physically co-present but not recognizable), and reserve (a state in which an individual may ignore the presence of others nearby) (Westin, 1967, as cited in Boyle & Greenberg, June 2005, p. 351). The anonymity piece involves the ability to be present but not recognizable in the online spaces.

Confidentiality refers to the keeping private or personal information safe from non-authorized access or disclosure. There are implications in information management, too, such as the collection of personally identifiable information. While a client may sign a "consent to disclosure" for some information in particular circumstances, without that, providers of such site information and services need to proceed with care. Aggregate information collection from the site may also have implications for privacy even if individually identifiable information is not collected.

Security

Security involves the protection of identities and user access. And liability involves the legal responsibilities associated with the provision of such information and services. There are laws related also to reporting (Ashford, 2005, p. 56) that need to be considered. Security issues work as a barrier to telemedicine and involve concerns about unauthorized access, data accuracy, and correct information handling (Wang, Phillips-Wren, & Forgionne, 2005, p. 409).

Liabilities and the Risks of Plaintiff Parents

Various institutions of higher education have concerns of so-called "plaintiff parents": "With one limited exception, the courts have consistently rejected parents' claims that schools have a special relationship with students that can lead to 14th Amendment due process liability. They have also rejected the theory that schools have intentionally or recklessly created the danger that resulted in the student's death" (Zirkel, May / June 2006, p. 10). Universities and schools have a vested interest in avoiding danger creation and avoiding foreseeable or direct harm. Whether a person has had specific training for suicide will potentially determine whether there was a breach of duty (Zirkel, Feb. 2006, p. 50). Educators working with pre-college students will have the additional factors of potential negligence, failure to evaluate, notify or refer.

This author suggests that an "undue fear of liability leads to over-reaction or paralysis. As a matter of professional discretion and ethical imperative, school leaders should be proactive in including suicide prevention as part of a co-ordinated and comprehensive program of a safe and secure environment for student learning and growth (Zirkel, Feb. 2006, p. 53). Schools are important settings for suicide prevention (Schroeder, May 2006).

CULTURAL FACTORS

Cultural factors affect the effectiveness of suicide prevention endeavors. Without a diversity of approaches, a range of students may be left out of the communications about suicide prevention and protective factors. The need for culturally tailored approaches exists at a time when various minority groups are showing increased risks for suicide.

The challenge in relying on demographic patterns of "at-risk" groups involves two limitation-it tells us who is at risk but not why (Rutter & Soucar, 2002) and it does not explain the recent jump in suicide rates among previously low-risk groups, such as ethnic minorities (Gutierrez et al., 2003). During the past decade, suicides among African-American and Latino youth have increased tenfold and fivefold, respectively (Canino & Roberts, 2001; Gould & Kramer, 2001) (Rutter & Estrada, Winter 2006, p. 89).

For example, suicide prevention for American Indian Youth usually must consider historical trauma, defined as "this disruption in family continuity, loss of land, and loss of languages." LaFromboise continues: "This type of trauma is passed from generation to generation through extended family-child interactions (Struthers & Lowe, 2003). According to Yellow Horse Brave Heart and DeBruyn (1998), symptoms of historical trauma include poor emotional tolerance, psychic numbing, substance abuse, depression, and identification with death. Within the framework of trauma, one would predict higher levels of suicidal behavior within a population that experiences such grief" (LaFromboise, 2006, p. 16).

The stress of acculturation stress adds a heavier load and involve "ethnicity-related issues such as historical distrust, prejudice, stereotype threat, and social conformity pressures (Beals et al., 2002). Acculturation stress can result in emotions and behaviors such as depression, anxiety, feelings of marginality and alienation, psychosomatic symptoms, and identity confusion. Turner and Lloyd (2003) assert that lifetime cumulative exposure to both distant and recent adversity predicts the risk of subsequent drug dependence, which is shown to be one of the risk factors for youth suicide. The litany of risk factors associated with suicidal ideation further includes: loss of cultural supports, hopelessness, psychological symptomatology (sic), weak cultural identity, strained interpersonal communication, limited social support, perceived discrimination, and school difficulties (Yoder, at al., 2006, as cited in LaFromboise, 2006, p. 17). This author points out that each tribe has its own uniqueness in addressing these various issues.

In a study of suicide prevention for Taiwanese college students, the researchers observed some unique factors that may be cultural.

The authors observed a positive linear trend between increased suicidal tendency and levels of neuroticism, harm avoidance, novelty seeking, psychopathology, and parenting styles of low affection, overprotection, and authoritarian controlling. Use of tobacco and alcohol and impaired family adaptation and cohesion were associated with high and moderate suicidal risks. Conclusions: Personality, psychopathology, substance use, and familial factors are important correlates of suicidal risks among college students in Taiwan (Gau, et al., 2008, p. 135).

The Culture of Online Sharing

Some online factors seem to encourage the sharing of some personal information online. There are some online disinhibition effects to share information (Joinson, 1998, 2001a, 2001b; Suler, 2004b) because of the lack of eye contact and sense of invisibility (Barak, 2007, p. 972). "Disclosing personal, intimate information seems to be related to the fact that many people, when communicating online, tend to expose concealed matters about their 'inner self' or 'true self' (McKenna & Seidman, 2005, as cited in Barak, 2007, pp. 972 – 973).

SITE DESIGN

The funded grant offers some indicators of the early premises for the site. Web-based communications technologies are a central part of college students' lives and may be tapped for a supportive virtual environment of co-learners. English, as the language of global commerce, culture and

Figure 1. A Screenshot of the Live University Life Café Site

science, would be used as a main communications method.

Initial Premises

The site would encourage professional help-seeking in the face of emotional distress, and it would not be therapeutic or offer "back-channel" communications for those who may be suicidal. The issues of emotional distress would be treated in a way so as to reduce stigma and to encourage more discussions. The information included would be based on timely research information, and it would be future-proofed as much as possible for longevity. The most timely and time-sensitive information would be campus and neighborhood events, which would tie students closer to the activities around them and discourage self-isolating.

The site would be designed around the user experience. At the heart of the site would be an interactive blog that students, staff and faculty may post to. The site would include podcasting,

music streaming and other "cool" features. The target audiences would mostly be Kansas State University students, but there would be support and education also for faculty and staff, and the general college student public through the public layer. The contents would clearly have to apply to a broad audience. The servers used would have to be robust to potentially support some 23,000 students as well as a large potential public.

In general, the site would be designed around the idea of a café, as an end destination. This is a recognizable metaphor for most college students. The look-and-feel of the site could surround this and would avoid the colors of the university to be branded in a broader way. While the URL for the site took some work (checking with the USPTO and Network Solutions; conducing general Web searches), that was also ultimately designed to be more general (http://www.universitylifecafe. org). It was hoped that the logo design and the overall vibe of the site would be edgy, young and engaging. Avoiding a commercial URL designation represented the non-profit aspect of the site.

The limits on .edu URLs meant that the best other option would be an .org.

It was clear early on that a robust and legally-sound Terms of Service would have to be created to protect the university. The site and its contents would also have to be accessible, so as to abide by federal 508 guidelines. This would include transcribing audio and video for textual versions, and adding alt text to images. This would have implications for the building of the site to allow annotations.

The site would have to evolve over time based on aggregated information from datamining, survey feedback, informal information channels and observations of the WWW's evolution. The high-value information will be identified and bolstered per the findings that site users needs' may be fulfilled by 20% of the high-value content (Chou, 2002, p. 25).

There would be plenty of partnering with campus entities. There would also be some social marketing using free coffee and advertising sleeves with messages about the site. A soft launch would be used to encourage learner usage, and a hard launch would follow later once the site had sufficient seeding of contents and an emergent ethos.

Student Feedback

Initial work on the site began with a two-day retreat in Fall 2007, of an advisory committee, which included plenty of students representing a diverse cross-section of the campus, faculty and staff. The meetings were videotaped, and transcriptions were made of the commentary. The students analyzed anti-suicide websites; they brainstormed ways to use Web technologies for community, self-help, and "hanging out."

The following figure, "Assumptions of the University Life Café Approach," depicts the strategies of empowering students to cope with a high-pressured life and their awareness of suicide risks (for themselves and their peers) are central

pieces to this site build. The need for a warm and mutually supportive virtual community is another linchpin to the site.

Site Versioning

Part of the site would be public and supportive of all college students, but part would be privately accessible for those with active electronic identifications (eID) to show their ties to the university. The need for user privacy along with authentication meant the need to build some designed anonymity on the site but still allow back-end tracking of users. Multiple accounts would not be possible because of the risks of abuse of the site, but one eID could be used to create one virtual persona that is anonymous. There would also have to be programming to allow an expeditious warning if someone posted information that might indicate an imminent risk of harm.

Synchronous Events

The advisory committee discussed the possible use of a "life pledge" contract for life that people could download and sign. There was discussion of having live synchronous events with well known speakers—possibly as a far-off functionality (created by integrated third-party software).

Tagging of Contents by Meaning and Form

A list of tags related to mental health would be a way to allow people to access resources from anywhere on the site. Another filter would allow access to multimedia types, for those who may want to experience the site through the prism of particular multimedia.

Self-Assessment Heuristics

Users of the site may experience self administered heuristics based on existing assessments created by

Figure 2. Assumptions of the University Life Café Approach (Hai-Jew, 2008)

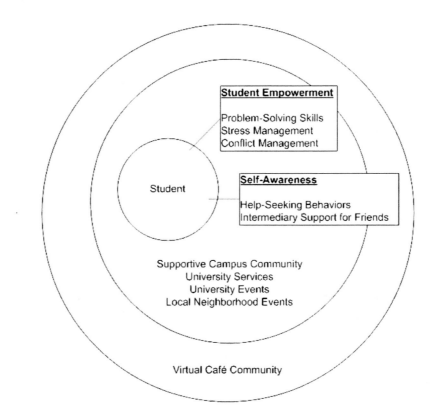

the K-State Counseling Services. These involved the College Learning Effectiveness Inventory, the Health Behavior Assessments, and the K-State Problem Identification Scale. These assessments are hosted on a separate secure server, and the results of the assessments are not linked to an individual per se. Only the users themselves will get the information from their assessments.

Back-End Technology

Given the needs of the Counseling Services, the site is hosted on campus for easier control, build and access in case of potential emergencies or need for access by law enforcement. More detailed back-end reporting and datamining also enhance the management of the site. The incoming webmasters for the site need a simple interface to maintain the materials. Also, if the contents are to

be archived, having in-house servers is important. For all these reasons, the back-end build required plenty of attention.

Creating Podcasts

To protect learner identities, it was decided that the video podcasts would be based on real-world challenges but would feature student actors and dramatizations vs. interviews. Initial scripts addressed scenarios of a military veteran returning stateside to return to school but still suffering residual effects of post-traumatic stress disorder (PTSD). Another deals with the problem-solving through the stresses of a higher education environment, maintaining a busy work life, resolving conflict with a colleague, getting along with roommates, managing a social life, developing a social support system, dealing with depression, supporting a suicidal friend, and studying effectively.

A range of ideas informed the creation of the guiding principles:

- Show a range of different student types. Avoid stereotyping.
- Keep this as real-world as possible in terms of real issues.
- Avoid "dating" the contents with particular recent events. Try to make this content last over time.
- Keep consistent voices within the scenario depicted in the videos.
- Offer helpful tips inside the body of the scripts.
- These podcasts should be about 3-5 minutes maximum.
- Show some optimism.
- Keep these within the guidelines of the University Life Café values and site.
- The actors may "improv" their acting based on their instincts and the setting.

Appendix A addresses some of the planning that has gone into the creation of some early videos and podcasts for this site.

Designing Content Streams

Plenty of work was put into cultivating faculty and others to support the building of contents for the site. Not only was a drama professor brought in to work with students for videotaping scenarios, but there were plans for various theme-based contests to solicit art, photos, essays, articles, stories, videos, and music, related to celebrating life. Technologically, a form was designed for easier submittal of contents through the site, and a group email was created with the alias of univlifecafe@k-state.edu to receive information and digital contents.

Terms of Service

The drafted terms of service offered the vision of the site and then a range of legal understandings. The age requirement for the site would have to be 18, the age of legal consent. Then, a range of factors were addressed: liability waivers, indemnification of the university from any claim based on submitted contents, the non-endorsement of linked sites, copyright releases in participating on the site, and a maiming / death clause. The Terms address the assumptions of participation on the site, including civility and care of others, maintaining authentic accounts, posting responsible messages, avoiding graffiti and defacement of the site, and the encouragement of professional help-seeking for those at risk of suicide. There were technology clauses warning against phishing schemes. Privacy rules were addressed with the discouragement of people from sharing private information. The university disclaimed any expectations for the maintenance of submitted information. It reserved the right to disallow participation based on any breakage of policies. Modifications (or discontinuance) to the service could be made at any time and without prior warning. Site heuristics are information only and not used for diagnosis, assessment, or advisement. Trademarks used do not suggest any dilution and may not be legally used.

Outsourcing the Build on Campus

The development of the navigational structure, the technological back-end, and some simple artificial intelligence functionalities would be "outsourced" to the Office of Mediated Education, an office that creates middleware. The site's graphic design would also be sent to them. A six-month (after launch) review would also be folded into the contract, for iterating the site based on user information.

Figure 3. Site Features in the Build

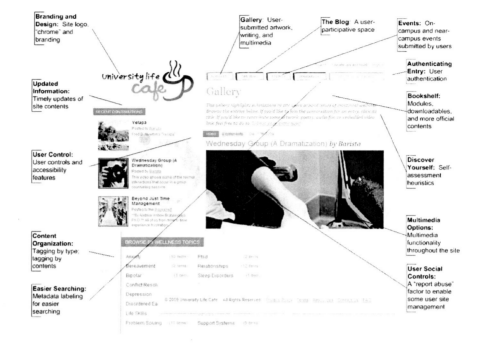

Maintenance Equipment Needs

The technologies needed to maintain the site: digital camcorders, tripods, digital cameras, memory cards, DV tapes, digital voice recorders, multimedia computers, external hard drives; software for editing photo imagery, video editing, the creation of interactive modules, and screen captures; and freeware programs for audio editing, converting DVDs to mp4s, screen capture software, and Web-based programs that allow for the sending of massive files. An upgrading cycle was attached to this list.

The phases from Ideation to Action

The research literature describes phases from suicide ideation to action. "Thoughts of killing oneself tend to occur fleetingly during times of distress; over time, suicidal ideation may become more persistent and expand to include thoughts about what it would be like to commit suicide and

how one would do so. As suicidal ideation progresses through increasingly significant identifiers (suicidal threat, suicidal gesture, suicide attempt, and completed suicide), students' behavior can range simply from speaking or acting in a way that is symbolic of suicide to creating and acting on a suicide plan. The degree to which a person experiences suicidal ideation or behavior is often categorized in levels of suicidal lethality. These range from no predictable risk of suicide now, to high risk of suicide now, to completed suicide" (Paladino & Minton, 2008, p. 644). Successful interventions to prevent suicide should interrupt this cycle.

The University Life Café may be seen as a place for initial supports for those who may be experiencing distress. In a sense, it exists between the two extremes of direct online psychotherapy with a client and a mental health professional at one extreme and that of self-help groups online (with "bulletin boards, chat rooms, news and discussion groups operated within health-related web pages, listservs…" (Gaggioli, Gorini & Riva, 2007, pp. 131 – 137) on the other. There is no implied therapeutic or maintenance use.

FOUR MODULAR BUILDS

The grant's Goal 2 addresses the creation of some learning modules "to increase awareness of protective factors that aid suicide prevention."

Four modules were created to support the more semi-formal learning on the site. These involve problem-solving, conflict resolution, developing a support system, and stress management. These would include some automated interactivity, multimedia, and campus videos and images. The contents would be fresh and not overlap any direct course materials. Each would be designed using SoftChalk™ Lesson Builder, so people would not have to jump outside the module and to various parts of the site to access the whole learning. The module may be experienced forwards or backwards. The pacing is determined by the student.

The modules consist of researched information about a range of protective features, with live links out to various resources. There are automated assessments: pretests, self-tests, and a post-test. Diagrams are created to illustrate particular concepts. Slideshows focus on unique topics within the larger modular topic. Some podcasts, acted out by on-campus acting students, show dramatizations of various "from-life" situations. A page of "Thrive" tips give suggestions on the topic by culling lessons and adding in images. Flashcards are made of related terms. The last screen of each module involves contact information to the university's counseling center and also a 24/7 access to The National Science Prevention Hotline and its toll free number, along with the respective URLs of the sites.

In addition to the formal modules, a diverse range of digital images were uploaded to the gallery for perusal. These included digital artworks, campus photos, student photos (with signed releases), nature photos, and other collections that people wanted to share. Some of these photos included ruminations on the meaning of life and the beauty and value of living in the world.

The back end offers a variety of functionalities and controls for the webmasters. Various types of contents may be uploaded. Featured items may be selected to showcase on the front page. Accounts of users may be approved or cancelled. Events may be updated for user value. Related videos may be embedded into the site. Contests may be launched for various types of contents and ideas. Core navigational structures may also be changed with the addition of new site features. In cases of

Figure 4. Some Intervention Phases with Suicide Prevention (Hai-Jew, 2008)

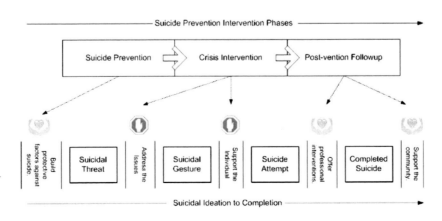

Figure 5. The Modular Structure (Hai-Jew, 2008)

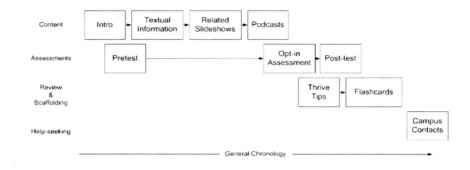

Figure 6. Diverse Imagery

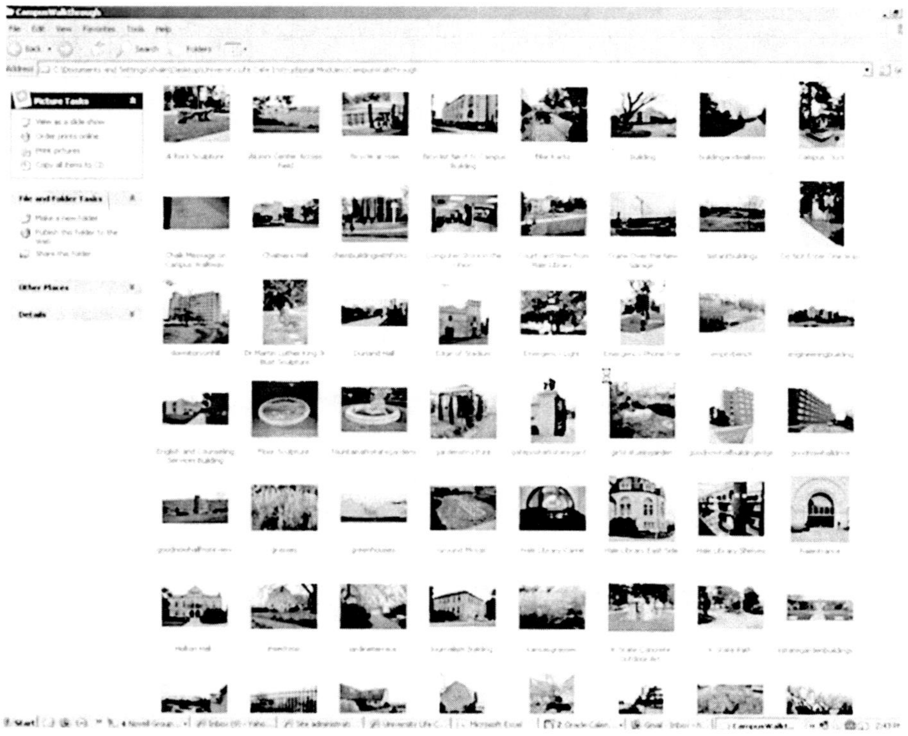

emergencies, the webmasters may also access the actual electronic identifications of those who may have posted messages that raise concern.

A training text was created with the site's policies, the back-end functions, the branding and design methodology, and the naming protocols of the digital files in order to help future webmasters support the site.

LIVE LAUNCHING AND ASSESSMENT

Launching

The team went with a soft launch initially (in February 2009) to make sure that there was sufficient contents to "seed" the site. Shortly thereafter, they

Figure 7. Screen Shot of the Webmaster Back End to the Site

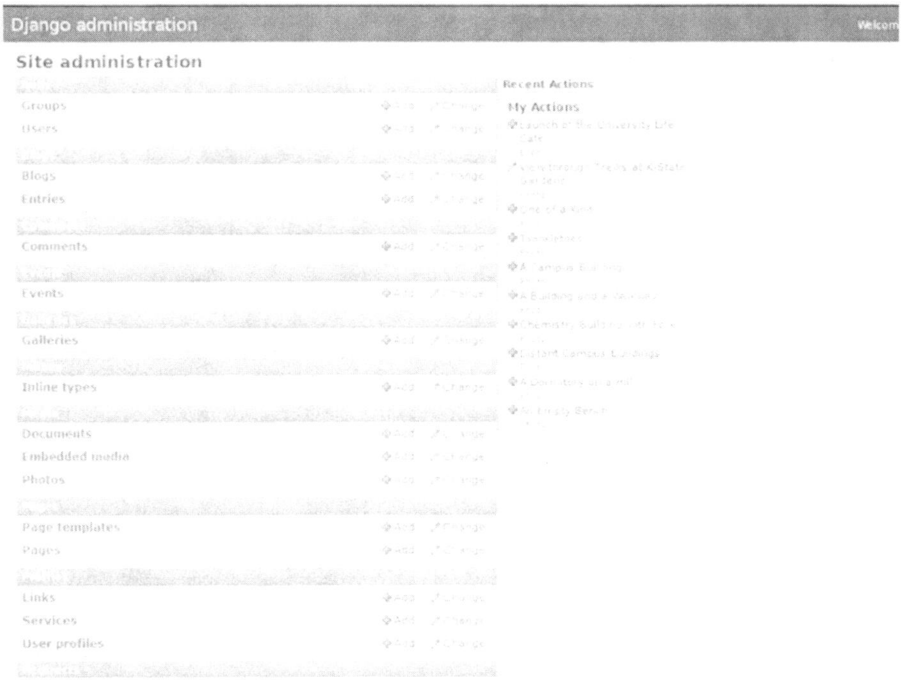

planned more of a media blitz on the WWW, in social networking sites, in immersive 3D social sites, and in the blogosphere. On a parallel track, there were presentations in professional conferences and postings to professional electronic mailing lists. The national publicity in a sense serves a consciousness-raising purpose on a larger stage and a rhetorical role in examining what benefits may emerge from socio-technical systems in the prevention of suicide.

Designing a Site Assessment

Shortly after the site's launch, there were plans for assessing the site for efficacy. This would involve user feedback surveys, user feedback via the site, datamining on the back end (using Google Analytics), and the collection of subject matter expert (SME) feedback. There would be assessments of both the information learning and the applied far transference learning. The channels for information would come from both formal and informal ones. Some early assessment design questions follow.

Datamining

- What parts of the site are most visited?
- What resources are downloaded most commonly?
- What sorts of textual feedback do users post (in the aggregate)?

User Experience

- How do users perceive the site? Its usability? Its informativeness? Its aesthetic design? Its main objective?
- What are cultural nuances in the user experience? (What are some strategies to make the site more international and culturally neutral?)

Near- and Far- Transfer Learning

- How effective is the factual learning?
- How likely is it for a site user to contact professionals for help-seeking?
- How likely is it for site users to support their friends or acquaintances who may be depressed?

The site's revision cycle is scheduled to happen six months after the launch, which occurred in February 2009. This redesign will focus on new ways to package digital contents for easier site use and showcasing of multimedia-based information, such as around issues of student financial health, post-traumatic stress disorder (PTSD), new student orientation, and stress management. The idea then is to evolve the site based on findings to make it more apropos to the evolving situations for its many users. Initial analysis of the site's usage in the first six months found visitors from over 60 countries around the world.

Near-future endeavors involve integrating this site with student retention endeavors on campus. There are also collaborative efforts to better serve the military community from nearby Fort Riley with information and tailored digital contents.

THE FUTURE

The future of the University Life Café site will depend on how it is received in both virtual and real spaces. As a user-driven site, it will depend on participation, digital information through-put, and social interactivity to work. Its success will also depend on how it is maintained and made receptive to and supportive of users. Ultimately, this resource must support users at their point of need, with the university intervening where necessary to support students in crisis. The university bureaucracy will have to protect this resource, and the site originators will have to find more grant funds to add continuing value.

ACKNOWLEDGMENT

Thanks to Dr. Barbara Pearson, project principal investigator, for her guidance and support. Thanks to Joshua Works, Andrea Mendoza, Brent Anders, and Garrett Pennington, all from the Office of Mediated Education at K-State, for their work designing the site's back end. Peter Paukstelis, campus legal counsel, gave relevant legal and practical advice to the team. Dr. Fred B. Newton served as senior advisor to the project. The advisory group, particularly the students, was critical in evolving this project. Thanks to all the contributors to the site and all current and future participants as well. My appreciation to R. Max.

REFERENCES

Ashford, E. (2005). The fight over screening students to prevent suicide. *Ed Digest, 71*(1), 52-56. Retrieved February 6, 2009, from http://www.eddigest.com

Barak, A. (2007). Emotional support and suicide prevention through the Internet: A field project report. *Computers in Human Behavior, 23*, 971–984. doi:10.1016/j.chb.2005.08.001

Bostic, J. Q., Rustuccia, C., & Schlozman, S. C. (2001). *The shrink in the classroom: The suicidal student.* Alexandria, VA: Association for Supervision and Curriculum Development.

Boyle, M., & Greenberg, S. (2005). The language of privacy: Learning from video media space analysis and design. *ACM Transactions on Computer-Human Interaction, 12*(2), 351. doi:10.1145/1067860.1067868

Chou, E. (2002). Redesigning a large and complex website: How to begin, and a method for success. In *Proceedings of the SIGUCCS '02,* Providence, RI (pp. 22-28). New York: ACM.

Fisher, D. (2006). Helping teenagers get through the worst: SUICIDE. *Education Digest, 72*(2), 9–13.

Friedman, E. (2008, November 21). Florida teen live-streams his suicide online. *ABC News.* Retrieved February 6, 2009, from http://abcnews.go.com/Technology/MindMoodNews/story?id=6306126&page=1

Gaggioli, A., Gorini, A., & Riva, G. (2007). *Prospects for the use of multiplayer online games in psychological rehabilitation.* Washington, DC: IEEE.

Gau, S. S.-F., Chen, Y.-Y., Tsai, F.-J., Lee, M.-B., Chiu, Y.-N., Soong, W.-T., & Hwu, H.-G. (2008). Risk factors for suicide in Taiwanese college students. *Journal of American College Health, 57*(2), 135–142. doi:10.3200/JACH.57.2.135-142

George, P. (2002). Student suicide and 9/11. *Education Digest, 77*(9), 12–15.

Gibbons, M. M., & Studer, J. R. (2008). Suicide awareness training for faculty and staff: A training model for school counselors. *Professional School Counseling, 11*(4), 272–276.

Gillman, J. L., Kim, H. S., Alder, S. C., & Durrant, L. H. (2006). Assessing the risk factors for suicidal thoughts at a nontraditional commuter school. *Journal of American College Health, 55*(1), 17–26. doi:10.3200/JACH.55.1.17-26

Gustafson, D. H., Greist, J. H., Stauss, F. F., Erdman, H., & Laughren, T. (1977). A probabilistic system for identifying suicide attemptors. *Computers and Biomedical Research, an International Journal, 10,* 83–89. doi:10.1016/0010-4809(77)90026-X

Haas, A., Koestner, B., Rosenberg, J., Moore, D., Garlow, S. J., & Sedway, J. (2008). An interactive Web-based method of outreach to college students at risk for suicide. *Journal of American College Health, 57*(1), 15–22. doi:10.3200/JACH.57.1.15-22

Helsel, D. C. (2001). Does your school track the suicidal student? *Clearing House (Menasha, Wis.), 75*(2), 2–95.

Hoover, E. (2006). Students: 'Giving them the help that they need': The author of a new book on student suicide says colleges need to think about a lot more than liability. *The Chronicle of Higher Education, •••,* A39–A41.

King, K. A. (2001). Developing a comprehensive school suicide prevention program. *The Journal of School Health, 71*(4), 132–137.

King, K. A. (2001). Tri-level suicide prevention covers it all. *Journal of School Health. Education Digest, 67*(1), 55–61.

Kurzweil, R. (2001). Promise and peril—the deeply intertwined poles of 21st century technology. *Communications of the ACM, 44*(3), 88–91. doi:10.1145/365181.365215

LaFromboise, T. (2006). American Indian youth suicide prevention. *Prevention Researcher, 13*(3), 16–18.

Levinsky, A. (2001). Are teen suicide and homicide related? *Education Digest, 66*(8), 49–53.

Milsom, A. (2002). Suicide prevention in schools: Court cases and implications for principals. *NASSP Bulletin, 86*(730), 24–33. doi:10.1177/019263650208663004

Newton, F. (2008). *Interview.*

Paladino, D., & Minton, C. A. B. (2008). Comprehensive college student suicide assessment: Application of the BASIC ID. *Journal of American College Health*, *56*(6), 643–650. doi:10.3200/JACH.56.6.643-650

Police foil teen's suspected Web suicide. (2008, December 2). Retrieved December 2, 2008, from http://www.cbsnews.com/stories/2008/12/02/national/main4642139.shtml?tag=topHome;topStories

Risk and Protective Factors. (2008). *Ulifeline*. Retrieved November 14, 2008, from http://www.ulifeline.org/main/page/55/RiskandProtective-Factors

Russell, S. T., & Marks, S. R. (2006). Preventing suicide risk among sexual minority youth. *Prevention Researcher*, *13*(3), 19–20.

Rutter, P. A., & Behrendt, A. E. (2004). Adolescent suicide risk: Four psychosocial factors. *Adolescence*, *39*(154), 295–302.

Rutter, P. A., & Estrada, D. (2006). Suicide risk and protective factors: Are there differences among young? *Guidance and Counseling*, *21*(2), 89–96.

Schroeder, K. (2006). Preventing suicide. *Education News in Brief: The Education Digest*, *71*(9), 49–50.

Schwartz, A. J. (2006a). College student suicide in the United States: 1990 – 1991 through 2003 – 2004. *Journal of American College Health*, *54*(6), 341–352. doi:10.3200/JACH.54.6.341-352

Schwartz, A. J. (2006b). Four eras of study of college student suicide in the United States: 1920 -2004. *Journal of American College Health*, *54*(6), 353–366. doi:10.3200/JACH.54.6.353-366

Suicide statistics. (2009). Retrieved February 6, 2009, from http://www.suicide.org/suicide-statistics.html

Wang, Y. D., Phillips-Wren, G., & Forgionne, G. (2005). E-delivery of personalised healthcare information to intermediaries for suicide prevention. *International Journal of Electronic Healthcare*, *1*(4), 396–412. doi:10.1504/IJEH.2005.006687

Willenz, P. (2008). *Suicidal thoughts among college students more common than expected*. Retrieved February 6, 2009, from http://www.apa.org/releases/suicideC08.html

Zirkel, P. A. (2006a). Student suicide and school liability. *Principal Leadership*, *6*(6), 49–53.

Zirkel, P. A. (2006b). Student suicide: An update. [from http://www.naesp.org]. *Principal*, *85*(5), 10–11. Retrieved February 6, 2009.

KEY TERMS AND DEFINITIONS

Anonymity (n): The state of being unrecognized because of a lack of personal identifiers .

Collective intelligence (n): The sharing of the combined wisdom of individuals in a group.

Confidential (adj): Not for public release or use, private, secret

Depression (n): Prolonged sadness or dejection.

Disinhibition (n): The lowering of inhibitions or restraints.

Liability (n): The state of being legally responsible.

Multimedia (n): Digital sound and video and other types of multiple media.

Protective factors (n): Aspects of skills and awarenesses that may defend against self-harm.

Substance abuse (n): Alcohol or drug addiction, the misuse or (over)consumption of alcohol or drugs

Suicidal ideation (n): The thinking of possibly committing suicide.

Suicidology (n): The study of suicide (its causes and prevention).

ENDNOTE

This chapter refers to work done under a Garrett Lee Smith Campus Suicide Prevention Grant under the administration of Substance Abuse and Mental Health Services Administration (SAMHSA), Grant #7H795M057871-02. The team would like to express their gratitude for this federal support.

APPENDIX A

DRAMATIC EDUCATIONAL FILM MAKING FOR THE UNIVERSITY LIFE CAFÉ WEBSITE

By Brent A. Anders, Kansas State University, USA

The Challenge

Sometimes video can be much more than simple moving pictures; sometimes, it can save a life. This is the main idea we are using to guide our video projects for use with the University Life Café website. The website is unique in that it is educational but is not limiting its presentation of educational content to the established dogma of classroom lectures or "talking head" videos. It is boldly looking at many ways in which it can get its many "wellness" messages across. The use of, or more correctly put, the dramatic use of video is one of the powerful choices they are going with. Videos are being written by current students as well as former students and then produced and directed into real miniature films. These films are using multiple locations, sets, music, sound effects, special effects, scripts, and lights. They have producers, directors, sound engineers and aspiring actors all trying to make it as good and as real as possible. Why so much effort? Because it is important and might just save someone.

At the time of this writing two videos have been produced to address two very important University Life Café "wellness" issues. The first is that of a soldier who has recently left the military and is now starting college, he is struggling with adjusting to his new surroundings as well as with all of the things he went through while serving. The film seeks to show incoming student soldiers that many of the problems they may be going through are normal and there are many free ways of dealing with them. The second video deals with group counseling. The video tries to show viewers that attending group counseling is quite beneficial and isn't that big of a deal. It is a supportive way to seek advice and help dealing with many issues that a lot of people go through. The film is designed to help reduce some of the stigma that is sometimes associated with group counseling or counseling in general.

Figure 8.

The Process

The creation process for the finished videos as well as future videos is one of meticulousness and inclusiveness based off of real world problems that students are actually struggling with. As an example, a former student wrote the student soldier film entitled "SUNSHINE ON THE Spiral," and various other current students made creative contributions. All the actors were current students with the actual video taping being done by a fulltime videographer with a student assistant. As for meticulousness, a heartfelt effort was made to take everything into consideration to maximize the power of the film. Music, lighting, colors, pace, location, even clothing and body posture were thought of so as to best present the film and the education within. Research was done on current wellness trends, educational film techniques, social network topics, Nielsen ratings, posttraumatic stress disorder, and various counseling techniques.

Figure 9.

Figure 10.

Figure 11.

The Difficulties

A stressful, yet interesting aspect of filming these "wellness" videos deals with trying to be current without being too trendy as well as working with student actors with very limited schedules. Special care was taken with the scripts to try and make conversations sound real, free flowing and not stiff and robotic. At the same time it was important to not date the film with too many specifics thereby limiting the videos usage. "SUNSHINE ON THE Spiral" can be viewed as a soldier returning from Iraq, Afghanistan, Bosnia or anywhere else or simply extremely hard training during his enlistment. Specifics were kept to a minimum so that soldier student viewers could more easily place themselves in the film. The student actors did a great job in giving of themselves and giving some very good performances but filming was very difficult. With students preparing for exams and working, filming that would normally take many hours over several days had to be done in extremely short filming sessions. "Guerrilla Filmmaking," is the term we came up with to describe some of the extreme techniques we used to maximize our time and effort in making the best "wellness" videos we could to educate, help and possibly even save others.

A third video endeavor at press time involves Suzy's Strategies, a webisode series about a student's strategies to stay focused on her goals as a student. This series humanizes the struggles of adjusting to student life with a large dose of humor.

Chapter 2
3D Design and Collaboration in Massively Multi-User Virtual Environments (MUVEs)

Steven Warburton
King's College London, UK

Margarita Pérez García
MENON Network EEIG, Belgium

EXECUTIVE SUMMARY

This chapter describes an exploratory study in the use of the virtual world Second Life as an innovative space for situating collaborative activity in the field of art and design. The authors identify eight key affordances of Second Life for learning and teaching and elaborate the educational approach based on group orientated design briefs, carried out over a three-week period by the students. The results of the study reveal both the negative and positive aspects of using Second Life as an educational space. These range from access difficulties and the steep learning curve in becoming familiar with the technology, to the expansive social and creative freedoms that the world allows. The conclusions draw together an analysis of the emerging themes and present a set of ten good practices for developing and running successful collaborative activities inside virtual worlds.

BACKGROUND

The following case describes a set of outcomes from the OpenHabitat[1] project, a study exploring the experiences of Art and Design students and tutors engaged in collaborative learning and teaching activities within the Multi-User Virtual Environment

(MUVE) Second Life[2]. OpenHabitat represents a 15-month JISC[3] funded project and collaborative partnership between three UK based institutions: University of Oxford, Leeds Metropolitan University and King's College London. The project has focussed on the extraction of good practices and meaningful design approaches for collaborative and dialogic teaching activities in 3D virtual spaces. The authors of this paper are part of the OpenHabitat

DOI: 10.4018/978-1-60566-878-9.ch002

project team, responsible for the research design and data analysis.

VIRTUAL WORLD LANDSCAPE

Virtual worlds such as Second Life (SL) are not a new phenomenon. Their roots can be traced back to the early days of MMOs (Massively Multi-player Online games) and the online role-playing games known as multi-user dungeons (MUDs) (Ludlow and Wallace 2007). The difficulty in defining virtual worlds reflects their continuous rapid evolvement, from text-based systems through to the graphically rich and multi-layered 3D worlds we find today. One of the most enduring definitions comes from Schroeder (1996, 2008) who has argued that virtual environments and virtual reality technologies can be described as:

"A computer-generated display that allows or compels the user (or users) to have a sense of being present in an environment other than the one they are actually in, and to interact with that environment" (Schroeder 1996: 25)

Here Schroeder identifies immersion as one of the key aspects of any virtual space, in other words, creating the sensation of the user actually 'being there'.

Within the relatively short time-span since their emergence, the number of Virtual Worlds (VWs) now in production or in the marketplace has grown rapidly, reaching upwards of ninety separate instances that cater for a variety of tastes and age groups (KZero Research 2008). From an educational perspective it is valuable to categorise these virtual environments to help make sense of their purpose and potential value. One way of doing this is to consider VWs as falling under one of four possible categorisations: Flexible Narrative (e.g. World of Warcraft); Social World (e.g. SL); Simulation (e.g. Google Earth); and 3D Workspace (e.g. Project Wonderland) (Warburton 2009).

These different types of VW have all received attention from educators. This encompasses the serious games movement through to more generalist educational approaches that have found value in more open ended, narrative free spaces that are the hallmarks of social worlds like SL.

VIRTUAL WORLDS FOR LEARNING

The recent Eduserv Virtual Worlds Watch (Kirriemuir 2008), a survey that casts its eye over educational activity in SL across UK institutions, reports that:

"Taking into account institutions who haven't responded but where there is reasonable evidence of Second Life activity, and institutions who are developing in SL but not in a public way, then a figure of roughly three quarters of UK universities are estimated to be actively developing or using Second Life" (Kirriemuir 2008, p.58)

The ongoing reports from Eduserv reveal a growing appetite for situating learning and teaching activities within immersive 3D spaces. It is also clear from comparisons of educational activity across a range of VWs that in terms of educator interest, the use of SL continues to dominate the landscape. From access and technical perspectives, the main attractions for using SL as an immersive educational platform can be summarised as follows:

- Basic SL accounts are free;
- SL is a hosted service and the mid-weight client download works across multiple operating systems;
- The system is relatively mature, having been launched in 2003;
- In-world tools for building, scripting and streaming media are sophisticated when compared to many of the other current offerings;

- SL boasts one of the largest support communities which includes the SLED (*Second Life* Educators) mailing list with over 6000 educators subscribed globally;
- Object ownership permissions mean that content authors retain intellectual property rights over their creations;
- Virtual space, or land, can be rented or bought at relatively low cost and provide a stable setting for controlling, building and creating a virtual educational environment.

SL also offers a set of educational possibilities that stem directly from the affordances (*after* Norman's 2002 definition of the term) of working within an immersive 3D space and these are described below.

SECOND LIFE AFFORDANCES FOR EDUCATION

SL exists as a non-narrative social space with no explicit goals or aims, unless users themselves impress these upon the environment. Within this open social space, SL offers a sophisticated set of tools for identity play, content creation, manipulation of objects, customisation of space and topography, and choice of communication modality. It is also driven by a tangible economy that underpins a business culture based on the sale of virtual goods and services. Within the scope of education eight key affordances can be identified that lend themselves to a number of learning and teaching approaches, extended here from Warburton (2009):

1. **Immersion** in a 3D environment where the augmented sense of co-presence, through virtual embodiment in the form of an avatar and the extensive modes of communication impact on the affective, empathic and motivational aspects of the experience;

2. **Extended or rich social interaction** between individuals and communities, humans and objects and also intelligent interaction between artifacts;

3. **Community presence** that promotes a sense of belonging and purpose that coheres around groups, sub-cultures and geography;

4. Exposure to **authentic content** such as works of art, and access to **cultures** that reflect linguistic and cultural diversity at local and national scale;

5. Opportunities for individual and collective **identity and role play**;

6. **Content production tools** that allow the creation and ownership of objects within the environment and respect an individual's intellectual property rights;

7. **Visualisation and contextualisation** through the production and reproduction of normally inaccessible content including artifacts that may be historically lost, imaginary, futuristic, or impossible to see by the human eye;

8. **Simulation** of existing real world contexts that may be too costly or dangerous to produce in real-life with the advantages that some physical constraints can be overcome.

In concrete terms these have been exploited across a number of disciplines to create educational opportunities that could be described as unique to virtual worlds and have allowed the deployment of the learning approaches that include both formal and informal aspects such as: roleplay and performative learning; experiential learning; cooperative learning; and game-based learning. The Preview[4] project has used a problem based learning approach to address issues in clinical management (Savin Baden 2008). By taking advantage of the creative role-playing opportunities that SL affords the project has produced a number of collaborative problem-based scenarios for students to learn how to deal paramedic emergencies. While the Moose[5] project has adopted the building capabilities of SL

Figure 1. Examples of design-based activities inside SL from the Art and Design pilot

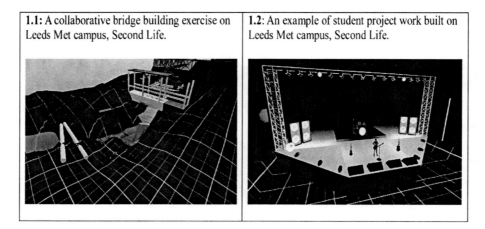

| **1.1**: A collaborative bridge building exercise on Leeds Met campus, Second Life. | **1.2**: An example of student project work built on Leeds Met campus, Second Life. |

to provide historical reconstructions of ancient artefacts that can be visualised and examined as part of classes in archaeology (Edirisingha et al. 2008). The opportunities for constructive collaborative activity are strengthened by the deep sense of co-presence combined with the in-world tool set and creative freedoms that SL affords. This is area that the OpenHabitat project has explicitly sought to investigate with its cohort of Art and Design students.

OPENHABITAT PROJECT APPROACH

The approach of the OpenHabitat project is based on the JISC User and Innovation Development Model[6] and comprises five main phases of activity: user needs analysis; instructional design; parallel pilots in the disciplines of Art and Design (Figure 1), and Philosophy; evaluation; and two final pilots using a redesigned instructional approach derived from analyses carried out during the evaluation phase. The value of collaborative work in learning is well documented (Johnson and Johnson 1990, 2003; McConnell 2000, 2006) and the conclusion from Johnson and Johnson's (1990) study of 323 cases indicated that cooperative methods resulted in better achievement than individualistic ones when measured across the four indices of: mastery

and retention of material; quality of reasoning strategies; process gains; and transference of learning. One of the key aims of the OpenHabitat project has been to examine collaboration in 3D worlds with Art and Design students and develop a set of validated guidelines for designing successful collaborative and dialogic teaching and learning activities in MUVEs.

SCOPE

This case study reports on the outputs from the design, piloting and evaluation stages of collaborative project work in the area of Art and Design and a post-pilot experts workshop. A total of eleven undergraduate Art and Design students at Leeds Metropolitan University were introduced to SL as a collaborative tool for project work in the area of 3D design. The students were led through an intensive three week programme of eleven face-2-face lab sessions and in-world meetings that spanned a period of three weeks in total (Table 1).

METHODOLOGY

To conduct and evaluate research inside SL demanded a multi-dimensional approach. To make sense of the data and triangulate the results a

Table 1. Activity schedule for the Art and Design pilot

SESSION	ACTIVITY
Week 1: *1 and 2*	Virtual world orientation using OpenSim[7]. These sessions used standalone instances of the reverse engineered and open source SL clone called OpenSim to expose students to the functionalities of SL but not the distractions of a populated world.
2, 3 and 4	SL induction and collaborative building activities (see Figure 1 above). A set of primer activities from avatar naming to preliminary building.
Week 2: *6 and 7*	Introduction to project brief and supported project work. Working individually or in teams to develop 2D design briefs through to their in-world 3D implementation with one-on-one support from the tutors (see Figure 2 below).
Week 3: *8, 9, 10 and 11*	Intermediate building skills classes. Continuation of work on the design briefs. Final review and evaluation of the student projects in SL.

range of quantitative and qualitative methods were deployed during the investigation.

- **Pre-pilot survey:** An online questionnaire targeted at the Art and Design students. This was aimed at uncovering their prior experience and competencies in 3D virtual worlds.
- **Pilot observation:** Participant observation during teaching sessions and recording of images and video.
- **Post pilot evaluation:** A focus group with students discussing their experiences during the activities of the pilot followed by semi-structured interviews with the course

tutors and the visual analysis of captured images and video.

- **Post pilot workshop:** An expert session based on a narrative inquiry methodology (Kohler Riessman, 2008). The group were brought together to uncover problem spaces in collaboration through storytelling and the identification of recurring issues via thematic analysis, leading towards the production of a set of guidelines for collaboration in MUVEs (see Figure 2). Stories were collected prior to the workshop using a template and were based on personal experiences in relation to the project and use of SL. The oral retelling of stories allowed for

Figure 2. Images captured during the experts storytelling workshop, attended by course tutors and the project team

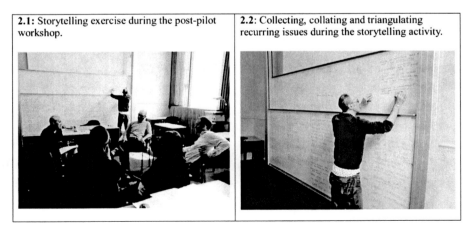

connections between narrated events to be established through the discussion, inquiry and commenting on the stories. Common problem spaces were legitimated using the rule of three i.e. where similar issues arose three or more times and these were noted as key problem areas. The workshop was used as a method for drawing together the analytic strands of the study and providing a set of guiding principles for collaborative design work in 3D worlds.

COLLABORATIVE ACTIVITIES IN 3D DESIGN

The students were asked to choose one design brief from a total of four possible projects and given two weeks to complete the activity. An example brief is shown in Table 2.

Evaluation of the student performance was carried out at the end of the three-week programme in form of a critical review, carried out in-world by the two course tutors. The best piece of student work was awarded a prize of L\$25,000[9] (Figure 3).

RESULTS

Pre-Pilot Questionnaire

The pre-pilot questionnaire revealed the students as a group of young digitally literate people who on average spend over 5 hours or more per week on the Internet:

- Eleven students in total all under 25 years old comprising six male and five female;
- Nine had played 3D computer games before but none had been inside SL;
- Nine spent more than 5 hours per week on the internet with three spending more than 10 hours per week on the internet;

- Eight used MSN, three used Facebook and three used Skype for communicating with friends;
- All students indicated they had a Facebook account with three occasionally using MySpace;
- Three indicated they spent more than 50% of their social life online.

Thematic Analysis of Student Focus Group and Tutor Interviews, Participant Observations and Visual Analysis of Captured Images

The transcripts from the interviews and notes from the participant observation were coded and analysed using a grounded theory approach (Glaser and Strauss 1967; Strauss and Corbin 1990). Extracts from the analysis, relating to the activities in both OpenSim and SL, are presented under the following six organising themes:

Theme 1: Technological and Related Barriers

1.1 The high demand on technical competences is a barrier to accessing virtual worlds
The majority of students found SL a complex environment to access, requiring a high level of technological ability to master effectively. For some it was a difficult environment to feel a sense of familiarity with. Among the main reasons given were:

- feelings of frustration during the first hours in-world because of the complex set of skills needed to perform basic navigation and movement. Searching for and finding objects was also reported as a difficult skill to develop. Some students commented that at the end of the pilot they still had problems moving their avatars with precision in the 3D space;

Table 2. One of the four possible design briefs given to the Art and Design students

Brief:	Design Brief Two
Type:	Collaborative
Title:	Reality Jam
Activity:	Reality Jam is a project that Cubist and Kisa are working on for the International Symposium on Electronic Art 2008. We are using the following quote from the isea2008 website to guide us. *"While the reality effects of photography had forced a re-evaluation of the conventions and concerns of painting as well as of perception in the mid 19th century, the realistic aspirations of recent visualization and experiential technologies (e.g. in animation, gaming, immersive environments, mixed/augmented reality) are forcing us to reconsider our registers of the 'real' in our media and our everyday lives. The confusing of the real and the virtual through seamless transitions and the perpetual obfuscation of the edges that demarcate them are increasingly the focus of scientific research as well as of creative works. The improvisational nature and interference potential of such 'reality jamming' - i.e. this pressing together of the real and virtual in a context where their distinctions are deliberately obscured - open further possibilities for research, scholarship and creative production. In this theme, we also seek to encourage artists and researchers to explore the ways in which the 'virtual' presences and experiences of folklore, religious beliefs, magical rituals and science and media-fiction interact with and counteract the lived experiences of the 'real'. Scholarly presentations, art works and research in the areas of virtual, mixed and augmented reality, not restricted to the technological platforms and equipment that enable such experiences, are especially encouraged."* see http://isea2008.org/page/30/ **Your task:** is to work together with one or more collaborators to produce artwork that follows the theme of the Reality Jam exhibition. You should use the dedicated collaboration area on LeedsMet Island[8] to develop this work.

Figure 3. Snapshots taken from inside SL during the various stages of the Art and Design pilot

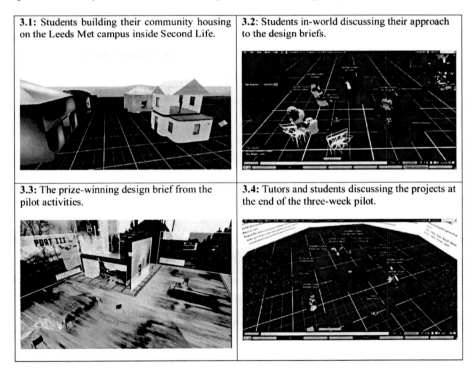

the majority of students stressed that the difficulty of mastering the interface, navigation and movement skills was compounded by the demands of social interaction and their inability to adequately answer solicitations via chat or IM . Communication and social interaction represent an added layer that is difficult to manage when students are not comfortable with basic skills.

It was apparent that very little of the student's past technological experience was useful in easing the above difficulties. There were few transferable skills identified by the students and none that derived from prior gaming experience either with video consoles or playing in PC games that required movement to be controlled by the keyboard. However, it was noted that over time, high levels of immersion and practice have a positive impact on the acquisition and development of basic competencies. Becoming accustomed to the client interface and being able to recall key-press shortcuts and procedures was seen as a key skill that was directly related to 'having a good memory'.

1.2 OpenSim offers a safe playground before entering Second Life
The design of the pilot explicitly used a standalone version of the OpenSim in advance of exposing students to SL to ease some of the difficulties observed by the tutors with previous student cohorts, related to the technical and social issues reported above. Within the closed world of OpenSim the students were able to concentrate on mastering the interface, particularly navigation and movement without being worried by the demands for social interaction. As the students commented:
   '[OpenSim] *eases you into it'*
   and is useful *'to find your feet in it'*
Some students felt on reflection that the OpenSim server provided a protective and safe space where:

'you can work in peace'.

OpenSim was regarded as a preparatory environment - a playground or training server - but in relation to SL the students were aware that this was not considered:

'the real thing'

To the students, SL appeared to be more personal, and:

'offers more opportunities for doing things when ones get bored'.

After the preparatory session in OpenSim, the students found that the multi-presence aspect of SL was more attractive as it offered possibilities for social interaction with other avatars and provided increased levels of sophistication in terms of avatar customisation:

'greater number of avatars, there are more people around'

'it is a more personal space because all the possible modification of avatars.

1.3 Physical togetherness can be a barrier to online computer-mediated cooperation
Some students articulated a tension between collaborating on a task in-world while physically located in the same room in real life. They described this as a confusion of communication channels when trying to cooperate in-world and be physically together in the real world (RL). Some students looked over their shoulders trying to find out what others were doing, but struggled to see their partner's screen. Others did not know if it was better to chat orally or to chat in-world with some conversations remaining mixed while others preferred to use in-world chat and IM exclusively. Chatting in RL was perceived as an annoyance as it forced them to turn their heads and move away from their screen and some complained at the fact that they could not see:

'... which buttons they're pressing when you're looking at what they're doing'.

Equally, some found it disrupting to use the in-world chat if they had the person they wanted to talk to handy:

'Just like we're working together, I thought, what's the point of like writing a message if we could just like talk to the person?'

A number of students concluded that they would have preferred to be at a distance to complete the tasks and remove the layer of confusion caused by real life co-presence.

Theme 2: Getting Social, but Progressively

2.1 The difference between real life and virtual spaces can be disruptive

The differences between real life and the virtual world created feelings of disorientation. SL provides a virtual space with many visual parallels to the real world and a strong sense of immersion through embodiment in an interactive 3D universe. But it also contrasts with RL in the diversity of communication modes, flexibility of representation and modelling of the environment. The students were surprised, and sometimes shocked by these commonalities and differences, and expressed feelings of confusion and surprise as they discovered SL. The extension of the self as an avatar, their 'strange' representation, and the concept of a parallel universe were a new experience to many students and remarked upon as 'weird' by some:

'Erm, to be honest I'm a bit freaked out by it and don't really know what to do.'

2.2 It is difficult to determine the purpose of communities and individuals in Second Life and to engage in wider social interaction

Despite the existence of several indications of the multi-user and community orientated nature of

SL, such as the number of active users, the world map and the local mini-map, the students found it hard to locate others and even if other people were in the immediate vicinity:

'they are not talking to you'

and *'they won't know you'.*

The students tried to interpret what people were doing in SL and how and why some people appeared to be simply:

'going round just like, having a laugh'.

The students highlighted appearance as an important factor in engaging with others, citing that at the beginning it was difficult to establish social interaction when ones' avatar did not look as if it belonged to the community:

'they've all got weird names, including us. Not like normal names, it seems',

'they have a "little world". Quite odd'.

Although some students were reserved, sceptical and even 'paranoid' about engaging in conversation with strangers, the level of engagement within the VW evolved over time and they recognised that older SL citizens had a level of engagement with the VW beyond theirs:

'they take the environment seriously [and] 'invest themselves in the creation of their avatars or alter egos'.

Theme 3: Building a Box is Easy, Designing a House is Difficult

3.1 Serious building in virtual environments is a complex and time-consuming process

Basic object creation and manipulation is a simple and rewarding activity. But the students found that it takes time and patience to develop good design skills and build something more serious such as their project brief. They also commented that things can get easily get damaged or destroyed. However, they felt that the sense of purpose imposed by a task that spanned several weeks could facilitate the learning experience. The students reacted to positively to idea of receiving guidance to accomplish more complicated tasks progressively over a period of time so they could respond by learning progressively and avoid becoming 'distracted'. The students found the tutors' desire to solicit creative acts from them at the beginning of their time in SL added a layer of complexity to the process of orientation around building tasks. They articulated a tension between the freedoms associated with being able to explore the world of SL and the sense of focus the design briefs brought to their in-world activity:

'And you just wander round, and everyone's got all this stuff. [...] You're not into this and that. You need money and it's just where do you get any stuff? And all this thing about land popping up on your land, and do this, do that [...]. I mean, that would be a barrier if you were doing this thing for real, and not building it. Plus the technical stuff if you were playing it really. The initial stages of what and how you're supposed to do it is next. I think I'd probably just walk around for a bit, and go, oh, this is shit. [...] But like you said, if you've got a bit of purpose with it, sort of three weeks to build something from when you get the brief, you can stick your mind to that then.'

Theme 4: A Virtual Space for Creative Acts

4.1 Virtual environments as social and creative spaces of freedom

The students saw SL as a space that offered freedom in terms of the almost unlimited possibilities for creation. They also recognised a social freedom that allowed the development and deployment of practices and behaviours beyond the social norms imposed by real life. Here they described behaviours not bound by conventions such as politeness, for example starting conversations with strangers or leaving a conversation by walking away and not feeling this was a rude gesture.

4.2 Virtual environments offer the possibility for bringing 2D design projects to realisation in 3D.

The students appreciated the fact that they could visualise their outputs. They stressed that among the advantages of using SL for 3D projects it was particularly good for developing design work at early stages. When compared to real life they could move from their initial ideas to mock-ups without the same level of associated cost and risk. For them it offered exciting possibilities for bringing 2D design projects to realisation in a 3D setting. They saw the opportunities for learning within the community, which included tutorials, in-world workshops and peer support in dedicated areas such as public sandboxes[10], as one of the advantages of using of SL as a workspace. It was noted that SL looked like a good tool to understand some real life concepts including for example the physical relation between object behaviours influenced by gravity.

4.3 Showcasing work has an impact on real life competences

Working in a public space like SL can serve as an inspirational arena for students where they can contact other creators and artists and be influenced by their work. Students recognised that showcasing their work in the SL had a positive impact on self-esteem. They were proud of their achievements and found it is rewarding that an unknown audience could see their work and they could receive feedback from this external audience – one that would normally be available to them within their institutional course setting:

'If you build something good, it can spread through the world like a virus, and everybody knows that it was you who built it and they can tell you they like it.'

Theme 5: Cooperation is not Easy

5.1 Virtual environments appear to be more suitable for individual work than for cooperative work

Students recalled feelings of isolation when in-world and a sense of being alone within their learning experience. They found themselves orientated towards individual work unless explicitly directed towards a collaborative task. Experience of co-building objects in SL demonstrated that the system of permissions that assigns individual ownership rights rendered a cooperative task more complicated than expected and it was easier to work individually as opposed to realising a common piece of work. Some tools like shared inventories and repositories of textures would have been highly appreciated, but as yet they do not exist. Collaborative building requires knowledge of and communication with others, and this was identified as a skill that went beyond the virtual world setting:

'following instructions seems easier than working with someone else at the same time'.

5.2 Second Life offers opportunities for informal learning

The students developed awareness that SL offered great potential to discover new things and meet people with whom they could interact informally and gain knowledge or help in further developing their skills.

5.3 Live demonstrations and mentoring are useful ways to help students succeed in achieving a task in Second Life

Some students confirmed that it was useful seeing video tutorials before doing the assigned tasks and that being able to count on the mentors support when needed was a factor of success:

'if I hadn't had Ian and Graham helping me, I probably wouldn't have done most of the stuff that I have done in that world'.

Though some students chose a different strategy and after being shown the basic features of the VW preferred to go ahead on their own, taking advantage of informal learning opportunities:

'building knowledge as you go alone'

'having to teach yourself solidly how to do it'

'you had to find your feet on it'.

Theme 6: What is the Added Value?

6.1 Transferability of knowledge and skills learned in Second Life

Students stressed that they lacked the experience to identify what knowledge and skills might be transferable: They felt that working within a VW was something:

'completely different from what they have done before and thus not immediately transferable'.

They did however appreciate that with a greater level of experience they might see the connection between the two spaces of real and virtual. The students viewed few of their technological skills acquired in other environments as transferable to working within virtual worlds.

DISCUSSION

The analysis of the project design work revealed many of the features of collaborative work that can be problematic. These stemmed from both the social and competency based nature of collaborative activity, as recognised by Irwin and Berge (2006), and the affordances of the environment in which collaboration was taking place. Designing for collaboration is not a straightforward process and as noted by McConnell (2000, 2006) requires attention to a range of factors to be successfully achieved. The added complexities of working within a virtual space with a steep overhead in terms of orientation and acclimatisation were also factors that distracted from the tasks in hand. The use of OpenSim as a pre-SL playground went some way to mitigating these problems but developing specific virtual world skills and competencies, an issue also identified by Minocha and Roberts (2008), remained present throughout the pilot.

The synchronous nature of the environment is an important element in any collaborative activity (Erlich and Chang 2006), yet stimulating productive patterns of behaviour for collaborative group work during the pilot proved difficult. Sustaining the necessary cycle of negotiation, discussion, agreement, work, research, collaboration and then production was made problematic by a host of factors. These included unfamiliarity with the environment through to distractions stemming from the open-ended nature of SL and the freedom to explore a rich parallel universe. Time played a major role in the pilot. With only three weeks in which to take students from induction to completion of their design briefs, the critical elements for cooperative work were only just starting to fall into place. As the pilot drew to a close the students were beginning to develop: self-awareness as learners; sense of purpose; intermediate/advanced in-world skills; and comfort with group working based on a shared sense of trust and security. But within the timeframe some of these competencies

and levels of awareness came too late to impact forcefully on the design activities.

The post pilot workshop, comprising a group of experts in the use of virtual worlds and observers of the pilot was used as method for both articulating and addressing these problems. The outcomes from this exercise are presented here as a set of ten guidelines that address the identified dimensions for fostering collaboration in a shared 3D environment:

1. **Socialisation before collaboration:** trust, identity and authenticity are key elements in any successful collaborative enterprise. Running a 'toy' task and a social event before the main activity can facilitate the building of relationships between the students and help establish purposeful dialog.

2. **Provide ground rules for communication:** dialog is fundamental to collaboration and VWs such as SL offer a variety of interactional modalities. People talk and type and different speeds and setting clear guidelines for the use of text or voice chat helps mitigate cognitive overload and confusion. Supporting persistent conversations across activities can be achieved using a combination of asynchronous in-world tools and external real-world tools.

3. **Revisit the concept of collaboration:** by identifying what tasks are in an activity there is the potential for assigning roles[11] as part of a collaborative team and creating skill based cooperation. Defining the different layers of collaboration can help overcome the complexity of sharing object permissions and the lack of any common inventories or repositories of objects and textures. It is important to negotiate cooperation strategies first and take into account the different level of building skills, techniques and conflicting aesthetics. Ideas can be exchanged between collaborators more easily than prims[12].

4. **Integrate collaboration into the pedagogical design:** check that collaboration is

intrinsic to the tasks being presented to the students. A common understanding of the meaning of collaboration should be reached by clarifying the type, level, suitability, people and need for collaboration. If collaboration is not intrinsic to the task then it needs to be signalled as optional and time needs to be factored into the course to allow for these group working skills to develop.

5. **Provide a safe training space:** a standalone VW, such as an instance of OpenSim, provides a 'safe' playground for experimentation before entering the more complex VW of SL. As a preparatory environment, or training server, students are able to concentrate on mastering the interface, the basics of building, navigation and movement without being worried by social interactions within the wider cultural community.

6. **Virtual collaborations can benefit from distance:** combining face-2-face and virtual co-presence can add confusion when establishing collaboration in a VW. Selecting a remote teaching setting allows students to concentrate on exploiting the in-world tools for collaboration. Face-2-face can be used for broad based decision making, for example where students need to reach agreements for their design briefs.

7. **Build a sense of purpose through narrative and step by step guidance:** provide inexperienced students with a flexible, individualised learning path to follow that serves as a set narrative, for example a cooperative game that allows the progressive acquisition of technical skills, identity building and engaging in diverse forms of social interaction with the community. Students reported that if they received guidance and briefing to gradually accomplish more complicated tasks over a period of time, they could learn progressively, and not become distracted and overcome what they perceived as the difficult process of responding to the tutor requests for creativity from the very beginning.

8. **Mentoring is a valuable approach to help scaffold student activities:** live demonstrations and mentoring are useful ways to help students succeed in the tasks set for them. As the students affirmed, it was useful seeing video tutorials before tackling the assigned tasks and being able to count on their mentors was a key factor in their sense of achievement.

9. **Take advantage of third party in-world devices for supporting collaboration:** there are a variety of tools and programming interfaces that have been created or can be taken advantage of to support collaborative processes. These include items such as shared whiteboards and to-do lists, communication managers and web-based protocol exchanges for browsing internet resources in-world.

10. **Cultural engagement should be encouraged:** reading the cultural codes inherent in social virtual world platforms can be challenging. Encouraging social activity within the broader community helps build a sense of digital identity and acclimatises students to the etiquette and norms of the VW. There is a tension evident in SL between the VW as a collaborative studio space, with sophisticated building tools and the VW as an inhabited and socially complex world. The inhabitants provide the external audience, positively appreciated by the students, but they also add an element of distraction and disorientation that stems from having to interpret extant cultural codes.

CONCLUSION

The results from the pilot have been valuable in highlighting the particular challenges that MUVEs present to designing collaborative activities. The guidelines outlined in the discussion above were integrated into the design of a second pilot where we have attempted to each address each dimension. The competency, social and time related elements have proved easier to integrate into the redesign when compared to the technological support needs. SL offers a minimal toolset for managing advanced collaboration between groups. Certainly, the repertoire of collaborative tools that can be found in most groupware applications is lacking. For example, group communication is essentially synchronous with no persistent in-world space for asynchronous group communication and no inbuilt task and workflow management. Some items can be sourced in-world, as indicated in the guidelines, above but more work is needed in this area to bring developers into the teaching arena to help build and test new tools.

Our overall conclusion is that virtual worlds such as SL can provide a rich and motivational environment for collaborative activities, when the aims of collaboration are clearly defined through group negotiation. The level of success in both creating and facilitating group activities is determined by making good design choices. To be of value these must cover the development of necessary skills and competencies for effective engagement with the virtual environment, as well as exploiting its' social and technical affordances.

ACKNOWLEDGMENT

OpenHabitat is funded by JISC under the JISC User and Innovation Programme.

REFERENCES

Edirisingha, P., Salmon, G., & Nie, M. (2008). Modelling of Second Life environments: 3-D multi-user virtual environments for socialisation in distance learning. In *Proceedings of the JISC Programme Project Presentations Association for Learning Technology Conference 2008* (pp. 20-24). Retrieved December 17, 2008, from http://www.jisc.ac.uk/media/documents/publications/altc2008presentationsv2.pdf

Erlich, K., & Chang, K. (2006). Leveraging expertise in global software teams: Going outside the boundaries. In *Proceedings of the IEEE International Conference on Global Software Engineering* (ICGSE '06) (pp. 149-158). Washington, DC: IEEE.

Glaser, B. G., & Strauss, A. L. (1967). *The discovery of grounded theory: Strategies for qualitative research.* Chicago, IL: Aldine.

Irwin, C., & Berge, Z. L. (2006). Socialistion in the online classroom. *E-Journal of Instructional Science and Technology, 9*(1). Retrieved December 17, 2008, from http://www.usq.edu.au/electpub/e-jist/docs/vol9_no1/papers/full_papers/irwin_berge.htm

Johnson, D. W., & Johnson, R. T. (1990). Social skills for successful group work. *Educational Leadership, 47*(4), 29–33.

Johnson, D. W., & Johnson, R. T. (2003). *Learning together and alone: Cooperative, competitive and individualistic learning* (8th ed.). London: Allyn and Bacon.

Kirriemuir, J. (2008). A spring 2008 snapshot of UK higher and further education developments in Second Life. *Eduserv VirtualWorldWatch.* Retrieved December 12, 2008, from http://www.scribd.com/doc/7063700/A-Spring-2008-snapshot-of-UK-Higher-and-Further-Education-Developments-in-Second-Life

Kohler Riessman, C. (2008). *Narrative methods for the human sciences.* London: SAGE.

Kzero Research. (2008). *K Zero Universe chart.* Retrieved December 10, 2008, from http://www.kzero.co.uk/blog/?page_id=2537

Ludlow, P., & Wallace, M. (2007). *The Second Life Herald – the virtual tabloid that witnessed the dawn of the metaverse.* Cambridge, MA: MIT Press

McConnell, D. (2000). *Implementing computer supported collaborative learning* (2nd ed.). London: Kogan Page.

McConnell, D. (2006). *E-learning groups and communities.* Maidenhead, UK: Open University Press.

Minocha, S., & Roberts, D. (2008). Laying the groundwork for socialisation and knowledge construction within 3D virtual worlds. *Association for Learning Technology Journal, 16*(3), 181–196.

Norman, D. (2002). *The design of everyday things.* New York: Basic Books.

Savin-Baden, M. (2008). From cognitive capability to social reform? Shifting perceptions of learning in immersive virtual worlds. *Association for Learning Technology Journal, 16*(3), 151–161.

Schroeder, R. (1996). *Possible worlds: The social dynamic of virtual reality technologies.* Boulder, CO: Westview Press.

Schroeder, R. (2008). Defining virtual worlds and virtual environments. *Journal of Virtual Worlds Research, 1*(1). Retrieved January 5, 2009, from http://journals.tdl.org/jvwr/article/view/294

Strauss, A., & Corbin, J. (1990). *Basics of qualitative research: Grounded theory procedures and techniques.* Newbury Park, CA: Sage.

Warburton, S. (2009). Second Life in higher education: Assessing the potential for and the barriers to deploying virtual worlds in learning and teaching. *British Journal of Educational Technology, 40*(3). doi:10.1111/j.1467-8535.2009.00952.x

ENDNOTES

[1] http://www.openhabitat.org

[2] http://www.secondlife.com

[3] Joint Information and Systems Committee, http://www.jisc.ac.uk

[4] http://www.elu.sgul.ac.uk/preview/blog/

[5] https://swww2.le.ac.uk/departments/beyond-distance-research-alliance/projects/moose

[6] http://www.jisc.ac.uk/whatwedo/programmes/programme_users_and_innovation.aspx

[7] OpenSim (http://opensimulator.org) is an open source reverse engineered version of Second Life that can be used either as a stand alone virtual space or connected to as part of a multi-user grid. OpenSim can be accessed using any of the standard Second Life clients.

[8] The Leeds Metropolitan University Island in Second Life

[9] Linden dollars (L$) are the official Second Life currency. US$1 is equivalent to approximately L$200.

[10] Sandboxes in Second Life are clearly marked areas where anyone can create and build objects that will remain visible for a set period of time, on average a few hours. Normally one can only build or create objects on private land or where one has been explicitly given permission.

[11] For example by using articulated roles such as those elaborated in the Belbin clusters of team behaviours, see http://www.belbin.com

[12] Primitives – the name for the basic shapes, such as cube, sphere and cylinder, that are used for building more complex objects in Second Life

Chapter 3
Music Matters:
A Unique Distance Education Opportunity for the Humanities

Rebecca Gould
Kansas State University, USA

Elizabeth Unger
Kansas State University, USA

"Never forget that music is much too important to be left entirely in the hands of professionals"
—Robert Fulghum

EXECUTIVE SUMMARY

This chapter describes how the introduction of a learning environment can stimulate creativity and innovation in learning and extend that innovation to students at a distance. The learning environment consists of a room, technology, and Internet assisted set of tools. This music environment is one of a series of learning environments created to enhance learning especially in the humanities. Capable of enhancing the instruction in music both for distance learning and for traditional students, this was accomplished at a Midwestern comprehensive research university. The learning environment created through a strong collaborative partnership between faculty and professional staff provided an enhancement to music theory instruction. It has served as a stimulus to innovation in music performance, band director's instruction at a distance, instruction of music teacher students at a distance and also in the dance program. The result to date is an environment that has encouraged learning, collaboration and outreach to the international world of music. It is being shared with another institution of higher education to enhance their music programs. Distance learning in music and music education programs began fall of 2008 and like the initial two years of uses to improve face-to-face instruction, the potential is limitless to develop innovation and creativity in students and faculty alike.

DOI: 10.4018/978-1-60566-878-9.ch003

SETTING THE STAGE

The university put a new spin on online and distance education for music providing unparalleled opportunities and demonstrating that music does matter. Innovative faculty in collaboration with media and design professionals took an old recording studio/radio transmission cluster of rooms and transformed these rooms into an environment that has encouraged greater interactivity for all students, allowed distance learning to evolve, and has increased creativity and collaboration. This new space was designed for enhanced music theory, for innovative traditional and distance education and to provide performing art researchers a robust environment in which to collaborate. The space plus information technology or that is, the learning environment was designed to enhance the music instruction experience of traditional and nontraditional students. It was envisioned, to empower students and faculty to participate fully in musical experiences by hearing while seeing the music. This learning environment (classroom and information) was not part of an effort to bring computing to the 'music appreciation' classes of the university; instead it was designed for music majors and for research in music education. The goal was to bring innovation, creativity and collaboration to the musical arts and beyond to the larger spectrum of the humanities.

The learning space has been highly successful in terms of encouraging music courses being offered at a distance to support other distance degree programs, to encourage the creation of a band directors program offered via distance, and to enhance and improve the learning experiences of on campus students. The stimulation of faculty to create and collaborate however is the greatest benefit to date. For instance, student teachers at a distance are now aided through synchronous two-way communication with their supervising professors on the campus, master's degree students are critiqued by experts anywhere in the world, local ensembles play simultaneously with musicians from around the world and the music faculty members provide continuing education remotely.

BACKGROUND

Distance learning programs were first offered on the Internet in the Fall of 1997 with a focus on graduate education to enhance the education of professionals already in the workforce. It was extended to undergraduate degree programs shortly after the turn of the century to serve those individuals place-bound or time-constrained who seek an undergraduate education. There are over 10,000 different individuals that currently take distance learning courses.

The strategy devised to stimulate the creation of distance learning was a by-product of an initiative to move to more interactive campus learning. The strategy consisted of a few important components. First create learning environments (room plus technology) in collaboration with faculty members; create tools and interfaces to make the technology easy to use; provide professional assistance without charge; capture the faculty creations from the face-to-face presentations and its materials and finally provide easy ways to edit this for reuse including use in distance learning.

The music learning environment has been very successful so far in meeting its initially perceived purposes and continues to stimulate individuals to do new and creative things for humanities learning.

The chapter is organized into sections describing the distance learning effort at the university, the process for creating this music learning environment and how it is designed to encourage visioning teaching and learning needs for music faculty and students, a description of the special music environment and finally the outcomes and the yet envisioned possibilities for this space.

Figure 1. The learning technology for music students

Distance Education at the University

To provide insight into the strategy for creating online academic programs, the following is a synopsis of the process used to encourage distance learning (online) experiences in music and to create the learning environment; we also provide the strategy for creating online academic programs and increasing communication and collaboration within all university courses.

About 10,000 unique individuals are participating in one of more than 40 academic programs via online distance delivery. Our success meshes with Allen and Seaman (2007), who document that the enrollment in online courses is exceeding overall enrollment in residential higher education. Distance education at this university began with online web-based learning in 1997 with a strategy that follows the basic principle that

A distance course will be the same course at a distance that is provided on campus.

This principle led to the design of classrooms capable of accomplishing equivalent educational experiences for the traditional and distant student. Some of the classrooms allow synchronous instruction simultaneously delivered to students on and off campus. Asynchronous instruction possibilities challenged not only information technology professionals and classroom designers and the impacted faculty members. After more than a decade of experience with online instruction, our data shows that the quality of distance learning rivals campus learning provided by the same instructor. Faculty members comment that the preparation and delivery of online instruction has enhanced their on campus instruction. The technology provided allows the reuse of previous courses. Instructors report that by being able to improve the presentation without recreation leads to better learning and cuts the effort required to participate in distance learning.

Creating a strategy to meet the challenge of assuring that a distance course equals or exceeds traditional instruction in quality required shared decisions among the faculty and other professionals. Quality instruction required collaboration about the design of the physical spaces and also the information technology environment. That is,

Providing the same course on and off campus necessitated the capture of class instruction as it occurred. This stimulated the redesign of classrooms creating learning spaces which most often are architecturally different and augmented with information technology to create learning environments.

An early step in the strategy was to meet with faculty members who regularly teach in the space and who are interested in the creation of a state-of-the-art facility. At this meeting a visionary presented the notions of thinking big, thinking best and thinking out of the box. A committee balanced with faculty, architects, facilities and technical staff is formed whose charge is to propose a learning environment that meets current and future needs without regard to funding and to follow through the first year of operation to assure the classroom functions as planned. Initially, this committee also was charged with review of the classroom every three years. This latter mission soon fell by the wayside however and a new group is appointed for redesign and major enhancement efforts. Co-chairs are appointed one from the faculty who showed interest in the remake and one from the technical staff. The committee develops a proposal complete with aesthetic, mechanical and information technological requirements, and a budget. If the project is approved and funding appropriated, the work of implementing the design is accomplished under the watchful eye of the original committee.

A component of the distance learning process is creating the best and most forward looking environment to meet the goals of the department(s) and faculty members involved.

Design of effective learning environments capable of encouraging interactive and collaborative learning as well as supporting online learning is accomplished through effective shared leadership - of faculty members and IT and facilities professionals.

Providing academic programs to individuals who are time or place constrained became a university goal in 1994. However, distance learning is no longer descriptive of the activities that began in 1994 with providing academic programs to a population that could not attend the university in the traditional way. Using media that can be distributed via the Internet for learning purposes is what we call Mediated Learning (ML). ML available in a synchronous (learner and instructor in the same time frame) or asynchronous (learner not live with the instructor's presentation) mode is a better description for what is still commonly called distance learning. The concept of "distance learning" has been broadened in two ways to include residential students and to move to providing "academic credit certifications" in addition to degree programs. This learning is now used for those students at a distance and those who are residential. ML is the acronym used in the rest of the chapter for the realm of opportunities in providing learning to students and researchers.

Online learning evolved from providing academic programs primarily in an asynchronous mode, to mixed mode programs using the newer Web tools, to the concept of partnering with other universities to collaboratively provide new academic programs online. Consortiums of universities have been formed to allow the faculty members skilled in an academic focus to come together over the Internet to offer new or better education. For instance, new programs have been offered by bringing faculty members together from up to 10 institutions. Ten institutions, in which no institution could offer the emerging programs, can react quickly without each taking the time and resources to create their own courses. Additionally, academic programs have been provided over Internet2 at the upper graduate level to bring together the world's experts in an area to teach students from multiple institutions.

The overarching goal has always been to provide to the nonresidential student the same or an equivalent learning experience as the residential student experience using the *Seven Principles of Good Practice* (Chickering and Ehrmann, 1996). The implementation of this principle meant that the essentials of an academic experience had to be provided which included the course or program offerings, collaboration with peers, and online academic and administrative services such as tutoring or financial aid, respectively.

Principles of Providing Online Learning to Distant Students

Mediated Learning (ML) at Kansas State University is predicated upon a set of principles, some of which are provided below:

- Teaching and learning experiences of distance students will be the same as that of the on campus student.
- Learning spaces on campus will be created for the enhancement of learning and simultaneously designed to capture and provide this experience or its equivalent to distance students.
- These learning spaces will have a common core of technology to reduce the faculty learning curve, facilitate ease of scheduling, and reduce the cost of refresh and maintenance.
- Online academic services will be provided in the course and those online services may be used by the traditional student, as well as, the student at a distance.
- The goal is to provide complete degree programs (or certifications) at a distance, not just courses unless those courses are a component of a distance degree program. Later in this chapter we discuss that music courses are now offered online but a music

degree program is currently not available. Thus, the music courses now offered are part of other degree requirements.

The first principle refers to the fact that the campus course presentations are normally recorded for use, and often edited, for mediated learning, ML. This class capture system is integrated with the learning management system, so that students may view and review the presentations. It also means that the process of uploading a class presentation or lecture by the instructor must be part of the learning design requirements. Traditional students find that being able to review a class presentation is a good learning tool. Some faculty members pre-record their class lectures and expect students to view the material before coming to the class. These faculty members are then able to move the "class meeting" to richer interactions with discussion and problem-solving.

In the early days of creating distance learning materials, capture of the classroom presentation material like power point slides was often overlaid with audio or visual subtitling and supplemented with written material. This then evolved to the capture of the classroom experience with single and multiple cameras with the feed to the presentation system in the classroom. The evolution now has moved to include video posting sites and virtual environments, podcasts and RSS feeds and other applications suitable for mobile devices.

The motivation associated with the second principle related to creation of physical spaces for more interactive learning. Changes to the physical environment should be as carefully considered as the information technology environment. For instance, if one expects small group discussions then tiered fixed seating is not conducive to this goal. Oblinger (2006) proved to be an important resource in guiding our thinking about technically enhanced learning spaces.

The third principle--providing a common core of information technology--is resource driven. Faculty time is a precious resource within universities. Any opportunity to assist faculty in freeing up time for teaching, research and outreach must be pursued. Therefore, the university standardized on a core set of technology tools and attempted to make these identical across classrooms. Other savings realized from these decisions included the flexibility of scheduling faculty in classrooms. Only faculty who needed specific rooms or equipment had to make special requests. A common inventory of rooms required fewer training sessions for users and maintenance of the room was simplified. In addition, now with more than 50 classrooms, negotiating larger quantity purchases brings lower prices.

The fourth principle, provision for online academic services, resulted in web-based academic services for students including office hour appointment scheduling and virtual office hours through e-mail, message boards, chats, blogs, etc. Other services like academic advising, obtaining library reserve materials, and career planning and placement are offered and can be used by all students—distant and traditional.

The fifth principle that only programs are offered online came from the desire to allow students to complete a degree or a credit certificate. Some residents of our state voiced their concerns that universities provided courses online but never enough to complete a program of study. This public relations debacle was a major factor in the decision that the university must enhance the student's ability to participate fully in the economic benefit of higher education by completing a degree.

Enhancements to Traditional Classroom Spaces to Evolve to Learning Environments

Information technology enhancements to classrooms have been implemented since 1995. Three major components of these classrooms include: 1) the physical space, 2) the information technol-ogy tools provided (includes software) and 3) the learning management system.

The common core of technology tools and applications in a technology classroom changes over time and the rooms are upgraded on a three-year refresh cycle. Currently the core contains a personal computer (PC or Mac or both), access to the Internet, sound system, classroom capture equipment, visual presenter, and a hot line for immediate assistance. Some rooms contain specialized equipment such as computers for students, ceiling mounted document cameras for the presentation of maps and charts in large high quality format, microscopes, music keyboards, multiple plasma screens for the presentation of sequences or of multiple sources of information, electronic balances, stress meters and specialized software.

The physical arrangement of the rooms varies but the goal is to provide flexible space when possible. Some classrooms include wheeled swivel chairs for ease of movement to form discussion groups or to participate at a station with a specialized type of equipment. Many classrooms have pods for small group activities. In biology, the pod is designed for two-four students to use while dissecting small animals, viewing microscopic organisms, simulating the life cycles of ecologies and learning through 3-D simulation how medications interact with organisms. The literature provides a wealth of information on designing learning spaces, a compilation of research and best practices is available from (Oblinger, 2006). Foster and Gibbons (2007), ethnography of students' study habits, and academic and library-related needs at University of Rochester has major implications for how students learn and is driving how the library is organized, the use of space, location of services, and the resources provided, and has broader implications about students' study habits and service needs.

Academic and Administrative Services for the ML Student

Good online academic services are critical to success of students. These include:

- Office hours which at minimum means access to the instructor. With the rise of synchronous communication such as instant messaging and VOIP systems students are provided constant access to the instructor.
- Advising is provided for all students via an online version of a degree audit that serves as a decision framework for programs of study. Non-residential students need additional guidance and a system of reminders coupled with access to an advisor encourages active participation in the advising process.
- Program progress monitoring and subsequent advising has proved invaluable in allowing students to monitor their own progress. It also provides information to departmental advisors for the non-residential students to encourage and advise them on a path that leads to a degree. Non-residential students often need more assistance in understanding the route to a degree than traditional students. Program coordinators in the division of continuing education have been trained to assist students choose the courses in the appropriate sequence.
- Library services are essential for all enrolled students and these services continue to be enhanced. Early on, the division of continuing education provided an individual who physically went to the library and copied the research materials for distance students. Now access to local digital library databases and resources and to the global library resources empowers the student to do their own research.
- Career assistance is available online for all students

- Limited tutoring is available for the distant student and more online tutoring is needed.
- Commencement is held online with messages from university officials with the opportunity for faculty, family members and friends to post congratulatory messages.
- Alumni status is acknowledged. Each graduate receives an alumni pin and a certificate from the university alumni association and the continuing education program.

Administrative services that must be enhanced are the ability to

- Register for classes and pay fees
- Add and drop courses
- Access grades and transcripts

The future blends the "distance student" with the residential student through the development of more services and enhanced learning environments using the rapidly evolving collection of tools The Music Matters project is a part of this evolutionary process.

CASE DESCRIPTION: MUSIC MATTERS

The project began with a faculty member in music approaching the Vice Provost for Academic Affairs and Technology with the idea to upgrade some old computers that were used for assignments in a beginning music theory class. Computers were old and the software had limited capabilities compared to currently available music composition and creation software that required newer and higher-end computing. Thus the collaborative approach to the design of a new learning environment for the music department was born. A team of interested faculty gathered with a few of the IT staff to brainstorm the uses of information technology in the music curricula and for research.

Preparatory work with the faculty who are chosen is critical to project outcomes. Creating a vision and enthusiasm for the things that can be accomplished in the learning environment is paramount for both the faculty and the facilities and IT professionals working on the project. First, the team is asked to design the best environment to meet the faculty goals for student learning outcomes and also to create a space in which the student and faculty can be creative and innovative. In this phase the costs of the planned environment are not considered. Thus, the first step is to dream big. In fact, dream well beyond what the educators may even think is possible technologically and without regard for costs.

A meeting was called for all music faculty members interested in helping to design a new learning environment and led the efforts to visualize the remake of the current facility by defining the departmental goals in the areas of new programs, dreaming of enhancements to current offerings and research that could be accomplished better, faster and with more collaboration in a renovated facility. During this dream phase, a new program in music production was considered and an addition to the classroom design was created to accomplish music production but neither the program nor the space has yet come to life. In one sense, the classroom stimulated strategic planning for the department based on Midwestern music educational needs for a program to teach the recording of music. In the early design phase, the burden was primarily on the faculty to vision, collaborate and agree on a vision.

Faculty members on the design team were challenged to visualize the best environment in which to teach their specialty without concern for resources needed to create that environment. This thought-provoking exercise resulted in a classroom equipped to teach music theory and practice and stimulated many of the faculty members to innovate new ways of instruction. This visualizing exercise continued by having the faculty members examine the long term curricular and research goals of the department. Questions were asked about challenges to the teaching in the department. Faculty members were asked to consider all the possible courses that might use the environment to enhance the learning experience.

The six members of the faculty met with IT staff members who demonstrated current available technologies. The faculty then characterized their needs, goals and dreams as the input to the initial design objectives. Visioning had a large role in the original design and planned enhancements. Student and faculty creativity for them meant an environment where collaboratively and individually, both could create, modify, hear, "see" and share their work. The original vision included a space to:

- Teach music theory classes and other areas of the core curricula – including composition; arranging; orchestration; part-writing; arranging for band; and marching-band techniques
- Allow students the ability to compose and arrange music from their desktop.
- Display music from the front of the room and remotely access students' desktops to assist with music notation and composition.
- Capture lectures and post them to the learning management system, using strategically-placed cameras and required software.
- Share and collaborate on music composition and creation with others in the learning space and around the world
- Offer a band directors master's degree program
- Provide an environment to allow off campus members of the Masters in Fine Arts committee to attend meetings via the Internet
- Foster creativity, innovation and collaboration

- Introduce a recording and music production studio to add a curriculum in music production.

The analysis of the vision against available technological solutions was then discussed among the 12-person committee – the six faculty members and six professionals. When this was complete, the vision became the room design and associated costs were determined. The faculty elected to pursue the classroom environment and delayed the creation of the production/recording studio because of funding and space restrictions. The classroom was created with a $130,000 investment in information technology and another $50,000 in facility upgrades, the classroom includes:

Student workstations -- 15 Apple MAC G5 machines with attached music keyboards interconnected with the instructor's keyboard, a large flat-screen monitor and earphones.

Instructor's station – a multimedia center with a touch screen control system, music keyboard, digital mixer, visual presenter, DVD player, classroom capture system, access to the Internet including Internet2 access, and printer.

Two large plasma panels (50 inches) for display from the instructor's podium and at the instructor's volition classroom display of the image from the student consoles.

Specialized software -Sibelius Music Notation software™, a digital mixer and other office suite software are provided at each workstation and the instructor's podium. To support teaching music theory, the students have programs that allow them to develop recognition of various tones, notes, musical instruments and to practice incipit creation and recognition

Providing an environment for innovation has increased the accomplishments of the faculty and the learning of students. The faculty members exhibit a mindset of originality and inventiveness. Yo-Yo Ma said, "Imagine having Einstein to talk to you, or Gandhi. In a concert, Mozart and Bach are talking to you. It's the best of them communicating with you through time and space. You're listening to the crystallization of great minds". This relatively small investment allows music to be composed, created on paper, performed and it connects minds. Communicating and learning with masters and nonprofessionals alike has been an unexpected benefit, which is a much different-side of distance education than conceived in the original design.

CURRENT CHALLENGES

Classrooms of this scope and design for a specific segment of the disciplines provide several challenges to the faculty and university. This section provides first a look at the vision and how that vision is not yet fully met. It provides examples of what has been done along with the challenges of extending this environment. Finally the costs of maintaining an environment for these disciplines that over the years continues to meet the learning goals as outlined. Nearly two years in the planning phase, construction of a state-of-the-art music studio was completed by August of 2005. Students now listen, compose, arrange and perform from one of the 15 workstations each housing an Apple G5 (TM Apple Corporation A), 20-inch flat-screen monitor, music keyboard, music composition and notation software, headphones and more.

The final vision for the music learning environment is captured in three general goals:

- Provide students with up-to-date resources for learning in a technology-based system for music theory and practice. And provide capabilities to capture the classroom experience for review by all students. Provide a facility to allow for capturing materials, lectures, etc. to be used in distance education classes.
- Provide a state-of-the art facility for in-services for public school teachers and for visiting musicians and to connect faculty

Figure 2. View of the student's workstation with music keyboard, earphones and Apple Mac computers

Figure 3. View of the instructor's console. Note the control panel next to the musical keyboard - with a touch the instructor can record various aspects of the presentation for distance learners

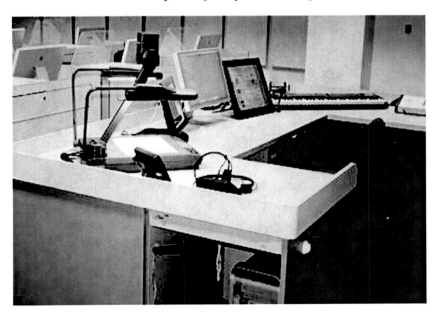

Figure 4. View of the musical score white board, large plasma screens that can work in tandem or independently of each other. Note the camera above the white board for capture from the front of the room

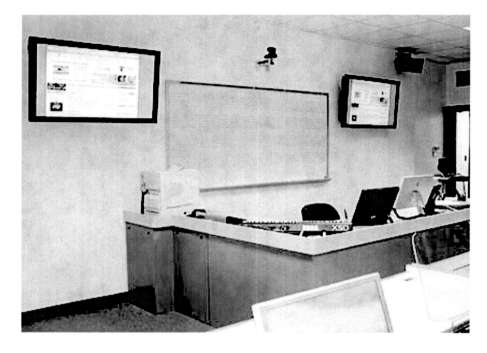

Figure 5. Another view of the instructor's console

and master performers from around the world, enhancing the learning for musicians at K-State.

- Standardize and upgrade many of the instructional resources in music education, including ear-training and aural skills, theory, composition, arranging, and orchestration using the interactive capability of the learning environment.

Some courses allowed the integration of distance students into the traditional classroom. Faculty members can capture lectures and post them to the learning management system, using the instructor controlled cameras strategically placed throughout the room. Faculty can display the music score being played via the two 50-inch plasma screens located at the front of the room, can remotely access students' desktops to assist with music notation and composition and can provide music instruction to a single student or to a team of students in the classroom. Faculty and students can perform at the university and simultaneously with musicians anywhere in the world. Student teachers can be observed and instructed as they teach at remote locations.

The current music department head, Dr. Gary Mortenson, says, "Music education has benefited tremendously from innovative new technologies. From music notation skills, to aural skills, to learning music theory, to mixing audition and demo recordings, music students learn to assimilate the nut-and-bolts of music quicker and with a higher degree of internalization when they work with the new software programs readily available. Teachers can use this technology to track students' progress and this in turn leads to greater efficiency in teaching musical concepts. Technology has changed our capacity to observe students in the field with the use of computers with integrated cameras and high-speed Internet connectivity. This means less time in the car and more time helping students through meaningful observation. With today's economic challenges, technology is more important than ever. So understanding, integrating, and expanding upon software and hardware innovations is a must right now, and will be even more important tomorrow. Human contact between teacher and student continues to be the "face" of meaningful music education. But technology's ability to help us teach basic concepts and to introduce advanced trends in the field is here to stay."

Imagine the learning that can occur when connecting an aspiring musician with a master performer. Dr. Kurt Gartner, Professor of Music, dreamed big during the exercise of dreaming about the best possible learning environment. He envisioned students being able to play along with professionals, get advice from professionals, the facility to play with other students around the world, to create new groups where the members are geographically separated and to perform with professionals in other locations. With the classroom in operation, he is able to connect students with professional musicians in their working environment to synchronously share knowledge and to participate in real-time performances and communications and real-time critique. This instance of remote collaboration of working professionals with students provides positive learning experiences and enhances the innovation aspect of the student's and professional's skill set. Extension of this concept to others courses is imminent.

Two examples illustrating the types of interaction that can take place with experts, in this case accomplished professional performers follow.

- **Example 1:** A student of percussion being able to exchange ideas with a well-known musician in New York, Chicago or Columbia: The Percussion Studio seminar assembles in the music classroom for a video conference with a virtual guest musician—Don Skoog in his home studio in Chicago. Skoog is a performer, teacher, composer, author, and scholar. Prior to the start of the session, the professor e-mails Skoog's handouts to stimulate discussion and innovation, to foster interactivity and to prepare students to ask questions of the expert. Students also are encouraged to visit the musician's website http://www.contemporarymusicproject.com. The session was on Bodhrán and Arabic drumming. Those students who brought their drums were able to try some of the techniques recommended by the master and even get instruction and feedback from him---all occurring at a distance.

- **Example 2:** Students in the Latin Jazz Ensemble performed in New York and Sweden -- without ever leaving Manhattan, Kansas. Using a laptop with a built in camera and chat software, the jazz group participated with Brooklyn College. Allan Molnar, an instructor at Brooklyn College in New York led the performance to demonstrate that music and instruction are possible at a distance. The students also participated in the "Days of Percussion" in Stockholm, Sweden. During the actual event, a slight glitch occurred when video was lost for a second. But when the video feed returned, the musicians on both continents were still in audio synchronization and the listeners heard an undisturbed performance.

While in the early stages of development, the planning team thought the studio would be used in very specific residential teaching ways, the music faculty has demonstrated that the possibilities require imagination and creativity on the part of the faculty and the university support staff. The faculty who oversees music education was looking to augment his assessment of student teachers as they practiced teaching across Kansas, without increasing the time he had to travel throughout the state. Prior to the introduction of the classroom capabilities, faculty members had to travel by car to observe their students a number of times over the course of the semester. In Kansas this often took up to six hours each way to observe student teachers. Using the facilities of the classroom and a laptop for the student teacher, observation can now be accomplished simply by scheduling time for each observation in each location, thus reducing the cost and time for travel and increasing the number of observations of student teachers.

Site visits are scheduled with the faculty who connect via the student's computer. The faculty observes the student teachers instruction, observe the student performers, and monitors progress of both throughout the semester. This saved significant faculty time and allows more observation sessions for a student teacher experiencing challenges in teaching. The instructor reports that, "We are MUCH more effective now in our observation of student teachers as our music education professors can view students in the field remotely". If for example, a student teacher is having a difficult time with classroom management, the faculty at K-State can say, "let me observe your classroom instruction" and connectivity and observation is handled remotely. The faculty then schedules a time to provide pointers to the student teacher to get over the hurdle allowing for rich, rapid feedback and quicker resolution. Fifty percent of new teachers leave the profession within five years. The faculty members are now looking for ways to use these technologies to enhance retention of teachers as they leave college and start their professional teaching careers.

The music department is exploring the use of the room to teach graduate level classes to students at other universities where there is not sufficient enrollment to warrant the development of a new course. In a distance capacity this helps both universities. The remote university is able to offer the course and the teaching university has additional students enrolled. The concept of team teaching with remote instructors is being considered and the department is sharing the space with a local university in exchange for new software. Such sharing of faculty and students is effective in providing a greater selection of courses and can provide more "experts" available to the students. It has it challenges however, first it takes a good deal of preplanning, coordination and communication for the faculty members and the IT support staff. Standard protocols, rethinking memorandums of agreement and in some cases policy changes are required by the participating institutions.

Another challenge is to broaden the disciplines that use the capabilities at the site. The learning space was created as part of a concerted effort to improve the information technology capability available to the social science and humanities faculty. Some discussion has ensued with the dance faculty who envision this environment as one capable of choreographing dance and of teaching by having the students visualize through simulation the dance instructions they create. The inclusion of one of the software systems to choreograph performances is all that is lacking to accommodate this enhancement and to allow set designers, directors, dancers and musicians to collaborate on performance productions instructions.

Inclusion of the visual arts in musical performances is anticipated and this research and development work could include the virtualization of stage settings for drama and dance using historical information from the visual arts. The potential for research and collaborative learning has just begun.

The cost of such a facility is high compared to a classroom with little technology and that cost is ongoing if the room is to continue to be state-of-the-art . There are daily maintenance checks by support personnel along with the software licenses and hardware upgrade costs that are ongoing if the room remains current technologically. Faculty time spent in creative uses of the facility is another cost but often this leads to better teaching so this is really an opportunity cost – as long as there is support staff is available to assist.

CONCLUSION

The humanities are often neglected at universities when technology enhancements for teaching, learning and research are considered. Departments in the humanities tend to be grossly underfunded and readily accepting of hand-me-down equipment, less than ideal space, cramped offices that doubles as the faculty studio for music lessons. Creation of a classroom designed initially to enhance the teaching of music theory and to allow the capture of classroom activity for use in distance learning, fostered many enhancements leveraging these capabilities for both delivery methods.

Music matters. Music, as well as, an appreciation of the humanities' disciplines enriches our lives. The greatest benefit of computing will conceivably come in the social sciences and humanities not the hard sciences. With the belief that humanities needs to be at the forefront of the university experience, K-State embarked on a process described in this chapter to provide creative music faculty with information technology tools to turn a dream into a reality. Although this project has created a learning space and environment for music, it serves as an incubator for the imagination of faculty in other humanities disciplines. This environment also has stimulated the first interdisciplinary course in the humanities where the teaching and learning is focused on a real world problem.

Three years since the completion of the room, faculty members continue to innovate. Now emerging technologies such as those identified in the Horizon Report (2008) – grassroots video, collaboration webs, mobile broadband, data mash-ups, collective intelligence and social operating systems will impact faculty and student work and our future environments. Augmented reality (Gartner, 2008) another emerging technology will allow musicians to play in an orchestra, a rock band or solo without the need to purchase an instrument or leave their desktop. In this participatory media culture, faculty will find a way to bring music to the masses, much like the live satellite simulcast of the Metropolitan Opera to the theatres around the world (Emelianov, 2007).

The lines between formal and informal learning (life-slc.org) are blurring, music is a perfect venue because it is universally understood with many genres and correlates to other humanities disciplines. Music does not require a translator to understand the language. Like art everyone translates to their own venue. Interdependent humanities education blending dance, theatre, music, art, architecture, history, literature and philosophy are seen as a wave of the future to bring greater understanding to everyone. This learning environment is seen as a first step to more interdisciplinary humanities education for both formal and informal learning.

The question remains can this model be sustained in terms of resources and faculty enthusiasm for new teaching and learning environments for students.

REFERENCES

Allen, I. E., & Seaman, J. (2007). Online nation: Five years of growth in online learning. *Sloan Consortium*. Retrieved January 29, 2008, from http://www.sloan-c.org/publications/survey/pdf/online_nation.pdf

Chickering, A., & Ehrmann, S. C. (1996). *Implementing the seven principles: Technology as a lever* (AAHE Bulletin). Retrieved May 28, 2008, from http://www.clt.astate.edu/clthome/Implementing%20the%20Seven%20Principles,%20Ehrmann%20and%20Chickering.pdf

Emelianov, M. (2007, December 18). *Metropolitan opera's first simulcast of 2007-2008 breaks attendance records*. Retrieved May 28, 2008, from http://pervegalit.wordpress.com/2007/12/18/metropolitan-operas-first-simulcast-of-2007-08-breaks-attendance-records

Foster, N. F., & Gibbons, S. (Eds.). (2007). *Studying students: The undergraduate research project at the University of Rochester*. Association of College and Research Libraries. Retrieved February 12, 2008, from http://www.ala.org/ala/acrl/acrlpubs/downloadables/Foster-Gibbons_cmpd.pdf

Gartner. (2008). Gartner report: Top ten disruptive technologies 2008-2012. Retrieved May 28, 2008, from http://www.gartner.com/it/page.jsp?id=681107

Learning in Informal and Formal Environments (LIFE) Center. (2009). Retrieved January 8, 2009, from http://life-slc.org

Oblinger, D. (Ed.). (2006). *Learning spaces*. EDUCAUSE. Retrieved May 28, 2008, from http://www.educause.edu/learningspaces

2008Report, H. (2008). *The EDUCAUSE Learning Initiative and the New Media Consortium*. Retrieved February 18, 2008, from http://connect.educause.edu/Library/ELI/2008HorizonReport/45926

Chapter 4

Virtual Worlds and Avatars for the Development of Primary Foreign Languages and Primary Foreign Languages for the Development of Real Children

Yongho Kim
Korea National University of Education, Republic of Korea

EXECUTIVE SUMMARY

The case study is a chronicle of Korean elementary students' efforts to gain autonomous control of a foreign language, English, from the top down, that is, through use of English in communication (as opposed to mere exposure to English through study or through the passive absorption of comprehensible input). This communicative use of English is realized through materials pertinent to their overall development and not just to their language development. The materials include a surrogate self or avatar within a virtual learning environment which can, in principle, though not in this study, connect them with children all over the world. The question for this study is how the use of an avatar in a virtual learning environment brings about not only the learning of vocabulary and grammar (similar to the piecemeal learning that happens in any classroom) but also interacts with and even activates the child's overall psychological development the way that play awakens developmental functions on the playground.

BACKGROUND

Vygotsky teaches us that the study of discrete elements rarely leads to a proper understanding of a complex phenomenon. Instead we need to understand how each element works in a unit that, like a cell, preserves the properties of the whole. For

example, we need to look at how word meaning is constructed in order to understand how mental developments such as ostension, indication, naming, and ultimately, conceptualizing can occur. Since meaning presupposes generalization, it is part of thinking. But since meaning is a part of a word, it is also part of speech (1987: 49). Through a meeting of lines of development and a dialectical mutual transformation between thinking and speech,

DOI: 10.4018/978-1-60566-878-9.ch004

Figure 1. Schematic flow of child's development

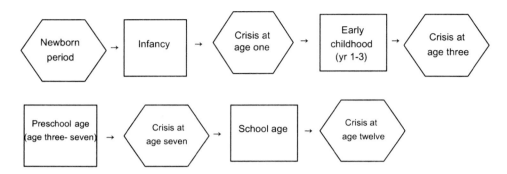

which, according to Vygotsky and Stern, occurs around the age of two, thinking becomes verbal and speech becomes intellectual (1987: 111 112, and 117).

But to say that the lines of development meet is not to say that they merge into a homogeneous mass. Instead, the lines of thinking and speech are differentiated into many threads. These threads are phylogenetically and ontogenetically distinct but culturally linked in a functional (that is, a functioning) unit, similar to the way that differently evolved organs (e.g., organs for breathing and organs for eating) are linked in the vocal tract.

Understood in this way, Vygotsky's developmental theory is not simply about how one line of development replaces another and becomes dominant, only to become again peripheral at the next level of development. Rather, it is about how a more dynamic relationship between past and future functions, between matured and maturing lines of development, contribute to reorganizing the child's whole position in the environment. This reorganization then creates a new social situation of development (SSD), leading previously undeveloped functions to mature in turn.

Vygotsky suggests that development is both an evolutionary and a revolutionary process. By this he means that radical changes occur in crises at birth, and then at ages one, three, seven, and twelve. We may represent the stream schematically as shown in Figure 1.

The periods between each crisis (represented by squares) are rather stable periods in which development of the whole is subordinated to the developmental rule of the parts.

From the very first day of birth, the baby is a social being since his or her needs are fulfilled only through others. But in differentiating between inner and outer experience, the child does not construct an individual self; instead, the infant constructs an undifferentiated "Proto-we" identity (in German, an *Ür-wir*) with the people around the infant (Vygotsky, 1997: 233). The child's predicament is that he/she lacks the main means by which communities are constructed among humans, namely speech. In response, without knowing grammar or vocabulary, the child attempts speech, based on the imitation of speech externals such as intonation, naseopharyngealized vowels (that is, crying), and simple labial consonants (babbling). This incomprehensible "autonomous speech" gives rise to a crisis at age one (Gillen, 2003: 76).

During the ages from one to three, the child replaces this babble with communicative speech, or rather reduces the role of babble to nonsense rhymes and onomatopoeia, where it remains as a kind of fossil. In this process, children begin to isolate the self from the environment. But often long before the emerging self is fully conscious, the child attempts to impose his or her will, often without needs and always without being able to satisfy needs independently of the adults.

One example of this is automatic "negativism" that is, the blind imitation of the word "no" even when this goes against the child's own desires and inclinations (Vygotsky, 1997: 283). But this use of the function of negation is eventually decisively subordinated to the child's recognition of necessity. And it is in this subordination to reality that we find a new function, which is the central object of our study. In order to find a way to fulfill desires that cannot be satisfied immediately, the child creates pretend play, a central line of development in preschool age children.

Children at play may be detached from their perceivable environment but they are still tightly bound to their internal experiences. The child who plays at being a fighting Shaolin monk may deliberately ignore that he is only a child, but the child who feels hungry does not so easily ignore that he is hungry. To sever consciousness from internal experience, the child must develop a metacognitive perspective. This emerges with the crisis at age seven as the child's affectation, posing, and acting out, and the appearance of the "imaginary friend".

School age is the period when a child builds on this emergent self by constructing self- love, self-esteem, and a conscious sense of purpose. At about middle school age, children start to critically examine social rules and customs, thus reaching a crisis at age twelve. This is the age when children consciously adapt the self to the rules and develop the seeds for the creation of social agreements in the future.

It is clear, then, that the general direction of development is for an individual to be free first from the unmediated dictate of needs and then from dependence on others. But the child can only be free of these by becoming fully socialized. This socialization happens because the child's mind, itself a microcosm of cultural meanings, finds itself in a social environment largely made up of meanings.

In assimilating these meanings through cultural tools and signs, the child finds it periodically necessary to completely reorganize his/her higher mental functions (Vygotsky, 1987: 199). When this happens, we can say that the child's mind, the cultural artifacts concerned, and the social environment of learning in which they are found constitute a "zone of proximal development." For Vygotsky, the very archetype of the zone of proximal development, at least at school age, is the construction of scientific concepts on the basis of every day concepts, and the construction of foreign language concepts on the basis of native language word meanings (1987: 213-221).

SETTING THE STAGE

Let us attempt to understand South Korea's struggle for autonomy and development in English education in Korea in much the same way we understand the child's struggle for autonomy and development; that is, from the outside in. In South Korea, the late 1990s saw the rapid growth of international relationships and the swelling of a huge economic bubble. English education was both a consequence of the economic bubble and part and parcel of it.

When the bubble burst and foreign companies began to leave Korea due to the instability of her finances, the Korean government almost simultaneously decided to inject a foreign monetary system (IMF loans) into the Korean economy and introduce English education to public elementary education. Although the former was a breakthrough from without and the latter was a breakthrough from within, both elements were foreign and neither was particularly well prepared.

The Korean government's trial to 'warm up' the public to the need for English education began in 1992 when the sixth national curriculum introduced English as a discretionary subject. But as the demand for English education greatly outstripped the supply, the financial burden of private English instruction became almost unbearable to Korean parents. The government realized that an overheated private education market could threaten equal access to education and went into action to stabilize prices. By 1997, English rose to the status of a regular (i.e., mandatory) subject. Elementary students from third- to sixth-graders started to study English as a regular subject for two class hours a week. Initially, sixteen different textbooks were privately published, and each school had a right to choose.

In the seventh national curriculum, which was put into action in 2001, a cooling-down process began. For example, English teaching was renamed 'foreign language (English)', in order to reinforce the idea that foreign language learning was for general educational purposes rather than specific language skills. By reducing third- and fourth-graders' English class hours to one hour a week, and replacing private publishers text books with one government published textbook, the government attempted to lessen the burden on students, teachers and parents.

After having a large portion of the nation's financial autonomy stripped away during the economic crisis (Sachs, 1997; Stiglitz, 2000), Korea has learned the painful lesson that "other" regulation does not automatically grow into self-regulation but can rather erode it. In contrast, the struggle to achieve self-regulation and local autonomy through public education has by and large paid off; after ten years of elementary English education, it has actually had a positive effect on students' English achievement in middle and high school (Kwon, 2006).

This struggle is ongoing, for example in teacher training. The teacher training system still aims at creating the ability of regular subject teachers to lead English class just as they deal with the other nine general subjects, providing local control of English education similar to what the responsible teacher is able to exercise in other classes. But at this point in time, unlike other subjects that are the responsibility of homeroom teachers, many

English lessons are taught by two or three designated teachers who specialize in English and who frequently do not learn all the children's names, hampering classroom interaction (Kwon and Kellogg, 2005).

In addition, about 30% of elementary schools in Seoul have assistant teachers from English-speaking countries. These teachers, who are on short contracts, will often not develop fully professional teachers, because they will return to their home countries. However, while they are in Korea, they have the effect of organizing English education around their own persons (Shin and Kellogg, 2007) and can often present an obstacle to the self-regulated control of English education based here in Korea.

This sketch of the history of Korea's English education over the last twenty years has been brief, but it is enough to reveal that, like the child's struggle for self-emancipation, the main direction has been that of a struggle to secure English education for local control by teachers and learners alongside other subjects and gain national control over the curriculum.

The next national curriculum is slated to replace the single national textbook with the multiple private textbooks. Private education is once again placing great pressure on national English education, and the class hours of English instruction are to be increased from 2010 hence two hours for third-and fourth-grades and three hours for fifth- and sixth-grades a week. Also there is serious talk of introducing English in first-grade.

At the moment, the central mediating tool for Korean elementary school children to learn English is their state-produced textbook and a subsidiary CD-ROM. The CD-ROM title provides animations and movie clips, model dialogues, songs and chants for practice, and also flash cards and other materials that teachers can print out. It's even possible to say that textbook acts as a program, articulating the organization of each lesson and each period, but in many classrooms the CD-ROM directly supports the actual performance.

In third- and fourth-grade books, we find 3-D characters, one of whom is an imaginary alien character named Zeeto. In contrast, fifth- and sixth-grade books only show real life characters in 2-D graphics. Although throughout the grades the main characters are normally Korean boys and girls, the situations are often concerned with family life in lower grades, whereas in higher grades, textbooks encompass a wide range of social life of children at school. For example, almost all the characters in third- and fourth-grade books have siblings, but only one character in the fifth- and sixth-grade books does.

The English lesson plan is also organized to extend the students' radius of subjectivity. If we roughly sketch the overall lesson, which consists of four periods, the plan progresses from introducing the characters in some new situation, to using the vocabulary and grammar they introduced in fixed dialogues, to freer activities based on that situation, to then "reviewing" the target expressions in decontextualized form (as a listening test, a reading/writing test, and a speaking activity) in "Let's Review". Underlying this progression is the so-called Presentation-Practice-Production (PPP) model (Johnson, 1996: 103).

This PPP model can also be seen within each period, since a typical period will begin with a presentation ("Look and Listen" or "Look and Speak") continue with some form of controlled practice ("Listen and Repeat" or "Let's Role Play") and end with a game ("Let's Play"). Even the individual activities may be said to have this PPP structure, since all must be presented by the teacher, exemplified in practice, and then handed over to the learner, if only in the form of a comprehension check. The three phases of each lesson roughly correspond to: (a) getting attention ("Look!"); (b) giving information ("Listen: 'Hello, I'm Zeeto' Repeat!"); and (c) checking integration ("Who is this?" "It's Zeeto!").

In this way, the overall functional structure is similar at the level of the lesson, the period, and even the activity. The logic of this is that at every level students are introduced to new language, they are allowed to use it under controlled conditions, and then encouraged to use it in a more independent fashion. Accordingly, it would appear that the students' mediating tools are organized to be more alienable (that is, adaptable to being removed from the classroom context for independent use).

The characters seem to reflect each grade's level of interest, so that they can more easily construct empathy. The situations expand from intimate relationships to wider social situations; the general structure of the lessons heads from guided practice to autonomous free production; the CD-ROM not only makes the material more manageable for teachers but also helps children when they go home and study by themselves.

However, there is a pitfall in the logic that autonomous production may be derived from other-presentation and other-controlled practice. We cannot expect students to develop autonomous control of language simply by providing the chance to practice the target expression and then reproduce what they've remembered without context. Unlike, say, mathematical skills, language is an interactional tool that loses much of its meaning when isolated from its context.

Part of the productivity of language stems from the fact that the same expression construes different meanings in different contexts. This productivity is developmentally necessary because different requirements are imposed by different contexts, and this instills in the users the necessity to have volitional control of grammar and vocabulary. Deprived of context that projects the verbal expression, the projected language itself is shorn of its practical usefulness, and thus, of its attractiveness to learners.

In presenting modal verbs like "can", the meaning "I can swim" must be distinguished from "I am swimming" or "I swim". If we attempt to present this through gestures, we find ourselves visually presenting actual swimming ("I am swimming") rather than the abstract capacity to swim ("I can swim"). The "Look and Listen" dialogues from the third-grade book, as performed using animated "avatars" in the CD-ROM, handle this in an interesting way.

(The alien Zeeto, his Korean friend Minsu, and an African-American boy named Thomas are frolicking in an indoor swimming pool. After seeing other children swimming, Zeeto thinks that he can do it too.)

Zeeto: I can swim.

Minsu: Can you?

Zeeto: Yes, I can. (Steps into a shallow pool for children) Come on, Minsu! (Although being confident at the beginning, Zeeto soon begins to flounder.) Help!

Minsu, Thomas: Wait! I'm coming! (They run to save the unconscious Zeeto. Minsu tries artificial respiration and Julie looks on. Zeeto wakes up and, embarrassed, runs away.)

Zeeto: Oh, no!

From the context, we can understand why someone might claim the abstract capability (using "can") and demonstrate the opposite in practice. The "Look and Listen" dialogue thus successfully differentiates the concept of capability ("I can swim") from the actual practice of swimming ("I swim" or "I am swimming").

But this understanding is much less clear when context is diminished, as in the dialogue given for "Listen and Repeat", where the contrast is not between saying and doing but simply between one thing children normally can do and another which they can't:

Julie: Can you jump?

Thomas: Yes, I can.

Tony: Can you fly?

Minsu: No, I can't.

Because normal children can jump and cannot fly, they do not normally talk this way. The children are simply repeating an almost meaningless part ("Can you…?") and contrasting it to a more meaningful lexical part ("…jump", "…fly"). We might predict that children walk away from this exercise with little more than lexical meanings in their heads, if that.

Unfortunately, when we consider the "Let's Play" activity which checks integration by getting all the children to actively produce the form, this tendency towards the death of pragmatic meaning becomes even more pronounced.

(Procedure of the activity)

1) Make groups of ten students
2) Each group come up to the front and stand in a line facing backwards
3) Teacher shows a card to a forefront student. The student will pass the meaning by miming to the next student. (e.g. by making swimming gesture)
4) Pass the gestures to the last students.
5) The student standing at the end of line will express verbally.

    S: I can swim.

6) First team which says the sentence wins.

Of course, the sentence "I can swim" becomes more portable as a discrete language item when the concrete context is reduced first to a "Listen and Repeat" dialogue and then to a simple sentence that can even be conveyed entirely without words.

But there is a price to this portability. Now the action "I am swimming" and the potential for action "I can swim" are completely indistinguishable, because the only thing left is the gesture, which as we have seen cannot differentiate between the act of swimming and the assertion of capability. Moreover, as the language loses its pragmatic meaning, it becomes impossible to explain who is saying what to whom, much less why they say it in this way and not in some other way. What are the students carrying if pragmatic meaning of language is removed? There is, perhaps, the external physical trait of sound. But this may well lost to memory soon after they stop practicing since there is neither a semantic nor a pragmatic trace to anchor it in the mind.

With the current utilization of technology, we cannot logically expect that in a decontextualized production phase students will 'produce' any new language. Really free production requires the recognition and adaptation to contextual constraints, and contextual constraints in the classroom yield only controlled practice. Thus the PPP model cannot deliver the final P for Production; it cannot allow students to break out of the confined circle of presentation and practice.

Current teaching practice has been very little help to resolving this fundamental contradiction. Because the classroom is a "real" context, teachers, now working with "native speaking" teaching assistants, have been encouraged to "teach English through English", by using only English to issue instructions to the children (e.g. "Open your books", "Look at page 22", "Listen…" "Repeat!"). This language, while thoroughly contextualized, is not alienable; it is not possible for the children to take it over for their own use, at least not in the classroom context, because children do not normally tell their teachers what to do.

The fixed framework imposed by the textbook-CD ROM format and the accompanying PPP teaching philosophy appear to assume that providing meaningful input in this manner will eventually lead to subconscious "acquisition" of the English rules of grammar. This has not, to date, occurred to any significant extent. What seems to occur instead is more or less what our "I can swim" example would predict; the children acquire the use of single lexical words (e.g. "swim") but shy away from grammatical constructions.

Below, we shall examine one possible alternative to this framework, namely the use of avatars in a virtual environment. We do not present a systematic, quantitative analysis of the (very large) database of our study. Following the case study method, we will instead select short segments of data to illustrate our more theoretical argument from three parts of the lesson that are functionally concerned with "getting attention", "giving information", and "checking integration" of new and old knowledge. Using these functional criteria, we'll compare data with and without the virtual avatars, and also data from those in lower grades (second-graders, in this case) and higher grades (fifth-and sixth-graders).

CASE DESCRIPTION

The crisis of the current utilization of technology, along with the teaching practice and philosophy that accompanies it, is a window of opportunity for educators. As we stated in our description of the developmental theory of Vygotsky, the school children are in a stage in which the concept of self oscillates; they are experimenting with images of self. According to Bakhtin, creating the concept of a self necessitates being momentarily freed from the self (that is, being an observer) to being an active participant (that is being an imaginary character) and then, return back to one's observational point of view (1990: 26). Instead of attempting to put the contextualized story into the children, by using elaborate storylines, we can put the students into the story, cutting away narrative and the inalienable and often inappropriately complex teacher talk and simply concentrating on alienable, appropriable dialogue.

For this purpose, we provide direct surrogates for the students themselves and a virtual environment in which they can create their own context. Naturally, when the students construct a role-play based on the avatar presentations, they can bring in their old knowledge of English outside of the teaching objective. From this experience in turn arises a critical viewpoint on other team performances, on other avatar presentations and eventually reflection on their own virtual role-plays. By foregrounding student-to- student interaction from the very beginning we expect the projecting language of teacher and students and projected language of the textbook to construct an integrated single classroom "zone of proximal development" in which the latter forms a lower limit and the former forms a higher limit (Guk and Kellogg, 2007).

During the summer vacation the school offered volunteering students the chance to review their first semester English textbook for ten days with the school English specialist teacher (the author). Students ranging from second-grade (7 to 8 years old) to sixth-grade (11to 12 years old) applied. Each grade was grouped into one class except for fifth and sixth graders, who were put together in one class with ten fifth graders and 6 sixth graders. Each class consisted of 16 students; gender ratio was not considered as a variable. As elementary school English begins in third grade in Korea, the second -graders in our research learned language from the third-graders' textbook and for the fifth- and sixth-grade integrated class, the fifth-graders' textbook contents were used.

The materials were developed around the 'Look and Listen' section. Students were presented with situations with the flash animation provided by the textbook CD-ROM. Corresponding to each textbook lesson, avatar 'Look and Listen' presentations were created by the author. The avatar presentation used same wave sound file as textbook CD-ROM but the situations were sometimes different. The characters were replaced by animated avatars, which were created by using photographs of the children.

Four lessons were studied with second and third graders and three lessons were done with forth, fifth and sixth graders. All grades were presented with the lesson's main dialogue in the textbook, once with the usual presentational CD-ROM and once with avatar material. The order of avatar and CD-ROM presentation was systematically altered from each lesson to eliminate any practice effect; if avatar material was used before the CD-ROM in Lesson One, the CD-ROM was presented before the avatar in Lesson Two. Each time, after the presentations, the students were asked questions about their understanding of the material. Some of the questions focused on relational processes ("What's this?" and "Who's this?"), some on material processes ("What is he/she doing?"), some on mental processes ("Is he/she happy?" "How does he/she feel?" "What is he/she thinking?"), and some on verbal processes ("What is he saying?"). There was also some use of meta-process questions (e.g. "Why?").

After questioning, the students were required to do a role-play using the language presented. The children produced two role-plays per each lesson; each group of students were assigned ten points if they reproduced every line presented in the materials, but got points deducted each time they omitted a line. Each time they changed the basic expressions or added new expressions, one point was added. Expressions such as 'yes' or 'no' and repetitions were not awarded points. Six children from each class carried voice recorders to track their private speech and his/her groups social interactions. It is from these recorders that the data examined below is taken.

Case Study

The first extract corresponds to the "Getting Attention" function we observed earlier. Some second grade children are being presented with Lesson One, "Hi, I'm Zeeto", of their future third grade materials for the first time. The material used is a student avatar version that created by the author using students' pictures. Below are students' responses to their friends' avatars. Korean utterances are translated into English and placed in italics in square brackets; English utterances are quoted as they appear in the recordings. Commentary on how language usage reflects a developing sense of self follows each line in parentheses. When the child's name is known, initials are used; unknown students are simply referred to as S, and the researcher appears as R.

S: 재밌어, 재밌어. 사진이... *[Interesting, interesting! The photographs...]* [This is apparently self-directed speech; it is not inflected for politeness and is not directed at the teacher.]

R: 자...여기봐...*[Now, look here]* ...who's this? (The teacher has to try to get the child's attention again. He begins with a direct command in Korean.)

S: 안 보여요. *[I can't see, Teacher!]* (Polite speech, directed to the teacher, concerned with regulating needs through others.)

S: 어 외계인이다. *[Huh—an alien!]* (This is again self-directed speech, not inflected for politeness and therefore not directed to the teacher. It is surprised and appreciative in emotional tone.)

MH: 어 SE이다. *[Huh—it's SE!]* (Self-directed speech, surprised and appreciative in tone.)

MH: 뭐야...내가 TV에 나왔어 *[Whaddis? I'm on TV?]* (Use of a non-humilific pronoun to refer to the self. The verb ending suggests intimate communication and some pride.)

S: 뭐래...*[Whazzat!]* (Here the tone and the grammatical form suggest irony about the previous speaker's overblown exultation.)

To describe the self-directed speech in this sample as "egocentric" or "noncommunicative" speech (Piaget, 1959) would be highly misleading. Much of this speech, although inflected as self-directed in Korean, is intended to be heard by everyone in the classroom, and is in that sense fully communicative. However, what the students are doing is not exchanging information but establishing a heterogeneous group identity through expressing shared and contrasting emotions. The actual informational content, largely redundant, serves as a vehicle for students' affective attitudes toward the material and towards each other's attitudes. Thus we find prominent exclamation tones, and bragging and complaining tones in the students' utterances. One student tries to show off by indicating his avatar starred in the material (뭐야~ "Whaddis?") but it is countered immediately with the same utterance with different emotional coloration (뭐래.."Whazzat!").

Contrary to Piaget, Vygotsky argues that "egocentric" speech is social in function from the outset (1987: 76). Sure enough, it is precisely through this self-directed speech that we can see the class operating as a whole. We can understand that students have produced this so-called "egocentric speech" not as discrete individuals but as a part of whole class, both to direct the attention of self and direct the attention of the group. But being thus socialized does not mean that the students feel and think all in the same ways. Rather it means that the classroom's attention is focused on the shared context and not atomized around individual students' interests. The students' different interpretations of the context stir the whole class emotion even more dynamically, and hence the ensuing exchange is saturated with emotional give and take.

The next data extract exemplifies the "Giving Information" function we remarked earlier. The avatar not only draws classroom attention, it also has students autonomously involved in the situation. In the following extract, children are arguing about the reason that Zeeto falls in love with SE, a student's avatar. One very good suggestion ("SE is beautiful?") is ardently resisted ("No!") and the debate gets so heated that even the teacher's arbitration ("Yes!") is rejected ("No!").

S: Zeeto like SE.

R: Zeeto likes SE! Yes! Why?

HJ: SE is beautiful?

R: SE is beautiful?

S: No!

R: Yes!

S: No!!

It is worth comparing this avatar-mediated data with data recorded using the CD-ROM that is in standard use in elementary English classrooms all over Korea. The students, the teacher and the lesson is the same, Lesson One "Hi, I'm Zeeto."

R: He likes

S: Julie

R: Julie likes him? Zeeto?

S: Yes.

S: You don't know.

R: OK, very good. Why does Zeeto like Julie?

S: ...

R: 몰라요..[You don't know...]

R: Is Julie pretty? 예뻐? [Pretty?]

S ...

R: Beautiful?

S: No.

R: OK.

From a strictly non-developmental, English language skills oriented point of view (following the traditional teaching philosophy which stresses providing comprehensible input) this might be satisfactory. The lack of Korean use is striking; the children studiously avoid responding to Korean utterances by the teacher. But from a developmental point of view, which sees the child's main task as building new foreign language concepts onto the largely affective stratum laid down by the first language, the data is rather distressing. We find no text-related self-directed utterances by the students, and this is the sign that the classroom's attention is not focused on the presentation context, although students might remember the language points. The result is no involvement to the situation, and probably only a very shallow understanding of it. No one seems to bother about whether Zeeto likes Julie or Julie also likes Zeeto. So the probing of the reason why Zeeto likes Julie draws no student attention. Instead, the teacher and students are doing a kind of comprehension test, in which students find answers that please the teacher, working more or less through trial and error.

In contrast, with the avatar presentation the children are not shy about demonstrating their autonomy from the teacher, and the dynamic atmosphere in the avatar presentation data has an active character. One way of understanding this is to look at the shift in controlling attention. While watching the avatar presentation, the locus of attention control gradually shifted to the students even to the degree that the teacher's intervention was not accepted. In the beginning the locus of control was obviously with the teacher (자, 여기 봐. ["Right. Look here."]). But as soon as the teacher showed the avatar and asked questions, the students took over and consolidated their collective emotional status, with only the general direction still controlled by the teacher's questions (e.g. "Why does Zeeto like Julie?").

The function of the next extract is checking on the integration of information by the children into the ongoing discourse. "Why" questions, as we've seen, represent metaprocess questions (Mehan,

1979: 46); they concern processes that underlie processes. By using metaprocess questions, the teacher leaves responsibility for integrating the material grammatically and semantically entirely with the children. The data below shows where this process of freeing the attention control from the teacher is heading.

R: He is laughing. Right! Why is he laughing?

Ss: He's a ...(unintelligible) Ha ha!

S: Happy?

S: Happy!

MH: Funny? Funny!

R: Funny! Why is he funny?

SC: 여자 친구하고 싶어하는 거야? [He wants to make a girlfriend, ya!] (Child uses the intimate form of address, addressing the other children.)

S: Ha ha.

R: Zeeto likes Julie and it's funny to MH, OK.

SS and S's responses are not exactly answers to the question. Rather, they are evaluating the relationship between Zeeto and Julie. In so doing, they are actually entering the story, because in the CD-ROM version of the story, this relationship provokes mirth from Julie's little brother, Tony. One way to put this is that the students are taking an observer's view, and then a character's view (MacNeill, 2005: 187). In Bakhtinian terms, the students are going out from and returning to self (1990). Of course, according to Vygotsky's developmental theory, the children are at the stage in which children start to establish cognitive layer that observe the internal status of themselves, the concept of self. Here, the key is detaching from an internal status of self and emphasizing with the

other's perspective thus being able to observe the self from the third person.

Does the heightened interest about English language using avatars stimulate the students' English use? Students' use of English occurs simultaneously as students assume the roles of the avatars; it does not exist as an independent process. The same thing, of course, is true of their use of Korean. English represents only one more tool for students to express their feelings and attitudinal evaluation about what is going on. Since language itself is a tool to organize our way of thinking about and seeing world, foreign language requires the learners to adapt the self to the newly organized conceptual system of a new self.

Teaching, however, is always specific to the developmental level of the child. In the above data, second- and third-graders seems to have little problem with taking the role of characters in context. In contrast, when we look at the following data from a fifth and sixth grade integrated class, even the avatar presentation seems not to draw very much interest from the students.

R: OK.. This is...

Ss: Mrs Smith,

R: 다시 한 번.. [One more time] JH...is JH happy or not?

S: Happy,

R: Happy? Why?

Ss ...

R: OK, where are they?

Ss: Park

R: Is she happy or not?

Ss: Happy

R: Why happy?

S: 기분 나빠 보이지 않아요. *[She doesn't look like she's in a bad mood.] (This utterance is politely inflected and addressed to the teacher as a formal reply.)*

We do not find any shared affect from the students and the understanding of the context is fairly superficial; the reason one avatar character feels happy is given as simply that "she does not look like she's in a bad mood", and there is no attempt to speculate about the processes which underlie the mental process.

This flat affect is also manifested in the fifth- and sixth-graders' improvised role-play data below. The students are making a role-play after watching a lesson about finding the way to a famous Seoul landmark illustrated by their avatars show.

S1: Excuse me, can you help me?

S2: Sure I can

S3: Where is Namdaemun?

S4: I'm sorry?

S5: Where is Namdaemun?

S1: I'm sorry, one more, please.

S2: Namdaemun, please.

S3: Oh, Namdaemun?

S4: Yes.

S5: Go straight and turn...

R: 잠깐만.. 너희가 물어보는 사람이고 너희가 대답해 주는 사람 아니야? *[Wait a minute. Are you the guy who asks or aren't you the guy who answers?]*

It's not the characters, but the concept of role that has really been lost here. The labor is mechanically divided line by line, and the role-play has been reconceptualized as language practice, along the lines of the "Let's Play" relay game we examined earlier. This is a clear example that shows what happens in language class when the students have lost their interest about the when, the where, the how, and the who; that is to say, when students are alienated from the context.

Remarkably, there were many requests from higher graders to the teacher not to use their personal avatars in language material presentation to the whole class. In contrast, there were no such requests from lower graders, and many requests by students to use their personal avatars for presentation. We cannot attribute the differences we find between lower graders' responses and 5,sixth graders' responses to individual or group abilities or even confidence, since the lower graders tend to be much lower in ability and confidence. We can, however, attribute these differences to development. Higher graders have already constructed a stable image of the self, which does not include stumbling around to put together simple sentences in a foreign language in order to express the most basic and even infantile thoughts. So it is natural for older children to be embarrassed to see a familiar avatar shows up and do things they can't or even don't want to do.

CONCLUSION

Vygotsky argued that at school age, children encounter a totally new situation where abstract concepts are formed and exchanged by using language (Vygotsky, 1987: 172). Simultaneously, and also for the first time in their lives, children encounter a situation where they become a member of a recognized social group outside their family and are expected to observe its norms of behavior. Previously dominant ways of using language such as face-to-face ostension, (Wittgenstein, 1958: 32-34; Moro and Rodriguez, 2008) no longer suffice. In this new social environment, even the preceding way of directly expressing themselves through face-to-face interaction is not acceptable anymore; children have to raise their hands and ask permission just to speak.

Of course, these new roles and rules do not drop on children out of the blue. Some children have more or less mastered playing different roles in preschool and in relationships with extended family and non-relatives. Similarly, the ability to signify about entities that do not physically exist (e.g. the concept of number) presupposes the ability to name objects which do exist, just as the ability to name objects presupposes the ability to direct attention using language; the conceptualizing function of language does not drop from the moon or even out of a teacher's hands but instead grows from the firm soil of experience via thick roots, such as nominalizing and indicating, i.e., naming and pointing.

But the school predicament is new enough for the child. Children must learn to operate with concepts as they do with concrete objects. This predicament requires children to gain the ability to distinguish between internal states (feelings and ideas) and external representations (expressions), and again between representations and internal reflections on those representations (understandings). Thus at the beginning of school age, children start to build an intellectual layer between internal and external experience (Vygotsky, 1998: 291). This new layer is itself a kind of avatar, an imaginary friend called the "self" (Taylor, 1999).

In this case study, we have seen that student learning occurs when they get interested and engrossed in characters and situations, and that virtual worlds are highly conducive to bringing this about in younger children. The languages produced (native and foreign) are loaded with emotional coloration and this is actually at the core of the students' motivation, with the communication of information serving a secondary role. Specifically, we found that avatar material prompted the emotional engagement of the 2~fourth graders, and that students easily shared attention as a group around the avatars. However, we did not find such deep involvement in the fifth and sixth graders even when these were provided with the avatar. This can be explained according to the students' development of the concept of self: the children feel preoccupied with a "real" self and no longer require or want an alien one that competes with it, particularly not if that "self" has to speak an alien language. Even for these higher-level children, therefore, the ability to think in concepts seems to be inextricably bound up with emotional, affective inclinations and the development of an evaluative, partisan, critical stance towards their social environment. With the younger children, we have seen the locus of control smoothly moving from teacher to students without the teacher's conscious intention. The intentional picking up of language only happened as a tool to express their emotional states in the ways the avatars did.

CURRENT CHALLENGES FACING THE ORGANIZATION

Of course, a little English use by the children during a ten-day English camp does not guarantee successful English learning. In the same way, the autonomous control of volition through avatar material does not guarantee the student's volitional development. Yet in both cases, we may say that learning awakens processes that must ultimately lead to abrupt leaps in consciousness. In the younger children, these processes are intensely social and easily shared; in the older ones, they are more personal and individual, and less susceptible to public display. As Vygotsky argued, the child is not born a personality. Even in English, the child's sense of "I" must be developed out of a sense of "we".

ACKNOWLEDGMENT

I appreciate the inspiration, guidance and support of professor David Kellogg in the writing and editing of this chapter.

REFERENCES

Bakhtin, M. M. (1990). *Art and answerability.* Austin, TX: University of Texas Press.

Freud, S. (1971). Desire expressed in children's dreams. In A.H. Munsinger (Ed.), *Readings in child development* (pp. 410-412). New York: Holt, Rinehard, and Winston.

Gillen, J. (2003). *The language of children.* London: Routledge.

Guk, I.-J., & Kellogg, D. (2007). The ZPD and whole class teaching: Teacher-led and student-led interactional mediation of tasks. *Language Teaching Research, 11*(3), 281–299. doi:10.1177/1362168807077561

Johnson, K. (1996). *Language teaching and skill learning.* Cambridge, MA: Blackwell.

Kim, Y.-H., & Kellogg, D. (2007). Rules out of roles: Differences in play language and their developmental significance. *Applied Linguistics, 28*(1), 25–45. doi:10.1093/applin/aml047

Kwon, M.-S., & Kellogg, D. (2005). Teacher talk as a game of catch. *Canadian Modern Language Review, 62*(2), 335–348.

Kwon, O.-R. (2006). *Suggestions for facilitating English education in elementary and middle schools on the basis of the analysis of ten years' elementary English education achievements.* Seoul, Korea: Ministry of Education and Development of Human Recourses.

McNeill, D. (2005). *Gesture and thought.* Chicago: University of Chicago Press.

Mehan, H. (1979). *Learning lessons: Social organization in the classroom.* Cambridge, MA: Harvard University Press.

Moro, C., & Rodriguez, C. (2008). Production of signs and meaning-making process in triadic interaction at the prelinguistic level. In E. Abbey & R. Diriwächter (Eds.), *Innovating genesis: Microgenesis and the constructive mind in action* (pp. 207-227). Charlotte, NC: Information Age Publishing.

Piaget, J. (1959). *The language and thought of the child.* New York: Routledge.

Piaget, J., & Inhelder, B. (1969, 2000). *The psychology of the child.* New York: Basic.

Sachs, J. (1997, December 11). The IMF is a power unto itself. *Financial Times.*

Shin, J.-E., & Kellogg, D. (2007). The novice, the native and the nature of teaching expertise. *International Journal of Applied Linguistics, 17*(2), 159–177. doi:10.1111/j.1473-4192.2007.00144.x

Stiglitz, J. (2000, April 17). What I learned at the world economic crisis. *New Republic,* 56-60.

Taylor, M. (1999). *Imaginary companions and the children who create them.* New York: Oxford University Press.

Vygotsky, L. S. (1987). *Collected works Vol. 1.* New York: Plenum.

Vygotsky, L. S. (1997). *Collected works Vol. 3.* New York: Plenum.

Vygotsky, L. S. (1998). *Collected works Vol. 5.* New York: Plenum.

Wittengenstein, L. (1958). *Philosophical investigations* (3rd ed.). New York: MacMillan.

FURTHER READING

Guk, Y.-J., & Kellogg, D. (2006). The ZPD and whole class teaching: Teacher-led and student-led interactional mediation of tasks. *Language Teaching Research, 11*(3), 281–299. doi:10.1177/1362168807077561

Kim, Y.-H., & Kellogg, D. (2007). Rules out of roles: Some differences in play language and their developmental significant. *Applied Linguistics, 28*(1), 25–45. doi:10.1093/applin/aml047

Kim, Y.-H., & Kellogg, D. (2009). Pulgasari: Ethics emerging from esthetics. *Mind, Culture, and Activity.* Kim, Y.-H., & Kellogg, D. (2008). Task and play in the words and minds of children. *Journal of Applied Linguistics, 3*(1), 25–47.

Lim, E.-S., & Kellogg, D. (2008). The ascent of the concrete: Grammatical reification in science teaching exchanges and episodes. *Language and Education, 22*(3), 206-222. Shin, J.-E., & Kellogg, D. (2007). The novice, the native, and the nature of language teaching expertise. *International Journal of Applied Linguistics, 17*(2), 159–177.

Chapter 5
Transpositions in Configurable Virtual Storyworlds

James J. Sosnoski
University of Illinois at Chicago, USA

Kevin Q. Harvey
University of Illinois at Chicago, USA

Jordan Stalker
University of Illinois at Chicago, USA

Colleen Monahan
University of Illinois at Chicago, USA

EXECUTIVE SUMMARY

BACKGROUND: *The Center for the Advancement of Distance Education (CADE) is a self-supporting unit within the School of Public Health at the University of Illinois at Chicago. The center's services range from online continuing education and professional training to multimedia Web-casting and research data management, analysis and presentation.* **TECHNOLOGY USED:** *In public health emergency response training, an isolation and quarantine situation is one of the most challenging. Second Life has the capability and potential to address many of the training and planning challenges associated with such a sensitive topic. It enables public health emergency responders to test and refine existing plans and procedures in a safe, controllable, immersive and repeatable environment.* **CASE STUDY:** *A quarantine scenario designed for emergency training. The authors designed "The Canyon Crossroads" as a key transit point between two quarantine areas and two uninfected areas. They placed a state border to divide the crossroads leaving quarantine zones in each jurisdiction. The local hospital was located in one of the quarantine zones and it is an official holding and treatment location for infected victims. The exercise involves transmitting persons in and out of the four areas.* **CHALLENGES:** *There are three challenges the authors are currently addressing: (a) how to increase the levels of engagement in the training process, (b) how to construct a virtual world that fosters collaboration, and (c) how to measure the levels of engagement in this collaborative environment.*

DOI: 10.4018/978-1-60566-878-9.ch005

BACKGROUND

The Center for the Advancement of Distance Education

The Center for the Advancement of Distance Education (CADE) is a self-supporting unit within the School of Public Health at the University of Illinois at Chicago. CADE partners or contracts with university, government, non-profit and for-profit organizations to provide innovative technological solutions to meet a variety of educational, training, research and administrative needs. These collaborations include the creation of interactive online training modules, the design and development of web sites, simulations, games and virtual worlds, mobile phone applications, multimedia production and webcasting, course registration and learning management system construction, web-based programming and database connectivity, and online data gathering and analysis. By expanding into new and emerging technological fields, CADE has managed to sustain continued growth in personnel, annual revenue, client base, and number of simultaneous projects.

Management Structure

Dr. Colleen Monahan, CADE's Director and Founder, has 20 years experience successfully managing a self-supporting unit. From 1986 to 1997, she founded and ran a self-funded Research and Development (R&D) unit within the UIC Division of Specialized Care for Children (DSCC). This unit focused on the development of proposals/projects that focused on children with special needs and their families.

Eventually the topics of interest broadened to include more public health populations and, in 1997 she transferred the unit and staff to the School of Public Health. CADE has a successful 10-year track record with revenues of over 22 million to date.

CADE employs more than 25 personnel - all full-time staff have college degrees; all higher-level staff have advanced degrees. Given the technical nature of CADE's activities, most of the staff have been recruited from their respective specialist fields: the Multimedia and Webcasting staff come from professional audio-video industries; the Web Design and Development group come from the graphic design, instructional design, programming, usability and project management professions; the Research Data Management staff have epidemiology, statistics, and programming backgrounds; the Network and Server Administration team have computer engineering, information technology and management and information systems expertise.

CADE mobilizes and integrates expertise across its production groups: Web Design and Project Management; Multimedia and Webcasting; Research Data Management; Data Systems Programming and Public Health Preparedness. This integration capacity permits the Center to deliver services that incorporate features drawing from a wide variety of specialized activities, which address the client's specific and specialized needs. CADE's projects blend programming, webcasting, web design, instructional design, data analysis, and learning/knowledge management

Figure 1. CADE organizational chart

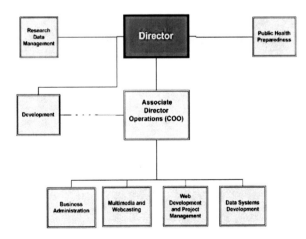

system creation and development in ways few other organizations can.

Type of Business

Products and Services

CADE services include:

- Support for online educational programs (e.g., skill building for faculty and staff, course development and remote communication strategies);
- Development of training/information/entertaining CD-ROMs and DVDs;
- Development of serious games and simulations, including virtual worlds;
- Development of facilitated virtual tabletop exercises using virtual worlds;
- Studio and Location Recording (e.g. HD video, Digital DVCAM or MiniDV in single or multi-camera productions, DAT and hard disk audio recording);
- Support for internet-based meetings (broadcasting/webcasting);
- Development of Internet-based applications to support business and educational systems. (e.g., online Course Evaluation Questionnaires, registration systems, online inventories, etc.);
- Assistance in writing grant proposals to include use of innovative online technologies;
- Development of informational web sites; and
- Research data management support for research projects.

SETTING THE STAGE

Use of Second Life Technology

Any activity that involves the emergency response field, from didactic training to drills and exercises, creates a significant cost structure for those involved. Often, local health departments, especially those that function with shrinking budgets and human resources, cannot fully implement processes that would create cost savings after a high initial cost.

In public health emergency response, an Isolation and Quarantine situation is one of the most challenging to rehearse and mitigate. Each state has the capability to exercise Isolation and Quarantine orders and every Pandemic Plan includes Isolation and Quarantine mitigation options, the issues surrounding these operations repeatedly trigger disagreements in strategy and ethics. It is also difficult, if not impossible, to exercise some of the possible scenarios, such as the quarantine of a school or a section of a community, in any realistic or meaningful way.

There are two major concerns at issue when dealing with Isolation and Quarantine scenarios: First is the ethical dilemma of protecting the public without violating their rights of privacy or liberty. Second, and probably most provocative, is the issue of enforcement, which can lead all the way to considerations of lethal force.

Second Life has the capability and potential to address many of the training and planning challenges associated with such a sensitive topic. It enables public health emergency responders to test and refine existing plans and procedures, or to assist in developing plans, if they do not yet exist; all in a safe, controllable, immersive and repeatable environment.

There are two major benefits: First, with the exception of the costs to acquire parcels of *Second Life* islands and employ builders, there is almost no expense to run the scenario, whether it is a medical supplies dispensation, a quarantine or mass fatality management. Second, there are no real, permanent consequences to the scenarios. If the users of the *Second Life* training course fail to effectively contain a major disease outbreak, such as pandemic influenza, they can, at CADE's discretion, retry the scenario until they get it right. This is of course unlike an offline disaster where the effects are permanent.

Second Life allows for organizations to create unique tutorial islands for their users. CADE has established one such environment that it calls Preparedness Island. The environment is a cluster of islands owned and maintained by CADE (the permission to build on these islands – to place objects in the environment – has been granted by Linden Labs, the creator of the *Second Life* platform.). The islands include an airport terminal, a shopping mall, a high school gymnasium, businesses and a hospital.

CADE uses *Second Life* to implement a set of best practices for training. In an effort to appeal to the widest number of clients, CADE provides access to *Second Life* in several formats. All of these combine to make for an enriching experience that increases efficiency and utility of the trainees.

Using *Second Life* enables the clients to immerse themselves in the Virtual Learning Environment (VLE) and interact with the environment and create an experience much closer to the real emergency situation for which they are planning. Hypothetical situations discussed in flow charts and PowerPoint presentations typically fail to capture the audience's attention in a way that fosters memorization.

The scenarios that utilize Auto-Bot Interaction (see Table 1) afford the opportunity to witness consequences, virtual though they are, of incorrect or inefficient response.

Advancement of Virtual Learning Environments

It does not seem totally out of line to place VLEs and Collaborative Learning Environments (CLEs) in the same lineage of educational technologies such as instructional television channels or open learning systems. Those technologies gained notoriety in the 1960s and especially took off in least-developed countries where large segments of the population had access to radio or televi-

Table 1. CADE's training techniques for collaborative learning environments

Training Type	Description
Groupthink	Large groups of trainees share a guided, simultaneous virtual world experience
Breakout Groups with "Designated Drivers"	Small groups assigned unique tasks guided by group leaders with virtual world experience
Benchmark Training	Expert CADE staff set benchmarks for training to identify understanding and knowledge gaps of the users
Command Team Training	Groups are assigned to respond and manage a disaster as first responders or materials dispensation
Incident Command System Reinforcement	Participants gain knowledge of the National Incident Management System through division of labor
Intelligent Environment	Uses in-world triggers to progress through the scenario
Auto-Bot Interaction	Involves interaction with pre-programmed objects, including Non-player Character (NPC) avatars, that enhances learning and training
Automatic Data Set Generation	Allows automated collection of data from scenario

sion signals but not classroom-based education (for a more detailed description of open learning systems, see Hawkridge, 1977).

One of the major drawbacks to large-scale open learning systems, as with any technology, is a very high startup cost. The client base, students from impoverished nations, makes for a difficult time recuperating those initial capital expenditures. *Second Life* provides a means for nearly free initial setup and a very low maintenance fee. With only very few exceptions, the costs associated with maintaining a presence in *Second Life* will never reach the same level as those of a material, physical model and training program. For example, if a vaccine is distributed in the offline world, the moment the vaccine is distributed and ingested by a patient that product no longer exists and more must be manufactured and brought to the distribution site. In-world, however, programmers can embed an island with the instructions to regenerate objects instantaneously or on a time release. Instantaneous regeneration allows the users of the scenario to try a different method of distribution and the benefit of a time-released object is of course that it better simulates what would happen in the field during an actual emergency while a response team waits for supplies to be replenished.

Teaching Practices

The CADE staff has used *Second Life* to design and demonstrate several types of emergency preparedness scenarios. Prior to engaging in the work related to the current grant under review that involves medication dispensation, mass fatality management and quarantining procedures, CADE developed, in consultation with the University of Illinois Hospitals, a functional scale model of the University of Illinois Hospital in Chicago, Illinois. The purpose of that scenario was to train the employees of the hospital what must be done in the case of a total facility evacuation.

In all three case studies, CADE developed a comprehensive training manual for the partici-

pants. The manuals combine an introduction to the *Second Life* VLE and included a series of learning objectives for the users. There were also several sets of exercise and evaluative questions in addition to step-by-step instructions that described how to proceed with the scenario.

Teaching Philosophy

CADE established its Readiness Training Group in 2005 with the vision that it could use new technologies like *Second Life* to deliver greater service and results to its immediate clients, which would in turn produce information about disaster situations that would facilitate recovery, response and prevention efforts for the affected populations. The user-generated content focus of *Second Life* enables CADE's team of programmers and designers to implement nearly limitless concepts for its clients. Given enough time to physically design objects for and write programming scripts for scenarios, CADE uses *Second Life*'s open platform technology to enhance training in and analysis of situations like those described in this chapter.

Like open learning systems of previous decades, VLEs enable CADE to service urban and rural communities and provide them with essential emergency preparedness training. The exercises meet the federally mandated standards set by the Centers for Disease Control and the Department of Homeland Security. This compliance with institutionalized standards and formalization enables the CADE staff to act and attract with a certain degree of reputation and stature that most non-university or non-governmental bodies – in other words, independent private sector entrepreneurs such as those who have long existed in *Second Life* – cannot have.

Those who agree to participate in VLE-based exercises and scenarios are expected to comply with a small but meaningful set of protocols. Trainees can take some solace in the fact that there are no right or wrong answers that must be set in stone. With VLEs, there is no need to "game the system" as might occur in other scenarios that attempt to use artificial methods to train people for crisis response. Each decision simply opens the path toward a set of new decisions. The trainees are also encouraged to engage the scenario with responses gleaned from individual user knowledge or institutional knowledge held by organizations like the CDC, DHS and CDPH. Lastly, the trainee must work to cooperate with and anticipate the needs and requests of agencies he or she may partner with in an actual emergency situation.

Teachers and Students

The CADE staff fills the role of the teacher in many of the scenarios with which it deals. Ideally they train a small core of individual clients to become adept enough so that the client can become self-sustaining to manage the project in the event of any continual or long-term processes.

"Teaching" in or about virtual environments is a bit of a misnomer. The term "facilitator" might be better. This is especially true in the early adopter stage. Although relatively new in development, given their cost effectiveness in emergency training, educational technology tools like Second Life are likely to be incorporated into future classrooms, especially when training exercises are costly and inconvenient. Most of the courses taught that make heavy use of *Second Life* are appearing in the catalogs at universities for the first time. Some of the instructors, even if they are adjunct lecturers who have careers building and utilizing *Second Life* or similar products, are sometimes only minimally more savvy than the students they intend to teach.

It is also difficult to standardize instructional elements in *Second Life*. The novelty of *Second Life* lies in the user's ability to change his or her appearance and to shape the environment. This can also pose a problem when it comes time to devise a syllabus that includes visits to different locations and islands. If an instructor assigns students to investigate a company's *Second Life* presence, the island has the potential to change in the interval between the instructor's visit to the island and a student's visit. The difference from a textbook is clear: the textbook does not change. Even revised translations or expanded editions must be treated as new texts. *Second Life* is decidedly more adaptive and responsive to the desires of the users and programmers who take it upon themselves to change the "text."

The *CADE* project is no exception to the scenario just described. An investigator's experience is dependent on the time when they encounter the island. A person familiar with the island as the hospital was being built will take away significantly different types of information than those of a person who visits it now. Both users would also have different experiences if they visited the island by themselves instead of visiting it as part of the pre-arranged training put on by the City of Chicago and CADE. Both sets of users have different preconceptions of how their experiences ought to be represented. Without proper preparation, both users run the risk of becoming frustrated with the scenario during their time spent meandering through the environment. Another important point is that a *Second Life* island, especially one that has a specific use in mind, is often a tightly controlled environment. The ideology and intention behind the structure and design of the islands is not always readily apparent. Without having the builders or experts to guide them through the experience, the chance to fully understand – and thusly fully appreciate – the reasons behind certain decisions is lost. We are still learning how to manage such differences.

CASE DESCRIPTION

[Note: the technologies involved are discussed in the section "Setting the Stage"]

The Isolation and Quarantine Exercise: Management and Organizational Concerns

In Pandemic Plans, the most extreme instances of quarantine (*cordon sanitaire*) are repeatedly regarded as improbable. However, lethal viruses or toxic agents suddenly increase the likelihood of quarantine not only for individuals but for communities. And setting up quarantine in a bio-event is still applicable for setting up cordons for other disasters like fire or flood.

Although with infectious diseases the question for communities is which side of the quarantine line you fall on. Are you keeping something out of your community or keeping it in? And due to the divisive nature of quarantine, can it ever work voluntarily?

These issues become even more complex when they occur at the borders of tribal reservation lands, especially if the quarantine direction creates a reservation versus state dynamic as in our case. Practicing collaboration between state and tribal representatives is critical to sort out the issues in such cases.

Tribal communities not only have special jurisdictional and legal concerns regarding quarantine, but they also have a history of tragic experience. We make an effort in this exercise to explore various scenario complications and balance the tribal needs with the state plans.

In this exercise, we begin with a sample response and allow trainees to change it according to the recommendations of their group.

Description of the Project

Quarantine Scenario

In this scenario, the Canyon Crossroads is a key transit point between two quarantine areas and two uninfected areas. However, the state border divides the crossroads leaving quarantine zones in each jurisdiction. The local hospital is in one of the quarantine zones north on Hwy A and it has become an official holding and treatment location for infected victims.

And just to make things a bit more complicated, a fruit stand is located on Canyon Road East, not far from the intersection. It is a mainstay supplier of

Figure 2. Canyon Crossroads map

food for local populations. The Health Department has carefully tested and inspected its employees for signs of infection and cleared them.

The quarantine exercise has several functions that, optimally, result in successful completion of a number of learning objectives. The first function is to establish criteria for the decision-making process that mirrors the local health officers' procedures to determine how to support those in charge of the quarantine process, including the appropriate steps to protect the local population.

Next, the exercise should identify hierarchy of control and leadership among and within the local health officers and partner agencies. This leadership transparency is especially important when conflict arises through encounters with individuals who try to leave the quarantine or isolation areas.

The exercise should also provide a demonstration of the steps necessary to limit the spread of the outbreak. These steps can include infection-control measures, adherence to jurisdictional issues that may arise in a crisis situation involving multiple groups – as seen in the mismanagement of the Hurricane Katrina aftermath – proper use of protective equipment. The use of decision trees and procedural maps is an integral part in successful detection, intervention and dissolution of infected cases.

The delegation of tasks across a core staff and the identification of suitable containment facilities is also made easier in *Second Life*. Across multiple iterations of the same scenario, users of the test program can switch roles and discover for which tasks they are best suited, without risking the lives of their team members or the citizens at risk in a crisis.

The quarantine exercises, as stated above, have numerous learning objectives attached to them. These objectives, for our purposes here, can be grouped into categories of information gathering and process streamlining.

Information gathering enables users to determine the capabilities and limitations of their current systems (as well as those of the *Second Life* VLE), which in turn improve the plans and procedures used. These limitations can include inadequate resources, ineffective or insufficient training and improper communication. The information should also enable the team to understand why previous isolation and quarantine systems were designed and implemented in prior cases.

Prior to execution, project members must reach consensus with each other. *Second Life* allows colleagues to evaluate and test out policies and procedures without danger and without waiting for an actual crisis. The employment of VLE technology enables the response team to test its preparedness at various levels of incident and degrees of severity.

As with any training scenario, it is important to recognize that the exercises in the real world do not exist in a vacuum. Responders must operate within the context of existing legal requirements and restrictions. A *Second Life*-based scenario is only as robust as the technological expertise of the builders. It is typically very difficult to incorporate all real-world variables into a scenario, especially those relating to the law. The upside is that, of course, there are no legal ramifications for failing in a *Second Life* scenario as there could be in an actual crisis situation. This freedom to act without penalty is a large potential criticism of the true usefulness of VLE programs. Careful research, however, can protect the integrity of the exercise.

After participating in the VLE-based exercise, the team should have sufficient information for meaningful discussion about shortcomings and successes. The evaluations that follow participation can include several points for improvement that optimally lead to a revised, expanded and more efficient plan of action to set up another scenario. The participants should also be able to perform additional reports and conduct further tests, using the information gathered from the scenario as examples.

The learning objectives described should have the intention of refining and retooling the *Second Life*-based scenario so that the responders are trained to the limits of their ability – or the limits of the software's ability to reflect the desired variables.

In order to accomplish these learning objectives, the *Second Life*-based exercises make the following assumptions of the user: (a) the user feels that the scenario is plausible and the events are realistic; (b) the user acts only as the local-level responder, operating independently from state and federal response teams that will have their own procedures and operations.

Related Issues: Commuters Play Large Role in Flu Spread

The potential for the avian influenza strain H5N1 – popularly known as bird flu – to spread into the human population and kill tens of millions of people has motivated researchers to study how influenza spreads. Some researchers at the US National Institutes of Health found through mathematical modeling that long commuter trips play a large role in spreading influenza.

Researchers at the National Institutes of Health (NIH) conclude that the regional spread of annual influenza epidemics throughout the United States is more closely connected with rates of movement of people to and from work than with geographical distance or air travels. They also found that epidemics spread faster between more populous locations. While it is not possible to know how the bird flu epidemic would affect people only using an interactive model, it is very appropriate to employ VLE approaches when the goal is to run risk assessments related to spread, especially given the opportunity to immediately generate data on long-tem hypothetical situations.

CURRENT CHALLENGES FACING THE ORGANIZATION

The Challenges

There are three challenges we are currently addressing: (a) how to increase the levels of engagement in the training process, (b) how to construct a virtual world that fosters collaboration, and (c) how to measure the levels of engagement in collaborating.

These challenges stem from CADE's most recent project—"Preparedness and Emergency Response Using Simulated Environments" (PERUSE)—which has recently been funded by the Centers for Disease Control and Prevention (COTPER/CDC) of the United States Department of Health and Human Services (HHS). The overall goal of this project is to determine whether the use of a Collaborative Virtual Environment (CVE) improves individual and system performance in public health preparedness and response planning. Though we believe that the use of Virtual Environments such as *Second Life* show great promise as a low cost ways to address some of the challenges we face, very little research has been done in their usefulness for training. . This project looks at the issues surrounding the use of Second Life to support a collaborative disaster response planning process.

The Aims of the project are:

1. To discover whether a Collaborative Virtual Environment (CVE) has the capabilities to improve administrative and operational collaboration and cooperation in emergency response planning.
2. To discover whether a CVE has the capabilities to increase awareness of the need to plan for vulnerable populations.

3. To discover whether increasing realism in the training exercise increase the effectiveness of planning.
4. To discover whether an agency, after introducing a tool like the CVE, will continue to use it.

Each of these aims depends upon the degree of engagement the trainees have in performing in the Collaborative Virtual Environment specific to their mission. By "engagement" we mean, the act of participating in the activities of a group, particularly when sharing a collective aim. Collaboration and cooperation are attitudes that engender dispositions to act in concert with others. Awareness of needs depends upon attentiveness to the conditions that call for them. The effectiveness of a group depends upon a commitment to shared concerns. The continued use of a tool depends upon the extent to which persons are committed to a purpose. Dispositions, awareness, commitment, and continuous practice all involve emotion (an integral aspect of motivation). Increasing the level of engagement in training exercises is a critical component of the project's aims.

Problems that the Organization Faces

Empirical evidence shows that the current public health system is severely lacking in the knowledge, skills, abilities that are required for an effective response. The *Nationwide Plan Review* (U.S. Department of Homeland Security 2006), the most comprehensive assessment of catastrophic planning yet undertaken in this country, found that the majority of the nation's current emergency operations plans and planning processes cannot be characterized as fully adequate, feasible, or acceptable to manage catastrophic events as defined in the *National Response Plan* (U.S. Department of Homeland Security, 2004). They also found that planning processes are outmoded, current tools and guidance are rudimentary, and planning expertise

is insufficient for catastrophic incidents. Further, states and urban areas are not conducting adequate collaborative planning, as a part of "steady state"' preparedness. The response to Hurricane Katrina uncovered major structural flaws in our current system for national preparedness. Most experts agree that a more collaborative approach is the best solution to effective disaster response (Waugh & Streib, 2006). So, the challenge is not only how do we engage persons to commit to a common purpose, but more specifically how do we motivate persons to collaborate with each other. It is one thing to share a common goal, but quite another to be disposed to work with others. In the light of these general circumstances, we are focusing on the three specific problems mentioned earlier: *increasing engagement* by *using story based models of virtual worlds* and finding *ways to measure the results*.

a) Increasing the level of engagement

Although virtual worlds that simulate real life experiences engage their visitors through several senses and although experiences in virtual worlds are recalled more readily than those encountered in conventional learning contexts, nonetheless, virtual worlds do not invariably induce significant *felt*-experiences. Since users do not necessarily identify with their avatars, learning in virtual worlds is often experienced as an exercise that mimics real life situations and thus is a less "serious" event. On the other hand, when users identify with their avatars to the point that they experience feelings as if they were actually in the situation, learning is intensified and the gap between the virtual world and the real world is bridged to varying degrees. In such instances, a transposition occurs during which participants in virtual worlds experience what they expect their avatars to feel in such circumstances.

Consider the differences among the most common types of virtual worlds with respect to participant reactions to them. A selective list of different types of simulated worlds would include:

a. Cinema-graphic Worlds (e.g., 3D films shown to audiences who react to their effects)
b. Computer Assisted Worlds (e.g., computer-aided design (CAD) programs on computers creating 3D artifacts and scenes)
c. Video Game Worlds (e.g., shooter games that provide interactivity with figures in the world)
d. Immersive VR Worlds (e.g., CAVEs—Immersive VR with an environment back-projected on several walls creating the sense of being inside the environment.)
e. Projected VR Worlds (e.g,. GeoWall technology—Computer assisted projections of 3D environments onto a screen.)
f. Habitable VR Worlds (e.g., Second Life)[1]

Each of these worlds was designed with specific goals in mind and for distinct audiences. Aspects of four of these virtual worlds are pertinent to our project because they intensify virtual experiences and have "as-if real" effects. However, different degrees of participant involvement depend on the medium and the type of virtual world. Each medium engages our senses in different ways. *Absorption* is a term suitable for readers of fiction because they become absorbed in the virtual world their imagination creates in response to the narrative. Movie audiences seem *entranced* by the audio/visual spectacles in front of them because films put their audience members in a trancelike state where they are controlled by the images and sounds they experience. Of course, the size of the screen and the deployment of sound alter an audience's experience. Seeing the same film in a fully equipped theatre is not the same experience as seeing it on TV. Visitors to VR CAVES are typically *immersed* in an environment with which they interact. Second Life scenarios can attain the highest degree of interactivity in a virtual world

where participants can be *transposed* and behave with considerable agency and creativity as if they were their avatars (Sosnoski, 2006, p. 40).

Depending upon the effectiveness of the narrative presentation, any of the media mentioned can *transport* its audience albeit to varying degrees. The phenomenon of "psychological transportation," is defined "as a state in which a reader becomes absorbed in the narrative world, leaving the real world, at least momentarily, behind" (Green & Brock, 2002, p. 317). Media can induce their participants to *transpose* themselves only on the condition that audiences identify with the desires or conflicts of a figure in a narrative. Relating these two phenomena to virtual worlds, it is critical to our project that transportation, together with transposition, warrants the highest degree of interactivity possible in an avatar-based environment and thus the highest degree of engagement.

b) Why a gaming model of a virtual world should be replaced by a *storyworld* model.

Based on their propensity to produce specific types of interaction, we can classify virtual worlds along the following lines:

1. Absorbed (attentive observation)
   a. Subjects enter a *simulated world*, which is a replica of real life (e.g., early versions of emergency situations such as Cease-Fire which replicated Chicago neighborhoods where gang activity is common).
   b. Feelings are typically projected onto figures in the world as concepts of what they might be.
2. Entranced (via immersion & interaction via partial agency).
   a. Subjects enter a *game world* (e.g., *The Disaster Game*, where participants must respond to an emergency situation)

    b.   Feelings are typically internalized and added to one's autobiographical memory.

3.   Transported (via immersion & interaction but without agency)

    a.   Subjects enter a STORYWORLD (e.g., a film, such as Christopher Stapleton and Charles Hughes's experiential entertainment trailers, which are designed to add narrative and entertainment elements to instructional scenarios).

    b.   Feelings are typically internalized and assimilated to previous ones in similar situations)

4.   Transposed (transported agency and creative involvement)

    a.   Subjects enter a CONFIGURATION (i.e., Configurable World) (e.g., "The Thing Growing," an immersive VR scenario designed to evoke anger.).

    b.   Feelings are typically accommodated—revising previous felt experiences stored in memory.

The typical differences in affordances (Gibson, 1977; Norman 1988)[2] among these four virtual worlds would be:

1.   *Simulated worlds* allow visitors to passively experience the environment.

2.   *Game worlds* add *interactivity*, allowing participants to alter the environment and to make choices about navigating it.[3]

3.   *Storyworlds* add *a plot* with twists and turns that requires resolution through problem solving.

4.   *Configurable worlds* add *creativity* and a greater *propensity for transportation & transposing.*

There is no doubt that virtual worlds are changing the way we think about learning, collaboration, and networking at intra- and inter-organizational levels, and in fact, how we think about learning

environments themselves (Dickey, 2005). A review of two distance learning projects using a virtual environment, concluded that a *virtual world* had significant potential for facilitating collaborations, community and experiential learning and that it allowed learners to become situated and embodied within the learning environment (Dickey, 2005).

It is clear that, due to the realistic nature of virtual environments, learners experience situations that are impossible or difficult to experience in the real world for reasons of safety, cost, time, etc. (Corti, 2006; Squire & Jenkins, 2003). In educational applications, studies have shown that an immersive learning experience creates a profound sense of motivation and concentration conducive to mastering complex, abstract material. (Swartout & van Lent, 2003). David Shaffer, Kurt Squire, Richard Halverson and James Gee (2005) argue that acting in virtual worlds makes it possible to develop situated understandings, effective social practices, powerful identities, shared values, and ways of thinking of important communities of practice.

Although *Second Life* does not render the level of fidelity (or high cost) found in high-end virtual reality systems such as military flight or medical patient simulators, there is evidence that it has enough verisimilitude to provide for an immersive experience. Research by Jan Herrington, Thomas Reeves, and Ron Oliver (2007) indicates that the "cognitive realism" of the task is of greater importance than its realistic simulation. They have found that it is the task itself that is the key element of immersion and engagement and that the technologies can be used as cognitive tools in constructivist learning to solve complex problems. But Shaffer, et al (2005) and Kurt Squire and Henry Jenkins et al (2003) assert that there needs to be more research into the use of CVEs in education.

New training approaches are needed that not only enhance preparedness skills, but create a culture of readiness. Daniel Barnett, George

Everly, Jr., Cindy Parker and Jonathan Links (2005) explain that "this may require innovative training and organizational development methods to enhance preparedness skills, and create a culture of organizational readiness among public health workers through a process of "syntonic" organizational change. In the syntonic model, organizational change is a nonthreatening, natural growth process that is more likely to be embraced by employees than resisted; key factors in syntonic change include anticipatory guidance and experiential learning. In addition to teaching competency-based factual information, preparedness curricula must also foster appropriate attitudinal "buy-in" from public health employees about their new professional readiness duties. The use of CVEs is consistent with the syntonic model of organizational change, as these can incorporate experiential learning to have an impact on knowledge and attitudes in a nonthreatening way. (2005). Competition is, in a number of respects, "threatening." Cooperation, by contrast, is nonthreatening.

In this context, it may be time to let go of the influence that video gaming has had upon the creation of virtual worlds and move toward a more "collaborative" type of situation. Games, after all are either won or lost, hence they induce competition more than collaboration.[4] Storyworlds, on the other hand, provide roles for participants and those roles can be collaborative rather than competitive.

A team of programmers and educational researchers from the Electronic Visualization Lab at UIC developed N.I.C.E: Narrative-based Immersive Constructionists-Collaborative Environments.

NICE is a project that applies virtual reality to the creation of a family of educational environments for young users. Our approach is based on constructionism, where real and synthetic users, motivated by an underlying narrative, build persisting virtual worlds through collaboration. This approach is grounded on well-established paradigms in contemporary learning and integrates ideas from such diverse fields as virtual reality, human-computer interaction, CSCW, storytelling, and artificial intelligence.[5]

We have a backlog of experience at UIC in constructing Configurable *Storyworlds* as collaborative environments. Consequently, we recommend a combination of the third and fourth types of virtual world mentioned above—a configurable story-world which Second Life technology makes possible. But, how can we measure the degree of engagement in a configurable *storyworld* designed as a collaborative environment.

c)   How do you measure engagement?

While virtual simulation environments provide a means to construct "artificial worlds" in which individuals can have experiences in a realistic interactive setting, the degree of control and observability that is feasible in these environments depends upon what is being measured. *While it is difficult to estimate engagement, nonetheless it can be measured with respect to the language used by participants to describe their virtual experiences.* Discourse Analysis provides a variety of tools for identifying emotional engagement. For this reason, we have chosen interview and ethnographic modes of assessment to track the degree of participant engagement.

Measures that will be collected include team performance evaluations, as indicated by such factors as the number of tasks successfully completed.[6] It is also possible to measure process variables that provide insight into decision strategies and team coordination, such as the speed with which different tasks are processed (including time to complete the exercise), the existence of uneven task loading across team members, the transfer of information among team members, and the transfer of resources among team members. Communication measures can also be collected. Text based communication measures and audio recordings will be collected and scored by project staff either in real time or from recordings. This data, collectively, provides an account of participant engagement.

In addition, measures will be collected from individuals participating in each planning group and from observers of each planning group.

Observer-Based Team Process Measures are obtained from trained observers who observe team performance and processes during a scenario run. The ratings they provide will pertain to individual members of the team, to subcomponents of the team, or to the team as a whole.

Participant-Based Knowledge and Perception Measures focus on individual respondents, other team members (individually or collectively), the team as a whole, and on factors associated with the scenario itself. These include subjective workload, mutual awareness measures, and team members' assessments of team processes and performance, as well as evaluation of the scenario. Participant-based measures will be obtained at the end of each scenario.

The particular measures that are collected in any given situation will depend upon the factors incorporated into the scenario and the goals of the training context in which the measures are collected. The purpose of the measures used in these efforts will be to assess how teams structure and how the use of the CVE affects the team's processes, and how those processes contributed to outcomes. See Table 2.

The Current Status of the Aforementioned Challenges and Problems

As we have mentioned above, the three challenges we are currently addressing concern: increasing the levels of engagement, fostering collaboration, and measuring the outcomes of our experiments. Currently, we are at the design stage. Our designs are based on a variety of virtual reality experiments and courses conducted at UIC in the communica-

tion department, in the electronic visualization lab, and the CADE labs.

With respect to increasing the level of involvement, we are addressing this problem on the basis of other VR scenarios that provided successful "experience transfers," e.g., the Round Earth Project. From a cognitive point-of-view, our aim is to generate an "experience transfer"—a transfer of virtual experiences in *Second Life* to real life (RL) experiences through the conduit of an avatar. The virtual experiences are thus remembered in RL situations and provide strategies for coping with them. Drawing upon recent developments in Cognitive Psychology and Neuroscience, we believe that virtual experiences that re sult in "deep" learning (significant changes in perspectives) depend upon the process of transposition wherein persons assume the identities of their avatars and experience a virtual environment as if they were their avatars. In this process, transposed virtual experiences are *felt experiences* and *generate emotions related to engagement*. Unless some degree of transposition takes place, persons entering virtual worlds only observe their avatars' behaviors, remaining detached from them.

Stories provide optimal conditions for transpositions because they predispose their audiences to feel the desires and the conflicts upon which they are structured (Green, 2002). For example, in the N.I.C.E. project participating children desire to grow plants. Conflicts ensue when they must share the sun and rain with other participants. They have to learn to work and share by allowing their avatars to cooperate with other avatars. Thus their avatars are the conduits of desires and conflicts. Configurable storyworlds, in our view, are more conducive to virtual deep learning experiences than other virtual worlds.

With respect to constructing a virtual world that fosters collaboration, we have designed a one in which collaboration is required because an emergency occurs in it. Hence the VW is configured as a collaborative environment. What does it mean to say that a virtual world is "configurable?"

Table 2. Types of data

Construct/Measure	Level of observation	Source of data	Description	Period
Demographics	Individual	Q, O	Demographics questionnaire.	Initial
Technology Acceptance	Individual	Q	Use the Technology Acceptance Model	Initial and Final
Individual Performance	Individual	Q	Behaviorally anchored ratings of quality of aspects of and individual performance, including number of tasks successfully completed	After each scenario run
Team Performance	Team	Q, O	Behaviorally anchored ratings of quality of aspects of and overall team performance, including number of tasks successfully completed.	After each scenario run
Team Processes/ Dynamics / Performance	Individual, team	Q	Enumeration of unobservable individual and team factors underlying team processes.	During scenario
Team work	team	Q, O	Behaviorally anchored ratings of quality of six dimensions of teamwork processes: communication, monitoring, feedback, back-up, coordination, and team orientation	During scenario and After each scenario run
Communication Measures	Individual	O	Records of type, sender and recipient, and frequency of communications	During scenario
Mutual Mental model congruence	Individual, team	Q	Assessment of the congruence of models team members hold of one another	Initial and Final
Organizational awareness	Individual	Q	Assessment of the accuracy or congruence of team members' situational and mutual mental models	Initial and Final
Evaluation of the scenario	Individual, team	Q	Ratings of aspects of scenario including level of difficulty, complexity, uncertainty, ambiguity for self, others, and/or team as a whole	After each scenario run
Attitude about the goal	Individual	Q	Assessment	Initial and After each scenario run
Emergency Plan Development	Individual	Q	Assessment of the contribution of the scenario to emergency plan development.	Final
Emergency Plan Modification	Individual	Q	Assessment of the contribution of the scenario to emergency plan modification.	Final
Emergency Plan Evaluation	Individual	Q	Assessment of how the scenario contributed to emergency plan evaluation.	Final
Cross-agency collaboration	Individual	Q	Assessment of frequency, types and novel communication across agencies attributed to intervention	Annual
Networking	Individual	Q	Number and type of new relationships formed due to intervention	Annual

Q=Questionnaire/Survey; O=Observation

Earlier we noted that configurable worlds (type 4 VW) add creativity and a greater propensity for transportation & transposing to a storyworld (type 3 VW). Every virtual world depends upon a visitor's imagination. The graphical dimensions of virtual worlds guide visitors' imagination but invariably they continue to be aware that the virtual environment is not the real world and do not take it seriously (no "felt" consequences in the experience). Nonetheless, visitors go through a process of mental modeling in "filling in" the construction of the virtual world in their imaginations according to the way in which the simulation provokes images that can be mapped to past experiences. Visitors in large part "flesh out" the graphical representation of an environment with details from their past experiences of similar objects and events.

A configuration is a term for this "construction" but it is a particular way of doing it. As with other virtual worlds, visitors perceive "figures"[7] in a representative situation located in a recognizable environment. In such perceptions, visitors can assume the perspective of one of the figures in virtual worlds—usually that of the avatar with whom they identify as a "self-figure."[8] Other figures are already in the scenario or enter it. It is not, however, an automatic occurrence that visitors assume the perspective of their avatars. Frequently visitors to virtual worlds maintain their real life perspective as "observers" of their avatars. They assume the perspective of their avatars *only when* they identify with them ("configure them"—perceive the situation as-if they were their avatars). Its condition is a "turning point" event, which is usually the realization that a particular action can solve a problem they encounter (see examples below).

Considering that many virtual worlds are seen only from the detached perspective of a person outside looking in (a perspective that most persons who are new to *Second Life* initially experience), we need to consider what happens when visitors "transpose" their perspectives with that of their avatars. Borrowing from Cognitive Science, we can say that a transposition occurs when visitors are no longer aware that they are not their avatars and merge their perspective with their avatar's. Part of this phenomenon is the effect of transportation. Configuring occurs at the moment of transposing perspectives once transportation has occurred. Some examples of this phenomenon drawn from the experiences in *Second Life* that students have reported. [Note: this data was collected from a course on *Second Life* but is relevant to the phenomena of being in a storyworld and thus is applicable to designing emergency training as a *storyworld* rather than a game.]

1. John does not care that his avatar is not as attractive as some of the other avatars in SL. Then at some point in time while exploring an *Second Life* environment, John feels that other avatars disregard his avatar and do not pay attention to "*him.*" As a result, John redresses his avatar and hopes for a more positive reaction to *his* embodiment.

2. Mary has been visiting various *Second Life* environments but finding them uninteresting on the whole because for the most part no other avatars are there. Suddenly a very attractive male avatar approaches her and asks if she would like to join him at a party. She realizes that "*she*" wants to do this.

3. Joan is a white woman whose avatar is also white. She meets another white avatar who tells her that in RL she is an African American. Joan is surprised to learn that many African Americans have white avatars to avoid the racial prejudice which exists in their virtual world. Joan decides to convert the skin of her avatar to resemble an African American. At a concert in *Second Life* to which she has frequently gone, she now experiences racial slurs, hatred, and malice. "*She*" is furious.

Each case begins with a virtual experience detached from the avatar representing the person at the computer terminal. Then some "turning point" event occurs and the person begins to experience the world through his or her avatar's perspective. This change in perspective can be a "deep learning" experience as it is in the fourth story. The *storyworld* is the critical factor because what makes a story a story is that an initial situation, as the result of some pivotal turning point (event), is resolved by inverting the initial situation. In Joan's case, her experience of *Second Life* is positive, she redresses herself as a black avatar, her next experiences are negative.

With respect to measuring the levels of engagement in this collaborative environment, after interviewing participants in the configurable storyworld we are designing, we will apply discourse analysis to the texts of the interviews to track expressions that imply identification with their avatars. This will result in a scale of the degrees of expressed identification.

CONCLUSION

Configurable worlds are storyworlds in which transpositions induce dispositions. In educational scenarios they can dispose learners to solve the problem that the virtual world presents. Changing perspective is the cognitive turning point. In a virtual world, this happens only when the world is configured and persons assume the perspectives of their avatars.

Creating a configurable virtual world depends upon creating a storyworld in which persons manipulating their avatars encounter a situation in which desires and conflicts are experienced and emotions are generated in them as if they were their avatars. The emotional component intensifies the virtual experience and deepens the learning.

Though we are persuaded that configurable *storyworld*s are a model for training in CVEs, we are at the preliminary stages of shifting from a gaming model, designing a *storyworld* for training, and learning how to assess the process of configuring.

REFERENCES

Barnett, D. J., Everly, G. S. Jr, Parker, C. L., & Links, J. M. (2005). Applying educational gaming to public health workforce emergency preparedness. *American Journal of Preventive Medicine, 28,* 490–495. doi:10.1016/j.amepre.2005.01.001

Corti, K. (2006). *Games-based learning: A serious business application.* PIXELearning Limited. Retrieved May 2, 2008, from http://www.pixelearning.com/docs/games_basedlearning_pixelearning.pdf

Dickey, M. (2005). Three-dimensional virtual worlds and distance learning: Two case studies of active worlds as a medium for distance education. *British Journal of Educational Technology, 36,* 439–451. doi:10.1111/j.1467-8535.2005.00477.x

Dickey, M. (2005). Brave new (interactive) worlds: A review of the design affordances and constraints of two 3D virtual worlds as interactive learning environments. *Interactive Learning Environments, 13,* 121–137. doi:10.1080/10494820500173714

Gibson, J. (1979). *The ecological approach to visual perception.* Hillsdale, NJ: Lawrence Erlbaum Associates Hawkridge, D. (1977). Communication and education in open learning systems. In D. Lerner & L. Nelson (Eds.), *Communication research: A half-century appraisal* (pp. 70-103). Honolulu, HI: University of Hawai'i Press.

Green, M., & Brock, T. (2002). In the mind's eye: Transportation-imagery model of narrative persuasion. In M. Green, J. Strange, & T. Brock (Eds.), *Narrative impact: Social and cognitive foundations* (pp. 315-341). London: Lawrence Erlbaum Associates.

Herrington, J., Reeves, T., & Oliver, R. (2007). Immersive learning technologies: Realism and online authentic learning. *Journal of Computing in Higher Education, 19*(1), 65–84. doi:10.1007/BF03033421

MacMillan, J., Paley, M. J., Levchuk, Y. N., Entin, E. E., Serfaty, D., & Freeman, J. T. (2002). Designing the best team for the task: Optimal organizational structures for military missions. In M. McNeese, E. Salas, & M. Endsley (Eds.), *New trends in cooperative activities: System dynamics in complex settings.* San Diego, CA: Human Factors and Ergonomics Society Press.

Norman, D. (2002). *The design of everyday things.* New York: Basic Books.

Parker, R. (2006). Commuters play large role in flu spread. *FuturePundit.com.* Retrieved from http://www.futurepundit.com/archives/cat_pandemic_isolation.html

Shaffer, D., Squire, K., Halverson, R., & Gee, J. (2005). Video games and the future of learning. *Phi Delta Kappan, 87*(2), 105–111.

Sosnoski, J., Harkin, P., & Carter, B. (2006). *Configuring history: Teaching the Harlem Renaissance through virtual reality cityscapes.* New York: Peter Lang Publishing.

Squire, K., & Jenkins, H. (2003). Harnessing the power of games in education. *Insight (American Society of Ophthalmic Registered Nurses), 3*(1), 5–33.

Swartout, W., & van Lent, M. (2003). Making a game of system design. *Communications of the ACM, 46*(7), 32–39. doi:10.1145/792704.792727

Waugh, W. L. Jr, & Streib, G. (2006). Collaboration and leadership for effective emergency management. *Public Administration Review, 66*(Suppl. 1), 131–140. doi:10.1111/j.1540-6210.2006.00673.x

FURTHER READING

April 27, 2008, from http://www.his.se/upload/19354/HS-%20IKI%20-TR-07-001.pdf

Atchison, C., Boatright, D., Merrigan, D., Quill, B., Whittaker, C., Vickery, A., & Aglipay, G. (2006). Demonstrating excellence in practice-based teaching for public health. *Journal of Public Health Management and Practice, 12*(1), 15–21.

Buckle, P., Mars, G., & Smale, S. (2000). New approaches to assessing vulnerability and resilience. *Australian Journal of Emergency Management, 15*, 8–14.

Daines, G. (1991). Planning, training and exercising. In T. Drabek & G. Hoetmer (Eds.), *Emergency management.* Washington: International City/County Management Association.

Decker, S., Galvan, T., & Sridaromont, K. (2005). Integrating an exercise on mass c casualty response into the curriculum. *The Journal of Nursing Education, 44*, 339–340.

Herman, D. (2002). *Story logic: Problems and possibilities of narrative.* Lincoln, NE: University of Nebraska Press.

Herman, D. (2003). Stories as a tool for thinking. In D. Herman (Ed.), *Narrative theory and the cognitive sciences* (pp. 163-192). Stanford, CA: Center for the Study of Language and Information.

Idaho Bioterrorism Awareness and Preparedness Program. (n.d.). Retrieved May 1, 2008, from http://irhbt.typepad.com/play2train/

Levchuk, Y., Pattipati, C., & Kleinman, D. (1998). Designing adaptive organizations to process a complex mission: Algorithms and applications. In *Proceedings of the 1998 Command and Control Research and Technology Symposium.* Mongerey, CA: Naval Postgraduate School.

Levchuk, Y., Pattipati, C., & Kleinman, D. (1999). Analytic model driven organizational design and experimentation in adaptive command and control. In *Proceedings of the 1999 Command and Control Research and Technology Symposium.* Newport, RI: Naval War College.

Littel, R., Milliken, G., Stroup, W., & Wolfinger, R. (1996). *SAS system for mixed models.* Cary, NC: SAS Institute.

Livingstone, D., & Kemp, J. (2006). Massively multi-learner: Recent advances in 3D social environments, virtual world environments. *Computing and Information Systems Journal, 10*(2).

MacMillan, J., Diedrich, F., Entin, E., & Serfaty, D. (2005). How well did it work? Measuring organizational performance in simulation environments. In W. B. Rouse & K. Boff (Eds.), *Organizational simulation* (pp. 253-272). Hoboken, NJ: Wiley.

Perry, R., & Lindell, M. (2003). Preparedness for emergency response: Guidelines for the emergency planning process. *Disasters, 27*, 336–350. doi:10.1111/j.0361-3666.2003.00237.x

Susi, T., Johannesson, M., & Backlund, P. (2007). *Serious games – an overview* (Tech. Rep. HIS-IKI-TR-07-001). University of Skövde, Sweden. Retrieved

U.S. Department of Homeland Security. (2004). *National response plan.*

U.S. Department of Homeland Security. (2006). *Nationwide plan review: Phase 2 report.* Washington, DC: Office for Grants and Training.

U.S. Department of Homeland Security. (2007, February). Homeland security exercise and evaluation program. In *Volume II: Exercise planning and conduct.* Retrieved May 1, 2008 from http://hseep.dhs.gov/

Virvou, M., Katsionis, G., & Manos, K. (2005). Combining Software Games with Education: Evaluation of its Educational Effectiveness. *Educational Technology & Society, 8*(2), 54–65.

ENDNOTES

1   By a "habitable" world we mean one in which the visitor to it is represented by an avatar who "lives" inworld. The other types of virtual worlds keep visitors outside of the world as observers of it.

2   Psychologist James J. Gibson originally introduced the term in his 1977 article *The Theory of Affordances* and explored it more fully in his book *The Ecological Approach to Visual Perception* in 1979. In 1988, Donald Norman appropriated the term *affordances* in the context of human–machine interaction to refer to just those action possibilities which are readily perceivable by an actor. Through his book *The Design of Everyday Things,* this interpretation was popularized within the fields of HCI and interaction design.

3   Guidelines for the use of gaming simulation (#2 above) in bioterrorism and emergency readiness were summarized by the ASPH/CDC Simulation-Based and Interactive Training Collaboration Group (chaired by Dr. Monahan) in January of 2007. The CDC commissioned this collaboration group of CPHP network participants to "review CPHP methods and identify measured benefits and successes related to such methods (simulation-based and interactive training) employed for preparedness training and education" (Association of Schools of Public Health, 2007). The group concluded that the learner using gaming simulation could be sensitized to roles and problems encountered during an emergency. "On the merits of these advantages, games and simulations should be an integral part of preparedness training in public health" (Ibid). Given limited training budgets, personnel resources and time constraints, the challenge is to provide guidance to health departments on how to approach an all-hazards training approach that not only addresses core readiness issues but is flexible, adaptive and effective.

4   Some cooperative scenarios are marketed as "video *games.*" For the purposes of this essay, we are not categorizing them as "games."

5   For more information on NICE, go to http://www.evl.uic.edu/core.php?mod=4&type=1&indi=371

6   It is very likely that there will be some modifications to the original measures.

7   Etymologically the word configuration suggests "figures with (*con*) other figures," that is, a recognizable situation.

8   This parallels the cinematic technique of having the perspective of the camera seeing the scene from behind it as if the camera were one's own eyes.

SUPPORT MATERIAL

Benchmarks of VW Training

We adapted Glynn and Duit's (1995) five conditions for learning meaningfully. Their schematic fits the parameters of "concept transfers" in Cognitive Psychology. We revised their "conditions" drawing upon recent developments in other Cognitive Sciences, principally from the research of Langacker, Lakoff, and Johnson in Linguistics, of Fauconnier and Turner in Cognition, and of Kosslyn and Koenig in "the New Cognitive Neuroscience." In addition, our adaptation was done with Don Norman's guidelines for VR design in mind. Whereas Glynn and Duit's benchmarks were consonant with experience transfers, we added the complementary notions about "experience transfers" in accordance what has been called "the embodied mind" model of cognition. The revised benchmarks are listed showing the concept transfer (CT) and the experience transfer (ET):

1. Existing memories are activated by the present situation (assimilation)
    a. CT—source of motivation is the problem encountered
    b. ET—[added value] recognition of disparities between past and present experiences.
2. Existing experiences are mapped to ongoing experiences
    a. CT—logical process of matching
    b. ET— [added value] "Cognitive blending," [1] a refinement of the activity of mapping.
3. Intrinsic motivation is developed
    a. CT—feelings are activated
    b. ET— [added value] dispositions are generated
4. New knowledge is constructed
    a. CT—accommodation (a conceptual change)
    b. ET— [added value] creative agency in constructing a mental model of experience
5. New knowledge is applied, evaluated, and revised Change in world views
    a. CT—change in conceptual framework
    b. ET— [added value] change in belief system
6. new experience is retained in memory
    a. CT—concept retained in memory
    ET— [added value] concepts, images, and feelings retained in memory

Defining Isolaton and Quarantine

The CDC differentiates between Quarantine and Isolation. Isolation is the separation of a person or group of persons from other people to prevent the spread of infection. Quarantine is the restriction of activities or limitation of freedom of movement of those presumed exposed to a communicable disease in such a manner as to prevent effective contact with those not so exposed.

Isolation

Isolation means separation, during the period of communicability, of a person infected with a communicable disease, in a place and under conditions so as to prevent direct or indirect transmission of an infectious agent to others. It may mean extremely limited contact with an ill person who is diagnosed with or suspected of having a communicable disease. The isolation can occur in a hospital setting in a negative airflow room (prevents potentially contaminated air from going back into the hospital) for very infectious airborne diseases. Isolation usually requires health care providers and visitors to use clothing protectors, masks or respirators, goggles and gloves as a means of protecting the visitors but also to protect the patient from exposure to new diseases that their weakened immune system may not be able to overcome.

Quarantine

Quarantine means restrictions, during or immediately prior to a period of communicability, of activities or travel of an otherwise healthy person who likely has been exposed to a communicable disease. The restrictions are intended to prevent disease transmission during the period of communicability in the event the person is infected. This period is commonly known as the "incubation" period of a disease. This means they have been exposed to an individual with a communicable disease and may be developing the disease as well. Some diseases are not communicable until symptoms appear; other diseases may be communicable for hours or days before the person shows any signs of the disease. Quarantine can be accomplished by a variety of means including having the person stay in their own home and avoid contact with others (including family members) to having the person or group of persons stay in a designated facility, to restricting travel out of an impacted area.

Sanitary Barrier

In extreme circumstances, public heath officials may consider the use of widespread or community-wide quarantine, which is the most stringent and restrictive containment measure. Strictly speaking, "widespread community quarantine" is a misnomer, since "quarantine" refers to separation of exposed persons only and (unlike snow days) usually allows provision of services and support to affected persons. Like snow days, widespread community quarantine involves asking everyone to stay home. It differs from snow days in two respects: 1) It may involve a legally enforceable action, and 2) it restricts travel into or out of an area circumscribed by a real or virtual "sanitary barrier" or "cordon sanitaire" except to authorized persons, such as public heath or healthcare workers.

NIH Report (*Interregional spread of influenza through United States described by virus type, size of population and commuting rates and distance*, The John E. Fogarty International Center for Advanced Study in the Health Sciences (FIC) - Wednesday, April 19, 2006) From Randall Parker Article (http://www.futurepundit.com/archives/cat_pandemic_isolation.html)

Primary Hypotheses to be Evaluated Include the Following:

Use of a Collaborative Virtual Environment (CVE) for emergency response planning will improve collaboration in emergency response planning. Based on a study by Dickey (2005), who showed virtual worlds have a significant potential for "facilitating collaborations, community and experiential learning" we predict that we will improve emergency response planning.

Use of a CVE will increase awareness of the need to plan for vulnerable populations. Based on Shaffer, et al, (2005), who argued that acting in virtual worlds makes it possible to develop situated understandings, effective social practices, powerful identities, shared values, and ways of thinking of important communities of practice, we predict that the use of CVEs will increase awareness of the need to plan for vulnerable populations.

Once trained on the use of the CVE, the participants' will continue to use the modality on their own. Based on Barnett et al (2005), who argue that the use of CVEs is consistent with a model of organizational change in that incorporates experiential learning that has an impact on knowledge and attitudes in a nonthreatening way and is more likely to be embraced by employees than resisted, we predict that once trained on the use of the CVE, the participants' will continue to use the modality on their own.

Increasing the realism in the training exercise, through the use of CVE, will increase the effectiveness of the planning. Based on claims by PIXELearning cofounder Kevin Corti (2006) and cultural theorists Kurt Squire and Henry Jenkins (2003) that, due to the realistic nature of virtual environments, learners experience situations that are impossible or difficult to experience in the real world for reasons of safety, cost, time, etc., we predict that increased realism in the training exercise, through the use of the CVE, will increase the effectiveness of the planning.

Chapter 6

Argumentative Interactions and Learning Through a Virtual Environment:
Lessons Learned from the Implementation of a Case in Science

Nathalie Muller Mirza
University of Lausanne, Switzerland

EXECUTIVE SUMMARY

In the scientific field, argumentative practices can, under certain conditions, help students to elaborate scientific concepts from everyday representations. However, setting up activities that enable learning in a classroom is not an easy matter. A technological environment may be useful in order to sustain argumentation and to "keep track" of the discursive processes. This chapter presents a pedagogical case in science in which the learners take part in an argumentative debate mediated by a technological environment, called Digalo. The chapter focuses on a socio-cultural perspective, thus assigning a central role to social interactions, symbolic and material mediation in development and learning processes. The author describes a case in Biology tested in two educational contexts, and discusses its psycho-pedagogical assumptions. From a qualitative analysis of the data, it appears that cognitive and argumentative processes are interconnected. This means that by articulating and making reference to the others' arguments, learners also develop a new understanding of the scientific content. The challenges for educational issues and the lessons that may be drawn from an analysis of this case are then discussed.

BACKGROUND

Introduction

Let me start by a question that may look a bit strange at first glance: "To your opinion, what is a tomato: a vegetable or a fruit?". People generally respond by saying that it is a vegetable. For botanists, however, tomato is a fruit, as it is the ovary, together with its seeds, of a flowering plant. It is thus a fruit, or more precisely, a berry. The term "vegetable" has even no botanical meaning, and is purely a culinary term.[1] For centuries, one of the scientists' main efforts is to try to "categorize" objects of the envi-

DOI: 10.4018/978-1-60566-878-9.ch006

ronment and to explain relationships, differences, and common points between them. However, objects are not so easily put into categories, and the definitions of categorizes evolve and change following new data or evidence. In our daily life, we, as laymen and laywomen, use categories that do not always fit with the ones the scientists have developed. Moreover, some objects of the reality can be considered as "ambiguous," as they share characteristics of two or more categories.

It is this kind of phenomenon that some researchers in education and pedagogy take as a starting point for designing pedagogical activities in teaching sciences. Their main assumptions are twofold: starting from an ambiguous object can lead learners in science to explore the specificities of the categories that are linked to the phenomenon; and starting with a kind of "controversy question" (is A part of X or Y?) may also allow participants to enter into an argumentative and dialogical work that is at the heart of scientific activity. It is one of these pedagogical scenarios or cases that I would like to present in this chapter. It is called "Digalized Euglena[2]", and is based on an inquiry-oriented and socio-constructivist pedagogical perspective, using argumentation as an exploratory and learning tool. In order to sustain and facilitate the dialogical processes, the activity is mediated by a computer-mediated learning environment called Digalo that provides a graphical map of the ongoing discussion. The case is constructed around the Euglena cell that presents interesting ambiguous characteristics with both vegetal and animal properties: it shows, for instance, an autotrophism function (like plants that "nourish" themselves via photosynthesis) and, under certain circumstances, a heterotrophism function, absorbing and digesting dissolved organic matter in the water (like animals). From a scientific perspective, the Euglena cell is part of the Protista kingdom of living that gathers all the mobile and unicellular living beings together.

My epistemological position in this chapter is not the one of a teacher in science nor even a researcher in teaching science, but rather the one of a psychosociologist in education interested in the contributions and limits of argumentation mediated by a learning environment in teaching sciences, and in its psychosocial issues.

Argumentation and Learning in Sciences

In science education, it is now recognized that argumentation, under certain conditions, helps students to elaborate scientific concepts from everyday representations: argumentation means to elaborate sophisticated processes of coordination with the other's perspective, of grounding in evidence one's own position and negotiating it in testing hypotheses (Baker, 1999; Erduran, Osborne, & Simon, 2005; Leitão, 2000; Osborne, Erduran, & Simon, 2004a; Schwarz, 2009). Through the confrontation with other positions and decentration processes[3] (Piaget, 2007), participants are lead to explore and construct new knowledge. This conception of argumentation and learning is based on a socio-constructivist model of learning and on a socio-cultural approach, inspired by authors like Vygotsky (1978), Mead (1934), and Bruner (1996), who claim the important role of language, social interactions, and socio-cognitive conflicts in thinking (Mercer, 2000; Perret-Clermont, 1980; Roth, 1995).

Argumentative designs in science classrooms refer to another important issue: they allow learners to become aware of the argumentative nature of scientific reasoning. In his/her everyday activity, the scientist is familiar with argumentation in the "dialogue" s/he establishes with nature (making hypotheses, testing their validity, modifying the first assumptions and models, etc.), and with her/his colleagues and audience, through the specific rhetorical discourse used in papers, talks, etc., aiming at the dissemination of scientific observations (Latour & Woolgar, 1988). Arguments in science are of several kinds: what kind and the amount of data to collect (for instance, whether the data will be valid and how much is needed to make it reliable); whether a given model is a satisfactory interpretation of the data (for instance, why the Bohr model of the atom is not a satisfactory model); the interpretation of data (for instance, do the rising levels of CO^2 mean that the global temperatures will rise?) (Osborne, Erduran, & Simon, 2004b). By arguing in the classroom, students understand that science is more about trying to construct and resolve problems in specific theoretical frames rather than "discovering" things that would have been hidden from the beginning of the world. Argumentation in teaching science allows students understanding and using the rules of reasoning that are used in the scientific community.

The Potentialities of Learning Environments in Argumentation Activities

Even if argumentation is conceived as a powerful practice in educational contexts, it rarely occurs spontaneously. Using argumentation in school raises questions and difficulties at different levels, institutional as well as psycho-sociological: argumentation is not a familiar discursive tool in classrooms, because teachers sometimes think that organizing debates could be time-consuming and do not feel comfortable with this kind of social dynamic in their classrooms (Cobb, Wood, Yackel, & McNeal, 1992). From the participants' side, argumentative communication may be perceived as a situation where their relationships with their schoolmates are at risk, because it involves confrontation and expression of conflicts. Designing argumentative activity is indeed a difficult matter. Research on this topic shows that disagreement seems both beneficial and detrimental concerning argumentation in learning. Conflicting positions may develop socio-cognitive conflicts that lead to learning, but disagreement also faces participants with a communicative situation that may be interpreted as a "danger" in terms of the relationship, and thus can inhibit learning gains (Van der Puil,

Andriessen, Kanselaar, 2004). The antagonistic dimension of debate may be an obstacle to learning: when two disagreeing arguers aim to win, the quality of their arguments may tend to decrease (Buchs, Butera, Mugny, & Darmon, 2004).

In the frame of European projects[3], researchers in education and software developers from different countries aimed to promote learning environments that would facilitate and sustain the argumentative processes in education contexts in the line of research showing the potentialities of computer-supported collaborative learning (Andriessen, Baker & Suthers, 2003; Andriessen & Schwarz, 2009; Baker, 2003). These projects have thus been the space for developing such environments by designing argumentative cases mediated by electronic environments and exploring the psychosocial issues of argumentation in learning sciences. Digalo was developed from this perspective in the DUNES project (Muller Mirza, Tartas, Perret-Clermont & de Pietro, 2007).

Currently, many different kinds of electronic environments may be found that help the design of productive argumentation. Andriessen, Baker, and Suthers (2003), in their analysis of computer-supported collaborative learning environments, propose the following division: the computer as channel of communication, the computer used for structuring interaction, the computer as a representational tool for representing arguments, and the computer as an active guide. Digalo is part of the third category and is meant to help participants to ground and articulate their positions through the visual frame in which they discuss (Andriessen & Schwarz, 2009).

Artifacts as Psychological Tools

Digalo has been developed from assumptions about its potential role on argumentative and cognitive processes. We must be aware, however, of the possible *decalage* between developers' intentions and actual uses (Muller Mirza, 2005). It will thus be important to observe how Digalo is actually used and interpreted by the students.

From a Vygotskian perspective, changes in tools bring about changes in thinking: the instrumental action is at the core of the thinking action that uses tools to achieve its ends. The triangular model of a complex, "mediated act" that links the triad of subject, object and mediated artifact, means a change of unit of analysis: it is not merely the individual alone but the individual-acting-by the means-of-cultural-artifacts that becomes the object of study. In his view, artifacts, provided by a cultural environment historically situated, do not serve simply to facilitate mental processes, but they fundamentally shape and transform them. Individuals use the tool-kit provided by culture to gain control of the world and of themselves, and in turn, through using tools, they change themselves and their culture. Vygotsky's view on the double side (material and ideal or semiotic) of artifacts and their cognitive transformative dimension, and the developments made to his concept of activity by others scholars (Cole & Engeström, 1993; Engeström, 1987; Leontev, 1978), are at the core of research and development in the field of education, and the use of technological mediation tools for teaching-learning purposes.

Currently, in some policy-makers' discourses, technology is believed to significantly enhance learning processes. We would claim or add to this assumption that a technology environment like the Digalo artifact, as other objects in the educational setting, needs to be «instrumentalized» in a complex meaning-making process: the object in itself has no function and does not change anything until it acquires the one of a "sign" through the student's action of giving meaning to it (Muller Mirza & Perret-Clermont, 2008).

In the following sub-chapter, I shall present implementations of one case called the "Digalized Euglena" case. It has been developed and tested in several educational contexts in Switzerland. In this account, I shall develop the specificities of the institutional and social context and describe the preparatory work of the research team, the

strategies and methods we have chosen, the main results we reached, and the teachers' and the learners' opinions about the whole process. From the analyses of the data gathered, I shall shed light on the "lessons learned" from an educational point of view.

SETTING THE STAGE

The General Context of Implementation

This contribution focuses on the description of the case Digalized Euglena which was implemented in two settings: in University of Neuchâtel (Switzerland), with the students who followed a course in Psychology and Education about psychopedagogical issues in argumentation, and in secondary schools. The data analyzed here come from observation made with one group of 25 University students (in Neuchâtel); and with 13-14-year-old students in one class of a secondary school (in Le Locle-Neuchâtel).

Testing the Euglena case with students in Psychology and Education in a University context had three main objectives: to evaluate the feasibility of the design, to gather data on which to develop methodological tools of analysis, and to allow students (many of whom are teachers or want to become teachers) to experience the argumentative processes "from the inside". Even though the cells as subject matter were not part of their academic curriculum, the students still retained notions from their secondary school classes. In the secondary school context, the preparatory work for the implementation consisted primarily of contacting science teachers who were known personally by the researchers. Once the teachers gave their personal agreements, the educational board of the district, the school officials, the parents and other authorities were contacted for their official agreement. It is interesting to note that the idea of implementing an argumentative scenario in their classrooms was enthusiastically welcomed by the teachers, even if an argumentative approach does not appear to be well-established in the school context. This kind of practice, however, seems strongly supported by the authorities. When discussing with the Neuchâtel school board director, he made reference to other experiences in sciences focusing on inquiry and debate practices that he wished to improve and develop, for instance the "Main à la pâte" program initiated in France in 1996 by Georges Charpak, Nobel Prize winner in 1992 (http://www.inrp.fr/lamap/; http://www. unine.ch/laquinzainedelascience/presentation. html). During the preliminary phase with the teachers, the general frame of research was presented to them together with its objectives and modes of implementation in their classes. We discussed and negotiated with them the content of the scenario that would fit their programs and their students' expertise and needs; the cases and their main phases were adapted according to their comments. A discussion was organized with the teachers after the case implementation to get their general feedback.

Digalo

The cases have been tested with Digalo as a mediation tool. Digalo is an interactive environment that allows visualization of the on-going discussion through an argumentative map. It is a graphical editor that allows the users to create and handle argumentative maps. Fed by the users' written contributions, the map increases through discussion and provides a picture of its evolution: who said what, when, to whom, etc.. On the shared screen, each participant or group is identified by means of a symbol. Each can select one of the predetermined shapes that designates the nature of the proposition: argument, idea, comment, information, question, etc.. Then, one can write down a main idea (in the "title" window) and develop it (in the "comment" window). With the help of a selected arrow, this shape can be linked to others

and signal the opposition, agreement or neutral orientation of the relationship (see Figure 1).

Digalo is a technological tool for facilitating argumentation practices in the learning environment, as it allows: keeping track of the discursive processes (learners can come back and reason about what has been said and why); supporting thinking processes in allowing the learners to write down, and thus to make explicit and externalize their ideas; taking time to reflect on the arguments of the other participants; justifying and grounding arguments (by means of the different windows of the software); sustaining articulation between arguments (with the use of the arrows); and diminishing the face-to-face stress of argumentation, which is mediated at a distance by writing with Digalo. The argumentative maps trace the discourse and keep it visible under the participants' eyes. In the process of argumentation, this allows for: (a) elaboration of arguments, because unlike an oral debate, participants have time to write down their arguments and reflect on them; (b) production of explicit speech acts; c) visibility of the arguments on the map, which helps students to concentrate on the evolution of the debate and prevent them from losing the thread of the discussion; and d) possibilities to make relations and links between the visible propositions, helping to maintain coherence during the discussion (Muller Mirza, Tartas, Perret-Clermont & de Pietro, 2007).

CASE DESCRIPTION

Psycho-Pedagogical Assumptions

The design of the case is grounded in a socio-constructivist approach, putting emphasis on the learner as an actor who constructs meanings and new knowledge in social settings. It is also developed on the basis of some of the previous results from research in argumentation and learning that shed light on the difficulty for children, and also adults, for engaging into argumentation (Golder,

Figure 1. Digalo Argumentative map

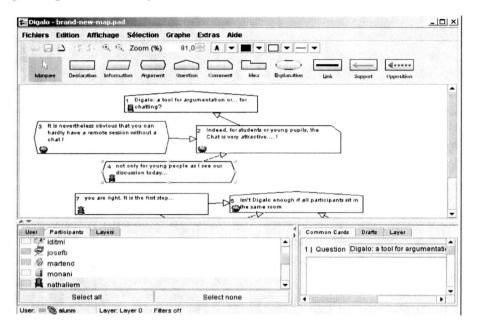

1996; Golder & Coirier, 1994). The studies show that students are not always willing to enter and maintain an argumentative posture (they quickly end what is interpreted as a "conflict" situation), and if they do, arguments are quite weak (Schwarz & Glassner, 2003). These findings stress the importance of carefully designing the argumentative activity, and in particular, taking into account:

(1) The *cognitive* dimension: to make sure that participants have knowledge about the topic, in providing, for instance, students with opportunities to make reference to "scientific" information; to make sure that the information is understood;

(2) The *affective* dimension: framing the argumentation phase such as it is focused on the content and not on the persons; preventing inter-personal conflicts;

(3) The *communicative* dimension: to agree on a "contract of communication"; framing a controversial and clear question for the debate phase; providing opportunities for interactions and confrontation of perspectives.

Our designing choices, as said previously, are also linked to the claim that learning environment tools provide opportunities for facilitating argumentation and learning.

A Phased Scenario

From these assumptions, and according to the topics and populations, we have adopted a main structure that involves a sequence of phases (Schwarz & Glassner, 2003), articulating collective, small group, and individual works. The argumentation phase is one among several steps. Throughout the sessions, the students are led to develop an inquiry approach by finding answers to some scientific questions, to look for arguments from textual resources, and to defend their points of view during the argumentative phase. In particular, they are asked, in small groups, to prepare and defend one position: Euglena is a vegetal cell vs an animal cell.

After a pre-questionnaire aimed at a better understanding of the learners' pre-existing knowledge and representations about the cell topic, the teacher presents the main features of the animal and vegetal cell, and the specificities of Euglena. Small groups are constituted: one will defend the position that Euglena is a vegetal cell and the other the position that it is an animal cell. During an "intragroup" phase of preparation of their main arguments, each group has some textual resources at their disposal. They prepare a first "argumentative map" (listing their arguments on a sheet of paper) that will serve as a tool for the debate phase. The debate, mediated by Digalo, follows: both groups try to convince the other and/or to reach a common understanding. Finally, the teacher discusses the results of the debate and presents the scientific categorization of this unicellular organism. The learners are asked to fulfill a "post-questionnaire", with the same questions as in the "pre-questionnaire".

The Digalized Euglena case focuses on two kinds of learning objectives: (a) a knowledge acquisition of specific contents in sciences, according to the students' age and their previous knowledge of the topic (a better understanding of what is a cell and what are the Euglena characteristics); and (b) the development of competencies and communication strategies in inquiry and argumentation (making reference to documents, referring to relevant information, grounding his/her perspective, taking into account the others' perspectives, asking questions, putting assumptions into questions, etc.). More precisely, learners, by exploring the characteristics of the Euglena cell, are expected to acquire new knowledge about the main features of an animal and a vegetal cell, the main differences between both, the existence of a class of organisms, Protista, which are neither animals or plants, and thus make them aware that kingdoms of living organisms are more than the two we usually know, the Animalia and the Plantae.

Data and Method of Analysis

The data gathered are audio recordings, Digalo argumentative maps, field notes, and pre- and post-questionnaires. Argumentation means an ability to justify and ground a statement in making reference to evidence or data in a discursive process, such as taking part in the development of scientific concept. In a Vygotskian perspective, the manner in which language is used in culturally organized activity settings interacts with the development of higher mental functions. Vocabulary used is thus an indicator of this development: scientific and relevant vocabulary is the sign of an interiorization of content. A more coherent and articulated thinking (links between items), and reference to other knowledge (rather than his/her personal experience) can also be considered as indicators of this development.

The focus thus will be on the vocabulary used by the participants, the arguments (their contents), and the argumentation processes (its relational specificities), namely: if and how participants take and maintain a position; if and how they make reference to evidence or data; if and how they anticipate contrary arguments; if and how they take into account the arguments of the other participants.

RESULTS

The Case in a University Setting

Twenty-five students took part in a first implementation of the Euglena case, in a course of Psychology & Education at the University of Neuchâtel (2006-07). At the end of the test, they expressed rather positive appreciation, as for instance, this student who wrote: "I found this activity interesting, trying to find arguments and counter-arguments opens for discussion of the tricky problem of Euglena. I would like to know more about it".

The analysis of the data show that learners actualized knowledge not only in the domain of the cell, and the Euglena in particular, but also in argumentative practices, and that both kinds of knowledge are actually interconnected. In terms of vocabulary, the participants used more of the *ad hoc* scientific vocabulary at the end of the test; we observed an increase in the specific vocabulary from pre- to post-questionnaire: in their response to the pre-questionnaire about their knowledge on plants and animals, students used common sense and did not generally use a scientific vocabulary in order to, for instance, define what an animal is: "The animal is a living being, like the mammals for example, it moves, it lives, while a vegetable is also alive, but does not move, like plants for example". In the post-questionnaire, the contents were more focused and better articulated, with the use of more scientific terms.

In the argumentative map, participants showed abilities to focus on relevant topics in order to go further into the debate, responding to the question. They formulated arguments linked to the following domains: internal structure (vacuole; chloroplast), ways of nourishing (hetero/autotrophy), external structure (membrane), and ways of moving (flagella).

In terms of argumentation, we can observe students playing their dialogical position (animal vs plant) as it was suggested by the moderator; it means that they formulated arguments related to the position they had to defend, and stayed focused on the task.

It is interesting to observe that the groups developed their arguments while taking explicitly into account what was said by the other group, articulating their claims with the one of the other, like in this intervention from the "animal group:" "As you have underlined it, very relevantly, the vacuole is CONTRACTILE. This is a tangible proof of the animalistic character of the small beast". This non-valid claim is countered by another intervention from the "plant group:" "the animal cell doesn't have a vacuole at all!!!". We

can also shed light on some interactions where the groups explore, in a collaborative way, the nature of the object they are discussing: "You say that the flagella and the vacuole are typical [of an animal], but can you explain why with more details? What can we say about the fact that the vacuole is a shared element of both animals and plants?". Or, in this exchange, which has a kind of inquiring spirit, when the "plant group" writes: "One does not know what the membrane is made of. If it is made out of cellulose, it is a plant". To which the animal group responds: "You did not understand properly, the vegetable cell has not got a membrane at all!". At the end of the discussion, the groups reached the conclusion that Euglena "is not a normal feature".

Digalized Euglena in a Secondary Classroom

Twenty students 15-16-years-old participated in the experiment at the secondary school level during a biology lesson. Researchers played the role of the teachers in the classroom. The biology teacher had prepared her students by giving two lessons about the cell topic before the case implementation. The students had, therefore, some pre-knowledge at the beginning of the case.

The implementation of the case took 45 minutes. After the researchers-teachers had introduced themselves to the class, they asked the students to take an individual written pre-test in order to establish their knowledge. The researchers-teachers told the students that the pre-questionnaire was not a test that would be marked. Then, they explained the next stage of the experiment, which would involve working in sub-groups and participating in debates. Afterwards, they introduced the topic and handed out documents that explained the particularities of a plant cell, an animal cell, and the Euglena. They then asked the students the following question: "Is Euglena an animal cell or a plant cell?" and, as previously advised, the researchers-teachers divided the class into two groups who had to defend each viewpoint. One sub-group worked with Digalo and was supervised by researchers-teachers, while the other group would debate orally.

The group that worked with Digalo was divided into two sub-groups: three students were put into the pro-animal group and two students into the pro-plant group. Each sub-group was then placed before a computer in order to be able to debate via the Digalo program. Before starting the debate, each group was given five minutes to prepare some arguments to support its position (pro-animal or pro-plant). The researchers-teachers also explained how the Digalo program worked. The debate via Digalo then took place for fifteen minutes. At the end of the debate, the students completed a ten minutes post-questionnaire. Finally, the researchers-teachers conducted a general concluding discussion with the class during which they talked about the particularities of the Euglena cell with the help of a Powerpoint presentation.

The students were able to use the *ad hoc* vocabulary (for defining a cell, for instance), from the beginning of the scenario. But they discussed among themselves and made reference to their notes when answering the pre-questionnaires. In the argumentative map, students formulated arguments linked to the following domains: internal structure (vacuole; chloroplast), ways of nourishing (hetero/autotrophy), external structure (membrane), and ways of moving (flagella). Thus they were focused on the task and used relevant concepts in order to explore and construct knowledge about the phenomenon.

As for argumentative practices, we can observe that in the Digalo mediated debate, students played their dialogical roles (Plant vs. Animal). They started by referring to the specificities following the position of their sub-group of either the animal cell or the plant cell ("Euglena has chloroplasts and animals do not"). The Digalo shapes are well interconnected by means of arrows, demonstrating an effort to make links between the interventions. However, the arrows show more of a preoccupation

with arguing in order to attack the other's position or ground the other group's, rather than trying to have a better understanding of the limits of an argument. We can read for instance for the Animal group: "Euglena doesn't have any cellulose wall, it is not a plant". Plant group reacts: "Euglena has chloroplasts, animals do not have any". The reasoning is interesting and valid as the participants seemed to say: if Euglena is a plant, it must have a cellulosic wall like all plants; since it does not have one, then is it an animal. This argument is countered by the other group, which seems to say: if Euglena were an animal, as you think, it would not have chloroplasts, so it is a plant.

They take into account the perspective of the opponents. The participants generally do not explicitly give arguments for their own position, but attack, in an anticipatory move, the position of the other, like in the following examples: "A plant cannot move by its own means" (Animal group). An intervention that is counter-argued by the Plant group, which claims: "And can a sponge move by its own means?". Or in this extract: "The animal cells are surrounded by only one membrane which allows the cell to be flexible".

It is interesting to observe a relationship between being at ease with the technical use of Digalo and involvement in the argumentation activity. The slowest students with Digalo were also the ones who hardly found arguments against the other group. The playful dimension of the software seems a positive factor that helps the students to get involved in the learning activity.

CHALLENGES AND LESSONS LEARNED FOR EDUCATIONAL ISSUES

Some Difficulties Encountered in the Tests, and Ways to Improve the Case

At the end of the experiments, we observe three main difficulties. Lack of time is the most important limit of these tests: learners did not have enough time to discuss and reflect on the activity and their argumentation; a longer phase must be dedicated to a conclusive feedback by the teacher at the end of the scenario. In order to avoid the antagonistic tendency to debate between two contradictory positions, the design should end with a final activity where all the participants are invited to share the same objective. The question of assessment-evaluation (when and what to evaluate from a teacher's point of view) also remains an important question that has not been addressed enough in our tests. A more general difficulty that faces technological implementations in the school context is the non-familiarity of many teachers with learning environments and the time-consuming organization of the technical setting.

Contributions from the Tests of the Case

In spite of some limits of the cases, it is interesting to see that learners, within the activity designed with Digalo, were able to focus on the task and play the role they were assigned, use and develop a scientific vocabulary that was made on purpose, articulate concepts (or try to), make reference in a relevant way to empirical data extracted from textual resources, and mobilize argumentation skills *and* construct knowledge in interaction at the same time. Some of the usual difficulties of argumentative activities in an educational setting (mainly the difficulty of entering into an argumentative dialogue and weak argumentation) appear less apparent here. However, we have to be cautious: the research design is still in an exploratory form; we have access to little data, mainly the argumentative maps and the researchers' notes.

Two main reasons (as hypotheses) may explain our observation:

(1) A "controversy" modality added with a "role playing" modality: learners have to

try to find relevant information and resolve a controversial question through dialogue. Many studies have shown the efficiency of this type of communication setting (for instance, Johnson & Johnson, 1995). That is, it is not really the learner's own opinion that is at stake but that of the "position" to which s/he is assigned. In that way, fear of entering into an interpersonal conflict might not be as strong (see also Muller Mirza, Tartas, Perret-Clermont, & de Pietro, 2007).

(2) Digalo's functionalities can also be seen to facilitate argumentation practices: they allow learners to formulate claims, make reference to them, and to articulate them. Its use is perceived as quite easy and friendly. From earlier studies we observed that the conditions for an effective use are to involve not too many users working at the same time on the argumentative map, and to adequately prepare the activity and the technical features of the setting before asking students to start the task.

The analyzes of the case show interesting findings and open new questions for researchers in education and for the teachers who wish to implement them in their classroom. Hereunder are listed several of them.

The status of "argumentation". Argumentation can hardly be considered as a set of reasoning skills and logical rules that would be defined *per se* independently from the social, technological, and institutional context in which it is used, and independently of a specific content (Andriessen, Baker & Suthers, 2003; Buty & Plantin, 2009; Muller Mirza & Perret-Clermont, 2008, 2009; Muller Mirza, Perret-Clermont, Tartas & Iannaccone, 2009). One does not argue on any topic with just anybody anywhere. It seems important, for example, that the individuals who engage in this way of communicating and learning can feel secure, as debating is a risky activity for at least three reasons that are probably interrelated: (a) for a relational reason (if I do not agree with my friend will s/he stay my friend?);(b) for an epistemological reason (if my opinions and beliefs are put into question, what is right? Who is right? What is the truth?); and (c) for an identity reason (if my opinions and beliefs are put into question, is it my own perception of myself, my identity that is at stake: who am I? How am I in an "uncertain" world?). And in the everyday practices of scientists, if argumentation can be located in different places, do students feel at ease questioning topics that have been the object of study by "scientists" for decades?

The personal position of the learners towards the topic under discussion. Some lines of research are studying the role and the impact of the personal beliefs of the learners on learning. About some topics, as for instance, natural selection, teachers are sometimes puzzled: are the difficulties faced by the students due to the inherent complexity of the topic or due to the personal perception of the conflict between science and their religious beliefs, or is it due to some combination of the two? Perspectives suggest that if learners recognize and become aware of the conflict between their existing knowledge and the scientific conception, conceptual change is possible, under certain circumstances (Sinatra & Pintrich, 2003). In argumentation activities, personal views are central when learners are asked to explicitly state their own perspectives on an object. In our designs, we made the pedagogical choice to assign a position (pro or con; Plant or Animal) to each participant, whatever her/his personal position. Debating from a perspective which is not the one of the student should allow to "mediate" the interpersonal relationship, even if s/he probably will still feel conflicted about a disconnect between her own beliefs and scientific claims. This dimension remains an issue to keep in mind when implementing an argumentative activity. In a more general discussion, the epistemic beliefs about sciences, their evolution, the status of hypothesis, truth, theories, etc., are of a central interest, both from the learners' and the teachers' points of view. It is obvious that the pedagogical choice of the teacher in using an argumentative activity for teaching science is linked to a view of science defined in terms of trying to construct and resolve problems in specific theoretical frames rather than "discovering" things.

The role of the teacher. In our design, the place of the teacher is not in front of the classroom yet her/his role is central. S/he not only has to mediate (give some scientific information and cues, suggest readings, ask counter-argument questions); but also to moderate (ask questions, guide the discussion, help to focus, etc.) the cognitive and discursive activities. S/he is the "guardian of the frame", in its cognitive and relational dimensions. At the end of the activity it is important that s/he concludes the activity both at the content and at the relational levels: to remind the learners of the meaning and the finality of the activity, come back to the main points and the process of the discussion, and give the "scientific" position(s) on the topic under discussion, and also to discuss what happened during the dynamic of the discussion.

The role of the software and its use. Our observation shows that Digalo is perceived as quite an easy to use and friendly tool. However, it is important not to underestimate the technical constraints of its use before, during and after the activity (setting up server, connections, firewalls, availability of the computer room and of the technicians, teacher's and students' familiarity with computers, configuration of Digalo, etc.). In our experience, it seems that Digalo may be used by the participants as a tool that to a certain extent leads them to externalize their thoughts and makes them "available" not only for the others but also for themselves. Its use also seems to be a motivational factor as it is still quite unusual for the students to use the computer in science classrooms, and because of its interactive and synchronous functions. It is important however to add that the artifact does not mediate the relationship between the learner and the object of knowledge "by itself."

It requires the elaboration of a complex activity (a design) by the teacher, and is the object of an active appropriation by the learner. In this dynamic process of appropriation and meaning-making, the tool "affords" interactions and argumentative practices. In that perspective, activity is not within the tool but a new complex activity is re-elaborated with the tool (Mercer & Littleton, 2007). It is less the technological software that transforms the pedagogical setting than the new activity, involving different and new roles for the actors who are co-constructing knowledge, other social configurations, and a new place for inquiry (Muller Mirza & Perret-Clermont, 2008).

For many years now, educational psychologists have agreed that knowledge is not acquired by transmission alone, but by co-construction. By putting the learners in argumentation settings, we proceed a step further showing that learners can be the agents of their own learning in a specific frame (Brown & Campione, 1994). In the kind of design we have tested, the learner does not behave as a receptacle of prior knowledge but as an actor who is able to act—seeking relevant information, making hypotheses, agreeing to be countered—who can reflect on his/her own productions as well as on those of others. The learner can thus experience, in this pedagogical frame, a decentration and reflexive position that may lead to a more meaningful and grounded learning.

ACKNOWLEDGMENT

The implementations of the case in the educational fields have been made with the collaboration of advanced students in psychology and education under the supervision of the author N. Muller Mirza, in the frame of the European project ESCALATE (coordinated by B. Schwarz, Hebrew University of Jerusalem), at the Institute of Psychology and Education (Prof. A.-N. Perret-Clermont), University of Neuchâtel, Switzerland. We thank them warmly for their collaboration and their contributions to the data gathering, analysis and reflection. Their enthusiasm provided a very important input towards the realization of this experiment. This text is therefore the fruit of the collaboration with Y. Benjelloul, F. Bonvin, N. Crélot, S. Davin, E. Fasan, M. Jeanneret-Atanasova, S. Kaelin, L. Lizano, C. Miserez, S. Moretti, M. Nansoz, E. Ndayiragije, A. Pylypenko, F. Rohrbach, F. Stettler, L. Teodoridis, N. Terrier, K. Vamavedan. We also thank the teachers and the students who participated in this experience. Some of the results presented in the chapter are part of the report "White Book" (edited by Baruch Schwarz and Anne-Nelly Perret-Clermont) prepared in the frame of the ESCALATE project.

I am grateful to the reviewers and to Dr Donna Russell for providing suggestions to revise the first draft of the paper.

REFERENCES

Andriessen, J., & Schwarz, B. (2009). Argumentative design. In N. Muller Mirza & A.-N. Perret-Clermont (Eds.), *Argumentation and education: Theoretical foundations and practices* (pp. 145-174). New York: Springer.

Baker, M. J. (2003). Computer-mediated argumentative interactions for the co-elaboration of scientific notions. In J. Andriessen, M.J. Baker, & D. Suthers (Eds.), *Arguing to learn* (pp. 47-78). Dordrecht, The Netherlands: Kluwer Academic Publishers.

Brown, A., & Campione, J. (1994). Guided discovery in a community of learners. In K. McGilly (Ed.), *Classroom lessons: Integrating cognitive theory and classroom practice* (pp. 229-270). Cambridge, MA: MIT Press.

Bruner, J. (1996). *The culture of education*. Cambridge, MA: Harvard College.

Buchs, C., Butera, F., Mugny, G., & Darmon, C. (2004). Conflict elaboration and cognitive outcomes. *Theory into Practice, 43*(1), 23–30.

Buty, C., & Plantin, C. (Eds.). (2009). *Argumenter en classe de sciences [Argumentation in science classroom]*. Paris: INRP.

Cobb, P., Wood, T., Yackel, E., & McNeal, B. (1992). Characteristics of classroom mathematics traditions: An interactional analysis. *American Educational Research Journal, 29*(3), 573–604.

Cole, M., & Engeström, Y. (1993). A cultural-historical approach to distributed cognition. In G. Salomon (Ed.), *Distributed cognitions: Psychological and educational considerations* (pp. 27-46). Cambridge, UK: Cambridge University Press.

Engeström, Y. (1987). *Learning by expanding: An activity-theoretical approach to developmental research*. Helsinki, Finland: Orienta-Konsultit.

Erduran, S., Osborne, J., & Simon, S. (2005). The role of argument in developing scientific literacy. In K. Boersma, O. de Jong, H. Eijkelhof, & M. Goedhart (Eds.), *Research and the quality of science education* (pp. 381- 394). Dordrecht, The Netherlands: Kluwer Academic Publishers.

Golder, C. (1996). *Le développement des discours argumentatifs* [The development of argumentative discourse]. Neuchâtel, Switzerland: Delachaux et Niestlé.

Golder, C., & Coirier, P. (1994). Argumentative text writing: Developmental trends. *Discourse Processes, 18*, 187–210.

Johnson, D. W., & Johnson, R. T. (1995). Positive interdependence: Key to effective cooperation. In R. Hertz-Lazarowitz & N. Miller (Eds.), *Interaction in cooperative groups: The theoretical anatomy of group learning* (pp. 174-201). New York: Cambridge University Press.

Latour, B., & Woolgar, S. (1988). *Laboratory life: The social construction of scientific facts*. London: Sage Publ.

Leontiev, A. N. (1978). *Activity. Consciousness. Personality*. Englewood Cliffs, NJ: Prentice Hall.

Mead, G. H. (1934). *Mind, self, and society*. Chicago: University of Chicago Press.

Mercer, N. (2000). *Words and minds: How we use language to think together*. London: Routledge.

Mercer, N., & Littleton, K. (2007). *Dialogue and the development of children's thinking: A sociocultural approach*. London: Routledge.

Muller Mirza, N. (2005). *Psychologie culturelle d'une formation d'adultes* [Cultural psychology of an adult training]. Paris: L'Harmattan.

Muller Mirza, N., & Perret-Clermont, A.-N. (2008). Dynamiques interactives, apprentissages et médiations: Analyses de constructions de sens autour d'un outil pour argumenter [Interactive dynamics, learning and mediation: Analyses of the construction of meaning around a tool for arguing]. In L. Filliétaz & M.-L. Schubauer-Leoni (Eds.), *Processus interactionnels et situations éducatives* (pp. 231-254). Bruxelles, Belgium: De Boek.

Muller Mirza, N., Perret-Clermont, A.-N., Tartas, V., & Iannaccone, A. (2009). Psychosocial processes in argumentation. In N. Muller Mirza & A.-N. Perret-Clermont (Eds.), *Argumentation and education: Theoretical foundations and practices* (pp. 67-90) New York: Springer.

Osborne, J., Erduran, S., & Simon, S. (2004). *Ideas, evidence and argument in science (IDEAS). In-service training pack, resource pack and video.* London: Nuffield Foundation.

Perret-Clermont, A.-N. (1980). *Social interaction and cognitive development in children*. London: Academic Press.

Piaget, J. (2007). *The child's conception of the world*. Lanham, MD: Rowman & Littlefield.

Roth, M.-W. (1995). *Authentic school science: Knowing and learning in open-inquiry science laboratories*. Dordrecht, The Netherlands: Kluwer Academic Publishing.

Schwarz, B. (2009). Argumentation and learning. In N. Muller Mirza & A.-N. Perret-Clermont (Eds.), *Argumentation and education. Theoretical foundations and practices* (pp. 91-126). New York: Springer.

Sinatra, G., & Pintrich, R. (2003). The role of intentions in conceptual change learning. In G. Sinatra & R. Pintrich (Eds.), *Intentional conceptual change* (pp. 1-19) Mahwah, NJ: Lawrence Erlbaum Associates.

Tomato. (n.d.) Retrieved August 6, 2008, from http://en.wikipedia.org/wiki/Tomato

Van Der Puil, C., Andriessen, J., & Kanselaar, G. (2004). Exploring relational regulation in computer-mediated (collaborative) learning interaction: A developmental perspective. *Cyberpsychology & Behavior*, *7*(2), 183–195. doi:10.1089/109493104323024447

Vygotsky, L. (1978). *Mind in society: The development of higher psychological processes*. Cambridge, UK: Cambridge University Press.

FURTHER READING

Andriessen, J., Baker, M., & Suthers, D. (Eds.). (2003). *Arguing to learn: Confronting cognitions in computer-supported collaborative learning environments*. London: Kluwer Academic.

Baker, M. (1999). Argumentative interactions, discursive operations, and learning to model in science. In P. Dillenbourg (Ed.), *Collaborative learning: Cognitive and computational approaches*. Amsterdam: Pergamon.

Leitão, S. (2000). The potential of argument in knowledge building. *Human Development*, *43*, 332–360. doi:10.1159/000022695

Muller Mirza, N., & Perret-Clermont, A.-N. (Eds.). (2009). *Argumentation and Education*. New York: Springer.

Muller Mirza, N., Tartas, V., Perret-Clermont, A.-N., & de Pietro, J.-F. (2007). Using graphical tools in a phased activity for enhancing dialogical skills: An example with Digalo. *Computer-Supported Collaborative Learning*, *2*, 247–272. doi:10.1007/s11412-007-9021-5

Osborne, J., Erduran, S., & Simon, S. (2004a). Enhancing the quality of argumentation in school science. *Journal of Research in Science Teaching*, *41*(10), 994–1020. doi:10.1002/tea.20035

Schwarz, B., & Glassner, A. (2003). The blind and the paralytic: Supporting argumentation in everyday and scientific issues. In J. Andriessen, M. Baker, & D. Suthers (Eds.), *Arguing to learn: Confronting cognitions in computer-supported collaborative learning environments* (pp. 227-260). Dorbrecht, The Netherlands: Kluwer Academic Publishers.

ENDNOTES

[1] Interesting note about the (legal and economical) issues of categorization: "This argument has had legal implications in the United States. In 1887, U.S. tariff laws that imposed a duty on vegetables but not on fruits caused the tomato's status to become a matter of legal importance. The U.S. Supreme Court settled the controversy in 1893 by declaring that the tomato is a vegetable, based on the popular definition that classifies vegetables by use, that they are generally served with dinner and not dessert. But due to the scientific definition of a fruit and a vegetable,

the tomato remains a fruit when not dealing with US tariffs. Nor is it the only culinary vegetable that is a botanical fruit: eggplants, cucumbers, and squashes of all kinds (including zucchini and pumpkins) share the same ambiguity" (http://en.wikipedia.org/wiki/Tomato, retrieved August 6, 2008).

[2]   A case called "Euglena" was initially developed by Osborne, Erduran, & Simon (2004b). In "Digalized Euglena" case we integrated the use of Digalo software and changed some points of the structure of the activity.

[3]   Decentration process is described by Piaget as the ability to consider the point of view of another person rather than just the child's own point of view as the centre of any representation of the world. The child cannot acquire the faculty of arguing until he or she has emerged from egocentrism, as "so long as the child supposes that every one necessarily thinks like himself, he will not spontaneously seek to convince others, nor to accept common truths, nor, above all, to prove or test his opinions" Piaget, 2007 p. 33).

[4]   Three European projects are involved: DUNES, ESCALATE and KP-Lab. DUNES (Dialogical argUmentative Negotiation Educational Software; http://www.dunes.gr/) is a European project coordinated by Baruch Schwarz, Hebrew University of Jerusalem, and funded by the Vth Program Frame of the European Commission (IST-2001-34153). It involved 9 participants, academic partners and software developers, from France, Germany, Greece, Israel, the Netherlands, Sweden, Switzerland and the UK. ESCALATE (Enhancing Science Appeal in Learning through Argumentative interaction; http://www.escalate.org.il/), is a Specific Support Action project sponsored by the 6th Framework of the European Commission (Contract No. 020790 (SAS6); 2006-2008), coordinated by Baruch Schwarz, Hebrew University of Jerusalem. Kp-Lab (Knowledge practice laboratory; http://www.kp-lab.org/), coordinated by K. Hakkarainen, University of Helsinki, funded by the Vth Program Frame of the European Commission. KP-Lab focuses on creating a learning system aimed at facilitating innovative practices of sharing, creating and working with knowledge in education and workplaces.

Chapter 7

Obesity Prevention in Second Life:
The International Health Challenge

Rebecca E. Lee
University of Houston, USA

Charles S. Layne
University of Houston, USA

Brian K. McFarlin
University of Houston, USA

Daniel O'Connor
University of Houston, USA

Sameer Siddiqi
University of Houston, USA

EXECUTIVE SUMMARY

In industrialized societies, between 50% and 75% of the population weigh in at overweight or obese health status (Low, Chew Chin, Deurenberg, 2009; Ogden, 2007). Ecologic models posit that heath behavior and outcomes are related to the environmental settings in which humans live, work and play; if environmental settings are not supportive, then poor health results. (Spence & Lee, 2003) Second Life is an interactive virtual world that is global, an ideal setting to reach international audiences who are real life residents of industrialized communities at high risk for obesity. Second Life provides a unique opportunity to increase knowledge, social support and behavioral skills necessary to reduce or prevent obesity with much broader reach than traditional face to face intervention strategies. Health behavior change interventions have had success in real life by exposing participants to interventions in virtual worlds, suggesting that information and skills learned in virtual worlds may translate to real life (Anderson, Rothbaum, Hodges, 2000). The International Health Challenge in Second Life began with the goal of extending the real life mission, goals and activities of the Texas Obesity Research Center of the University of Houston into Second Life. What emerged was a fun, exciting, interactive, multicultural, multilingual, theoretically grounded, virtual setting where resident avatars of Second Life learned about

DOI: 10.4018/978-1-60566-878-9.ch007

healthful living, met others like them, and had virtual experiences that in turn contributed to real life health improvement. This chapter investigates the utility of applying the ecologic model of health to virtual worlds to reduce the public health burden of obesity, with the case example of the International Health Challenge.

BACKGROUND

The Ecology of Overweight and Obesity

Obesity affects one in three Americans (Ogden et al, 2006) and has become a global epidemic in all industrialized societies (Low, Chew Chin, Deurenberg, 2009). In the United States alone, 64% of non-Hispanic whites, 76% of non-Hispanic blacks, and 76% of Mexican Americans are overweight or obese, with higher rates of overweight among men, and higher rates of obesity among women (Ogden et al, 2006). The overweight and obesity epidemic is primarily attributed to lifestyle and environmental changes that have occurred in the industrialized world in the last three decades, and is largely preventable with early and broad based intervention efforts. Overweight and obesity are associated with numerous chronic health illnesses, including coronary heart disease, cancer, stroke, and diabetes, four out of the ten leading causes of death identified by U.S. sources (Department of Health and Human Services [DHHS] 2008), and echoed by international bodies (World Health Organization [WHO], 2008). In the USA, roughly 300,000 deaths and $120 billion in medical expenses are attributed to obesity and obesity-related conditions annually. Over half of these expenses are paid for by Medicare and Medicaid, with each U.S. taxpayer responsible for about $200 per year for obesity-related medical costs. From an employer's perspective, medical costs are 77% higher for obese employees than healthy employees, costing employers over $8,000 per person per year (Centers for Disease Control and Prevention [CDC], 2008).

Numerous individual approaches to weight control have been tried, and found effective, but typically only for a very short period of time. People find it hard to stick to restrictive diets and rigorous exercise programs, suggesting that lifestyle approaches that emphasize moderation may be a more realistic way to live a healthful life. However, even moderate approaches may be ineffective when there is little support for healthful living and are few opportunities to eat healthfully and be physically active. Ecologic models provide a structure to account for multiple levels of influences and the linkages and processes among them. Ecologic models encompass everything both internal and external to the individual and have recently begun to show promise for guiding research and practice across a variety of health domains. Spence and Lee (2003) have described the Ecological Model of Physical Activity that conceptualizes influences on physical activity as micro-, meso-, exo- and macro-environmental and suggests individual level health behavior and disease states as outcomes. Lee and Cubbin have provided an updated, visual model in their recent work (2009) to help consider how ecologic models can be broadened in scope to consider not only physical activity but also dietary habits and obesity as outcomes.

Micro-environments are the immediate environments in which humans live, work and play and may include the home, work, school, cafe, store, restaurant, park and many more. The micro-environments may be thought of as relatively static, but these are linked by dynamic meso- and exo- environmental linkages and processes. The linkages and processes may be social interactions, such as a conversation, or actual physical linkages.

Meso-environmental elements directly connect two or more micro-environments together, such as the physical roadway between the home and the park. Exo-environmental factors indirectly link micro-environments. For example, dietary habits that occur in the cafeteria at a child's school (micro-environment of the child, but not the parent) may impact the dietary habits of parents and friends of parents in the workplace (micro-environment of the parent but not the child), by way of a shared conversation between the child and parent. The macro-environmental factors are broad overarching factors such as municipal designs, policies, transportation systems, social and cultural norms and many other factors. All of these environments lie within the ecologic milieu and are influenced by extra-individual forces of change (e.g., technological innovation), and intra-individual factors that are biological and psychological in nature. Ecologic models provide a useful heuristic to conceptualize and investigate the multiple physical, social and virtual environmental factors that influence health behaviors.

Virtual Learning Environments

Virtual learning environments are three-dimensional, computer-generated places that are interactive and appear realistic to users (Inoue, 2007). Technology has advanced so much that users actually perceive themselves as being in the virtual learning environment and as interacting as if they are in real life with other people and objects. If we superimpose an ecologic model on top of virtual environments, many of the same factors that occur in real life are also found in virtual environments. Virtual environments have micro-environmental places, meso- and exo-environmental linkages and processes, and overarching macro-environmental factors. As technological innovation increases, it impacts on the entire ecologic milieu in the virtual world. Further, unlike real life, in virtual environments people can more rapidly change and manipulate micro- and macro-environments.

Thus, virtual environments are able to provide more health promoting opportunities more rapidly that one would be able to find in real life.

Users in virtual learning environments are represented by avatars. Attributes of the user, or avatar, represent the intra-individual factors of a virtual ecologic milieu. The word "avatar" is derived from the Hindu term that refers to an earthly incarnation of a god. Avatars represent a person virtually and can take on many forms, human, animal or object. The use of avatars to represent humans has inspired virtual manifestation from the serious to the very silly. Some companies have instituted "appearance codes" to ensure that avatars look similar to their real life human. Appearance codes regulate avatar type, shape, size, attributes and wardrobe (McArthur, 2008). Thus, a human white woman with blond hair who wears a suit at work would need to appear similarly in avatar form, as a human white woman with blond hair wearing a suit. If she appeared as a non human or a human of another ethnicity, or perhaps as a man, or wearing inappropriate attire, that would be a violation of the appearance code. The fact that appearance codes are now widely used by corporations in virtual environments underscores the fact that there can be true anonymity in virtual worlds.

The anonymity offered in virtual worlds can be a great asset for providing an opportunity to educate about sensitive topics. In the case of obesity, avatars can appear slender or obese, regardless of the real life weight status of the human behind the avatar. People can gain information free from judgment. The sense of anonymity may promote greater interaction and learning opportunities (Boulos, Hetherington, & Wheeler, 2007). People, in their avatar form, may feel freer to talk to others whom they might not know well, or ask "stupid" questions that actually may not be so stupid. Complex social communities develop in virtual worlds, just as in real life, fostering sense of community, affiliation and attention to specific places and people.

The social element found in virtual worlds is a vital and dynamic representation of the meso and exo-environmental factors found in the virtual ecologic milieu. Virtual communities provide the same sense of community as real life communities, fostering sense of membership, influence, needs fulfillment, and shared emotional connection that is vital in order to prevent and reduce the epidemic burden of obesity. Because the majority of the population in industrialized societies are overweight or obese, the majority of virtual world users, although represented by apparently healthy avatars, are likely overweight or obese or at real risk for developing these conditions in real life. Public health approaches, which aim to reach as many of the target population as possible in order to both *prevent* and *reduce* obesity, may benefit through the use of virtual environments to reach that population.

In addition to anonymity and unique social opportunities, virtual learning environments provide opportunity to navigate and browse information in three dimensional and multimedia formats. Users can visit virtual enactments of historical events, visit cultures and places that are far away geographically, and participate in events that they might not have access to in real life. As a reflection of the powerful opportunities presented in virtual worlds, enterprising avatars and corporations have set up businesses offering the sale of virtual goods and services. Some projections have suggested that the Internet itself will eventually become a three dimensional space, in contrast to its current two dimensional manifestation, and all browsing and online interaction will become fundamentally different.

SETTING THE STAGE

Organization Implementing the Project

The Texas Obesity Research Center is located in the Department of Health and Human Performance at the University of Houston and established in 2007. The Texas Obesity Research Center employs an interdisciplinary, holistic model that combines the traditional individually-focused, behaviorally-based approaches found in psychology, with the environmentally-focused, macro-based approaches of research grounded in an ecologic model together with the biologic and physiologic understanding of obesity from health and human performance. The mission of the Texas Obesity Research Center is to promote interdisciplinary research, education and training and foster local community collaborations to develop state-of-the-art obesity prevention and control methodologies through cross sectional and longitudinal research investigating psychosocial, environmental and biologic determinants of obesity and its consequences. The Texas Obesity Research Center has one director and an executive committee comprised of three active faculty members of the Texas Obesity Research Center. Other faculty in related fields may join the Texas Obesity Research Center faculty upon review and approval of the director and executive committee.

In the first year of its existence, faculty of the Texas Obesity Research Center became interested in the potential of virtual learning environments as a medium for research, education and community collaboration. The relatively low cost of implementing projects and programs in virtual learning environments in the face of uncertain economic times held great appeal, especially given the broad reach of virtual learning environments, in particular Second Life.

Second Life

Second Life is a three dimensional virtual world created in 2003 by Linden Lab Corporation (Boulos, Hetherington, & Wheeler, 2007). Second Life is a multi-user, interactive, stimergic, boundless game that has grown well beyond a simple game for many users. Users are called "residents," and membership is free. As of February 2009, there were nearly one and a half active users, defined as users who had logged on in the past 60 days (Linden Labs, 2009). To join the game, one must register and select a name, download the program client software, and complete a brief tutorial in the game, or "in world." First names are selected by the user, and last names are selected from a list of existing last names provided by Second Life. Names that duplicate an existing resident are not allowed. The use of a finite list of existing names provides a sense of affiliation with others in world that shares the same last name, creates a history, as older names are retired and new names are introduced, assures some level of confidentiality and anonymity, and prevents names from overuse. It is possible to purchase a name, if a specific name is desired, but this is rarely done. Personal identification information has not been collected as part of the Second Life registration process; however, concerns of minors accessing the game have lead to strategies using a third party age verification process. Regardless, a guiding directive of Second Life is to provide an opportunity for a true "second" life, where one can be anything one wants to be free from the limits of real life.

The International Health Challenge in Second Life was funded through an initiative called, *Second Life and the Public Good*, as part of the Network Culture Project, from the USC Annenberg School for Communication. The project was awarded through a competitive process along with two other projects aimed at increasing awareness and information about various topics in Second Life. The International Health Challenge was designed to be a multinational effort aimed at increasing awareness, knowledge, skills, and support for healthful living including daily physical activities and healthful dietary habits—in short, an effort at preventing or slowing the rapidly escalating rates of obesity in the industrialized world. Avatars were recruited using both virtual and real life strategies, and invited to virtually practice physical activities, try new foods and

learn about healthful living strategies while having opportunities to visit with other avatars from around the world. To increase accessibility, materials were translated from English to French and Spanish. Financial incentives were offered in the Second Life currency, the Linden dollar. Residents received small payments for visiting the site and participating in activities daily.

CASE DESCRIPTION: THE INTERNATIONAL HEALTH CHALLENGE

The International Health Challenge is an elaborate health promotion study conducted entirely in the virtual world of Second Life. The goals of the International Health Challenge are aimed at improving health knowledge, attitudes, and behaviors in real life. Theoretically grounded educational content on physical activity, dietary habits and behavioral strategies to adopt and maintain health behaviors was adapted for use in Second Life. Resident avatars learn, practice and interact in activities centered on these topics, and all activities are incentivized, a method of content delivery familiar to Second Life residents. The International Health Challenge initially started as a strategy to extend the activities of the Texas Obesity Research Center by developing an interactive, multilingual, and multicultural health promotion project in Second Life, as evidenced by a full service virtual build, activities, and participating residents.

As of March 2009, the International Health Challenge has enrolled over 120 of the goal of 500 residents of Second Life. Resident participants are recruited using established real life recruitment strategies translated to Second Life. Residents of Second Life who had agreed to be contacted as part of previous outreach methods were invited via in world, Second Life announcements. Announcements were posted in the classified advertisements in Second Life and on group lists and in collaborating Second Life locations. Also, recruiters traveled throughout Second Life to tell avatars about the project. All potential recruits were given an International Health Challenge Welcome Kit, that included (a) an International Health Challenge t-shirt, (b) a high fly wrist band that allows avatars to fly high enough to reach the International Health Challenge in Second Life sim located thousands of meters above the virtual ground, (c) a notecard describing the project, (d) a smile attachment that allows avatars to smile—a universal symbol of happiness and fun.

After resident avatars complete the tutorial on "learning island," the virtual world of Second Life has nearly unlimited virtual resources available. The "world" of Second Life is housed in a three-dimensional matrix that appears as blocks of territory comprised of land and water similar to real life earth, complete with virtual latitude and longitude and the possibility for "islands in the sky". Resident avatars can explore different islands and sims (simulations of places in real life), meet and socialize with other residents, participate in activities, and create and trade items and services with one another. Residents can purchase land and build objects to play on, in and with. Animation scripts can be added to objects and "worn" by avatars to simulate real life activities ranging from activities as mundane as housecleaning to exotic and complex dance steps, likely beyond the abilities of many residents in real life. It was in this unique virtual world that the International Health Challenge developed into an elaborate and exciting research project.

Residents of Second Life who wished to enroll in the project were invited to complete an online consent form as required by the Internal Review Board of the University, and then to complete a short (20 min) survey. Survey instruments collected important information about health attitudes, knowledge and habits in real life, to help evaluate the effects of the project. Residents were then enrolled in the International Health Challenge, where they selected an affiliation country (Canada, Mexico, Switzerland, USA) or no affiliation, and had the opportunity to "camp" (explained below), complete informational quiz games, and sampled fruits and vegetables. For each of these activities residents earned valuable Linden dollars ($L) and International Health Challenge Points for their affiliation country, if they had affiliated with a country. Linden dollars are the currency in Second Life, and although $50L in Second Life goes a long way in Second Life, in real life it is about $.20US. Thus, health promotion and research in Second Life is cost effective relative to the science yield while being rewarding and engaging for participating residents.

Participating residents had the following opportunities available to them over a four week period:

1. Consent & Survey Time 1 ($50L)
2. Country affiliation selection ($5L)
3. Educational quiz games ($5L per week)
4. Weekly monitoring of physical activity and dietary habits ($10L per week)
5. Camping doing physical activity ($6L per 28 days)
6. Eating fruit and vegetables ($1L per 28 days)
7. Survey Time 2 ($50L)

Survey

The survey was conducted online, using established protocols from previous work similar to the popular survey tool, Survey Monkey. Because all information, including surveys, collected from resident avatars represented private information protected by US Federal Law, a separate, password-protected database was developed using a mixture of custom and open-source scripts that utilize XML-RPC protocols to relay information between in-world input (where avatars completed activities) and protected databases. Survey questions, along with all materials, were available in English, French and Spanish, and included language preference, basic demographic characteristics, physical activity beliefs and habits, dietary habits and beliefs, weight and height, computer use and psychosocial measures. The survey was about 20 minutes in length.

Country Affiliation

Resident avatars could affiliate with Canada, Mexico, Switzerland or USA to compete with the other country teams. We aimed to reach not only a US national population of residents, but also an international population by developing Spanish and French language resources based on our existing research collaborations in real life in Canada, Mexico and Switzerland. Residents who participated in the International Health Challenge could affiliate with any one of our four collaborative countries to log their health habits and weight status or they could choose no affiliation. The country that had the most improvement over time as described by total number of Challenge Points was declared the winner. After completing the consent and Time 1 survey, residents were asked to select one of four countries with which to affiliate, or no country. Each country could have up to 100 residents join its team. All materials were available in English, French or Spanish, so even if the country with the closest predominant language team were closed, residents could still participate with a separate team still using their favored language. Upon selecting their country Challenge team or no country, residents were paid $5L.

Challenge Points

Challenge points accrued by a resident avatar for completing any of the activities were allocated to their affiliated country. Four large flagpoles were displayed prominently on the International Health Challenge site. A Challenge Point scoreboard showed how each country progressed in the challenge for all to view. The scoreboard was updated as each resident completed her or his activity that accumulated points. At the end of the Challenge, the team with the most points would win the Challenge.

Information Delivery

Throughout the Texas Obesity Research Center sim, in highly visible places, rotating content slide shows provided information about physical activity, dietary habits and healthy weight. Content was presented in English, French and Spanish, and updated weekly to increase interest with novel content. Topics of information that were provided included information on physical activity recommendations, appropriate levels for beginners, what counts as physical activity, neighborhood safety, injury prevention, dietary habits recommendations, safe food storage, serving sizes, goal setting, improving self efficacy, increasing social support, relapse prevention, self monitoring, body mass index calculation, health benefits, and other topics.

Weekly Quizzes and Monitoring

We adapted information and activities provided in our real life interventions for Second Life use with the goals of improving health knowledge, attitudes and skills necessary to prevent and reduce obesity. Accurate scores on games and participation in activities were incentivized with Lindens to increase participation. We provided group membership for people who were interested in learning about healthy habits and obesity prevention and control to promote social connectedness around healthful living.

Behavioral Monitoring

Residents who participated in the International Health Challenge were able to complete dietary habits and physical activity logs as both a measure of success and to accumulate Challenge points. The Check And Line Questionnaire (CALQ) was developed by this team for use in real life interventions to promote physical activity, the Fruit and Vegetable (FV) Log was developed for use in real life interventions to improve fruit and vegetable consumption, and both were adapted for online use. Both the CALQ and the FV Log asked participants to check boxes to indicate the type and amount of physical activities done or fruit and vegetables eaten in real life. Participants could complete the CALQ and the FV Log each week, and receive $10L for completing it correctly. Thus, if residents completed all CALQs and FV Logs throughout the study, they could accrue a total of $80L along with Challenge Points for their country.

Sampling Fruits and Vegetables

Each day, residents could go to the café area of the International Health Challenge site and virtually sample a fruit or vegetable. Along with the fruit or vegetable of the day, the avatar received a short informational note card about the fruit or vegetable that included a brief history, seasonality, storage information and a recipe suggestion.

Camping

Residents had the opportunity to practice virtually different types of physical activity while earning valuable Lindens. This type of activity, where a resident affixes her or himself to a particular location for money is called, "camping." It is very popular and widely done throughout Second Life. At the International Health Challenge site, residents earned $2L per every 10 minutes of camping. After they have been camping for 15 minutes, they were prompted to determine whether they wished to continue camping. Residents could camp up to 30 minutes on any camping spot, to match the amount of time of physical activity recommended for good health by the US Surgeon general, and simulate time limits on cardio machines at popular fitness clubs in real life. Because resources for this

project were limited, the total amount of camping that could be done by each unique avatar was 30 minutes per day for a total of $6L.

Sim Monitoring

All residents who visited the site were logged to compute the number of unique visitors and number of repeat visitors. Each time an avatar visited the Texas Obesity Research Center sim it was uniquely counted. The amount of time each avatar spent on the sim every day was counted. These two measures provided a strong gauge of not only how many people visit the sim, but how long they spent there.

Build

Space for the International Health Challenge in Second Life was provided above the main site of the Department of Health and Human Performance sim. Space for the International Health Challenge in Second Life was a 30 m X 30 m platform that could be easily accessed via teleport from the main HHP teleport pad. The platform was enclosed on four sides with clear walls, to avoid residents inadvertently falling off. The roof was open so that residents could fly in or out if they desired. Unlike in real life, where four walls and ceilings are necessary to create security and intimacy, in Second Life, open spaces are preferred by avatars, and security can be provided invisibly with transparent barriers and scripts that remove avatars that are not controlled by a human. Upon arrival at HHP, residents could teleport to the International Health Challenge, where they could access the following locations: (a) physical activity camping area, (b) café food sampling area, (c) survey and study information area, and (d) the Challenge points monitoring area.

The physical activity camping area was an open square building that houses four treadmills, four stationary bicycles, four trampolines and four dance pads. Each of the 16 physical activity resources could be used for camping. In the physical activity camping area there was a large slide show screen where residents could see rotating educational content as well as profile pictures of residents who have camped there within the last 24 hours.

The café food sampling area was an open air café where residents might sit at café tables or go to the bar. The residents could select the fruit or vegetable of the day and receive a Linden and note card along with their selection. Residents could also select fruits and vegetables from previous days, with which they received a note card, but no Lindens. In this area there was a large slide show screen where residents could view rotating educational content.

The survey and study information area provided opportunities to complete educational quizzes and gain information on a variety of topics that mirrored the information presented on the slide show in other areas of the sim. Information was presented via note cards that accessible at this information area. As well, information was provided about the existing project, the funding agency, the Texas Obesity Research Center in real life, the investigators, the Health and Human Performance department and the University of Houston.

CURRENT CHALLENGES FACING THE ORGANIZATION

The challenges faced in the International Health Challenge centered primarily in the domains of technology and staffing. The project itself appeared straight forward in the application, but as the project got underway, it quickly became apparent that the team would need a substantive amount of technical support to lead the project to fruition. As well, ongoing recruitment efforts were steady, but slower than expected. It is noteworthy that recruitment is nearly always the most difficult part of any research and promotion project.

SIGNIFICANCE AND FURTHER READING

Reducing obesity translates to a greatly reduced public health burden. Other data suggest that it might also reduce the burden to the planet via reducing the needed food supply and costs associated with feeding and transporting overweight and obese individuals who eat and weigh more than lean individuals. Readers are referred to extensive information on the topics provided on the *Centers for Disease Control and Prevention* (http://www.cdc.gov) and *World Health Organization* (http://www.who.int) web sites, where detailed information is available on these topics.

Virtual learning environments and interactive three-dimensional worlds are evolving into meaningful places for work related education and networking as well as playing, making them an undertapped resource for health promotion projects. Novel, peer-reviewed, special interest journals in the arena of virtual worlds and health are quickly becoming premier sources of information on virtual environments. Readers may turn to many strong publications on this topic, including, *ACM Transactions on Graphics* (ISSN: 0730-0301), *Annual Review of CyberTherapy and Telemedicine* (ISSN: *1554-8716), CyberPsychology & Behavior (ISSN: 1094-9313), Journal of Medical Internet Research (ISSN:* 1438-8871), *Journal of Virtual Worlds Research* (ISSNISSN: 1941-8477), *Simulation and Gaming (ISSN: 1046-8781), Studies in Health Technology and Informatics (ISSN: 0926-9630), Telemedicine and e-Health* (ISSN: 1530-5627). Given the novelty and rapid growth of virtual worlds, in particular, Second Life, the proceedings of health or education related, professionally organized, in Second Life and/or real-world conferences are among the most valuable sources of information on current best practices, findings, and collaborative opportunities. Recent conference proceedings include, *Virtual Worlds Best Practices in Education Conference* (http://www.vwbpe.org/), *Second Life Com-*

munity Convention (http://www.slconvention. org/), *New Media Consortium Summer Conference* (http://www.nmc.org/), *Games for Health Annual Conference* (http://www.gamesforhealth. org/), *Medicine Meets Virtual Reality* (http:// www.nextmed.com/), *Special Interest Group on Graphics and Interactive Techniques* (http://www. siggraph.org/). Last, more and more virtual world projects and collaborators are turning to "open source" code, projects, and information sharing strategies, resulting in numerous wiki-based databases describing previous and ongoing in-world projects. These include, *RezEd* (http://www.rezed. org/), *University of Oregon's SaLamander Project* (http://eduisland.net/salamanderwiki/index. php), *SimTeach* (http://www.simteach.com/wiki/ index.php), *SimTeach Educational Content and Presence Database* (http://simteach.com/sled/ db/), *Nonprofit Commons* (http://npsl.wikispaces. com/), and *Multimedia Educational Resource for Online Learning and Teaching (*http://www. merlot.org/)

Reducing obesity is an international health priority, and Second Life provides a portal to an international community of people who are at risk, promising broad based reach for improving the health of the public. Ecologic approaches that focus on providing environments that are supportive for healthful lifestyles stand to enhance health, and virtual environments are a nearly untapped resource for this kind of work. There are few scientific investigations to test the efficacy of applying an ecologic model to a virtual environmental setting. The rapid development and broad-based adoption of virtual worlds both by health promoters and the general public, make knowledge and understanding of virtual worlds a valuable channel for obesity prevention and health promotion. The International Health Challenge is innovative, theoretically grounded and among the first of its kind.

ACKNOWLEDGMENT

Authors would like to gratefully thank Ashley Medina for her assistance in the preparation of this manuscript. This project was supported in part by an award from the USC Annenberg School for Communication Network Culture Project.

REFERENCES

Anderson, P., Rothbaum, B., & Hodges, L. (2000). Virtual reality: Using the virtual world to improve quality of life in the real world. *Menninger Winter Psychiatry Conference, 65*(1), 78-91.

Boulos, M., Hetherington, L., & Wheeler, S. (2007). Second Life: An overview of the potential of 3-D virtual worlds in medical and health education. *Health Information and Libraries Journal, 24*(4), 233–245. doi:10.1111/j.1471-1842.2007.00733.x

Centers for Disease Control and Prevention (CDC). (2008). *Economic consequences of overweight and obesity*. Retrieved March 13, 2008, from http://www.cdc.gov/nccdphp/dnpa/obesity/ economic_consequences.htm

Inoue, Y. (2007). Concepts, applications, and research of virtual reality learning environments. *International Journal of Social Sciences, 2*(1), 1–7.

Lee, R. E., & Cubbin, C. (2009). Striding toward social justice: The ecologic milieu of physical activity. *Exercise and Sport Sciences Reviews, 37*, 10–17. doi:10.1097/JES.0b013e318190eb2e

Linden Labs. (2009). *Second Life economic statistics*. Retrieved February 28, 2009, from http:// secondlife.com/statistics/economy-data.php

Low, S., Chew Chin, M., & Deurenberg, M. (2009). Review on epidemic of obesity. *Annals of the Academy of Medicine, Singapore, 38*, 57–65.

McArthur, V. (2008). Real ethics in a virtual world. In *Proceedings of the Conference on Human Factors in Computing (CHI)* (pp. 3315-3320).

Ogden, C. L., Carroll, M. D., Curtin, L. R., McDowell, M. A., Tabak, C. J., & Flegal, K. M. (2006). Prevalence of overweight and obesity in the United States, 1999-2004. *Journal of the American Medical Association, 295*, 1549–1555. doi:10.1001/jama.295.13.1549

Spence, J. C., & Lee, R. E. (2003). Toward a comprehensive model of physical activity. *Psychology of Sport and Exercise, 4*, 7–24. doi:10.1016/S1469-0292(02)00014-6

U.S. Department of Health and Human Services, Centers for Disease Control and Prevention. (2008). *Deaths-leading causes*. Retrieved March 13, 2008, from http://www.cdc.gov/nchs/FASTATS/lcod.htm

Chapter 8
Dissection of a Desktop Microworld

Christine S. Marszalek
Northern Illinois University, USA

Jacob M. Marszalek
University of Missouri-Kansas City, USA

EXECUTIVE SUMMARY

Despite the long history of the use of dissection in biology coursework, it has and continues to be, very controversial (Hart et al, 2008; Kinzie et al, 1993; Langley, 1991; Orlans, 1988; Nobis, 2002; Strauss, 1991; Madrazo, G, 2002). This case study evaluation was conducted in an affluent suburban middle school in the Upper Midwest as a response to the problem of finding an alternative means of instruction that would yield the same cognitive knowledge development, address the issue of science anxiety, and accommodate different learning modalities. Several alternatives were compared in 14 seventh-grade biology classrooms, including physical dissection, virtual dissection in a desktop microworld, and content instruction through an interactive CD-ROM tutorial. Although differences were observed in immediate retention, none were observed in retention after three months. Differences in science anxiety are discussed, and comparisons made of retention and anxiety among various learning styles. Implications for classroom instruction are discussed from an instructional perspective. The smell of formaldehyde was in the air as students tenaciously poked with dissection probes at the frogs pinned to their dissection trays. The familiar comments of "Gross!" "I don't want to cut him," and "Hey, Mrs. M, what do I do now?" punctuated the air. It was the start of the annual climax of the seventh-grade biology curriculum, dissecting a frog. The teacher, already dealing with notes from parents objecting to their sons/daughters participating and the logistics of helping 30 students simultaneously, could not help but think that there had to be an alternative way of presenting the experience to the students. This case study was born from that familiar, frustrating scene, which occurs annually throughout school systems everywhere. The teacher in the scenario above was one of three from the Biology department at a middle school in northeastern Illinois. Her team came to Christine with the problem of finding an alternative means of instructional delivery that would yield substantially the same cognitive knowledge development in the students, help address the declining frog population, address the issue of science anxiety among students at the middle school level, and accommodate the learning modalities of the students.

DOI: 10.4018/978-1-60566-878-9.ch008

BACKGROUND

In 1946, four one-room school districts merged to form a single elementary school district covering approximately 20 square miles in northeastern Illinois. Since that time, the area has changed from mainly rural farmland with a few small towns to six well-populated, growing suburbs. The suburbs themselves are among the most affluent in terms of per capita annual income in the US. The student body has changed little since the time of the study as shown by the following indicators of its makeup. It is still predominantly White (1996: 88%; 2007 81.2%), but the Asian/Pacific Islander population has increased from 1.7% in 1996 to 7.6% in 2007. Still, only a small percentage of students are Black (1996: 1.7%; 2007: 1.4%), Hispanic (1996: 2.4%; 2007: 3.7%), low-income (1996: 2.1%; 2007:3.8%), and/or categorized as having limited English proficiency (1996: 2.3%; 2007: 3.6%). Most district students continue their education at a nearby public high school consistently identified as one of the top 100 in the country over the past decade.

Perhaps influenced by the prestige of the high school, the district's stated vision is to become the premier elementary school district in the nation, and it appears to be well on its way. Teachers have an average of 13.8 years of experience, and 60.6% hold graduate degrees. The student:teacher ratio is 17.8:1. District performance on the Illinois Standards Achievement Test is strong. For example, 97.7% of district third-graders and 98.5% of district fifth-graders meet or exceed Illinois learning standards in mathematics, and 96.4% of district fourth-graders and 93.8% of district seventh-graders meet or exceed state standards in science. Five district schools–including the middle school that is the focus of this chapter– were named in March 2007 to the *Chicago Sun Times* Top 50 Suburban Public Schools list. In recognition for academic excellence, the middle school at the heart of this case study was named

a Blue Ribbon School by the US Department of Education in October 2007.

The surrounding communities greatly support the district's educational efforts. In the past 14 years, three building referenda and an educational fund referendum have been passed. The district's own Foundation for Educational Excellence, and each school's Parent/Teacher Organization (PTO), help fund innovative teacher development activities and the purchase of computer and other educational and recreational items to enhance student learning. In 1999, the district constructed a new elementary school and a new middle school, and made major renovations to three existing school buildings. That same year, it reorganized into one building designated as an early childhood/Kindergarten center, four buildings as elementary schools housing Grades 1-5, and two buildings as middle schools housing Grades 6-8.

SETTING THE STAGE

At the middle school that is the subject of our case study (let's call it Smith School), the curriculum is designed and managed by teams of teachers from each core subject area (i.e.: math, science, English language arts) for each grade level. There are also three additional teams, one of which is Special Services, that design and manage the curriculum outside of the core subjects (i.e.: music, art, physical education). The members of the Special Services team included school counselors, social workers, speech therapists, and the Learning Center/Technology Director (LCTD) of the school.

Christine was employed as the LCTD from 1994 to 2008, and reported directly to the school principal. The district has a Technology Coordinator, but the areas of responsibility merely overlapped in some areas rather than having a hierarchical relationship. In other words, the LCTD did not report to the district Technology Coordinator, but had to seek cooperation/

collaboration from time-to-time regarding the implementation of certain technologies. As the LCTD, Christine coordinated all of the school's multimedia, print, and technology purchasing and distribution. She was also responsible for implementing all technology infrastructure improvements, modifications, and troubleshooting. As a former computer science teacher, she was also used as a valuable resource both in formal (e.g., district-level committees) and informal settings (e.g., teachers seeking advice).

The biggest challenge for the LCTD is providing training and guidance to teachers in the proper use of educational and communications technology within their curriculum. By the mere nature of technology, this is best approached using active training techniques, which most often arrives when teachers come seeking personal advice. As illustrated by the scene at the beginning of this chapter, it was just such an occurrence that served as the seed for this case.

CASE DESCRIPTION

Despite the long history of the use of dissection in biology coursework, it has and continues to be, very controversial (Hart et al, 2008; Kinzie et al, 1993; Langley, 1991; Orlans, 1988; Nobis, 2002; Strauss, 1991; Madrazo, G, 2002). The Florida legislature passed a bill in 1988 protecting the rights of students who do not wish to participate in dissection, and nine other states have followed suit, including Illinois in 2000. However, at the time of this study, with no such law in existence, the teachers of this school saw the need to explore alternatives to their current conventional practices. To explore potential new approaches, it was first necessary to look at the various alternative forms of delivery available, and secondly, to find the appropriate alternative means of instruction for this grade level and the depth of coverage desired.

Technology Concerns and Components

The team contacted the National Anti-Vivisection Society (NAVS) in Chicago to see what alternative learning materials were available for this age group. The following were reviewed:

1. Anatomical models, such as a lifelike bullfrog model with removable parts available on a free loan basis from NAVS, a three-dimensional vinyl zoological model of a frog from Nystrom, and vinyl relief models of a frog with removable flexible organs from National Teaching Aids.
2. Charts of frog anatomy and development from Denoyer-Geppert and Nystrom.
3. Laserdiscs such as *Principles of Biology* from Optical Data Corporation's Living Textbook Series.
4. Reference books such as *Pictorial Anatomy of the Frog* from University of Washington Press.
5. Advanced coloring books such as *The Marine Biology Coloring Book* from Harper Collins.
6. Computer programs presenting simulations or tutorials of frog dissection such as *Operation Frog* from Scholastic, *Visifrog* from Ventura, and *Digital Frog* from Digital Frog International;
7. Internet sites on the World Wide Web (WWW) presenting the anatomy and dissection of a frog, such as *Virtual Frog Dissection Kit* (http://froggy.lbl.gov/virtual) from the Lawrence Berkeley National Laboratory, and *NetFrog* (http://frog.edschool.virginia.edu/) from the University of Virginia.

Although there are many alternatives to dissection, the extent to which computer models, videotapes, or other nonanimal materials can replace it remains open to question. For example, in one survey of a group of American teachers (Mayer

& Hinton, 1990), 74% of middle-school teachers and 94% of high school teachers still reported the use of physical dissection in classes. Many of the alternatives are faulted for their low levels of realism or for limited opportunities for active student participation (Strauss & Kinzie, 1991). Whether or not the alternatives are interactive appears to be an important factor in ensuring success (Strauss & Kinzie, 1994). With this in mind during the search for a comparable alternative to an actual frog dissection, various forms of instructional material were examined involving computers as the delivery medium. Computers were chosen because of their inherent constructivist and hands-on elements, which would more closely parallel the essence of an actual dissection activity. These delivery systems fell into one or more of the following general categories (Piskurich, 1993):

1. *Hypertext:* The ability to link any place in text stored in a computer with any other place in the same or different texts, permitting rapid access through buttons and other tools across nonlinear pathways.
2. *Hypermedia:* Similar to hypertext, but hypermedia allows free linking of different media (e.g., text, graphics, video, voice, and animation).
3. *Simulation:* An operating representation of central features of reality; a portrayal of a real-life situation or episode.
4. *Multimedia:* The use of two or more instructional media together. Technically, examples include audiotape and slides. However, this term has come to represent optical disc technology combined with computer power.
5. *Virtual Reality:* A computer-generated environment that simulates reality sufficiently enough for the human senses to experience it.
6. *Microworld:* A computer-based simulation with opportunities for manipulation of content and practice of skills.

The biology team ruled out the computer program *VisiFrog* because of its high school level target audience, and because the content that it presented did not meet the objectives the team used with real dissection: 1) knowledge of a frog's anatomy; 2) comparison between the functions of the major organs with those in the human anatomy; and 3) performance of a dissection instead of merely watching one being performed.

Problems also arose with using the Internet sites as the sole delivery method. One problem was the time needed to create movies and perform dissection. For example, within *Virtual Frog*, signals issued by the user must go out to California to be rendered, then downloaded to the user's computer. Such a time lag would prohibit use of Internet sites within a typical class period of 43 minutes. A more acute problem was that access to the Internet sites would not be consistent or reliable when working within time constraints mandated by a fixed class schedule and limited lab access. For example, the network could go down or the students might be accessing the site at a time when there was heavy demand, resulting in even slower times or with access to the site being denied.

The computer tutorial program *Digital Frog* could be adjusted to the level of a middle school audience and was the favorite of existing alternatives among the biology team. However, the team did have concerns due to the lack of interactivity of *Digital Frog* during the dissection sections; students were watchers rather than participants in the process. The computer program *Operation Frog CD* covered the material desired by the biology team and also offered a hands-on simulation mode for delivery of instruction. However, the biology team felt that the depth of material covered was inadequate for the level of understanding desired.

The biology team was concerned about all of the alternatives to dissection because of their lack of a three-dimensional quality in the graphics presented. They felt this lack of 3D quality would limit the students' perceptions of how specific body parts related to the anatomical systems of which they were a part (e.g., the heart related to the circulatory system). It soon became clear that no one delivery system existed which would cover the subject matter needed, at the grade level needed, or with a constructivist hands-on approach to parallel that of an actual dissection. It also became clear that there had been few efforts to evaluate the learning effectiveness of alternatives to dissection (e.g., Langley, 1991). It became necessary to combine elements of each delivery system category to form a virtual learning environment (VLE) of frog dissection in which to immerse the students. This microworld was made up of the computer multimedia simulation *Operation Frog* CD, movies of the various stages of frog dissection, 3D movies of frog anatomy, sounds, and digitized images. The combination of these elements are referred to as a *desktop microworld*.

The biology team decided to compare two alternatives to frog dissection in order to look at the proposed benefit of a hands-on approach to learning: (a) the desktop microworld with *Operation Frog* providing the hands-on element, and (b) a CD tutorial, *Digital Frog,* that had no hands-on element. Technology is developing more rapidly than public research can examine it, and the technological base will continue to change. Multimedia evolved into hypertext. Hypertext evolved into hypermedia. Hypermedia coupled with simulations evolved into virtual reality. Although software and technology firms conduct research into their own products, it is difficult, and some would say wasteful of scarce research dollars (e.g., Iodannis, 2007), to rigorously evaluate every new technological product purported to be educational. However, the basic principles of representation, learning, and interaction will transfer across many technologies. While an understanding of how to use the media effectively is being developed, work must continue. Without a broad research base in the foundations of these learning systems, educators will be blind to the how and why of their inner workings, and cannot hope to predict their outcomes.

Educational Concerns

Many teachers believe that careful performance of dissection has the potential for increasing student understanding of the organism, encouraging a greater appreciation of human anatomy, and developing higher-level thinking skills. They believe dissection also has the potential for increasing student interest in science due to its inherently hands-on approach (Kinzie et al., 1993). Many of these same teachers believe that the knowledge that students gain from dissection has more impact, is retained longer, and is understood better than the knowledge gained when teachers substitute models, charts, or materials from textbooks (Orlans, 1988). Smith (1994) found that most teachers do not see the replacement of live animals for classroom study by alternative means of instruction to be desirable.

With the richness of computer-based microworlds comes many questions about how these environments compare with actual reality. Some research has been done in microworlds with regard to: (a) comprehension and recall of material (Sinclair, Liljedahl, & Zaskis, 2006); (b) how the classroom teacher can harness the power of these computer-based environments (e.g., Bellemain & Capponi, 1992; Dreyfus & Halevi, 1990; Jackiw, & Sinclair, 2002; Jiang & Potter, 1994; Roth, 1996); and (c) how students and teachers interact with a microworld (e.g., Jackiw, & Sinclair, 2002; Roth, 1996; Roth, 2001; Xinogalos, Satratzemi, & Dagdilelis, 2006). However, our recent search of the entire ERIC database revealed no studies (aside from the current one) that examined microworlds with regard to whether all learners, or only those with certain learning styles, can follow the conceptual model. Similarly, no other studies were found specifically in the area of alternatives to physical dissection and their impact on cognitive development gains, long-term retention, science anxiety, and differing learning styles. We were unable to find examples of studies formally comparing the two "realities."

It was our purpose to investigate and compare the level of learning and long-term retention of the frog's internal anatomy between seventh-grade students using an interactive CD tutorial, a hypermedia simulation, and conventional frog dissection. Students' anxiety toward science was also compared across the three treatment groups. Additional data was collected on the students' preferred learning modality to explore any relationship between the level of learning or long-term retention and their respective instructional activities.

Much of the literature related to computer-generated microworlds has focused on their use as a presentation vehicle for information (e.g. Becker, 1989; Heller, 1990; Lamb, 1991). However, microworlds have the potential to alter the roles of teacher and learner, and the interactions between them, by allowing students to create their own interpretations of information through modeling, coaching, fading, reflection, exploration, and encouragement to debug his/her knowledge. The microworlds that we used, an interactive tutorial and a desktop microworld, offered a chance to test how they measure up as alternatives to conventional dissection.

With advances in technology expanding the boundaries of computer-generated microworlds, we felt that we should be taking a close look at how best the technology could be put to use for the learning of our students. To do this, we had to also gain a better understanding of how our children learn best in relation to technology. We anticipate that many of these general principles should apply to future technology and future applications even if the specifics change in unforeseen ways.

Evaluation Design

The comparison of the desktop microworld, interactive CD tutorial, and conventional frog dissection was conducted within the seventh-grade prescribed curriculum following the completion of the unit on cold-blooded vertebrates, which is the last unit of the school year. Students had already performed dissections on earthworms during the course of the year and were familiar with dissection instruments and general lab procedures and safety precautions.

The biology team was interested in seventh-graders for two reasons. First, a unit on frog dissection was part of the mandatory biology curriculum as stated by the district. Second, seventh-graders are at the maturational level when they begin to be able to ignore nonessential information and become capable of self-directed study (Carnine, Kameeniu, and Coyle, 1984; Kline, 1971). The technology we were examining involved hypermedia, which relies on these two cognitive considerations.

In addition, in studies to investigate the relationship between age and the learning environment, incidental learning was found to increase with age. As children mature, they are more capable of hypothesis scanning and structuring presented information. When studies were made to pinpoint the age at which children are more able to ignore nonessential information, researchers found that the skill appeared in early adolescence (Nix & Spiro, 1990). Older students use context clues more frequently and effectively than younger students, and preadolescent students cannot be assumed to have adequate contextual skills. Because of these findings relating to maturational age level and ability to ignore nonessential information, as well as the capability of self-directed study, it is appropriate to limit generalization of our case to students no younger than seventh-grade.

Each of the fourteen seventh-grade science classes in Smith School was randomly-assigned an instructional delivery system subject to scheduling constraints (each teacher was to have at least one class of each treatment to help control for bias) and availability of conventional or computer lab space. This process resulted in four classes using the interactive tutorial, six classes using the desktop microworld, and four classes using the conventional dissection method. No class exceeded 30 students. Prior to the actual dissection activity, teachers received training in manipulating the computer treatments, using the same lab worksheets as the students would use.

The students in the experimental sections conducted their alternative dissection activity using the interactive tutorial or desktop microworld in the auxiliary computer lab at the school. This lab contains 15 Macintosh computers, which necessitated the partnering of subjects, two to a computer. This was appropriate, as the control group was also partnered, two to a dissection pan, as they historically had been grouped within the school. This partnership allowed the students to share the dissection tasks, taking turns on the computer or with the dissection tray, as they discussed their observations and results, and collaborated on what to write on their separate packets. Each student was assessed individually on the lab activities. The partnerships were formed from intact lab partner groups assigned by their teachers in their regular classrooms. There were several strengths to conducting the self-study in this way:

1. Research was conducted in the actual educational setting to which we wished to generalize our findings, namely, future seventh-grade students at the school (and for the purposes of this book, seventh-graders with comparable demographic characteristics).

2. Environmental variations were incorporated into the design of the experiment. Specifically, not just one teacher but three teachers used the new instructional methods.

All teachers were trained in the new means of instructional delivery and all had previous experience with conducting conventional frog dissections. All teachers taught both control and experimental groups.

3. The teachers observed what their students actually did during the experiment; for example, whether the research participants were attentive to a particular treatment or appeared to be distracted by other events. These observations were helpful in interpreting the results and in planning future research. The classroom teachers recorded their observations in the form of notes taken during the dissection unit.

4. Teachers noted the social context in which the experiment was being conducted, as certain events that occurred in the schools might have affected experimental treatments. In this case, the timing of the experiment during the last remaining weeks of the school year might prove to be a distraction to the learning environment due to the students' heightened anticipation of the approaching summer vacation and "end-of-the-year" school activities taking place during the day.

5. Teachers prepared participants for the experiment by giving brief instruction and a few minutes' training prior to the start of the experiment to ensure a smooth transition from each participant's current mental state to the one required by the experimental tasks.

6. A control treatment allowed participants to use their customary approaches to learning, forming a naturalistic baseline against which the behavior and learning of the experimental groups could be evaluated.

For all groups, the dissection took place over a span of four consecutive days with each class having a 43-minute instructional time period each day. The testing, preparation and closure took place during three class periods. All achievement tests used the same instrument, the Frog Dissection Test. The pretest and preparation occurred on the day before the dissection activity began. The immediate posttest occurred on the day following the dissection activity. The class period for administration of the delayed posttest was three months following the dissection activity during the opening days of the following academic school year. A science anxiety survey, Science Survey, was administered in each class two days prior to the start of the dissection activity to establish a baseline for comparison, and then again on the second day following the conclusion of the dissection activity. A self-assessment of learning styles had occurred a month prior to the start of the study as part of the study skills teacher's curriculum.

Technology Conditions

It is important to keep in mind that our purpose in this self-study was to determine how to incorporate technology into the frog dissection unit and evaluate whether it could replace frog dissection entirely. The media for creating a desktop microworld and an interactive tutorial of a frog dissection, our two options, had to be readily available, relatively easy to use, and able to run on existing platforms within an average educational setting. After careful consideration of existing media for frog dissection, as discussed previously, *Digital Frog* from Digital Frog International was chosen as the instructional delivery system for an interactive tutorial. However, a combination of programs appeared to be best suited for creating a desktop microworld environment.

Digital Frog *interactive CD-ROM. Digital Frog* is an interactive CD-ROM that incorporates full-motion video, animations, sounds, narration, in-depth text, full color photographs and a comprehensive workbook in three modules: Dissection, Anatomy, and Ecology. The dissection module uses a tutorial approach with the dissection proceeding in a step-by-step presentation manner.

Users can access multimedia files to view a frog dissection being performed, but do not actually perform a dissection themselves. The help screen allows the user to click on a button to be taken to the appropriate section:

1. Dissection, where the tutorial dissection takes place.
2. Anatomy, where various parts of the frog's anatomy are explained and shown using graphics and digitized photos as well as animations.
3. Ecology, where the life cycle, behavior, and biodiversity of the frog are discussed.
4. Getting Started, where general instructions on how to navigate through the program are given.

The dissection section of *Digital Frog* basically operates in the same manner throughout the various stages of the dissection process. The user is presented with an opening screen of the anatomical section being dissected, which contains hotspots. A hotspot colors a particular part of the system as the cursor passes over it, and at the same time, puts a check mark by the appropriate name for that anatomical part in a list on the left-hand side of the screen. The user is then given information on the steps in the dissection process with the incisions that are needed outlined in white on the graphic. Finally, the user is shown a digitized movie of the described dissection procedure within the frame on the screen. The student is able to cancel the movie by clicking to the next screen or can view the movie again by clicking on the frame within the screen.

The dissection section of *Digital Frog* is arranged by the following body sections: (a) head (mouth, brain, eye, tympanum); (b) abdomen (heart, liver, lungs, stomach, intestine, fat bodies); and (c) legs. The bodily systems of the frog are addressed within the Anatomy section of the interactive tutorial with the main sections being that of circulatory, respiratory, digestive, urogenital, and control/nervous systems. With the use of the navigational toolbox, the user is able to go back and forth between the systems, but there is no way to bookmark where you have been. The student is given a warning message if he/she tries to progress in the dissection in an out-of-order manner, such as removing the stomach before the heart. However, they may still proceed with their choice by clicking the organ a second time. Note also that two modes of viewing are given at the beginning of the tutorial: basic level and advanced level. However, there is very little difference between the two modes, with the advanced version offering only a few additional screens of information.

Desktop Microworld

The desktop microworld environment was built around *Operation Frog on CD* with other programs serving as auxiliary forms of instructional delivery. *Operation Frog on CD* contains a tutorial simulation of the dissection of a frog, male or female, with three built-in guides: (a) OptiFrog, a picture reference that displays the three layers of frog organs; (b) the Frog Files Database, to inform students about individual organs and their systems; and (c) a Help Index, a how-to guide to the program features.

Unlike *Digital Frog*, *Operation Frog* allows students to perform the dissection, not just view it. Unlike a real dissection, students also can reconstruct the frog. Using surgical scissors, a probe, forceps, and a magnifying lens, students use the computer to probe and snip body organs, to remove organs to the examination tray, and to investigate frog body systems close-up. Hints help guide students through the program. For example, holding down the probe instrument on the frog temporarily displays yellow dots indicating the spots on the frog's body where the next incisions should occur.

During the simulated dissection, the student has access to the Frog Files, which contain informa-

tion about the frog's organs. There are two ways to open a Frog File; either by choosing it from the reference menu, or by using the magnifying lens to click an organ in the examination tray. Once a Frog File window is opened, it presents the students with various ways to learn more about the specific organ. A graphic shows the student a close-up view of the organ or a diagram of how the organ fits into one of the frog systems. Scrolling text contains information about the organ in either basic or enhanced (more detailed) mode, which is controlled via the preference menu. By clicking one of several buttons, the student can access different features: (a) with the compare button, the student can see how the frog organ compares to the same organ in a human; (b) with the animate button, the student is shown an animated sequence of the organ; (c) with the movie button, the student is shown a full-motion video sequence; and (d) with the photo button, the student is shown a digitized photo of the frog's organs. The student may access a small reference section that includes OptiFrog, which shows the three layers of the dissection process, and Frog Files, which allows the student to view any of the digitized images and movies. However, there are few images and movies to view in comparison to *Digital Frog*.

There are a number of differences between *Operation Frog* and a real dissection that should be pointed out. For example, in the *Operation Frog* dissection, students don't work with all of the frog's body parts, only the main organs in the head and torso areas. Also, when the student snips the closed frog's skin to begin the dissection, the skin automatically disappears, revealing the main body organs. In a real dissection, students would need to snip and remove both the skin and the underlying abdominal muscles before reaching the frog's internal organs, which leads to another distinct difference. Instead of showing the dozens of different bones and muscles in a real frog, *Operation Frog* includes no bones and shows the muscles as a system, rather than individually. This limitation did not affect the present self-study, however, because the curriculum being addressed focused on the internal organs of the frog's anatomy and not the musculature or skeletal frame. An additional difference is that the body organs in *Operation Frog* are colored to make them easier to find, while in a real dissection the exact color, size, and location of the organs will differ from one frog to the next.

To help compensate for some of the limitations of *Operation Frog*, and to build a stronger desktop microworld environment, the students were given additional modes of instruction to use, downloaded from the Internet to each computer's hard disk prior to the dissection: (a) 3D QuickTime movies of the frog at various stages of the dissection from the Web site, *Virtual Frog*; (b) QuickTime movies of the stages of dissection being performed from the Web site *NetFrog*; and (c) other digitized pictures and sounds. These components were accessible to students at given times during the dissection process as indicated on their worksheets by icons matched with file names, which could be called up via the Apple (system) menu.

Conventional Frog Dissection

The conventional physical dissection method was used as the control treatment within this study. It was comprised of the traditional method of providing a preserved specimen of a frog for every two students within the class. Students used traditional dissection trays and related tools. The dissection activity was conducted within the regular science classrooms, which contained lab tables for science activities. Teachers guided students through the dissection process aided by the worksheets given to students.

Computer Set-Up

This study utilized a lab of 15 Macintosh computers. The program *Digital Frog* was loaded onto all the hard drives in order to minimize ac-

cess time, enabling the program to run smoothly without long pauses between displays. The same approach was used with the *Operation Frog* CD. The access program installed on each computer was configured so that when a student signed in for use of *Digital Frog*, access was denied to *Operation Frog* and its auxiliary material, and vice-versa for those signing in for use of the desktop microworld. Additional application programs were used to display various other elements of the desktop microworld such as sounds, QTVR movies and digital images. These programs were freeware or shareware programs downloaded from the internet and installed on each computer and would be called up automatically when a student clicked on the appropriate icon.

Results and Discussion of the Formal Evaluation

Relative Effects on Student Achievement

Results were mixed. It was found that students participating in physical dissection and the CD tutorial had higher gains in learning than students in the microworld condition one day later. However, the effect size of this difference was small. In fact, students gained about two standard deviations in test score under each condition. However, no difference was found between the conventional treatment and the CD-tutorial treatment. Therefore, if the desired outcome is immediate gain of knowledge, the preferred delivery system would appear to be either the conventional dissection or the CD-tutorial.

The question arises as to why students within the microworld treatment scored slightly lower than both other treatments. If the hands-on component is thought to provide better encoding of information, then the logical conclusion would be that both the conventional and the microworld treatment groups would outperform the CD-tutorial group on the immediate post-test. Perhaps the reason lies in the findings of Thomas and Hooper (1991). They believed that the effects of simulations were revealed not by tests of knowledge but by tests of transfer and application. Another explanation can also be given when looking at the students' experiences with the various forms of instructional treatment. All students had previous dissection experience, and all students had experienced working with CD-tutorials, albeit not those in which an entire science unit was delivered. However, the microworld environment was completely new to their range of experiences and may have resulted in a lowering of their immediate achievement gain due to unfamiliarity with the format.

Students in the physical dissection condition had higher learning achievement scores than either virtual condition three months later. When looking at the mean gain score over time from the pretest to the delayed posttest, students in the conventional dissection method showed significantly better retention than those in either the microworld or the CD-tutorial treatment. But again, the effect size was small, and students declined about one standard deviation in test score under each condition. This seems to give an advantage to the conventional method of dissection, but this advantage disappears when looking at the gain scores from posttest to delayed posttest. There, the differences favoring the conventional treatment disappeared, as no one treatment proved to be significantly better for retaining knowledge gained over the long term than either of its counterparts. In other words, the knowledge decrement (Grieve, 1992) was not significantly different across treatments.

When looking at the retention of knowledge gained over the long term, this self-study's results supported the view that alternative forms of dissection are as effective in instructional delivery as the actual practice of physical dissection. This lends support to the National Association of Biology Teachers (NABT) official policy supporting alternatives to dissection and vivisection in the biology curricula wherever possible, as long as those alternatives satisfy the objectives of teaching scientific methodology and fundamental biological concepts.

In the debate over animal dissection in the classroom, a number of studies (Downie & Meadows, 1995; Kinzie, Larsen, et al., 1996; Leonard, 1989; Quentin-Baxter & Dewhurst, 1992; Strauss & Kinzie, 1991; Strauss & Kinzie, 1994) have attempted to find suitable alternatives to animal dissection. Our findings show that two forms, a CD-Tutorial and a desktop microworld, are viable alternatives to physical frog dissection in retaining knowledge gained over the long term.

Relative Effects on the Level of Science Anxiety

When looking at the results of the science anxiety survey, the physical frog dissection group showed significantly lower levels of anxiety both before and after the unit. While at first glance this appears puzzling, closer inspection reveals two possible explanations. The first concerns the timing of the unit of instruction and the arrangement of lab facilities. Because the frog dissection unit was conducted at the end of the academic year, and this was the first time that two alternatives to conventional dissection were to be offered, the biology team needed an uncommon level of coordination to plan use of lab facilities. Unfortunately, these same teachers had no common planning period, and therefore, coordination of facilities had to occur before and after school, as well as in the halls between class periods. All these discussions took place at times when students could have been present and overheard the planning, which could have resulted in students having an idea of which treatment their class would receive, skewing the initial findings of pre-treatment anxiety levels.

Another explanation for the physical frog dissection group exhibiting the least amount of anxiety both before and after treatment can be seen when looking at the experiences of our students. All seventh-graders had had previous exposure to dissection activities during the course of their life-science curriculum. Conversely, the students had received no prior exposure to a unit of instruction delivered entirely through a desktop microworld or a CD-Tutorial. Koballa (1993) stated that activity-oriented science instruction can help develop favorable attitudes toward science. Previous exposure to a similar activity could have skewed the results of the science anxiety measurements in favor of the physical dissection activity. When looking at the pre- and posttest change in anxiety across technology groups, no single group showed a significantly different change in anxiety compared to the others. Apparently, the type of treatment received had no bearing on the level of science anxiety.

It is interesting to note the relatively low levels of anxiety reported by students across the board. All but one of the mean anxiety level scores fell below 2.00 on a response scale of 1 (not at all nervous) through 5 (very nervous). This finding may be a result of the timing of the study at the end of a year-long seventh-grade life-science curriculum that stressed active participation by students. This follows the conclusion of Hill, Atwater, and Wiggins (1995) that overall attitude toward science improves significantly over time when students are engaged in active participation within a seventh-grade life-science curriculum. Our study falls within their call for additional research to focus on particular connections among specific science instructional activities, such as in this case, a frog dissection unit.

It was in looking at the results of the science anxiety measures by gender that some interesting patterns began to emerge. Females reported significantly higher initial science anxiety than males. After treatment, although anxiety levels declined for both genders, females continued to report significantly higher science anxiety than males overall. Varying results were displayed by the three technology groups when looking at differences in anxiety levels by gender. The initial difference within the CD-tutorial group was

no longer present after treatment, suggesting a beneficial effect for treatment in reducing female science anxiety. For subjects in the microworld treatment, the difference was not significant either pre-treatment or post-treatment. However, after treatment, the difference between males and females in the microworld group did approach significance, with anxiety declining more among males than females. It appears that this treatment was more beneficial for males. Finally, for the conventional dissection group, the difference between genders was significant both before and after treatment. The experience of conventional dissection had no effect on the disparity in science anxiety between males and females.

It is interesting to note that the CD-tutorial treatment seemed to reduce the level of science anxiety displayed by female students, while just the opposite was occurring within the microworld treatment group as the level of anxiety decreased for males after treatment. This might be due to the fact that students in the microworld treatment were active participants in their use of the computer and had much more control over the flow of information presented than those students in the CD-tutorial treatment, who merely observed a dissection taking place. Because the microworld group actually performed a frog dissection utilizing representations of dissection tools, they faced the very real possibility of making a mistake in the dissection process. This possibility did not exist for students in the CD-tutorial treatment, because they merely watched as the various dissection activities were performed by the computer. Additional research to pursue the interaction effect of active versus passive roles and their relationship to gender regarding anxiety would shed valuable light on technology implementation in the classroom.

Overall, this study demonstrated that science anxiety is clearly related to gender, which confirms the findings of Wynstra (Wynstra, 1991; Wynstra & Cummings, 1993, 1995). Wynstra reported that females exhibited significantly higher science anxiety than males, and suggested that in classes involving activities that could make one squeamish, alternative delivery systems could be used. In this way, students would have the option of working with charts, models, or interactive computer software instead of having to dissect once-living creatures, such as frogs or pigs. The results of our study support Wynstra's findings.

Our world has rapidly become one based on scientific inquiry that crosses all economic, political, and geographic boundaries. Educators have long called for a fuller, stronger, and more fundamentally sound science curriculum within our schools and the development of ways to encourage students to pursue a scientific career path. Atwater, Wiggins, and Gardner (1995) concluded that the less anxious a student was toward science, the more positive that student was toward the sciences in general. In their review of the research, Koballa, Crawley, et al. (1990) found that the years 8 to 13 are the critical ages for influencing science attitudes. By understanding which components of a science unit produce anxiety, middle-school teachers can better mitigate those negative emotions and facilitate the learning process more effectively. Our study demonstrates that technology can play a central role, but that different technologies may benefit different groups.

Preferred Learning Style and Achievement

The data from this study did not support any claims of a general effect on achievement for the students' preferred learning style. This was true when looking at differences in achievement for pretest scores, the posttest scores and the delayed posttest scores. Within this study, learning style alone does not appear to be related to achievement. It was only when looking at differences in gain scores by preferred learning style within technology group that differences began to emerge. The conventional dissection group seemed to have the least effect on those students with a prefer-

ence for the visual-kinesthetic learning style. These students significantly under-performed peers taught with the same dissection activity who displayed a preference for the auditory, the auditory-kinesthetic, the kinesthetic, or the visual learning styles.

The microworld treatment seemed to have particular merit for students who preferred any of the auditory learning styles (auditory, auditory-kinesthetic, and auditory-visual), they outperformed their peers with a kinesthetic preference from the pretest to the posttest. In fact, students with a preference for the auditory-visual learning style had the best performance overall in any of the dissection activities. They also showed significantly higher gain-scores than students using the microworld technology who preferred the visual learning style.

Both the conventional dissection activity and the desktop microworld activity offered not only visual and auditory channels, but also kinesthetic channels in the form of actually participating in the dissection process. However, the CD-Tutorial students merely observed the dissection process take place. The findings of this study support the contention of researchers (Craik & Tulving, 1975; Ellis & Hunt, 1983; Korwin & Jones, 1990; Seifert, 1995) that hands-on activities help to encode knowledge acquired into long-term memory, and that knowledge decrement (Grieve, 1992) is less following activities that address all the varying styles of learning. However, these hands-on activities must not be exclusively kinesthetic, but incorporate all learning styles.

CURRENT CHALLENGES

Several limitations were evident within our self-study. To assess the preferred learning style of a student, we were limited to data from the school's study skills teacher. The instrument used to obtain the data allowed for categorizing students into groups, reflecting a balance between the three major learning styles: auditory, visual, and kinesthetic. This resulted in small numbers of subjects falling into the shared categories of auditory-kinesthetic (12), auditory-visual (30), and visual-kinesthetic (21). Taken by themselves, the numbers reflected in these groupings would not pose a problem, but when they were further divided by the instructional technology received, the numbers in some cases were very small. Teachers attempting a similar evaluation of the implementation of technology should either utilize an instrument for assessing preferred learning that would not allow for cross-groupings, or increase the overall number of students.

Our study was conducted at the very end of the school year, and problems inherent with this timing were the built-in distractions to students of end-of-the-year activities, anticipation of summer vacation, and attrition due to students leaving school early for family vacations and/or relocation. All these factors can play a role in the level of concentration attainable by students and a reduction in the number of student participants. As stated earlier, the timing of the study left little time for the biology team to coordinate the use of facilities. This led to a possibility of students over-hearing teachers discussing arrangements during periods of the day when students were present. If this evaluation were to be replicated, care should be given in the discussion of implementation plans to ensure that students are unaware of their technology group prior to the actual start of the instructional unit.

In the course of conducting our self-study, many questions arose that provided a varied base for further consideration. In order to offset the effects of previous experience on the levels of science anxiety reported, our future evaluations/studies will be conducted comparing the various instructional technologies earlier in the year. This approach will also make it so that our students would have no experience in completing a seventh-grade scientific unit of study through conventional dissection, desktop microworld or CD-Tutorial. We also plan to conduct ethnographic studies to provide insight into particular connections between instructional technology, science instruction, science attitudes, science achievement, and cultural background.

The studies of Ester (1994) and Messick (1976) revealed a significant interaction between instructional approach and student learning style. This study supports those findings in the case of the microworld group but not for the conventional group or the CD-tutorial group. The question that naturally follows is, why didn't the pattern that appeared within the microworld treatment also appear within the conventional treatment, if both treatments incorporated all the styles of learning within their environments? We intend to conduct further research in this area in order to answer this question.

Addressing the gender interaction with science anxiety suggested several directions of inquiry. If females exhibit a higher level of science anxiety overall than males during the middle-school years, will that difference increase, decrease, or remain the same in subsequent years? And if there is a change, what are the forces that caused the change? We would love to track the students on our current study as they progress through high school, but the challenges of negotiating with two different district administrations, not to mention parents, are very daunting. We may have to settle for voluntary completion of periodically mailed questionnaires.

The belief that the effects of simulations are not revealed by tests of knowledge, but instead revealed by tests of transfer and application, suggests further study. How would the microworld compare with the CD-tutorial if observations were made on the students' performances in later dissection procedures or life-science exercises? Would tests of transfer and application show that the learning achieved within the microworld frog dissection be greater than that attained through the CD-tutorial dissection activity?

The level of knowledge retention displayed from the posttest to the delayed posttest also merits further investigation. While most tests within the school curriculum are geared toward immediate achievement gains, the goal of most educational institutions is to help students not only learn but to retain that which they have achieved, which leads to the following questions. Once knowledge is gained, how much is lost over time? And which methods of instructional delivery help the most in the retention of that knowledge? Further research into these areas is a must given the rapid advance of technological innovation and the increasing need for a technologically literate and educated workforce.

There is a definite need for more research in the area of desktop microworlds. With access to the Internet increasing throughout our schools and spurred on by government initiatives, questions arise as to what can be done with all the information so readily available. This is particularly true for multimedia elements such as digitized pictures, sound, and movies. Desktop microworlds, composed of these downloaded elements and run by shareware programs, offer a relevant and easily upgradable instructional environment. There are then many questions concerning these desktop microworlds and their role in the instructional process. How best can they be incorporated into today's learning environments? Will they be effective vehicles for information transfer for all students? Are they more effective if created by students for students? Do they allow for student control over the pacing of information flow and the pathways followed? If so, do they allow for the molding of the program to the student's preferred learning style? Just how do teachers and students interact with a microworld to gain the greatest benefit?

EPILOGUE

The biology team hoped that an effective alternative to physical frog dissections could be identified for use within the seventh-grade life-science curriculum. With that objective in mind, we set out to investigate and compare the level of learning and long-term retention of the frog's internal anatomy between seventh-grade students using an interactive CD tutorial, a desktop microworld, and conventional frog dissection. Anxiety levels toward science were also compared across the three technology groups. In addition, data were collected on the students' preferred learning styles to explore any relationship between the level of learning or long-term retention and the respective instructional activity.

While strict qualitative data were not collected, the team wrote down daily comments and notes about how they perceived the classes progressing and any problems they encountered during the process. Some of the more relevant comments were as follows:

1. "I personally felt that for the average 7th grader, the Simulation [microworld] was better suited to their learning needs. The packet and program kept them on task and actively engaged."
2. "It took them longer to finish this pathway [microworld] than the CD program classes."
3. "The CD program was too challenging for some of my slower students - too easy to get through for others."
4. "I hope the results will prove that the most learning and retention occurred with the Simulation [microworld], because that's the way I wish to do it next year."
5. "The program [microworld] practically runs itself."
6. "My classes [involved in the microworld environment], even the immature students, are very much on task. I truly feel like the

'guide on the side' and not the 'sage on the stage'!"

After analyzing the data and the mixed results obtained within this study, the team elected to discard individual physical frog dissection in favor of the alternative of the desktop microworld. Because of the mixed results obtained within this study, the team did not totally abandon the conventional method of frog dissection. Instead, they incorporated the conventional dissection of one frog per class period as a class demonstration prior to students participating in the desktop microworld.

Although the team's reasoning was not explored, their decision to go with the desktop microworld as the primary instructional unit for the dissection of a frog could be explained by Rogers' Perceived Attributes as outlined by Surry (1997) and further defined by Rogers (2003). Rogers states that potential adopters judge an innovation based on their perceptions of five attributes of the innovation. If the potential adopters perceive that the innovation incorporates these attributes, that innovation will experience an increased rate of diffusion.

The first of these attributes, *trialability,* insures that the innovation can be tried on a limited basis before adoption. In this self-study, both the alternative forms of dissection were tried before a decision to adopt an alternative was made. The second attribute of *observability* assures that the innovation will offer observable results. Once again, both alternatives within this study have this attribute. The third attribute, *relative advantage,* means that the innovation offers an advantage to the status quo. The results of this study showed the status quo, the conventional dissection, to be significantly better than the alternatives in many instances and on even par in others. However, one clear advantage of the alternative methods was the avoidance of many dissection controversies. The fourth attribute of *complexity* simply means

that the innovation is not overly complex. All the technologies used seemed to fit this attribute.

The fifth and last attribute is that of *compatibility,* which means that the innovation is compatible with existing practices and values. The desktop microworld offered the hands-on component of the conventional dissection while the CD-tutorial did not. Hands-on science activities are the norm within the school's science curriculum. It is this attribute coupled with the observed engagement of students that seems to have weighed the most heavily in the selection of the desktop microworld over the CD-tutorial treatment as the desired alternative to conventional dissection.

Since the conclusion of this study, the science department continued to employ the desktop microworld dissection within their 7th grade science curriculum until the 2005/06 academic year when they adopted a new science textbook and accompanying curriculum, which did not include dissection. However, the dissection controversy continues (Hart et al, 2008), and new desktop microworlds are being developed (University at Buffalo, 2008), all of which creates new opportunities for further examination of the results from this study.

REFERENCES

Becker, H. J. (1989). The effects of computer use on children's learning: Limitations of past research and a working model for new research. *Peabody Journal of Education, 64*(1), 81–110.

Bellemain, F., & Capponi, B. (1992). Specificities of the organization of a teaching sequence using the computer. *Educational Studies in Mathematics, 23*(1), 59–97. doi:10.1007/BF00302314

Carnine, D., Kameeniu, E., & Coyle, G. (1984). Utilization of contextual information in determining the meaning of unfamiliar words. *Reading Research Quarterly, 19*(2), 188–204. doi:10.2307/747362

Craik, F. I. M., & Tulving, E. (1975). Depth of processing and the retention of words in episodic memory. *Journal of Experimental Psychology. General, 104*(3), 268–294. doi:10.1037/0096-3445.104.3.268

Downie, R., & Meadows, J. (1995). Experience with a dissection opt-out scheme in university level biology. *Journal of Biological Education, 29*(3), 187–196.

Dreyfus, T., & Halevi, T. (1990). QuadFun: A case study of pupil computer interaction. *Computers in Mathematics and Science Teaching, 10*(2), 43–48.

Ellis, H. D., & Hunt, R. R. (1983). *Fundamentals of human memory and cognition* (3rd ed.). Dubuque, IA: Brown.

Ester, D. (1994). CAI, lecture, and student learning style: The different effects of instructional method. *Journal of Research on Computing in Education, 27*(2), 129–140.

Grieve, C. (1992). Knowledge increment assessed for three methodologies of teaching physiology. *Medical Teacher, 14*, 27–32. doi:10.3109/01421599209044011

Hart, L. A., Wood, M. W., & Hart, B. L. (2008). *Why dissection?: Animal use in education*. Westport, CT: Greenwood Press.

Heller, R. (1990). The role of hypermedia in education: A look at the research issues. *Journal of Research on Computing in Education, 22*(2), 431–441.

Hill, G., Atwater, M., & Wiggins, J. (1995). Attitudes toward science of urban seventh-grade life science students over time, and the relationship to future plans, family, teacher, curriculum, and school. *Urban Education, 30*(1), 71–92. doi:10.1177/0042085995030001006

Iodannis, J. P. A. (2007). Why most published research findings are false. *PLoS Medicine, 2*(8), 696–701. doi:.doi:10.1371/journal.pmed.0020124

Jackiw, N., & Sinclair, N. (2002). Dragon play: Microworld design in a whole new class context. *Journal of Educational Computing Research, 27*, 111–145. doi:10.2190/RYW7-EG6H-QU6V-8REC

Jiang, Z., & Potter, W. D. (1994). A computer microworld to introduce students to probability. *Journal of Computers in Mathematics and Science Teaching, 13*(2), 197–222.

Kinzie, M. B., Foss, M. J., & Powers, S. M. (1993). Use of dissection-related courseware by low-ability high school students: A qualitative inquiry. *Educational Technology Research and Development, 41*(3), 87–101. doi:10.1007/BF02297359

Kinzie, M. B., Larsen, V. A., Burch, J. B., & Baker, S. M. (1996). Frog dissection via the World-Wide-Web: Implications for widespread delivery of instruction. *Educational Technology Research and Development, 44*(2), 59–69. doi:10.1007/BF02300541

Kline, A. (1971). A study of the relationship between self directed and teacher directed eighth grade students involved in open ended supplementary ESCP. *Journal of Research in Science Teaching, 8*(3), 263–271. doi:10.1002/tea.3660080310

Koballa, T. R. (1993). *Synthesis of science attitude research for elementary grades*. Paper presented at the 1993 annual meeting of the National Association for Research in Science Teaching, Atlanta, GA.

Koballa, T. R., Crawley, F. E., & Shrigley, R. L. (1990). A summary of research in science education- 1988. *Science Education, 74*(3), 252–407. doi:10.1002/sce.3730740304

Korwin, A. R., & Jones, R. E. (1990). Do hands-on, technology-based activities enhance learning by reinforcing cognitive knowledge and retention? *Journal of Technology Education, 1*(2), 26–33.

Lamb, A. C. (1991). *Emerging technologies and instruction: Hypertext, hypermedia, and interactive multimedia: A selected bibliography.* Englewood Cliffs, NJ: Educational Technology.

Langley, G. R. (1991). Animals in science education: Ethics and alternatives. *Journal of Biological Education, 25*(4), 274–279.

Leonard, W. H. (1989). A comparison of student reactions to biology instruction by interactive videodisc or conventional laboratory. *Journal of Research in Science Teaching, 26*(2), 95–104. doi:10.1002/tea.3660260202

Madrazo, G. (2002). The debate over dissection: Dissecting a classroom dilemma. *Science Educator, 11*(1), 41–45.

Mayer, V. J., & Hinton, N. K. (1990). Animals in the classroom: Considering the options. *Science Teacher (Normal, Ill.), 57*(3), 26–31.

Messick, S. (Ed.). (1976). *Individuality in learning.* San Francisco: Jossey-Bass.

Nix, D., & Spiro, R. (Eds.). (1990). *Cognition, education, and multimedia: Exploring ideas in high technology.* Hillsdale, NJ: Lawrence Erlbaum Associates.

Nobis, N. (2002). Animal dissection and evidence-based life-science and health-professions education. *Journal of Applied Animal Welfare Science, 5*(2), 157–161. doi:10.1207/S15327604JAWS0502_06

Orlans, F. B. (1988). Debating dissection. *Science Teacher (Normal, Ill.), 55*, 36–40.

Orlans, F. B. (1991a). Forum: Dissection. The case against. *Science Teacher (Normal, Ill.), 58*(1), 12–15.

Orlans, F. B. (1991b). Use of animals in education: Policy and practice in the United States. *Journal of Biological Education, 25*(1), 27–32.

Piskurich, G. M. (1993). *The ASTD handbook of instructional technology: American society for training and development.* New York: McGraw-Hill.

Quentin-Baxter, M., & Dewhurst, D. (1992). An interactive computer-based alternative to performing a rat dissection in the classroom. *Journal of Biological Education, 26*(1), 27–33.

Rogers, E. (2003). *Diffusion of innovations.* (5th ed.). New York: Free Press.

Roth, W. (1996). Situating cognition. *Journal of Science Education and Technology, 5*(3), 171–191. doi:10.1007/BF01575302

Roth, W. (2001). Situating cognition. *Journal of the Learning Sciences, 10*, 27–61. doi:10.1207/S15327809JLS10-1-2_4

Seifert, T. (1995). *Human learning and motivation: Readings.* St. John's: Memorial University.

Sinclair, N., Liljedahl, P., & Zaskis, R. (2006). A coulored window on pre-service teachers' conceptions of random numbers. *International Journal of Computers for Mathematical Learning, 11*(2), 77–203. doi:10.1007/s10758-006-0002-y

Smith, W. (1994). Use of animals and animal organs in schools: Practice and attitudes of teachers. *Journal of Biological Education, 28*(2), 111–118.

Strauss, R., & Kinzie, M. B. (1994). Student achievement and attitudes in a pilot study comparing an interactive videodisc simulation to conventional dissection. *The American Biology Teacher, 56*(7), 398–402.

Strauss, R. T., & Kinzie, M. B. (1991). Hi-tech alternatives to dissection. *The American Biology Teacher, 53*(3), 154–158.

Surry, D. W. (1997). Diffusion theory and instructional technology. *Instructional Technology Research Online*. Retrieved from http://intro.base.org/docs/diffusion/

Thomas, R., & Hooper, E. (1991). Simulations: An opportunity we are missing. *Journal of Research on Computing in Education, 23*(4), 497–513.

University at Buffalo. (2008, February 21). 'V-Frog' virtual-reality frog dissection software offers first true physical simulation. *ScienceDaily*.

Wynstra, S. (1991). A study of high school science anxiety including the development of a science anxiety instrument (Doctoral Dissertation, Northern Illinois University). *Dissertation Abstracts International, 53-01A*, 0116.

Wynstra, S., & Cummings, C. (1993). High school science anxiety. *Science Teacher (Normal, Ill.), 60*(7), 18–21.

Wynstra, S., & Cummings, C. (1995). High school science anxiety: Easing the common classroom fears. *The Queensland Science Teacher, 21*(4), 5–6.

Xinogalos, S., Satratzemi, M., & Dagdilelis, V. (2006). An introduction to object-oriented programming with a didactic microworld: "object-Karel. *Computers & Education, 47*(2), 148–171. doi:10.1016/j.compedu.2004.09.005

Chapter 9
Using Digital Communities to Enhance Student Persistence and Retention

Charles S. Layne
University of Houston, USA

Rebecca E. Lee
University of Houston, USA

Daniel P. O'Connor
University of Houston, USA

Catherine L. Horn
University of Houston, USA

Brian K. McFarlin
University of Houston, USA

EXECUTIVE SUMMARY

Achieving student persistence and retention at the University of Houston has often been a challenge for the university. This chapter concerns using Second Life to develop a digital community of students from a single academic department to enhance student persistence toward graduation. It was postulated that the development of a digital community could strengthen the social cohesion of the students and thereby promote academic persistence. Students joined Second Life voluntarily or as part of their course requirements and then were invited to participate in various social and educational activities led by their classmates. The amount of time spent in Second Life was tracked and will be compared to academic performance.

BACKGROUND

As of February 2009, there were over 26,500 members of the University of Houston's *Face-*

DOI: 10.4018/978-1-60566-878-9.ch009

book digital community according to the network statistics provided by provided by *Facebook*. Over 30,000 individuals with profiles on *MySpace* identify themselves as affiliated with the University of Houston and approximately 3000 videos about the university and/or its student's activities have been posted on *YouTube* according to each website's statistics. Participation of this magnitude indicates both the interest and comfort level that today's students have with Internet technology as a means to develop and maintain relationships that until very recently have been conducted primarily through face-to-face interactions. The rise of the Internet has substantially modified the form of interpersonal relationships for students who have grown up with the world literally at their fingertips through digital means. These students are often comfortable sharing relatively personal or intimate knowledge with millions of people, but may be uncomfortable interacting with their classmates or professors in a face-to-face setting. This face-to-face discomfort, busy schedules, family obligations, and job responsibilities, are a few of the reasons why the development of traditional learning communities are becoming more and more difficult to foster. This is particularly true of universities, where a large percentage of the student population commute, such as at the University of Houston (UH). At commuter campuses this may cause challenges to the development of strong communities that, in the past, have been based upon solid interpersonal interactions – a key factor contributing to student persistence (Astin, 1993).

Student persistence, the degree to which students are able to complete all of the requirements necessary to achieve a college degree, is of great importance not just to educators but to many local and state governments interested in developing well educated workforces and productive citizens. For instance, the Texas Higher Education Coordinating Board (THECB) is organized around two themes, one of which is participation and success in higher education (THECB, 2008). At commuter campuses, innovative strategies are needed to foster active and nurturing communities with regular student interaction with faculty, and mentoring (Braxton, 2000) in order to achieve student persistence (i.e., participation and success). The development of technologically innovative

programs designed to improve student persistence and retention is consistent with the need to develop an educated and successful citizenry. We are using Second Life as a platform to develop a digital community composed of majors from the Department of Health and Human Performance (HHP) at the University of Houston, monitor their involvement in the community during their time at UH and examine the relationship between their involvement in the Second Life community and their academic performance.

University of Houston

The University of Houston currently enrolls approximately 34,000 undergraduates (or 27,000 full-time-equivalent students). Among those, approximately 3,200 enter each year as first-time-in-college freshmen (University of Houston Office of Institutional Research, 2008). Figure 1 indicates that the fraction of first-time University of Houston freshmen requiring remediation in 2002 (the most recent year for which public data are available) exceeds the need for remediation at other Texas four-year postsecondary institutions across all race/ethnicity categories. Remediation rates for White, Hispanic, and Black UH freshmen are 25, 39, and 48 percent, respectively. In the context of the retention and persistence literature, such data suggest that a reasonable proportion of students entering the University of Houston likely do so at a disadvantage.

In particular, much research suggests the number of developmental classes a student is required to take – a strong proxy for academic preparedness – negatively relates with the likelihood of completion (Bettinger & Long, 2004; Rosenbaum & Person, 2003), a conclusion perhaps not surprising given that typically the most academically under-prepared students are enrolled in such courses. There is some evidence pointing to the benefit of a structured open access model, though, where mandatory sorting strategies determine the extent to which a student must participate in remedial

Figure 1. Proportion of first time freshman who entered texas public higher education institutions underprepared, 2005

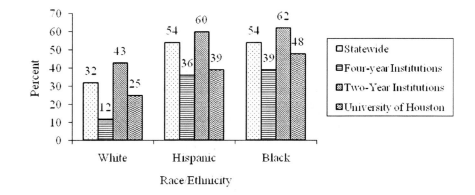

education (Beatty-Guenter, 1994; Fonte, 1997; Moss & Yeaton, 2006). Specifically, universities that allow most or all applicants to the institution to enroll need a mechanism for determining those students' preparedness for college-level coursework and structuring appropriate interventions in response. Developmental efforts seem to function most effectively, however, in the context of collaborative learning communities (Grubb, 1999; Miglietti & Strange, 2002; Tinto, 1997) and institutional programs with tutorial services with trained tutors and with advising and counseling (Boylan, Bliss, & Bonham, 1997).

Student Persistence

Current college participation rates are the highest of the last 30 years (Snyder, Tan, & Hoffman, 2006). In spite of such increases in the proportions of high school graduates continuing on to postsecondary education, college completion rates have been largely stagnant - around 66 percent for those who achieve at least 10 credits at a baccalaureate-granting institution and substantially less for the full population of postsecondary entrants who aspire to a baccalaureate degree (Adelman, 2006). For example, of the freshman who enroll at the University of Houston, only 39 percent graduate with a bachelor's degree within 6 years of entry

(author calculations, National Center for Education Statistics, 2008). Moreover, graduation rates remain significantly lower for minorities and for those who come from low economic backgrounds than for White and relatively advantaged students (Kurlaender & Felts, 2008).

In understanding that complex dilemma, research suggests several personal and structural conditions that contribute to why students who begin college do not earn a bachelor's degree. First, the extent to which a student has had a rigorous academic experience in high school is the single best predictor of college completion (Adelman, 1999; 2006), however research suggests that more than one-quarter of all first-time freshmen are enrolled in some remedial course (Parsad & Lewis, 2003). Money is a second barrier to college completion. Much research has documented the relationship of cost and college enrollment, particularly identifying that reduction of costs increases enrollment (e.g., Bound & Turner, 2002; Kane, 1994).

A third factor influencing college completion is individual campus practice. A substantial body of research suggests that campus-level conditions and interventions, including student interaction with faculty, a shared sense of community among students, active engagement with the institution, and mentoring all contribute to higher rates of persistence (e.g., Astin, 1993; Mertz, 2004; Pascarella & Terenzini, 1991; Tinto, 1993).

Finally, within the institutional setting, course instruction is perhaps the most intimate academic structure available to extend retention practice. While there are many tactics that cultivate successful experiences, one innovative approach to class-based strategies is the learning community (Zhao & Kuh, 2004). Such a practice "intentionally links or clusters two or more courses, often around an interdisciplinary theme or problem, and enrolls a common cohort of students. At their best, learning communities practice pedagogies of active engagement and reflection" (Smith, MacGregor, Matthews, & Gabelnick, 2004, p. 67). It is in this framework, then, that this project was initiated.

The current project consists of using Second Life as a platform to develop a digital community composed of majors from the Department of Health and Human Performance (HHP) at the University of Houston. Once the students have joined Second Life, they complete academic assignments in Second Life and are invited to voluntarily participate in both social and educational activities. The use of online chatting within Second Life to complete assignments and to socially interact promotes the development of the student community. The cumulative time the students spend in Second Life is monitored automatically and tracked within a data base. Based upon participation they can earn free gifts, access to 'elite' student lounges or given Linden dollars, the currency used in Second Life. Ultimately the relationship between the student's involvement in the Second Life community and their academic performance will be examined.

SETTING THE STAGE

Group dynamics theorists have posited that social cohesion, the emotional bonds of attraction to a community and the goals and activities of the community enhance retention and performance (Carron, Bray, Eyes, 2002; Friedkin, 2004: MacCoun, Keir, & Belkin, 2006). A community is socially cohesive to the extent that its members like each other, prefer to spend their social time together, enjoy each other's company, and feel emotionally close to one another (MacCoun, Keir, & Belkin, 2006). Communities with strong social cohesion tend to be more effective in accomplishing both individual and shared community goals. Intervention strategies such as setting shared community goals, clarifying individual roles, developing a group name, and wearing distinct apparel (e.g., group t-shirts) leads to a positive and distinct group environment resulting in increased group cohesion (Estabrooks, 2000). Shared community goal setting facilitates adherence to specific behavioral norms such as completing home work assignments, enrolling in a set number of courses per semester and seeking assistance when needed, which are all activities associated with retention. Developing individual roles or goals for behavior that will assist in attaining the collective goal increases individual identifiably and eliminates social loafing. Generating specific group goals and norms, along with individual roles within the group, contributes to the development and sustainability of a group's structure and productivity (Dzewaltowski, Eastbrooks, & Johnston, 2002; Estabrooks, 2000).

The initial step in developing a method to enhance student persistence among the students in our department was to assemble an interdisciplinary team of academic and technical experts. Specialists in social cohesion theory, student persistence, statistical methodology, and curriculum development were invited to meet to discuss how to enhance the overall sense of student community. Given the large number of commuters in the student body, it was decided that creating a digital community offered the best opportunity to engage the students. Second Life was selected as the digital platform because of its overall functionality and creative opportunities. The fact

Second Life was of no cost to the students was also a consideration.

The second step was to purchase a Second Life island and replicate the buildings and services that are available at the physical campus. Buildings were created that are identified with each degree program. For example, there is a Nutrition, a Kinesiology, and a Health academic building. Services such as academic counseling with contact information for academic advisors that operate both within Second Life and through face-to-face contact, and published degree plans are available. Social activity opportunities were also added to the island such as bowling, swimming and helicopter rides. Following the physical development of the island, educational information was added to the classrooms. For example, digital monitors that display a series of informational slides are available in addition to video and audio playback units. These units can play educational videos as well as internet radio stations.

Simultaneous with the above activities, the research team discussed the methods to monitor student participation and the reward systems to encourage participation. Additionally, measures of student persistence, retention and success were chosen and the statistical methodology used to determine if participation in Second Life influenced student persistence were adopted. Finally, the project was initiated when we began actively recruiting students to join the department's island in Second Life.

CASE DESCRIPTION: BUILDING THE DIGITAL COMMUNITY

Second Life

Second Life is a 3-dimensional 'world' in which individuals create avatars, or virtual identities, that can interact with fellow avatars through text and/or voice chat. The 3-D world is composed of parcels of land referred to as islands. Since

Second Life has all of the features of a real world (ex. buildings, transportation within and between islands, personal interactions, monetary system, links to the text, video and PowerPoint delivery systems both within Second Life or through the internet) and is available 24 hours a day, seven days a week, it is an ideal digital environment in which to engage students in a non-traditional manner. This non-traditional learning tool is being introduced to students early in their academic careers to facilitate the development of an interactive and socially supportive environment.

Targeting New Students Entering the Department of Health and Human Performance

In the Department of Health and Human Performance at the University of Houston there are three undergraduate career degrees: Kinesiology, Nutrition, and Health. Each of the degree plans has a key class that is always taken in the first academic year. Those classes are Foundations of Kinesiological Studies, Introduction to Human Nutrition, and Personal Health, respectively. To foster student involvement in Second Life, a lecture-learning module was developed that is presented in all three classes. Students are given a tour of the HHP at UH island in Second Life and provided information concerning basic virtual world etiquette. Students are offered extra credit or required by their instructors to create a Second Life Avatar and complete a basic scavenger hunt on the island. These activities are designed to spark student interest in the HHP Island and plant the seeds for fostering an online community in Second Life.

In addition to the above approach a series of at-large meetings were held with UH health and human performance undergraduate students to promote interest in joining Second Life. These meetings, at which a free lunch was provided to increase attendance, were conducted by the department chair and faculty who are actively engaged in Second Life for educational purposes. These meetings also consisted of an overview of Second Life and a tour of the HHP island with an invitation to contact us if they were interested in more information.

Student 'Camp Counselors'

The department also hired two undergraduate students who are earning degrees from our department to serve as 'camp counselors'. These camp counselors are tasked with contacting HHP students through traditional means (ex. face-to-face, flyers, hallways posters, and emails) and through Second Life to notify students of opportunities to learn how to operate within Second Life. As such, they conducted training sessions in our student computer laboratory on topics such as how to create Second Life accounts, obtain an avatar, change the appearance of your avatar, navigate, communicate, find objects, places, and people and other basic functions within Second Life. Additionally the camp counselors served to host events in Second Life such as 'pool parties, scavenger hunts, shopping trips, concerts and trips to museums, art galleries, and innovative educational sites. The research team believed it was important that student colleagues take the lead in the development of our Second Life community since many students are often unsure of their role vis-à-vis professors and instructors in settings that are predominately social.

Faculty Participation

Once a thriving community of HHP students is established, the next phase of the project depends heavily on student interaction with professors in the department. Given the goal of the project is to determine if non-traditional learning experiences and interactions with professors is associated with increased student success and persistence, the involvement of HHP professors is essential. Several professors have spent considerable time learning the nuances of Second Life. These professors serve as Second Life mentors to other professors in the department who express interest in becoming involved in Second Life activities. These same professors also hold regular 'office hours' within Second Life to encourage student use of the HHP at UH island. Several professors are developing extensive learning modules for individual courses that enable them to take advantage of the unique three-dimensional properties for exploratory purposes. For example, one professor has built an artery in which students can 'walk' into and explore fundamental differences between healthy arteries and those experiencing atherosclerosis. Many other 'hands on' learning activities are currently in development.

Building Student Community

Upon their initial arrival at the HHP at UH island, students are offered the chance to join the HHP Community Group. Once a student joins, they receive an HHP t-shirt that their avatar can wear and $100L (~$0.50 USD)—a 'Linden' ($L) is the Second Life currency unit. Students who log at least 15 hours a month (~0.5 hours per day) on the HHP Island are provided a monthly stipend of $50L (~$0.25 USD). Other rewards are provided to the students once they have logged certain benchmarks of hours on the island. (See Table 1.).

As students reach one of the above benchmarks, a group email is sent in Second Life, acknowl-

Table 1. Student Incentives for Participation in Second Life

Hour requirement	Second Life delivery item
None	HHP T-shirt
60 hours	Building Access for Sandbox
75 hours	Access to Entry Student Lounge
120 hours	$500L
150 hours	Access to Elite Student Lounge

edging their accomplishments. Through the use of the rewards program we are able to reward the students for their time spent in community building activities, while maintaining a low real life cost. For instance if a student put in the minimum of 10 hours each month for an entire year, they would be paid $500L, or about $2.50 USD.

HHP at UH 'island' in Second Life

The Second Life HHP at UH island is composed of 16 educational buildings, parks, benches, waterways, a pool, and helpful signage containing transporting features to allow avatars to travel easily to selected areas of the island. We have also completed the two student lounges and a sandbox to encourage practice building objects, and we have developed an extensive site that contains our International Health Challenge (IHC) project. The IHC site was built as a result of being selecting as one of the three semifinalists in the Network Culture Project contest, sponsored by the University of Southern California-Annenberg School for Communication. The IHC site is used to prevent and treat obesity through education, skills training and outreach. On the HHP at UH island, each of our curriculum areas (ex. health, nutrition, kinesiology) has a building devoted to it that serve as a portal to online classes within their degree program and provide information about their specific degrees, course information, student organizations and other material of interest to a major of that particular degree. We envision these buildings, the Quad area, and the tree-lined parks to be popular places for our students to congregate when visiting the island. At this time we are not offering complete courses within Second Life but rather materials and opportunities for engagement supplemental to the traditional experience. We anticipate that this interaction will result in the development of relationships that promote the free exchange of information among fellow students and professors and thereby provide a 'value added' experience for our students beyond the traditional

face-to-face or online class setting. We anticipate that students who are engaged in the Second Life Experience are more likely to both enjoy and value the education they are receiving at UH, and therefore, persist in obtaining their degree.

Establishing Student Small Groups

We use orientation meetings and camp counselor follow-up to promote the idea that there are educational advantages to spend at least some time on the island associating with those avatars that are earning the same academic degree. We encourage avatars from each of our undergraduate degrees to regularly visit the buildings exclusively devoted to their particular academic major. We emphasize that we would like for the avatars of each of the academic degrees to 'take ownership' of their particular building by suggesting ideas for interior decorating, educational resources and activities. The purpose of this is to link students with similar educational experiences and career expectations in a way that is consistent with social cohesion theory. It is our hope that in time, the students will develop their own groups based upon scholarly and social interests beyond their academic major; however, initially we are developing the framework for the students to develop a sense of comfort and community. Students who actively engage and participate in the activities of their academic major group receive an extra $10L stipend per month.

ASSESSING THE DIGITAL COMMUNITY

Structure of Surveys

Upon joining the HHP community group, students are asked to complete an entry survey, which they take using a testing section in WebCT, an online learning system. All surveys include a combination of Likert scale and open-ended questions.

Students receive their initial $100L (described above), after they have completed the initial survey. Similar follow-up surveys are offered every six months. We employ a series of Second Life analytics to track: (1) number of logins, (2) amount of time spent each visit, and (3) resources visited/utilized.

Major Survey Themes to Assess Student Persistence

The themes explored in our surveys focus on two broad areas: (1) the use of Second Life as a platform to develop a digital community, and (2) the students' perception of the effectiveness of the HHP Second Life community in influencing their educational persistence.

Students that do not login to Second Life for 60 consecutive days are sent an email through their student account asking them to 'rejoin' their digital community. If an additional 30 days go by without activity in Second Life we speak with the students in 'real life' (assuming they have not dropped out of the university) and ask them to complete a modified 'drop-out' survey used by the University of Illinois – Urbana Champaign (Graziano, 1971) to assess common reasons for dropping out of school. Although this survey was not designed to gather information regarding persistence in the use of Second Life per se, it does assess a number of areas that would have direct relevance to dropping out of the Second Life community. The portion of the survey that is used focuses directly on their experience in Second Life. Responses to questions as to whether there were 'Too many requirements outside their field of interest, 'Poor intellectual environment', and 'Irrelevant (to social problems/real world)' are useful indicators of the students perceptions of their experience in Second Life. Information gained from our surveys are used to enhance the features of the Second Life experience as they relate to the building of social cohesion and persistence and will enable us to identify reasons why people withdraw from the digital community. Work by the research team is continuing on the development of a more complete assessment survey to identify both the perceived strengths and weakness of using Second Life in an academic setting.

The survey results are analyzed to evaluate the relation of students' perceptions of the Second Life environment and their persistence in university studies. The relations between each survey question and grade point average, years to graduation, and drop out are examined to determine whether student perceptions of Second Life are associated with measures of student persistence. Grade point average, years to graduation, and drop out rates are compared to the respective university values for age- and degree-matched students to determine whether the Second Life experience may have affected student persistence. Survey summary scores (i.e., sets of survey questions representing different factors related to persistence) and demographic information are used in discriminant function analyses to identify and evaluate the perceptions and characteristics of four groups of students: (1) those who both continue participation in Second Life and persist/succeed in university studies, (2) those who continue participation in Second Life but do not persist/succeed in university studies,(3) those who discontinue participation in Second Life but persist/succeed in university studies, and (4) those who both discontinue participation in Second Life and do not persist/succeed in university studies. These ongoing analyses provide not only provide feedback with which to improve the Second Life environment to enhance the student experience, but assist us in identifying those students for whom the Second Life experience is most and least likely to enhance persistence.

Preliminary Results

The current project describes an innovative use of an immersive digital community to enhance the success of college students. The procedures and policies described above are proving reasonably

Table 2. Preliminary Descriptive Statistics Indicating HHP at UH Island Use

	Total visitors	Total visits	Total duration	Mean total duration	Mean visits
A	353	1561	339 hours	58 min	4.4
B	197	1405	326 hours	99 min	7.1

*Row A reflects data that includes all students who visited the HHP at UH island between September and mid-November, 2008. Row B reflects the data after the removal of avatars that only visited the island a single time.

effective at developing a community of students with a shared sense of identity tied to their degree program and department. Three months after the initiation of the program, 353 students of the approximately 1400 students in the department have visited the island and received their free HHP t-shirts. (See Table 2.)

In general the responses to the open ended questions the students answered when they first joined Second Life have been varied. Some students find the experience worthwhile, interesting, and feel positive about having joined the community. Other students feel spending time in Second Life is not a productive use of their time, find the mechanics of the experience difficult and master, and generally feel negative about Second Life. The more positive students have mentioned that they enjoy the interaction with their fellow students and in some case, faculty members, in an unusual and more relaxed environment than while they are at the university during the day. A consistent point that has been made clear is that all new users find the operation of their avatar fairly cumbersome which detracts from the overall experience. Currently, efforts are underway to provide additional assistance to those that have recently joined Second Life so that they master the basic operational functions and focus more on the educational and social opportunities presented by Second Life. Ongoing efforts are directed at monitoring student participation in Second Life activities and academic progress toward degree completion to determine if the two are positively associated. Finding such a link has implications for the manner in which universities might use

Second Life to enhance the educational experiences of their students.

CURRENT CHALLENGES FACING THE ORGANIZATION

The greatest challenge facing the project is to increase the number of students who regularly participate in our island's Second Life activities. Although at this point, we have had an acceptable number of students join Second Life, few routinely spend significant amounts of time on the HHP at UH island. This lack of full engagement likely is a function of the fact that the student Second Life community is still in the developmental stage combined with the fact that we currently only offer a limited variety of activities for them to participate in. Additionally, the lack of face-to-face interaction with their classmates in real life is also probably contributing to their lack of interaction within Second Life. To address these issues the camp counselors offer lessons in navigating, changing appearance, shopping trips and a variety of other social activities in other parts of the Second Life world. Additionally, we are actively working to develop Second Life learning modules that will be used by our instructors as part of mandatory class activities and we are enhancing our island's academic advising center. Through these activities we hope that the students will begin to explore on their own and begin to realize the possibilities that Second Life affords.

Another challenge is that of convincing some of the instructors that Second Life offers innovative learning experiences that cannot be duplicated in real life situations. While we have had a number of early adopting professors, many remain reluctant to provide the value added experiences offered by Second Life. We are currently exploring the possibility of providing additional demonstrations to the faculty that emphasize the unique learning opportunities in Second Life and how easy it is to take advantage of these opportunities. It is anticipated that as more students have positive experiences in Second Life they will begin to ask their instructors to provide more educational opportunities in Second Life.

Related to the above two challenges, we are working to increase the absolute numbers of students who join Second Life. The Department of Health and Human Performance has over 1400 students of which approximately 350 have joined Second Life. This represents 25% of the potential students we would like to see engaged in Second Life. We are trying to increase our membership by hosting free lunch events for the students where we demonstrate Second Life and encourage them to join, providing extra credit in some of the lecture format courses, and posting banners and flyers throughout our academic real life building. Faculty members are beginning to incorporate mandatory Second Life experiences within their courses that will result in an increase membership. It is anticipated that as more faculty make use of Second Life, more students will join the HHP at UH island. Additionally, we are planning to use *Facebook* advertisements of our planned Second Life activities, providing space in the HHP 'sandlots' to allow students to build and develop their own subcommunities and possible financial incentives to professors who utilize Second Life in their courses. We will also be promoting our HHP at UH island on the island being developed by the University of Houston in anticipation of increasing the visibility of both islands.

Due to the short time that the project has been in existence it is not possible to relate student success as measured by time to graduation and grade point average and the use of Second Life. Since

the project is easily sustainable, these relationships will be evaluated as data becomes available.

FURTHER READING

A search of *YouTube* for 'Second Life Educational' approximately 1850 videos devoted to educational uses of Second Life. In our opinion, one of the best introductions to Second Life for educators is titled *Educational Uses of Second Life* (Mary AnnCLT, 2007) which has been viewed over 69,437 times in just over a year. We also recommend *Education in Second Life: Explore the Possibilities* (xxArrete2xx, 2007), which has been viewed 58,887 times since May, 2007. In addition to these videos, there are many discipline specific videos filled with creative ideas on how to use Second Life as an educational tool. The users of Second Life for educational purposes are generally experienced computer users and often share their ideas through both blogs and listservs. Two of our favorite blogs are *eLearning Technology* (http://elearningtech.blogspot.com/) and *Kapp Notes* (www.karlkapp.blogspot.com). The Second Life website (http://secondlifegrid.net/slfe/education-use-virtual-world) offers links to many excellent sites devoted to assist educators in incorporating Second Life into their teaching. Additionally, we have found the *Second Life Educator list (SLED)* (http://www.sl-educationblog.org/) to be of great value when seeking information about a variety of topics ranging from technological to philosophical issues concerning the use of Second Life in the classroom. As immersive environments become more common and technologically innovative it is anticipated that more educators will begin to use them to promote social learning. As students become more familiar with these environments and the social networks that emerge from their use, students and teachers will have the opportunity to interact in ways as never before. This interaction could very well promote learning styles that are just now being imagined.

Fortunately for those interested in learning more about the use of Second Life as an educational tool or the impact of immersive environments on the educational process, there are a number of books, listservs, blogs, *YouTube* videos and conference Powerpoint presentations that cover these topics. In February, 2009 Amazon.com offered 102,441 books for sale devoted to the uses of second Life. Although not all of these books were exclusively concerned with possible educational uses of Second Life, the magnitude does reflect a strong interest in the platform. We have found *Second Life For Dummies* by Sarah Robbins and Mark Bell (2007) and *How to Do Everything with Second Life®* by Richard Mansfield (2008) to be very useful resources.

Student persistence toward graduation is a major concern for both universities and state legislators. The spiraling costs of college, the graying of the American workforce, and the lack of a well-trained workforce in many states makes college student persistence an important topic (Department of Education, 2006; Kahlenberg, 2004). We have initiated a project that explores the relationship between student involvement in the Second Life community and their academic performance as measured by grade point average and time to graduation. It is hypothesized that students who are actively engaged in Second Life departmental communities will also demonstrate improved measures of student success including decreased times to graduation, relative to their classmates who chose not to actively engage in Second Life.

To gain additional information concerning the use of the Second Life platform to enhance social learning and knowledge acquisition the experience at the University of Houston has revealed several challenges. The foremost challenge is that not all students posses the same computer-based skill sets. Some students quickly learn to create avatars, navigate, change their appearance, and begin immersing themselves within the environment. Conversely, some students have great difficulty getting started with the technology despite both face-to-face and online assistance. Our experience is that this difficulty results in frustration and an unwillingness to continue with the Second Life experience which can be difficult for the instructor to overcome. Additionally, the Second Life platform is relatively unstable and occasionally goes 'offline' which also increases the frustration level of the students. A final difficulty is the need to develop enough Second Life interactive activities that capture and hold the student's attention during the time the social community is in its infancy. We have found interactive activities such as swimming, bowling, helicopter rides, and dancing promotes communication between the students and is essential for community building.

REFERENCES

Adelman, C. (1999). *Answers in the tool box: Academic intensity, attendance patterns, and bachelor's degree attainment.* Washington, DC: U.S. Department of Education.

Adelman, C. (2006). *The toolbox revisited: Paths to degree completion from high school through college.* Washington, DC: U.S. Department of Education. Retrieved June 30, 2006, from http://www.ed.gov/rschstat/research/pubs/toolboxrevisit/index.html

Astin, A. W. (1984). Student involvement: A developmental theory for higher education. *Journal of College Student Personnel, 25*(3), 297–308.

Astin, A. W. (1993). *What matters in college: Four critical years revisited.* San Francisco: Jossey-Bass.

Beatty-Guenter, P. (1994). Sorting, supporting, connecting, and transforming: Retention strategies at community colleges. *Community College Journal of Research and Practice, 18*(2), 113–130. doi:10.1080/1066892940180202

Bettinger, E. (2004). Is the finish line in sight? Financial aid's impact on retention and graduation. In C. Hoxby (Ed.), *College choices: The economics of where to go, when to go, and how to pay for it* (pp. 207-233). Chicago: Chicago University Press.

Bettinger, E., & Long, B. T. (2004). *Shape up or ship out: The effect of remediation on underprepared students at four-year colleges* (NBER Working Paper Number 10369). Washington, DC: National Bureau of Economic Research.

Bound, J., & Turner, S. (2002). Going to war and going to college: Did the G.I. bill increase educational attainment. *Journal of Labor Economics, 20*(4), 780–815. doi:10.1086/342012

Boylan, H. R., Bliss, L. B., & Bonham, B. S. (1997). Program components and their relationship to student performance. *Journal of Developmental Education, 20*(3), 2-8. Braxton, J. (2000). *Reworking the student departure puzzle*. Nashville, TN: Vanderbilt University Press.

Carron, A. V., Bray, S. R., & Eyes, M. A. (2002). Team cohesion and team success in sport. *Journal of Sports Sciences, 20*(2), 119–126. doi:10.1080/026404102317200828

Conklin, M. S. (2007). *101 uses for Second Life in the college classroom*. Retrieved February 11, 2009, from http://facstaff.elon.edu/mconklin/pubs/glshandout.pdf

Department of Education. The Secretary of Education's Commission on the Future of Higher Education. (2006). *A test of leadership: Charting the future of U. S. higher education*. Retrieved December 2, 2008, from http://www.ed.gov/about/bdscomm/list/hiedfuture/reports/final-report.pdf

Dzewaltowski, D. A., Estabrooks, P. A., & Johnston, J. A. (2002). Healthy youth places promoting nutrition and physical activity. *Health Education Research, 17*(5), 41–51. doi:10.1093/her/17.5.541

Estabrooks, P. A. (2000). Sustaining exercise participation through group cohesion. *Exercise and Sport Sciences Reviews, 28*(2), 1–5.

Fonte, R. (1997). Structured versus laissez-faire open access: Implementation of a proactive strategy. *New Directions for Community Colleges, 100*, 43–52. doi:10.1002/cc.10004

Friedkin, N. E. (2004). Social cohesion. *Annual Review of Sociology, 30*, 409–425. doi:10.1146/annurev.soc.30.012703.110625

Graziano, A. F. (1971). *Drop out survey at the University of Illinois at Urban Champaign* (Report No. HE 004302). Champaign, IL: University of Illinois at Urbana Champaign. (ERIC Document Reproduction Service. No. ED 078750)

Grubb, W. N. (1999). Innovative practices: The pedagogical and institutional challenges. In W. N. Grubb (Ed.), *Honored but invisible: An inside look at teaching in community colleges* (pp. 245-279). New York: Routledge.

Hayes, E. R. (2006). *Situated learning in virtual worlds: The learning ecology of Second Life*. Retrieved February 25, 2009, from http://www.adulterc.org/Proceedings/2006/Proceedings/Hayes.pdf

Kahlenberg, R. D. (2004). *America's untapped resource: Low-income students in higher education*. New York: The Century foundation Press.

Kane, T. (1994). College entry by blacks since 1970: The role of college costs, family background, and the returns to education. *The Journal of Political Economy, 10*(5), 878–911. doi:10.1086/261958

Knapp, L. G., Kelly-Reid, J. E., & Whitmore, R. W. (2006). *Enrollment in postsecondary institutions, fall 2004: Graduation rates, 1998 & 2001 cohorts; and financial statistics, fiscal year 2004* (NCES 2006-155). Washington, DC: U.S. Department of Education. Retrieved October 1, 2006, from http://nces.ed.gov/pubsearch/pubsinfo.asp?pubid=2006155

Kurlaender, M., & Felts, E. (2008). Bakke beyond college access: Investigating racial/ethnic differences in college completion. In P. Marin & C. Horn (Eds.), *Realizing Bakke's legacy: Affirmative action, equal opportunity, and access to higher education* (pp. 110-144). VA: Stylus Publishers.

MacCoun, R. J., Keir, E., & Belkin, A. (2006). Does social cohesion determine motivation in combat? *Armed Forces and Society, 32*(4), 646–654. doi:10.1177/0095327X05279181

Mansfield, R. (2008). *How to do everything with Second Life.* New York: The McGraw-Hill Companies.

MaryAnnCLT. (2007, August 10). *Educational uses of Second Life* [Video File]. Video posted to http://www.youtube.com/watch?v=qOFU9oUF2HA

Metz, G. W. (2004). Challenge and changes to Tinto's persistence theory: A historical review. *Journal of College Student Retention Research Theory and Practice, 6*(2), 191. doi:10.2190/M2CC-R7Y1-WY2Q-UPK5

Miglietti, C. L., & Strange, C. C. (2002). Learning styles, classroom preferences, teaching styles, and remedial course outcomes for underprepared adults at a two-year college. *Community College Review, 26*(1), 1–19. doi:10.1177/009155219802600101

Moss, B. G., & Yeaton, W. H. (2006). Shaping policies related to developmental education: An evaluation using the regression-discontinuity design. *Educational Evaluation and Policy Analysis, 28*(3), 215–229. doi:10.3102/01623737028003215

National Center for Education Statistics. (2008). *Integrated postsecondary education data system.* Retrieved October 15, 2008, from http://nces.ed.gov/ipeds/

Parsad, B., & Lewis, L. (2003). *Remedial education at degree-granting postsecondary institutions in fall 2000* (NCES 2004–010, Table 4). Data from U.S. Department of Education, NCES, Postsecondary Education Quick Information System (PEQIS), *Survey on remedial education in higher education institutions, fall 2000.*

Pascarella, E. T., & Terenzini, P. T. (1991). *How college affects students.* San Francisco: Jossey-Bass.

Robbins, S., & Bell, M. (2008). *Second Life for dummies.* Indianapolis, IN: Wiley Publishing.

Rosenbaum, J. E., & Person, A. E. (2003). Beyond college for all: Policies and practices to improve transitions into college and jobs. *Professional School Counseling, 6*(4), 252–260.

Smith, B. L., MacGregor, J., Matthews, R. S., & Gabelnick, F. (2004). *Learning communities: Reforming undergraduate education.* CA: Jossey-Bass.

Snyder, T. D., Tan, A. G., & Hoffman, C. (2006). Table 181: College enrollment and enrollment rates of recent high school completers, by race/ethnicity: 1960 through 2004. In *Digest of education statistics, 2005.* Washington, DC: U.S. Department of Education, National Center for Education Statistics.

Texas Higher Education Coordinating Board. (2008). *Closing the gaps by 2015: Texas' strategies for improving student participation and success.* Retrieved February 14, 2009, from http://www.thecb.state.tx.us/reports/PDF/1669.PDF

Tinto, V. (1993). *Leaving college: Rethinking the causes and cures of student attrition.* Chicago: University of Chicago Press.

Tinto, V. (1997). Classrooms and communities: Exploring the educational character of student persistence. *The Journal of Higher Education, 68*(6), 599–623. doi:10.2307/2959965

United States General Accounting Office. (2003). *College completion: Additional efforts could help education with its completion goals.* Washington, DC: United States General Accounting Office.

University of Houston Office of Institutional Research. (2008). *Statistical handbook 2007-2008.* Retrieved October 12, 2008, from http://www.uh.edu/ir/index.php?id=139

Venezia, A., Callan, P. M., Finney, J. E., Kirst, M. W., & Usdan, M. D. (2005). *The governance divide: A report on a four-state study on improving college readiness and success.* San Jose, CA: The National Center for Public Policy and Higher Education. xxArete2xx. (2007, May 29). *Education in Second Life: Explore the possibilities* [Video File]. Video posted to http://www.youtube.com/watch?v=TMGR9q43dag

Yee, N., & Bailenson, J. N. (2008). A method for longitudinal behavioral data collection in Second Life. *Presence.* Retrieved February 15, 2009, from http://www.mitpressjournals.org/doi/abs/10.1162/pres.17.6.594

Zhao, C., & Kuh, G. D. (2004). Adding value: Learning communities and student engagement. *Research in Higher Education, 45*(2), 115–138. doi:10.1023/B:RIHE.0000015692.88534.de

Chapter 10
Designing for Social Interaction and Social Competence in a 3D-VLE

James Laffey
University of Missouri at Columbia, USA

Matthew Schmidt
University of Missouri at Columbia, USA

Janine Stichter
University of Missouri at Columbia, USA

Carla Schmidt
University of Missouri at Columbia, USA

Danielle Oprean
University of Missouri at Columbia, USA

Melissa Herzog
University of Missouri at Columbia, USA

Ryan Babiuch
University of Missouri at Columbia, USA

EXECUTIVE SUMMARY

The purpose of the iSocial project is to support the development and practice of social competence for individuals with Autism Spectrum Disorders (ASD) through a social-skills curriculum and online social interaction delivered via a 3D virtual learning environment (3D-VLE). This chapter describes the background and rationale for developing iSocial, gives an overview of the system, and reports some of the results from a field test of a partial system implementation. The field test provides lessons about the initial system design and recognition of challenges to be faced. The key challenges include (1) finding best approaches for adapting effective teaching approaches to a 3D-VLE, (2) supporting online social

DOI: 10.4018/978-1-60566-878-9.ch010

interaction for a target population challenged to be social, and (3) amplifying the engagement of youth in support of achieving desired learning outcomes.

BACKGROUND

The iSocial project is a collaboration by two faculty members and a number of students and represents a joint effort between the Thompson Center for Autism and Neurodevelopmental Disorders (TC) and the School of Information Science and Learning Technologies at the University of Missouri (MU). One faculty member, Janine Stichter, is a researcher in the field of social competence for youth with ASD and has developed a curriculum for teaching social competence to these youth. The 10-week curriculum, Social Competence Intervention based on a framework of Cognitive Behavioral Intervention (SCI-CBI), applies cognitive behavioral strategies to the development of social competence for youth with ASD. The second faculty member, Jim Laffey, is a researcher in the field of learning technologies and human-computer interaction. His research has included the development of a number of digital media systems and networked learning environments and includes a focus on social ability among members of these environments. As with many joint efforts in life, the collaboration began with a few casual conversations about their mutual interests and then escalated to a commitment to work together. In a 12-month period Stichter and Laffey wrote 4 failed proposals (two to MU-based granting agencies, one to the U.S. Department of Education and one to the National Science Foundation) in efforts to establish funding for the project. However, with each failed proposal the idea for iSocial came into sharper focus. The team continued to write funding proposals, but saw an opportunity with some personal and departmental resources, as well as a doctoral student ready to embark on his dissertation (Matt Schmidt), to begin development of a prototype system.

These initial stages with a fairly ad hoc collection of volunteers and some paid hours by a student programmer spanning a set of tasks that included identifying and building competence with a development environment, designing ways to adapt a face-to-face instruction into a 3D-VLE, and teaching ourselves how to succeed at both the collaboration and the development work. In the spring of 2008 two awards were made on the second submissions of revised proposals to the MU-based granting agencies which provided seed money to turn our prototype work into a pilot system for one unit of the social competence curriculum. As of fall 2008, funding support has come from the Thompson Center's Scholars Fund, the University of Missouri Research Board and Autism Speaks, a non-profit foundation devoted to autism research. This funding enables the project to continue developing a key design concept of "social orthotics" and to test for system efficacy. Support for building a full implementation of the curriculum and for providing the iSocial system to youth outside a controlled field test context is being sought.

As the iSocial project demonstrates, a university is fertile ground for building and refining ideas for innovation. However, external funding is needed to develop and sustain a project, and the level of funding needed to develop complex systems is hard to achieve. The team's commitment to persevering through the many steps needed to get the project started and the rationale for external funding come from the potential of 3D-VLE to address a substantial need for helping youth with ASD develop social competence. Participation in iSocial will engage members in curriculum activities that target the remediation of core deficits in social functioning. According to the Center for Disease Control (2007), from 1994 to 2005 the number of children and youth ages

6–21 years receiving services for ASD increased from approximately 20,000 to 200,000. Children identified with ASD have deficits in social competence that can lead to problematic social behavior and social isolation (Stichter et al., 2007). The outcomes of these deficits, if untreated, can lead to a lower quality of life as well as deficits in other developmental areas such as language and cognition. To date there is an extensive body of research that supports using cognitive behavioral strategies for social skills training that are typically implemented in face-to-face instruction for individuals with ASD (Rogers, 2000). However, access to evidence-based interventions for youth with ASD for social skill instruction is limited. The iSocial project is an effort to test the potential of new technologies, such as internet-based 3D-VLEs to provide access to interventions, qualified guides, and social cohorts; all while maintaining fidelity to core features of the curriculum and intervention programs.

SETTING THE STAGE

Much of the initial excitement about 3D-VLEs is based on the potential to add social and physical attributes to traditional computer capabilities for supporting learning. As humans, we are naturally social and physical, and thus, 3D-VLEs can be intuitive and engaging in ways that mirror natural experience. 3D-VLEs also provide the benefits of computerization in that learning can be delivered anytime and most any place, can provide feedback in an endlessly patient fashion, can be adaptive so as to provide multimedia and varieties of representation, and can record behavior for diagnosis and assessment. It is a substantial challenge to design all of these capabilities into a 3D-VLE, and there is much to be learned in order to make good design decisions; however, there is great potential to provide well designed student activities and experiences that can be richly cognitive, social, emotional and physical in these

environments. Our case report is about the design process and early lessons for a 3D-VLE where we cannot assume natural and intuitive social and physical appropriation. Indeed, the purpose of the environment is to teach social, and in some ways physical, competence to youth who often perceive and interact with their environments differently than neuro-typical youth. Participation in iSocial will engage youth in curriculum activities that target the remediation of core deficits in social functioning. We use the term "social orthotics" to focus attention on building an environment and mechanisms within the environment that are purposefully social when being social cannot be taken for granted. While this is of special importance for the youth we target with iSocial, we suspect that social orthotics is a design construct that has potential for all computer-mediated learning contexts.

Some efforts have been made to use 3D-VLEs to teach social competence. These studies have demonstrated that participants with ASD can use and interpret VLEs successfully and use VLEs to learn simple social skills (Cobb et al., 2002; Mitchell, Parsons, & Leonard, 2007). For the most part, prior work has focused on limited skill sets taught in isolation of other skills and have addressed teaching of skills, but not structures and mechanisms (orthotics) for actually being social in a 3D environment. For example Parsons et al. (2006) report using a café scene to teach skills of finding an appropriate seat, but the scene is a single user context and only implements a set of rules for finding a seat, rather than possibly providing opportunities for greeting others, leaving others or practicing how to act in a café with peers taking on other roles in the scene. Additionally, this prior work has viewed VLEs as an experience of a single user sitting at a computer to take on a specific task with a physically-present adult assistant. They have not imagined what it might be like to immerse the youth in a VLE for multiple and integrated experiences as well as how these youth might learn collaboratively with and from other members of the VLE. However, Mitchell and colleagues (2007) suggest that using collaborative virtual environments could be a means to provide virtual social interaction for ASD-affected individuals and may promote improvements in social skills in the real world. In addition, some reports in the popular press (Loftus, 2005) suggest that immersion in VLEs can enable social interaction for very high performing individuals with ASD (known as Asperger's Syndrome) in their use of an island in the Second Life 3D virtual world.

iSocial seeks to adapt and implement, in a 3D-VLE, a curriculum with demonstrated impact for improving social competence when implemented in a face-to-face small group setting. The 10-week SCI-CBI curriculum challenges thinking patterns and includes the use of meta-cognitive strategies, as well as various exposure and response situations designed to promote the use of self-monitoring and self-regulation. In each unit, the lesson plan follows a consistent structure of learning and rehearsing skills. Initial results from work to develop the face-to-face version of SCI-CBI indicate promising trends for growth (across pre- and post-intervention assessments) among youth with ASD.

CASE DESCRIPTION

iSocial is being developed using Sun's Wonderland virtual world toolkit. Wonderland provides tools for building multi-user virtual environments (MUVEs) with a promise of being secure, scalable, robust and functional. Perhaps equally importantly, Wonderland is Free Software, released under the GNU GPL, meaning that the software is free to use, modify and distribute according to the license terms. Using Free and Open Source software creates opportunities for dissemination of iSocial and collaboration with Wonderland developers that would not be possible using proprietary products. For example, the iSocial development team was able to examine

and modify Project Wonderland's underlying source code and collaborate with Wonderland developers in order to change how avatars look and behave. The iSocial development team also worked closely with Wonderland developers to extend the functionality of the in-world video player. These enhancements were then released to the entire Wonderland community, benefiting not only the iSocial development effort but also anyone who uses Wonderland.

Our initial efforts to develop a first implementation of iSocial attempted to use an open source development toolkit for building 3D-VLEs called Open Croquet. Croquet has many attractive features including a robust architecture for scaling implementations, but we eventually settled on Wonderland based on perceived ease of development, Java programmers being more readily available than Smalltalk programmers, and our perception that advancements to the toolkit were happening at a faster pace with Wonderland than with Croquet signifying a more active development community. Using a common avatar representational scheme, the Wonderland software provides for multiple communication channels between users and implements both voice and text, even allowing participants to connect to the virtual environment via telephone. In addition, desktop applications such as web browsers and word processors can be shared seamlessly among multiple users within Wonderland environments.

Using an Open Source toolkit to build a completely customized and customizable virtual world was a high priority to the iSocial project for two key reasons. First, the ability to regulate access and manage the security of the system and the security of the youth within the system was important, especially as we anticipate that schools will be one source of access to iSocial for youth and we will need to meet varying but strict security standards. We did not want to assume than an environment like the Second Life 3D virtual world would be able to meet those criteria. Secondly, little is known about using single-user 3D-VLEs with the ASD population, and virtually nothing is known about using multi-user 3D-VLEs. Having complete control of all aspects of the environment allows us to manipulate the environment at a deep level, change default behaviors to be most appropriate, re-conceptualize and reconfigure the entire interface if warranted, and constrain or expand interactivity modalities as needed. The ability to customize and expand our development platform on a fundamental level allows us to research the impact of alternative approaches and to custom fit the iSocial environment to how our user population will best be able to interact with and through it.

Adapting the SCI-CBI curriculum into a 3D virtual space requires that all physical aspects of the curriculum be modeled and the potential for all activity as well as how the space responds to activity be programmed. For a brief introduction to what the iSocial experience might be like, imagine a youth, John, sitting at a computer in his school or at home. A local facilitator (teacher or parent) is nearby, but has already sat with John during previous sessions for orientation and prior lessons and allows our youth to work with minimal supervision. A communication channel between the online guide (a teacher trained in the implementation of SCI-CBI online and who interacts with the youth during their online sessions) and the facilitator allows the online guide to request assistance if John falls behind the group or does not participate as expected. Upon login John sees that others are already online and is greeted by the online guide. John can go to his virtual room which holds trophies and awards for previous accomplishments in iSocial. These awards also provide a mechanism for reviewing earlier lessons if desired. However, his online guide is calling the youth together to start the "rules of the road" activity. In this one-hour session John and his four peers receive instruction and modeling from the guide and by watching media, can try out skills in game-like contexts, rehearse skills through interacting with teammates, and test themselves.

The tryouts, rehearsals and assessments are both cognitive and behavioral. The youth and guide are represented by 3D avatars (digital representations of self in the virtual world) that allow them to move around, virtually interact with objects and others, and have a sense of their presence and the co-presence of others in the environment. Figure 1 shows some sample scenes from iSocial. In one part of the lesson (left) students must take turns to try to match faces. Turns are managed by students telling each other that they have finished their turn and that it is now the other person's turn. Students offer each other encouragement and hints in order to beat the game. The game provides an opportunity to practice skills and an opportuntiy for the guide to help the youth build a cognitive understanding of the purpose and value of the skill. In another part of the lesson (right) students review appropriate and inappropriate conversational manners, and are required to produce examples of each. In one lesson students plan a trip to Los Angeles together, and in another students play a role-playing game where they are lost at sea. These forms of collective practice require a skilled guide to manage the behavior of the youth, a well designed environment to encourage some behaviors and constrain others, and mechanisms such as voice, text, and gesture to enable communication and shared understanding.

Our chapter is a case report about the iSocial project, but our implementation to date is a single unit on "conversational turn-taking" from the five-unit SCI-CBI curriculum. Whereas a commercial organization might develop specifications for iSocial, undertake some usability testing to verify assumptions of human computer interaction and build alpha and beta versions of the system as means to debugging and eliminating flaws, and then build out a version of the system for implementation; as an academic institution our efforts serve research goals as well as development or product goals. Our next section of the chapter describes a field test of an initial implementation of one unit of the SCI-CBI curriculum, and

Figure 1.

some of the lessons we are learning through this trial effort.

CURRENT CHALLENGES

A field test of a single unit from the five-unit curriculum was undertaken during the fall of 2008. Two separate virtual groups undertook the unit and each consisted of two youths (boys on the autism spectrum, ages 11-14), an online guide, as well as a technical "helper" in the VLE, and a facilitator for each youth. The facilitators sat physically at the youths' computers as the lesson was carried out. For each group, the unit consisted of two training sessions of one hour for learning to use the 3D VLE system and then four one-hour lessons from the curriculum unit delivered over a two week period. The key purposes of the field test were to (1) assess the efficacy of design decisions for adapting the face-to-face based curriculum into the new medium, (2) identify issues with system usage and (3) generate ideas for needed social orthotics. Data collected during the field test consisted of a technology competency survey administered at the beginning of the study, social presence surveys, adapted from Bailenson, Beal et al. (2001), administered at the end of each session, screen and audio recordings of all participants' sessions within the VLE and videotaped recordings of participants with their facilitators physically

using computers for each session. In the following sections we address the lessons learned from the field test under four categories: (1) challenges of adapting face-to-face instruction into 3D-VLE medium, (2) challenges of enabling and shaping appropriate social interaction within the medium, (3) easing transitions and reducing distractions and (4) leveraging the engagement and enthusiasm of youth for being a part of iSocial toward achieving the desired learning outcomes.

Challenges of Adapting a Face-to-Face Curriculum into 3D-VLE Medium

The prototype iSocial turn-taking unit used in the field test was adapted from the face-to-face SCI-CBI curriculum delivery. The benefits of using a curriculum with empirically demonstrated improvements in social competency are obvious, but lead to challenges for how to adapt to a virtual environment. An identical implementation of the face-to-face curriculum in the VLE was neither feasible, nor likely desirable. For example, having learners use worksheets face-to-face is a task with low complexity and provides for relatively simple classroom management; however, in iSocial, distributing a dynamic turn-taking worksheet and using it effectively is highly complex. Many face-to-face activities relying on paralinguistic cues such as eye contact cannot be supported currently in the VLE and require adaptation. However, equally compelling is the belief that what may make sense in a face-to-face group, such as using worksheets to learn from problem solving what to do on a deserted island could be replaced by putting youth on a virtual deserted island and giving them more authentic exposure to the problems. It was necessary and desirable, therefore, to redesign certain aspects of the curriculum to make them more suitable for virtual instruction.

One of the more successful adaptations was a replacement for a face-to-face logic puzzle. The logic puzzle from the face-to-face instruction was predominantly text based and relied heavily on learners being able to work collaboratively with paper and pencil and receive feedback from the instructor. The activity provided learners opportunities to practice the conversational skills of the lesson such as staying on topic, using appropriate tone of voice, initiating conversation and using proper turn-taking strategies. Such an activity is amenable to the affordances of classroom instruction but does not translate directly to virtual instruction. We designed a substitute activity that lacked the managerial complexity of the logic puzzle and leveraged the visual affordances of the 3D-VLE while at the same time providing opportunity for verbal practice of targeted skills. Learners participated in a structured "spot the differences" game in which two similar pictures were displayed with subtle differences. Learners took turns, encouraged and helped one another to find the differences in the pictures while remaining engaged and on-task.

F.N. and U.B. made up one of the dyad groups who participated in the spot the differences game. Both learners expressed a liking for this type of game and engaged in finding differences with very little instructional prompting. In fact, the majority of prompts from the online guide were usually managerial (i.e., reminding the learners that their time was almost up) or encouragement (i.e., "Great comment, U.B."). The game neces-

sitated that the learners negotiate for meaning, which spurred conversation and hence provided many opportunities for practicing turn-taking, staying on topic, etc. For instance, U.B. was unsure about a particular part of the picture:

U.B.: Is that ice cream?

F.N.: I think it looks like salad.

U.B.: OK, salad. [Pause] Well whatever it is, one has one pink thing in it and the other one has two.

F.N.: [Pause] That's pretty good.

U.B.: Yeah, that one is pretty hard to find.

F.N.: Yeah, it took me a while to see it.

In this example we see a relevant example not only of negotiation for meaning but also of proper conversational turn-taking. In addition, the learners encourage one another, something which occurred throughout the activity; for example, "Hey, I didn't see that," or "Ooh, that's a hard one." What we did not anticipate was that the structure and nature of activity facilitated learners being patient as they waited their turn. After they pointed out one difference, they had to tell the partner it was their turn and wait until the partner was finished and conceded their turn before they could go again. Learners would quickly spot differences between turns, but were forced to wait before they could contribute. When a participant would forget to concede his turn, the partner would often prompt him to do so, e.g., "OK, so tell me it's my turn," or "Is it my turn now?" Such interaction is highly desirable with our user phenotype because it indicates executive functioning through awareness of the basic rules of conversational turn-taking. It remains an open question, however, the extent to which and in what ways such behavior might transfer to contexts beyond the spot the differences game.

A less successful example of curricular re-design was an activity in which learners were to plan a hypothetical trip to Los Angeles. In the face-to-face classroom, this activity is supported by handouts and worksheets. When we replaced handouts and worksheets with static posters and images, the interactivity of the classroom activity seemed to get lost in translation. When learners worked through this activity they exhibited little motivation, were easily distracted, engaged in off-task activity and showed little cooperation or spontaneous conversation with each other.

O.A. and U.Z. made up one of the dyad groups who participated in the Trip to Los Angeles activity. During the activity both participants were distracted and engaged in off task activity, such as looking out the window, looking at the video camera and trying to talk with the helper. They were not engaged and only rarely spoke without instructor prompting. In fact, nearly the entire activity was instructor driven. The online guide's suggestions, such as "O.A., maybe you'd like to tell U.Z. why you want to stay in that kind of hotel," would often be followed by long pauses. The online guide would resort to direct prompts, e.g., "Why do you want to stay there, O.A.?" Ultimately, the instruction resembled more of a question-and-answer format between the online guide and individual participants than a conversation between participants. In addition, there was some difficulty understanding the premise of the activity as evidenced by U.Z. asking the online guide, "So are we really going to Los Angeles? [...] I can't afford that. I'm waiting to get Iron Man." This is not surprising, as individuals with ASD are known to have difficulties in understanding pretend play and imaginative play (Jordan, 2003). Nevertheless, given the affordances of 3D-VLE technology, the capabilities exist to mediate pretend play and imagination by providing an activity that more firmly situates learners in the virtual role of someone who is going to Los Angeles, for instance, a visit to a virtual travel agent's office. To be sure, we knew that our trip to Los Angeles activity could have been replaced by more authentic tasks, but working on rushed timelines to meet the field test dates and working within financial limitations gave us little alternative but to attempt to fit a learning activity that relies on handouts and worksheets to the 3D-VLE. While it appears somewhat obvious that one would want to have more money and more time to build more authentic experiences, this too must be done with caution because it is possible to build a highly engaging experience that misses the cognitive and behavioral requirements of the lesson, which indeed is the purpose of the activity and the human activity warranted by previous research on the intervention.

Challenges of Enabling and Shaping Appropriate Social Interaction within the Medium

Our findings for system usage show iSocial to be easy to use. The participants readily adopted the avatar representations of themselves. As part of our design research we compared variations in physical representation from less realistic block figures to more realistic human-like avatars and variations in behavioral representations from limited motion to more freedom in movement and gesture (i.e., walk, nod, wave, shake hands, etc.). See Figure 2 for examples of the human-like and block-like avatar figures making a waving behavior. While the full range of data have not yet been analyzed along these dimensions, our observations are that the youth valued the behavioral capabilities as, when possible, there was frequent and enthusiastic use of gestures. When gesturing capabilities were removed, learners frequently asked why the gesturing no longer worked and when they would be able to use gestures again. Orienting the avatars so that they seemed to represent eye contact in the 3D world also was important to a number of the participants as they would initiate

Figure 2.

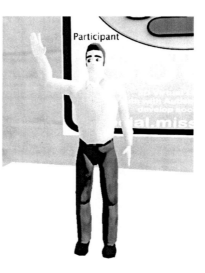

a conversation, i.e., "Why don't you look at me?" and express intentions, i.e., "I'm trying to look at him." While these gestures were a fun part of the experience for the youth, the level of gesture and behavioral expression were fairly limited as no real eye contact could be made nor could subtle cues for emotions be conveyed. Similarly, while we noted the prominence of behavioral over physical representation, the physical representations were also fairly limited. As stated above, participants demonstrated a clear preference for avatars that were able to exhibit human-like gestures, and were perturbed by avatars that had no behavioral animations, often asking why their avatar could not wave or walk. At the same time, participants did not demonstrate as obvious a preference for realistic-looking versus non-realistic-looking avatars. To be sure, they noticed and commented on the visual difference in appearance, but did not appear to be very bothered by it. To illustrate this point, we juxtapose two sessions with U.B. and F.N. In both sessions, participants' avatars were represented as blocky, cartoonish figures. In the first session the avatars had gesturing capabilities. In the second session they did not. As participants began the first session, they immediately noticed

that gesturing was enabled. U.B. exclaimed, "Hey, they [the gestures] work today!" In addition, participants seemed amused at the way their avatars looked:

F.N.: I'm a block! I'm a block! I'm a block! I'm a big muscular block! I am a stinking block! Why am I... Why am I a block?

U.B.: Why am I a block?

[...]

FN: Wheee! I'm a walking block!

This amusement with the avatars continued into the second session. F.N. jokingly said, "Helper, tell me why we're still blocks... I demand!" However, U.B. was not pleased with having the gesturing capabilities turned off:

Guide: Now, you can't shake hands, but you can use your words.

U.B.: Yeah we can.

Guide: No you can't... I don't think so today.

U.B.: [Presses key for shaking hands. Nothing happens. Begins banging on keyboard.] UGH!

Guide: It's OK, it's just, today your avatar's going to be different.

These anecdotes provide some indication that learners prefer behavioral realism in their avatars, but not necessarily photographic realism. We are currently investigating the degree to which these observational findings are in agreement with the research on neuro-typical individuals that indicates that photographic realism of avatars does not appear to be as influential a factor socially as behavioral realism (see Bailenson, Blascovich et al., 2001).

In spite of the intriguing findings about gesture and behavioral representation, our members experienced noticeable difficulties in coordinating activity. This was especially prominent for the online guide who was charged with keeping the youth engaged and on track with the curriculum activities. Our online guide sometimes had trouble managing instruction in the VLE, due to the lack of nonverbal and paralinguistic prompts. For example in the classroom the guide notices subtle cues from students as they are starting to drift from instruction, and she can use those cues to start processes to bring the student back to attention. This form of control was more difficult to exert online. Further, communication with the facilitators who physically oversaw learners was limited. Facilitators could hear and see what was happening in the VLE but could not communicate with the online guide. Hence, when learners would engage in undesirable behavior such as gazing out the window or excessively clicking mouse buttons or keyboard keys, the online guide lacked effective tools to coordinate with physical facilitators to bring learners back on task both physically and virtually. In addition, the prototype environment was built with minimal tools to control what learners could and could not do within the environment. As a result, learners had the same control over many functions of the environment that the online guide had. This became problematic when learners chose to explore the limits of the VLE and inadvertently caused problems such as closing shared windows, taking control of a collaborative application when it was not their turn or stopping a video. Such issues were distracting, which typically slowed the rate of instruction and

impeded the flow of the lessons. Consequentially, the online guide was unable to address the same amount of instruction in one hour in the VLE as is typical in a face-to-face class, causing instruction to be sometimes rushed. It may well be the case that virtual instruction necessarily proceeds at a different pace than face-to-face; however, supporting coordination and reducing distractions with social orthotics is an obvious target for future iterations of iSocial.

The role and need for social orthotics to fit the targeted population is underscored by U.B.'s performance in iSocial. In face-to-face instruction U.B. is characterized by a general lack of impulse control and a tendency to exhibit disruptive behavior. This type of behavior persisted during the study as he was reluctant to participate in cooperative tasks and often moved his avatar away from the rest of the group. In addition, he would often defy the online guide's instructions when he was unable to be in control of activities. In face-to-face training special educators have control mechanisms for influencing these types of behavior, such as limiting the ability to move away from the group and cueing the learner from off-task or errant behavior. iSocial needs mechanisms geared towards behavioral management and change. For example, enhanced access controls could effectively lock certain functions from being accessed and would presumably decrease distractions. Having social orthotics focused on improvement of targeted individual social deficits could provide just-in-time feedback based on identified learner needs. However, U.B.'s behavior was not entirely due to a lack of programmatic mechanisms that limit access and control and enhance social competencies. U.B. brought with him a bias in that he perceived iSocial to be a video game. He often referred to iSocial as a game and would sometimes defend his actions within iSocial as being those of an experienced gamer, e.g., "I know how to do that. I play games all the time."

We envision social orthotics as software tools and customizations to the environment which are integrated into the interface and virtual world in such a way as to support social interaction and mediate acquisition of social competency from coaching, on-demand assistance and just-in-time feedback. A goal of these orthotics is to enable learners to engage in effective social practice for which they do not have full competence. Our vision of orthotics includes mechanisms that are permanent features of the environment for the youths and mechanisms that may serve as temporary scaffolds. The permanent orthotics are to support social interaction for youth who do not have the needed competence and may always be challenged by the lack of social capability. The temporary orthotics are for social functions that the youth can learn, but support is needed until the youth has demonstrated sufficient capability. Once the youth has made progress in learning the social function the support can be faded or removed. Ultimately, the orthotics should be mapped to individual youth and needs and be adaptive to the youth's behavior and progress. Preliminary findings and feedback from facilitators has provided the design team with three target categories for development of orthotics. These categories have to do with directing learners' attention appropriately, mediating conversation and managing proximity.

Directing learners' attention appropriately is needed because learners exhibited difficulty in orienting to tasks, especially when they were distracted. Sometimes learners would not comply when asked to participate, or they would engage in off-task activities. To address this issue, we envision a class of software tools that we name "iFocus." Because it can be difficult for learners to orient their avatars to an item of interest since there are no indicators to show what specifically is being referred to, iFocus can provide visual cues for the instructor to indicate what is being referenced, such as a virtual laser pointer and the ability for objects to shake, glow, etc. In addition, iFocus can provide activity notifications, indicating when something should be attended to, and

will also provide mechanisms for coaching and providing on-demand and just-in-time assistance. For example, when the instructor is speaking a user might receive a notification such as, "When you are listening to the teacher it is polite to face her and make eye contact. If your back is turned, the teacher will think you are not listening."

Providing mechanisms to mediate conversation is necessary because individuals with ASD struggle with many of the subtle rules of basic conversation, such as proper turn-taking, maintaining appropriate volume and tone of voice, etc. To address this challenge, we envision a class of tools which we call "iTalk." iTalk will provide learners with an interface that explicitly models the implicit rules of conversation. This tool will monitor conversational turns using a token-passing system, will inform learners when it is their turn to speak and will constrain their ability to speak out of turn. Learners will also be able to "see" others' moods in thought bubbles above their avatars and provide indication of their own mood. In addition, iTalk will provide coaching and assistance using indicators such as, "Martin has changed his mood to bored. Maybe he is no longer interested in this topic. You could ask him if he wants to talk about something else." We provide a sample of what this orthotic might look like in figure 3.

Managing proximity is important because learners can get lost in the 3D-VLE or they may stray from the group. When learners move their avatars away from the group, they cannot hear others and tend to engage in off-task behavior. We envision a class of tools called "iGroup" to approach this issue. iGroup will provide a number of features for group management. For example, a circle could be displayed on the floor of the 3D-VLE indicating where the group is to congregate. The circle varies in color from green to red. When the circle is green, learners can move freely in and out of the circle. When the circle is red, learners cannot leave the circle. In addition, iGroup will provide automated grouping features. For instance, the instructor can use a "follow me" mode which

Figure 3. iTalk's prototype conversation console

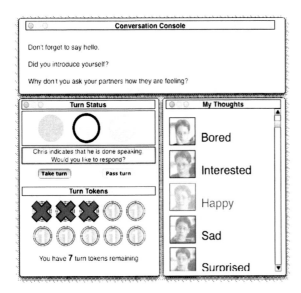

forces all users' avatars to follow the instructor's avatar. Other grouping features might include settings for a single speaker with all avatars oriented towards him/her, group discussion with all avatars in a circle, or a semi-circle around a presentation or video. iGroup can also provide notifications such as, "You are too far away from the group to hear. Follow the green arrow above your avatar's head to re-join the group."

Easing Transitions and Reducing Distractions

Distractions in iSocial are a particularly relevant challenge, as evidenced by the difficulty that the online guide and physical facilitators had bringing learners back on task after they had been distracted. Transitioning between activities can be difficult for ASD-affected youth and can result in problem behaviors (Sterling-Turner & Jordan, 2007). In addition, set-shifting (moving back and forth between tasks, activities or cognitive activities) can pose a challenge for these individuals (Hughes, Russell, & Robbins, 1994; Rinehart, Bradshaw,

et al., 2002). In iSocial, moving from one activity to the next was difficult because, for each part of the lesson, learners had to physically move their avatar from the space in which they were working to a new part of the virtual space. This is different than in face-to-face SCI-CBI instruction in which the physical context stays the same but the activity context changes (e.g., the instructor introduces a new activity in the same room). As such, it is not surprising that learners had difficulties staying engaged when moving from one task to the next. These difficulties were magnified when learners would lose the group, have audio problems, experience avatar glitches, etc.

Keeping learners cognitively engaged is an important part of the learning process. In many instances, learners were deeply engaged in their iSocial experience. However, when learners are distracted such as when transitioning between tasks due to other reasons, they are less engaged. This is evidenced by the exploratory study of an immersive virtual environment for individuals with ASD by Max and Burke (1997) in which the researchers found that ASD-affected individuals were more prone to distractibility in complex visual environments than a neuro-typical control group (Max & Burke, 1997). A challenge we faced during the iSocial field test was keeping distractions to a minimum. Some distractions were anticipated, such as learners getting disoriented in the environment and requiring assistance to find the group again or learners accidentally pressing an incorrect key on their keyboard. These issues became less prevalent over time as learners developed competence in using the iSocial software. However, some distractions were unanticipated. For example, the headsets that learners wore for communication were uncomfortable, and learners would frequently reposition them or even remove them to take a break. The noise from these frequent movements was captured on the headset microphones and transferred to everyone in the 3D-VLE, which was loud and unpleasant. In addition, the headsets had audio controls on them.

When learners would reposition the headsets, they would often inadvertently mute their audio or turn their audio up or down, requiring that a technical assistant interrupt the lesson to fix the problem. In this case, what was perceived as a simple purchase of headsets had a significant impact on learning, as when learners became distracted, they had difficulty re-orienting to the task. Consideration must be given to not only the environmental and educational design of a 3D-VLE, but also to the tools that facilitate use of the virtual world.

Easing transitions and reducing distractions is a clear target for future design work. Providing cues and prompts for smoothing transitions and preparing learners for transitions is desirable, but equally important is anticipating the problems that occur during transitions such as getting lost or distracted and developing social orthotics and curricular supports to diminish these issues.

Leveraging the Engagement and Enthusiasm of Youth Toward Achieving Desired Learning Outcomes.

Participants enjoyed their experience in the iSocial field test. Even U.B., who appeared at times to be frustrated, disconnected, and wanted the experience to be more like the games he was familiar with found iSocial enjoyable. His mother spoke of his wanting to continue to participate even as the field test was ending. The online guide and physical facilitators noted that learners showed evidence of being differently engaged in the virtual SCI-CBI lessons than in face-to-face lessons. They noted that some participants showed more patience in the 3D-VLE and that others got along better in the virtual space than in the classroom. They also maintain that learners may have paid more attention in iSocial than face-to-face because they tend to like video games. While these observations need further examination, we find these preliminary hypotheses intriguing and potentially promising. We approach these assertions with

caution, as engagement in iSocial could be due to participants merely being enamored with the technology. We need to be cautious about attributing enthusiasm for the medium and experience to design characteristics of iSocial. It may have just felt novel and been a curiosity which could diminish in appeal over time. Yet the field test did last over multiple sessions with no apparent decline in interest from the early stages to the latter, and the youth expressed their desire to keep participating. A next stage for our research and design work is to examine which aspects of the iSocial experience seemed most engaging or engendered the most enthusiasm and then to see how those elements can be enlisted in the pedagogical design. For example, the youth clearly enjoyed being able to gesture. Thus gesturing might be a tool to leverage engagement in activities that otherwise might be tedious. As an illustration, imagine the youth in the turn-taking exercise where they need to say "it's your turn" before the next youth can start, making a hand gesture when releasing his turn. Additionally the capability for new gestures might be a reward for mastering a competency so only youth who have made it through a particular lesson can "high five" with cohorts.

SUMMARY

The early findings outlined above provide numerous points of departure for further design, development and research into utilization of 3D-VLE technologies for facilitation of collaborative virtual social competence instruction for individuals with ASD. Perhaps most encouraging is the observation that, despite shortcomings, learners' experiences in iSocial were enjoyable and their perceptions were positive. Generally speaking, learners were able to operate within the environment with minimal difficulty, engage in instruction, follow directions and interact with others. Upon completion of the field test, all participants expressed dismay that they would not be participating in more lessons and indicated a desire to continue using iSocial. Participants also asked that they be invited to participate in future studies.

There is also much to be explored about the design and implementation of social orthotics which is a key element of our design for our specific audience but which also has potential as a design construct more generally across the use of 3D VLE. As discussed in previous sections we anticipate benefits from the implementation of social orthotics but also recognize that there is much to be learned. We must also bear in mind that orthotics have the potential to be distracting in and of themselves. Given the uniqueness of our user phenotype, it is therefore important for us to understand how learners will use and react to the instructional and environmental supports that we provide. Hence, much of our upcoming research will focus on usability and usage of the social orthotics. In addition, revisiting the design of the virtual SCI-CBI curriculum and investigating how it can better leverage the affordances of the 3D-VLE should lead to tasks that are appealing and interesting and take full advantage of the capabilities of 3D-VLE. We believe that the lessons learned from the field test provide a basis for improved authentic and meaningful instruction in 3D-VLE, and provide a foundation upon which to build and improve virtual technologies for individuals with ASD.

REFERENCES

Bailenson, J. N., Beall, A. C., Blascovich, J., Raimundo, M., & Weisbuch, M. (2001). *Intelligent agents who wear your face: Users' reactions to the virtual self.* Paper presented at the Intelligent Virtual Agents: Third International Workshop, Madrid, Spain.

Bailenson, J. N., Blascovich, J., Beall, A. C., & Loomis, J. (2001). Equilibrium theory revisited: Mutual gaze and personal space in virtual environments. *Presence (Cambridge, Mass.), 10*(6), 583–598. doi:10.1162/105474601753272844

Center for Disease Control and Prevention. (2007). *Prevalence of autism spectrum disorders (ASDs) in multiple areas of the United States, 2000 and 2002* (No. MMWR SS 2007; 56 (SS1)(12)). Atlanta, GA.

Cobb, S., Beardon, L., Eastgate, R., Glover, T., Kerr, S., & Neale, H. (2002). Applied virtual environments to support learning of social interaction skills in users with Asperger's Syndrome. *Digital Creativity, 13*(1), 11–22. doi:10.1076/digc.13.1.11.3208

Hughes, C., Russell, J., & Robbins, T. (1994). Evidence for executive dysfunction in autism. *Neuropsychologia, 32*(4), 477–492. doi:10.1016/0028-3932(94)90092-2

Jordan, R. (2003). A review of the role of play in theory and practice in autistic spectrum disorders, *Autism: the International Journal of Research and Practice, 7.*

Loftus, T. (2005). *Virtual world teaches real-world skills.* Retrieved February 27, 2007, from http://www.msnbc.msn.com/id/7012645/

Max, M., & Burke, J. (1997). Virtual reality for autism communication and education, with lessons for medical training simulators. *Studies in Health Technology and Informatics, 39*, 46–53.

Mitchell, P., Parsons, S., & Leonard, A. (2007). Using virtual environments for teaching social understanding to 6 adolescents with autistic spectrum disorders. *Journal of Autism and Developmental Disorders, 37*(3), 589–600. doi:10.1007/s10803-006-0189-8

Parsons, S., Leonard, A., & Mitchell, P. (2006). Virtual environments for social skills training: Comments from two adolescents with autistic spectrum disorder. *Computers & Education*, *47*(2), 186–206. doi:10.1016/j.compedu.2004.10.003

Rinehart, N., Bradshaw, J., Tonge, B., Brereton, A., & Bellgrove, M. (2002). A neurobehavioral examination of individuals with high-functioning autism and Asperger disorder using a fronto-striatal model of dysfunction. *Behavioral and Cognitive Neuroscience Reviews*, *1*(2), 164–177.

Rogers, S. (2000). Interventions that facilitate socialization in children with autism. *Journal of Autism and Developmental Disorders*, *30*, 399–409. doi:10.1023/A:1005543321840

Sterling-Turner, H., & Jordan, S. (2007). Interventions addressing transition difficulties for individuals with autism. *Psychology in the Schools*, *44*(7), 681–690. doi:10.1002/pits.20257

Stichter, J. P., Randolph, J., Gage, N., & Schmidt, C. (2007). A review of recommended practices in effective social competency programs for students with ASD. *Exceptionality*, *15*, 219–232.

FURTHER READING

Blascovich, J., Loomis, J., Beall, A. C., Swinth, K. R., Hoyt, C. L., & Bailenson, J. N. (2001). Immersive virtual environment technology as a methodological tool for social psychology. *Psychological Inquiry*, *13*, 146–149. doi:10.1207/S15327965PLI1302_03

Brown, D. J., Kerr, S., & Wilson, J. R. (1997). Virtual environments in special-needs education. *Communications of the ACM*, *40*(8), 72–75. doi:10.1145/257874.257891

Gee, J. P. (2003). *What video games have to teach us about literacy and learning*. New York: Palgrave Macmillan.

McLellan, H. (2004). Virtual realities. In D. Jonassen (Ed.), *Handbook of research on educational communications and technology* (pp. 461-498). Mahwah, NJ: Lawrence Erlbaum Associates.

Parsons, S., Mitchell, P., & Leonard, A. (2005). The use and understanding of virtual environments by adolescents with Autistic Spectrum Disorders. *Journal of Autism and Developmental Disorders*, *34*, 449–466. doi:10.1023/B:JADD.0000037421.98517.8d

Schmidt, M., Laffey, J., Stichter, J., Goggins, S., & Schmidt, C. (2008). The design of iSocial: A three-dimensional, multiuser, virtual learning environment for individuals with autism spectrum disorder to learn social skills. *The International Journal of Technology . Knowledge and Society*, *4*(2), 29–38.

Standen, P., Brown, D., & Cromby, J. (2001). The effective use of virtual environments in the education and rehabilitation of students with intellectual disabilities. *British Journal of Educational Technology*, (32): 289–299. doi:10.1111/1467-8535.00199

Standen, P. J., & Brown, D. J. (2006). Virtual reality and its role in removing the barriers that turn cognitive impairments into intellectual disability. *Virtual Reality (Waltham Cross)*, *10*, 241–252. doi:10.1007/s10055-006-0042-6

Chapter 11

Maximizing Collaborative Learning and Work in Digital Libraries and Repositories:
A Conceptual Meta-Case

Shalin Hai-Jew
Kansas State University, USA

EXECUTIVE SUMMARY

Digital libraries and repositories aren't often thought of as virtual learning environments. However, in function and designs, they are. A wide range of digital artifacts are archived on both private and public open-source digital libraries and repositories. There are digital collections of texts, maps, photos, sound files, geospatial resources, video, and 3D objects. There are repositories for particular fields of study as well as multi-discipline ones. These may be structured as ontologies or taxonomies in particular knowledge (or cross-discipline) domains. Recently, designers of digital libraries and repositories have been focusing more testing and design on making such spaces usable for collaborative learning and building networks of communities. This chapter will explore how to maximize collaborative learning and work in digital libraries and repositories by applying pedagogical strategies.

INTRODUCTION

Digital libraries and repositories have been growing in popularity as virtual learning environments (VLEs) and sites for collaborative learning and work. These resources may manage terabytes of information and make these available anywhere through the Web and even into wi-fi enabled ambient spaces. These are a critical part of the overall information space.

Those working in education and training may benefit from using the built-in tools of various such digital libraries to encourage learner development. These systems sometimes involve tools to promote collaboration. These include embedded workflows, artificial intelligence (AI) and intelligent agentry, and other types of collaboration support. A number of pedagogical strategies may enhance the virtual collaborations made possible in contemporary digital libraries. Collaborative assignments may be created for uses with digital libraries and repositories. These include assignments involving co-research,

DOI: 10.4018/978-1-60566-878-9.ch011

informational treasure hunting, informational resource sharing, and the identification of themes and trends in a knowledge domain field. Learners may co-create an emergent curriculum with their work on digital libraries and repositories. Student-created artifacts may be presented to others in digital galleries. New knowledge may potentially be created in such endeavors with digital repositories.

BACKGROUND

Digital libraries and repositories tend to be collections of digital materials. A digital library consists of "collections" of materials usually based around particular topic areas; however, the definitions of "collections" do vary (Krafft, Birkland, & Cramer, 2008, p. 315). A digital repository is a storehouse for various types of digital contents, without an organizing hand through curatorship or content editing.

In the past decade and a half, digital libraries and repositories have grown in importance with the massive proliferation of new knowledge creation. Every 15 minutes, the world churns out the equivalent of the knowledge that took 200 years to create to fill the US Library of Congress in Washington, D.C.: "29 million books and periodicals, 2.7 million recordings, 12 million photographs, 4.8 million maps, and 57 million manuscripts" (Smith, 2005, p. 22).

This new information is predominantly digital: texts, maps, photos, sound files, geospatial resources, emails, weather data, video, 3D, and other objects. There may be live data streams of spatio-temporal information from satellite, infrared cameras, remote sensing, and scanning. Some collections are location-based, and others are distributed and widely dispersed through the Internet and WWW.

SETTING THE STAGE

Some contents in digital libraries and repositories are public and socially relevant; some are private. In the latter set, there are individual repositories of journals, notebooks, and family histories formed over a lifetime of computer usage (Callan, Smeaton, Beaulieu, Borlund, Brusilovsky, Chalmers, Lynch, Riedl, Smyth, Straccia, & Toms, 2003). Such repositories may be subjectively categorized and sufficiently scalable to handle tens of thousands of documents, photos, papers, emails, and books for individual document collections (Janssen, 2004). Private businesses maintain repositories of corporate records, patent specifications, designs and blueprints, computer coding, datasets, and reports. Some repositories are interoperable with a variety of systems and are networked for wider resource offerings; many of these are free and accessible via the WWW and the Internet. Others are proprietary, closed, subscription-only, and accessible only to those who've been vetted and approved. Most inaccessible are those that are "dim" or "black" databases for consumption by those with security clearances.

Born 0s and 1s

The information may be "born digital" or purely created in digital form. "Lazy preservation" of website resources aids in website reconstruction and the protection of data in a volatile preservation environment (McCown, Smith, Nelson, & Bollen, 2006, pp. 67 – 74). Electronic records may be digitally archived with full authenticity and integrity "from a recordkeeping system to a preservation system" (Glick, Wilczek, & Dockins, 2006, p. 359). There are endeavors to archive all things digital, too, such as born-digital blogs which are "valuable records of current social and political events" (Hank, Choemprayong, &

Sheble, 2007, p. 477). Another project also captures high-level snapshots of the WWW and has since its inception.

Atoms to 0s and 1s

At the same time, physical objects are migrating to digital formats for cultural preservation, research, learning, and appreciation. Sculptures and artworks may be captured in terms of digital imaging modalities: visual appearance, surface, texture, shape, and subsurface characteristics. "Techniques such as photography, video, X-ray, 3-D scans, infrared, UV, and laser scans have been used successfully for different art recording purposes" (Chen, Wactlar, Wang, & Kiernan, 2005, p. 278).

To preserve cultural artifacts like "paintings, sculptures, and other works of art and fragile handwritten records in a plethora of styles and scripts on clay and stone and wood and canvas and cave walls, on parchment and paper and papyrus, not just in libraries and museums, but also in churches, temples, and mosques, and in the living museums of the longest inhabited cities and villages throughout the world" as a preserve against time and natural disasters; theft, vandalism, and terrorism (Chen, Wactlar, Wang, & Kiernan, 2005, pp. 275 - 276). Spoken-word audio collections may be captured for historical use (EU-US working group on spoken-word audio collections).

Ironically, digital preservation has its own frailty, in terms of potential degradation and "slow fires" obsolescence. "Whereas books can be preserved for years and even centuries, the preservation of digital data is dependent on the technologies on which it is stored. In the next 100 years, storage technologies will advance tens of generations, and the digital collections preserved on up-to-date storage technologies will need to transition through each new generation, and many times over" (Berman, n.d., p. 3). Abandoned technological protocols, lack of political will, non-

funding, and public non-use or non-interest also present risks to digital collections and artifacts. Long-term sustainability and protectionism are important planning concerns.

Current repositories in use include those focused around fields like medical libraries (Nikolaidou, Anagnostopoulos, & Hatzopoulos, 2003); a health education assets library (McIntyre, Dennis, Uijtdehaage, & Candler, 2004), archaeology (Gorton, Shen, Vemuri, Fan, & Fox, 2006), and engineering knowledge over the life spans of airplanes (Wong, Crowder, Wills, & Shadbolt, 2006).

Other informational repositories contain usable interface coding for mobile devices (Paelke, Reimann, & Rosenbach, 2003) and non-public data such as the Web Characterization Repository of log files used by researchers "to analyze and improve on the architecture of the Web" (Suleman, Fox, & Abrams, 2000, pp. 228 – 229). Others archive digital versions of physical objects like newspaper clippings (Calvanese, Catarci, & Santucci, 2000). There are thematic repositories such as one based around global climate change (McCaffrey & Weston, 2005).

For higher education, there are repositories of syllabi (Tungare, Yu, Cameron, Teng, Pérez-Quiñones, Fan & Fox, 2007), repositories of digital learning objects, a library for undergraduates to draw connections across disciplines in the sciences (Yaron, Davenport, Karabinos, Leinhardt, Bartolo, Portman, Lowe, Sadoway, Carter, & Ashe, 2008), and others. An ethnomusicology digital repository may capture the ethnographic fieldwork of researchers in audio and video "to help document and understand the musical practices of people all over the world. Ethnomusicologists have used a variety of recording technologies over the years to capture film and video, and much of this footage lies in researchers' offices and home basements. No systematic mechanism exists for preserving and providing access to this video for other students and scholars" (Dunn & Cowan, 2005, n.p.).

CASE DESCRIPTION

This conceptual case reviews the extant literature on digital libraries and repositories, with a special focus on those designed for education and training. It explores how the archived resources are captured or "ingested"; labeled with metadata; organized and stored for search and use; protected for intellectual property rights, and shared with open source provisions. This will explore some of the interface designs for easier use by a range of stakeholders. The tools used to promote user collaboration around learning, research, problem-solving, project-based learning, and other tasks, will be explored. This case will present practical strategies for supporting collaborative work in digital libraries. This will show how such data repositories may be integrated with learning in learning/course management systems (L/CMSes). This will offer ideas on how such virtual communities may be supported within repositories for growing networks- and communities-of-practice. Also, this will address how new knowledge may be created and added to the repositories by users. This is written from the instructional design perspective of supporting faculty in the design of e-learning and capitalizing on the many digital library resources on the public and the invisible Webs.

The main repositories of interest here will be those focused on education and training. These may involve interoperable digital learning objects, such as virtual microscopes, simulations, case studies, lectures, academic videos, music, maps, and 3D objects. How people will use such repositories for learning is a very new field. Indeed, distributed digital libraries have been eyed for training and learning because of the potential cost savings.

CURRENT CHALLENGES: THE CORE FUNCTIONS OF DIGITAL LIBRARIES AND REPOSITORIES

The design of digital libraries and repositories draw from "information retrieval, human-computer interaction, computer supported collaborative work, machine learning, user modeling, hypermedia, and information science" (Callan, et al., 2003, p. 2). A variety of professional roles may contribute to digital library design: librarians, archivists, data curators, information managers, technologists, and instructional designers. Digital libraries are complex entities that require plenty of effort and resources and time to build. "What is desired is a simplified modeling process and rapid generation of digital libraries" (Zhu, Goncalves, & Fox, 2003, para. 1).

Within the design-based disciplines of human-computer interaction and educational technology, researchers are grappling with developing methodologies and theories capable of both: (1) informing the design and creation of new artifacts and (2) providing mechanisms for knowledge sharing within a design and research community. Digital libraries, as complex forms of educational technology, inherit these evaluation and research challenges as well as pose new and confounding ones of their own (Sumner & Marlino, 2004, p. 170).

Digital libraries and repositories have general functions: the identification and "ingestion" of appropriate contents, their labeling, and the proper delivery of appropriate contents to users on demand. Many back-end functions occur that users may not be aware of in terms of intellectual property rights protections, user authentication, and system security. The collaboration tools offer creative interactivity solutions for learning. The following features apply to many digital libraries and repositories, but it's important to note that each unique repository is different.

Contents: Selection, Ingestion and Labeling

Information may be seen as having a life cycle in a digital library.

1. "Ingestion / creation – also known as capturing or digitizing of those physical objects (painting, artifacts) into digital representation,
2. Editing—includes the normalization, standardization and cleansing of the captured data, including color and brightness adjustment,
3. Analysis – includes various metadata extraction such as low-level features (color histogram, textures, shapes, geometries, etc.), high-level features, and potentially correlating with other 'related' content,
4. Management – includes the management of both metadata and content, such as developing indices for aster retrieval, addressing issues such as data integrity, consistency, and versioning,
5. Distribution – addressing issues related to content dissemination for the consumption by the end user and require I/T infrastructures (such as caching), copyrights management, etc." (Chen, Wactlar, Wang, & Kiernan, 2005, pp. 285 - 286).

Virtually all digital libraries have standards for materials acceptance. These guidelines may relate to topics, content providence, originality, or multimedia file types. There are likely standards for archival, metadata, and accessibility (Tech-Dis, 2005). They may be permanent or temporal. Knowledge itself may be persistent or evolving. Some libraries are heterogeneous and cut across various information domain fields while others focus on particular topics.

Digital libraries collect contents in various ways. Some digital collections are topical only, and may be by invitation. These collections are curated, with a focus on quality, formal validation, originality, and freshness. Some are submitted by people without any editorial vetting. The interchange of data, going into the repository and being delivered based on others' requests, should have a low barrier for participation to encourage participation (Baker, Gold, & Sudholt, 2003).

Still, others include automatic "ingesting" of materials. One example is the automatic captures of video lectures for deployment on a digital repository (Abowd, Harvel & Brotherton, 2001, pp. 467 – 474). "Automating the creation of useful digital libraries—that is, digital libraries affording searchable text and reusable ("re-purposable") output—is a complicated process, whether the original library is paper-based or already available in electronic form" (Simske & Lin, 2004, para. 1).

Data streams may be captured in an automated way:

Saving data streams in digital libraries add the advantages of using digital libraries from archival, preservation, administration, access control, etc to this information. For this specific type of digital libraries, event-based retrieval provides an alternative, yet a very natural way of retrieving information. People tend to remember or search by a specific event that happened in the stream better than by the time at which this event happened (Kholief, Shen, & Maly, 2000, para. 1)

Granularity

The optimal size of contents (or granularity) may vary depending on the uses of the contents. Some digital libraries prefer "flexible content that is small, modular, and adaptable" for "distributed reusable and multilayered information" for educational purposes (Morris, Hembrooke, & Rayle, 2006, p. 354). Larger grain resources tend to be less usable in a variety of contexts because of internal dependencies; "conversely, small, self-contained resources afford greater teacher improvisation and adaptation in a wider range of situations" (Recker & Palmer, 2006, p. 241). There are risks of too tight coupling of digital objects for end-user usability (Li, Liu, & Yu, 2007, n.p.). Digital learning objects need to be mix and matchable and nestable (able to be placed within other digital objects in a hierarchy for e-learning purposes) for learning value.

Metadata and Labeling

Metadata (unstructured and distributed) may also be mechanically harvested. Digital contents may be labeled at the point of submission by the authors. If a collection is curated, the curator(s) then decides how to formally label each artifact. Automatically ingested contents may be labeled through the use of artificial intelligence 'bots. No matter the method of labeling, there will be difficulties and risks to misclassification.

The act of labeling opens up opportunities for disagreements and inconsistency. "The three most commonly reported problems with description were: consistent application of the chosen metadata scheme within a project, identification and application of controlled vocabularies, and integration of sets of data, schemes, and vocabularies either within an institution or among collaborators. In addition, there were clear tensions between local practices and what was perceived as the best for interoperability" (Palmer, Zavalina, & Mustafoff, 2007, p. 393).

To avoid having multiple versions of a particular file, the different technological systems use different methods. Efforts to avoid duplication of contents for a more efficient repository (deCarvalho, Goncalves, Laender, & da Silva, 2006, pp. 41 – 50). Eliminating "different URLs with similar text" (or "DUST") reduces indexing overhead, provides more effective crawling or browsing through a digital library, and improves the quality of popularity statistics (Bar-Yossef, Keidar, & Schonfeld, 2007, pp. 111 – 120). Shape and image comparing software helps identify similarities between digital images (Ko,

Maekawa, Patrikalakis, Masuda, & Wolter, 2003). In multi-billion page repositories, documents are "fingerprinted" for uniqueness and identified using these (Manku, Jain, & Sarma, 2007, pp. 141-149). Some systems use persistent identifiers or "handles" to label each digital source. This provides a stable and lasting point-of-reference. In situations where digital artifacts are nested for different uses, serializations of scholarly papers occur, and the reassemblage of artifacts may occur, such globally unique identifiers may be especially useful in discerning provenance (Bekaert, Liu, Van de Sompel, Lagoze, Payette, & Warner, 2006, p. 368).

Such repositories often multimedia contents which may range in the hundreds of megabytes to over a terabyte (Reuning & Jones, 2005, p. 396). Technologies used to find particular files (often in sub-seconds)—by text, by image, by audio or voice extraction, and by video key frames—may be used to compare digital objects to eliminate repeated files. Having clean content ingestion processes and content tracking and management should enhance the effectiveness of the data repository.

Info Structure

Some contents may have inherent form while others have domain-based structures, which may be expressed as ontologies, taxonomies and knowledge structures. These structures identify objects or entities, and the relationships between them. These organizational schemas may offer ways to place digital items in categories (Nelson, Marchionini, Geisler, & Yang, 2001, pp. 310 – 311). Machine learning may tap into human browsing behaviors and create automated taxonomies built using machine learning to support future human browsing in the digital library scenario (Krowne & Halbert, 2005, pp. 246 – 255). Well-structured hierarchies—such as thesauruses and ontologies—may support users with topic clarification and effective searches through synonym selections (Soergel, 2005, p. 421). Topic mapping or "the

Figure 1. An Overview of the Digital Resource Ingestion and Management Process

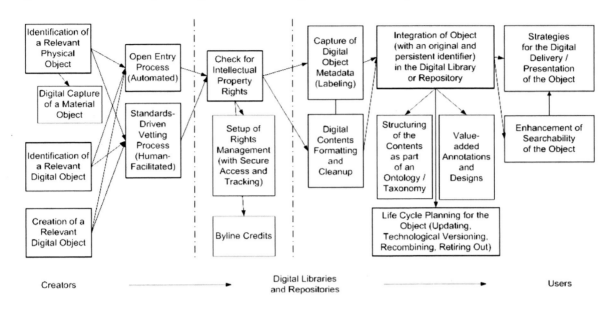

subject-based organization of information" is a common organizational structure for information (Yang, Han, Oh, & Kwak, 2007, pp. 106 – 110). This may be done textually or visually / spatially.

A visualization structure may be a tree map to show the relationships between certain topics. "Our prototype designs use color to represent content type. The size of the leaf nodes can be constant (showing the relative density of different sections of the repository) or encode access or rating data to emphasize popular or useful sections or documents" (Clarkson & Foley, 2006, p. 361). Others capture typical trails through the contents based on user objectives or profiles and record those for future users.

A concept-mapping application in an integrated digital library enhances the ability for users to create "clear pathways through the resources linked together on a concept map and the ability to control the sequence in which resources are viewed" (Kumar, 2007, p. 510).

Other digital contents may not fit into a larger context or form. Some repositories then merely

house information. Some libraries store the digital materials on their own servers while others (referatories) merely "point" to the contents while housing only the metadata of the digital contents

Info Sharing

The searchability of the contents of a digital library directly relates to its value as a resource. There must be an ability to search documents and query them independent of the digital formats in which they are represented (Malizia, 2004, para.1). While there are open published standards for the interoperability of various digital objects and the standards for such systems to interchange digital objects, to avoid a "digital tower of Babel" (Smith, 2005, p. 27), many authoring tools output digital objects with different standards, and collections have their own proprietary coding. Home-grown metadata may result in localized data, linkable to other contents through social tagging and folksonomies (Palmer, Zavalina, & Mustafoff, 2007, p. 393). The high variance in the uses of labeling terminology may degrade the quality of amateur tagging, however.

The Open Archives Initiative – Object Re-use and Exchange (OAI – ORE) strives to "develop, identify, and profile extensible standards and protocols that allow repositories, agents, and services to interoperate in the context of use and reuse of *compound digital objects* beyond the boundaries of the holding repositories" (Lynch, Parastatidis, Jacobs, Van de Sompel, & Lagoze, 2007, p. 80). Shared standards are a core strategy for interoperability (Bainbridge, Ke, & Witten, 2006), which would then allow objects to be exchanged and stored in different storage systems.

The need for interoperability between digital libraries is especially important to avoid the problem of missing documents (Zhuang, Wagle, & Giles, 2005). There are endeavors to ingest digital artifacts into multiple repositories simultaneously (Rani, Goodkin, Cobb, Habing, Urban, Eke, & Pearce-Moses, 2006) for greater efficiencies. Indeed, data spaces are "bootstrapped" with various tools for connectivity and a "semantic Web" of knowledge and information for federated digital repositories.

Researchers have been developing cross-system personalization, which shares individual information across different systems to enhance the sensitivity of the various systems to the unique data needs of unique users (Wang, Zhang, & Zhang, 2007). Various strategies are being used to understand how different users use the digital library and how to close the "intention gap" (Vuorikari, 2007, p. 207). Collaborative filtering is based on what people with similar profiles chose or liked in the past and is often domain independent. This information may be used to help users of a digital repository find applicable resources. However, such systems have few ways to capture or understand subjective elements like quality and taste (Torres, McNee, Abel, Konstan, & Riedl, 2004). Given the difficulty of knowing whether a resource met a particular goal-based need or for some other purpose, one researcher introduced "a personal bookmarking and tagging tool" (Vuorikari, 2007, p. 208) to capture more of that subjective user information.

Cross-lingual Query

Unknown cross-lingual search query terms may draw from the WWW as a corpus of terms to help a system understand the query. This system mines bilingual search result pages obtained from a Web search engine. This approach can enhance the construction of a domain-specific bilingual lexicon and benefit CLIR (cross-language information retrieval) services in a digital library that only has monolingual document collections. Very promising results have been obtained in generating effective translation equivalents for many unknown terms, including proper nouns, technical terms and Web query terms (Wang, Teng, Cheng, Lu, & Chien, 2004, p. 108).

Search Interfaces

Because of the variety of digital contents archived in digital repositories, new strategies have been designed for locating the desired contents. Traditional interfaces used text for searches. Others have visual metaphors to explain the interrelationships of various types of information in the digital repository. One such visual interface is the "islands of music" metaphor where related music is seen as clusters of similar-sounding music based on rhythm-based fluctuation patterns (Knees, Schedl, Pohle, & Widmer, 2006, p. 17).

Instead of just using metadata, key details in images may be used for querying digital "artwork collections, tele-sensing images, aerial photographs, astronomic databases, etc. The basic feature of the method is the capability of detecting and locating anyway rotated details with reasonable computational costs" (Capodiferro, Neri, Nibaldi, & Jacovitti, 2004). Their content-based image retrieval and classification techniques strengthen usability of large-image databases.

Searching music data may involve the use of solo digital voice extraction: "The paradigm is built on the automatic extraction of information of interest from music audio signals. Because the vocal part is often the heart of a popular song we focus on developing techniques to exploit the solo vocal signals underlying an accompanied performance. This supports the necessary functions of a music digital library, namely, music data organization, music information retrieval/recommendation, and copyright protection" (Tsai & Wang, 2005, pp. 197 – 206).

Geospatial information "represents the location, shape of, and relationships among geographic features and associated artifacts, including map and remotely sensed data" (O'Sullivan, McLoughlin, Bertolotto, & Wilson, 2003, p. 79). For geospatial and georeferenced resources, the main method of accessing data may come by "specifying the location of the information on the surface of the Earth" (The Alexandria Digital Library Team, 2004, p. 410) and for the oceanic and coastal environments (Marincioni & Lightsom, 2002). Geo-spatial image databases may be accessed based on task-based annotation of resources, based on "intelligence operations, recreational and professional mapping, urban and industrial planning, and tourism systems" (O'Sullivan, McLoughlin, Bertolotto, & Wilson, 2003, pp. 78 – 87).

Personalized Responses

Personalization and recommender systems have been built into digital libraries to address specific user needs, based on user profiles, user behaviors, and user-initiated search actions. Artificial intelligence agents may enhance user searches. Autonomous agents may offer even more directive supports, with users abdicating the role of directing the system to particular contents in an intelligent system (Leong, Howard, & Vetere, 2008, p. 716).

Value-Added Outputs

Some systems offer the same contents as was uploaded, and often with additional metadata and annotations (in text, voice, or video)—to add value. Still others may create contents on the fly for original presentations. "Systems for digital libraries should be able to select the appropriate type and amount of information from a comprehensive pool and compose it on the fly for a meaningful and coherent presentation which might have never occurred before or never will again after this event because it is customized to the current situation" (Hűser, Reichenberger, Rostek, & Streitz, 1995, p. 49). Helpful adding of resources and "chaining" of digital contents may enhance retrieval context (O'Sullivan, McLoughlin, Bertolotto, & Wilson, 2003, p. 86).

The integration of insightful annotations to digital objects may enhance their value. Annotations may well go beyond text: "We study the possibility of annotating multimedia documents with objects which are in turn of multimedial nature. Annotations can refer to whole documents or single portions thereof, as usual, but also to multi-objects, i.e. groups of objects contained in a single document" (Bottoni, Civica, Levialdi, Orso, Panizzi, & Trinchese, 2004, p. 55). There's learning value, too, in the act of annotation, of highlighting important parts of digital objects and adding ideas.

Another value-added aspect may be the inclusion of bibliometric metadata, the capturing of referencing information to analyze the impact of a particular digital resource. Such relationships may spark fresh insights: "Through the use of efficient extraction and inference techniques, complex relations between data items can be established. In this paper we explain the importance of the co-relation in enabling new techniques to rate the impact of a paper or author within a large corpus of publications" (Tarrant, Carr, & Payne, 2008, p. 471).

Some libraries have started packaging their digital contents—such as through creating subject-specific syllabi—to enhance the coherence of the digital contents for the learning context (Pérez-Quiñones, Fox, Cassel, & Fan, 2006).

Value may be added, too, with more full-surround service, such as alerts about certain resources of interest (Buchanan & Hinze, 2005, pp. 131 – 140). Social computing tools to connect those with like-interests may also enhance digital libraries and repositories.

Multi-Device Access

Some digital libraries are designed for access by mobile devices (Callan, et al., 2003). This means that portable devices may be used in ambient (wifi-enabled) spaces to access mobile knowledge with time efficiencies (Aridor, Carmel, Maarek, Soffer, & Lempel, 2002). Digital library contents may be mapped to ambient spaces such as a museum installation with 3D soundscapes linked to museum displays (Hatala, Kalantari, Wakkary, & Newby, 2004).

A Variety of Stakeholders

Different groups of individuals may have different needs from the various repositories. "Individuals, teams, organizations, and networks can be thought of as tiers or classes within the complex grid of technology and practice in which research documentation is both consumed and generated. The panoply of possible classes share with the others a common need for document management tools and practices" (Gold, Baker, LeMeur, & Baldridge, 2002, pp. 287 – 288). Considering users' needs is an important part of designing the information sharing of digital libraries and repositories. Users may need information on a short-term and sporadic basis, for example, or on a long-term continuous one.

The whole information journey involves three stages: "*information initiation, facilitation* (or *gathering*) and *interpretation*. The study shows that, although digital libraries are supporting aspects of users' information facilitation, there are still requirements for them to better support users' overall information work in context. Users are poorly supported in the initiation phase, as they recognize their information needs, especially with regard to resource awareness; in this context, interactive press-alerts are discussed. Some users (especially clinicians and patients) also require support in the interpretation of information, both satisfying themselves that the information is trustworthy and understanding what it means for a particular individual" (Adams & Blandford, 2005, pp. 160 – 169).

Security

Security for digital libraries and repositories is needed because of legal, cultural, competitive advantage and information vulnerability issues. Legal issues include concerns around intellectual property rights. Systems need to be accurate in representing ownership of digital materials and ensure that the levels of access to that information are correctly represented in the system. Open access archives and new copyright release systems that promote sharing of intellectual property have promoted more author self-archiving of works and sharing in the information commons. The use of user's personally identifiable information (PII) should be guided by user privacy protections (Callan, et al., 2003, p. 10). "Privacy (or the lack thereof) is of a special concern in subscriptions to large data repositories with heterogeneous information, where the service provider can easily profile its users and sell that information to third parties" (Blanton, 2008, p. 217). Another aspect of privacy relates to what information may be accessible to which level of data repository users. For example, some annotations and notes about certain resources may remain private to the authors using the various annotation tools in a digital repository.

Figure 2. Stakeholders to Collaborative Digital Libraries and Repositories

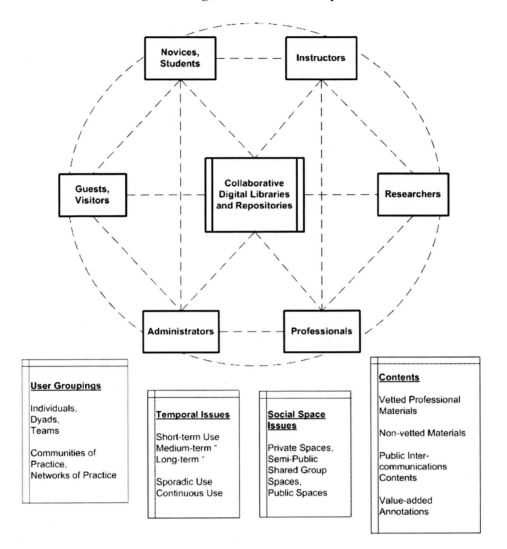

Social and cultural sensitivities may arise with the dissemination of particular digital artifacts that depict history or realities in different ways. Other information may have implications on competitive advantage and research and development (R&D). Yet other information may be restricted and not for mainstream consumption or distribution.

Back-end endeavors have worked to prevent non-repudiation, which prevents an individual or an entity from denying of having performed an action. "There are different types of non-repudiation---non-repudiation of origin, delivery, submission, roles, request, etc. In the context of digital libraries, non-repudiation of record genera-tion, distribution, verification and retention are important. The usage of digital signatures, third party signatures, recipient acknowledgements, de-livery reports, etc., provides a means of enforcing non-repudiation" (Vemulapalli, Halappanavar, & Mukkamala, 2002, n.p.). The authors elaborate on the uses of private keys used for signing, secure time-stamping, digital notarization services, and the use of trusted third party services for non-repudiation.

The distributed nature of digital libraries makes security harder to manage. Federated searches tap into a variety of digital libraries and repositories to cull requested information. "Increased dependence on agent-based architectures for digital libraries and peer-to- peer communications makes them more vulnerable to security threats. Thus, evolving a comprehensively secure distributed digital library system is challenging. In addition to the security guarantees, performance guarantees such as convenience in usage, minimal response time, and high throughput are also required of these systems" (Vemulapalli, Halappanavar, & Mukkamala, 2002, n.p.). The downstream use of digital objects is even harder to manage, if not impossible, even with the resources of watermarking (Tsolis, Tsolis, Karatzas, & Papatheodorou, 2002, p. 56) and spider tracking of authored digital items. Some systems deploy 3D images in pieces so as to protect them from being downloadable but still letting them be manipulable (for viewing different angles) on the original repository.

The importance of data will also make digital libraries the target of malicious attacks "by people seeking unauthorized information, and by terrorists seeking to disrupt the global information infrastructure and the physical infrastructures built upon it, it is both timely and essential to study the cybersecurity characteristics future digital libraries will have to support" (Birnbaum, 2004, p. 169). This reality will up the ante for those who would create and host digital repositories.

COLLABORATIVE DIGITAL LIBRARIES

In the same way that four-walls libraries are centers of research and learning, digital libraries may provide scholarly virtual spaces where people collaborate, share knowledge and resources, co-learn, and co-create. Repositories now are evolving to have features of knowledge networks, which are people-to-people. "The fundamental advantage

Figure 3. Some Security Issues in Digital Libraries and Repositories

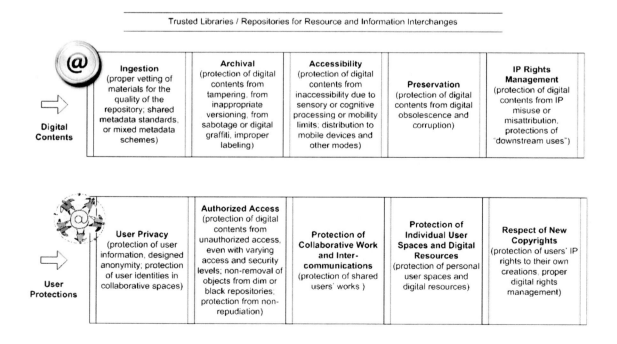

of this approach is that people who do not know one another can share potentially diverse and novel insights, ideas, and expertise. Moreover, since there is no central repository for archiving knowledge, it is more likely that the knowledge accessed through the network is up to date. These benefits can be realized without having to codify difficult-to-articulate tacit knowledge" (Bush & Tiwana, 2005, p. 70). Some of these changes may be attributed to industry: "Business models for digital libraries evolve from mere content providers to sophisticated service suppliers. They offer a rich variety of information services combined with collaboration, e-learning and portal features. Traditional classification schemes for digital libraries do not sufficiently take this development into account or fail to meet it at all" (Markscheffel, Fischer, & Stelzer, 2006, pp. 457 – 464).

Iverson describes "a vision of the digital library as the hub of a personalized, integrated information management environment," with asynchronous and synchronous interactions between users and data. He describes an integration between library services and tools for using the digitized informational resources. He suggests a data model that can handle resources at various levels of granularity: "structured, semi-structured or unstructured" and with user annotations integrated as metadata. He proposes "a data security model that provides full support for a range of private to semi-public to fully public data and metadata for users and user communities; and simple, flexible and integrated control of privacy, security, and integrity of all such data and metadata (Iverson, 2004, p. 380).

Sumner & Marlino (2004) suggest the following:

- "Accommodate and support different types of participant interactions, both human and technology-mediated
- Foster knowledge building and community development through specific forms of interactions

- Enable participants to choose varying thresholds of entry and ongoing participation
- Support participants to make use of captured interactions to inform their current activities
- Affect participants' views of themselves, their knowledge and skills, and their changing role in the community
- Grow and sustain themselves" (Sumner & Marlino, 2004, p. 176).

"The class *community* describes business models of digital libraries that expand their services by providing collaborative services for customers. Users of digital libraries in the class community may share information with other users by applying synchronous or asynchronous communication platforms" (Markscheffel, Fischer, & Stelzer, 2006, p. 463).

Some research has explored promising participant models for digital repositories. "Participant involvement is a critical factor not only in developing educational digital libraries, but also in sustaining the resources, the technology and most importantly, the communities who use them. Without converting casual or onetime users into recurring, involved participants, or even members of a community, educational digital libraries will simply be yet another example of, "If you build it, will they come" (Muramatsu, Giersch, McMartin, Weimar, & Klotz, 2004, p. 396).

A collaborative digital library is necessarily user centered: "This Digital Library scenario establishes a unique workspace for each particular community, supporting not only search and access but also process and work-flow management, information exchange, and distributed work group communications" (DELOS / NSF Working Group, 2003, p. 12).

Various tools have been integrated into digital libraries for a collaborative sub-structure and overlay. For example, blogs and wikis offer a way for content creators to interact with content users via the digital library. "Blogging provides a low barrier opportunity for time-constrained teachers to connect to busy scientists. Scientists, in turn, can share their knowledge and zeal through a blog, using it to debate the results of studies or events in real time, organize information, and relate their work to background materials, relevant areas of science, and the real world" (Krafft, Birkland, & Cramer, 2008, p. 319). A wiki allows for collaborative authoring of "resources with simple structured metadata" (Krafft, Birkland, & Cramer, 2008, p. 320).

Interactive, immersive, and discovery-based microworlds are being explored to add value to digital library contents but have been time-consuming and difficult to produce. "One proposed solution for accelerating production has been the creation of repositories of reusable software components or learning objects. Programmers would use such components to rapidly assemble larger-scale environments. Although many agree on the value of this approach, few repositories of such components have been successfully created. We suggest some reasons for the lack of expected results and propose two strategies for developing such repositories. We report on a case study that provides a proof of concept of these strategies" (Laleuf & Spalter, 2001, p. 33).

Intuitive content creation and annotation must be included in immersive spaces for co-learning: "Annotations in virtual spaces may include features such as comments on objects in the environment, guided tours through the virtual space, and a history mechanism so that the evolution of objects or portions of the space can be replayed and examined. In general terms, an annotation is simply a relationship between one object and another and we examine several methods of displaying these relationships. To extend annotations across communities, the system architecture supports naming and packaging object and meta-information and integration of content into a shared digital repository. By distributing to users the power to create,

edit, store, and retrieve objects and annotations, we promote development and re-use of meaningful content. Such systems can have great utility for the development of virtual environments for learning and research" (Kadobayashi, Lombardi, McCahill, Stearns, Tanaka, & Kay, 2005, p. 255).

Shared mental models may be co-created in information-rich digital libraries and repositories. Inherent in this perspective is the idea that digital libraries can provide users with interfaces, tools or services that help them to engage with, and make sense of, information provided across multiple, mixed media resources (e.g., text, videos, audio clips, interactive visualizations, etc.) that are made accessible in the libraries' large information spaces. In the distance learning literature, this is often referred to as 'resource-based learning,' which strives to offer learners choices in their learning materials and to accommodate individual differences through the provision of a wide selection of topically related, multimedia learning resources (Sumner & Marlino, 2004, p. 173).

Under this cognitive tool model, digital libraries provide scaffolding for both novices and experts in a field for resource-based learning. The interactive tools help learners interact with each other and the resources in creative ways. Media and informational literacies are built into the interactions within the digital libraries.

Workflow

Some digital libraries help structure user interactions with the affordances created by various technologies. Such workflows may enhance research strategies, source citations, and informational and media literacy.

A note-taking tool may help learners orient "search activities around student-generated guiding questions" (Sumner & Marlino, 2004, pp. 173 - 174). Part of the workflow may involve the annotation of the digital artifacts in the repository. "Such annotations manifest themselves in different forms and dimensions, ranging from simple highlighting of text and personal notes through (typed) links between documents up to nested and shared annotations with which collaborative discussions about a specific topic are realized" (Frommolz & Fuhr, 2006, p. 55). Using the contents of such annotations that were created before may tailor digital library services closer to learner needs. Even fragments or portions of documents cited by an annotation as a target . The workload may be lightened with simultaneous searching and reference linking across bibliographic resources on the Web (Mischo, Habing, & Cole, 2002).

User goal-directedness may enhance their use of an AI-enhanced digital library: "While valuable, this approach is most effective when people's interactions with digital libraries are purposefully driven by the need to quickly and accurately produce a singular and definitive result. Similarly, situations addressed by decision theories deal best when our choices are goal directed in the presence of options. It assumes that people know what they want in their interactions" (Leong, Howard, & Vetere, Apr. 2008, p. 716).

Users may be encouraged to build their own "digital libraries" as a sense-making task. "This naturally applies to students wishing to learn how to build DLs (digital libraries) or those who will need familiarity with their underlying nature" (Nichols, Bainbridge, Downie, & Twidale, 2006, pp. 185 – 186). Digital library toolkits may be employed for users to rebuild and re-index resources. For example, there may be an "interface to allow learners to explore and associate hypertext content with knowledge maps of their own creation" (Lawless, Hederman, & Wade, 2008, p. 167).

One aspect of workflow may involve the creation of private personal spaces in which users may organize resources and personalize that virtual space (Fernández, Sánchez, & García. 2000). There may be persistence to these spaces for long-time use. A central assumption is that learners own the contents to these spaces. There may be options to share private digital data for

collaborative research (Ye, Makedon, Steinberg, Shen, Ford, Wang, Zhao, & Kapidakis, 2003).

The encouragement of discovery and browsing by users may be built into the user interface and structure of the digital library. Ideally, serendipity as "the meaningful experience of chance encounters" will be part of this experience (Leong, Howard, & Vetere, 2008, p. 719).

Mediated Communications

Long-term evolution of collaborative digital repositories will require "the interplay of human relationships in order to promote the success of knowledge networks as 'social apparatuses'" (Bush & Tiwana, 2005, p. 68). There must be designs to promote efficiency "in ad hoc, self-supervising peer-to-peer search networks in information repositories" (Cooper & Garcia-Molina, 2005, pp. 169 – 200). Participants need to be able to build persistent identities and telepresences in these repositories and allow for individuals to interact virtually with a blend of shared interests and "swift trust."

User Contributions

User-created digital objects may be vetted and accepted into the various digital repositories to add value and freshness to the overall collection. Prototypical users may include researchers, instructors, and learners, and individuals from the various user groups may share new learning. Works may be versioned, with derived works connected to the fresher created works. Such new creations may be made semi-public or fully public, depending on the release status of the work.

Connections to Learning / Course Management Systems

Some digital libraries and repositories have been made interoperable with digital learning / course management systems. Some plug in as content cartridges based on particular subject matter. Other repositories are linked in through straightforward user interfaces. Many such systems have interoperability gaps (Arapi, Moumoutzis, & Christodoulakis, 2006, para. 1).

PEDAGOGICAL APPROACHES

Digital libraries have been evolving as sociotechnical systems, to build the patronage of their various stakeholders. Various pedagogical theories may be applied to the conceptualization of these as knowledge acquisition and knowledge building spaces: situated cognition, communities and networks of practice, inquiry learning, self-discovery learning, problem-based learning and project-based learning.

To actualize these spaces, digital libraries must move beyond the mere provision of access to relevant resources.

Digital libraries can provide effective support in the curriculum areas of presentation, exploration of material, and assessment. Support from digital libraries will aid educators in development of the curriculum. The improved curriculum will provide students with clearer presentations, more focused exploration of the material, and integrated assessments. Issues in digital library support of curriculum development include ways to address the needs of different users, the importance of complexity management, the requirements for digital libraries, the difference in student capabilities, and the emergence of national-level digital libraries (Carver, Hill, & Pooch, 1999, pp. 12c2-18 to 12c2-23).

How faculty approach using such repositories may vary. Digital libraries may be integrated with face-to-face, blended, or fully online learning—to support the assignments. They may provide resources for typical research. They may be used to fill gaps in the learning, related to media literacy. A new layer of virtual collaboration has been designed into digital libraries.

A pedagogical strategy for using a digital library needs to take into consideration the types of desired learning outcomes. At a basic level, the co-learning may involve knowledge ingestion and simple sharing of learning. This level may involve basic information, media literacies, and straightforward research. A higher level of learning may involve applied knowledge or the use of information to problem-solve and form strategies. An even higher level may lead to the co-creation of new knowledge through innovative applications of the information. This level assumes potential contribution to the digital library or repository.

Assessing Digital Libraries

The usability of digital libraries may be assessed with user testing through empirical techniques and usability personnel analysis using established methods. "However, none fit seamlessly with existing digital library development practices, highlighting an important area for further work to support improved usability" (Blandford, Keith, Connell, & Edwards, 2004, p. 27). Datamining of users' behaviors within the system may be analyzed for design improvements.

Digital libraries strive not only to provide access to information and knowledge but also the high impact of the materials, as captured in research citations and educational outcomes. This information may be captured and analyzed.

Traditional measures of research impact are citation counts for the article, citation counts for the researcher, and co-citation or co-text maps; we draw citation images and other networks to reveal invisible colleges, research fronts, and influences in a discipline. Traditional measures of educational impact include student scores on standardized tests and increased learning outcomes. They can also include web usage measures as well as case studies and stories of improved cognitive thinking, increased scientific reasoning behaviors greater motivation and the development

Figure 4. Collaborative Assignments Using Digital Libraries and Repositories

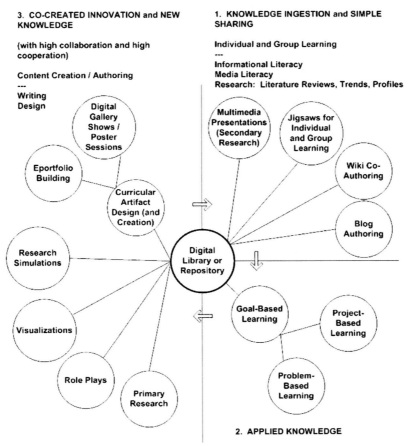

of similar habits of mind (Coleman, Bartolo, & Jones, 2005, p. 372).

Digital libraries will likely have to perform on a range of metrics in order to be competitive in the Webosphere, with their contents, information handling, security, and services to users at the center.

FUTURE ISSUES

Digital libraries and repositories of the future will likely be more complex. They may spawn centers of excellence in knowledge sharing and innovations, with star patrons and participants, in a global setting. They may involve ever more complex multimedia objects; they may be more common in ambient spaces through the uses of mobile devices. They may involve deeper layers of protection for unpublished individual contents and the contents created by teams. There may be more seamless connections between digital repositories and learning / content management systems (L/CMSes). More from-life contents may be archived digitally, through the automated capture of artifacts and the bequeathal of digital resources from public and private individuals and entities. Optimally, new efficiencies may arise in terms of ease-of-use, speed, and value-added contents. Such libraries may be direct publishers of prestige (multimedia) publications in academia and beyond.

CONCLUSION

Digital libraries and repositories are proliferating in a variety of fields and in many forms. These tools are critical aspects of competitive advantage. Many repositories are now being integrated into collaboratories built for researchers to conduct their collaborations and research (Baecker, Fono, & Wolf, 2007). In the Information Age, much collaboration occurs around valid, fresh and actionable information, and digital repositories and libraries will be critical virtual learning environments (VLEs) of the present and future. How users of today exploit these digital libraries and repositories will affect how these socio-technical systems evolve and the interactive functionality built into them. Their activism today will also affect the quality of the informational contents.

ACKNOWLEDGMENT

Thanks to Dr. Howard W. Beck for the introduction to an educational repository and some of its many possibilities, back in 2006, under the auspices of a biosecurity project. Thanks to Dr. Beth Unger, Rob Caffey, and Scott Finkeldei of K-State, for the first "yes" that started this line of inquiry. Thanks to Donna Schenck-Hamlin for her ability to see possibilities and make connections between people, technology, and information. I am grateful to all the supervisors and colleagues through the years who've taught me about handling information. I am thankful, too, to R. Max, always.

REFERENCES

Abowd, G. D., Harvel, L. D., & Brotherton, J. A. (2001). Building a digital library of captured educational experiences. In *Proceedings of the International Conference on Digital Libraries: Research and Practice, 2000, Kyoto* (pp. 467-474). Washington, DC: IEEE.

Adams, A., & Blandford, A. (2005). Digital libraries' support for the user's 'information journey.' In *Proceedings of the JCDL '05* (pp. 160-169). New York: ACM.

Arapi, P., Moumoutzis, N., & Christodoulakis, S. (2006). ASIDE: An architecture for supporting interoperability between digital libraries and elearning applications. In *Proceedings of the Sixth International Conference on Advanced Learning Technologies (ICALT '06)*. Washington, DC: IEEE.

Aridor, Y., Carmel, D., Maarek, Y. S., Soffer, A., & Lempel, R. (2002). Knowledge encapsulation for focused search from pervasive devices. *ACM Transactions on Information Systems, 20*(1), 25–46. doi:10.1145/503104.503106

Baecker, R. M., Fono, D., & Wolf, P. (2007). Toward a video collaboratory. In R. Goldman, R. Pea, B. Barron, & S. J. Denny (Eds). *Video research in the learning sciences* (pp. 462). Mahwah, NJ: Lawrence Erlbaum Associates, Publishers.

Bainbridge, D., Ke, K.-Y., & Witten, I. H. (2006). Document level interoperability for collection creators. In *Proceedings of the JCDL '06* (pp. 105-106). New York: ACM.

Baker, K. S., Gold, A. K., & Sudholt, F. (2003). FLOW: Co-constructing low barrier repository infrastructure in support of heterogeneous knowledge collection(s). In *Proceedings of the 2003 Joint Conference on Digital Libraries* (pp. 397). Washington, DC: IEEE.

Bar-Yossef, Z., Keidar, I., & Schonfeld, U. (2007). Do not crawl in the DUST: Different URLs with similar text. In *Proceedings of the WWW 2007 / Track: Data Mining, Mining Textual Data. International World Wide Web Conference Committee (IW3C2)* (pp. 111-120). New York: ACM.

Bekaert, J., Liu, X., Van de Sompel, H., Lagoze, C., Payette, S., & Warner, S. (2006, June). *Pathways core: A data model for cross-repository services.* In Proceedings of the 6th ACM/IEEE-CS Joint Conference on Digital Libraries (pp. 368-368). New York: ACM.

Berman, F. (n.d.). One hundred years of data. In *Proceedings of the 2006 International Conference on Digital Government Research* (pp. 3-4). New York: ACM.

Birnbaum, J. S. (2004). Cybersecurity considerations for digital libraries in an era of pervasive computing. In *Proceedings of the JCDL '04* (pp. 169). New York: ACM.

Blandford, A., Keith, S., Connell, I., & Edwards, H. (2004). Analytical usability evaluation for digital libraries: A case study. In *Proceedings of the 2004 Joint ACM / IEEE Conference on Digital Libraries (JCDL '04)* (pp. 27-36).

Blanton, M. (2008). Online subscriptions with anonymous access. In [New York: ACM.]. *Proceedings of the ASIACCS, 08*, 217–227. doi:10.1145/1368310.1368342

Bottoni, P., Civica, R., Levialdi, S., Orso, L., Panizzi, E., & Trinchese, R. (2004). MADCOW: A multimedia digital annotation system. In *Proceedings of the AVI '04* (pp. 55-62). New York: ACM.

Buchanan, G., & Hinze, A. (2005). A generic alerting service for digital libraries. In *Proceedings of the JCDL '05* (pp. 131-140). New York: ACM.

Bush, A. A., & Tiwana, A. (2005). Designing sticky knowledge networks. *Communications of the ACM, 48*(5), 67–71. doi:10.1145/1060710.1060711

Callan, J. Smeaton, Al., Beaulieu, M., Borlund, P., Brusilovsky, P., Chalmers, M., Lynch, C., Riedl, J., Smyth, B., Straccia, U., & Toms, E. (2003, May). *Personalization and recommender systems in digital libraries* (joint NSF-EU DELOS working group report). Retrieved February 6, 2009, from http://dli2.nsf.gov/internationalprojects/working_group_reports/personalisation.html

Calvanese, D., Catarci, T., & Santucci, G. (2000). Building a digital library of newspaper clippings: The LAURIN Project. In *Proceedings of the IEEE Advances in Digital Libraries 2000, ADL 2000* (pp. 15-26). Washington, DC: IEEE.

Capodiferro, L., Neri, A., Nibaldi, M., & Jacovitti, G. (2004). Robust detail recognition and location technique for image retrieval in digital repositories. In *Proceedings of the Eighth International Conference on Information Visualization (IV '04)*. Washington, DC: IEEE.

Carver, C. A., Hill, J. M. D., & Pooch, U. W. (1999). Emerging curriculum issues in digital libraries. In *Proceedings of the 29th ASEE / IEEE Frontiers in Education Conference*. Washington, DC: IEEE.

Chen, C.-C., Wactlar, H. D., Wang, J. Z., & Kiernan, K. (2005). Digital imagery for significant cultural and historical materials: An emerging research field bridging people, culture, and technologies. *International Journal on Digital Libraries, 5*, 275–286. doi:10.1007/s00799-004-0097-5

Clarkson, E., & Foley, J. D. (2006). Browsing affordance designs for the human-centered computing educational digital library. In *Proceedings of the JCDL '06* (pp. 361). New York: ACM.

Coleman, A. S., Bartolo, L. M., & Jones, C. (2005). Impact: The last frontier in digital library evaluation. In *Proceedings of the JCDL '05* (pp. 372). New York: ACM.

Cooper, B. F., & Garcia-Molina, H. (2005). Ad hoc, self-supervising peer-to-peer search networks. *ACM Transactions on Information Systems, 23*(2), 169–200. doi:10.1145/1059981.1059983

De Carvalho, M. G., Goncalves, M. A., Laender, A. H. F., & da Silva, A. S. (2006). Learning to deduplicate. In *Proceedings of the JCDL '06* (pp. 41-50). New York: ACM.

Dunn, J.W., & Cowan, W.G. (2005). EVIADA: Ethnomusicological video for instruction and analysis digital archive. *TCDL Bulletin, 2*(1).

EU-US working group on spoken-word audio collections. (n.d.) Retrieved February 6, 2009, from http://www.dli2.nsf.gov/internationalprojects/working_group_reports/spoken_word.html

Fernández, L., Sánchez, J.A., & García, A. (2000). MiBiblio: Personal spaces in a digital library universe. In *Digital libraries* (pp. 232-233). New York: ACM.

Frommolz, I., & Fuhr, N. (2006). Probabilistic, object-oriented logics for annotation-based retrieval in digital libraries. In *Proceedings of the JCDL '06* (pp. 55-64). New York: ACM.

Glick, K. L., Wilczek, E., & Dockins, R. (2006). The ingest and maintenance of electronic records: Moving from theory to practice. In *Proceedings of the JCDL '06* (pp. 359).

Gold, A. K., Baker, K. S., LeMeur, J.-Y., & Baldridge, K. (2002). Building FLOW: Federating libraries on the Web. In *Proceedings of the JCDL '02* (pp. 287-288). New York: ACM.

Gorton, D., Shen, R., Vemuri, N. S., Fan, W., & Fox, E. A. (2006). ETANA-GIS: GIS for archaeological digital libraries. In *Proceedings of the JCDL '06* (pp. 379). New York: ACM.

Hank, C., Choemprayong, S., & Sheble, L. (2007). Blogger perceptions on digital preservation. In *Proceedings of the JCDL '07* (pp. 477). New York: ACM.

Hatala, M., Kalantari, L., Wakkary, R., & Newby, K. (2004). Ontology and rule based retrieval of sound objects in augmented audio reality system for museum visitors. In *Proceedings of the 2004 ACM Symposium on Applied Computing* (pp. 1045-1050). New York: ACM.

Hűser, C., Reichenberger, K., Rostek, L., & Streitz, N. (1995). Knowledge-based editing and visualization for hypermedia encyclopedias. *Communications of the ACM, 38*(4), 49–51. doi:10.1145/205323.205333

Iverson, L. (2004). Collaboration in digital libraries: A conceptual framework. In *Proceedings of the JCDL '04* (pp. 380). New York: ACM.

Janssen, W. C. (2004). Collaborative extensions for the UpLib System. In *Proceedings of the JCDL '04* (pp. 239-240). New York: ACM.

Kadobayashi, R., Lombardi, J., McCahill, M. P., Stearns, H., Tanaka, K., & Kay, A. (2005). Annotation authoring in collaborative 3D virtual environments. In . *Proceedings of the ICAT, 2005*, 255–256. doi:10.1145/1152399.1152452

Kholief, M., Shen, S., & Maly, K. (2000). Event-based retrieval from digital libraries containing streamed data. In *Proceedings of the International Conference on Information Technology: Coding and Computing* (pp. 234). Washington, DC: IEEE.

Knees, P., Schedl, M., Pohle, T., & Widmer, G. (2006). An innovative three-dimensional user interface for exploring music collections enriched with meta-information from the Web. In [New York: Association for Computing Machinery, Inc.]. *Proceedings of the MM, 06*, 17–24.

Ko, K. H., Maekawa, T., Patrikalakis, N. M., Masuda, H., & Wolter, F.-E. (2003). Shape intrinsic fingerprints for free-form object matching. In [New York: ACM.]. *Proceedings of the SM, 03,* 196–27.

Krafft, D. B., Birkland, A., & Cramer, E. J. (2008, June). NCore: Architecture and implementation of a flexible, collaborative digital library. In *Proceedings of the JCDL '08* (pp. 313-322). New York: ACM.

Krowne, A., & Halbert, M. (2005). An initial evaluation of automated organization for digital library browsing. In *Proceedings of the JCDL '05* (pp. 246-255). New York: ACM.

Kumar, A. (2007). Visual understanding environment. In Proceedings of the JCDL '07 (pp. 510). New York: ACM.

Laleuf, J. R., & Spalter, A. M. (2001). A component repository for learning objects: A progress report. In *Proceedings of the JCDL '01* (pp. 33-40). New York: ACM.

Lawless, S., Hederman, L., & Wade, V. (2008). Enhancing access to open corpus educational content: Learning in the wild. In [New York; ACM.]. *Proceedings of the HT, 08,* 167–174.

Leong, T. W., Howard, S., & Vetere, F. (2008, Apr.). Choice: Abdicating or exercising. In *CHI 2008 Proceedings – Sound of Music* (pp. 715-724). New York: ACM.

Li, K., Liu, H., & Yu, H. (2007). VegaDLib: A service-oriented platform for building digital libraries. In *Proceedings of the The Sixth International Conference on Grid and Cooperative Computing (GCC 2007)*. Washington, DC: IEEE.

Lynch, C., Parastatidis, S., Jacobs, N., Van de Sompel, H., & Lagoze, C. (2007). The OAI-ORE effort: Progress, challenges, synergies. In *Proceedings of the JCDL '07* (pp. 80). New York: ACM.

Malizia, A. (2004). A cognition-based approach for querying personal digital libraries. In *Proceedings of the 2004 IEEE Symposium on Visual Languages and Human Centric Computing (VLHCC '04)*.

Manku, G. S., Jain, A., & Sarma, A. D. (2007). Detecting near-duplicates for Web crawling. In *Proceedings of the WWW 2007/ Track: Data Mining, Similarity Search. The International World Wide Web Conference Committee (IW3C2)* (pp. 141-149). New York: ACM.

Marincioni, F., & Lightsom, F. (2002). Marine realms information bank: A distributed geolibrary for the ocean. In *Proceedings of the JCDL '02* (pp. 399). New York: ACM.

Markscheffel, B., Fischer, D., & Stelzer, D. (2006). A business model-based classification approach for digital libraries. In *Proceedings of the 1st International Conference on Digital Information Management* (pp. 457-464). Washington, DC: IEEE.

McCaffrey, M., & Weston, T. (2005). The climate change collection: A case study on digital library collection review and the integration of research, education and evaluation. In *Proceedings of the International Conference on Digital Libraries. Proceedings of the 5th ACM / IEE-CS Joint Conference on Digital Libraries*, Denver, Colorado (pp. 392).

McCown, F., Smith, J. A., Nelson, M. L., & Bollen, J. (2006). Lazy preservation: Reconstructing websites by crawling the crawlers. In [ACM.]. *Proceedings of the WIDM, 06,* 67–74.

McIntyre, S. A., Dennis, S. E., Uijtdehaage, S. H. J., & Candler, C. S. (2004). A digital library for health sciences educators: The Health Education Assets Library (HEAL). In *Proceedings of the JCDL '04* (pp. 387).

Mischo, W. H., Habing, T. G., & Cole, T. W. (2003). Integration of simultaneous searching and reference linking across bibliographic resources on the Web. In *Proceedings of the 2nd ACM/IEEE-CS joint conference on digital libraries* (pp. 119-125). Washington, DC: IEEE.

Morris, C. M., Hembrooke, H., & Rayle, L. (2006). Finding a metaphor for collecting and disseminating distributed NSDL content and communications. In *Proceedings of the JCDL '06* (pp. 354). New York: ACM.

Muramatsu, B., Giersch, S., McMartin, F., Weimar, S., & Klotz, G. (2004). 'If you build it, will they come?' Lessons learned from the workshop on participant interaction in digital libraries. In *Proceedings of the 2004 Joint ACM/IEEE Conference on Digital Libraries (JCDL '04)* (pp. 396). Washington, DC: IEEE.

Nelson, M. L., Marchionini, G., Geisler, G., & Yang, M. (2001). A bucket architecture for the Open Video Project. In *Proceedings of the JCDL '01* (pp. 310-311). New York: ACM.

Nichols, D. M., Bainbridge, D., Downie, J. S., & Twidale, M. B. (2006). Learning by building digital libraries. In *Proceedings of the JCDL '06* (pp. 185-186). New York: ACM.

Nikolaidou, M., Anagnostopoulos, D., & Hatzopoulos, M. (2003). Using a medical digital library for education purposes. In *Proceedings of the 16th IEEE Symposium on* Computer-Based Medical Systems (CBMS '03).

O'Sullivan, D., McLoughlin, E., Bertolotto, M., & Wilson, D. C. (2003). Capturing task knowledge for geo-spatial imagery. In [New York: ACM.]. *Proceedings of the K-CAP*, *03*, 78–87.

Paelke, V., Reimann, C., & Rosenbach, W. (2003). A visualization design repository for mobile devices. In *Proceedings of the 2nd International Conference on Computer Graphics, Virtual Reality, Visualisation and Interaction in Africa* (pp. 57-61). New York: ACM.

Palmer, C., Zavalina, O., & Mustafoff, M. (2007, June). Trends in metadata practices: A longitudinal study of collection federation. In *Proceedings of the JCDL '07* (pp. 386-395). New York: ACM.

Pérez-Quiñones, M. A., Fox, E., Cassel, L., & Fan, W. (2006). Work in progress: Personalizing a course website using the NSDL. 36th ASEE / IEEE Frontiers in Education Conference. San Diego, California. IEEE. M3F-3 to M3F-4.

Rani, S., Goodkin, J., Cobb, J., Habing, T., & Urban, R. Eke, Jn., & Pearce-Moses, R. (2006). Technical architecture overview: Tools for acquisition, packaging and ingest of Web objects into multiple repositories. In *Proceedings of the JCDL '06* (pp. 360). New York; ACM.

Recker, M., & Palmer, B. (2006). Using resources across educational digital libraries. In *Proceedings of the JCDL '06* (pp. 240-241). New York: ACM.

Reuning, J., & Jones, P. (2005). Osprey: Peer-to-peer enabled content distribution. In *Proceedings of the JCDL '05* (pp. 396). New York: ACM. DELOS / NSF Working Group. (2003). *Reference models for digital libraries: Actors and roles*. Retrieved from http://delos-noe.iei.pi.cnr.it/activities/internationalforum/Joint-WGs/actors/Actors-Roles.pdf

Simske, S., & Lin, X. (2004). Creating digital libraries: Content generation and re-mastering. In *Proceedings of the First International Workshop on Document Image Analysis for Libraries (DIAL '04)*. Washington, DC: IEEE.

Smith, M. (2005). Eternal bits: How can we preserve digital files and save our collective memory? *IEEE Spectrum.*

Soergel, D. (2005). Thesauri and ontologies in digital libraries. In *Proceedings of the JCDL '05* (pp. 421). New York; ACM.

Suleman, H., Fox, E. A., & Abrams, M. (2000). Building quality into a digital library. In *Proceedings of the 5th ACM Conference on Digital Libraries* (pp. 228-229). New York: ACM.

Sumner, T., & Marlino, M. (2004). Digital libraries and educational practice: A case for new models. In *Proceedings of the JCDL '04* (pp. 170-178). New York: ACM.

Tarrant, D., Carr, L., & Payne, T. (2008). Releasing the power of digital metadata: Examining large networks of co-related publications. In *Proceedings of the JCDL '08* (pp. 471). New York: ACM.

TechDis. (2005, April). *Guidance on accessibility for JISC exchange for learning and digital libraries in the classroom projects.* Joint Information Systems Committee.

The Alexandria Digital Library Team. (2004). The Alexandria Digital Library and the Alexandria Digital Earth Prototype. In *Proceedings of the JCDL '04* (pp. 410). New York: ACM.

Torres, R., McNee, S. M., Abel, M., Konstan, J. A., & Riedl, J. (2004). Enhancing digital libraries with TechLens. In *Proceedings of the JCDL '04* (pp. 228-236). New York: ACM.

Tsai, W.-H., & Wang, H.-M. (2005). On the extraction of vocal-related information to facilitate the management of popular music collections. In Proceedings of the JCDL '05 (pp. 197-206). New York: ACM.

Tsolis, D. K., Tsolis, G. K., Karatzas, E. G., & Papatheodorou, T. S. (2002). Copyright protection and management and a Web based library for digital images of the Hellenic cultural heritage. In *Proceedings of the 2001 Conference on Virtual Reality, Archeology, and Cultural Heritage* (pp. 53-60). New York: ACM.

Tungare, M., Yu, X., Cameron, W., Teng, G. F., Pérez-Quiñones, M. A., & Cassel, L. (2007). Towards a syllabus repository for computer science courses. In [New York: ACM.]. *Proceedings of the SIGCSE, 07,* 55–59. doi:10.1145/1227504.1227331

Vemulapalli, S., Halappanavar, M., & Mukkamala, R. (2002). Security in distributed digital libraries: Issues and challenges. In *Proceedings of the International Conference on Parallel Processing Workshops (ICPPW'02).* IEEE.

Vuorikari, R. (2007). Can social information retrieval enhance the discovery and reuse of digital educational content? In [New York: ACM.]. *Proceedings of the RecSys, 07,* 207–210. doi:10.1145/1297231.1297276

Wang, C., Zhang, Y., & Zhang, F. (2007). User modeling for cross system personalization in digital libraries. In *Proceedings of the First IEEE Symposium on Information Technologies and Applications in Education, ISITAE '07* (pp. 238-243). Washington, DC: IEEE.

Wang, J.-H., Teng, J.-W., Cheng, P.-J., Lu, W.-H., & Chien, L.-F. (2004). Translating unknown cross-lingual queries in digital libraries using a Web-based approach. In *Proceedings of the 2004 Joint ACM/IEEE Conference on Digital Libraries (JCDL '04)* (pp. 108-116). New York: ACM.

Wong, S. C., Crowder, R. M., Wills, G. B., & Shadbolt, N. R. (2006). Knowledge engineering—from front-line support to preliminary design. In . *Proceedings of the DocEng, 06,* 44–52.

Yang, J., Han, J., Oh, I., & Kwak, M. (2007). Using Wikipedia technology for topic maps design. In . *Proceedings of the ACMSE, 2007*, 106–110.

Yaron, D. J., Davenport, Y. L., Karabinos, M., Leinhardt, G. L., Bartolo, L. M., Portman, J. J., et al. (2008). Cross-disciplinary molecular science education in introductory science courses: An NSDL MatDL collection. In *Proceedings of the JCDL '08* (pp. 70-73).

Ye, S., Makedon, F., Steinberg, T., Shen, L., Ford, J., & Wang, Y. (2003). SCENS: A system for the mediated sharing of sensitive data. In [Washington, DC: IEEE.]. *Proceedings of the Joint Conference on Digital Libraries, 2003*, 263–265.

Zhu, Q., Goncalves, M. A., & Fox, E. A. (2003). 5SGraph Demo: A graphical modeling tool for digital libraries. In *Proceedings of the 2003 Joint Conference on Digital Libraries (JCDL '03)*.

Zhuang, Z., Wagle, R., & Giles, C. L. (2005). What's there and what's not? Focused crawling for missing documents in digital libraries. In Proceedings of the JCDL '05 (pp. 301-310). New York: ACM.

KEY TERMS AND DEFINITIONS

Aggregation: An assemblage of objects

Collaborative Digital Library: A user-centered resource that provides services and access to digital multimedia resources

Collaboratory : A digital center for researchers with access to digital libraries, software sharing, high-interactivity communications, and "the ability to control remote instruments" (Baecker, Fono, & Wolf, 2007, p. 462)

Collection: A grouping of objects of a type, usually for a particular purpose, with semantic meaning

Data Stream: A sequence of data units captured often with timing information, from remote sensors, satellites, cameras, and other digital capture technologies

Digital Library (Electronic Library, Virtual Library, and E-Library): A collection of digital objects that are organized and labeled in a coherent and usable way

Georeferencing: A way of pointing to information based on the location of the data on the earth's surface, captured through aerial photography, satellite, and other forms of digital image and information capture

Intelligent Agent: An often-autonomous computerized entity that has been coded to act upon an environment

Metadata: Information about information, derived information nested aggregation (n): An assemblage of digital objects within other digital objects, in a hierarchical structure

Ontology: A rigorous structure of defined objects / entities and their relationships that describe a domain field or an aspect of a knowledge domain. A hierarchy of information

Repository: A storehouse for digital objects, with tools for submittal, archival, labeling, search, and extraction / download

University-Based Institutional Digital repository: A system for the management and dissemination of digital materials created by the institution's members, including theses, dissertations, journals, instructional materials, and other contents (often to help the campus retain copyright to some of the intellectual property output of their faculty and staff)

User interface: A communications system through which users may access a digital repository or library

Chapter 12
Creating a Motivated Online Graduate Community

Joan E. Aitken
Park University, USA

EXECUTIVE SUMMARY

The purpose of this chapter is to provide a case study of the problem solving processes of a faculty who developed a new graduate program in communication studies. Students could take all courses online, all onground, or use a combination of the two delivery formats. For the totally online program, a key desire was to help students and faculty achieve a sense of a collaborative community. Students needed to get to know each other and feel a part of the whole program, even though course delivery for some students was totally online. Further, the faculty sought to motivate students to engage in a challenging program of research and application.

CREATING A MOTIVATED ONLINE GRADUATE COMMUNITY

A student forwards fun animal picture emails to her professor. A professor sends out postcards to students directing them to the online café where they can "Expresso" themselves. A student sends hatching eggs to classmates on Facebook. Two students conduct class discussion via Skype. These are a few of the ways students and faculty are creating a sense of community in a new graduate program.

Communication technologies can provide networking opportunities for individuals to build and maintain relationships (e.g., Boase, 2008; Stern, 2008). Social networking sites are popular among college students, and they can be used to build relationships online (Tufekci, 2008). One study in China, for instance, suggested that an online community could accomplish "maintenance of harmony, revelation of identities, articulation of nostalgia, and reiteration of values" (Zhang, 2008). Many people like to use social networking sites, as evidenced in the relationship building with the political candidates during the 2008 political campaign for President of the United States (Erikson, 2008). Social network-

DOI: 10.4018/978-1-60566-878-9.ch012

ing gives people easy access to each other in interpersonal ways. When someone is "poked" on Facebook, for instance, the process is similar to saying "hi" when seeing a colleague in the hallway. This kind of mediated small talk may be quite useful in building and maintaining relationships (Miller, 2008). Thus, social networking sites can provide new communication channels so students and faculty can get to know others.

Teaching communication studies online can be challenging (Vanhorn, Pearson, & Child, 2008). Communication technologies can provide networking opportunities for students and faculty so that they can stay motivated. Collaborative learning—which may be one of the most effective learning strategies for the widest number of students--through groups has been successfully used in the distance learning process (Cho & Lee, 2008; Staggers, Garcia, & Nagelhout, 2008). Another advantages is that communication technologies can be used to motivate students (Edwards, Bresnahan, & Edwards, 2008; Mazer, Murphy, & Simonds, 2007).

Research suggests that online groups use a form of interpersonal communication (Wang, Walther, & Hancock, 2009), which can create community. Communication technologies can provide social networking opportunities for students and faculty so that they can create a feeling of community. News websites, for instance, can be used to help build a sense of community (Fisher, 2008). People use various communication channels in their effort to achieve interpersonal communication with people they do not know (Westerman, 2008), which suggests that such channels could be useful in building feelings of community between students in distance locations. These communication technologies are transforming higher education in ways that provide both prospects for improvements and challenges (Slevin, 2008). Thus, the purpose of this chapter is to discuss the use of communication technologies and the opportunities and challenges faced during the development of a new online and onground graduate program. By explaining

strategies used in this case, the reader may gain insights into community building approaches that may prove useful in other contexts.

BACKGROUND

This section provides a historical orientation to the case.

The University in this case had an established undergraduate program in communication studies, which uses traditional, face-to-face, distance location, and online courses. The administration of the university has actively worked to encourage faculty to develop more online courses, as has happened in other universities (Applegate, 2002). A key faculty member in the department developed the proposed graduate program, which was designed to be available onground and online, or through a combination of courses.

The University attracts many nontraditional and transfer students. Although distance education, continuing education, and online courses have been available at the institution for many years, the online graduate programs are relatively new. The new program means that faculty continue their traditional work while learning how to develop and teach effectively in both formats at the graduate level. Faculty have needed encouragement to engage in the diverse work and administrative complexities of putting a program online, which is consistent with findings at other universities (Matthews, 2008; Panda & Mishra, 2007).

With an expectation of rigor, the University's faculty have been particularly concerned about the quality of instruction and learning in the new program. Like at other universities (Matthews, 2008), the faculty seem divided on how to best employ learning technology in instruction.

Online Groups

With the advent of electronic listservs and the Internet, opportunities for support and information-sharing have increased through the use of online communities (Shedletsky & Aitken, 2004). These groups have permeated education, business, and social interactions. One important feature of the new graduate program in communication studies was to create a sense of a supportive learning community and to use research-based techniques to do so. Online communities have provided a new area of research interest. Ye (2006) found that international students in an online support group received more information and felt less stress. Kuster (2007) also found information value in online groups.

Research has sought to determine the reasons people select online classes, just as scholars have sought to determine why people join an online discussion group instead of a face-to-face group (Meyer, 2003). These reasons may include frequency of interaction, availability, a sense of anonymity, convenience, and the lack of pressure to talk in a group. The online choice works well for students who are highly motivated, learn well through reading and writing, or need flexibility for work, travel, or other reasons. Scholars continue to wonder if the personality of online students is different from onground students. Mesch (2006), for example, suggested that people with low self-esteem were more likely to be frequent Internet users.

In recent years, online collaboration and support have been areas of research that interest academics in higher education (e.g., Barker, VanSchaik, & Famakinwa, 2007; Baer, 2000; Curtis & Lawson, 2001; Petrides, 2002; Whatley & Bell, 2003). Online groups provide opportunities for learning and empathy for people who share interests or concerns. In fact, the value of online support groups can be as important to the members as a face-to-face support groups are to their members (Turner, Grube, & Meyers, 2001). This finding suggests that online community may be extremely important to students too.

For online students, e-learning can be successful and provide some advantages (Luppicini, 2007). In fact, some faculty believe that the online format works extremely well for reflection and opinion discussion. Further, the sense of anonymity in the nature of online interaction may actually increase the quality and depth of member responses through personal disclosure, reciprocity, and personal acceptance (VanLear, Sheehan, Withers & Walker, 2005).

Every teacher knows that each class develops a personality. The social construction of the learning collaboration creates something unique based on the people who interact together. This personality or social construction seems less clear in the online environment. Scholars have discussed the need for students and teachers to determine where they will locate themselves in the social space of the classroom (Anagnostopoulos, Basmadjian, & McCrory, 2005). They suggest the following:

Not only does the virtual classroom lack the shared expectations and social conventions associated with the face-to-face classroom, it also lacks markers that root it in any particular place. Unlike face-to-face classrooms, virtual classrooms are radically disassociated from the locales in which teachers and students live their everyday lives. Identifying the textual devices teachers and students use to construct social presence in online classrooms is a step towards understanding how teachers and students respond to the delocalized classroom space. (p. 1700)

Faculty may be able to create some social conventions and locate the classroom in a space. One would suspect that a possible outcome, however, might be that unless faculty and students can create a collaborative learning environment, online learning may be less meaningful, less engaging, or less motivating than the face-to-face environment.

SETTING THE STAGE

Technology and management considerations are discussed in this section. Collaborative solutions in program development were arrived at with the help of staff, faculty, and students. The University uses course environment software—such as Blackboard, Blackboard, WebTycho, eCollege, or First Class—which is available to all faculty who teach onground or online. This system contains communication technologies capable of instant messaging, document sharing, and other standard features. Scholars have discussed the importance of effectively facilitating online discussion (Rovai, 2007), which was a key element of each online course. Because the course platform allows chat, a discussion board, website sharing, and document sharing, students can and do converse in various ways. Instant messaging, for example, tends to be popular among college students (Flanagin, 2005). This kind of nteractivity between students and faculty is essential to the success of a collaborative learning community (Mabrito, Dyrud, & Worley, 2001).

Each course package was prepared in a style so the course could be taught by other faculty. The University pays each faculty member who wants to develop an online course as an incentive for putting the course online and keeping it up-to-date. Staff from the online instruction department facilitated all administrative aspects of the course development, course copying, and similar duties. A wider array of learning strategies were provided as the courses evolved. Although the course environment is the centerpiece for instruction and communication, additional technology use is an important part of the program's success.

Institutional Support

Faculty worked with staff to obtain high quality library research databases for all students to use. The University's separate email system can be used through the course environment or externally.

An online syllabus system required faculty to post their syllabi one month before classes began. Course development faculty can put a template syllabus up for the course, which any faculty can copy and modify for his or her use in teaching. A colleague reviewed each syllabus, so there was a sense of transparency and preparation for a larger audience.

Teleconferencing

In the beginning stages, all faculty were located on or near the main campus, and faculty did sometimes meet together via teleconferencing. Teleconferencing has been shown to be an effective method (Rourke & Kanuka, 2007). Some teleconferencing was used to enable students at a distance to participate in a traditional face-to-face course. Class meetings for one course were held in real time using Skype. Although faculty encouraged the students to come to campus for the final defense of their thesis, committee meetings for online students were provided via teleconferencing.

WebPages

Faculty can create tutorials, which they put in the course environment or external web services. The University also provides access to its own webpage system for faculty, plus faculty can use their own private webpage services. The university requires that their IT staff upload all information to regular university system webpages. While this creates consistency for an attractive web resource, the process fails to have the flexibility needed for faculty pages. One faculty member set up a series of webpages on the faculty member's private website. These pages had several purposes.

One faculty member set up a fun page for the graduate students. A fun webpage with pictures of students allowed students and faculty to see each other. The faculty member asked students to provide photos and information about themselves.

In some cases, the students provided photos of themselves, while others provided pets, grandchildren, or artwork. The idea was to provide some kind of personal information to help students know each other.

The faculty created several tutorials, including ones for submitting to the Institutional Review Board, using American Psychological Association writing style, and conducting research using the University library's online databases.

In addition, a faculty member created an information page for expectations for Graduate Theses.

Computer Support

The University owns several laptop carts, which can be wheeled into on-campus classrooms. Each laptop contains a wireless card, and the carts contain enough laptops so each student in the face-to-face course can have a laptop to use during the class. In some cases, students bring their own power adapter to make sure they will have computer access for long classes. In other cases, students bring their own laptop computers to use during the class. This way the face-to-face class can be used as a lab environment when appropriate.

Free Internet Services

Faculty may take advantage of the many free Internet services in their classes. One faculty member encouraged students to create a group for students in Facebook.com. Facebook has been shown to be potentially effective in enhancing motivation and classroom climate (Mazer, Murphy, & Simonds, 2007). Faculty can use Facebook.com, for example, to set up a Facebook group to add another dimension to the course. Extensive free online services can be used for student communication during courses. Free services used by faculty include the following: Google Blog, Webpages at Glogster.com, and wikis at Pbwiki.

com. Today, blogging, webpages, and wikis are part of the Blackboard service.

Integrating Communication Methods

One faculty member was extremely effective in using email and telephone calls to students. For another faculty member, handwritten personal notes sent to students seemed to engage their spirit of community.

One faculty member encouraged students to write private snail mail notes to a student who was deployed to Iraq during the course and thus unable to communicate with the class via email for a week.

Although not part of the typical technology, one faculty member had several different advertising-type postcards printed that could be sent easily to students, while adding a personal note on the back. Postcards were designed to be reminders or encouragement for students at a distance.

When one student had a baby the last week of class, one faculty member sent a gift on behalf of the department. When another student had a seriously ill child, a faculty member arranged for a gift to be sent to the hospital.

One faculty member encouraged online students to participate in a gift exchange of inexpensive gifts—such as a bookmark—between students via postal mail.

A faculty member made a point of visiting a distance education student in Alaska, while on vacation. The face-to-face meeting allowed the faculty member to meet the student and talk about the program. The student said the encounter made him feel more connected to the program. The University also paid for another faculty member to visit students at an international distance location.

CASE DESCRIPTION

In this section, an overview of the example program is described.

Unlike a graduate program that evolves from a group of faculty who teach undergraduate students, there was only one full-time faculty member teaching this general content. The faculty member spent years planning the course goals and courses until the University received approval to begin the new graduate program. After the faculty member developed the structure for the program, full-time and part-time faculty were hired to teach in the program. Only the basic courses were setup in the beginning. Over the years, additional courses were approved through the Curriculum Committee and developed for online instruction. Typically, faculty taught the course onground to develop materials, then used those materials to develop the online course.

Universities often design a program, then hire faculty to meet those needs. One of the advantages of an online program is that faculty can be recruited at a distance. The challenge then becomes: How do full-time faculty make part-time faculty feel a committed part of the program? This program was able to find excellent local part-time faculty from neighboring institutions, who were willing to teach online. The main advantages here is that these highly-skilled faculty members had considerable flexibility in teaching part-time online, and they were able to develop additional electives for the program.

Starting Any Term

Online students may seem more impulsive about trying a program than do the onground students. Some online students typically enroll in this graduate program at any time and register for courses at the last minute. When starting an online program, there are too few students to stick with a logical sequence approach to taking courses. This flexibility means that a student may start a course without the basic information needed. Although a program in communication, students come from engineering, health care, business, and psychology, so the new students do not necessarily have what they

need in background theory, research skills, and academic perspectives. One of the strengths and challenges of the field of communication is that this interdisciplinary field attracts people from an array of academic areas.

1. Advertising
2. Business
3. Cultural Studies
4. Education
5. English
6. Ethnic and Women's Studies
7. Health
8. Information Systems
9. Linguistics
10. Political Science
11. Sociology
12. Psychology

Communication is seen as an approach within many fields because nearly all employees can benefit from more effective communication skills. What happened in this communication program was that some students came from diverse backgrounds, without previous experience in communication as an academic field. Students came from psychology, engineering, business, health, and other fields. These students had never conducted any research in communication, lacked knowledge of communication theories, and never read a journal in communication. This lack of academic experience meant that while some students had an undergraduate degree in the field of communication, others had no background. When students were in a course where they had to write a research paper with a review of literature, some students failed to use a single peer-reviewed article from the field of communication. These students had their own field and seemed to lack the motivation to learn the theories and perspectives of a new field.

To solve the problem of insufficient academic backgrounds in the field, a one-hour introductory course was added to every term of the schedule so that each student could learn the basics for success. Students needed to feel comfortable with the field of communication studies in order to make sense of materials and stay motivated in their other courses. The new course was designed to introduce students to the skills necessary to do well in the program. The class focused on the structure of the discipline, library research, reading communication research, types of research methods, APA style, and writing. The class is offered each term in the online format and designed to be taken concurrently with the student's first course in the degree program. As described in the rationale for the course:

Material making up this course has been spread across multiple classes. Because students "jump in" at varying times, it is impossible to know if they have been exposed to training in these introductory skills. We believe this hurts student performance in classes when they have missed the core courses. Pulling the material into one short course will lighten the load on the core courses and allow students to perform better in their coursework. This will prepare students to do the library research and writing that is required in our courses.

8-Week Format

The graduate program primarily offers an 8-week course format five times a year. Other formats include 16-week, 2-week, and weekend formats. For the graduate program, students are encouraged to take one course per term, although some students take more and others take less. After trying different formats with limited success, the faculty decided to use only the 8 week accelerated courses. Basically, the administrative requirements of course coordination and student preferences for efficiency and predictability suggested the 8-week format works best in this program.

Pay for Part-Time Faculty

When the program began, part-time faculty were paid per student, based on the size of enrollment in week three of the term. The rationale for this approach was that faculty who taught well and worked hard to retain students would be rewarded for their efforts. For a new online graduate program, however, that meant that part-time faculty were paid too little to make teaching worth their while. Thus, a new system was put in place that would require a certain number of students to enroll in a course for it to make, then the faculty member would be paid a flat fee. This approach seemed much more effective for everyone involved.

The program is dependent on part-time faculty for teaching courses, and students often make strong connections with some of those faculty. Particularly in an online format, students see all faculty as equals. Many students ask part-time faculty to serve on their committees, advise their thesis or project, and more. For the full-time faculty member service is part of his or her load. For part-time faculty, they need some kind of additional incentives. A stipend is paid for any independent study student, including project and thesis advising.

Graduate Research Projects and Thesis

Part of the challenge of developing a quality program is whether or another program exists that can be serve as a template for the new program. In this case, there was no established program that required a research component. When distance students began to conduct research, the faculty needed to figure out how they could be confident that procedures for researching human subjects could indeed be followed. Students at a distance would write up what they planned to do. At a distance, they would be trusted to conduct the research according to the proposal plan.

An additional strength and challenge of the field of communication is that this interdisciplinary field uses an array of research methods. The department began by trying to teach the basics of many different research methods.

1. Analysis of dynamic processes
2. Computational modeling
3. Content and textual analysis
4. Critical and cultural analysis
5. Discourse analysis
6. Ethnographic research
7. Ethnography and field observation
8. Experimental research
9. Feminist methods
10. Historiography
11. Mathematical modeling and simulations
12. Media effects analysis
13. Narrative writing
14. Network analysis
15. Organizational audit
16. Rhetorical criticism
17. Survey research

Two research courses were designed to introduce students to the research process: Qualitative Research Methods and Experimental Research Methods. The Experimental Methods course was broadened to introduce quantitative methods. Online instruction meant that a faculty member who had never seen a student, had no idea of what the research context would be like, and had a limited sense about the student's ability to comply with federal and school regulations would be conducting research on human subjects. This procedure gave a whole new meaning to the idea that the research method had to be planned out sufficiently so that anyone could pick up the proposal and conduct the research. As a safety precaution, faculty typically followed these expectations.

1. No participants under 18.

2. No participants who are members of a protected population (e.g., minors, pregnant females, incarcerated, or infirm).
3. No research that provides any financial gain to anyone.
4. No collection of health information.
5. No collection of names or any demographic information (e.g., age, ethnicity, religion).
6. No research that involves anything beyond minimal risk.
7. No use of deception.
8. No use of video or audiotaping.
9. No use of a sensitive topic (e.g., drug use, sexual practices, aggressive behavior, criminal activity).

Course Development

With a new program, new courses, and a small faculty, the Program Director recruited faculty to teach the courses. Each course had to be developed online in a way that would provide content consistency, while allowing faculty flexibility. One way of creating consistency was to create a master list of the books and materials permitted for each course.

When the program first began, the course environment was being tested in a Beta stage, which had an array of bugs that frustrated many faculty. Often the software did not work. When a problem arose, the screen would say the problem had been reported, when in fact it was not. When new versions of course environment software are installed, additional operation quirks and changes can develop, which may be frustrating for faculty. A system for listening and responding to student and faculty problems is essential. If students cannot get the course environment to operate in a new version of their favorite course browser or on a new computer, for example, this problem may affect their frustration levels.

Assessment

The faculty have decided to use the comprehensive exams as a program assessment tool. What this requires is developing a rubric that all faculty can use in grading comprehensive exams. Faculty need to determine whether or not to create a pool of questions to be distributed from one faculty member or to use the comprehensive exams as part of the Project and Thesis Committee function. There also is collaborative discussion about whether questions should seek to be directly tied to the program goals. The comprehensive exams, theses, and projects are tied to the program assessment process. The magnitude of responsibilities for building a successful program from scratch has been a challenge. Faculty believe they need ways to work smarter and more efficiently to help students succeed and meet their program goals.

CURRENT CHALLENGES FACING THE ORGANIZATION

Although the program is well underway, there are still decisions that face the people involved. There seems to be a move on the part of the online instruction department to have online courses developed so extensively—regarding content and procedures--that faculty are primarily facilitators. Scholars have discussed the importance of effectively facilitating online discussion (Rovai, 2007). This approach is consistent with the findings of Anagnostopoulos, Basmadjian, and McCrory (2005):

We think it is important for online teachers to consider the challenges and potential of being decentered in the classroom. Our study suggests that because of the separation of time and space, students can position the individual teacher on the sidelines, or on the backstages, of the classroom, even as they engage in the tasks created and assigned by the teacher. (p. 1726)

At this point, faculty have not received approval to use blended learning despite the perceived advantages of the approach suggested in research literature (e.g., Boyle, Bradley, Chalk, Jones, & Pickard, 2003; Darian, 2008; Oravec, 2003; Schweizer, Paechter, Weidenmann, 2003). Blended learning in the future may be a way of integrating a wider array of communication technologies for effective learning. In a time of economic constraints, faculty may want to use freeware or inexpensive technologies to enhance the sense of community. Using freeware requires faculty to find the software on their own and implement its use without support from the institution. Making the right technology selections is complicated (Minocha & Roberts, 2008). The implementation may take extra work and be a temporary experiment or solution. Creating and maintaining a sense of community is distance education graduate programs can be full of challenges (Laru & Jarvela, 2008).

At the time the new graduate communication program began, the entire University was restructured. Because of those changes, there was little tradition or understanding of the lines of responsibility. This lack of clarity has caused some problems regarding collaboration while faculty and administrators try to figure out who should be doing what. By keeping everyone involved in the collaboration, a sense of cooperation continues to develop among the faculty. Since that time, faculty have worked with administrators to clarify the lines of responsibility and who needs to be consulted from areas outside the department (e.g., Online Instructional Department, Graduate School, Dean, Registrar). Clarity on responsibilities will be helpful for launching any new program.

As the program expands, keeping track of student progress, committees, projects, and thesis will become more complicated, so that a clear student advising and mentoring process is in place. The difficulties in motivating students in this program seemed most challenging when students first began the program and again near the end of the program. Some students were frustrated with the adaptation to the online format in early stages. Some students felt confused, overwhelmed, and disconnected. All student advising was given to one faculty member so there was consistency in contacting and encouraging students to stay on track. As the program expands, new administrative procedures may be essential.

LESSONS LEARNED

In contemplating the lessons learned, they seem to fall into a few categories. Perhaps the two overriding principles for effectiveness are to plan and adapt. As soon as one problem is worked out, another idea or decision will be needed. The faculty continue to face challenges on many levels. Here are some of the lessons learned during the first years of the program.

1. Encourage students to take the format they prefer given their needs at the moment and consider using a blended approach to instruction. The program has local students who prefer to take courses online, so the program has difficulty filling onground courses.
2. Make connections with all parties involved. Inconsistent management, lack of needed support from the online staff, and employee turnover sometimes make it difficult for students and faculty to have questions answered.
3. Work toward a collaborative environment. Conflict between online staff and faculty arose because the online staff made decisions without consulting faculty and vice versa.
4. Adapt to the needs of nontraditional students. The average age of the University's students is 32, so these are students who have many external demands on their time. Students came and went and came back according to personal demands, so in this program students are allowed seven years to completion.

For students who work well independently, the online approach can work well (Pearson & Lewin, 2005).

5. Set admission standards and expectations for quality from the beginning of the program. A few students who came from less rigorous programs had an attitude that they just needed to enroll in a course to receive a high grade.
6. Find ways to reward part-time faculty and avoid faculty burnout. The program has many part-time faculty, who need to feel appreciated and rewarded.
7. Show appreciation to students who give feedback for improving the program and show patience about improving the program. Given the university is a predominantly undergraduate institution, the first students had to pave the way for completing comprehensive exams, designing research projects, preparing theses, and meeting evolving university and department guidelines.
8. Find ways to make sure students know the nature and expectations of the program. Because courses are free for employees, a large number of students enrolled were University staff, which sometimes caused questions about roles or inter-campus work.
9. Find ways to increase enrollment in order to secure the program's future. Economic pressures meant that small classes could not make, and previously promised faculty hires had to be postponed.

CONCLUSION

As one faculty member said: "Some classes are just hard to teach online!" A student enrolled in one course online during the summer and dropped the course. He then enrolled in a face-to-face (onground) session, and after the first night said to the professor: "I've learned more in one night than during weeks online during the summer." One could say that this comment has more to say about the student's learning style than anything else, but it also suggests something about the immediacy of faculty-student interaction in the onground section, which was lacking in the online section. Sometimes teaching and learning online seem particularly challenging.

This chapter has discussed the overall strategies used for developing a new graduate program in onground and online formats in hopes of generating ideas for other faculty facing similar challenges. In this case, the faculty in this program are beginning to feel a sense of stability and success. The intricacies of a new graduate program seem complicated by the online format, but the students and faculty have been motivated to make it work. As students, faculty, and administrators work to improve the foundation laid for this program, they feel motivated to work collaboratively for student success.

REFERENCES

Anagnostopoulos, D., Basmadjian, K. G., & McCrory, R. S. (2005). The decentered teacher and the construction of social space in the virtual classroom. *Teachers College Record, 107*(8), 1699–1729. doi:10.1111/j.1467-9620.2005.00539.x

Applegate, J. (2002). Chairs and deans develop strategies to motivate faculty and engage programs. *Spectra, 38*(2), 5.

Baer, W. (2000). Competition and collaboration in online distance learning. *Information Communication and Society, 3*(4), 457–473. doi:10.1080/13691180010002341

Barker, P., VanSchaik, P., & Famakinwa, O. (2007). Building electronic performance support systems for first-year university students. *Innovations in Education and Teaching International, 44*(3), 243–255. doi:10.1080/14703290701486530

Benoit, P. J., Benoit, W., Milyo, J., & Hansen, G. (2006). *The effects of traditional vs. Web-assisted instruction on student learning and satisfaction.* Columbia, MO: University of Missouri.

Boase, J. (2008). Personal networks and the personal communication system. *Information Communication and Society, 11*(4), 490–508. doi:10.1080/13691180801999001

Boyle, T., Bradley, C., Chalk, P., Jones, R., & Pickard, P. (2003). Using blended learning to improve student success rates in learning to program. *Journal of Educational Media, 28*(2/3), 165–178. doi:10.1080/1358165032000153160

Cho, H., & Lee, J. (2008). Collaborative information seeking in intercultural computer-mediated communication groups: Testing the influence of social context using social network analysis. *Communication Research, 35*(4), 548–573. doi:10.1177/0093650208315982

Curtis, D. D., & Lawson, M. J. (2001). Exploring collaborative online learning. *JALN, 5*(1), 21–34.

Darian, S. (2008). Preparing for blended e-learning. *Technical Communication, 55*(3), 285–287.

Edwards, C., Bresnahan, K., & Edwards, A. (2008). The influence of humorous positive computer-mediated word-of-mouth communication on student motivation and affective learning. *Texas Speech Communication Journal, 33*(1), 1–8.

Erikson, E. (2008). Hillary is my friend: MySpace and political fandom. *Rocky Mountain Communication Review, 5*(1), 3–16.

Faiola, A., & MacDorman, K. (2008). The influence of holistic and analytic cognitive styles on online information design: Toward a communication theory of cultural cognitive design. *Information Communication and Society, 11*(3), 348–374. doi:10.1080/13691180802025418

Fisher, D. (2008). Building community online: A twice-weekly's experience extending its reach with the Hartsville Today citizen-based news site. *Grassroots Editor, 49*(4), 12–18.

Flanagin, A. (2005). IM online: Instant messaging use among college students. *Communication Research Reports, 22*(3), 175–187. doi:10.1080/00036810500206966

Jaya, R. (2008). Skype voice chat a tool for teaching oral communication. *Language in India, 8*(12), 9.

Kuster, J. (2007). Facilitating group therapy and support meetings. *ASHA Leader, 12*(7), 30–31.

Laru, J., & Järvelä, S. (2008). Social patterns in mobile technology mediated collaboration among members of the professional distance education community. *Educational Media International, 45*(1), 17–32. doi:10.1080/09523980701847131

Luppicini, R. (2007). Review of computer mediated communication research for education. *Instructional Science, 35*(2), 141–185. doi:10.1007/s11251-006-9001-6

Mabrito, M., Dyrud, M., & Worley, R. (2001). Facilitating interactivity in an online business writing course. *Business Communication Quarterly, 64*(3), 81–86. doi:10.1177/108056990106400308

Matthews, N. (2008). Conflicting perceptions and complex change: Promoting Web-supported learning in an arts and social sciences faculty. *Learning, Media and Technology, 33*(1), 35–44. doi:10.1080/17439880701868846

Mazer, J., Murphy, R., & Simonds, C. (2007). I'll see you on "Facebook": The effects of computer-mediated teacher self-disclosure on student motivation, affective learning, and classroom climate. *Communication Education, 56*(1), 1–17. doi:10.1080/03634520601009710

Mesch, G. (2006). Online communities. In C. Milofski & R. Cnaan (Eds.), *Handbook in sociology of communities.* New York: Lower Academic/Plenum Books.

Meyer, K. (2003). Face-to-face versus threaded discussion: The role of time and higher-order thinking. *JALN, 7*(3), 55–65.

Miller, V. (2008). New media, networking and phatic culture. *Convergence: The Journal of Research into New Media Technologies, 14*(4), 387–400. doi:10.1177/1354856508094659

Minocha, S., & Roberts, D. (2008). Social, usability, and pedagogical factors influencing students' learning experiences with Wikis and blogs. *Pragmatics & Cognition, 16*(2), 272–306. doi:10.1075/p&c.16.2.05min

Oravec, J. (2003). Blending by blogging: Weblogs in blended learning initiatives. *Journal of Educational Media, 28*(2/3), 225–233. doi:10.1080/1358165032000165671

Panda, S., & Mishra, S. (2007). E-learning in a mega open university: Faculty attitude, barriers and motivators. *Educational Media International, 44*(4), 323–338. doi:10.1080/09523980701680854

Pearson, M., & Lewin, C. (2005). Online education and learner autonomy: Reports from the field. *Learning, Media and Technology, 30*, 259–261.

Petrides, L. (2002). Web-based technologies for distributed (or distance) learning: Creating learning-centered educational experiences in the higher education classroom. *International Journal of Instructional Media, 29*(1), 69.

Rourke, L., & Kanuka, H. (2007). Computer conferencing and distance learning. In H. Bidgoli (Ed.), *The handbook of computer networks, vol. 3* (pp. 831-842). Hoboken, NJ: John Wiley & Sons.

Rovai, A. P. (2007). Facilitating online discussions effectively. *The Internet and Higher Education, 10*(1), 77–88. doi:10.1016/j.iheduc.2006.10.001

Schweizer, K., Paechter, M., & Weidenmann, B. (2003). Blended learning as a strategy to improve collaborative task performance. *Journal of Educational Media, 28*(2/3), 211–224. doi:10.1080/1358165032000165699

Shedletsky, L. J., & Aitken, J. E. (2004). *Human communication on the Internet.* Boston: Allyn & Bacon/Longman.

Slevin, J. (2008). E-learning and the transformation of social interaction in higher education. *Learning, Media and Technology, 33*(2), 115–126. doi:10.1080/17439880802097659

Staggers, J., Garcia, S., & Nagelhout, E. (2008). Teamwork through team building: Face-to-face to online. *Business Communication Quarterly, 71*(4), 472–487. doi:10.1177/1080569908325862

Stern, M. (2008). How locality, frequency of communication and Internet usage affect modes of communication within core social networks. *Information Communication and Society, 11*(5), 591–616. doi:10.1080/13691180802126778

Tufekci, Z. (2008). Grooming, gossip, Facebook and Myspace. *Information Communication and Society, 11*(4), 544–564. doi:10.1080/13691180801999050

Turner, J., Grube, J., & Meyers, J. (2001). Developing an optimal match with in online communities: An exploration of CMC support communities and traditional support. *The Journal of Communication, 51*(2), 231–251. doi:10.1111/j.1460-2466.2001.tb02879.x

Vanhorn, S., Pearson, J., & Child, J. (2008). The online communication course: The challenges. *Qualitative Research Reports in Communication, 9*(1), 29–36. doi:10.1080/17459430802400332

VanLear, C. A., Sheehan, M. A., Withers, L. A., & Walker, R. A. (2005). AA online: The enactment of computer mediated social support. *Western Journal of Communication, 69*(1), 5–26. doi:10.1080/10570310500033941

Wang, Z., Walther, J., & Hancock, J. (2009). Social identification and interpersonal communication in computer-mediated communication: What you do versus who you are in virtual groups. *Human Communication Research, 35*(1), 59–85. doi:10.1111/j.1468-2958.2008.01338.x

Westerman, D. (2008). How do people really seek information about others?: Information seeking across Internet and traditional communication channels. *Journal of Computer-Mediated Communication, 13*(3), 751–767. doi:10.1111/j.1083-6101.2008.00418.x

Whatley, J., & Bell, F. (2003). Discussion across borders: Benefits for collaborative learning. *Educational Media International, 40*(1/2), 139. doi:10.1080/0952398032000092189

Ye, J. (2006). Traditional and online support networks in the cross-cultural adaptation of Chinese international students in the United States. *Journal of Computer-Mediated Communication, 11*(3), 863–876. doi:10.1111/j.1083-6101.2006.00039.x

Zhang, M. (2008). Connecting alumni around the world: A study of harmony, memory, and identity online. *China Media Research, 4*(4), 85–91.

FURTHER READING

Huang, Y., Kuo, Y., Lin, Y., & Cheng, S. (2008). Toward interactive mobile synchronous learning environment with context-awareness service. *Computers & Education, 51*(3), 1205–1226. doi:10.1016/j.compedu.2007.11.009

Huett, J., Kalinowski, K., Moller, L., & Huett, K. (2008). Improving the motivation and retention of online students through the use of ARCS-based e-mails. *American Journal of Distance Education, 22*(3), 159–176. doi:10.1080/08923640802224451

Lorenzetti, J. (2008). Encouraging faculty to go online: New study points to reasons why faculty may shy away from incorporating distance education technology in their classrooms. *Distance Education Report, 12*(18), 4–6.

Miller, R., & Benz, J. (2008). Techniques for encouraging peer collaboration: Online threaded discussion or fishbowl interaction. *Journal of Instructional Psychology, 35*(1), 87–93.

Monahan, T., McArdle, G., & Bertolotto, M. (2008). Virtual reality for collaborative e-learning. *Computers & Education, 50*(4), 1339–1353. doi:10.1016/j.compedu.2006.12.008

Puzziferro, M. (2008). Online technologies self-efficacy and self-regulated learning as predictors of final grade and satisfaction in college-level online courses. *American Journal of Distance Education, 22*(2), 72–89. doi:10.1080/08923640802039024

Rodriguez, M., Ooms, A., & Montanez, M. (2008). Students' perceptions of online-learning quality given comfort, motivation, satisfaction, and experience. *Journal of Interactive Online Learning, 7*(2), 105–125.

Shedletsky, L. J., & Aitken, J. E. (Eds.). (2010). *Cases on online discussion and interaction: Experiences and outcomes.* Hershey, PA: Information Science Reference.

Shroff, R., Vogel, D., & Coombes, J. (2008). Assessing individual-level factors supporting student intrinsic motivation in online discussions: A qualitative study. *Journal of Information Systems Education, 19*(1), 111–126.

Wang, S., & Wu, P. (2008). The role of feedback and self-efficacy on Web-based learning: The social cognitive perspective. *Computers & Education, 51*(4), 1589–1598. doi:10.1016/j.compedu.2008.03.004

Chapter 13
Developing Collaborative Problem–Solving in an Online Training Program for Insurance Agents

Patrick Connolly
Director of Operations and National Training Manager, USA

Donna Russell
Arete' Consulting, LLC, USA

EXECUTIVE SUMMARY

This case is a narrative of the design, review, revision and implementation of an online training program for insurance brokers. The goal of the online training program is to develop advanced problem-solving knowledge and skills including communication abilities in trainees. The case is narrated from the perspective of the training manager with the reviewer's comments included during the review cycle of implementation. The evaluative review is completed using cultural historical activity theory to identify contradictions in the training process. The purpose of the case is to identify the development of advanced knowledge and skills resulting from the online training program. The results of implementing an online training program include 1) reduction in turnover, 2) cost savings and 3) training benefits for the regional branch offices and the trainees.

BACKGROUND

The company is a nation-wide service partner in the residential and commercial property and casualty sectors of the insurance industry. Our company has about 1,400 field representatives and approximately twenty-four branch offices, which presented its own unique challenges, since we were greatly relying on

manager buy-in and support of any training program. I would estimate that the company's managers were largely comprised of technology immigrants, many of which could not perform basic functions in Excel. This is not to say that they were not good managers of their prescribed region, they just weren't very computer savvy.

I think that it's important to consider the size of the company. Although we are the largest company

DOI: 10.4018/978-1-60566-878-9.ch013

performing the work for the insurance industry that we do, not to mention the only true nationwide company, we are still a medium sized company. At this point in time, total company revenue was approximately $80 million. I think this is important to share because I felt that we were just large enough to fund a strategic technology solution and also small enough to not have too much bureaucratic red tape that would stymie creative ideas.

Think back to the first day of your job or former job. Do you remember the feelings that you had in the pit of your stomach while you meticulously ironed your clothes and left home early to be in before 8AM? The first day of work can be a daunting experience, especially when your new job will require you to digest a considerable amount of knowledge just to be able to function successfully. Nothing is routine on a first day of work. Many studies show that it can be one of the most stressful times in a person's life.

"This job will require a lot from you," I can remember my manager informing me. "Many people work very hard to learn this job, but succumb to the learning hurdles. They just can't seem to get past the learning curve to become productive, which is important because you will be paid by the hour for every job that you complete – like piece work." I was challenged by his words of caution, but I have to say that I really just felt that he was describing the performance of the average new hire. Besides, who really considers themselves as being average? Not to mention that I have always been successful at commission based jobs, raising money for non-profits, and I even remember winning prizes for selling the most candy bars in elementary school candy drives. I was quickly deflated, however, as I carried my box of newly assigned training books out to my car. I instantly became overwhelmed with the sheer amount of information that was required for someone to digest and understand to succeed in this role within the insurance industry. The company that I was just hired to work for was a fortune 500 company providing risk management, auditing, and loss control information to the insurance industry.

I was probably one of very few who actually made a valiant attempt at reading the array of manuals, which resembled a few law firm bookshelves. This was prime bedtime reading – the kind of material that dizzied the mind with foreign terminology and new concepts that had to be prescribed to memory. Thankfully, I did manage to learn the job over time and I have since held many management positions in my 14 years of service to the company. Although I was not in a role to directly impact the training and development of an employee, I remained passionately committed to lessening the learning curve and the training experience of my new hires. I was a fan of providing my employees with "cheat sheets" to simplify concepts so that learning would become easier.

Years later as a manager, I watched the company migrate away from the "box of books" training program to a 2-week classroom training session. During the classroom training session, the trainer would literally reviewed a total of about 2,000 text-heavy slides, many with enough text to warrant the use of new paragraphs. The slides were essentially read to the learners, which would have driven the most moral people to a good, stiff drink by the end of the week. I often likened this approach to the movie The Matrix where Keanu Reeves, as Neo, was connected to a computer that downloaded fighting strategy and skills directly to his mind. At the end of the download, Neo opens his eyes and exclaims, "I know Jujitsu." How much like The Matrix were we treating our new employees as we led them into a class and plugged them into the annals of insurance rules and concepts? We expected to plug them up to the 2,000-slide PowerPoint presentation and essentially hit the upload key. Needless to say, this training platform was not the most effective manner in which to prepare our employees to be as successful as possible and to equip them for their job in the field.

Ultimately, this realization spawned the need for a creative solution that was found in a virtual, interactive online learning series. I always felt strongly that there was a better way for the company to train its employees, considering the large amount of knowledge that had to be delivered coupled with a large geographically dispersed workforce. For many years as a manager I bounced various ideas off of my boss and he seemed open and supportive of the idea of a progressive change in our training methodology. We began discussing videotapes that the rep could watch via VCR and television. Technology progressed, as did our discussions, which now focused on using DVD's and CD's that could be played on the new hire's laptop. Ultimately, I progressed in my career to a position where I could lead the charge to make a change in our training methods and by this time, my focus was online delivery of a comprehensive training program. The solution was an online university that provided a well-rounded, 8-week curriculum for new hires to our company.

I understood that this training platform would not cater to those who do not flourish in a self-paced and self-starting learning environment. I would be narrow-minded to believe that this particular style of learning would benefit all learners. Adult learners tend to expect learning to be delivered in a traditional, teacher-led way, and to expect the faculty member to do the "work" of the learning. The adult learner is there to absorb the learning. Now, this does NOT say that this is an effective way to teach adults. This is saying that most of us, for years, have been taught via a certain method, namely, faculty-led instruction. We have not been expected to be part of the hands-on learning process. This is a pattern that is in the process of being broken down; however, we are talking about breaking down a pattern that has been in existence for decades, even centuries. This mindset is not going away easily, and to expect adult learners to automatically embrace a brand new way of learning immediately, or without proper orientation, is expecting too much. This is particularly important for me to understand because we have to begin with the hiring process of selecting the right candidate that will flourish in this type of learning environment. The program can be put together as effectively as possible, but if we are presenting it to a new hire that only benefits from learning in a classroom environment, we have already failed.

SETTING THE STAGE

My overall goal was to design the program in a manner that made it fun and engaging while using real-life scenarios in a multi-media format. While I did want the learning platform to be fun and engaging, I also wanted for it to be effective; This was the focus. "The rush to internet-based CBT has produced some great looking, yet awful training. Despite a history of failures with learning technologies, IBM's Tony Driscoll suggests that many trainers are still obsessed with "technolust," which drives them to try the latest technological gizmo—the Internet being the latest iteration. Ignoring the tenets of instructional and information design amidst fervor over technology usually results in lots of Web wizardry that often doesn't teach anything of value. This can be a costly lesson" (Rosenberg, 2001).

Curriculum for the learning series was designed in a constructivist format, requiring the trainee to actively participate in their learning. I figured that since the job required the new hire to be able to be self-starters and to work from their home then they should also be able to participate in web-based virtual learning environment that was led by a virtual mentor. If the new hire struggled to keep up to task or to be a self-starter, then there is a strong possibly they were not cut out for the job to begin with. I considered the correlation between being a self-starter in an online learning environment and being a self-starter in the real world and felt that those who were disciplined to keep themselves on schedule with their training plan would be more likely to be self-starters when they completed their training. I also considered the possibilities of the company actually saving money by identifying poor performers earlier in the training process.

All of the skills that we expect from an experienced employee were considered and strategically included in the overall curriculum path. Furthermore, a primary goal of the online program was use technology as a means to lengthen the total training period from a 2-week classroom program to a 10-week to 13-week program. This allowed for the rep to learn without being overloaded with information. This approach was also important because we would be able to deliver knowledge to the learner in a measured manner, which coupled with other on the job training, would become more meaningful to them. This online solution fit well for us as a company when we considered the number of new hires that were trained and developed each year and the geographical diversity. The online training program would allow the new hire to work at their own pace in an interactive format, which placed them in the very situations that they would be experiencing in the field once trained. They would also have to participate in their learning through interactive scenarios. The training program is scenario-based and recursive.

The training program for new hires is to be administered by a local manager who would outline a training program for the newly hired rep and manage the rep through the process. The manager would provide ride along experiences for the new hire using an experienced rep that was usually closest to the new hire. The ride along mentoring experiences were viewed as the backbone of the training program because mentors would be able to provide the new hire with a hands-on training experience while performing actual work in the field. This sounds good in theory, but we were not seeing the desired results from our trainees. In fact, many new hires complained about their ride along experiences. I had a theory as to what

the root cause of the complaints was and I also had some potential solutions through use of the now online training program.

My hypothesis was that the direct manager of the rep was bogged down with responsibility in their usual day-to-day and really didn't have the time to dedicate to developing the new hire, although this is their primary job responsibility. I felt that the manager's view of their own role was distorted by the fact that they rarely saw the new hire because of geography. I also felt that they relied heavily upon the experienced "mentor" to train the new hire. The problem was that these "mentors" weren't trained to mentor, nor were they even managers. They were typically just successful field reps for our company that were able to get through the training process and progress their earnings through field productivity…they are producers. The "mentors" are producers for 48 weeks out of the year, except for when a new hire was assigned to them. When this happened, the concept was that they would slow down and provide the new hire with a meaningful, hands-on training experience. I strongly felt that this critical process was destined for failure because the experienced "mentors" were programmed to produce for their paycheck each week.

Understandably, it would be hard for them to shift gears mid-stream and then become teachers. For this reason, I felt that it was critical to shift the "mentoring" process to a virtual mentor in the online learning series that would guide the new hire through the online learning series and also through the virtual scenarios. It was also critical to re-establish the concept that training responsibility lies with the local manager. This type of program would not only be cutting edge for our company, but it would also be cutting edge for the insurance industry.

"To achieve comprehensive learning goals, training must consider using every delivery format and medium available. Products and programs must integrate labs, simulations, interactions, and technology to improve the efficiency and effectiveness of the training delivery process. Alone, traditional instructor-led training, video-based instruction, and computer-based training have limits. In combination, they offer real opportunity to evolve" (Connor, M., Wright, E., Curry, K. DeVries, L., Zeider, C., Wilmsmeyer, D., & Forman, D. 1996). After completing the online training series, each new employee will have to complete a Capstone Course, which will be held each month in Kansas City, to consider their training program complete. My goal for having a face-to-face training class was to offer a blended approach to the employee's learning. In an effort to make the Capstone Course more interactive and engaging and to collect valuable information from the learner, I purchased and infused a Classroom Performance System into the program.

Classroom Performance Systems are used in the Capstone Course to engage the learner and to track individual performance. Specific questions will be asked in more detail related to the virtual auditing scenarios that they viewed in the online program. The audit trainees will be instructed to bring their completed audits to class with them. The class will view the virtual scenario again and the trainee will be given time to make any adjustments to their audit. Then, we will begin asking specific questions related to the audit to see if they, in fact, understood the concepts presented in the online program. After they answered the questions using the CPS clickers, the trainees will break into small discussion groups to discuss the questions as a group. Then, they will return to their individual seats to enter their answers to the same questions again.

The Capstone Class will conclude with the learner providing me with subjective information related to their manager's involvement in their training plan, various items of communication between the learner and their manager, as well as their ranking of the online course's effectiveness. By doing this, I hope to make deficiencies of the training program more transparent than ever before.

Success of the training program will be measured by the proficiencies of the trainee after completion of the online program as compared to the former program, the reduction in employee turnover related to employees learning their job more quickly, cost savings to the company from reduced travel expenditures, industry, and manager support.

CASE DESCRIPTION

Development of the program took roughly one year, which was an arduous process of first considering the desired outcomes, building a curriculum path that would produce those outcomes, and then considering how we would assess the learner's skills in both a formative and summative manner. I became more and more excited as the program roll-out day approached. I knew that the program was well-rounded and prompted the new hire to action in a self-directed manner. The program also engaged the learner; promoted new hire initiated interaction with the new hire's manager; provided many virtual experiences where the learner could apply their newly found knowledge as a skill; accepted the fact that our previous mentoring processes were not hands-on training experiences; and we extended the overall learning process from 2-weeks to 10 to 13 weeks. I had ensured that the new program included all of the material and experiences that I needed when I was hired 14-years ago. I considered all of the mentoring experiences that I felt were valuable when I was a "mentor" and had a newly hired rep ride along with me. I also considered the training programs that I had created and managed for my new hires when I was a branch manager. I thoughtfully considered all of the successes and failures that I witnessed with new hires and training programs in my 14-years of experience with the company and I made sure that the online program was ready to address them. I was very excited about the program rollout and how it would shape the face of training and continuing education in our company and for the industry. Certainly, everyone else was excited about this new program too, especially after all of the marketing and kick-off programs that I sponsored. They were excited, right?

I quickly learned that no matter how much you prepare a new program for easy implementation, a lot of the overall success is dependent upon others. In my case, the person that my program was dependent upon was the local manager. To the local managers the online learning program was a change from the norm – it was "out there" and it was ultimately viewed as a way in which to limit the human element from the training experience. Although, this perception could not be further from the true intent of the program since it's designed encouraged manager contact and support. However, I learned that perception can sometimes become reality, so I steadied myself for the inevitable backlash on the horizon. The backlash did come, like an organized coup or revolt. I realized early on that in order to make this program a success I would have to remain extremely objective and welcome criticism. I decided to implement a systemic evaluation of the online training platform with a focus on improving the program for end users. Donna Russell of Arete' Consulting, LLC was hired to review the online training program based on concepts of expansive learning in Cultural Historical Activity Theory.

Case Study Evaluation

The evaluation of the online training platform used Cultural Historical Activity Theory to understand the contradictions in the design of the training program. The goal of the online course is to develop advanced problem solving and decision making abilities in the trainees. The learning processes of 1) advanced decision making, 2) critical evaluation of information needed to solve the problem, and 3) problem-solving are designed into the interactions in the online university. Their acquisition will be evaluated by the reviewer based on 1) attribution

rates, 2) successful on job activities as evaluated by the local manager, 3) formative and summative surveys of the trainees, and 4) assessments of content knowledge in each scenario.

Problem-Based Learning (PBL) is an instructional method that addresses the complex knowledge and skill applications learners will face in the future by participating as problems solvers. Problem-based learning is dependent upon the interdependent attributes of meaningful learning including authentic, intentional, active, constructive, and cooperative learning involve meaningful application of knowledge and skills (Jonassen, Peck, and Wilson, 1999). Consequently as a result of the online training scenarios, the trainees should consider themselves active members of their community of learners within the context of the problem, but respond with less risk than in actual business situation, a phenomena Lave and Wenger (1991) called legitimate peripheral participation (LPP). Additionally the problem-solving scenarios should be as realistic as possible to reduce the possibility of low motivation, low transferability, and rapid forgetting (Bereiter and Scardamalia, 1996). It is essential for the online training scenarios to develop advanced learning processes that a series of meaningful authentic interactions be included in the training program. In studies of online learning environments, research has shown that learners can develop higher levels of awareness and knowledge as a result of their dialog and interactions in online environments (Russell, 2005). The design of the online training program should, therefore, involve the trainee in collaborative problem-solving processes developmentally scaled to support the development of high-level problem-solving processes necessary for the training program to be successful.

Learning as defined by sociocultural theories of learning includes the concepts of the zone of proximal development (Vygotsky, 1978). The zone of proximal development (ZPD) is the actual developmental level as determined by independent problem solving under guidance or in collaboration with more capable peers (Wertsch, 1991). Thus the understanding of cognitive development based on a sociocultural perspective emphasizes "the transition from primitive remembering and involuntary attention to the higher mental processes of voluntary attention and logical memory" (Vygotsky, 1986, p.166). This perspective on learning identifies the learning process as an interactive process that is impacted by the tensions in the learning system itself. The level of learning is an outcome of the successful negotiation of these tensions as learners move through their zone of proximal development to attain new knowledge and skills.

Based on sociocultural theories of learning the reviewer of this online learning environment will use Cultural Historical Activity Theory to evaluate the effectiveness of the design. Cultural Historical Activity Theory (CHAT) involves defining the influences on the system that cause contradictions to arise between the identified aspects of the system. Activity systems are connected models of interactions within which equilibrium is the exception and the tension, disturbances, and local

innovations are occurring and cause change over time (Salomon, 1993). Once an activity system is defined, then patterns of change can be identified and evaluated in relationship to the interactions in the learning environment. CHAT provides a systems-based model with methods to understand the patterns of relationships among the systems (Banathy, 1991). By analyzing these complex social interactions, Dr. Russell identified patterns of contradictions in the design of the training program that were conflicting with the development of advanced problem-solving skills and knowledge in the trainees (Engestöm, 1987).

An activity system contains a variety of different viewpoints as well as patterns of division of labor). Identifying the tensions that result in contradictions between the goals of the activity system and the interaction is the basis for the review (Il'enkov (1977). In the triangular model (Figure 1) of activity the Subject works to develop the Object, in this case successful completion of the online training program.

The remaining interactive components include:

Figure 1. Activity Theory Model

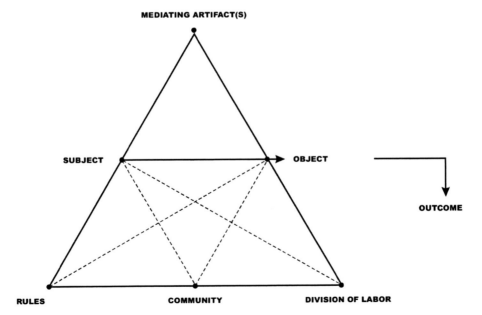

1. Tools: new tools used to support the development of the object. For this study this includes 1) the online interface for training and 2) the curriculum
2. Subject: the characteristics of the trainee identified as critical for successful training
3. Object: the goal of the subjects in the activity system. In this case it is to successfully complete the online training program
4. Outcome: the ultimate result of the training- the development of problem-solving skills including the ability to do effective decision-making in the field
5. Context issues; Rules: Rules are aspects of training program that impact the success of the object. In this case rules include 1) the schedule for the online and face-to-face training, and 2) the training requirements e.g. contact requirements.
6. Context issues; Community: Community is those people that give support to the training and can impact the success of the training. In this case this includes the branch managers, online support personnel and field mentors
7. Context issues; Division of Labor: This includes those people needed for the trainee to be successful. In this case this included field mentors and managers.

To encourage successful completion of the Object, these aspects of the work activity system should be supporting the object and the advanced learning processes that are its potential outcome. In order to review the work activity it is important to identify the aspects of the activity system are supportive of the development of the object and the learning outcomes and which aspects are not supportive of the development of the object and learning outcomes. Those aspects identified as not supportive are labeled as contradictions and, if not addressed, lead to a narrowing of the object including 1) trainees unable to complete the training, and 2) a high attrition rate if trainees are unable to function in the field after training. It is the goal of this review to identify contradictions so they can be addressed in the redesign of the training process.

The reviewer interviewed the designer and manager of the trainee program. She also reviewed the online training program using the activity theory model to identify contradictions. As a result, the reviewer identified the components of the training program that were not supportive of the training object and learning outcome goals. The resulting activity theory model for the training program is shown below as Figure 2. Contradictions in the training program are identified as broken arrows in model. There were four contradictions identified including:

1. There is a contradiction between Subject, the characteristics of the subject identified as important to field-based work, and Outcome, the development and assessment of these characteristics in the training program. In this case these characteristics include communication and interpersonal skills.
2. There is a contradiction between the Division of Labor, the collaboration of the trainee and their field mentor, and the Object, successful completion of the training. The trainees do not receive consistent feedback from the mentors during their training resulting in higher levels of attrition during and after training.
3. There is a contradiction between Tool, the online interface, and the Outcome, successful problem solving and decision-making processes. In this case the online curriculum does not include interactive components and correlating formative and summative assessments that develop high-order learning processes.
4. There is a contradiction between the Community, the online support systems, and the Object, successful completion of the training. In this case, the interactive

Figure 2. Review CHAT Model

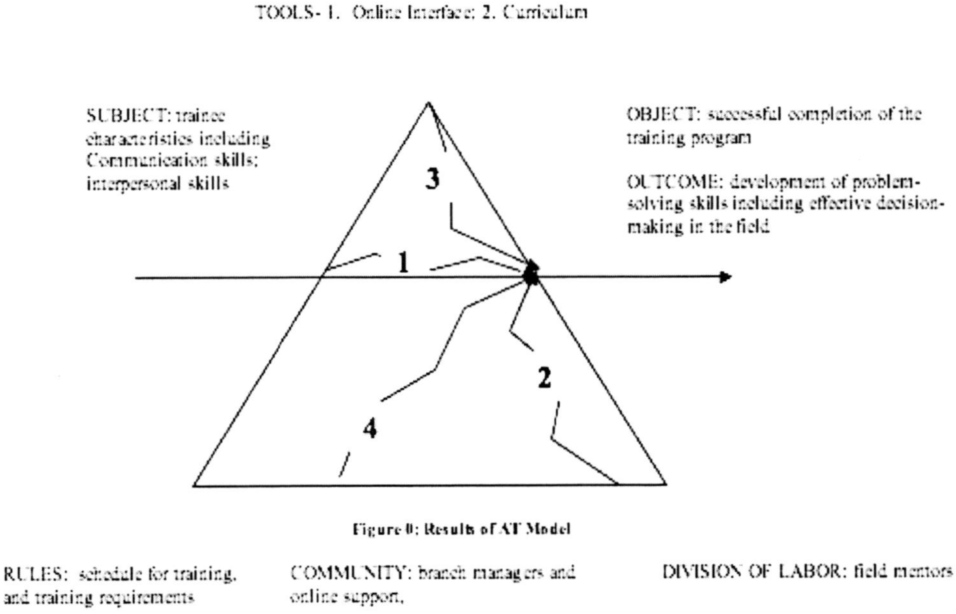

TOOLS- 1. Online Interface: 2. Curriculum

SUBJECT: trainee
characteristics including
Communication skills;
interpersonal skills

OBJECT: successful completion of the
training program

OUTCOME: development of problem-
solving skills including effective decision-
making in the field

Figure 0: Results of AT Model

RULES: schedule for training,
and training requirements

COMMUNITY: branch managers and
online support,

DIVISION OF LABOR: field mentors

support was inadequate to provide timely and responsive feedback to the trainees.

As a result of the review of the training program the following recommendations were made to increase the productivity of the training program.

- **Contradiction #1:** It is recommended that the training have defined assessment points to identify those subject characteristics that are developed during the training. These assessment points would include:
  1. a pre-survey of trainees that addresses their interests, background and motive including their ideas about training online.
  2. A post-survey that asks them to identify productive or less productive aspects of the online training program.
  3. A post survey at the end of each course asking trainees about the productive and less productive aspects of the course related to course learning goals

and objectives. This consistent self-evaluation provides feedback to the designers of the training program and also identifies the learning goals for the course so the trainees understand the learning goals for the program and can potentially develop these cognitive processes.

- **Contradiction #2:** It is recommended that the field mentors be compensated for their work with the trainees. This can include a money amount or by making these interactions part of their work assessment. Additionally it is recommended that these mentors be given a set of guidelines including a schedule for mentoring their trainees.

- **Contradiction #3:** It is recommended that the online interface include problem-solving scenarios as ongoing processes in the courses. These scenarios can be developmentally scaled for levels of response including recall of information, analysis of information (identification of useful and less useful information) and problem solving. These progressive learning processes can be formatively and summatively assessed by designing interactions between the trainees and the scenario such as open ended scenarios for the trainees to complete and justify.

- **Contradiction #4:** It is recommended that the online interactions between the online mentors, currently they included an ongoing video mentor, and a discussion board, be developed by adding a live collaborative process among the online trainees and the mentor that should coincide with decision making in the scenarios. Also it is recommended that the trainees have an asynchronous contact such as an email contact with a mentor.

CURRENT CHALLENGES FACING THE ORGANIZATION

As a result of the above evaluation and feedback from the trainees and field personnel, redesign of the online university was initiated. Some of the manager complaints stemmed from design issues that needed to be re-worked or accomplished in a different manner. Other items were related to technical issues, which would require a plan of action to address but will not require a specific change in the curricula. The designer maintained a very positive attitude with the managers and continued to consistently communicate to them openly about the program's failures. The root cause of the program not being as effective as anticipated include the 1) the program assessments, 2) the lack of virtual audit scenarios, 3) need for interactive technology in the training process and 3) manager participation/buy-in.

Assessments

Assessments are a great tool to provide summative results to evaluate what knowledge the learner has retained. The complete learning platform is comprised of eight individual courses, containing a total of 31 individual modules. The culminating event for each course is an assessment where the learner is required to answer 25 questions, usually multiple choice, related to the content presented in the course. The courses are designed to be taken sequentially and require one course to be passed before the learner is able to progress to the next course. The intent was to make the learner unable to progress further into the learning series until they have passed the assessment for the current course. I assumed that a trainee who was unable to pass an assessment at the end of a course would realize that they did not truly understand the course content and would contact their manager to assist them in understanding the material. Besides, this is what they had been instructed to do if they had trouble passing the assessments. Our goal was not to frustrate the trainee or discourage them in any manner. After all, we did want a blended approach to learning, especially since the content is heavy. We wanted to promote more interaction between the learner and their manager, not less. However, what we found was that the exact opposite was more of the practice of our learners.

This was exampled as many would take assessments, receive a non-passing score and then just re-take the assessment immediately by guessing at the questions answered incorrectly during the first attempt. The trainee is able to manipulate the integrity of the assessment process the majority of the time by using this approach to non-passing assessments. What has been intriguing to me is that the trainee would rather guess or take another stab at passing the assessment instead of simply interacting with their direct manager for assistance, even though they were going to be responsible for applying the concepts that they learned in their day-to-day job. Additionally, comprehension of the material would potentially equate to more money for the trainee since they are being paid on a production basis. When the employee did interact with their manager, as the program was designed, the manager was unable to identify which of the questions were incorrect, as the Learning Management System did not report information at this level. Managers were also found to be neglectful in monitoring the progress of their trainee to proactively determine if their employee was having difficulty with an assessment, as was the intent. The trainee's responses to the assessments remind me of placing a mouse in a maze; they may wander around for awhile but they'll eventually find their way out.

The approach that we used for the assessment really didn't work very well either. We assessed knowledge, not the overall skill that we need them to perform when they were no longer in training. I feel that the assessments, which are currently multiple choice and typically based upon a rule or principle, should be separated into two distinct categories; Learning Process Assessments and Performance Assessments. Additionally, I discovered that only 26 of 52 total managers have even enrolled in a course. Enrollment into a course doesn't mean that they have completed the course, nor does it mean that they have taken and passed the assessment. It only means that they have signed up for the course. My initial expectation that managers would enroll in the course and experience it first-hand to be able to effectively mentor a trainee through the program was found to be in error. Unfortunately, this impacts the trainee as they are faced with taking courses and passing assessments that are challenging with little manager involvement.

Learning Process Assessments will be littered throughout the course, not just at the end of the course. The primary function of the learning process assessments is to track compliance with specific tasks assigned in the learning series. This would include various checkpoints that would require them to state that they have read the material assigned or that they have reviewed a company policy, not an assessment of whether they understood the reading assignment or policy. The learning process assessment would be used as a motivating tool since they are being asked to verify that they have completed a particular reading assignment and since their manager would be able to monitor responses to these questions.

Performance Assessments would be used at the end of each module to ensure that the trainee understood the learning objectives. Currently, the assessments are taken at the end of each course, which may contain five modules each with a different overall learning objective. The performance assessments would be a formative assessment where they are provided with a quiz or specific task that summarizes the overall learning objective for the module. I will also provide an activity that is directly related to the skill we are trying to develop in the course, graduating the level of complexity commensurate with the course content. My intent will be to have the tasked performance assessments be combined to create a complete audit that the trainee can defend or present in some manner during our face-to-face Capstone Course. I can see this culminating activity being realistic even over a 10-week to 13-week period of time since each course's concepts build upon the prior course's concepts.

Learning process assessments were added to each module of the course as checkpoints to ensure that the learner completed a specific task or reading. The revised course also implements the use of an advanced organizer at the beginning of each module to prepare the learner's mind for the upcoming learning topic. Compliance with acknowledged learning process completion would be easily identifiable within the learning management system.

Performance assessments will still be used at the end of each course to assess whether or not the learner understands the material presented. The performance assessments are not simply a 25-question, multiple-choice test. More focus has been placed on the quality and relevance of the question, rather than the number of questions presented. Some assessments only have 8 to 10 questions, but the questions are more effective and really gauge the learner's understanding. We have made the questions more thought provoking to assess understanding rather than their ability to look up the definition of a word. Many of the questions are even educational in that they review a principle with the learner and then ask them to apply that same principle to a question. For instance, we know that the rule for "X" states that we must "Y." Considering this, select the best response to the following questions.

Virtual Audit Scenarios

The Virtual Audit Scenarios have seen lackluster results with root cause stemming mainly from topic complexity. The Virtual Audit Scenarios were never intended to be completed without any mentoring and guidance from the employee's direct manager. Conversely, they were designed to promote interaction with a manager or mentor. It is my experience now that a trainee will generally not engage their manager to let them know that they are experiencing a problem with the virtual audit scenarios. The causative factors probably stem from the employee knowing that they can pass the assessment without obtaining the correct answers in the virtual scenarios and also because they don't want to appear that they don't understand the topic at hand. Additionally, a call to ask their manager for assistance has sometimes been met with a manager response like, "I'm not familiar with the scenarios in the online course."

My goal would be to create a help feature for all skill related tasks where the learner can click on a button and see a menu of topics to learn about that are similar to the tasks they are being assigned. The necessity of manager and mentor interactions cannot be overstated, but I need to provide a feasible alternative to satisfy the looming

issue of uninvolved managers. This will have to be the approach until the manager can be properly trained on how to manage a new hire through the online course. The lack of manager involvement is more of a cyclical issue with our company than one directly related to this course. It is a training issue that will be resolved over time with proper communication and education.

I do, however, believe that it will also be important to somehow provide a method of feedback to the learner if they are having difficulty, possibly through the use of a "Virtual Buddy," which explains and leads them through a similar task as the one being assigned. I've realized that the "test" or "assessment" isn't as important as the overall learning experience and whether or not I can engage the learner to construct and develop their own knowledge through the application of a given skill. I may be giving them assistance to complete the task at hand, but I really believe that their learning experience will be improved because of it. Potentially, we can integrate an assessment with the task too. By doing this, we can have the trainee self-assess whether or not they should be prepared to use the "Virtual Buddy" to assist them in completing their task.

Interactivity

We have also implemented the use of a "virtual buddy" to assist the auditors complete their virtual audits. Conceptually, we originally thought that the virtual buddy would be designed like an A.I. bot that the learner could click on to gain decision-making information. Keep in mind that the original intent was for the learner to interact with their manager to gain this level of support. However, we found that our learners would either not engage their manager at all when they had a question or concern, or they would engage the manager with their question or realize that their manager was not familiar with the material to be able to help them. Ultimately, this left the learner with the only alternative of partially completing the assignment and guessing at assessment questions related to the task. The virtual buddy idea, provided by Dr. Russell, was an excellent solution to the problem. The solution was much easier than anyone could have anticipated. We are still providing the learner with a virtual auditing experience where they will virtually visit a business and gather the necessary information to complete their audit, but we are not dropping the learner after they view the scenario to complete that audit on their own. After information had been gathered in the virtual audit, the learner would access records and open their auditing program and complete the audit from scratch. This process has been replaced to provide them with a partially completed audit to open and finalize. The partially completed audit spotlights blanks that need to be populated with the correct figures. By doing this, the learner now is able to see how our company prefers for worksheets to be set up and filled out. It also provides them with a resource for self-help if they get stuck. Instead of simply admitting defeat or giving up when they don't know what to do next, the learner can view how a similar employee's payroll was handled and where the information was gathered. By using this framework, the learner will hopefully be able to reason through their questions to produce a completed audit. The amount of "blanks" in the supplied audit framework will gradually increase with every virtual audit completed. Ultimately, the learner will complete their last audit without any assistance.

Technology Issues

It is often said that technology is great but it can also be extremely frustrating when it doesn't work properly. The online program has seen its fair share of technology related issues, from scores not posting at all for anyone's assessments, to courses not launching at all. One of the most time consuming issues pertained to the assessment scores not posting. This technology issue literally took months to diagnose and ended up being a flaw with the

assessment tool itself not properly communicating with the Learning Management System. Most of the technology issues were more of a headache for me and for the learner than anything else.

The only viable solution to the current nagging technology issues was to consider using a different vendor company to re-create and host the entire program. The main driving factor for re-tooling the entire project is the need to create a generic online learning program to satisfy our customer demand for the product. This overall need to provide or charge our customers a fee to participate in the online learning platform for their own employee training forced us into a position where we were required to purchase ownership rights to the original project. Purchasing ownership rights and pursuing the learning series as a viable product to sell meant that we also had to develop a solution for our delivery methods since we were currently storing all of the heavy content on the hard drive of the employee's computer and the web interface was making calls to the pull and play the appropriate content files at the correct time.

This methodology was justified since it was a cost savings because of the minimal bandwidth required. However, if we had to move to a total online-hosted solution, we would have to convert and compress every file so that it would be sized properly and in the correct format to play via the web. We later learned that the content and structure that we used for the online project was not Vista compliant…another set back since our company is currently ready to convert to Vista and is being delayed by this learning series. We knew we had to make changes to our current platform to convert to web delivery, purchase the licensing, and resolve the issues with Vista. We didn't understand, however, that it would cost us double the money to stay with the current vendor and keep the same project rather that literally starting all over. It really didn't make sense to me that this would be possible, but it was more cost effective to fully depreciate the original project and literally scrap it and begin all over again. We also considered that this would allow us to make considerable changes in our content and allow us to correct items that were not working as effectively as we had anticipated they would. Because of this, we strongly felt that the prudent thing for us to do would be to enter into another agreement with a separate vendor and totally re-work the online project.

Ultimately, I feel that our end product will be much improved because of this re-tooling process and because of the many program enhancements that we will be able to make.

The technology issues were all worked out within 6 (painful) months of rollout. However, we carefully considered the pros and cons to revising the program to be available in an online platform rather than storing heavy content files locally on the individual's hard drive. We felt that our current multi-media company's charge estimate was much higher than competitive bids to reproduce and re-shoot the entire program. Because of this, we moved to re-shoot and reproduce the entire program whereby we could correct any disconnects and enhance the program while ultimately meeting our overall goal of switching to an online platform for hosting. I entered into negotiations with the current vendor to purchase all video files. They agreed, and we were able to minimize the video shots required to complete the program reconstruction/revision while making improvements and enhancements to the program.

Mentoring

I initially expected tremendous manager buy-in and participation in the online training program. I assumed that it would be welcomed by all of our managers, as it was taking a lot of responsibility off of their shoulders with new hire training. If I had to do it all over again, I would have made sure that managers had much more time to understand the program than two weeks. I guess that I just figured that they were just as excited about the

program as I was. I definitely felt like I did my fair share of communicating to the managers in many different ways to promote hype about the new training platform. Little did I know that most of the hype generated was among the people who were working on the program. I began marketing the idea of an online virtual platform for training immediately after I knew that the company had committed to funding the project. Some of the marketing efforts included a presentation at a face-to-face manager's meeting, numerous corporate communications, several webinars, and even a personal invitation to preview the program two weeks prior to release.

I was sorely disappointed in how few managers participated in the program during the initial two week manager testing phase. This was critical since managers were responsible for creating training plans for the trainee. If they didn't know the program, which was designed to initiate conversation and questions between the trainee and the manager, how would they be able to support the program? This realization was sobering for me as I had poured and entire year and a half into planning and developing the program and I felt that the program's success resided largely in the hands of managers who really didn't make the time to learn about the program. My frustration was compounded by the fact that the training platform that was released was designed to release much of the burden of training from the manager. Every problem has a solution and we felt that our solution was to continue heavy communication campaigns to ensure that all managers were on the same plan with the program.

It didn't take long to see that these communication efforts were not working well. The program was designed to provide 8 to 10 week of online training. The trainee would ultimately complete their training program at our Capstone course, which is a face-to-face meeting where we collaboratively explore the virtual scenarios presented in the learning series. We were extremely disappointed when trainees were attending the course so incredibly stressed out because their manager only gave 8 days to complete the 8 courses of the learning series, which was supposed to be spread out over an 8 to 10 week period. We knew that we needed to intervene to protect the integrity of the program and to also protect the trainee's learning experience and morale.

A meeting was organized with all of the Senior Vice/Presidents to consider immediate solutions. It was suggested that we construct a sample training calendar and then ask managers to use the same format but customize the training calendar for the specific trainee. The plan would have to be submitted to my team for approval prior to the start date of the new hire. Managers became very upset about this requirement and viewed it as a control tactic and to some extent it was, but it was only put into place to bridge the disconnect of managers who were not familiar with the online program constructing the new hire's training plan. To put some teeth into the requirement, we did not allow any training reimbursements to be paid to the branch office until we had received and approved the new hire's training plan. The concept was to provide one plan, one format and an overall outline of minimum requirements that each plan must meet. The sample plan was in a calendar format and it was very clear and easy to read. A color coding scheme was also used for certain tasks so that the trainee would be able to easily identify similarities between days/weeks, etc.

The goal was to provide one style across the nation that was customizable for each manager, but still met minimum requirements. Any plans that did not meet minimum requirements were sent back to the manager for revision. The most common disconnect that we saw from the manager's plans that were submitted was an overall lack of understanding how much time was associated with each course and module. The program was designed to impart new content and knowledge to the trainee over a measured period of time, but the experience to the trainee would still be like drinking from a fire hose if their manager didn't

properly space their module and course completion expectations. This disconnect was directly related to the manager's lack of engagement with the online courses. To provide an immediate band aid to this problem, we created a manager's training guide that provided high-level information about the content of each course. The guide also provided responses to probable questions the manager would be asked by the trainee at the end of each course/module. Because we saw so many disconnects between the manager's expectations outline in the training calendar and the actual amount of time the trainee would invest into the course, we decided to include the actual computer seat time for all modules and an estimated amount of associated offline time per module for the trainee to complete all offline tasks and readings.

We also immediately began to offer a live, moderator-hosted, 12-week re-occurring webinar training library that is designed to serve as an immediate stand in for manager interaction and as an accompaniment to the online program. Webinars are held each Friday at 2:30, central. We try to keep webinars to 45 minutes to ensure that we keep the trainee's attention and we never exceed 1-hour. Webinars provided support to the trainee's online experience while also providing them with an opportunity to ask questions and make comments. We also created polling questions to be used during the webinar so that we could provide an engaging experience for the employee. Survey questions were automatically sent to webinar attendees after the exited the webinar to evaluate how their training was progressing. This was a very important motivator for the managers because they knew that there would be transparency in their performance with the trainee. All comments from trainees are shared with all managers across the nation, while comments that expressed any concern on behalf of the trainee were also sent to their manager for immediate handling and interaction. The surveys provided us with a chance to gain actionable information related to trainee performance and perception each week of the trainee's training plan. Below is an example of our survey questions that trainees receive after each webinar. Polling questions change with each webinar topic, so they have not been provided.

How many training weeks have you completed?

Possible Answers

Can input a short phrase answer

My field mentoring has been effective and "hands-on."

Possible Answers

Yes; No; It's been so-so; I have not had any field mentoring yet

I need for my manager to help me with the scenarios presented in the ELITE Learning Series.

Possible Answers

Yes – I feel lost; Yes – I can use some assistance; No – I'm Fine; N/A – I haven't had to complete any yet. Select all that may apply:

Possible Answers

This job isn't what I thought it would be; I'm concerned about my compensation after training; I'm really not getting the help that I need; My training plan doesn't seem to align with my day-to-day; I may not be cut out for this type of work

Rank the effectiveness of this webinar.

Possible Answers

Waste of my time; I'm not a fan, but I learned from it; I would rate this webinar as average; Good webinar; I really learned a lot!

Additional Comments:

Possible Answers

Can input up to a paragraph

In addition to the weekly, topic-based webinars, we also began offering an orientation webinar to prepare the new hire for their blended learning experience. The orientation webinar was added to set expectations for the employee. "Adult learners tend to expect learning to be delivered in a traditional, teacher-led way, and to expect the faculty member to do the "work" of the learning. The adult learner is there to absorb the learning. Now, this does NOT say that this is an effective way to teach adults. This is saying that most of us,

for years, have been taught via a certain method, namely, faculty-led instruction. We have not been expected to be part of the hands-on learning process. This is a pattern that is in the process of being broken down; however, we are talking about breaking down a pattern that has been in existence for decades, even centuries. This mindset is not going away easily, and to expect adult learners to automatically embrace a brand new way of learning immediately, or without proper orientation, is expecting too much" (Smith, 1997).

The coupling of the required training plan approval and the weekly webinars provided an immediate turn around in trainee performance, comprehension, and instantly improved the overall experience for the trainee. We recognized the weaknesses of the program and adjusted our method of operations to respond to the issues.

Capstone Course Findings

My findings have revealed that most of my trainee's come to class with incorrect audits and misconceptions of how to handle specific situations presented in the virtual audits of the learning series. I have found that most score poorly on the initial round of questions related to the audit that they printed and brought with them, but their score improves after the small group discussion. The interesting item that this brings to light is that the trainee has found a way to save their incorrect answers in their course assessment for the specific questions related to the virtual audit. This allows them to pass the assessment without having correct answers on the audit that they complete. It also makes the lack of manager participation and involvement with the trainee more transparent. Additionally, many of the trainees have answered that they have not even received a training plan when they were asked about their local training with their manager. This was one of the most alarming items that became evident is that some managers are hiring the employee and then just allowing them to sink or swim. In many instances, they have shown little ownership of the trainee in facilitating their training plan.

Considered Solutions

Implemented above resolutions that addressed the Capstone course issues. See quantitative progress below as a result of changes implemented.

Research Findings

Representation of class averages. About ¼ of the questions posed to the trainees specifically relate to the audits that they conducted on their own and brought to class with them. This graph will show the progression of grades scored by employees attending the Capstone Course progressively getting better with the implementation of program support methods, as discussed.

Other Learner Responses to the Program

Manager comment to his trainee:

I enjoyed speaking with you last Saturday.

I have looked at your first few cases submitted to review. Two out of 3 passed; not bad at all!

All 3 descriptions of operations were excellent! Writing a good description catalyzes excellence throughout the entire auditing process. The first few tracks in the snow tell a lot about what is to come; very impressive.

Thanks for your hard work during your 8 weeks of field training with Robert Holley your mentor. Robert is amongst the best auditors in the business and you will be too! Nelson and I entrusted you to our very best and you guys have hit a grand slam!

You diligently completed all 8 Learning Courses and were amongst the cream of the crop at the Capstone in Kansas City. I have no doubt the combination of the Learning Series and the field mentoring has shortened the learning curve and that you are a direct beneficiary of the combination of technology, education, and human resources devoted to your success as the newest team member of the Charlotte Branch.

Figure 3. Capstone Course Averages

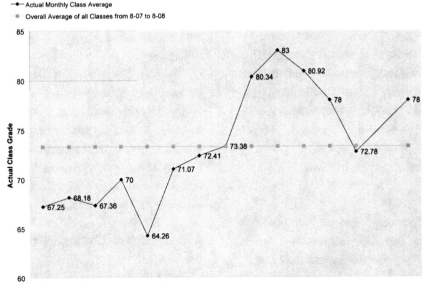

Nelson and I look forward to working with you as you enter the next phase of your development.

Learner Responses

Just wanted to stop and make a note here about how this training is going... For those of you who have not worked in the financial field or 'corporate-world' before, this is the best method of training I have ever encountered. It is a credit to the company to make such a concentrated effort on educating their auditors - and on providing them with immensely valuable resources in order to effectively complete their duties. That being said, everyone knows you only get out of something what you put into it. With everything the company has provided (training, this very discussion board, mentors, involved managers, online support, etc.), I feel very confident that I will be able to effectively do my job. As scary as something new may seem, we are really lucky to have this opportunity with a company that has invested so much into our success.

Patrick,

Thank you so much for the incredible training class you have put together. So many things make sense now in regards to why things are done a certain way. I am very excited about my future with the company. I have already started to implement what I need to do to make my goals.... If I can get my audit manager as excited as I am that would be FABULOUS!!! Thank you again for putting together such an awesome program.. Can't wait to see the new one.

CONCLUSION

Based upon my research, I have concluded that the online training program is effective, but is highly dependent upon the active participation of managers to support it. The content is complex and, in many cases, cannot be fully digested without human interaction. The complexity of the content is not a product of the online program; rather it's the topic of study itself that is complex.

I have found that participants in the program are better prepared to do their job when they get out of training than in the past. They ask better questions, perform better audits, etc. I believe that this will be enhanced further as changes to address each issue are implemented.

The program was built to enhance and promote interactions between the trainee and their manager. It was also built assuming that a manager would work with a trainee to explain many of the concepts that were being discussed. What I did conclude, much to my surprise, is that managers were not participating in the program themselves to position themselves as someone who could support the program. I was amazed that more managers didn't eagerly enroll and participate in the online program.

A common misconception was that the program would do all of the training for the manager and the manager would just have to hire the rep and introduce them to the program. Although manager participation was communicated from the conception of this project, either managers didn't take it seriously or they felt that they did not need to be involved in the rep's training. I believe that this same mindset that had always perpetuated within our company but it had finally become transparent.

Overall, I believe that the online program is an excellent tool for training in this industry. I realize now more than ever before that program rollouts do not go smoothly in most cases and that I have to remain adaptable to change. Things will not always go as planned and in many cases, effective solutions will need to be considered to support the learning technology.

Affect of the Overall Project

The effect of the project will be measured using the following criterion:

1) Reduction in Turnover
2) Cost Savings Related to the Online Learning Platform
3) Benefits for the Regional Branch Offices & the Learner

Turnover has typically averaged in the 30 percentile range. I believed that a certain percentage of the turnover could be directly related to the lack of proper training. A recent HR study in 2006 showed that one of the top three reasons why employees left the company was because they did not feel that they were adequately trained to perform their job. The online program provides a training experience for the new hire that our company has never seen before. Not only will the trainee learn about the company but we have also used this opportunity to impart a sense of corporate culture while teaching the trainee basic principles of auditing and actually engaging them in virtual audit scenarios that are typical to what they will experience when they are finished with their training. To date, our overall turnover percentage has decreased from 30% to 27% since the online learning platform was introduced. This is a sizable decrease for a 9-month period of time.

Cost savings has been realized, as projected in the initial ROI (Return on Investment). The cost savings included in the ROI considered soft costs and cost avoidance but only factored the actual hard costs into the justification for the initial investment. Projected hard costs savings for 2007 were estimated at $123,500 and $247,000 for 2008. These estimates are in line with current savings since the online program was able to replace one week of a 2-week classroom session with online learning over an extended period of time. Cost savings were estimated based upon historical averages of cost per head for airfare, hotel accommodations, meals, etc. We felt that it would be much cleaner if we based the cost justification of the program on hard costs alone since so many other factors contribute to the overall success of a trainee.

Benefits to the Regional Branch Offices were vast, since this was the first formal training program instituted across the nation. There are a total of 24 branch offices throughout the nation and each one runs much like its own entity. The company does have overall branch expectations and guidelines to follow, but the branch managers have a considerable amount of flexibility in how they run their branch. This is true for their day-to-day management style and also for administering a training program for a new hire to the company. So branch offices were very good at training and mentoring new employees, although they were few. Other branch offices really did a poor job of training and would place most all of the responsibility to learn the job on the trainee. One of the best features of this training plan is that it immediately brought continuity to each branch's training methodology since the online program embraced a trainee from their first day and welcomed them to the company to the actual virtual audit scenarios where they were engaged to perform an audit in a virtual environment.

In addition to the uniformity of training plans, the branch offices also benefit from the online learning program and its supporting component parts since it is intended to provide actionable information to managers so that they readily know the misconceptions that the new hire has or items that the new hire is struggling with. This valuable information is obtained via weekly webinars with the new hires and also through survey questions in our face-to-face Capstone Course. Providing actionable information to the manager is critical and an extremely important intent of the online learning program.

Another benefit to our branch offices is that they are better equipped to identify a trainee who is not cut out for the job or who is not applying themselves since the training program requires participation/assessments to complete. Overall, the program is designed to "weed out" bad hires so that less money is spent on a candidate who is not cut out for the job. The online platform incorporates a lot of the day-to-day aspects of the job, including a self-directed work environment, an employee who is comfortable in a technically demanding position which requires reasonable computer skills, one who can manage their time and follow a schedule, and more. Because the skill set required to successfully progress through the online program is the same as the ones required to be successful after training, it was evermore important to focus our attention to ensuring that our recruiting department clearly understood the training expectations. By selecting candidates that would fair well in this type of demanding learning environment, they were actually focusing in on those employees who would ultimately flourish in this type of job.

The overall benefit for the learner is that they are being provided the best training currently available in the industry for insurance premium auditing. They are provided with a self-paced, engaging program that allows them to practice their skills of insurance premium auditing in a virtual environment.

REFERENCES

Banathy, B. (1991). *Systems design of education: A journey to create the future*. Englewood Cliffs, NJ: Educational Technology Publications.

Bereiter, C., & Scardamalia, M. (1996). Rethinking learning. In D. Olson & N. Torrance (Eds.), *Handbook of education and human development: New models of learning, teaching, and schooling* (pp. 485-516). Cambridge, MA: Basil Blackwell.

Connor, M., Wright, E., Curry, K., DeVries, L., Zeider, C., Wilmsmeyer, D., & Forman, D. (1996). *Learning: The critical technology*. Retrieved September 25, 2007, from http://learnativity.com/download/Learning_Whitepaper96.pdf

Engeström, Y. (1987). *Learning by expanding: An activity-theoretical approach to developmental research*. Helsinki, Finland: Orienta-Konsultit.

Engeström, Y., Miettinen, R., & Punamaki, R. (Eds.). (1999). *Perspectives on activity theory*. Cambridge, UK: Cambridge University Press.

Il'enkov, E. V. (1977). *Dialectical logic: Essays in its history and theory*. Moscow: Progress.

Jonassen, D. H., Peck, K. L., & Wilson, B. G. (1999). *Learning with technology: A constructivist perspective*. Upper Saddle River, NJ: Merrill-Prentice Hall.

Lave, J., & Wenger, E. (1991). *Situated learning: Legitimate peripheral participation*. Cambridge, UK: Cambridge University Press.

Rosenberg, M. J. (2001). *Building successful online learning in your organization*. Retrieved September 25, 2007, from http://books.google.com/books?hl=en&lr=&id=hI8643XS3SIC&oi=fnd&pg=PR10&dq=effectiveness+of+online+learning&ots=mA76zgSdtS&sig=Lql5wAUKPeffeNOsmtLxOebw6SY#PPA44,M1

Russell, D. (2005). Implementing an innovation cluster in educational settings in order develop constructivist-based learning environments. *Educational Technology and Society, 8*(2).

Salomon, G. (1993). No distribution without individuals' cognition: A dynamic interactional view. In G. Salomon (Ed.), *Distributed cognitions: Psychological and educational considerations*. New York: Cambridge University Press.

Smith, J. (1997). *Adult learning styles*. Retrieved September 25, 2007, from http://adulted.about.com/cs/learningtheory/a/lrng_patterns.htm

Vygotsky, L. S. (1978). *Mind in society: The development of higher psychological processes*. Cambridge, MA: Harvard University Press.

Wertsch, J. (1991). *Voices of the mind. A sociocultural approach to mediated action*. Cambridge, MA: Harvard University Press.

FURTHER READING

Books on sociocultural learning and Cultural Historical Activity Theory: Engeström, Y., Miettinen, R., & Punamaki, R. (Eds.). (1999). *Perspectives on activity theory*. Cambridge, UK: Cambridge University Press.

Leont'ev, A. N. (1978). *Activity, consciousness, and personality.* Englewood Cliffs, NJ: Prentice-Hall.

Vygotsky, L. S. (1978). *Mind in society: The development of higher psychological processes.* Cambridge, MA: Harvard University Press.

Wertsch, J. V. (1998). *Mind as action.* NY: Oxford University Press

Chapter 14
Ethical and Legal Issues in Teaching and Learning in Second Life in a Graduate Online Course

R. S. Talab
Kansas State University, USA

Hope R. Botterbusch
St. Petersburg College, USA

EXECUTIVE SUMMARY

As a growing number of faculty use SL as a teaching platform, outside of anecdotal articles and the legal literature, no research exists on the many legal and ethical issues that affect course development. Ethical issues include abuse ("griefing") nudity and lewd behavior, and false/misleading identities. Legal issues include creation and use of copyrighted and trademarked items, faculty intellectual property rights in objects and course content, and criminal behavior. Following the experiences of the instructor and 5 students, their 12-week journey is documented through interviews, journals, weekly course activities, SL class dialogs, and in-world assignments. Additionally, 5 faculty and staff experts who teach or train in SL at this university were interviewed and consulted, as well. This study provides insight for designing courses that foster exploration of rich learning opportunities outside a traditional classroom-both real and virtual.

BACKGROUND

As of December 1, 2008, the number of universities, colleges, and community colleges, participating in Second Life, reached over 300 institutions in the U.S. and the combined total for the U.S. and overseas was well over 500 (SimTeach, 2008a). Educational institutions, schools, and associations have created private islands and immersive environments where students practice new building design concepts, become familiar with the components of operating rooms, perform dangerous experiments in safety, learn to plan events, and explore the history in 3-D (Romme, 2003).

DOI: 10.4018/978-1-60566-878-9.ch014

The number of education groups, libraries, museums, associations and institutions, both national and international, participating in Second Life (SL) grows monthly (SimTeach, September, 2009), with over five thousand educators on the Linden Labs Educators Mailing List as of 2008 (SimTeach, 2008b). Educational associations in SL include the International Society for Technology in Education, Sloan-C Consortium, The New Media Consortium, Eduserv, and many special interest user groups in educational associations (Wong, 2006). SL also maintains a wiki for nonprofit resources - the SL and Nonprofits listserv, and SimTeach. Various research and ethics groups and listservs have been created around Second Life and virtual worlds, such as Second Life Grad Student Colony, Social Second Life Educators (SLED), Real Life Education in Second Life, RezEd, Educators Working with Teens Mailing List, Second Life Researcher, Slrl Digest, etc., as well as two new journals, the *Journal of Virtual Worlds Research* in 2008, and the Journal of *Virtual Worlds Educational Research* Journal in 2009. The International Journal of Cyber Ethics in Education will be forthcoming in 2011.

In response to educator and researcher requests, SL also provides free space (an island with its own intranet) for research programs through the SL Campus Life program, which accepts eight research proposals a semester. The Second Life Campus region is the main hub for classes participating in the Campus: Second Life program. It has public meeting area, a sandbox for temporary building, and a public picture board for sharing photos, among other features. However, in order to take full advantage of all SL has to offer, venturing out into the various SL regions can be fulfilling and frightening. Just as with any exploration, there are dangers which good teaching strategies can be used to avoid in order to enhance student learning and minimize risk, both ethically and legally.

Ethical Issues

"Ethics" is a set of beliefs about right and wrong behavior. Ethical behavior conforms to generally accepted social norms, many of which seem universal (Reynolds, 2007). SL has created its own ethics code, called the "Community Standards" (Second Life, 2009). Professional educational associations with presences in Second Life that have codes of ethical behavior are the National Education Association, Association for Computing Machinery, Association of Information Technology Professionals, and EDUCAUSE.

There are many ethical issues in virtual worlds, yet, outside of the legal literature and legal blogs, most discussions of ethics are to be found on legal and educational blogs (Acello, 2008; Kittross, 2003; Romme, 2007). More than one author has noted that these user-initiated actions seem to be detached from the fear of consequences in the "real world" so that teleportation to various places may or may not be allowed or even desirable in certain instances due to the behaviors and practices of various people and groups (Kerbs, 2005).

"Griefing" is defined as "purposefully engaging in activities to disrupt the gaming experience of other players" (Mulligan & Patrovsky, 2003). Griefing is fairly common in the public regions of SL, particularly against "newbies"- those new to SL (Boostrom, 2008). Ethical issues arise when educational groups, including universities, schools, state groups, associations, and companies own land or host events and seminars. Nudity is not allowed in public in SL, except on nude beaches and private spaces. Avatars must not "bump into" other avatars, etc., according to the Terms of Service Agreement of SL. Moreover, ethics and legal issues intersect in SL, since to violate the SL community standards is to also violate the agreement (Second Life TOS, 4.1, 2009), for which the user can be banned and not be able to log in again (Bragg v. Linden Lab, 2006).

Legal Issues

Though several articles and papers have been written about ethics and virtual worlds (Elliot, 2008; Gunkel & Hawhee, 2003; Horsfeld, 2002; Roper, 2001; Schroeder, 2007; Wainio, 2002), little has been written and no research has been conducted on legal issues affecting teaching and learning in education in virtual worlds (Annetta, et al., 2008; Duranske, 2009; Kittross & Gordon, 2003; Legal and Ethical Group, 2007; Shutkin, 2004; Talab, 2008) and little case law has been applied to education (Botterbusch & Talab, 2009). Teaching and learning in SL involves intellectual property issues, such as copyright infringement in the purchase, sale and use of items with trademarked logos (such as Gucci purses). Criminal issues, such as theft, prostitution, gambling, pornography, the buying and selling of virtual goods using Linden dollars, and other issues loom large when faculty develop courses and activities which make use of the many elements in SL (Legal and Ethical Group, 2007). For example, when students in a class are sent on field trips, scavenger hunts, purchasing expeditions for avatar clothing, textures, furniture, or other items, or are invited to private parties or events through chatting with other avatars, or to a region that changes from a bookshop to a bar, anything can happen.

Faculty and students should be aware of what these legal issues are with respect to teaching and learning in SL, and then be prepared how to handle them when they occur (Talab, 2008). Crime has entered SL. "Recognizing there is money to be made and disturbances to cause, criminals and attackers have entered into virtual worlds such as SL" (Elliot, 2009, p. 3).

SL, as defined by the Digital Millennium Copyright Act and is not an "internet service provider" (ISP), since by definition ISPs can't make judgments about users or their behavior, benefit materially from trademarked products, virtual stores, or other goods and services (Duranske, 2009; Talab, 2008; Talab & Butler, 2007).

Linden dollars are geared to the U.S. dollar, which fluctuates, but is 240 to 250 Lindens per U.S. Dollar. In 2009 over 5 billion Linden dollars were available for sale to over 14 million inhabitants of SL (Second Life.com). All this virtual money translates into real money, as well as merchandise counterfeiting and design theft (Duranske, 2009; Kane, 2007). Since each virtual world has its own policies toward real money/virtual money, this study is confined to SL.

"Business and law in virtual environments is a rapidly growing field" (Shannon, Judson, & Nuara, 2008). Use of copyrighted materials on SL will be of increasing concern as more courses are offered "in-world". For example, only 10 seconds of audio may be uploaded in public spaces, but movies, images, and music can be viewed in private spaces without detection, currently, and policing of these rules seems lax, possibly due to SL's enormous growth.

Legal issues in SL involve all forms of communication. SL, as other virtual world environments, saves them to a file for an indeterminate period and SL conversation logs have been used in court (Duranske, 2009). Snapzilla, part of SL Universe, also at the time of this writing contains over sixty million screenshots (April, 2009). Chat logs, instant message logs, screenshots, in-world video, webcam captures, transaction logs, object histories, friend lists, audio recordings and authenticated documents can all be used as evidence in court cases (Duranske, 2009) and as ways to track student work in courses.

Second life, Virtual Law, and The Magic Circle Test

The "Magic Circle" proposed by Huizinga (1998) on the separation between play and the real world, later elaborated upon by Castranova (2005), has evolved into the "Magic Circle Test" which basically means that when a user undertakes an activity in a virtual world and does or should reasonably understand that the activity has real world implications, then the activity is subject to real world law (Duranske, 2009). Arguments for recognizing virtual property involve the extent to which virtual goods have value to consumers and match most property definitions in real life. In SL, unlike in some other virtual worlds, "these types of objects are indistinguishable from real world property interests", since they can be purchased with Linden dollars and converted into currency (Lastowka & Hunter, 2004). Nota Bene, for example, operates a virtual notary business in SL that supports in-world business.

Theory used in this study included current United States copyright and trademark law, ethical codes of behavior developed by the educational organizations in which the students participated, and the published Community Standards of Second Life. Reverse engineering, open source code, competitive intelligence, pornography, except to the extent that it affects teaching and learning, and "cybersquatting" were outside the scope of this paper.

SETTING THE STAGE

The setting is a land grant university with 22,000 students, located in a college town in the Midwest. The university offers the traditional majors, options, and specializations in undergraduate courses and graduate levels. Alongside traditional on-campus courses, it also offers distance education opportunities to students at both the undergraduate and graduate levels. Most of these distance education courses use internet-based technologies for delivery of course materials and communication among students and teachers.

Almost the entire campus has wireless internet access. The *Princeton Review* and *PC Magazine* published a list in 2008 of "America's top wired colleges", and this university was highly ranked (Griffith, 2008). While not all the classrooms are equipped with technology tools, most colleges have university-designated technology class-rooms and mobile labs – carts that can be pushed by one person. These mobile labs are equipped with up to 24 laptop computers, video projector, visual presenter, cassette and DVD players, and speakers.

University support of Second Life has been resisted due to legal liability issues, cost, and upkeep issues, although some faculty and programs have islands and property through grants and unfunded projects. A Second Life Users Group was begun in late October, 2008. This group has monthly meetings and is pursuing university-wide initiatives.

CASE DESCRIPTION

Methodology

This case study can be considered, in part, as a "netnography" (Kozinets, 2002) and a descriptive case study using Miles and Huberman's analytic strategy (1994). Kozinets defined a netography as "qualitative research methodology that adapts ethnographic research techniques to the study of cultures and communities emerging through computer mediated communications" (p. 62). Netnography has emerged within the last decade as an important means of studying and understand virtual communities (Fox & Robert, 1999; Kozinets, 1997). Participants were the researcher, the instructor, 6 graduate students enrolled in twelve weeks of the spring semester online graduate Educational Technology course, "Second Life and Virtual Learning Environments in Education", and other 5 faculty and staff who teach or train in Second Life at the university and were members of the university SL users group. They served as the expert panel. All but one had building and scripting experience with the construction of a sim and three with constructing an island in SL, including the instructor, though one worked only on the Teen Grid.

The course met weekly in Second Life. Course materials and grades were made available through Second Life and through a proprietary learning management system equivalent to Blackboard. Students in this course had advanced computer experience. All students were new to SL. Though all students had advanced computer knowledge, only three had previous experience with virtual worlds, one female had been in Sim Online and two males were in World of Warcraft.

The course used a virtual classroom on a private island for all in-world weekly class meetings. This island had tutorials, which were used by the class to get acquainted with SL. The instructor would meet with the class for about ten minutes at the beginning and then take the class on virtual field trips to explore various regions. These excursions also provided opportunities to observe educational conferences, events, shop for hair, clothing and other objects. Each assignment was designed to provide information on a legal or ethical aspect of SL activities. Topics included in the assignments were commerce (clothing, jewelry and other virtual items built in SL), copyrighted materials use (art, music, graphics, images), building and scripting (using copyrighted textures) and role playing (books and ethical issues). Students had three major projects during this period, as well as smaller assignments: a role playing assignment that required students to work in other regions, one assignment that focused on legal and ethical issues, and the class art gallery opening. For the art gallery opening, students were required to contact potential artists, arrange for installations for the exhibition and the gallery opening event. Students also kept journals to chronicle their experiences in class and to record observations in SL. Other documents, designed to triangulate the data and increase trustworthiness (Yin, 2003), were student and instructor notecards, objects, notecards, and PPTs.

Special issues existed in data collection involving ethics and legal issues in Second Life. Since many legal issues are unclear to educators and they may be reluctant to provide this information, to strengthen the validity of the research multiple data collection techniques were employed. Researcher, instructor, and student observations, in-world assignments and in-world class activities, journals student interviews, and course documents, including archived SL communications, class dialogs and chat logs (permission obtained beforehand) were also included.

Students were asked to document legal and ethical issues found in SL by taking photographs of copyright and trademark violations, such as event "handouts", to take pictures of graphics, PPTs, images, or other materials pertaining to legal and ethical issues, save them to a file and provide them to the researcher. The legal and ethical issues assignment used an instructor-provided checklist, provided for research purposes.

One of the most common forms of data collection in qualitative inquiries in education is interviewing (Merriam, 1998). A protocol similar to that used by Ostrander (2008) was used for interviewing purposes. Interview protocols were developed for the instructor, students, and university experts. Interviews were conducted by telephone, were transcribed and checked by the interviewee for accuracy. Interviews lasted approximately 20 minutes to 45 minutes for students, and 45 minutes to an hour for university experts and the instructor. Trustworthiness of the research was developed through the use of multiple sources of evidence to provide data triangulation and enhance construct validity.

FINDINGS

Depending on the degree to which they ventured out of the educational regions of SL, the class, instructor, and faculty/staff university experts had much the same experiences with ethical issues with "griefing", lewd behavior, and avatar identities, though male and female avatars did receive different treatment. The students were instructed in basic SL skills, community standards, how to read profiles, how to handle "griefing", how to teleport home and taken on weekly field trips to enhance their SL skills. The following section outlines some of the main findings about student experiences in SL.

Ethical Issues

Overall, the students had positive experiences in the class, largely due to the many field trips that they took and the project-based in-world assignments. The instructor knew that there would be ethical issues encountered as they attended conferences, purchased clothing, visited role playing sims, and visited Help and Orientation Islands and the Mainland, so each class she would prepare them for their trip.

Nudity and lewd behavior, "griefing" and other forms of abuse, and false/misleading/alter identities were sometimes problems for the students, but most had no problems with others' asking to share personal information or do unethical things, in general. However, the more they ventured out into SL the more rich the environment was perceived to be, the more varied their experiences were, and the more incidents of ethical breaches of the Community Standards they saw, as well. All students saw the benefit in taking the fullest advantages of the many regions that there are in SL.

The instructor developed an exercise for the students to do before beginning the field trips to help them acclimate.

I told them to huddle into a group and then I put a cage on them and told them to get out. Once there were ones who were out, I asked them to ask the ones that were still in problem solving questions and give them hints. "What were we told to do when we are in a tight situation?" "Teleport home!", she answered. Then she got out of the cage.

Nudity and Lewd Behavior

I teleported to where you start the [educational] conference and 5 people were walking around nude. I was supposed to interview people and I lost my train of thought. I stayed there. They stayed there, and then they walked on. Everybody's avatars turned and watched them and stopped talking until they walked away.

The class barely missed lewd behavior in a field trip when it visited one historical role-playing region.

About every time we'd go out in-world we'd find somebody doing something.... We were going to be taken into a group bath house in our tour of Rome, but we never went inside because the instructor asked the guide why we were going in there and stopped it. It was an adult bath house.

One expert, in SL since 2003, had this to say:

It's been called the "wild west". How do you police it? The wild west towns were so far apart, and you might see the marshal once a year.

"Griefing" and Other Forms of Abuse

No students in this class experienced griefing, likely due to luck and wise field trip choices made by the instructor. Orientation and Help Island had a large number of griefers that some students commented on, though none approached them. They liked the orientations on ISTE, Angel Island (private) and New Citizens Island. On one outing on Help Island the researcher and instructor experienced griefing as pornographic pictures rained down from the sky.

In the public areas (of Help and Orientation Islands) there are a lot of people talking, so people talking take up your audio channel and your chat is taken up by that, too. You have 30 people standing around and everyone is trying to figure out what to do, so it's distracting.

To some extent, the above student's experience may have been the result of more experiences in SL than other students and more exploratory behaviors. This student, below, was more careful.

I had positive experiences everywhere I went. When I talked to people, I made a lot of friends. I did teleport somewhere accidentally when I was looking for a build shop. It was a nude male place so I tp'd home. I didn't have any negative experiences, but I try to stay on track and stick to the educational sites.

Everybody I've met has been very friendly, particularly the educators...

False or Misleading Identities

Students chose avatars that matched their sex. However, they were made aware that other avatars might not be who they seemed to be. Experienced university SL experts often had more than one avatar, such as one male and one female. About half of them had them for varying reasons. Those that had both sexes had different kinds of encounters, both positive and negative, but mostly positive. However, this identity discrepancy could be disconcerting. The instructor had this to say about not knowing who the person behind the avatar was:

It causes problems. You think you are relating or communicating with a girl and it's a guy. You might say something to a girl that you would not say to a guy or vice versa.

Males who create female avatars were shocked at the different responses that their avatars receive in SL, both positive and negative.

In SL I asked people ...about the difference [three women and three men in a group] ...they said they use female avatars when they teach classes because their initial reception as a presenter is better, they get better reactions, people are more involved, and people are more apt to give them feedback. They are not ignored. ...when a female avatar comes in it's always how nice their outfits are and how pretty they look, but when guys come in they don't say anything.

The difference in male/female perception is born out by a male university expert who made both male and female avatars and caused distress to a group of women in a professional group.

From the standpoint of coming from a feminist point of view, myself, I was surprised at their reactions to my female avatar. They were shocked at my female avatar. They didn't think that I should have a beautiful avatar. They were attacking me, saying "beauty is on the inside, don't be a part of this", etc. I didn't get the same reaction with my male avatar as I did with my guy avatar and he is equivalent to my female avatar looks. Was it because it was a guy avatar and I'm a guy, or was it because I shouldn't be allowed to sit behind a beautiful female avatar as a guy? I think it's more the idea, "Oh, my gosh, here's another guy and this is what he thinks beautiful should be." But everyone has the opportunity to make a beautiful avatar. I appreciate beauty in all its forms, in a sunset or in another human being, male or female. I also don't use that as my sole judge of beauty in another. If they would have taken the time to get to know me as a person they might have thought differently.

The same university expert had this to say about harassment:

I've been sexually harassed in SL....I've actually been harassed in ways that I have been dumbfounded by. The one time I knew someone and he did it, I was surprised, since he knew who I actually was and that I was a guy. It happens quite a bit with people you don't know. It seems to be a problem with male avatars to female avatars.

Instructors should choose regions for their educational benefits, realizing that the educational regions are safest. However, students that make fullest use of the various SL regions need to be trained in the importance of teleporting to a safe place, and handling themselves in SL in much the same way that they need to in real life. One university expert summed it up, thusly:

In terms of protocol and behavior it takes some time to get into SL and interact with others to see what is acceptable and welcome and what is not..... We all come to SL and real life with our own expectations and we carry them into SL. We become offended and proud, just as in real life.... Most people try to follow the rules and do what others expect in a virtual environment.

Legal Issues

Students were taught to observe legal issues through their various assignments, field trips and projects. Since regions vary and the educational sites were the ones that students frequented most, the incidences of copyright and trademark infringement and other crime observed by the class, as a whole, were very rare. University experts and the instructor observed that student experiences of legal issues, much like ethical ones, were a function of their lack of experience in SL commerce, building and scripting. Also, leasing from or owning a private island, rather than the Mainland, which has no covenants, also provided a measure of security from these types of infringements, since sim owners could require

covenants against certain types of establishments and behaviors that would lend themselves to this type of activity.

Copyright Infringement

A lot of people talk about uploading files. When I was looking around The galleries I saw quite a few images that they probably didn't get permission to put them there....Where is the line between stealing and acquiring? Other than the visual arts I didn't see anything that was copyrighted....I'm not big on shopping and haven't frequented a lot of stores.

What if we have an IM conversation and we put it on a notecard? I had a conversation with (artist) and I wanted to remember particulars about that conversation so I cut and pasted it onto a notecard. I'm saving that for myself, only, and not sharing it with anyone.

Saving this notecard would be the equivalent of saving an e-mail to us. We can't pass it on without permission, but we can store it and refer to it for our own use or paraphrase it.

University experts had this to say about copyright infringement:

In terms of [copyright] violations, they happen all the time....Most of the time when you say, "Hey, when you post this chat, even to me, it's a violation of the terms of SL and you can be banned..." They are surprised....

In terms of building and scripting, most university experts agreed that infringement and theft were problems, as noted by Elliott (2008), with these observations.

One of the bigger problems is copyright and intellectual property. There are a lot of problems there. I've been involved with different designers in SL that have tried to work with LL to protect IP. In terms of browsers, people can actually use them to create a script in SL that allows them to steal scripts in SL, textures, objects. If you realize that something has been stolen then you can file a Digital Millennium Copyright Act violation with Linden Labs and they will clear the databases of the stolen objects.... a group of designers filed against someone who had stolen textures (buildings, clothing)....They won...

The instructor, who also did a lot of building and scripting in SL, confirmed this perception of copyright and trademark infringement, as well.

Copyright issues - people have imported movie posters, masterpiece Art (Mona Lisa, etc.), etc. Name brand products like Nike shoes, Prada Purses, that kind of thing....performing copyrighted plays in SL....When I went to the SL Bar Association meeting I was talking to a vocalist there ...on changes to the law on live streaming on the internet. They might only be able to perform their own music on SL and not someone else's.... There are a lot of storytelling places. They are reading copyrighted stories. It's happening on public land.

In summary, copyright and trademark infringement appear to be a factor of how involved the user is SL, and how much the user does building and scripting. The more one is involved in constructing a space in SL and furnishing it the more interaction there would be with SL commercial endeavors potentials and hazards. Students, as a whole, at this level, found few legal issues of note.

CURRENT CHALLENGES IN GRADUATE ONLINE TEACHING

When students are expected to take full advantage of SL, not just sitting in a replica of an in-world

classroom, then they need the tools to explore SL in their learning and avoid potential legal and ethical issues. Some of this learning is gradual, according to the experts and the instructor, and comes with experience. However, other information needs to be taught, along with some strategies. Adventures have an element of risk, yet they allow for the exploration of the rich palette that SL has to offer. Some implications for future classes would be:

1. Teach students about the SL Community Standards and other legal and ethical issues before leaving the SL classroom.
2. Do exercises with students in which they must problem solve about difficult situations, such as being harassed, captured, or griefed, so that they can handle themselves when going into SL alone.
3. Teach them how to teleport home or to a safe place should unpleasantness occur.
4. In order to teach students about the many regions, problems and wonders of SL, begin by taking students on virtual field trips before sending them out on their own.
5. Use SL for what the instructor has called "three-dimensional representations of difficult or expensive concepts". It's cheaper, easier, and faster than in real life, though it's best done on private land, due to theft issues.
6. When learning to teach or build in SL for the first time or in developing immersive learning environments, the university experts and instructor recommended having a mentor.
7. Teach them to appreciate what SL has to offer through what the instructor has called "the power of play". SL was originally designed as a game, and it's social networking opportunities abound. As one student said:

I've met people from all parts of the world, Germany, England, Canada, and I don't travel there every day.

REFERENCES

Acello, R. (2008, October). As worlds collide: ABA groups ponder "real" law rules and applications in virtual environments. *ABA Journal.* Retrieved December 5, 2008, from http://www.abajournal.com/magazine/as_worlds_collide/

AITP. (2009). *Association of Information Technology Professionals (AITP) code of ethics.* Retrieved on August 9, from http://www.aitp.org/organization/about/ethics/ethics.jsp

Annetta, L., Murray, M., Laird, S., Bohr, S., & Park, J. (2008). Investigating student attitudes toward a synchronous, online graduate course in a multi-user virtual learning environment. *Journal of technology and teacher education, 16*(1), 5-34. ACM Council. (2009). *Association for Computing Machinery (ACM) code of ethics and professional conduct.* Retrieved August 9, from http://www.acm.org/about/code-of-ethics

Boostrom, R. (2008). The social construction of virtual reality and the stigmatized identity of the newbie. *The journal of virtual worlds research, 1*(2), 2-19.

Botterbusch, H., & Talab, R. (2009). Ethical and legal issues in teaching with Second Life. *TechTrends.*

Bragg vs. Linden Research Inc. (n.d.). Retrieved April 7, 2009, from http://dockets.justia.com/docket/court-paedce/case_no-e:2006cv04925/case_id-217858 [subscription required]

Castranova, E. (2004). The right to play. *New York Law School Review, 49.* Retrieved from http://ssrn.com/abstract=733486

Castronova, E. (2005). *Synthetic worlds.* Chicago: University of Chicago Press.

Charmaz, K. (2006). *Constructing grounded theory: A practical guide through qualitative analysis.* London: Sage Publications.

Duranske, B. (2008). *Virtual law: Navigating the legal landscape of virtual worlds.* Chicago: American Bar Association Publishing.

Elliot, J. (2008). Help-somebody robbed my Second Life avatar! *Journal of virtual worlds research,* 1(1), 1-11.

Ethical and legal group. (2007). *Second Life feasibility study: Government, crime and Second Life.* Retrieved April 5, 2009 from http://manfromporlock.wetpaint.com/page/Ethical+and+Legal+Group

Fetscherin, M., & Lattemann, C. (2007, June). User acceptance of virtual worlds: An exploratory study about Second Life. Retrieved December 7, 2008 from http://www.fetscherin.com/UserAcceptanceVirtualWorlds.htm

Gunkel, D., & Hawhee, D. (2008). Virtual reality and the reformatting of ethics. *Journal of Mass Media Ethics, 18*(3/4), 173–194.

Horsfield, P. (2002, November). *Continuities and discontinuities in ethical reflections on digital virtual reality.* Paper presented at the Virtual Reality International Conference, University of Illinois at Urbana-Champaign.

Huizina, J. (1998). *Homo ludens: A study of the play element in culture.* New York: Taylor & Francis.

Kane, S. (2007, November). Merchants decry copyright chaos. *Reuters.* Retrieved March 30, 2008, from http://secondlife.reuters.com/stories/2007/11/07/merchants-decry-second-life-copyright-chaos/

Kerbs, R. W. (2005). Social and ethical considerations in virtual worlds. *The Electronic Library, 23*(5), 539–547. doi:10.1108/02640470510631254

Kittross, J., & Gordon, D. (2003). The academy and cyberspace ethics. *Journal of Mass Media Ethics, 18*(3), 286–290. doi:10.1207/S15327728JMME1803&4_9

Kozinets, R. V. (1997). I want to believe: A netnography of the X-Philes. *Advances in Consumer Research. Association for Consumer Research (U. S.), 25*, 470–475.

Kozinets, R. V. (2002). The field behind the screen: Using netnography for marketing research in online communities. *JMR, Journal of Marketing Research, 39*(1), 61–72. doi:10.1509/jmkr.39.1.61.18935

Lastrowka, G., & Hunter, D. (2004, January). The laws of virtual worlds. *Cal. L. Rev., 1,* 49. Retrieved from http://ssrn.com/abstract=402860

Merriam, S. B. (1998). *Qualitative research and case study applications in education* (2nd ed.). San Francisco: Jossey-Bass. Miles, M., & Huberman, M. (1994). *Qualitative data analysis* (2nd ed.). Thousand Oaks, CA: Sage Publications.

Mulligan, J., & Petrovsky, B. (2003). *Developing online games: An insider's guide.* Boston: New Riders. Ostrander, M. (2008, March 4). *Interview protocol. Second Life interviews.* Retrieved on December 5, 2008 from http://librariandreamer.wordpress.com/?s=interview+protocol

Romme, A. (2003). Learning outcomes of microworlds for management education. *Management Learning, 34*(1), 51–62. doi:10.1177/1350507603034001130

Schroeder, R. (2007). An overview of ethical and social issues in shared virtual environments. *Futures, 39*(6), 704. Second Life. (2009). *Community standards.* Retrieved March 5, 2009, from http://secondlife.com/corporate/cs.php

Second Life. (2008, April 29). *Second Life economic statistics.* Retrieved April 30, 2008, from http://secondlife.com/whatis/economy_stats.php

Second Life. (2009). *Terms of service.* Retrieved April 7, 2009 from http://secondlife.com/corporate/tos.php

Shannon, J., Judson, J., & Nuara, L. (2008). Pirating the metaverse. Second Life as a context for a business/law seminar. *Virtual worlds at Seton Hall.* Retrieved on December 4, 2008, from http://tltc.shu.edu/blogs/projects/virtualworlds/

Shutkin, D. (2004). Virtual community and ethical differences in the field of education. *JCT, 20*(4), 91–113.

SimTeach. (2008, December 1). *Universities, colleges & schools* (October 19th, 2007). Retrieved December 7, 2008, from http://simteach.com/wiki/index.php?title=Institutions_and_Organizations_in_SL

SimTeach. (2009). *Institutions and organizations in SL.* Retrieved September, from http://tinyurl.com/2fen2s http://www.simteach.com/wiki/index.php?title=Second_Life:_Educators_Working_with_Teens

Talab, R. (2008). Using digital materials in online courses: A cautionary tale of Georgia State University. *TechTrends, 4*(52), 30–35.

Talab, R., & Butler, R. (2007). Shared electronic spaces in the classroom: Copyright, privacy, and guidelines. *TechTrends, 1*(51), 12.

Yin, R. (2003). *Case study research: Design and methods.* Thousand Oaks, CA: Sage Press.

Chapter 15
Second Life® Project Development as a Venue for Interdisciplinary Collaboration

Susan Toth-Cohen
Jefferson College of Health Professions, USA

Pamela R. Mitchell
Kent State University, USA

EXECUTIVE SUMMARY

The increasing complexity of health service delivery, along with rapid growth of the older population, increased survival of premature births and serious accidents, and retirement of baby boomer healthcare workers have created a critical need for health care professionals who can function as team members and leaders who collaborate to deliver effective, individualized care. Yet, while collaboration between disciplines is considered an ideal, many barriers impede its implementation, including geographic isolation and limited information exchange opportunities (Kilgo & Bruder, 1997). As a result, students in health disciplines frequently are educated without exposure to the professionals with whom they will work when entering the workforce. The need for interprofessional education was highlighted by concerns noted by the Committee on the Health Professional Education Summit for the Board of Health Care Services of the Institute of Medicine in 2003, that reported a major disconnect between the isolated professional education approach in health care and increasing expectations for interdisciplinary team-based care. The Center for the Advancement of Interprofessional Education indicates that benefits of such an educational approach can cultivate closer collaboration between professions, organizations and service users, which can improve quality of care (Center for the Advancement of Interprofessional Education, 2002). The ability of health-related programs to implement interprofessional project-based learning is often hampered by distance, time and programmatic constraints. Virtual worlds such as Second Life can help address these constraints. Virtual worlds like Second Life® (SL) provide unique venues for fostering collaboration by closing the gaps created by distance and lack of information exchange. In this chapter,

DOI: 10.4018/978-1-60566-878-9.ch015

the authors describe the process of collaboration by occupational therapy (OT) and speech-language pathology (SLP) students and faculty in developing an educational event in the virtual environment of SL. The event planning and implementation provide an example of project-based learning (Donnelly & Fitzmaurice, 2005) and interdisciplinary community-building that provides insights and "lessons learned" with application to future project development in virtual worlds. The authors discuss the applications of project-based learning for interdisciplinary team building, describe student and faculty roles and specific steps in planning, management, and production of an event for current and prospective OT and SLP students, and analyze challenges and supports in project implementation

BACKGROUND

The present chapter details the interdisciplinary collaboration of two faculty members from university programs in the health professions: one from a SLP department in a Midwestern university and the other from an OT program at a university on the East Coast. These two professions commonly interact closely on interdisciplinary teams in the workplace and may engage in co-treatment, in which an OT and SLP work simultaneously with a patient.

Occupational therapists help patients improve their ability to perform tasks in living and working environments. They work with individuals who suffer from a mentally, physically, developmentally, or emotionally disabling condition. Occupational therapists use treatments to develop, recover, or maintain the daily living and work skills of their patients. The therapist helps clients not only to improve their basic motor functions and reasoning abilities, but also to compensate for permanent loss of function. The goal is to help clients have independent, productive, and satisfying lives. (Bureau of Labor Statistics, 2008)

Speech-language pathologists, sometimes called speech therapists, assess, diagnose, treat, and help to prevent disorders related to speech, language, cognitive-communication, voice, swallowing, and fluency. Speech-language pathologists work with people who cannot produce speech sounds or cannot produce them clearly; those with speech rhythm and fluency problems, such as stuttering; people with voice disorders, such

as inappropriate pitch or harsh voice; those with problems understanding and producing language; those who wish to improve their communication skills by modifying an accent; and those with cognitive communication impairments, such as attention, memory, and problem solving disorders. They also work with people who have swallowing difficulties.(Bureau of Labor Statistics, 2008)

The OT and SLP faculty members had both been engaged in virtual learning initiatives in Second Life® starting in early 2007 with funding from their respective universities. However, while supported by their universities, these faculty conducted the initiatives largely as individual efforts. Their status as innovators in this effort (Rogers, 2003) was notable in that none of their colleagues had yet begun to explore or utilize the potential for virtual environments as venues for learning by students in health professions. Thus, each faculty had begun developing initial programs for their respective students at the time they met at an event at the OT faculty's Center on SL; this formed the basis for discussion and common interest that initiated their collaboration. The first group effort by SLP and OT faculty and students was to expand an exhibit on adapting environments for daily life; this was followed by a joint exhibit for the SL Fifth Birthday Celebration, which highlighted the importance of interdisciplinary collaboration through informational displays and virtual objects. These initial efforts then expanded to the focus of the present case study, an event for current and prospective SLP and OT students collaboratively planned by SLP and OT students and faculty from the two universities.

SETTING

Both key project faculty recognized the potential of SL as an immersive project-based learning environment, particularly for students in disciplines characterized by the application of science and technology to everyday challenges of people facing disease, injury, or challenging life situations. Each had established a virtual center to serve as a test-ground for projects, classes, and meeting space and determine feasibility and best applications for their respective institutions. Additionally, both faculty had begun collaborative projects with others in SL who were geographically distant and in working in disciplines very different from (though complementary to) their own. The SLP faculty had started a group on interdisciplinary practices in an effort to promote further efforts to exchange information and develop collaborative projects, unbounded by time and location constraints that can hamper real world collaborative efforts. It was at this point that the two principal faculty met during an event held at the OT faculty's center; each was thus "primed" for collaboration as each had students already in-world and previous experience with group work in SL.

CASE DESCRIPTION

Primary participants in the case project included three undergraduate and two graduate students in speech-language pathology, and five graduate students in occupational therapy. Under faculty direction, the 10 students planned, implemented, and participated in a virtual information fair (the Interdisciplinary Open House in SL), designed to provide information about OT and SLP in a social and enjoyable atmosphere. The case illustrates key

characteristics of project-based learning, including the emphasis on:

- creating teams of three or more students to work on an in-depth project for three to eight weeks;
- introducing a complex entry question that establishes a student's need to know, and scaffolding the project with activities and new information that deepens the work.
- providing timely assessments and/or feedback on the projects for content, oral and written communication, teamwork, critical thinking, and other important skills. (Pearlman, 2006)

Planning consisted of a multi-stage process that occurred over an eight-week period. We presented students with the challenge of creating the Interdisciplinary Open House event. The project faculty held regular meetings in SL with students from their own discipline, and interdisciplinary group meetings with speech-language pathology and occupational therapy were held to plan the Interdisciplinary Open House event. During these meetings, students engaged in brainstorming about activities and content for the event, many of which were very challenging as they involved skills in translating ideas that worked well in real life into the virtual world. Students experimented with various ideas and constructed objects for the event that would be interesting for participants interacting with them and that would also inform participants about the disciplines of OT and SLP (Figure 1).

The virtual space was set up with a carnival theme, with rides, games, a maze, skating, and information booths (see Figure 2 and Figure 3). The atmosphere was very casual and playful, with about 30-35 avatars in attendance. During the last 1 to 1 ½ hours of the event, participants listened and danced to a live concert provided by a SL performer (Figure 4). On the evening of the event, we administered an online survey to the students

Figure 1. Organizing for the Event

Figure 2. Interdisciplinary Open House Fairground

on the interdisciplinary virtual project to evaluate their perceptions of the Open House event and on the value of interdisciplinary training experiences in SL. The survey consisted of 16 questions, with 12 requiring closed choice ordinal responses and four requiring open ended narrative responses. Students completed the survey within two days of the completion of the Open House event.

Nine students (90%) on the project completed the survey to report on their perceptions of their experiences in interdisplinary practice in OT and

SLP. Five were OT students, three were in SLP and one was a graduate student project intern. The majority of the event group students were graduate level (7) and two were undergraduates, and the students varied in their pre-service clinical preparation, ranging from zero to six semesters of clinical practica. When asked to rate the importance of interdisciplinary training experiences in real life and SL, 44.4% rated real life interdisciplinary experiences as "essential", and 55.6% rated them as "very important". Student perceptions of

Figure 3. Information Booths

Figure 4. Concert Performance

the importance of interdisciplinary training in SL were rated somewhat lower, with 55.6% indicating the value of such experiences as "very valuable" and 44.4% indicating it to be "moderately valuable". The majority of respondents perceived the career relevance of interdisciplinary work in SL as "moderately relevant" (55.6%) and 33.3% felt it

was "somewhat relevant". One respondent rated the item as "extremely relevant".

Students were asked about their overall experience planning for and implementing the Interdisciplinary Virtual Open House project. Most students perceived the experience to be "very valuable (66.7%) or "moderately valuable" (33.3%). Since a major goal of the project was to engage students in the planning and implementation of the event to facilitate interdisciplinary collaboration, they were asked to rate their opinion of the quality of their experience in planning and organizing the open house event. The majority of students rated the experience as "very good" (55.6%), while 33.3% rated the experience as "excellent". One student rated this item as "good". Students were asked to indicate what they found most enjoyable about the interdisciplinary virtual open house project from a closed set of outcomes identified by the project directors as desired outcomes. See Table 1 for detail on this item. Since reliability and access to SL can be an issue for students who may not have computers meeting the basic requirements, the project students were asked about their experience with this. There was a range on this item from "fair" to "excellent", with the most frequent response "very good". Please see Table 2 for a categorization of responses to this item.

Table 1. Ratings of "Most Enjoyable" Aspects of Project Participation

Enjoyed	Number of responses
Opportunities to collaborate	8
Learning about the other discipline	7
Socialization	5
Planning process	4
Building things for the project	4

Table 2. Ratings of Second Life® Technology

Please rate your experience related to the Second Life® technology platform	
Excellent	2
Very good	5
Good	1
Fair	1
Poor	0

CHALLENGES AND SOLUTIONS

Project Platform

Experience in SL by students was varied, from no previous experience to approximately one year, although the majority had less than two months of experience in SL. This presented an immediate challenge on the project. In order to address this issue, a Master's level intern was recruited within SL to provide orientation and training. The intern had over two years of experience in SL, and was assigned to the interdisciplinary project five to ten hours per week throughout a 16-week academic semester. The intern's activities consisted of small group and individual training sessions addressing individual student questions and providing specific training in navigation and communication in SL. In addition, students were encouraged to develop individual goals on anything they wanted to learn related to SL that could be addressed in the small group sessions or in individual tutoring sessions. Student goals for these individualized development sessions included the following skills: building, dancing, using avatar gestures, finding a virtual pet, making T-Shirts and finding locations around SL for bargains on clothing. Once the initial concept for the Interdisciplinary Open House was developed, the intern also assisted with coordinating the planning for the event.

Student Interaction

Initial brainstorming sessions were characterized by somewhat low rates of communication and uneven participation by students. In addition, limited interaction occurred in the early project brainstorming meetings between students across the two disciplines. In order to support increased participation by students, faculty utilized wait time and leading questions to increase student participation. On occasion, students were sent in pairs consisting of one SLP and one OT to complete planning activities to report ideas back to the group. Once the initial plans for the event were agreed-upon, large group meetings decreased and OT and SLP students were paired to meet independently to finalize their assigned project activities.

Scheduling

Since most students were on different schedules, it was sometimes difficult to arrange meeting times that were convenient for all. To address this issue, we alternated days of the week when meetings were held. Additionally, when students were paired as above, scheduling became easier. Another strategy was to do as much as possible individually and outside of the virtual environment. Many planning and organizational tasks were well adapted to this strategy.

EPILOGUE AND LESSONS LEARNED

Students and faculty viewed the planning and implementation of the Open House event as a successful venture that helped OT and SLP students to better understand each other's discipline and have fun doing so. The opportunity to collaborate and learn was the most common benefit that students listed in their survey responses. Sample quotes included:

- Can learn about different areas of the other discipline in a fun, creative, & convenient way
- Getting to learn about other disciplines and to learn to collaborate and work with others

The creative aspect of collaborating with one another to plan and implement an event also appeared to be a valued benefit.

As one student said:

The creative process is limitless and both disciplines can hone in on specific adaptations needed.

These comments suggest that the Open House project provided students with an opportunity to develop key skills considered necessary in the 21st century marketplace: the ability to think creatively, evaluate and analyze information, and communicate effectively (Silva, 2008). Results from the post-event evaluation supported this conclusion, and indicated that the vast majority of students on the project viewed the quality of the opportunity as very good or excellent.

Lessons Learned

1. Realize that students from different disciplines or different levels within the same discipline may need considerable encouragement as well as time to develop a collaborative relationship. Pairing students and having them work as independent teams after initial guidance by faculty is an effective method for facilitating higher levels of participation. However, faculty should be prepared to provide considerable mentoring in the initial stages of a project.

2. Take technological aspects of virtual environments into consideration when planning educational experiences in-world. Also, do not assume that because students are so-called digital natives, that they will learn how to navigate and work within virtual worlds at rapid speed and high levels of skill immediately.

3. Identify a student mentor—someone who is at a higher skill level in navigating and working within a virtual environment. This can help to bring the rest of the student group up to speed so that they can fully participate in the collaborative effort.

4. Make learning fun by framing projects in a playful yet substantive and focused manner.

This interdisciplinary project used the unique affordances of Second Life® to enable collaboration between faculty and students in occupational therapy and speech-language pathology at geographically distant universities. A project-based format helped to promote students' creative thinking, communication skills, and their ability to evaluate and analyze information. Special considerations for conducting projects in virtual environments include the additional time required to become familiar with the environment and to establish collaborative relationships as well as the need by faculty to facilitate participation and provide structured mentoring, especially at the beginning of a project.

REFERENCE

Bureau of Labor Statistics, U.S. Department of Labor. (2008). *Occupational outlook handbook, 2008-09 edition, speech-language pathologists.* Retrieved November 30, 2008, from http://www.bls.gov/oco/ocos099.htm

Bureau of Labor Statistics, U.S. Department of Labor. (2008). *Occupational outlook handbook, 2008-09 edition, occupational therapists.* Retrieved November 30, 2008, from http://www.bls.gov/oco/ocos078.htm

Donnelly, R., & Fitzmaurice, M. (2005). Collaborative project-based learning and problem-based learning in higher education: A consideration of tutor and student roles in learner-focused strategies. In G. O'Neill, S. Moore, & B. McMullin (Eds.), *Emerging issues in the practice of university learning and teaching.* Dublin, Ireland: AISHE.

Edutopia. (2001). *PBL research summary: Studies validate project based learning.* Retrieved October 19, 2008, from http://www.edutopia.org/project-based-learning-research

Institute of Medicine. (2003). *Health professions education: A bridge to quality.* Washington, DC: National Academies Press.

Kilgo, J. L., & Bruder, M. B. (1997). Creating new visions in institutions of higher education: Interdisciplinary approaches to personnel preparation in early intervention. In P. J. Winton, J. A. McCollum, & C. Catlett (Eds.), *Reforming personnel preparation in early intervention.* Chapel Hill, NC: SCPP.

Pearlman, B. (2006). *News skills for a new century: Students thrive on cooperation and problem solving. Edutopia.* Retrieved November 10, 2008, from http://www.edutopia.org/new-skills-new-century

Rogers, E. M. (2003). *Diffusion of innovations* (5th ed.). New York: Free Press.

Silva, E. (2008). Measuring skills for the 21st century. *Education Sector.* Retrieved November 2, 2008, from http://www.newtechfoundation.org/press_research/MeasuringSkills_11-08.pdf

APPENDIX 1. COMMENTS FROM STUDENT SURVEY

Biggest Challenges:

- Coordinating schedules to meet and finding people to collaborate with
- Achieving the same the goals and demonstrating how professions compliment each other
- It is hard to represent yourself effectively and gain all the information I want to hear from people.
- Setting up in-world meeting times,
- Communication and the time everyone is available to meet.
- Finding times that everyone can meet, and meetings with large groups can be tough in SL when a lot of people are talking at once.
- Unexpected technological difficulties, and acclimating to the system/VR world
- Times were everyone can meet

One Thing Learned:

- I learned about some of the assistive devices used in the field of Occupational Therapy.
- SLP deal with a lot of medical diagnoses like trachs
- That OT and speech therapy interventions often intertwine
- Unsure
- How the leg lifter is used
- Adaptive devices used outside a school based setting
- Specifics about the usage of adaptive devises in OT to increase independence with ADLs
- That OT and SLP are very similar in their approach with clients

Biggest Benefits:

- Getting to learn about other disciplines and to learn to collaborate and work with others
- Creative process is limitless and both disciplines can hone in on specific adaptions needed
- You can leave self image of the RL behind! You can get to know the discipline through people you may never actually communicate with in RL.
- Can learn about different areas of the other discipline in a fun, creative, & convenient way
- Learning about other disciplines, as well as learning more about the different aspects within SL.
- Meeting new people, and SL connections.
- Makes the issue of geographical location non existent
- Having perspectives of other disciplines
- Appreciating other's point of view

Technology Aspects:

- I learned a lot of new technology relevant to SL. I learned a lot of of building techniques and new experiences that I haven't heard in SL before.
- I like being in SL. I feel like it will give me an edge technology-wise as well as a knack for OT consultation in the future. In addition, I think it's a great avenue to educate people who would not try to seek advice in real life.
- I am still getting used to Second Life.
- There is just so much potential for creativity.
- Feel very comfortable with most aspects of SL. The areas I am not comfortable with include scripting and extensive building.
- I find it hard to to learn here being someone who is not good with computers.
- I believe that the SL technology platform is very user friendly and allows for alot of creativity when planning events.
- Easy to learn and even if having trouble there are a lot of outlets for help

Open Comments:

- Maybe the timing could have been better...i think with Halloween next week a lot of people are having parties tonight. Maybe if the event was held on a weeknight the turnout may have been better??
- As a new student, I did not have a big role in the planning for this project, but look forward to helping out more with events like this in the future. Everyone did a great job with planning and building, I'm still very impressed.
- This was a very unique event and it was interesting to participate in both the creation and execution of it.
- Overall, this was a very valuable experience. The experience from this project will allow me effectively plan future programs in virtual worlds. I realize the importance of communication throughout the project, as well as making sure everyone is contributing equally to the various aspects.
- I am a first year student and I did not help too much with the planning. I am hoping to be able to help more in the future
- This was a great learning experience and would love to work on another one again soon!

Chapter 16
Critical Thinking in Discussion:
Online versus Face-to-Face[1]

Leonard Shedletsky
University of Southern Maine, USA

EXECUTIVE SUMMARY

This chapter explores the question: does online discussion produce critical thinking? It presents a selective review of the literature concerned with critical thinking and/or interaction during online discussion. It presents an experimental study of the effects of instructional media and instructional methods on critical thinking. The study tests the influence on critical thinking of online vs. face-to-face discussion, individual vs. group consensus in summarizing discussion, and discussion of examples of concepts vs. discussion of more abstract analysis. The purpose for reviewing the literature and carrying out the study is to increase awareness of variables that may influence the quality of discussion.

BACKGROUND

In general we define *discussion* as an alternately serious and playful effort by a group of two or more to share views and engage in mutual and reciprocal critique. The purposes of discussion are fourfold: (1) to help participants reach a more critically informed understanding about the topic or topics under consideration, (2) to enhance participants' self-awareness and their capacity for self-critique, (3) to foster an appreciation among participants for the diversity of opinion that invariably emerges when viewpoints are exchanged openly and honestly, and (4) to act as a catalyst to helping people take informed action in the world (Brookfield & Preskill, p. 6).

A close look at online discussion in education takes us headlong into a heated battleground of strongly held beliefs about the classroom. Some maintain that the traditional, face-to-face classroom is an environment of debate and interaction and immediacy between human beings and that the online classroom is a cold and inhuman landscape. Others hold that the online discussion forum extends the classroom interaction and makes the online experience worthwhile, that in fact, discussion online surpasses discussion face-to-face. Which is it?

DOI: 10.4018/978-1-60566-878-9.ch016

Discussion as a way of learning has been extolled by numerous scholars. Gergen (1995) wrote of ongoing exchange as part of the collaborative construction of knowledge, where students are involved in " . . .engaging, incorporating, and critically exploring the views of others" (p. 34). Curtis and Lawson (2001) wrote: "Interactions among students make positive contributions to students' learning (Laurillard, 1993; Moore, 1993; Ramsden, 1992) (p. 21). In their book, Discussion as a Way of Teaching, Brookfield and Preskill (2005) write:

Whether labeled "discussion," "dialogue" or "conversation," the liveliest interactions are critical. When participants take a critical stance, they are committed to questioning and exploring even the most widely accepted ideas and beliefs. Conversing critically implies an openness to re-thinking cherished assumptions and to subjecting those assumptions to a continuous round of questioning, argument, and counterargument. One of the defining characteristics of critical discussion is that participants are willing to enter the conversation with open minds. This requires people to be flexible enough to adjust their views in the light of persuasive, well-supported arguments and confident enough to retain their original opinions when rebuttals fall short. Although agreement may sometimes be desirable, it is by no means a necessity (p. 7).

One major argument offered for teaching online is the increased opportunity for discussion and collaboration (Murphy, 2003; Swan, 2006). Meyer (2003), based on her review of over 30 studies comparing web-based and traditional courses, said that " . . .if there is one strong area where the Web is used to consistent effect, it is by making ample interaction feasible, including students interacting with the course material, faculty or other experts, as well as other students" (para. 4). The constructivist model is often invoked to argue for the power of online discussion. Lapadat (2002) maintained that discussion promotes critical thinking and that asynchronous online discus-

sion, because it is written, even further enhances the higher order thinking processes. Pena-Shaff and Nicholls (2004) explained that:

Dialogue serves as an instrument for thinking because in the process of explaining, clarifying, elaborating, and defending our ideas and thoughts we engage in cognitive processes such as integrating, elaborating and structuring (Brown & Palinscar, 1989; Johansson et al., 1995; Norman, 1993). Therefore, it is in the process of articulating, reflecting and negotiating that we engage in a meaning making or knowledge construction process. This process can become even more powerful when communication among peers is done in written form, because writing, done without the immediate feedback of another person as in oral communication, requires a fuller elaboration in order to successfully convey meaning (Koschmann, Kelson, Feltovich, & Barrows, 1996, pp. 244 -245).

Time and again we are presented with the idea that discussion is especially well suited for online environments, that students inter-act with one another and the teacher, they debate, they collaborate and offer constructive feedback and engage one another in ideas. At the same time, we hear from teachers that they are disappointed with the level of discussion in their online environments. In discussing just this topic-- online discussions in his courses-- one college professor said that "sometimes they seem to go nowhere/ everywhere." Another concurred with this: "I, too, like the idea of using the Discussion Board to promote thoughtful and organized discussions. However they seem to fall flat for the same reasons that Harry mentioned." And another said: " . . . often students use these to simply respond to others and/or just complete an assignment. Thoughtful reflections and substantiated arguments are often lacking in the posting. Does anyone have a way of increasing either?"

Numerous teachers have made the same observation: Online discussion is often lifeless. You can add my personal teaching experience to those who have been disappointed with the level of discourse in the online discussions in the courses I have taught. It would appear that the disappointing level of discourse may be a function of some pervasive influence. In this chapter, I would like to explore the state of online discussion in college classes. Are some models for running a discussion more likely to lead to a better outcome—i.e., more productive, engaged, involved students--than other models?

One experimental study of online discussion set out to discover if managing or designing specific discussion behaviors would improve the level of critical thinking skills displayed by students. Duphorne and Gunawardena (2005) compared three groups of students engaged in online discussion. The students were randomly assigned to either (condition 1) " . . . a problem-posing, critical inquiry approach to discussion with specific roles supporting critical thinking that were assigned to members" (p. 42); (condition 2) ". . . a five-step problem-solving approach: (a) formulate the problem, (b) generate or find alternate strategies or explore possible strategies, (c) choose a solution, (d) discuss how one might carry out the solution, and (e) evaluate potential consequences or implications" (Duphorne & Gunawardena, 2005, p. 42). Roles were assigned to individuals, such as Leader, Gatekeeper, Summarizer, and (condition 3) a control group that was not given a specific critical thinking strategy. Dependent measures consisted of a measure of the S's critical thinking ability. The results showed no significant difference in critical thinking skills employed in the three conditions.

Garrison, Anderson, & Archer (2001, 2000) found little evidence of any critical discourse in students' online discussion. While there was some brainstorming (42%), there was only 13% Integration (construction of a possible solution) and only 4% of responses in the highest stage of critical discourse, Resolution (assessment of a solution). One review of the literature (Rourke & Kanuka, 2007) reported that "Observers of interaction as it

takes shape in computer conferencing rarely report significant instances of critical discourse, dissenting opinion, challenges to others, or expressions of difference" (p. 835). This makes it difficult to assess the relationship between the various models of running online discussion in comparison to running classroom discussion.

Meyer (2003a) performed a content analysis of the threaded discussions of graduate level students. She coded each posting as one of the four cognitive processing categories derived from Garrison, Anderson, & Archer, 2001. Triggering refers to posing the problem; Exploration refers to a search for information; Integration refers to construction of a possible solution; and Resolution refers to critical assessment of a solution. She reported the following results: " 18% were triggering questions, 51% were exploration, 22% were integration, and 7% resolution" (para. 1). Clearly, evidence of critical or higher-order thinking was scarce.

In one study of undergraduate pre-service teachers, the participants were asked to link field experiences to their readings and to discuss their ideas in an online discussion (Angeli, Valanides & Bonk, 2003). They were told to describe an interesting experience in their teaching and to respond to at least four other student descriptions and to summarize a peer's posting. Case discussions were analyzed for the quality of postings. Only 7% of the students' replies were supported ideas, while 49% were unsupported advice and personal opinions. The authors concluded: "The results showed that students' online discourse was mostly an exchange of personal experiences and did not reflect well-supported reasoning" (p. 31).

There are some notable exceptions to this pattern of disappointing online discussions. Heckman and Annabi (2005) compared 120 seniors in a capstone course in Information Management, using the same facilitator for both online and face-to-face discussions of case studies. The study was careful to make the behaviors of the

Table 1. Summary of findings: Comparison between FTF and ALN case study discussions (table taken from Heckman and Anabi, 2005)

• Teacher presence was much greater in FTF discussions.
• Virtually all student utterances in FTF were responses to the teacher. In ALN discussions nearly two-thirds of student utterances were responses to other students.
• FTF discussions used more informal language and active voice.
• Student utterances were longer in ALN, while teacher utterances were shorter.
• The major interactive operation in ALN was continuing a thread, while in FTF it was asking a question (usually by the teacher).
• There was a greater incidence of direct instruction in the FTF discussion. This was true of confirming understanding (a feedback function), presenting content, and focusing the discussion.
• There was a greater incidence of drawing in participants, especially through cold calling on students, in the FTF discussions.
• More than half of the instances of Teaching Process in the ALN discussion were performed by students rather than the teacher.
• In the average FTF discussion there were nearly twice as many instances of Cognitive Process as in the average ALN discussion.
• In FTF discussions, the instances of Cognitive Process were predominantly in the lower order exploration category.
• In contrast, the ALN discussions contained more high-level Cognitive Process instances, both in absolute and relative terms.
• Student-to-student interactions contain a greater proportion of high-level cognitive indicators.

instructor as consistent across modes as possible, and to randomly assign students to one of eight groups for comparison, controlling for order effects. An extensive content analysis was done on the transcriptions of the discussions. Numerous categories were applied to the data, such as

- **Cognitive Process:** components of critical thinking (triggering, exploration, integration, & resolution);
- **Social Process:** characteristics of the social interaction, such as cohesiveness;
- **Teaching Process:** design of the learning experience, as well as its delivery and facilitation [either student or teacher behaviors];
- **Discourse Process:** responses between learners and learners and learners and instructors;

Heckman and Annabi reported dramatic differences between the online (what they call asynchronous learning networks or ALN) and face-to-face modes. With regard to critical thinking, they found that the online discussions contained

nearly twice as many instances of high level analysis compared to the face-to-face discussions. However, the highest level of cognitive processing, Integration, was identical in both modes. Some key findings in Heckman and Annabi (2005) are shown in Table 1.

The Heckman and Annabi study gives us reason to be cautious in coming to conclusions on the comparison between online and face-to-face discussion. They report numerous qualitative differences in the process of communication between the two modes. The teacher seeking to facilitate a discussion characterized by student engagement should be encouraged by the active involvement of Heckman and Annabi's students. Some other studies also find the online discussion to generate more critical thinking than the face-to-face discussion (Garrison, Anderson, & Archer, 2003; Vess, 2005). As for critical thinking, Heckman & Annabi's results are a bit mixed as far as which mode is better, although encouraging for the use of online discussion.

Most of the studies reviewed, unlike the Heckman and Annabi (2005) study, did not observe the classroom side of discussion, but only reported on levels of critical thinking and other categories for the online discussion. Just how much interaction is in classroom discussion and how high a level of discussion is found in most classroom discussions? One suspects that often we imagine the classroom discussion contains more engaged students than it actually does contain. Heckman & Annabi's results would not support such an optimistic view of classroom discussion.

The teacher-centered climate of the classroom is what Heckman and Annabi find, even with college seniors in a capstone course. To this writer, a classroom teacher with a history of some 30 years of experience, this is not surprising at all. When you stop to think about it, how often are students willing to disagree with one another in the public setting of the classroom, where students challenge one another's statements, seek clarification, or elaboration and ask one another questions? In my experience, students are more likely to back off or possibly roll their eyes than to challenge one another in the classroom. It is unfortunate that so often judgments of online discussion are offered against the backdrop of an imagined classroom discussion, with all its imagined give and take.

We would be remiss if we did not notice what appears to be two different and contradictory stories being told here. On the one hand, it appears that online discussion does not really live up to the promise of engaged students applying critical thinking to their online discussions. On the other hand, some evidence demonstrates a dramatically more involved student online than in the classroom. How do we resolve this apparent contradiction?

Rourke & Kanuka (2007) offer an important idea that may answer this conundrum. They propose that computer conferencing that results in increased critical thinking takes place in conditions of collaborative meaning making. Features that characterize this design are small group size and purposive collaboration (e.g., case-based learning, problem based learning). The design that produces low levels of interaction and low levels

of critical thinking is the open-ended forum of the whole class, with little structure. Pena-Shaff and Nicholls (2004) point to the need for students to reach consensus in the collaborative small group that encourages the interaction. Without this need, disagreements can be ignored. Rovai (2007) reviewed the literature on running effective online discussions, and concluded that "Online courses need to be designed so that they provide motivation for students to engage in productive discussions and clearly describe what is expected, perhaps in the form of a discussion rubric" (p. 77). This study attempts to take into account instructional methods and instructional media.

SETTING THE STAGE

The students in the junior/senior level course on discourse analysis, Meaning and Communication, were randomly divided into 4 equal size groups. Each group discussed a transcribed conversation of two people engaged in a natural and spontaneous conversation. The conversations were tape recorded and transcribed the previous semester by students[2] in the Meaning and Communication course as part of the course. Over the semester, due to attrition of students, group 1 had 7 students, group 2 had 5 students, group 3 had 5 students, and group 4 had 6 students (N = 23). To determine the influence of Medium (Online vs. Face-to-Face classroom environment), Analysis (analysis based or case-based vs. example based, i.e., examples of concepts to discuss) and degree of collaborative interdependence or Report (consensus vs. individual posting of the summary of the discussion), the study was designed as shown in Table 2.

The teacher did not run the discussions. The face-to-face groups met in two separate rooms, with two groups per room, to provide ample space so that tape recording was not diminished. The teacher floated among the groups to make sure all was going well but he did not take part in the discussions. Similarly, in the online discussions

Table 2. Research Design Experimental Groups (2X2X2) Factorial Design

	INDIVIDUAL DRIVEN		CONSENSUS DRIVEN	
To Discuss	FACE-to-FACE [4 groups]	ONLINE [4 groups]	FACE-to-FACE [4 groups]	ONLINE [4 groups]
Case Based	Transcript 2, group 1 Transcript 1, group 2	Transcript 1, group 1 Transcript 2, group 2	Transcript 2, group 3 Transcript 1, group 4	Transcript 1, group 3 Transcript 2, group 4
Example Based	Transcript 4, group 1 Transcript 3, group 2	Transcript 3, group 1 Transcript 4, group 2	Transcript 4, group 3 Transcript 3, group 4	Transcript 3, group 3 Transcript 4, group 4

the teacher did not take part in the discussions.

Two students were non-traditional age and were in different groups from each other, but all the rest were traditional college age students. During the fifth week of the course, students got to practice a face-to-face discussion of a transcript and an online discussion of a transcript. The first face-to-face discussion for the purpose of collecting data for this study took place in the classroom eight weeks into the semester. By then, the students were familiar with course concepts and the idea of analyzing a transcribed conversation. The same week as the first face-to-face discussion, the online discussion started for each group. The online discussion was given eleven days in which to be completed. The second face-to-face discussion took place during the twelfth week of the course and again the online discussion began the same week and lasted for eleven days.

The face-to-face discussions were transcribed and analyzed for levels of critical thinking and the online discussions were also coded for levels of critical thinking. Analyses were carried out to determine the influence of medium (online vs. face-to-face), report (individual vs. consensus) and analysis (examples of concepts vs. case analysis) on levels of critical thinking and interaction.

CASE DESCRIPTION

This study was undertaken to determine whether or not online discussion produces a higher level of critical thinking among students in a college

course than face-to-face discussion [MEDIUM]. In addition, this study sought to determine whether or not having to report on discussion outcomes (a summary) as an individual or a group consensus would influence levels of critical thinking displayed in the discussion [REPORT]. And finally, this study sought to determine whether or not students asked to discuss at the level of finding examples of course concepts versus asked to find a more abstract analysis of course materials (what is going on in a conversation) would influence levels of critical thinking displayed in the discussion [ANALYSIS].

The three independent variables were:

- Medium, with two levels, online discussion versus face-to-face discussion;
- Report, with two levels, subjects are told prior to discussion that each individual will write a summary of the discussion versus one written group consensus summary;
- Analysis, with two levels, subjects are told prior to discussion that they are to find examples of specific concepts in the transcription of a conversation versus they are to discuss broadly what is going on between the communicators in the transcribed conversation;

The dependent variables were four levels of critical thinking and other:

- Triggering, messages that evoke thinking about issues, that evoke a response;

- Exploration, messages that relate and connect with one another but are not supported;
- Integration, messages that build on previous messages and are supported;
- Resolution, messages that develop a hypothesis and suggest ways to test and defend the hypothesis;

Other, messages that are social in character, such as "Did you watch the game last night?"

The two raters spent several months practicing using the critical thinking coding system taken from Garrison, D. R., Anderson, T., and Archer, W. (2001), and modifying it (see Appendix A, Modifications). They chose an arbitrary discussion from the data to independently code and found substantial interrater reliability, using Cohen's Kappa (1960), a chance-adjusted measure of agreement (K = .718), with 81% agreement.

Univariate analysis of variance was performed on the data using SPSS. Main effects were found for the medium of discussion (online versus face-to-face), report (individual summary versus group consensus summary), and analysis (examples discussed versus abstract or case analysis). In addition, a number of interactions were statistically significant: report * analysis; report * medium; analysis * medium; report * analysis * medium. Interactions will be discussed separately.

TRIGGERING

The medium of discussion had a statistically significant effect on the dependent measure, triggering (F = 23.986, df = 1, 50, p <.000). Triggering messages occurred significantly more often in face-to-face discussion (Mean = 2.423) than in online discussion (Mean = .192). The type of analysis (example or case) had a statistically significant effect on the dependent measure, triggering (F = 20.406, df = 1, 50, p <.000). Triggering messages occurred significantly more often in abstract analyses of

Figure 1. Mean Frequency of the Triggering Response During Face-to-Face and Online Discussion

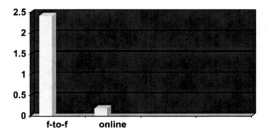

Triggering Messages F-to-F vs. Online

the transcript (Mean = 2.337) than in discussion of examples of concepts found in the transcripts (Mean = .278). The type of report (individual or consensus) had a statistically significant effect on the dependent measure, triggering (F = 12.324, df = 1, 50, p <.001). Triggering messages occurred significantly more often in consensus summaries of the discussion (Mean = 2.107) than in individual summaries of group discussion (Mean = .508).

EXPLORATION

The medium of discussion had a statistically significant effect on the dependent measure, exploration (F = 20.310, df = 1, 51, p <.000). Exploration messages occurred significantly more often in face-to-face discussion (Mean = 9.065) than in online discussion (Mean = 1.141). The type of analysis (example or case) did not have a statistically significant effect on the dependent measure, exploration (F = 2.721 df = 1, 51, p >.05). The mean score for exploration messages in abstract analyses of the transcript was 6.554 and the mean for exploration messages during discussions of examples was 3.653. The type of report (individual or consensus) had a statistically significant effect on the dependent measure, exploration (F = 6.665, df = 1, 51, p < .013). Exploration messages occurred significantly more often in consensus summaries of the discussion (Mean = 7.373) than in individual summaries of group discussion (Mean = 2.833).

INTEGRATION

The medium of discussion did not have a statistically significant effect on the dependent measure, integration (F = 20.310.022, df = 1, 51, p >.05). Integration messages did not occur significantly more often in face-to-face discussion (Mean = .129) than in online discussion (Mean = .111). The type of analysis (example or case) did not have a statistically significant effect on the dependent measure, integration (F = 1.612 df = 1, 51, p >.05). The mean score for integration messages in abstract analyses of the transcript was .042 and the mean for integration messages during discussions of examples was .199. The type of report (individual or consensus) did not have a statistically significant effect on the dependent measure, integration (F = .841, df = 1, 51, p > .05). Integration messages did not occur significantly more often in consensus summaries of the discussion (Mean = .063) than in individual summaries of group discussion (Mean = .177).

RESOLUTION

The medium of discussion did not have a statistically significant effect on the dependent measure, resolution (F = 0, df = 1, 51, p >.05). Resolution messages did not occur significantly more often in face-to-face discussion (Mean = 0) than in online discussion (Mean = 0). The type of analysis (example or case) did not have a statistically significant effect on the dependent measure, resolution (F = 0, df = 1, 51, p >.05). The mean score for resolution messages in abstract analyses of the transcript was 0 and the mean for resolution

messages during discussions of examples was 0. The type of report (individual or consensus) did not have a statistically significant effect on the dependent measure, resolution (F = 0, df = 1, 51, p > .05). Resolution messages did not occur significantly more often in consensus summaries of the discussion (Mean = 0) than in individual summaries of group discussion (Mean = 0).

OTHER

The medium of discussion had a statistically significant effect on the dependent measure, other (F = 22.449, df = 1, 51, p < .001). Other messages occurred significantly more often in face-to-face discussion (Mean = 6.317) than in online discussion (Mean = .163). The type of analysis (example or case) had a statistically significant effect on the dependent measure, other (F = 7.050, df = 1, 51, p <.011). Other messages occurred significantly more often in abstract or case analyses of the transcript (Mean = 4.964) than in discussion of examples of concepts found in the transcripts (Mean = 1.515). The type of report (individual or consensus) had a statistically significant effect on the dependent measure, other (F = 6.921, df = 1, 51, p <.011). Other messages occurred significantly more often in discussions where students were instructed to produce a consensus summary of the discussion (Mean = 4.948) than in discussions where students were instructed to produce an individual summary of the group's discussion (Mean = 1.531).

INTERACTIONS

Report X Analysis

The interaction between type of report (individual or consensus) and type of analysis (example or case) had a statistically significant effect on the dependent measure, triggering (F = 12.096, df = 1,

50, p < .001). The level of triggering was highest for the combination of consensus and abstract or case analysis (M = 3.929).

Report X Medium

The interaction between type of report (individual or consensus) and type of medium (online vs. face-to-face) had a statistically significant effect on the dependent measure, triggering (F = 18.939, df = 1, 50, p < .001). The level of triggering was highest for the combination of consensus and face-to-face (M = 4.214).

Analysis X Medium

The interaction between type of analysis (example or case) and type of medium (online vs. face-to-face) had a statistically significant effect on the dependent measure, triggering (F = 16.336, df = 1, 50, p < .001). The level of triggering was highest for the combination of abstract or case analysis and face-to-face (M = 4.373).

Report X Analysis X Medium

The interaction between type of report (individual or consensus), type of analysis (example or case) and medium (face-to-face vs. online) had a statistically significant effect on the dependent measure, triggering (F = 15.630, df = 1, 50, p < .001). The level of triggering was highest for the combination of consensus report, case analysis and face to face (M = 4.373).

Multivariate Analysis

The data were entered into a multivariate analysis of variance and the results obtained with the univariate analysis were confirmed. Statistically significant main effects were found for medium, report and analysis with regard to dependent measures, other, triggering, and exploration, but no effect was found for integration and resolution. Interactions were found for report * medium, report * analysis, medium * analysis, and report * medium * analysis.

Word Count

It appeared from observing the students participate in the face-to-face discussions and the online discussions that far more interaction took place in the face-to-face discussions. Online, students waited for days after the discussion opened to post anything. It did not appear to be active at all online, nor to be interactive. To verify and document this observation, we took a count of how many words were uttered by each student in each condition. What we found was that online in the two discussions, the average number of words written per student was 262 words. Face-to-face the average number of words spoken by each student in the two discussions was 439 words. The difference between the means was tested with a oneway ANOVA and found to be statistically significantly different (F = 4.194, df = 1,55, p < .05). As stated above, the face-to-face discussions produced significantly more Other talk than the online discussion (F = 22.449, df = 1, 51, p < .001). Other messages occurred significantly more often in face-to-face discussion (Mean = 6.317) than in online discussion (Mean = .163).

CURRENT CHALLENGES FACING THE ORGANIZATION

This paper began with a question: Does online discussion produce increased interaction and critical thinking? The main purpose in asking this question was to try to learn what we can to help the teacher in running discussions. So, what can we say?

To begin with, there is no evidence here for saying that online discussion produced increased critical thinking. In fact, we saw that there was a statistically significant difference between the online and face-to-face discussions, with the face-to-face discussions showing a higher level of critical thinking. But perhaps more importantly, neither environment, online or face-to-face produced very high levels of critical thinking, and this was consistent with other studies reviewed. And that takes us to another question: Is there increased interaction in online discussion?

In the case presented in this chapter, where online discussion was compared to face-to-face discussion with 4 groups of students compared across these 2 environments, face-to-face produced a greater amount of interaction and a higher level of critical thinking. What sense can we make of all this and what advice might we offer the teacher?

We saw that instructional methods (type of analysis and type of reporting out) have an effect upon two of the levels of critical thinking, triggering and exploration, and upon the relational communication (other). Instructional media also showed an effect on the first two levels of critical thinking and relational communication.

It appears that there is a low level of student-to-student interaction in the online course discussions we studied and the level of critical thinking is also quite low. These are two major findings and they are entirely consistent with what others have reported in the research literature.

What we think we need to look at more closely are the following sorts of concepts: personal significance of the topic, perceived anonymity, trust, motivation to learn, and confidence about one's knowledge of the topic under discussion.

Recall the extreme difference of opinion referred to at the outset of this paper: Some maintain that the classroom is an environment of debate and interaction and immediacy between human beings and that the online environment is a cold and inhuman landscape. It would seem that the research does not support the extreme view that the face-to-face discussion is an environment of

active engagement, nor that the online environment is a cold and desolate domain of inhuman communication. We observed a greater amount of interaction face-to-face, but it was filled with Other category utterances and a fairly low level of critical thinking. Online discussion produced even less critical thinking than face-to-face and less overall discussion. At this point, it would appear that neither one can be counted out, but the new guy on the block, the online discussion, did not live up to the expectations of those who see it as the strength of online education. We have a ways to go in understanding the variations in communicative behavior in discussion. It may turn out that online discussion, under the right conditions, can produce student-to-student interaction but with the conditions studied here we have not found that to be the case. Keep in mind that in this study the face-to-face groups and the online groups were discussing without the teacher leading. We would like to know more about what sort of outcome derives from these discussions. For instance, do students write better papers after the discussion when the level of critical thinking is higher? Do students write better papers after the discussion when the amount of student-to-student interaction is greater? In some studies now underway, those questions will be answered.

Finally, there are a number of variables which this study did not measure but which require close scrutiny and reflection. Many or all of these come under the headings of intrapersonal and interpersonal dynamics, such variables as trust, respect, autonomy, motivation, openness to ideas and appreciation for one another's ideas and personal relevance of topics. We cannot forget to take a close look at these attitudinal variables. While the empirical study presented here did not measure any of these variables, a close look at discussions suggests that the willingness of participants to say what they think and to listen to others is tied to their perceptions of a safe environment, a collaborative attitude, and motivation to give and take. Such forces likely transcend other aspects of the discussion. We can say with confidence that some of the conditions under which a discussion takes place do influence the behavior of discussants. In addition to instructional variables of group size and purpose and so on and media variables, we need to keep an eye on the attitudinal variables. Further study ought to explore just how these attitudinal variables operate in online and face-to-face discussions.

REFERENCES

Angeli, C., Valanides, N., & Bonk, C. (2003). Communication in a Web-based conferencing system: The quality of computer-mediated interactions. *British Journal of Educational Technology, 34*(1), 31–43. doi:10.1111/1467-8535.00302

Brookfield, S. D., & Preskill, S. (2005). *Discussion as a way of teaching* (2nd ed.). San Francisco, CA: Jossey-Bass.

Cohen, J. (1960). A coefficient of agreement for nominal scales. *Educational and Psychological Measurement, 20,* 37–46. doi:10.1177/001316446002000104

Curtis, D. D., & Lawson, M. J. (2001, February). Exploring collaborative online learning. *JALN, 5*(1), 21–34.

Duphorne, P. L., & Gunawardena, C. N. (2005, March). The effect of three computer conferencing designs on critical thinking skills of nursing students. *American Journal of Distance Education, 19*(1), 37–50. doi:10.1207/s15389286ajde1901_4

Garrison, D. R., Anderson, T., & Archer, W. (2000). Critical inquiry in a text-based environment: Computer conferencing in higher education. *The Internet and Higher Education, 2*(2–3), 87–105. doi:10.1016/S1096-7516(00)00016-6

Garrison, D. R., Anderson, T., & Archer, W. (2001). Critical thinking, cognitive presence, and computer conferencing in distance education. *American Journal of Distance Education, 15*(1), 7–23.

Garrison, D. R., Anderson, T., & Archer, W. (2003). Critical thinking, cognitive presence, and computer conferencing in distance education. *American Journal of Distance Education, 15*(1), 7–23.

Gergen, K. (1995). Social construction and the educational process. In L. Steffe & J. Gale (Eds.), *Constructivism in education* (pp. 17-39). Hillsdale, NJ: Erlbaum.

Heckman, R., & Annabi, H. (2005). A content analytic comparison of learning processes in online and face-to-face case study discussions. *Journal of Computer-Mediated Communication, 10*(2), article 7. Retrieved from http://jcmc.indiana.edu/vol10/issue2/heckman.html

Lapadat, J. (2002, July). Written interaction: A key component in online learning. *Journal of Computer Mediated Communication, 7*(4). Retrieved July 12, 2007 from http://jcmc.indiana.edu/vol7/issue4/lapadat.html

Meyer, K. (2003). Face-to-face versus threaded discussion: The role of time and higher-order thinking. *JALN, 7*(3), 55-65. Retrieved October 13, 2008 from http://64.233.169.104/search?q=cache:ax5fuY3nKGQJ:www.aln.org/publications/jaln/v7n3/pdf/v7n3_meyer.pdf+JALN+Meyer+2003&hl=en&ct=clnk&cd=1&gl=us

Murphy, E. (2003). Moving from theory to practice in the design of Web-based learning from the perspective of constructivism. *The Journal of Interactive Online Learning, 1*(4). Retrieved October 13, 2008, from http://www.ncolr.org/jiol/issues/PDF/1.4.4.pdf

Pena-Shaff, J., & Nicholls, C. (2004). Analyzing student interactions and meaning construction in Computer Bulletin Board (BBS) discussions. *Computers & Education, 42,* 243–265. doi:10.1016/j.compedu.2003.08.003

Rourke, L., & Kanuka, H. (2007). Computer conferencing and distance learning (pp. 831-842). In H. Bidgoli (Ed.), *The handbook of computer networks, vol. 3* (pp. 831-842). Hoboken, NJ: John Wiley & Sons.

Rovai, A. P. (2007). Facilitating online discussions effectively. *The Internet and Higher Education, 10*(1), 77–88. doi:10.1016/j.iheduc.2006.10.001

Vess, D. L. (2005, October). Asynchronous discussion and communication patterns in online and hybrid history courses. *Communication Education, 54*(4), 355–364. doi:10.1080/03634520500442210

ENDNOTES

* Other: An "other" category was developed in order to provide coding criteria for utterances made that do not fit into any other category. These include messages that are social in context; "Did you watch the game" message that are vague; "very thought provoking, thanks" and messages that are mechanical or organizational; "I'll type the summary."

[1] I am indebted to two wonderful students who worked closely with me on this research project. I owe thanks to Laura Woods and Alice O. Goodwin for their many hours of collecting data and talking with me as we worked through these studies. I am grateful to the University of Southern Maine for granting me a sabbatical leave, which allowed me to travel to NYC to present this research at the Center for New Media Teaching and Learning at Columbia University in October, 2008.

[2] Each student granted their permission for their transcript to be used in this research and the names of the interactants in the transcripts were changed to maintain anonymity. All interactants in the conversations were asked their permission to use the recordings. All students in the online and face-to-face discussions gave their permission to use the data.

[3] Taken from Garrison, D. R., Anderson, T., and Archer, W. (2001) and modified. Book Title Emphasis Followed Hyperlink HTML Acronym HTML Cite HTML Code HTML Definition HTML Keyboard HTML Sample HTML Typewriter HTML Variable Intense Emphasis Intense Reference Line Number Placeholder Text Strong Subtle Emphasis Subtle Reference

SUPPORT MATERIALS: APPENDIX A: MODIFICATIONS[3]

Table 3. Triggering events

Descriptor	Indicators	Sociocognitive Processes	Modifications
EVOCATIVE	Recognizing the problem	Presenting background information that culminates in a question	*Asking questions does not necessarily indicate triggering.
	Sense of puzzlement	Asking questions	If the person is using questions to try and evoke a response, triggering may be the appropriate code.
		Messages that Take discussion in a new direction	If the questions are asked in an assertive or rhetorical way, coding up might be more appropriate.

Table 4. Exploration

Descriptor	Indicators	Sociocognitive Processes	Modifications
INQUISITIVE	Divergence: *within the online community*	Unsubstantiated contradiction of Previous ideas	
	Divergence: *within a single message*	Many different ideas/themes presented in one message	*If the multiple ideas/themes presented in one message relate and connect with one another and are laid out in a logical, flowing manner the message should not be coded down solely due to divergence.
	Information exchange	Personal narratives/descriptions/facts (not used as evidence to support a conclusion)	*Personal narratives are utterances about one's personal life that could easily be omitted without altering the message being sent. Personal narratives alone, without the support of other exploration indicators, should not be coded as exploration.
	Suggestions for consideration	Author explicitly characterizes Messages as exploration – e.g., "Does that seem about right?" or "Am I way off the mark?"	
	Brainstorming	Adds to established points but Does not systematically defend/justify/develop addition	*Indicators of brainstorming include Messages such as: "I think" "Maybe" "Might be" "We could.."
	Leaps to conclusions	Offers unsupported opinions	*Author can support their own opinions with additional opinions if they develop a justifiable and defendable argument. Otherwise, additional information from various sources are needed. Look for terms such as "I believe" "I think" "My opinion"

Table 5. Integration

Descriptor	Indicators	Sociocognitive Processes	Modifications
TENTATIVE	Convergence: *among group members*	Reference to previous message. Followed by substantiated agreement, e.g., "I agree because...."	*Agreeing/disagreeing with a previous message applies if, and only if, it is followed by substantiated and developed reasoning as to why they have come to that conclusion. If simply disagreeing or agreeing the student must justify as to why they are taking that stance.
	Convergence: *within a single message*	Building on, adding to others' ideas	*Re-phrasing what another student has said does not fall under this category (even if the unit being re-phrased did) unless there is a clear and developed addition
	Connecting ideas, synthesis	Justified, developed, defensible, yet tentative hypotheses	*Simply referencing a source does not qualify unless there is a developed connection
	Creating solutions	Integrating information from various sources: *textbooks, articles, personal experience*	*Personal experience is something that the student has gone through that has a clear and distinct connection to the content being discussed.
		Explicit characterization of message as a solution by participant	*The student should be using at least 2 sources. For personal experience to count as a source it must be clearly related to a theory, idea or subject that relates to the assignment and also be accompanied by a different source.
			*The main factors used to distinguish between exploration and integration were unsupported vs. supported statements/opinions.

Table 6. Resolution

Descriptor	Indicators	Sociocognitive Processes	Modifications
COMMITTED	Vicarious applications to real world	None	*Resolution mimics the research process. Participant must first develop a hypotheses, test their given solutions and then defend and explain the results.
	Testing solutions		
	Defending solutions	Coded	

Chapter 17

Enhancing Intelligence, English and Math Competencies in the Classroom via *e@Leader* Integrated Online Edutainment Gaming and Assessment

Anthony R. Dickinson
Academic Research Laboratory, People Impact International Inc, Hong Kong

Diane Hui
The University of Hong Kong, Hong Kong

EXECUTIVE SUMMARY

Whether online edutainment gaming can enhance intelligence, student learning, or scholastic performance remains hotly debated in education research circles. In response to this academic issue, and in order to address a number of educational policy questions asked of the authors by several government organisations, the authors have developed the online e@Leader edutainment gaming platform as a solution. Their e@Leader program is the first comprehensive 'learning by gaming' system to also be designed according to the findings of advanced machine learning and cognitive developmental neuroscience research. In 2008, the first empirical evidence was generated with its use, and together with its built-in assessment system, integrated into the school curriculum. Beyond this existence proof of concept, and practical program application for educational use, results of beta-testing with the e@Leader system across primary schools in two countries support the claim for tutored online educational gaming in enhancing intelligence, active student learning, and scholastic performances in English and math.

DOI: 10.4018/978-1-60566-878-9.ch017

CASE BACKGROUND

Introduction

Online edutainment gaming has both its vociferous advocates and critics, and the issue concerning whether the use of computer- and video-based gaming can really enhance intelligence and active student learning as may truly correlate scholastic achievement, has remained hotly debated in education research for more than a decade (e.g., Gee, 2005; Prensky, 2006; Walsh, 2004; see also Fishman, Marx, Best, & Tal, 2003). This issue has not, however, remained solely the interest of academics, developmental psychologists and education researchers, and has been of more than a passing interest to educational policy-makers and curriculum designers.

In 2005, the current authors were approached by several commercial and Governmental organisations with a view to the possibility of developing an online gaming system integrated into (or at least compatible with) existing academic primary school curricula, whilst also extending those curricula to include the enhancement of general intelligence and the learning of socio-emotional 'soft' skills. In accepting this challenge, we embarked upon the project with a view to combining our expertise in intelligent systems and task design, curriculum development, and assessment. Within 18 months of beginning what was to become an unexpectedly entrepreneurial 'eduventure' in itself, we were ready to test the resulting platform, now known as the online *e@Leader* edutainment gaming platform. Built fully in-house at the Academic Research Laboratory of Global Choice Psychometrics (Hong Kong), the *e@Los* operating system, with more than 300 games, (a subset of which we will describe as case examples below), all graphics and a fully integrated player monitoring assessment system, were designed and built in accordance with the most forward-looking research findings of experimental psychology and cognitive learning theories (McGonigle, 1991).

The resulting *e@Leader* program is thus a unique tool for student cognitive enhancement, and is the very first fully comprehensive 'learning by gaming' system to be built based upon the findings of some thirty-plus years of advanced intelligent machine learning and cognitive developmental neuroscience (e.g., Calton, Dickinson, & Snyder, 2002; McGonigle, Chalmers & Dickinson, 2003; Minsky, 1988). However, and in order to begin our optimal program design architecture, it was first necessary to acquaint ourselves with the finer details of the existing debate concerned with the pro and con arguments for video-gaming, and the putative claims for its effects upon mainstream school student learning.

A Need for Development-Based Task-Design, Remote Online-Access, and Empirical Outcome Studies

Amongst the current generation of young students attending our schools, it is frequently reported that one of the most popular activities distracting them from their studies is the persistent use of computerized video games (e.g., Walsh, 2004). Accounting for as much as 20 minutes to 3 hours of choice behavior activity per day/week (e.g., Henry J. Kaiser Family Foundation, 2002), this modern development has become of increasing concern to both parents and educators alike, many of whom are of the belief that such activities may interfere with students' more traditional scholastic study methods and homework completion. However, little if any empirical data has as yet been put forward in confirming the fears of computer gaming activity critics (e.g., Walsh, 2004) who claim that student's use of computerized video gaming is having a negative effect upon either scholastic achievement, or the development of core academic, cognitive or social intelligences. However, even within the modern classroom, traditional 'chalk and talk' methods of direct instruction are themselves becoming replaced by newer methods (including the increasing use of computer-based teaching and learning tools) for enhancing the multifariously scaffold intelligence of pupils from kindergarten through to their high school years (e.g., Gee, 2003; Prensky, 2006). Of critical importance right now, is the determination of whether, and to what extent, the use of such alternative computer-based teaching tools (and in this case the use of a novel game-play edutainment program) may afford the optimal nurturing and development of our pupils for the coming challenges of the 21st century, which clearly requires an increasing diversity of curricula components which can cater to the more holistic development of all students, and which may be used to complement any schools' existing curriculum (e.g., Tan & Boon, 2007).

The question of whether, and how, such technology may be used to both increase and enhance student learning is thus a growing area of interest in educational research, and much needed empirical results are keenly awaited by both its champions and critics (e.g., Dickinson, 2008).

In this chapter, we set out to explore the new opportunities (and solutions to extant problems for educators), provided by the construction of a self-paced, artificial intelligence (AI)-driven literacy, learning and intellectual enrichment activity program of our own design. If successful, *e@Leader* would be the world's first purpose-built online (remote) edutainment system to incorporate real-time auto-regulatory psychometric assessment for the enhancement of individual student's general intelligence and scholastic aptitude. Through the use of a virtual access site of this sort, students would be encouraged to engage, interact and learn in a fun, interesting, non-threatening environment, whilst also being exposed to a variety of academic, social and intellectual learning challenges, new subject matter, and thus new knowledge. We describe this kind of learning as experiential learning. As has already been proposed by Coiro (2003), frequent classroom use of the Internet, together with other web-based learning environments can promote higher levels of engagement, enhanced personal

knowledge gain, and more diverse knowledge gains in terms of potential learning opportunities for pupils, although Coiro stops short of informing us how this might be achieved (for the engagement of online learning for teachers within informal online professional communities, see Hui, 2006). With the proposed purpose-built *e@Leader* tool at our disposal, this hypothesis may be tested; the perceived benefits for students' using a web-based learning system to include measures of any increased general intelligence, motivation, scholastic achievement, social and intellectual knowledge development, technology skills, and pupil's increasing ease with accepting tasks of increasing levels of challenge and difficulty.

As Laird (2007) has suggested, such an online edutainment program as *e@Leader* may "make a rich laboratory for developing intelligent and socially autonomous agents." However, this type of claim also remains to be tested, and there has as yet been no controlled studies which address specified student learning aims with respect to any independent measures of scholastic achievement, intellectual, social or emotional learning content, as may be derived from interactive online game-play. Indeed, prior to the current *e@Leader* development, no complete online edutainment system has proven *capable* of both the delivery of scaffolded tasks of increasing levels of difficulty (according to student performance success and thus auto-regulation of learning challenge), together with the automated assessment of their performance (but see McGonigle (1990) for an early architecture proposal), with such tasks being built into its core hierarchical operating system *e@Los* (also of our own design). We have now built this system, (the *e@Leader* edutainment program), and it is completing its first year of beta-testing, with correlate scholastic data collection for review as we write this chapter. Some preliminary results have already received wide attention following their presentation to international conferences (e.g., Dickinson & Hui, 2008a; Dickinson & Yung, 2008), both in the popular and academic press (e.g., Dickinson & Hui, 2008a, 2009; Lee, 2008; Tan & Boon, 2007).

More specifically, knowing that tests of general fluid intelligence (Gf) have previously been found to correlate with scholastic aptitude (at least with regard to performance in school-based language and mathematics tests (e.g., Pind, Gunnarsdottir, & Johannesson, 2003), and computer-based cognitive learning tasks with adults (e.g., Jaeggi, Buschkuehl, Jonides, & Perrig, 2008), indicants of student's intelligence quotient (IQ) levels need also be made to ensure that general fluid intelligence might not, in and of themselves, be sufficient to account for any significant variations in performance recorded (e.g., Dickens & Flynn, 2001). The beta-testing results so far available, cover the first full calendar year of student's daily *e@Leader* system use across three countries, and we will briefly review some of the key (and rather surprising) differential findings towards the end of this chapter. The results to date show unambiguous differences between the higher scholastic performance of *e@Leader* program users versus non-users (as measured by periodic standardised in-class primary school tests of English and Mathematics), and surprisingly so, their further (but non-confounding) differential performance, in relation to independent measures of individual student's general fluid intelligence. *e@Leader* is thus already proving to be a revolutionary development, and if such results prove replicable across newly explored population samples across the World, will potentially serve a wide community of both casual, scholastic, and academically-motivated users, with the explicit goal of enhancing their intelligence, however such may be expressed by them in their future personal, social and working lives.

We now outline the evolution of the characteristic features included in the development and operationalisation of the *e@Leader* system as it now exists, how it came to have its component rationale(s), and its unique, integrated, hierarchically-driven auto-regulatory assessment engine.

SETTING THE STAGE

Putting the 'Edu' Into Edutainment Gaming for Student Learning

Originally designed and built for the explicit purpose of enhancing intelligence by users' experientially 'learning to learn', the *e@Leader* program has its roots in learning theories developed since the new 'cognitive revolution' era and the exponential growth of knowledge derived from cognitive neuroscience and intelligent systems (e.g., Bruner, Goodenough, & Austin, 1956; McGonigle, 1991; Miller, 2003). The *e@Leader* system would thus be designed with a very robust artificial intelligence engine which constantly monitors the performance of its student users, and 'scaffolds' the level of learning (and thus difficulty level of challenge), according to task/activity success, in real-time. Student users are thus able to exert a very real degree of personal control over certain component features of their learning environment (and in turn the learning opportunities such might afford), in a self-regulatory way. Such a learning environment would be designed to accommodate not only much needed academic and scholastic (content/skill) learning opportunities but could also readily include social and socio-emotional skill development activities, for use in both formal (classroom) and informal (home or cybercafe) learning environments. The *e@Leader* program would thus be designed to enhance a wide variety of intellectual and social skill developments, whilst also addressing a number of pedagogical issues of recurrent interest to education practitioners and policy-makers (e.g., Bruer, 1993). The following section will address a series of discussion questions increasingly being aired at recent educational, government policy-making conferences, and direct approaches to the authors in consultations, together with our responses to them as were to be later incorporated into the critical *e@Leader* architectural design evolution, as became manifest throughout the development stages of the *e@Leader* platform in determining some of its content, game play and assessment features. *e@Leader* is also now available in multiple languages, including English and Chinese (in both traditional and simplified Chinese characters).

Getting Started With *E@ Leader* Development: A Response to Cognitive Learning Theory and Pedagogy

With the need for public education delivery systems to include clear and explicit learner expectations, and to convey such to the relevant institutional and end-user parties, it was incumbent upon us to provide, for each and every *e@Leader* game/task/activity, its own unique introduction and instruction set, which may be examined at any time prior to, or reviewed during, its use. Further to this requirement, the design of a truly integrated learning system needs provide target for assessment, using criteria which must be both observable and measurable. In addressing this pedagogic need, we set out to design all *e@ Leader* games/tasks (now totalling more than 300 games in number), to be capable of their real-time user monitoring and assessment, with measures of all reaction times, choice object selections, sensorimotor neglect, task management and sensory-motor control, being recordable (in real time) as frequently as every 25 mini-seconds. Individual challenge scores, progress options and *ePoint* rewards (good student progress motivators !) were also to be updated in real time, and shown by request to each individual student as they continued to interact with each game/task environment. The design and construction of our custom-built *e@Leader* core operating system architecture (*e@Los*), dealt with these front-end coding issues from the start. Next addressing the issue of *e@Leader*'s value in potentially contributing to students' academic achievements as 'the key outcome of public education' (as mandated

to us by the then Education Bureau of the Hong Kong (SAR) Government), the *e@Leader* knowledge content was explicitly designed to provide a variety of learning opportunities which could complement, if not replace, traditional classroom teaching materials and practices. Such inclusive features were to include the provision of student exposures to a wide selection of tasks/challenges situated in different cultural and community contexts through experiential learning. These additional features were to be delivered together with customized knowledge-based *Brainboxes* of our own design (and their built-in, language comprehension assessment tools), and would cover topics inclusive of information concerning different world cultures and their typical artifacts (including Geography, History, Mathematics, Biology, Physics and Astronomy, Computing and Technology, The Arts (Musical and Visual), Humanities and Social sciences. Such relatively classical academic knowledge content, would thus be provided for student learning within the course of their daily game-play, and developed on a continual basis throughout their regular interaction with the *e@Leader* program.

A Truly Global Psychometric Measurement System

Further to such content provision, a fully operational assessment engine was built into the *e@ Leader* system which fully integrates the AI-driven game-play difficulty level as an auto-regulatory network, whilst also providing regular feedback (to both the student/player and their teachers/parents) upon request. An example screen shot illustrating this feedback in graphical form across four key domains of expertise, may be seen in Figure 1.

This feature reveals the relative strengths and weaknesses of individual player attentions (during game-play, and in real time) to the following 'core developmental areas' of interest, each demonstrating a different expression of their intelligence through behavioural interaction with the chosen

Figure 1. Example of real-time 'Core Development Area' feedback available to individual students, parents and classroom teachers

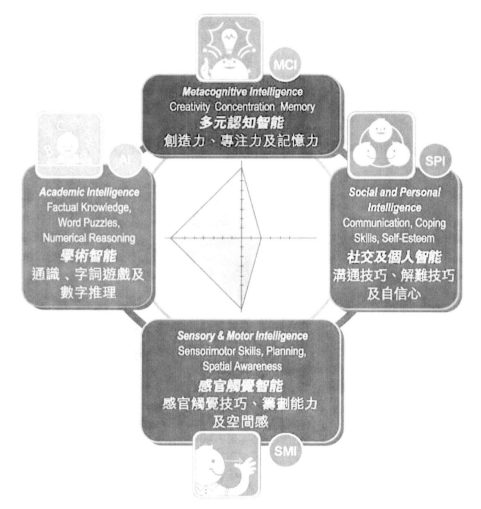

e@Leader system options:

(i) Academic domain (e.g., factual knowledge, linguistic and numerical reasoning)

(ii) Metacognitive domain (e.g., creativity, concentration, memory)

(iii) Sensorimotor domain (e.g., eye/ear-hand co-ordination, planning, spatial awareness)

(iv) Socio-emotional domain (e.g., communication, coping skills, self-esteem)

The relative 'success level' achieved by each student in the course of their ongoing game-play, is indicated in two rather novel ways. Firstly, the graphical feature shown in the centre of Figure 1 illustrates the extent of achievement within each dimension according to the distance from the centre of the extending line quadrant marker. Secondly, due to the restriction of the line sizes' linear versus logarithmic extension with cumulative success over the duration of a year's course of *e@Leader* usage, a novel graded color replacement feature was designed to reveal continuous growth in achievements (from the lowest, red, through orange, yellow, green, blue, and indigo, to the highest violet, according to the light frequency color sequence found in the electromagnetic spectrum). Another unique learning assessment feature to be built into the *e@Leader* program was the *Brainbox* knowledge acquisition tool, which affords further assessment of each student user's individual knowledge content identification, comprehension, information manipulation and application skills. This additional learning tool feature would itself again be automatically adjusted for level of difficulty according to success, and each individual student's task achievement history (for more on *Brainboxes*, see the next section below). With some of these indicants of individual game-players achievements being transparent to other users, students would, we predicted, become even further self-motivated by knowing their personal rankings with respect to their fellow *e@Leader* user colleagues attending the same classes, school, region and country. This was also to be updated and available to all users of the system, and in real time.

CASE DESCRIPTIONS

Beyond Academic Content Learning for 21st Century Edutainment Gamers

The once futuristic views of Toffler's predictions of ever increasing (and quickening) changes for society are clearly bearing upon the current generation, as they prepare for their careers, and the now increasingly realistic view that tomorrow may see the demise of many of the more 'traditional professions' (e.g., Howe, 2006, 2008). The need for good adaptive skills to allow optimal coping with an uncertain, unpredictable future (together with its equally surprisingly unpredictable opportunities!), will require tomorrow's students to enter the workplace with a new, and highly flexible, dynamic tool kit readily available to hand and mind. This tool kit will need contain not only the traditional academic and practical skills in order to remain competitive, but will

also include newly developed skill sets more finely tuned to the development of 'character education' and 'soft skill' acquisition. A first shopping list of such new skills, as are already becoming proposed in the education policies of several countries, might include training designed to enhance the individual student's self-esteem, anger management, emotional valence stability, assertiveness, coping skills, communication abilities and leadership potential. Already staples of many a corporate organization's Human Resources and staff training development programs, these and other like-oriented course content and skill areas are becoming increasingly proposed for incorporation into school classroom curricula. Indeed, it soon became one of our goals to include such training within the design of the core educational foundations of the *e@Leader* program environment (e.g., Yung & Dickinson, 2008). Amongst other dimensions of their personality, the enhancement of such student skills as those listed above would inevitably lead each student user of the *e@Leader* program towards their increased awareness, respect and contribution to the harmony of the communities within which they would live and conduct their business, through their 'game play' activities.

Of the mid-level 'hard skills' between the academic/scholastic and soft skill arenas, we soon sought to design additional training components into the *e@Leader* program which would enhance students' preparation and abilities in coping with these demands. A variety of different *e@Leader* tasks/challenges were specifically designed to therefore exercise, practice, monitor and develop a variety of abilities, many of which are essential to all basic academic, business and social skill management for use in the home, public and workspaces alike. A non-exhaustive listing that we drew up included the desire for our edutainment-gaming user students to inclusively enhance their *sensory-motor coordination* (e.g., eye-hand co-ordination, visual and sound-driven multi-tasking); *visuo-spatial intelligence* (including serial and exhaustive search, planning, navigation, congruency, geometry); *verbal intelligence* (e.g., vocabulary, spelling, syntax, semantics, pragmatics, comprehension, practical communications, foreign language words/phrases); *logical intelligence* (e.g., inference, induction, deduction, hypothesis testing, conclusion formation); *mathematics skills* (e.g., numbers, counting, simple math, calculation, estimation, probability, algebra, geometry, matrixes); *cognitive skills* (e.g., critical thinking, categorisation, active search, creative thinking, productive thinking, attention, identification, lateral thinking); *memory* (e.g., linear, combinatorial, spatial, temporal, pictorial, object, event, short and long term); *socio-emotional awareness* (e.g., detection of emotional valence, expression and interpretation, ambiguity, conflict resolution, communication and control). Explicit rationales for all of the above (and more) were drawn up, defined, tasks designed and implemented, and assessment protocols put in place for each. Example game-play descriptions and accompanying *Brainboxes* with regards some of these task/skill spaces will be shared below in a later section.

The Evolving *E@Leader* Task-Design Architecture: New Client-Driven Rationale Considerations

The ways in which such hard and soft skills were now becoming requested integrated into existing curricula was clearly manifest during the earliest phases *of e@Leader* development, and may be exemplified by the interest shown in our evolving system by the respective educational oversight authorities of the Education Bureau of the Government of Hong Kong (SAR), and the Ministry of Education in Singapore. Representatives from each of these bodies consulted with us following their policy review paper preparations regarding the introduction of new topic proposals and methods of educational content delivery within their mainstream public school curricula. A further

consideration, this time hailing from Australia, concerned a need to provide for remote, online educational content provision, training-delivery and assessment for communities located at considerable distances from major towns or cities, with relatively poor access to libraries or standard educational materials and facilities updated in a regular basis. For example, in our prepared response to a government paper, *MOS Lui Tuck Yew on Holistic Education, FY 2007 Committee of Supply Debate*, we addressed a request for the possibility of *e@Leader*'s assisting with training for students' "Strength of character [that] makes the difference in how we respond to trials and tribulations, and in how well we [the students] ride out the storms that buffet us,...". As discussed above, all *e@Leader* tasks and challenges were to be driven by our artificial intelligence system built into the *e@Los* operating system architecture, which continuously monitors and automatically shifts the level of task difficulty presented to each student, in real time. A sub-set of the tasks to be made available, would now be also specifically designed to introduce features which challenge the student to cope with unexpected, yet significant, changes occurring within their interaction environment(s). The results of each student's coping skills and challenge management ability would also be included in their *Brainbox* challenges, usage patterns and assessment scheduling, in order to address this concern. The same request then continued, "...while values, like respect and care for others, add value to who we are and what we do. How we can better communicate ideas and connect with a wide spectrum of people, the ability to persuade and motivate those we work with give Singaporeans the edge when they are thrust into positions of leadership at home and abroad?". To address this related issue, a subset of *e@Leader* tasks/activities (and their accompanying *Brainboxes),* were specifically designed to challenge (and assess each student's understanding of) the diversity and interpretation of personality, character analysis, emotional valence, cultural identity and citizenship, so assuring that we might facilitate teachers and policy-makers that we had succeeded in, "Making sure that [we] achieve the right balance between these 3 aspects - academics, character and skills -- an on-going effort and no easy task."

The e@Leader architecture and operating system was thus specifically redesigned to work as an automated task-interaction monitoring and updating program, using sophisticated artificial intelligence driven algorithms which increase the levels of task difficulty, with the growth of each individual student's abilities in each of multiple domains of assessment. In this way, students would be continually challenged to develop their best performance across a much wider variety of relatively soft, hard and academic skills, all within the single integrated operating platform of the *e@Leader* edutainment system architecture.

Enhancing Teacher and Student Engagement in Learning via Classroom-Based Gaming

With the further task of needing to both facilitate and continually engage students for extended periods of time in order to achieve maximum, sustained effectiveness (e.g., Hui, 2006, 2009), it was essential that a new technology-based development being introduced to the classroom be fully integrated into a robust curriculum. The *e@Leader* system thus had to be appealing to both students and their parent/teachers alike, whilst remaining capable of motivating teachers who aim high, for a rigorous and transparent assessment system which could be regarded and recognised by other educational institutions outside their own, and ideally, all over the world. To facilitate this, we constructed a cryptic summary output illustration of some of the built-in assessment features of *e@Leader*, which would be simultaneously available to any user, independent of nationality and location of operation, and wherever they may be using the system, anywhere in the world. Such a transpar-

ent facility would allow for fair and accurate assessment(s) to be made of the relative performance of individual students (match-controlled for age and levels of task difficulty achieved), across a variety of performance measures. Results would be posted to the *eleaderonline.com* website, and ranked by individual student (chosen) login name, school and country of origin. These scores are now updated live, online, 24 hours a day, and may be seen by anyone, anywhere in the world with Internet and secure-login site access. These types of results can also indicate/correlate concurrent progress with ingoing mainstream classroom teaching, whilst also showing individual classroom teachers the way(s) in which any particular student's *e@Leader* interaction development is being used to achieve existing school curriculum goals. Monthly progress reports for each student are also now available to parents and teachers by request (generated automatically), and may be sent direct to email account addresses if preferred. Teachers may also request automated email notice/receipt of their student's results from any *e@Leader Brainbox* interactions which they may have selected and required completed for the purposes of class homework assignments. We now introduce a sample subset of 10 *e@Leader* task/challenge sets (from a total of now more than 300), with a view to illustrating some of the wide diversity of aims and target skill domains that we now address as described above. A few example *Brainbox* features will also be shown here in the case of the first task to be presented.

A Diversity of Skills and Game-Play Challenges for the Enhancement of Student Intelligence

1. Based upon a well-established and robust correlate finding of high self-esteem with social situational understanding, the *e@Leader* 'Miles for Smiles' task/game requires students to identify and select images of smiling faces from amongst an array of

Figure 2. Example screenshot of 'Miles for Smiles' task activity

otherwise unhappy or neutral facial expressions as quickly, and as accurately as they can.

Figure 2 shows an example screen shot of a choice 'Miles for Smiles' array for a relatively simple trial for primary school students. High levels of self-esteem and relative emotional stability have been repeatedly shown to correlate with both performance accuracy and short reaction times (RT) with a task of this kind (e.g., Hansen & Hansen, 1988). Students typically improve both their accuracy, and accompanying reduction in their RT, with repeated exposure to search task images this kind, even as the level of difficulty continues to increase (from small 3x3 to 5x5 arrays, and from cartoon images towards the use of sets with moving objects, and increasingly human-like faces). Task *Brainboxes* relevant to smiles and smiling were designed to address a variety of factual knowledge acquisition covering the specific icons/images used in game play, and

explore issues of significance to one's becoming able to interpret the emotions of both oneself (self-esteem), and those of others (empathy). This task design also assesses each child's comprehension and knowledge of the implications for their understanding of facially-expressed emotional cues per se (including: Smiling, Human faces, Emotional expressions, Clowns, Mona Lisa, Smiley icon, and so forth). Table 1 shows a relevant *Brainbox* example as we designed and provided them for use in this task domain only – from a total of more than 1,200 *Brainboxes* now available.

Looking at this example task more carefully, allows one further feature of the *Brainbox* to also be seen. The six questions provided for each of the *Brainbox* sets (presented to the student one at a time, without presence of the original text) are designed to reflect three different 'depths' of cognitive processing, each of which requires a different level of understanding and consideration of the text content provided. The first level requires little or no significant depth of process-

Table 1.

BRAINBOX: *Emotional Faces:*

Factual Knowledge

The human face provides a great deal of information about a person's emotional state. Facial expressions further provide messages concerning somebody's attitude and thoughts, but can also tell us something about their, and our, internal feelings. Being able to quickly and correctly detect the emotional state of another person helps us to choose which people of a group we might prefer to spend our time with. Smiling friends will often be easier to get along with, and are often a good choice of work and play partner.

Questions:

1. *What might looking at human faces tell you about a person ?*
   - a. Intelligence c. Nationality
   - b. Emotional state d. Cleverness
2. *The internal feelings of a person can be guessed at by looking at their ....*
   - a. Clothes c. Diaries
   - b. Homework d. Facial expressions
3. *What facial expression would indicate that you are a happy, friendly person ?*
   - a. Showing teeth c. Frowning
   - b. Showing eyes d. Smiling
4. *How might you try best to attract the attention of another person ?*
   - a. Looking away c. Hiding facial expressions
   - b. Smiling d. Shouting
5. *What behaviour might indicate our openness to being approached and admired ?*
   - a. Smiling in a mirror c. Returning a smile
   - b. Not smiling d. Smiling when alone
6. *How might smiling with someone benefit others ?*
   - a. Smiling causes smiling c. Mirror effects
   - b. Smiles cannot be seen d. Smiling faces

Example Brainbox Text and Question Set for Knowledge Acquisition, Comprehension and Assessment of Individual Student's Depth of Information Processing: Facial Expressions

Please refer to Tables A1-A3 in Appendix A for additional *Brainbox* examples.

ing or understanding of the text beyond simple pattern-matching (looking 'at' the text) in order to ascertain the 'correct' answer. The second pair of questions require at least some degree of semantic processing and comprehension. The third level necessitates students to make use of the information provided (by looking 'for' the most salient information), possibly manipulating or re-representing the same information, in order to determine the correct answer. Various of the examples below show illustrations of this text comprehension assessment feature, the latter two providing information of distinctively socio-cultural learning interest. *Brainbox* exploration is, in and of itself, neither a compulsory nor necessary feature for the students to engage with during game-play, but they are richly rewarded for doing so (via their noticing its effects upon their bonus scoring increments), and can lead to the opening of new 'level-up' gaming options – a highly significant motivator for most young and

enthusiastic game players (e.g., Gee, 2005). Deep learning opportunities are thus initiated by those *e@Leader* users coming to look 'for' *Brainbox* opening clues during game play, choosing to self-interrupt their gaming in order to examine their contents, and thereafter willingly engaging in trivia question and answer challenges. This supervised, yet auto-regulated success, with students deliberately and pro-actively taking responsibility for their own learning opportunities, is one of the very skills we are successfully facilitating the student to experientially learn-to-learn, without explicit tutoring.

2. The 'Dragon Boat Festival' task (set in China), requires each student to identify unique characteristic features of on object (in this case a boat figurehead) and to locate an exact match from amongst similar looking objects. In conducting this task the student will learn to make economical and strategic

use of their memory resources, whilst also learning to trade speed for accuracy in making their decisions. Additional *Brainbox* knowledge targets include: Dragon, Dragon Boat, Paddle, Drum, Qu Yuan (name of a drowned poet associated with dragon-boat racing legends).

3. The 'Tsing Ma Bridge' task invites students to identify and locate a sequence of adjacent letters which may be used to form a 'target' English word. Whilst expanding student vocabulary and context-specific knowledge, this task also exercises the skills of optimal search and an understanding of the spatial reorientation of familiar components set in novel arrangements. Additional *Brainbox* knowledge targets include: Bridge, Cable, Span, Towers, Suspension, Arch, Aqueduct, Inca Rope Bridge, Bascule, Footbridge, Moon Bridge.

4. The 'Money Maze' task requires the student to plan a series of optimal paths through the same space of opportunity in a way dependent upon the specifically stated goals to be attained. For example, the same set of paths may be traveled, but will be more or less 'optimal' depending upon whether one is attempting to take the shortest, longest, cheapest, most expensive, most direct, including location 'x', route. Students thus learn to plan their critical paths according to identifiable criteria, including short term goal acquisition, obstacle avoidance, sequential planning considerations and choice discriminations, whilst also learning about the effects that their decision making can have upon their future option selection. Additional *Brainbox* knowledge targets include: Numbers 1-10, plus 20 or so specific locations according to the context of challenge – e.g., HK or Singapore roads, Museums, Sites of Interest, Key Landmark Buildings, and so forth.

5. 'Overcoming Hurdles' is a relatively fast action sensory-motor attention task. Students are required to negotiate a series of visual obstacles, whilst developing an object tracking, guidance and avoidance strategy in the face of partially-predictable changes in their operating environment(s). Eye-hand coordination and speed Vs accuracy trade-off ability is also being exercised in this task. Additional *Brainbox* knowledge targets include: Horse, Racecourse, Saddle, Jockeys, Cap, Shoes. Figure 3 shows an example screen shot of a choice 'Overcoming Hurdles' array for a relatively simple trial for primary school students.

6. The 'Panda Mathology' task is designed to help students learn the difference between short- and longer-term planning outcomes and optimal solution finding in the presence of a competitor of equal or greater ability. Using a simple mathematical challenge, students are required to discover and select options from amongst a number of alternative, immediate, correct numerical reasoning solutions, each of which will have different consequences for their long-term success. Learning to plan in this way will allow students to experientially learn that the 'best' solution at any given point in time, may not necessarily prove to be the 'best' solution with respect to their longer term goal(s). Additional fun *Brainbox* knowledge targets include: Panda, Bamboo, and the numbers One, Two, Three, Six, and Ten.

7. The 'Great Wall and Inventions' task invites students to select matching icons according to logical principles whilst negotiating a spatio-temporal 'elimination maze'. Students will learn to both identify and plan the analysis of visual data which may be processed in a variety of more or less optimal ways. *Brainbox* knowledge targets include a series of inventions specific to the country of interest - e.g., for China: Abacus, Paper, Gunpowder, Compass and Tangram.

Figure 3. Example screenshot of an 'Overcoming Hurdles' task activity

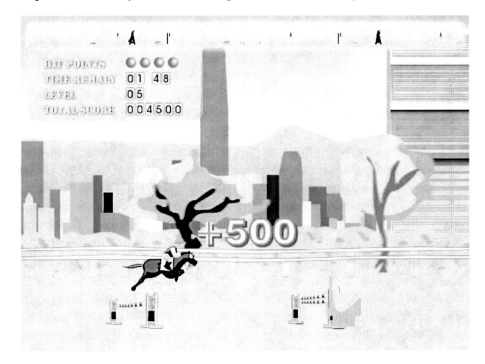

8. 'The Forbidden City' is a communication and word search task which requires students to locate 'hidden' target words from amongst a distractor sentence which has multiple meanings. The skill being developed here is that of each student learning to pay simultaneous attention to both the meaning of the particular words used, and also to the (unrelated) categorical nature of the target being searched. Such multi-tasking and focused split-attention will enhance verbal intelligence abilities, a skill crucial to the development of accurate and efficient communication across a wide range of domains. *Brainbox* knowledge targets include: Great Wall, Forbidden City, Xian, Communication, Listening, Attention.

9. The 'Korean Mobile Phone' task challenges each student's ability to learn symbolic associations between familiar and unfamiliar objects or events. This particular task (and others) may also be used to strengthen the learning of a foreign language (in this case the written English-Korean equivalents for the numbers 0-9), or any other novel system of symbolic representations, such as International safety codes, road signs or the chemical table of elements. *Brainbox* knowledge targets include: Telephone, Switchboard, Various Numbers, Dial, Tone and Ring.

10. 'Leader Sheep' requires students to keep track of, and intentionally direct a group of moving objects which must kept in close proximity in order to enter a visible target. Success with this task involves each student developing the ability to independently locate and regulate the mobile interactions between members of their 'team', and to lead them towards the same goal, whilst also paying keen attention to their communication skills in meeting individual team member's needs and behaviours. Figure 4 shows an example screen shot of a choice

'Leader Sheep' array for a relatively simple trial. Additional fun *Brainbox* knowledge targets include: Leadership, Sheep, Tree, Food, Grass and Goal.

A total of more than 200 tasks (see Figure 5 for further example screenshots) have now been beta-tested for a period of one academic year, in several schools, and in four countries, the first data from which has allowed preliminary answers to be provided to the lingering questions discussed above, and still awaiting their first empirical research findings.

Having now begun to collect the results of game-play scoring, measures of independent psychometric testing (including intelligence and emotional quotients, and creativity), and correlate standardized, scholastic school test results, we can now for the first time begin to determine whether there really might be any measureable effect of structured, supervised game-playing upon student learning outcome – and most importantly, whether it will manifestly appear to be a positive, or negative one.

Effects of *e@Leader* Edutainment Gaming Upon Scholastic Performance: Exposure and Preliminary Research Findings

As part of the current beta-testing of *e@Leader* as integrated into the mainstream school curriculum, the effective use of the program over a 12 month period has been monitored with primary school pupils in Singapore. The research was conducted by Academic Scholars of the Singaporean Ministry of Education wishing to test the explicit hypothesis that the use of an online edutainment program might enhance the intelligence of pupils, as may be reflected in their academic results, as well as in changes in other psychometric measures of their individual intelligence, in comparison with a sample-matched, non-user control group. The results showed unambiguous differences between

the higher scholastic performance of *e@Leader* program users versus non-users (as measured by periodic standardised in-class primary school tests of English and Mathematics), and surprisingly so, their further (but non-confounding) differential performance, in relation to independent measures of individual student's general fluid intelligence (e.g., Tan & Boon, 2007). Subsequent follow-up studies have confirmed, and strengthened the extent of these claims (e.g., Dickinson & Hui, 2008b, 2009; Dickinson & Yung, 2008), and especially so with regards the depth of English comprehension learning as indexed by *Brainbox* usage and response successes (e.g., Dickinson & Hui, 2008a). No significant effects were determined with regard to data partitioning for age or gender, but putatively confounding outcome measure differences were found with regard to the study cohort's individual general fluid intelligence levels (IQ[Gf]). Not surprisingly, students of higher general fluid intelligence levels scored significantly higher in both their pre- and post-program measures of English and Math competences. More specifically, the high general fluid intelligence students engaging with the online *e@Leader* edutainment program showed even greater increased scoring in their post-course tests (in comparison to matched high general fluid intelligence students in the control group).

In Hong Kong, data collection is still in progress at the time of writing, with the *e@Leader* edutainment program now integrated into the Information and Communication Technology Association (ICTA) Computer Technology in Education curriculum, being made available to more than 400 publicly-funded primary schools in the region. The *e@Leader* program has most recently been recognized by the Information and Communication Technology (ICT) Awards 2008, and was awarded certificates of the highest merit levels, including 'Best Edutainment Software', and the Gold Award for 'Best Digital Entertainment (Digital Entertainment Software)', with the judges noting that, "This was the most interesting

Figure 4. Example screenshot of a 'Leader Sheep' task activity

Figure 5. Example e@Leader task activity screenshots

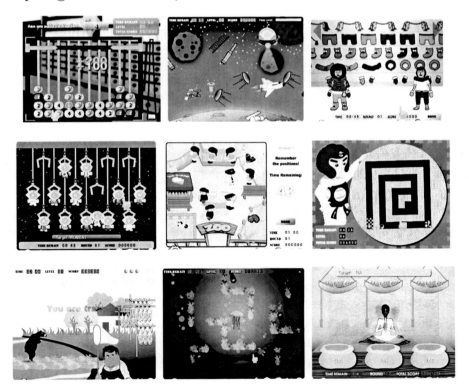

edutainment software with a professional content platform for the self-development of students. The platform has great potential for deployment in the mainstream educational environment." (e.g., HKDEA, 2009).

Concluding Remarks

Designed and built for the explicit purpose of enhancing students' intelligence by their experientially 'learning to learn', computer-gamers and gaming enthusiasts are now able to access a new means of acquiring a wide range of knowledge, academic and social skills. Drawing on learning theories derived from the educational and brain sciences, the *e@Leader* system employs the very latest techno-interactive design features, and artistic displays to form an integrated edutainment learning platform, for use in both formal (classroom) and informal (home/cybercafe) learning environments. Further to achieving an existence proof of concept and practical application, we have begun to empirically determine whether active student learning and performance can indeed be enhanced by the use of a purpose-built online edutainment gaming system, as had been proposed by Gee (2003). A second question addressed in the course of developing this program, has involved an attempt to examine the claims for online gaming expertise transfer as may be measurable by scholastic performance (e.g., Prensky, 2006), and concomitant enhancements (or correlate increments) in the development of individual student intelligence as previously suggested possible (e.g., Jaeggi et al., 2008; Pind et al., 2002).

The empirical results available to date include independent measures of scholastic performance change, individual student psychological trait development, and the enhancement of socio-emotional valence and intelligences as recently cited above. These results are consistent with the view that the use of the *e@Leader* online edutainment gaming platform can indeed be associated with enhanced scholastic performance, as measured by differentially enhanced scores for standardized primary school classroom-based tests of English and Mathematics. Based on the empirical findings provided in this case description chapter, we conclude that active student learning and scholastic achievements can be enhanced by the use of (at least one) online edutainment gaming systems, with pupils of higher general intelligence showing even further elevated performances in contrast to other pupils. It is our current belief that the environmental effects of providing specific training and curriculum content via the remote server-driven *e@Leader* online computer-based edutainment gaming system can indeed lead to increases in students' scholastic performance by the transfer of core cognitive skills learnt whilst engaging with this novel educational tool, wherever in the world they might be. Indeed, resituating learning within a purpose-built online learning program specifically designed to nurture student-centered, self-regulatory learning with social and cognitive skill development, affords a new collaborative context which provides for more equitable learning opportunities for *all* students.

Methodologically, the current case study as provided in this chapter has provided an existence proof of concept much awaited (e.g., Fishman et al., 2003), and an exemplar for education researchers to replicate in order to provide for additional findings within their own contexts, so further exploring the claims of the current findings as cited above. In addition, these findings now present the *e@Leader* platform as a first solution for teaching practitioners and government education policy-makers in search of a novel research-based practical guidance for enriching curriculum and pedagogy amidst assessment reform through the use of a cultural tool (i.e., online educational games) for improvement of students' scholastic achievements, socio-emotional and general intelligences which will in turn affect their future differential selection for school application success and life-long learning.

ACKNOWLEDGMENT

Our thanks are to be extended to the core program coding colleagues in the lab - Louis Lor Jnr., Alan Lee, William Lau and Silver Yu; graphic designers/artists in residence – Kim Lo and Alan Wong; fellow game designers – Nelson Wong and Julia Hui; and the many children attending the various *People Impact Intelligence Centres* around the world who tested and commented upon the attractiveness of various *e@Leader* tasks and game-play. The research mentioned in this case chapter was supported by a group of dedicated volunteer educators in Hong Kong and Ministry of Education scholars. Our special thanks to the Principal of our research primary school in Singapore, Dr Ng Yeow-Ling, the class teachers, Ms. Rhoda Tan, all the pupils and parents who participated in the study, and to Ms. Yolanda Yung, Ms. Rosena Ho and their team of attending psychologists from Global Choice Psychometrics, who assisted in data collection and psychometric testing throughout the research process.

REFERENCES

Borko, H. (2004). Professional development and teacher learning: Mapping the terrain. *Educational Researcher*, *33*(8), 3–15. doi:10.3102/0013189X033008003

Bruer, J. T. (1993). *Schools for thought: A science of learning in the classroom*. Cambridge, MA: MIT Press.

Bruner, J. S., Goodenough, J., & Austin, G. (1956). *A study of thinking*. New York: Wiley.

Calton, J. L., Dickinson, A. R., & Snyder, L. H. (2002). Non-spatial motor-specific activation in posterior parietal cortex. *Nature Neuroscience*, *5*(6), 580–588. doi:10.1038/nn0602-862

Coiro, J. (2003). Reading comprehension on the Internet: Expanding our understanding of reading comprehension to encompass new literacies. *The Reading Teacher*, *56*, 458–464.

Dickens, W. T., & Flynn, J. R. (2001). Heritability estimates versus large environmental effects: The IQ paradox resolved. *Psychological Review*, *108*(2), 346–369. doi:10.1037/0033-295X.108.2.346

Dickinson, A. R. (2008). Critical review of Prensky, M., "Don't bother me mom – I'm learning!" *Metapsychology Reviews*, *21*(5).

Dickinson, A. R., & Hui, D. (2008a, December). *Enhancing school performance in English and mathematics through online educational games*. Paper presented at the 1st international conference on Popular Culture and Education in Asia, Hong Kong.

Dickinson, A. R., & Hui, D. (2008b, December). *Role of e-leader in the globalization of a business institution based in Hong Kong*. Paper presented at the first international conference on Globalization: Cultures, Institutions and Socioeconomics, Hong Kong.

Dickinson, A. R., & Hui, D. (2009, June). *Effects of online educational games on students' scholastic achievements*. Paper accepted at the ED-MEDIA 2009 world conference on Educational Multimedia, Hypermedia & Telecommunications, Honolulu, HI.

Dickinson, A. R., & Yung, Y. (2008). Being gifted: Enhancing school performance via online educational games. In *Proceedings of the 10th Asia Pacific Conference on Giftedness*, Singapore.

Fishman, B. J., Marx, R. W., Best, S., & Tal, R. T. (2003). Linking teacher and student learning to improve professional development in systemic reform. *Teaching and Teacher Education*, *19*, 643–658. doi:10.1016/S0742-051X(03)00059-3

Gee, J. P. (2003). *What video games have to teach us about learning and literacy.* New York: Palgrave MacMillan.

Gee, J. P. (2005). *Why video games are good for your soul.* Melbourne, Australia: Common Ground Publishing: The Learner.

Hansen, C. H., & Hansen, R. D. (1988). Finding the face in the crowd: An anger superiority effect. *Journal of Personality and Social Psychology, 54,* 917–924. doi:10.1037/0022-3514.54.6.917

Henry, J. Kaiser Family Foundation. (2002, Fall). *Key facts: Children and video games.* Retrieved February 22, 2008, from http://ww.health08.org/entmedia/loader.cfm?url=/commonspot/security/getfile.cfm&PageID=14092

Hong Kong Digital Entertainment Association or HKDEA. (2009). Hong Kong information and communication technology (ICT) awards ceremony program. *Best Digital Edutainment and Entertainment Awards, 2,* 10.

Howe, J. (2006). The rise of crowdsourcing. *Wired (San Francisco, Calif.), 14*(6).

Howe, J. (2008). *Crowdsourcing: Why the power of the crowd is driving the future of business.* [Audiobook read by Kirby Heyborne]. New York: Random House Audio.

Hui, D. (2006). *Engagement in supporting new teachers: A role for computer-mediated communication in teacher learning within informal professional communities.* Unpublished doctoral dissertation, Washington University in St Louis, Missouri.

Hui, D. (2009). *A dialogic framework for evaluating the effectiveness of teacher engagement within online professional communities.* Manuscript submitted for publication.

Jaeggi, S. M., Buschkuehl, M., Jonides, J., & Perrig, W. J. (2008). Improving fluid intelligence with training on working memory. In *Proceedings of the National Academy of Sciences.* Retrieved February 22, 2008, from www.pnas.org/cgi/doi/10.1073/pnas.08012681056

Laird, J. E. (2007). *Using computer games to develop advanced AI.* Retrieved February 22, 2008, from http://ai.eecs.umich.edu/people/laird/papers/Computer01.pdf

Lee, C. (2008, December 13). Web games 'aid learning'. *South China Morning Post, Education Supplement.*

McGonigle, B. O. (1991). Incremental intelligent systems by design. In J. Arcady-Meyer & S. Wilson (Eds.), *From animals to animals.* Cambridge, MA: MIT Press.

McGonigle, B. O., Chalmers, M., & Dickinson, A. R. (2003). Concurrent disjoint and reciprocal classification by Cebus Apella in seriation tasks: Evidence for hierarchical organization. *Animal Cognition, 6,* 186–197. doi:10.1007/s10071-003-0174-y

Miller, G. A. (2003). The cognitive revolution: A historical perspective. *Trends in Cognitive Sciences, 7*(3), 141–144. doi:10.1016/S1364-6613(03)00029-9

Minsky, M. (1988). *Society of mind* (Touchstone ed.). New York: Simon & Schuster Inc.

Pind, J., Gunnarsdottir, E. K., & Johannesson, H. S. (2003). Raven's standard progressive matrices: New school age norms and a study of the test's validity. *Personality and Individual Differences, 34,* 375–386. doi:10.1016/S0191-8869(02)00058-2

Prensky, M. (2006). *Don't bother me mom – I'm learning!* St Paul, MN: Paragon House Publishers.

Tan, R., & Boon, C. T. N. (2007). e@Leader: Engaging pupils in active learning through a self-paced online edutainment programme. In *Celebrating Learning Through Active Research, NZ CLEAR III*. Singapore: Ministry of Education.

Walsh, D. (2004). *Why do they act that way? A survival guide to the adolescent brain for you and your teen.* New York: Free Press.

Yung, Y., & Dickinson, A. R. (2008). Being and becoming gifted: Enhancement effects of socio-intellectual study programs. In *Proceedings of the 10th Asia Pacific Conference on Giftedness*, Singapore, (pp. 86).

APPENDIX A

Table A1.

BRAINBOX: *Smiles and Smiling:*

Factual Knowledge

Smiling is infectious (like yawning, or the flu), and research has shown that smiling at someone can result in that person also beginning to smile in response. Smiling is also associated with coming to feel 'lighter', more comfortable, and relaxed, as the brain begins to release natural stress-relieving chemicals such as endorphins. Smiling also requires the use of fewer face muscles than are required to make a frowning or sad face!

Questions

1. *Like the flu, what can be the cause of our smiling at someone?*
    a. Exposure to infected birds c. Seeing somebody else yawning
    b. Seeing somebody else smile. d. Seeing somebody with a sad face
2. *What feeling can occur as a result of smiling?*
    a. Cold c. Sleepy
    b. Heavy d. Relaxed
3. *How many facial muscles are used to create a smile, compared to showing a sad face?*
    a. More c. Same
    b. Less d. None
4. *Which part of the body releases chemicals that make us calm when we smile?*
    a. Lips c. Mouth
    b. Brain d. Heart
5. *What is released in the nervous system when we smile?*
    a. Endorphins c. Diamorphs
    b. Endoscopes d. Dolphins
6. *What extra benefit may result from smiling, even when alone?*
    a. Reduced stress c. Attracts birds
    b. Get the flu d. Attracts honey

Table A2.

BRAINBOX: *Mona Lisa:*
[INSERT FIGURE 001]
Factual Knowledge

In the year 1506, the Italian Leonado de Vinci painted the Mona Lisa on a piece of wood – a portrait painting that has become one of the most famous, recognizable images of our time. The reason that it has aroused so much interest is because of its 'enigmatic' (puzzling) smile. Although most observers agree that it is indeed a smile – most people looking at the smile report a difficulty in stating the emotional state of the lady (artist model) in the picture. Some researches claim there was no real model, the face (smile) being that of the artist himself ! What do you think ?......

Questions

1. Who was painter of the Mona Lisa ?
    a. Leonado de Caprio c. Leonard Vincent
    b. Leonado de Vinci d. Leo the Lionheart
2. What feature of the Mona Lisa painting has attracted so much attention ?
    a. Enigmatic eyes c. A puzzling smile
    b. Not sure who the lady is d. The De Vinci Code
3. The puzzling smile of the Mona Lisa is painted on what material ?
    a. Paper c. Canvas
    b. Wood d. T-shirt
4. When was the Mona Lisa and her enigmatic smile painted ?
    a. 1906 c. 1956
    b. 1609 d. 1506
5. What does the Mona Lisa's smile make it difficult to 'read' ?
    a. The De Vinci Code c. Emotional feelings
    b. Facial features d. State of health
6. In which country was Leonardo de Vinci born ?
    a. Europe c. Spanish
    b. Italy d. Italian

Table A3.

BRAINBOX: **Smiley:**

[INSERT FIGURE 002]

<u>Factual Knowledge</u>

The familiar text message-based 'smiley':) and 'winky' ;) follow use of the "Smiley face" ☺ image. The smiley face craze, if not necessarily the smiley face itself, is thought by some to have been the work of two brothers in Philadelphia, Bernard and Murray Spain, who were in the business of making would-be fashion items in the 1970s. They added the slogan "Have a happy day," and soon they and their many imitators were cranking out badges, posters, greeting cards, shirts and car stickers. The *original* smiley face is said to have been created either in 1963 for a subsidiary of the advertising campaign of an insurance company by Harvey Ball, or by David Stern who claims to have designed it for a savings and loan company 1967.

Questions

1. What was the 'smiley' face originally used for in the 1970s ?
   a. A fashion icon (image) c. Make people smile
   b. Make people happy d. Looks like the sun
2. What phrase (slogan) came to be associated with the 'smiley' face in the 1970s ?
   a. Have a Happy Birthday c. Be Happy Today
   b. Have a Happy Day d. Happy Days are Here
3. When was the 'smiley' face thought to have been designed ?
   a. 1560-1570s c. 1760-1770s
   b. 1860-1870s d. 1960-1970s
4. Who was thought to have first produced the 'smiley' face in 1970s ?
   a. The Wright Brothers c. The Marx Brothers
   b. The Philadelphia Brothers d. The Spain Brothers
5. What was the 'smiley' face said to have been originally used for in the 1960s ?
   a. Inventing c. Eduventuring
   b. Advertising d. Edutainment
6. What is another name for a 'craze' ?
   a. Crazy c. Nit-wit
   b. Chi Xin d. Fashion

Chapter 18
Herding Cats:
Striking a Balance Between Autonomy and Control in Online Classes

Donald N. Philip
University Of Toronto, Canada

EXECUTIVE SUMMARY

Teachers using online learning environments have found that traditional classroom control techniques do not work when applied online. Instead, other approaches need to be used. This chapter introduces the concept of knowledge-building as an approach that is effective in online learning, and the concept of protocological control as a means of controlling the communications networks that evolve during the learning process. Data from a study involving students in a gr. 5/6 hybrid (online and face-to-face) class are used to illustrate how the teacher controls the learning process when the students all work independently of each other. The use of social network analysis as a tool for visualizing the communications networks that form is demonstrated.

INTRODUCTION

Online learning is growing by leaps and bounds throughout North America. Christensen, Horn, and Johnson note that student enrolment in online classes has risen from forty-five thousand in 2000 to about one million by 2008 (2008, p. 98). Further, their extrapolations indicate that by 2019, fully fifty percent of U.S. secondary school classes will be online. Even if these predictions fall short, online education is positioning itself to be a potent factor in North American education.

One of the more popular and successful ways to conduct online learning is via the *blended* or *hybrid* class model (Palloff & Pratt, 2001). Such classes feature both live-class interactions in a traditional classroom, and online interactions through some form of online learning environment. However appearances are deceiving: such classes cannot be run in the manner of a traditional class, even though they may take place, at least partially, in a traditional classroom setting. Due to the asynchronous nature of online learning environments, traditional means of control of the learning process quickly reveal themselves as unworkable, and the teacher has to

DOI: 10.4018/978-1-60566-878-9.ch018

adjust to news ways of working. As Palloff and Pratt note, "Teaching in the cyberspace classroom requires that we move beyond traditional models of pedagogy into new practices that are more facilitative." (2001, p. 20)

This chapter explores how one teacher in a Gr. 5/6 hybrid class manages the learning process through a combination of knowledge-building pedagogy (Scardamalia & Bereiter, 2003b) and *protocological* control, a way of controlling networks (Galloway & Thacker, 2007).

NASA's Problem

Space exploration in general, and Mars exploration in particular provide good examples of challenging control problems. Some years ago, when NASA was designing the now-famous Mars Rovers, it was presented with such a problem: Mars is a long way from Earth, and to communicate with the rovers, scientists needed to use radio. Radio waves are part of the electromagnetic spectrum (like light), and suffer from the same limitations—radio waves travel at a finite speed. Mars is so distant that there is a ten minute lag between the time a signal is sent from the Earth to when it is received on Mars; twenty minutes for the round trip (Intelligent Systems Division, 2008). Now imagine the problem: the rover is on Mars and a landslide starts downhill toward it. If traditional hierarchical control is applied, then the rover's video signals would have to be monitored twenty-four hours each day, seven days a week, looking for problems. When the video of the landslide is transmitted, it would take ten minutes to reach the control technician. Assuming the technician is alert, and not on a break, the message telling the rover to move out of the way would arrive at Mars ten minutes later, completing the twenty minute round trip. Landslides move more quickly than that, even in low gravity. The rover would be destroyed. Traditional control won't work, and another solution had to be found.

Figure 1. A Mars rover (NASA, 2008)

The solution was to *not* control the rovers directly. Instead, the rovers were built with *bug-level* intelligence. Insects routinely engage in goal-seeking behaviors (as when bees forage for flowers), avoid dangers, and so forth. Giving the rovers artificial intelligence of this level gave them sufficient autonomy to control themselves. NASA could specify the goal: move to a rock or other Martian feature, but the rovers *decided for themselves* how to move to that goal. The overarching goal was specified, but the specific path to that goal was not.

Most robots in current use (such as the military's mine clearing robots) are sort of like puppets. An operator directly controls every movement. This is called *short-leash* control (Stanovich, 2004). There is no intelligence in the machine, only in the operator.

The rovers operate by what is called *long-leash* control (Stanovich, 2004). They make some autonomous decisions, but scientists provide the overall direction. Named *Spirit* and *Opportunity*, they are among the most successful and famous of NASA's current missions, and are, to a degree, autonomous machines. At the time of writing, they have been operating about five years, and are still functional.

A teacher in an online class is a little like the scientists at NASA. They are in the position of having to create a learning community among the students, but at the same time, allow the students to pursue their own ideas–a clash between autonomy and control. While traditional classes operate in a hierarchical control mode, with little or no autonomy on the part of the students, online classes need to allow the students considerable autonomy and yet the teacher still needs to maintain some form of control over the learning process. This is the subject of this chapter: how to control the learning process, while still providing the necessary autonomy.

BACKGROUND

The School and Study Group

ICS is a private school in the inner city area of a large city in Canada. It has a highly multi-ethnic, multi-cultural co-educational population. The students are not specially chosen in any way, and are accepted on the basis of their ability to pay. Established in 1925, the school currently works actively with various educational research projects. A current focus of a number of teachers at the school is *knowledge-building* pedagogy in an effort partnering with the *Institute for Knowledge Innovation and Technology* (IKIT; www.ikit.org), part of the *Ontario Institute for Studies in Education* (*University of Toronto*).

The particular study group for this case was a Gr. 5/6 class who at the time were working on a unit on Ancient Civilizations. The class was chosen because both the teacher and students were experienced with knowledge-building, and with the *Knowledge Forum*™ knowledge-building software system created by IKIT (see below). The physical classroom was in an older part of the building, and consisted of two rooms connected by a workspace. Importantly, the class had a set of laptop computers, and was comfortable with their use, as was the teacher. Twenty of the twenty-two students (ten boys; ten girls) and the teacher agreed to participate in the study.

Observations took place over a two-month period, and included observations of students working with computers, without computers and in full-class discussions.

Knowledge-Building

Knowledge-building is a process by which a community engaged in the solution of a common problem creates new knowledge and new understandings of knowledge (Scardamalia & Bereiter, 2003b). There are a number of points of interest in that simple statement.

The first is the notion of community in the solving of problems, something closely related to the concept of *community of practice*. Lave and Wenger describe a community of practice thus (1999, p. 98):

A community of practice is a set of relations among persons, activity, and world, over time and in relation with other tangential and over-lapping communities of practice. A community of practice is an intrinsic condition for the existence of knowledge, not least because it provides the interpretive support necessary for making sense of its heritage. Thus, participation in the cultural practice in which any knowledge exists is an epistemological principle of learning. The social structure of this practice, its power relations, and its conditions for legitimacy define possibilities for learning ...

A community of practice contains within it the cultural practices necessary for the support and use of the specialized knowledge of the community. This is an important concept, as in the context of a school, it embeds the students in a community–a network–of other individuals, and the artifacts and practices necessary for the work of the community. However, not all communities of practice are knowledge-building communities (Hewitt, 1996). Knowledge-building communities are something that have been quite rare in the world's societies until recently (Bereiter, 2002). For example, Lewis, speaking principally of the Ottoman Empire and their view of knowledge noted, "Knowledge was something to be acquired, stored, if necessary bought, rather than grown or developed" (2002, p. 39). A similar statement could be made for almost every past civilization. The deliberate creation of new knowledge is quite recent. How then do knowledge-building communities differ from communities of practice?

Arguably the best explanation of this can be found in the work on how the current model of science developed and how scientific revolutions occur. Schaffer (in an interview with Cayley, 2008), discusses the importance of a *community* in the establishment of scientific truth. He notes one of the big advances chemist Robert Boyle made was to create a community of observers who watched as an experiment was performed and later attested to the results. Boyle also encouraged the publication of detailed descriptions of the experiment and details of how any apparatus used could be built, allowing others interested in the work to perform the experiment and verify it themselves. This was the nascent stirring of research communities that explored ideas, created and validated new knowledge, and shared the results among the community. A key idea here was that the community was developed not for the purpose of continuing previous practices, but of creating *new* knowledge and *new* practices–very different from a traditional community of practice. How do such communities work?

Kuhn, in his exploration of how scientific revolutions occur, gives a very clear picture of this. He introduces the concept of *normal science*, which, "… does not aim at [paradigm shifting] novelties of fact or theory …" (Kuhn, 1996, p. 52). Most research communities of any type typically engage normal science-type work; work that attempts to extend, clarify, and elaborate the current best paradigm. This is original work, and produces new insights and new knowledge, but about an already existing paradigm. However,

over time, problems with the paradigm begin to crop up, and in solving these, new knowledge is created that results in the famous *paradigm shift* in which a new model becomes the focus of the activity of the community. Kuhn examined paradigm shifts that were World changing, but paradigm shifts can occur at any scale from very small to very large.

Knowledge Forum

Knowledge Forum™ has been created to facilitate the knowledge-building process by providing an online networked environment containing supports for the knowledge-building process. Ideas about the problem under study are contributed in the form of notes posted to a communal database. Knowledge Forum™ has a suite of tools that allow students to revise their notes, critique the notes of others by responding to them (building-on), referencing others, organizing the notes into conceptual groupings, and synthesizing knowledge. Within a note itself, there are tools to metacognitively scaffold ideas, to identify the problem under study, to create searchable keywords, and to allow multiple authorship. Through these tools, the focus of the class shifts from individual knowledge to group knowledge. As well, an evolving suite of analytic tools allows teachers and students to more closely examine facets of the knowledge-building process.

An introductory tour of Knowledge Forum™ can be found at: http://www.knowledgeforum. com/Kforum/Products/Intro/audioon/tour1.html, and contains images and more detail.

Working in a Knowledge-Building Class

In a knowledge-building class, the focus is on student ideas, students' naïve paradigms (Scardamalia & Bereiter, 2003a) or mental models (Vosniadou, 2002). The teacher presents a problem of real substance that provides the long-leash, overarching goal for the class. Students advance their ideas about the problem in public (usually in an online discourse space), and read about other students' ideas. In so doing, problems with the ideas are noticed, and the students begin to research in the manner of normal science to support their ideas, extend them, and apply them to the problem under study. As this process continues, however, gradually the students' original ideas begin to change until there are paradigm shifts (writ small) within the class. This work to continually improve and extend ideas becomes a continuous flow of inquiry. The knowledge produced is often new only to their community (Bereiter, 2002), but that is often true for other research communities. The teacher's problem is this: What controls the class when each student's ideas are different, when each student, like the Mars rovers, has to find their own path and do different research to improve their ideas? In a traditional class, the teacher controls the learning process by having everyone do the same activities at the same time, but that isn't possible in a knowledge-building class. In common parlance, the teacher has to 'herd cats'. To better understand this, we need next to turn our attention to the nature of networks.

NETWORKS AND THE CONTROL OF NETWORKS

In recent years, stories about networks (especially in the popular press) have reached a crescendo that is hard to ignore. Much of the discussion has revolved around social networking sites like Facebook (www.facebook.com), MySpace (www.myspace.com), Twitter (http://twitter.com), LinkedIn (www.linkedin.com), and so forth. There are two reasons for this: (1) the power of social networks has become evident, and economically and socially important; and (2) we now have the tools available to analyze these networks, helping us to understand them better. For these reasons, the study of networks has become critical.

The first thing to be aware of in studying networks is that there are ubiquitous properties of networks that appear in very diverse networks: physical, chemical, biological, ecological, and communications as well as social (Ball, 2004; Barabási, 2002; Buchanan, 2002). Briefly put, there are certain patterns which tend to form in networks, and these show up over and over again in different types of networks. Further, networks are built on other networks, so networks interact and affect each other. As stated by the Committee for Network Science for Future Army Applications (2005, p. vii), "Networks interact with each other and are recursive. Social networks are built upon information networks which are built upon communications networks which in turn are built on physical networks." Therefore, a disruption in the physical network affects the social network. This is not limited to computer-based communication, but again can be much more widely applied. Traffic patterns (a social interaction) are networks of interactions among drivers of cars, but these interactions can be severely altered by disruptions in the physical networks of streets and highways over which the traffic travels (see Surowiecki, 2005, for a good discussion of this). We literally live immersed in a sea of networked interactions of which we have largely been unaware because of the practical difficulties of gathering data and the computational difficulties of the analysis. With automated data collection and new analytic tools, the networked underpinnings of our civilization are gradually being made explicit.

A network can be described as a set of actors or nodes and the relations among them (Krebs, 2007). In social networks, the nodes are people, and the relations (connections) among them are communications or social interactions of some kind. In order to study social networks, various statistical measures are used, but the most intuitive tool is the creation of a *sociogram*, sometimes called a *network map*, that visualizes the nodes as dots or squares and the relations among them

Figure 2. Sociogram of the response network in a knowledge-building class

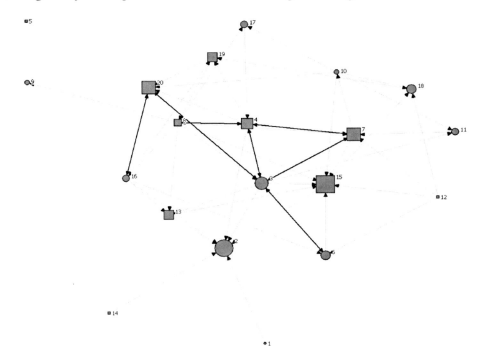

as lines called arcs or edges. Figure 2 shows a sociogram.

Network science is a rapidly growing field at this time, and there are many ways in which a sociogram can be presented. In Figure 2, square nodes represent boys; round nodes, girls. The size of a node indicates the frequency with which people have responded to that individual. Darker lines indicate reciprocal interactions; lighter lines, one-way interactions. A node with no connections (as in the upper left) indicates a non-participant in responding. As can be seen, a lot of information can be packed into a sociogram. Sociograms allow what is essentially an invisible network of interactions to be made visible and susceptible to analysis (Cross, Borgatti, & Parker, 2003).

Very well, we can analyze social networks, and they tell us something about human interaction patterns, but as noted by Galloway and Thacker (in one of the first serious works on this), we don't understand networks very well at all–we have no real *theory* of networks (2007). (Our

current theories are largely about how to *analyze* networks, which is quite a different thing). As Galloway and Thacker state, networks make us uncomfortable because of their *nonhuman* nature (2007, p. 5):

The nonhuman quality of networks is precisely what makes them so difficult to grasp. They are, we suggest, a medium of contemporary power, and yet no single subject or group absolutely controls a network. Human subjects constitute and construct networks, but always in a highly distributed and unequal fashion. Human subjects thrive on network interactions (kin groups, clans, the social), yet the moments when the network logic takes over–in the mob or the swarm, in contagion or infection–are the moments that are the most disorienting, the most threatening to the integrity of the human ego. Hence a contradiction: the self-regulating and self-organizing qualities of emergent networked phenomena appear to engender and supplement the very thing that makes us human, yet one's ability to superimpose top-down control on that emergent structure evaporates in the blossoming of the network form, itself bent on eradicating the importance of the distinct or isolated node. (Emphasis added)

How Does this Affect a Knowledge-Building Class?

As noted above, in knowledge-building classes, each student creates their own path to knowledge under the overall guidance of a research question. The teacher facilitates this, but does not directly control the students' paths; in fact, *cannot*, because of the asynchronous nature of the online environment. In the course of their research, the students interact, either in the live class setting, or online. In so doing, they create communication networks that are emergent in the sense of complexity theory: interactions that *self-organize* into stable networks. There has been much recent work on the nature of the innovation process, and one thing that is very clear is that innovation happens among individuals embedded in a supportive social network (Berkun, 2007; Gloor, 2006; Johansson, 2006; Ogle, 2007; Rogers, 1995; Sawyer, 2007). Thus, *the creation of a networked community is essential to the knowledge-building process, but control of that network cannot, because of the nature of networks, happen through traditional hierarchical means.*

Protocological Control

Galloway and Thacker: "*The quandary is this: no one controls networks, but networks are controlled*" (2007, p. 39, original emphasis). So what do we really know about controlling networks? Galloway and Thacker respond with the term *protocological control.*

They borrow the term *protocol* not from diplomacy, but from the life sciences and computer science. For them, protocol, "*...refers to all the technoscientific rules and standards that govern relationships within networks. Protocols abound in technoculture. They are rooted in the laws of nature, yet they sculpt the spheres of the social and the cultural. They are principles of networked interrelationality ...*" (2007, p. 28, original emphasis). They are the constraints on the system, physical, social, technological, and other. These place limits on the outer boundaries of the activity, but allow for considerable freedom of action within those boundaries. They give the characteristics of protocols (2007, pp. 29-30):

- Protocols emerge through the complex relationships between autonomous, interconnected agents.
- To function smoothly, protocological networks must be robust and flexible; they must accommodate a high degree of contingency ...
- Protocological networks are inclusive rather than exclusive; discrimination, regulation, and segregation of agents happen on the inside of protocological systems (not by the selective extension or rejection of network membership to those agents).
- Protocols are universal and total ...
- Protocol is the emergent property of organization and control in networks that are radically horizontal and distributed.

Let's Unpack this and see what it Means

The first point is that protocological networks are emergent phenomena of complex systems, and in knowledge-building classes, students function as autonomous, interconnected agents. Emergence is a term taken from complexity theory (Holland, 1998; Waldrop, 1992), and refers to behaviors of interest that arise spontaneously through self-organization. Typically, emergence occurs when independent (autonomous) agents interact in a system with a considerable degree of horizontal interaction: hierarchical interaction tends to inhibit emergence, and in fact, is intended to do so. In a knowledge-building class, it is important then to create the conditions in which emergence can take place. Johnson (2001) notes the importance of random interactions among group members (p. 79), and notes why there is a sudden interest in non-hierarchical forms of organization among businesses (p. 223):

[E]mergent systems can be brilliant innovators, and they tend to be more adaptable to sudden change than more rigid hierarchical models. Those qualities make the principles of bottom-up intelligence tantalizing ones for businesses struggling to keep up with the twenty-first century rate of change. A number of companies, concentrated mostly in the high-tech industry, have experimented with neural-net-like organizational structures, breaking up the traditional system of insular and hierarchical departments ... Units can assemble into larger clusters if they need to, and those clusters have the power to set their own objectives. The role of traditional senior management grows less important in these models—less concerned with establishing a direction for the company, and more involved with encouraging the clusters that generate the best ideas.

If we take that statement and replace 'departments', 'companies', managers', and 'management' with 'classes', 'schools', 'teachers' and 'administrators', then we have a pretty good description of what a knowledge-building class is trying to do. Living as we do in a period of rapid and accelerating change, the adaptability of such systems is a very attractive way to manage education.

The second point is that protocological networks need to be robust and flexible, and in particular accommodate a high degree of contingency. This is one of the really critical points: contingency. *Since a teacher in a knowledge-building class never knows exactly which ideas the students will pursue and how enthusiastically, they have to make all of their plans contingent on the actions of the students, and these cannot be predicted in advance.* An understanding of the contingent nature of control in knowledge-building classes is critical, and the process can be somewhat nerve-wracking, especially to teachers new to the process.

The third point, that protocological networks are inclusive, is simply consistent with good teaching practice. A network that excludes parts of the class isn't functioning properly, knowledge-building class or not.

The fourth point regards the universality of protocols. In terms of a knowledge-building class, they apply universally to all members–including the teacher. The teacher cannot expect to proceed hierarchically, and then expect that the students will be able to function as an effective knowledge-building community.

Finally, the fifth point is something already discussed: the protocols are emergent, and occur among non-hierarchical groups of people. Knowledge-building teachers have to resist the impulse to impose top-down organization on the class, and have to monitor their behavior to see if they are doing it.

The concept of protocological control is difficult to grasp at first, and is counter-intuitive to those of us who have been educated in traditional hierarchical classes. The remainder of this paper will use a case study to illustrate how one teacher managed it.

CASE STUDY METHODOLOGY

As noted above, this was a case study of a Gr. 5/6 class in an urban setting in Canada in which ten boys, ten girls and their teacher participated. There were two kinds of data collected: qualitative data, including ethnographic observations, video and audio interviews, surveys, and questionnaires; and quantitative data from the server log files from the *Knowledge Forum™* online environment. Of particular note here are the ethnographic observations, as these provided the details of what the teacher did in the traditional setting to facilitate the work in the online environment. Special attention was paid to the typical student behaviors, how the teacher used technology, and what forms of control were applied to the class.

Social network analysis using data obtained from the online environment was used to examine some of the communication networks that formed. Analysis was done using the Ucinet social network analysis program (Borgatti, Everett, & Freeman, 2002).

Results

We will first look at a typical knowledge-building session, then focus on how the teacher used the various technologies in the class, and how the teacher applied protocological control to the class.

Typical Knowledge-Building Sessions

The teacher used the time at the very beginning of these sessions to deal with administrative concerns, and to remind students of relevant class policies. For example, on one occasion, the teacher reminded the students that problems with individual computers should not be addressed during 'whole class' time, but instead should be brought to the teacher privately.

The teacher began the knowledge-building part of the session by reminding the students of what topics they were studying and why. The teacher, as noted above, did not *assign* topics–these were self-assigned by the students. But the teacher did remind the students of what they were working on. In some cases, this was actually a set of multiple reminders to multiple groups of students, who were all working on different things.

In reminding the students of what they were working on, the teacher often tried to phrase the

reminder in the form of a question or problem. For example, when reminding the students that some were working on whether or not certain societies had a written language, he said, "What if you're interested in how language affects a civilization?" He then suggested that students might start on this by searching the KF database for any notes relating to the keyword 'language', and that they might create a rise-above note to contain any notes they found. However, this was phrased as a suggestion, and essentially reinforced the normal classroom practice.

In some sessions, the teacher would review the use of functions like responding or note collections called *rise-aboves*; in others he dealt with other concerns. In the aforementioned case, the teacher reviewed the creation and use of rise-above notes in case any students decided to use them.

\When the teacher had dealt with the preliminaries, he instructed the students to start their work. For most, this involved getting their computers, a procedure that would differ in other locations, depending on the computer set-up of the class. In this class, laptop computers were located on a cart, and the students had to move to the cart and get their own computer, one per child. Usually there were a few students who did not get their computers, but instead got books or other materials from the classroom supply.

The laptop arrangement provided considerable flexibility for the students. They could move their computers from desk to desk, depending on with whom they were working.

As the class progressed, the teacher moved constantly about the class, answering student questions, clarifying concepts, solving technological problems, etc. Since the classroom was composed of two rooms joined together, the teacher moved between the spaces frequently.

Children are children, and one of the teacher's jobs was to keep the students focused on task. The girls, for example, had a tendency to start rhythmic clapping, as this excerpt from the field notes demonstrates:

Table 4 discusses ancient Japan (and one student does a little dancing).

Table 1 calls [a student] over (for the 2nd time).

Rhythmic clapping erupts at table 4 (two girls). The clapping is complex rhythmically, and involves hand waving as well. It is obviously rehearsed.

There is a general huddle at table 1 as the students from tables 1 and 4 try to solve a technological problem.

More clapping. [Teacher] negotiates a cessation.

Now table 1 starts clapping the identical complex pattern as the table 4 group. ...

The boys tended to engage in horseplay, such as playing with some of the classroom props (plastic swords) provided for a discussion of the Roman army. In each case, the teacher would move quickly to bring the students back on task, but these events were infrequent and for the most part, the students kept themselves on task.

The knowledge-building sessions occurred three times per week for about ninety minutes at a time. This is about four and a half hours, or about 18% of school time each week. The time Google (www./google.com) allots for knowledge-building-type activities (new learning and working on employee's own ideas) is about 30% of an employee's time (Ignatius, 2006), so the time allotted for knowledge-building was not excessive—indeed, one could argue that it was insufficient compared to knowledge age businesses. About 70% of classroom time was spent in more traditional pursuits.

Because of the extended inquiry time, it was possible to observe the students frequently forming groups to work on problems, and having solved these (and usually placing a note about it in Knowledge Forum), move on to something else, often forming new groups in the process. This was very fluid and flexible.

Another aspect of the class was communal note reading. In this excerpt, the students at various tables read notes aloud to others, or suggested notes for others to read:

At table 3, the students negotiate some note reading. One student tells another to read her "Norse" note. The other students says, "OK, you read 'Inca' [referring to her note]."

At table 1, a student reads a "Weapons" note aloud to the group.

Table 3 also has some reading aloud.

At table 2: "Listen to what Charlotte [her note] says." The note is then read aloud and causes some merriment. The teacher asks them to focus on knowledge-building.

A student shows a note to another student [on the computer screen.]

A further aspect of the knowledge-building sessions was knowledge-building talk sessions. In these, the teacher had the students rearrange the room so that chairs could be placed in a circle. The teacher himself sat in one of these chairs in a non-hierarchical position. He then invited the students to begin discussion their ideas. Usually the discussion was quite free-ranging, and the student who last spoke generally decided who would speak next. However, if something came up that engendered a lot of interest, the teacher changed the procedure and went around the circle to give everyone a chance to speak. Knowledge-building talks were not held on a regular basis, but were frequent enough to be a typical class activity.

Teachers' Comments

Earlier, it was noted that the process of releasing hierarchical control and moving to protocological control is disconcerting to teachers. Here's what the teacher had to say about it. (These comments were an e-mail communication regarding an interview):

Well, I have to say it's challenging for many reasons. You need to be comfortable with the fact that many different inquiries are occurring simultaneously by the students, inspired by their research interest in the chosen topic, making it impossible to teach in a tradition way in which you control all the information students are accessing in a uniform way. We were trained as teachers to plan and deliver lessons for the whole class, kidding ourselves into believing that this uniformity ensured equality of learning opportunity for each student. Then we would design assessments that complemented what we taught – grading our teaching more than the students' learning. All this gave us a sense of security, albeit a false one. Yet, in a knowledge-building classroom, you are never completely certain where the inquiry will lead, how deep the study will go. You must trust the students.

I grappled for years with how much agency and responsibility of the design of the inquiry to hand over to them. There were moments where I, early on in my experiences, doubted the ability of the students to be self-directed, questioning if any learning would actually take place, underestimating their abilities. For example when you have students designing their own experiments to test

their theories, that takes time. Enough time to make you worry if this is working or worth it. Or when you have a group of students laughing as they watch a video of a probe on Mars they found on the web, you wonder if time is being used productively. And then they surprise you, with a knowledge advance, new knowledge learned in a meaningful way because they were able to direct it, to connect it to their own questions and share it with the community to construct a deeper collective understanding.

I struggled with misconceptions that were unchallenged. Although I knew that simply correcting these misconceptions would not be ultimately beneficial and that instead creating a situation where the students themselves were able to identify them would be best, this was definitely the most painful part of my teaching. It is so easy to correct a mistake and feel we have eliminated it forever...

...you also are forced to admit that your own understanding of the material will be challenged as you realize you cannot and should not limit the inquiry based on your own comfort or understanding of the material. As the students refine their theories through research and experimentation, they develop new problems of understanding that delve deeply [into a topic], questions that you may not be able to answer. Your role changes from that of "information provider" to "co-learner" in the community as you acknowledge the limits of your understanding. Your own misconceptions will be revealed and this is definitely disconcerting as we were trained as teachers to be "curriculum experts", as if knowledge were a finite thing and the curriculum expectations are the sum total of all that is needed to be learned. The role of teacher in a KB classroom is that of a facilitator, assisting students in identifying their questions, stating their initial theories, testing and research-

ing them and sharing their "new information" with the community for others to build upon to improve their theories.

Even experienced teachers find it difficult to let go of hierarchical control, to *trust* their students. It's scary and difficult, especially when a teacher has to start clean with a class of inexperienced knowledge builders who themselves are accustomed to hierarchical control.

Zhang, Scardamalia and Reeve (2006), in a three-year longitudinal study of a knowledge-building class, found that the release of control was not immediate. Instead, the teacher began with a specialized-group model in the first year, moved to an interacting-group model in the second year, and in the third year, moved to an opportunistic-collaboration model as in the study class. This progression demonstrates that release of control can be a gradual process as the teacher becomes accustomed to and experienced with the knowledge-building process. Simply put, greater degrees of freedom can be allowed the students as the teacher's understanding of the process grows.

Another comment of note has to do with making class plans contingent on student ideas. In this excerpt, a pre-service teacher talks about this in relation to some questions they planned to pose the students:

[W]e didn't create those questions as links to other [workspaces], which was my initial [idea] ...and it was suggested not to do that ... because we don't know what's going to explode, what's going to be the key area of interest ... So I guess ... we have an idea of what we'd like the Big Ideas to be, but even we're not sure what the Big Ideas will necessarily be.

The implication of this comment is that not knowing which Big Idea will motivate the students to do more research forces the teacher to not direct the process, but be ready to exploit the Big

Idea when it arrives. This exploitation sometimes forces the teacher to become a co-learner in the class, because the students can easily get into an area the teacher does not understand and has to research. This is what is meant by contingent control: being ready to exploit the Big Idea when it arrives, and teacher preparation is often playing catch-up to the students, a kind of *just-in-time* lesson planning.

What the Teacher Did

This is a delicate section to write because it lists what techniques this particular teacher in this class did to control the knowledge-building network. It is delicate because there is a danger that it could be read proscriptively: Do this and no other, in this order, and a knowledge-building community will result. Unlikely. It is best, then, to keep in mind that this is protocological control contingent on student ideas. Any of these techniques could be used, or none. Entirely new techniques could emerge on the part of the teacher in response to student behaviors. That having been said, here are the techniques used by this teacher during the observation period:

- *Monitoring*: The teacher constantly monitors student activities, not just to keep them on track, but to better understand what they are working on and what materials and resources they might need next. In wholly online classes, this would involve reading postings, etc., and using any available analytic tools provided (see below).
- *Modeling*: The teacher frequently demonstrated the features and functions of Knowledge Forum, especially when they were relevant to something the students were working on. Even though the students were experienced, they sometimes needed a nudge to make effective use of the online environment.

- *Reading Aloud of Student Notes*: If the teacher found a note he thought particularly good, relevant, or interesting, he would get the student author to read it aloud to the others. This is a subtle technique. Using it, the teacher, without entering notes into the database or injecting his own ideas into the class, directed students to points he considered important.
- *Technology Choices*: All of the students had access to laptop computers, and Knowledge Forum. However, the teacher was careful to model *effective* use of technology, not just technology for its own sake. In one instance, the teacher asked the students to write information on flip charts; on another, they wrote on a white board. Both were persistent and visible to all students. So while Knowledge Forum was available, it wasn't just used because it was there–it was used when it was the most effective tool. However, sometimes, the most effective tool is something old-fashioned (and this is often cheaper). This is in line with the recent UNESCO report on ICT competency standards for teachers. They suggest that teachers need to know when and how to use technologies, which must be appropriate to the pedagogy (UNESCO, 2008).
- *Organization of Knowledge-building Talk Sessions*: Discussed above, these were organized to emphasize the non-hierarchical nature of the discourse, and to allow all students to participate. Discourse focused on student ideas and the teacher functioned as a moderator, not a director of the discussion. Ensuring equal participation has a side effect: *the students have to listen because they know they will be asked to speak*. This increases engagement with the material.
- *Knowledge-building Terminology*: The teacher encouraged the use of knowledge-building terminology to constantly reinforce

that this was a knowledge-building class. This included using and encouraging students to use terms like 'build-on', rise-above', 'theory', and 'idea' frequently.

These were the observed techniques, and there are most probably others that were not observed. Other researchers have noted different techniques being used (Bielaczyc, 2007; Bielaczyc & Collins, 2005). Binding commonalities are the focus on the improvement of student ideas and the absence of hierarchical control of the knowledge process.

The Emergence of Stable Networks

Using social network analysis, it is possible to examine the emergence of stable networks among the students. One facet of the current study was an examination of the build-on (response) network that formed over the course of the class. Figure 3 shows this network as it develops. 3a shows the network after the first week, and subsequent sociograms show the network at the end of each month of the extended inquiry.

The sociograms in Figure 3 show the growth of the building-on network from rather sparse beginnings to a more complex and inclusive network later on. Of particular note is that by the time of Figure 3c, the network had achieved a configuration that didn't change much in the next month, as evidenced by Figure 3d–it achieved a dynamic, but stable configuration. With the exception of one student (special needs), the entire class was involved in the build-on network.

It should be noted that while social network analysis and sociograms can tell us what communication patterns formed, it cannot tell us anything about the content of the communications. Thus we can say that the *pathways* that would allow knowledge-building to occur are present, but cannot say definitively that knowledge-building *did* occur. For that we would need multiple forms of analysis.

Figure 3. The growth of the network of build-ons over the inquiry period

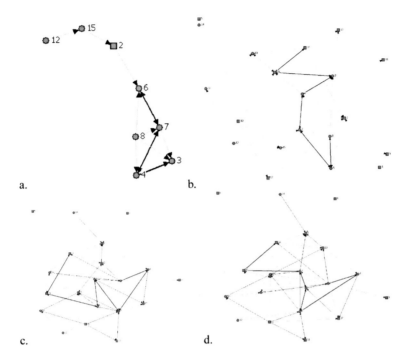

a.   b.

c.   d.

Knowledge Forum currently has a social network analysis tool built in, and it allows the teacher to quickly and easily perform such analyses. One value of this tool is to provide the teacher and students with feedback as to how the network is developing. It can show if the network is inclusive, and if the students are freely interchanging ideas without clumping into non-communicating groups. This can help to reinforce the protocological control of the network. By making the invisible networks visible (Cross, et al., 2003), they become objects for reflection and guidance for teachers and students.

Current Challenges

ICS has the ongoing problem that is plaguing most schools that use technology heavily: where to get the money to replace aging equipment when it has reached the limits of its lifespan. The laptop computers that were used in this case study came from a grant, but that has now run out and new computers

are needed for the class. At the time or writing, it is unclear how this challenge is being met.

Another challenge is to inculcate new teachers into the knowledge-building culture of the school. Partly handled through the interview process by which new staff are hired, the main process is through a carefully maintained culture of supportive collaboration among the teachers. It's not just the students who proceed in a knowledge-building manner; the staff also brings it into every aspect of their teaching. Thus, a teacher at a staff meeting will raise an issue that is troubling them, and the whole staff will work on how to proceed in a knowledge-building manner. The culture of knowledge-building is pervasive in the school at all levels.

CONCLUSION

This chapter has dealt with the concept of protocological control, a quite new concept about how networks are controlled. Protocological control replaces hierarchical control when we deal with the emergent networks that form when classes move online and form knowledge-building communities. Protocological control is a difficult concept to grasp because it is very different from the experience of most teachers and, and because it is contingent–something that most teachers find quite nerve-wracking at first.

Protocological control is contingent: it depends on feedback loops. For that reason, many of the teacher's activities in a knowledge-building class involve making sure they have adequate feedback to ensure that the knowledge-building community forms properly and keeps its focus. This involves monitoring students' progress and providing appropriate materials in a just-in-time fashion, and monitoring the progress of the community. New tools such as the social network analysis tool are being developed to aid in that process. It also, in the teacher's words, involves having trust in the students.

Part of the reason that protocological control is nerve-wracking is that until recently there hasn't even been a word to describe the process. It has been the purpose of this chapter to give the process a name and to describe how it works in practice. Persons new to knowledge-building will hopefully find this useful as they begin their journey.

This work has been supported in part by a generous grant from the Social Sciences and Humanities Research Council.

REFERENCES

Ball, P. (2004). *Critical mass. How one thing leads to another*. New York: Farrar, Straus and Giroux.

Barabási, A.-L. (2002). *Linked. The new science of networks*. Cambridge, MA: Perseus Publishing.

Bereiter, C. (2002). *Education and mind in the knowledge age*. Mahwah, NJ: Lawrence Erlbaum Associates.

Berkun, S. (2007). *The myths of innovation* (1st ed.). Sebastopol, CA: O'Reilly.

Bielaczyc, K. (2007). *Informing design research: Examining the ways that teachers design social infrastructure*. Paper presented at the Building Knowledge Institute, Toronto, Canada.

Bielaczyc, K., & Collins, A. (2005). Fostering knowledge-creating communities. In C. E. Hmelo-Silver, A. M. O'Donnell, & G. Erkens (Eds.), *Collaborative learning, reasoning, and technology*. Mahwah, NJ: L. Erlbaum Associates.

Borgatti, S. P., Everett, M. G., & Freeman, L. C. (2002). *Ucinet for Windows: Software for social network analysis*. Harvard, MA: Analytic Technologies.

Buchanan, M. (2002). *Nexus. Small worlds and the groundbreaking science of networks*. New York: W. W. Norton & Company Inc.

Cayley, D. (Producer). (2008, April 30). Simon Schaffer [Episode 1]. *How to think about science*. Podcast retrieved from http://www.cbc.ca/ideas/features/science/index.html

Christensen, C., Horn, M. B., & Johnson, C. W. (2008). *Disrupting class. How disruptive innovation will change the way the world learns*. New York: McGraw Hill.

Committee for Network Science for Future Army Applications. (2005). *Network science*. Washington, DC: The National Academies Press.

Cross, R., Borgatti, S. P., & Parker, A. (2003). Making invisible work visible. In R. L. Cross, A. Parker, & L. Sasson (Eds.), *Networks in the knowledge economy* (pp. 261-282). New York: Oxford University Press.

Galloway, A. R., & Thacker, E. (2007). *The exploit: a theory of networks*. Minneapolis, MN: University of Minnesota Press.

Gloor, P. A. (2006). *Swarm creativity. Competitive advantage through collaborative innovation networks*. Oxford, UK: Oxford University Press.

Hewitt, J. (1996). *Progress toward a knowledge-building community*. Unpublished doctoral dissertation, Ontario Institute for Studies in Education of the University of Toronto, Toronto. Holland, J. H. (1998). *Emergence: From chaos to order*. Reading, MA: Helix Books.

Ignatius, A. (2006, Feb. 20). In search of the real Google. *Time* (Canadian ed.), 20-32.

Intelligent Systems Division. (2008). *The mission. Destination: Mars*. Retrieved May 13, 2008, from http://ti.arc.nasa.gov/destination/mars/our_part.php

Johansson, F. (2006). *The Medici effect. What elephants and epidemics can teach us about innovation*. Boston, MA: Harvard Business School Press.

Johnson, S. (2001). *Emergence. The connected lives of ants, brains, cities, and software*. Toronto, Canada: Scribner.

Krebs, V. (2007). *Social network analysis, a brief introduction*. Retrieved August 16, 2007, from http://www.orgnet.com/sna.html

Kuhn, T. (1996). *The structure of scientific revolutions* (3rd ed.). Chicago, IL: University of Chicago Press.

Lave, J., & Wenger, E. (1999). *Situated learning: Legitimate peripheral participation*. Cambridge, UK: Cambridge University Press.

Lewis, B. (2002). *What went wrong?: Western impact and Middle Eastern response*. New York: Oxford University Press.

NASA. (2008, Aprril 23). *Spirit and Opportunity. Mars exploration rovers*. Retrieved May 1, 2008 from http://marsrovers.nasa.gov/home/index.html

Ogle, R. (2007). *Smart world: Breakthrough creativity and the new science of ideas*. Boston, MA: Harvard Business School Press.

Palloff, R. M., & Pratt, K. (2001). *Lessons from the cyberspace classroom. The realities of online teaching*. San Francisco: Jossey-Bass.

Rogers, E. M. (1995). *Diffusion of innovations*. New York: The Free Press.

Sawyer, K. (2007). *Group genius: The creative power of collaboration*. New York: Basic Books.

Scardamalia, C., & Bereiter, M. (2003a). Beyond brainstorming: Sustained Creative work with ideas. *Education, 43*, 4–44.

Scardamalia, C., & Bereiter, M. (2003b). Knowledge building. In J. W. Guthrie (Ed.), *Encyclopedia of education, second edition* (pp. 1370-1373). New York: Macmillan Reference, USA.

Stanovich, K. E. (2004). *The robot's rebellion. Finding meaning in the age of Darwin*. Chicago: University of Chicago Press.

Surowiecki, J. (2005). *The wisdom of crowds* (1st Anchor books ed.). New York: Anchor Books.

UNESCO. (2008). *Policy framework. ICT competency standards for teachers*. New York: United Nations Educational, Scientific and Cultural Organization (UNESCO).

Vosniadou, S. (2002). Mental models in conceptual development [Electronic edition]. In L. Magnani & N. Nersessian (Eds.), *Model-based reasoning: Science, technology, values* (Vol. 2005). New York: Kluwer Academic Press.

Waldrop, M. M. (1992). *Complexity. The emerging science at the edge of chaos and order.* New York: Touchstone.

Zhang, J., Scardamalia, M., & Reeve, R. (2006, April 8). *Designs for collective cognitive responsibility in knowledge building communities.* Paper presented at the American Educational Research Association, San Francisco, CA.

Chapter 19
The Critical and Historical View in Communities of Practice (CoP) for the Development in Education

Neli Maria Mengalli
Pontifical Catholic University – PUC-SP, Brasil

José Armando Valente
Pontifical Catholic University – PUC-SP, Brasil

EXECUTIVE SUMMARY

This chapter describes the training course for school managers for the use of information and communication technology (ICT) that was developed at Sao Paulo Pontifical Catholic University, (PUC-SP), Brazil. This was a blended course, using face-to-face and online activities, providing school managers with the experience of using ICT to share experiences, and to learn about effective ways of using ICT for school management. Even though the school managers had no previous experience with technology they succeed in changing their working reality and understanding the use of ICT to interact, exchange documents and organize their ideas. This experience has produced two other important results. One is the interaction that enables the formation of collaborative networks and partnership among school managers. Social and cultural practices were considered for analysis concerning the subjects that contributed to the creation of the ICT culture in the school. The authors have considered this network and the building of this community as the seed of a community of practice (CoP), as proposed by Wenger (1998a). Second, it was possible to see a close relationship between Wenger's theory and Freire's (2003) educational approach, which showed that social transformations are constructed on the basis of participants' will and in the presence of leadership in a historic moment.

INTRODUCTION

The development of virtual communities as part of the learning process starts to gain momentum after the publication of the studies conducted by Etienne Wenger (1998a) on communities of practice (CoP). The creation of these communities has been facilitated by the dissemination of information and communication technologies (ICT) and, in particu-

DOI: 10.4018/978-1-60566-878-9.ch019

lar, by the increased number of online courses offered. These technologies have enabled learners to interact, exchange ideas and experiences and reflect on the contribution that each individual brings to the community and, as a result, provide the possibility of reconsidering their experience and build new knowledge.

As noted by Wenger, besides the way how groups of people and learning are formed, the communities of practice (CoP) are defined according to three dimensions: the institutional, the functional and the dialogic. The first dimension relates to how the institution is understood by professionals and how they continuously renegotiate their daily practices so that they can solve problems, make decisions and generate information related to the institution to be later conveyed to those working in the institution. The second one addresses how the pedagogical and administrative practices related to their social aspects are shared (Wenger, 1998a; Wenger, 1998b). The third is related to how the shared repertoire of routines, responsibilities, vocabulary, styles and technological resources is set up (Wenger, 1998a).

These three dimensions of the communities of practice greatly resonate with the work developed by Paulo Freire in relation to the school as an institution. Freire points out that learning is a social phenomenon and that it is connected to experience, history, and daily practice, as a creative act intended to gain a critical understanding of the social practice and as a contributor to the learning process, both collective and that used for the purposes of action (Freire, 1981).

Thus, this work attempts to use the ideas of communities of practice (CoP) developed by Wenger in an educational context, related to the training of school managers via an online course. Although this course relies on Freire´s educational principles as its theoretical basis, it seeks to create conditions so that those managers may engage in activities that can be regarded as the seeds of a community of practice (CoP). With that, in addition to showing how the course supports the develop-

ment of this community, the chapter also aims to establish the connections between Wenger's and Freire's views.

This chapter presents an overview of the relationship between Wenger's ideas on the communities of practice and how these ideas relate to Freire's educational tenets. The chapter also describes the manager training delivered and its results, in addition to how a community came to be formed although this outcome had not been previously foreseen.

RELATIONSHIP BETWEEN WENGER'S AND FREIRE'S IDEAS

The work of Wenger (1998a) shows that the construction of an active and successful community depends on a person or a core group that assumes the responsibility for the development of the community. As self-organizable systems, the communities of practice (CoP) bring about collective learning and the professional qualification of its members, according to the interests of the institution and the will of the participants.

On the other hand, one of the aspects that differentiate the communities of practice (CoP) is how the connection is made because interest and geography for their own sake are not enough to gather people together. The important thing is working with shared practices and that such practices are accepted willingly. In this regard, Freire's work can greatly contribute because it shows that social transformations come about based on the will of the participants and on the presence of leadership in a proper critical and historical moment (Freire, 2003). This willingness can be that of helping yourself and helping the institution solve its problems, a historic opportunity and a social meaning which justifies the time spent and the intimacy with the events, or the contradictions found in the context (Freire, 2003).

Moreover, as noted Freire, learning is subject to political and social purposes (Freire, 2003). The collective learning process is a result of practices and of social and cultural relationships which are properties of the members of the communities when sharing occurs, thus representing the communities of practice (CoP) as a way for learning to occur in educational institutions.

Knowledge is an integral and inseparable aspect of social practice (Lave & Wenger, 2006). However, as noted Freire, individuals become qualified and then become part of it (Freire, 2001). The places where members are found in the communities of practice (CoP) are regarded as peripheral or central, though not accurately identified from the geographical viewpoint, because the spaces where interlocutors who record and/or generate information or knowledge are located are not specified. Participation must be effective in the sense that there must be involvement and accountability, so that the collective knowledge or practice may be constructed by the members. Peripheral is regarded as the core in which the participant learns more than he teaches. In the central core are the experts: people who teach and learn from the peripheral.

The need to understand the historical-sociological influence of knowledge in order to verify the context, so as to reinvent, recreate and record the path of the subjects is important to the group. This knowledge is in the sharing and, from that perspective, the participants of communities of practice (CoP) must have critical attitudes when interfacing with the constructed knowledge and when establishing the interconnection with the world (Freire, 1979; Freire, 1981; Freire, 2003), as well as in their relationship with technology, to the extent that it provides a 'globalizing', temporary and reflective view that the technological resources and methodology are not neutral.

Dwelling in the virtual space requires commitment and criticism in relation to the partial dimensions of the space shared. You can live in the community adopting a critical attitude after overcoming the initial difficulties of belonging and technological fluency, even if it is known that

every proposition requires an intervention of the central group in relation to the peripheral. The participation of the peripheral group towards the central group is evidenced in the act of thinking, rethinking and negotiating the meaning of social practice (Freire, 1981), since those who make up the core are invited by the institution and defend, to a certain extent, the prevailing position.

The records of the daily practices can be understood as structuring elements for the discussions and for the decisions, provided that there is a proposal that the peripheral should be legitimized by the central. The difference existing in the communities is the way the tools and technological interfaces are used when dealing with information. The information, styles, language, stories, records, storage, dissemination (Wenger, McDermott & Snyder, 2002) and the ideologies have different meanings in the communities because each community has its central core. It may happen, nevertheless, that the same person should belong to different cores. However, each central core is unique, as Freire highlights, because the emphasis is on *praxis* - the practice is part of the typical knowledge that the community develops and shares.

The creation of virtual learning communities has been a strategy seldom used in the educational context, and that includes the communities of practice (CoP) that occupy a wider space in corporations. This strategy is clearly used in companies which understand that this knowledge-based management tool is crucial for the institution members to exchange ideas and search for a common goal in order to improve the activities of all those who make up the organization. Nevertheless, education must unlock this learning potential through actions, and through continuous training as a lifelong process, as well as provide the possibility of being effective for the knowledge-based management at the educational institutions.

In education, communities of practice (CoP) primarily focus on professional development and on the exchanges among participants. The effective information and knowledge depend on the degree to which each member has access to it and offer his/her contributions and, in addition, one must consider that they are limited by the level of legitimacy of the institution for the records to become effective parts or the community activities and that a new routine can be set up. Although the use of technology in the community development can assist the institutions to become less bureaucratic and encourage leadership (Freire, 1981), the members whose decisions are made at high levels of the institutions seek ways to encourage communication between core and peripheral groups, but there are no assistants who regard the communities of practice (CoP) as a means of making the work with public policies in education feasible.

Therefore, it is essential that the feasibility and the development of virtual communities of practice (CoP) should be contemplated in the initial training and in the training programs devised for educators so that opportunities can be created for new knowledge and new possibilities to be applied at dialogic, professional and institutional dimensions, similarly to what took place during the training of school managers intended for the use of information and communication technology (ICT), as described below:

THE TRAINING AND SCHOOL MANAGEMENT AND TECHNOLOGIES PROJECT

The School Manager Training course for the use of Information and Communication Technologies (ICT), as part of the School Management and Technologies Project, was initially delivered in a partnership between the Pontifical Catholic University of São Paulo - PUC-SP, the Department of Education of the State of São Paulo - SEESP - and Microsoft in Brazil that later established partnerships with education departments of other states.

This chapter will be limited to the partnership formed with the State of São Paulo.

The purpose of the training was to incorporate the technologies to the school management, taking into consideration the specific roles of the managers, the problems found in the school context and the value that these technologies can add to the work of the manager. The main objective of the training of managers of public schools linked to the Education Department of the State of Sao Paulo was to encourage the use the existing technological resources in schools as part of the activities of school management, as well as to enhance and enrich the quality of management itself.

The ideas was to make the manager perceive the importance of bringing about favorable conditions for the teachers to integrate technology to teaching practices, resulting in a more meaningful learning experience to students of these schools (PUC-SP, 2004). Moreover, the manager would be capable of "setting up" internal and external networks to streamline the sharing of ideas, experiences and practices that would advance the development of collaborative work, thus enabling the establishment of mechanisms for interactions at school involving the various players who are included in curriculum.

The course was developed in four modules. In all modules, work teams were encouraged to be set up in and out of the school, favorable situations to reconsider school contexts were created, the roles that technologies should play were examined and an understanding about the links between the political pedagogical project of the school and the technological resources was gained.

The approaches to learning were based on the reflection-in-action and on multidirectional interaction networks which were made possible by the technological network (Almeida & Prado, 2005). The employment of technological resources was helpful in the sense that records, storage, retrieval possibilities, interactions and dissemination of information could be used throughout the course. The foundations that supported the course were the theories of knowledge-based management (Nonaka & Takeuchi, 1995), the training based on daily practice (Freire, 2003) and the dialog between theory and practice (Valente, 2002; Valente, 2005; Almeida, 2005).

The contents and activities were related to the managers' practices so that they could be offered the opportunity to reflect upon the action and the reality itself. The idea was that they should recognize the school technologies, ponder over how they are used in the local context and identify the possible contributions of the available technologies for the purposes of recording, storing and disseminating the knowledge produced at school. All these would include the identification of the strengths of the school and the individual path of each member of the team, proposing actions to change the contexts detected in the curriculum.

The managers identified the "hallmark" of the school investigating the most striking characteristics, seeking to reflect upon the "I" with "my area" of work. This approach created the "input" for meaningful learning using technological "tools".

In this sense, the theory and practice were mediated by technological resources through interfaces that allow interconnections. The tasks actually performed by the managers enabled the implementation of new daily practices and the creation of the meaning of the network at school and in the community, as shown in Figure 1. During the course, it was possible to realize that the seeds of communities of practice (CoP) could be detected in the records of educational managers in the interfaces for interaction, that is, some managers have shown similar interests, similar daily practices and some of their comments reached beyond the course. In this sense the online course has helped the creation of the school manager communities of practice.

The network illustrated in Figure 1 is composed of managers who work with the course content and the school context and, discuss about the daily practices with their peers in forums, chats and in the mail. The forums are portrayed in the brief description of the course. The chats, dialogs with the teacher, with the monitors and the peers were means to solve specific problems and the mail was the tool they had available to send messages to colleagues. The teacher knew only the content they had submitted, s/he did not intervene in the interactions among peers.

The scenarios presented in the course attempted to show the reality of other schools. However, they were not totally unrealistic, because they were certainly present in the schools of each manager. They have been theorized in commented readings that stimulated discussions in forums and sharing of experiences. This initiative not only led the managers to change the way they described their own realities but also encouraged the investigation of the actual context by means of scientific knowledge. These elements provided the basis for the actions related to the use of technology in the management developed at the schools. One example is the second module, whose final product was the preparation of a poster per school which was presented in the face-to-face meeting of the third module.

In the last module, the school management and technologies project was developed collectively by each school and was supervised by the course professors. The final project, which was used as a tool to assess the manager's performance during the course and which was intended to be later implemented at the schools had as its main purpose to meet the needs of the school community, which is present in the school network.

It is interesting to observe that the managers live in physical networks such as schools, and networks of belonging, such as social groups and problem-solving and decision-making groups. Some, however, are unable see themselves as the "we" that make up this social and historical network at the beginning of the course. To change the realities found that do not include the models of the schools, the course emphasized the intended

Figure 1. Dynamic Network - Taken from the course environment

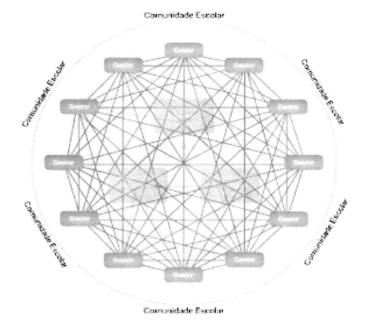

structure, as regards the type of training and the different roles assumed by the trainers.

After the course, the managers displayed "mastery" of the technological resources and were also able to reflect upon the role performed by the trainer and the responsibilities connected to their position or function as well as exercise reflection over the development of actions according to the reality and based on the school community. Such statement is based on the weekly face-to-face meetings and on the recorded testimonials by teaches and the tutors of the Pontifical Catholic University of São Paulo.

The next topic displays a brief description of the course, providing details on the groups formed to streamline the course logistics and a quick overview of the four planned modules and shows the activities to be recorded in forums and in the portfolios open for the managers to offer their contributions to their peers.

THE LEARNING DYNAMICS IN A BRIEF DESCRIPTION OF THE COURSE

The purpose of the course description is to identify the axes required for the establishment of communities as regards the activities and the methodology. The School Manager Training for the use of Information and Communication Technologies (ICT) started in the second semester of 2004 and ended in the second semester of 2006, in a partnership with the State Department of Education – SEESP. It involved managers at several levels: schools, educational workshops and boards of education, which then amounted to 89 (eighty-nine) boards of education that were split into 03 (three) groups:

- **Group 1:** 31 (thirty-one) Boards of Education in 3937 (three thousand, nine hundred and thirty-seven) participants;
- **Group 2:** 31 (thirty-one) Boards of

Education in 3937 (three thousand, nine hundred and thirty-seven) participants;

• **Group 3:** 27 (twenty-seven) Boards of Education in 3429 (three thousand, four hundred and twenty-nine) participants.

Altogether the number of educational managers trained was 11,303 (eleven thousand, three hundred and three). In order to implement the course, each of these groups was divided into groups of about 40 (forty) student-managers, and in each group there was 01 (one) professor of PUC-SP; 02 (two) monitors, supervisors from the education network of the State of São Paulo; 01 (one) ATP monitor of the NRTE[1].

The managers produced a great number of data in forum and in individual portfolios. In spite of the fact that titles were duly defined in the activities, it is possible to come across postings which provide evidence of how the management is carried out at schools. However, only the activities devised to be discussed in forums that display the features of the communities of practice (CoP) will be approached. In addition to the forums, the managers show evidence of management in reflective memoirs. However, in this topic, the digital data are related to the mentioned forums.

The learning offered in module 1 relates to the use of the basic software and Internet navigation, the use of the digital platform for distance education, the activities suggested to be done individually or in groups in order to use the technologies by the school managers and the School Administration (SA). In this module the activity No.4 required the managers to describe how they work with the school technologies, as shown in Figure 2.

Module 1

Activity 4: Socializing experiences with ICT

With this activity we begin a discussion on "What are the contributions of ICT to your school / School Administration?" – proposed in activity 3. This discussion will continue in the Forum during Module 2.

1. Discuss with your group the question raised about the possibilities and limitations of ICT.
2. Access the **FORUM – "Socializing experiences with ICT"** and share with the members of the group your thoughts and ideas about the question.

The forum "Socializing experiences with ICT" (Figure 2) started with the question: "What are the contributions of ICT to your school/SA?" In this field, the manager wrote about the initiatives related to the educational and administrative practices which relied on technology to assist the management process. The managers were invited to work on the activity which, after the posting of some messages, turned into assistance which was used by the peers and into records of the daily practice.

Forum 1: **Socializing experiences with ICT**

GROUP 1 – Created on: **May 10, 2005**
GROUP 2 – Created on: **August 30,2005**

Welcome Message: The purpose of this forum is to share reflections with your class colleagues on "What are the contributions of ICT to your school/SA?" according to the guidelines of activity 4. It is highly important that everybody should participate so that the discussions can be fruitful and the group can develop properly.

Module number 2 was further divided into two parts: module 2a and module 2b. The first, approached individual learning and the second was based on the theory related to management. Such module reviewed and discussed the management experiences lived at school and the School Administration. The scenarios referred to situations in which technologies or technological resources were used so that the management could be carried out. The contribution of the technological tools or data systems to the educational or administrative practice was considered as well as the theory-

Figure 2. Socializing experiences with ICT

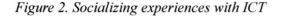

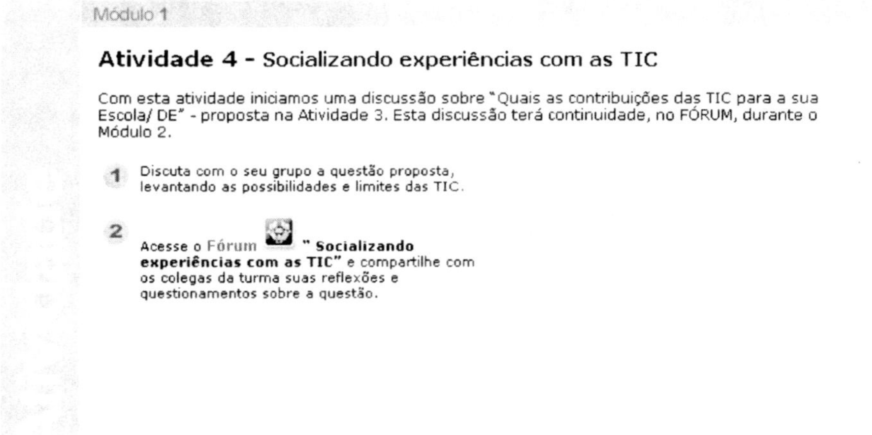

Módulo 1

Atividade 4 - Socializando experiências com as TIC

Com esta atividade iniciamos uma discussão sobre "Quais as contribuições das TIC para a sua Escola/ DE" - proposta na Atividade 3. Esta discussão terá continuidade, no FÓRUM, durante o Módulo 2.

1 Discuta com o seu grupo a questão proposta, levantando as possibilidades e limites das TIC.

2 Acesse o Fórum " **Socializando experiências com as TIC"** e compartilhe com os colegas da turma suas reflexões e questionamentos sobre a questão.

practice movement related to the concepts of school management and technologies.

As the student-managers checked upon the hallmark of the school or of the School Administration, they perceived reality and had the chance to ponder over the role of the manager relying on significant learning, both theoretical and practical. The activities were turned into opportunities for reflection. They could then assign meaning to the network existing in the daily work, which is a network set up before the course started but likely to continue existing and become stronger after this training course. The student-managers analyzed 06 (six) scenarios which represented real situations of technologies used at schools. The participants read the recommended texts and, after the reading, they offered their contributions. These activities of context reading contributed to the reflection on the daily practices, and the recording of those reflective considerations was posted in the forum and referred to as Commented Readings.

Module 2

Activity 4: Understanding and interpreting the theoretical aspects

The purpose of this activity is to organize and share the reflections of each participant of the course on the theoretical aspects covered in the 6 (six) related scenarios and texts linked

to the management practice when using ICT in the context of school / SLAB. After reading and individually analyzing each situation (scenario, text and practice), post your contribution in the forum.

1. Go to Forum "Commented Readings" and share your considerations, questions and interpretations from the reading of the texts and the reality of your school / SLAB with your colleagues.

! Important

After the analysis of scenarios and readings, share the doubts, considerations and interpretations in a forum.

Forum 3: **Commented Readings**

GROUP 1 – Created on: May 04, **2005**
GROUP 2 – Created on: September 19, **2005**

Welcome message: The purpose of this forum is to provide opportunities to share questions, considerations and interpretations based on the reading of scenarios and the reality of your School / SA, according to the guidelines of activity 4 of module 2b and of the schedule. This is to remind you that everybody should participate so that

Figure 3. Understanding and interpreting the theoretical aspects

the discussions can be fruitful and the group can develop properly.

In Module 3, the shared experiences were reported as a result of the implementation of the management using technology at school and in the School Administration. These experiences were described based on the reflection on the activities of Module 2a and 2b which approached the difficulties, progress and innovations arising from the new possibilities of using technologies in the managers' daily lives.

Finally, Module 4, the last and the most important one, focused on keeping the records of the project. It dealt with the development of a project both for school management and technological management, using enhancing technological resources to set up the network or the community so as to establish a partnership that would enable interactions to take place whenever possible aiming at the production, construction and management of knowledge. In this module, the managers discussed the project intended to be implemented at school. The activity aimed at linking the theoretical and practical aspects (Figure 4) by collectively devising the school management and technologies project which was related to the political pedagogical project of the school.

Module 4

Activity 2: Linking the theoretical and practical aspects

The purpose of this activity is to link the **theoretical and practical aspects** covered in the course. To do so, during the development of the School Management and Technologies Project and the ICT, we will resume the discussions over the concepts formulated in Module 4 and the development of the project by the management team of the school / Board of Education.

1. Go to Forum Partnerships and Projects and discuss with your class colleagues the theoretical aspects raised from the reading of the texts and their relationship with the School Management Project and the ICTs.

>> Learn more

The purpose of the activity was to discuss the theoretical aspects in connection with partnerships so as to search for partners in and out of the school to actually implement the project.

Forum 4: **Partnerships and Projects**

GROUP 1 – Created on: July **29, 2005**
GROUP 2 – Created on: November **18, 2005**

Figure 4. Linking the theoretical and practical aspects

Módulo 4

Atividade 2 –Articulação dos aspectos teóricos e práticos

O objetivo desta atividade é a articulação entre os **aspectos teóricos e práticos** abordados no decorrer do curso. Para isto, durante a construção do Projeto Gestão Escolar e as TIC, vamos retomar a discussão entre os conceitos trazidos no módulo 4 e a construção do projeto pela equipe gestora da Escola/DE.

1 Acesse o Fórum 🖼 **Parcerias e Projetos** e discuta com os colegas da turma os aspectos teóricos suscitados a partir da leitura dos textos e sua relação com o Projeto Gestão Escolar e as TIC.   ▶▶ Aprofunde-se

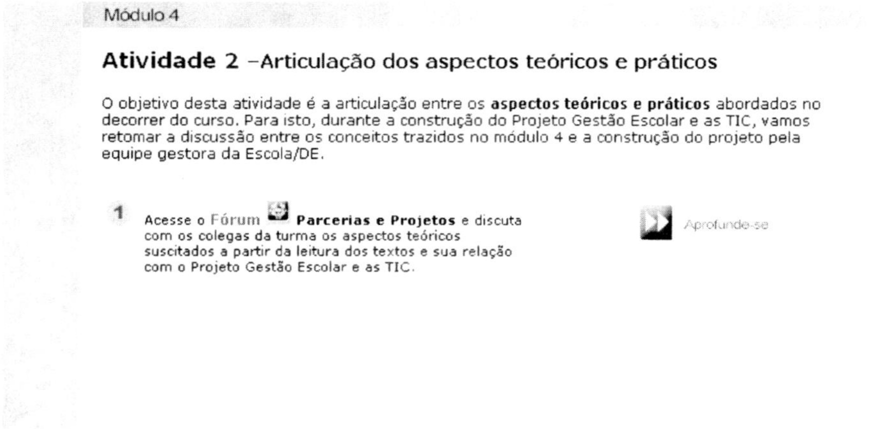

Welcome message: Discuss with your class colleagues the theoretical aspects related to partnerships and their relationships with the School Management Project and the ICTs, according to the guidelines of the activity.

In the topic that follows, some digital data taken from the forums mentioned above will be addressed in an attempt to illustrate the beginnings of communities of practice (CoP) - still in their informal configuration - as regards the sharing of ideas, experiences, and criticism related to the theoretical and practical aspects in the use of technologies in the management and in the educational activities at school. It shows that if the Department of Education of the State of São Paulo should provide legitimacy to this initiative, it would have the means to spot talents and have more information and digital data available to learn more deeply about the school systems from the viewpoint of a networked curriculum. This curriculum enables us to follow the path of history, culture and the movement grounded on experiences and events that are properly recorded for the participants and for the educational institute, so that there will be no need to reinvent what can already be found out there in the public network.

THE ANALYSIS AND INTERPRETATIONS OF DIGITAL DATA

The results which are reported here are very limited if compared to the wealth of digital data that are recorded in the environment. These records provide evidence that the theory of Lave and Wenger (2006), and Wenger, McDermott and Snyder (2002) are justifiably applied in the field of education in a management of knowledge based on Freire's teachings written in a number of books.

The following accounts, which display the records in the forum interface that transcend the course, are the seeds of the communities of practice (CoP) which are created at the schools. The reader will notice that the dates are different and that the account was not provided by the same subject. Each record shows the dialog between his/her peers and reports how each person works at school. Even though each description is quite unique, everybody shares volunteerism, the social history, and institution and the search to provide professionalism to the collective elements. The educational managers see participation as a means for performing the actions planned at the institutional level.

All subjects will be referred to as educational managers, considering the irrelevance of specifying the name, the gender or ethnicity, but rather how those who we call seeds of the community of practice (CoP) work. The first manager to be addressed shows how he worked to improve the learning and teaching process at school. The manager points out that [...] *the current collective educational working hours ("HTPc – horário de trabalho pedagógico coletivo"), during the night shift, was highly productive. The coordinator is working on the Networked High School with the teachers and used the opportunity to integrate the teachers' activities with the ICT. As a consequence, we ended up with three or four teachers who, together with the students, were planning to enter the activities in the PCs. For example: a magazine about Biology, the establishment of a pool with the students using the information resources to set up a data bank, for Mathematics. All this planned to start this coming week [...]. We were quite glad because we also managed to start the project "Numbers in Action", at the Elementary/ Secondary levels* [16/6/2005 22:20:37].

The manager writes to his colleagues describing how, at the time, he went about including two projects for the state school network and how he incorporated the technological resources in the school planning. He was not heading the initiative, but there arises the educational teacher coordinator representing the managing team of the school and belonging to the central core and who meets the teachers on a weekly basis to deal with educational topics related to the students' learning and teaching processes.

Another manager reports how the deals with the school educational issues and refers to him/herself as "we" to show that there is a team involved, that is to say, the central core comprises more people. His/her accounts starts with [...} *the actions we are developing* (at school) *is primarily to make teacher aware of what ICT is and we are trying to develop a strategy to find enough time to do both the school activities and implement our project in action. [...] The coordinators are expediting some activities in the HTPc and we have also taken some steps to make the people involved in our daily school routine aware of the meetings held, through the Board, so that we, managers, can be qualified to streamline our activities so that we can move more directly towards all school community* [23/5/2005 21:42:51]

The actions developed by the manager are related to the incorporation of technological resources into the teachers' activities and it is reported that the project is in the implementation stage because it is mentioned that the project is in action. Once again, the educational coordinator teacher arises, but now the purpose is to help the teachers reflect, during the HTPc, on the use of the technologies in the teachers' activity. In addition to the teacher, other people start to join the peripheral core to learn more about the use of the technology. The aim of this manager is to attract the school community into this dynamic network where the school lies.

The peripheral movement towards the center can also be perceived in the records prepared by one manager who writes about how he started to understand the use of technologies more clearly and how he is performing in his own reality. The manager starts writing about himself, [...] *after reading a number of texts, I came across a number of accounts of positive experiences, suggestions of use and clarifications about the application of ICT. This course was crucial to broaden my knowledge, acquire practice in its uses [...] Currently, the use of this technology is undoubtedly enriching, facilitating and speeding up the way our students are learning [...] We are paving the way for the inclusion of ICT at school and, as a manager, I am also taking on the responsibility for the maintenance of the equipment so that when we use the information technology environment room (SAI), the students do not face problems when using technology in their school activities* [26/8/2005 12:14].

This manager tells his colleagues that he knew very little about the use of technologies, but that the course helped facilitate the classes of students who took students to the information technology room. Because he was aware that the computers needed proper maintenance, he writes to his colleagues in the forum about how he managed to reduce the infrastructure problems found in the information technology environment room at school. He understood the fact that computers without maintenance would hinder learning. Considering that he was in the central core of the school and by relying on the constructed knowledge, he decided to change the school reality.

The information technology environment room is a place for teaching and learning which is typically equipped with 10 to 20 computers (desktop) which are used to enhance the teaching and learning processes by means of basic or educational pieces of software as well as the resources found on the Internet. Another manager mentions the information technology room and the changes which were made after people became more aware of the need to preserve the school assets.

He starts with [...] *the process of making people aware of the importance of the information technology environment room (SAI) as an asset to be preserved occurs gradually and, little by little, in each action, the need to care and, preserve it is stressed so that they can always have these resources available. It is easy in relation to SAI because it belongs to them, it is the ideal place to share knowledge with colleagues and, at the same time, learn new things with the teachers. [...] The students who currently attend morning and afternoon classes are also working with SAI projects, helping teachers and manager teams in the use of technologies as well as incorporating the resources that ICT offer and experiencing all the difficulties that they bring along* [25/6/2005 15:28:58].

In this record, the manager describes how he works with the preservation of the public asset and with the inclusion of technological resources

for purposes of teaching and learning. He mentions how the students with higher technological proficiency help and assist the teachers and the managing team in the use of the technologies. This becomes the central core and receives help from the peripheral group so that changes can be brought about at school: joining interests for the common goal of teaching and learning.

With this same goal, in the forum interface there is another account that shows how the technologies are being incorporated at school. [...] *the use of the ICT is radically changing the school environment. It is not just another piece of equipment, but rather a new look, a new challenge, new dynamics. We said goodbye to the teacher who holds all the knowledge. Our space presently belongs to the educator who helps the student find paths [...] The director is no longer locked inside his room, trapped in the red tape. We are more democratic and participative [...] we are not just the support, we also found the "shoulders" in our school [...] We live in a new school that invites the community in and, with that, we have fewer discipline-related problems. With the community in the school [...] students are involved and understand the importance of what they are learning. What is most rewarding is the fact that I am part of this process, even when there is pain resulting from all these changes, at least I now believe that a better citizen will arise (either the teacher or the student) and that my work (and my pleasure) is not in vain* [28/6/2005 22:45:14].

The account implicitly describes the paradigm shift taken place at school to deal with discipline issues and the manager's satisfaction for being a member of the team that is transforming the school and opening the doors for the school community to help solve problems which do not belong exclusively to the school. In the account, there is evidence that the school changes its way of management and the way the teachers work. Those ways of managing the school are also linked to the inclusion of technology in the school environment. This *new dynamics* referred to by the manager changes the way the manager sees the school and the sharing with peers is part of this change. It is the change of the central in order to include the peripheral to manage the school.

Very timidly, another manager attributes Module 2 of the course to the change in the understanding of what technology is and suggests that his colleagues should not allow the information gathered in the course to get lost. He suggests that the texts should be printed so that they could be used at school. First, he explains why he wishes to share information, [...] *the readings of Module 2b really helped us broaden our knowledge and stressed the importance of ICT for us, MANAGERS. Helping share the actions at school, by the managers with the school community and the local community, in the use of these new information technologies is also the purpose of the printed texts of Module 2b and have greatly contributed to the development of our activities at school, so much so that I believe we must print those texts because they can provide support for us in the school routine* [26/9/2005 11:31:51].

As described by the manager, he was interested in learning more about and on the importance of the technologies at school and when he noticed that the readings related to Module 2 would be helpful in the school activities, he suggests that his colleagues should do the same: print and communicate to the teachers and to the other members of the managing team. With this, these colleagues would have the theory to support their daily practice and the reflections over the use of technological resources. This manager expresses his will to disseminate the information which was relevant to his own learning process.

Ranging from shy to daring managers, we can perceive the movement of the school central core in favor of learning. Another manager describes the importance of the readings of the course and how he can change the reality based on the texts. [...] *taking into consideration the readings and the daily practices, in an joint effort with the School*

Unit, we are led to think that each member of the school team has his/her own role and tasks [...] We develop our activities and challenges [...] when we learn more deeply about the use of the ICT [...] and, as a result, new horizons are opened up in our students' teaching and learning process [23/8/2005 15:00:55].

To this manager, delving into the theory is one way of overcoming the difficulties found in the students' teaching and learning process. After unraveling the technology, the readings started to become part of the changes that take place at school. Although he does not provide details about his way of working, in the account he describes his daily practice and his belief that the use of technology cannot occur without a theoretical basis. It is one way to share with his colleagues the learning he acquired.

In the forum there were records which reached beyond the mere act of collaborating or collaborating simply, there was also an offer of a piece of software to the teacher's library. A manager explains that [...] *we installed the software of the teacher's library, where more than 2,000 titles may be found, all with reviews which will be used in researches and consultations by all students and teachers [...] Today we started to keep records of all the books and borrowers, and next week we are likely to have all the system organized in computers [...] Should you need software from the library, get in touch with me and I will be more than pleased to help you* [26/9/2005 19:42:51].

This manager aims at preventing his colleague from doing re-work. Therefore, he offers the solution that it should be installed at his peer's school. He describes how he is working and offers help so that his colleague's school can have the same software in its teacher's library. Such reduction in re-work is a feature of knowledge-based management. This manager offers all the participants of the forum this reduction and the implementation of new look in the library.

In education, technology is the reflection of the technique (Silva, 2001) and cannot be understood as the way the working class operate machines as we can see in the movie Modern Times in which the work involves merely tightening screws in mass production as criticized by Chaplin (1936) and ratified by Freire (2003). The manager position in relation to technology depicts the professional evolution in relation to his own activities.

Exchanging ideas, sharing and criticizing theoretical and practical aspects related to the use of technologies in the school management and activities is simply the beginning of the inclusion of the communities of practice (CoP) in education to address the dynamic networks existing in the physical, historical, cultural, political and economic spaces typically occupied by work a "troublemaker" idealism. In these forums, the managers went beyond that, they told their colleagues that they were changing the realities and in each of those changes, it is possible to perceive the emergence of a new community.

In a voluntary manner and without any systematic method, the manager describes how he works. In spite of the fact that each manager has his own way of expressing, all of them unveil the start of a community emerging in the schools. The communities of practice (CoP) are regarded as a way of working in which all the members have a space of time and a geographical or technological space to discuss and understand the institution and negotiate meanings with other participants. They can relate at the institution to work on topics related to work and share routines, responsibilities and technological resources, records, vocabulary and styles.

Although the external guidelines may influence the activities performed in the communities, they do not prevent the members from getting involved in the social practices because they are self-organizable systems. The communities of practice (CoP) may exist in every institution, in view of the fact that society is based upon the participation and does not require a strict hierarchy to exist. There are development stages that start with the groupings which are formed because the members share interests or needs, then they move on to an informal organization and reach their peak with the members engaged in the development of shared practices, later on some participants get interested in the continuity and, provided it is supported by technological resources, they are able to welcome new members and record what has been built so far.

Because they are organized in spaces used for collective learning, they have new members that learn from more experienced members. All the time knowledge in the community is constructed about a domain – the main topic – and professional learning in such a manner that participants are able to analyze and reflect upon their own work and propose innovative solutions to the institution. The limits of the communities of practice (CoP) are more flexible than those of the organization and, as such, people may contribute in different manners and at different levels. The peripheral members have opportunities to learn because the master the practice in concrete terms and the core participants can work on concepts and practices with the newer members.

FINAL CONSIDERATIONS

The number of people who become involved in and accountable for these groups has continuously increased along the years, and the records and the professionals of the central core take on the responsibility of establishing new peripheral cores as the participation in this institutional learning process gains more acceptance. The contributions to the institution are more significant in the communities of practice (CoP) because the endless starting-over of courses and in-job training is put to an end.

Freire's inclusion in Wenger's concept of communities of practice (CoP) encourages the development of communities for education which offer with more possibilities for interaction with and reflection over each contribution. The institutional dimension is seen as a defined notion which aims at the assertion of men as subjects, and as such, these beings operate in the functional dimension by means of dialogs that lead to action in the social reality in order to transform it (Freire 1979).

With shared repertoires of the routines whose responsibilities have been properly assigned, with the domains, with the social practice and with the incorporation of the technology into the networked curricula, learning becomes more meaningful, acquires a social nature and is more closely related to the historical and cultural experiences. It is a creative act for the discussions and for the criticism of the institutionalized world in favor of the training in the learning process in a collective manner in which the central core works together with the peripheral core towards a common goal; several interests converge into the social practice.

The dynamic network addressed in the course is a potential to be developed and legitimized in the communities of practice (CoP) in the convergence of Wenger's writing to an active construction for the social transformations described by Freire in the paths connected to education. Initially, the core group takes the lead in a proper historical moment, but such moment is not eternal and does not keep knowledge and the institution memory to itself. They are self-organizable systems at the service of a knowledge-based management in education.

In the managers' discussions in the forum interface, after these are analyzed and interpreted, knowledge is seen and written as an integral and inseparable part of the social practice which qualifies the political, social, cultural and economic subjects to their daily activities. Technology serves a purpose and is subject to human beings. If it is viable on the one hand, on the other it is no longer neutral.

The recovery of the incorporation of dynamically networked curriculum technology lies in the criticism and in the use of reasoning through the effective participation that educational managers have in the course by means of several interfaces in the learning environment. The incorporation of techniques is a result of a joint and collective effort that demands the performance of experts in central cores. In the forum interface, managers report how they bring about changes at schools so that they let the reader perceive the beginning of the establishment of at least one community of practice (CoP) in each school reported by the manager.

Both in the course and in the community, the first activities are related to the subject so that they may at a later time, be expanded into the contextual world so that people can develop their views and produce the readings resulting from the initial formations. Recording the path is a step to contribute to the memory and to the collective organization so that participants can perceive the signs of convergence during knowledge acquisition.

Being in the course and in the community is a turning point for those who can intervene in the basic elements inherent to the context of the work so that they can think, rethink, negotiate and renegotiate the meanings of the social practice. The daily life is the framework for the development of the language and for unveiling prevailing ideologies. In Freire, it would be the continued training as a means of making the knowledge-based management effective.

The framework of the communities of practice (CoP) for training purposes is legitimized by the institution and made effective by the participation of each member (Freire, 2003). Instead of only considering courses which end on established dates, one must think about the continuity of the courses so that opportunities for a new learning format can be created involving the collective players of the dynamic network. This translates into the possibility of working on the institutional and professional structure in a dialogic infrastructure, allowing school managers to be continuously trained in the use of information and communication technologies.

REFERENCES

Almeida, M. E. B. (2005). O relacionamento entre parceiros na gestão de projetos de educação a distância: Desafios e perspectivas de uma ação transdisciplinar. In *Proceedings of the II Congresso Mundial de Transdisciplinaridade*, Vitória, Brazil.

Almeida, M. E. B., & Prado, M. E. B. B. (2005). A formação de gestores para a incorporação de tecnologias na escola: Uma experiência de EAD com foco na realidade da escola, em processos interativos e atendimento em larga escala. In *Proceedings of the Congresso ABED, 2005* (pp. 10).

Chaplin, C. (Producer). (1936). *Modern times* [Motion picture]. USA: United Artists, MGM Tower.

Freire, P. (1979). *Conscientização: Teoria e prática da libertação. Uma introdução ao pensamento de Paulo Freire*. São Paulo: Cortez & Moraes.

Freire, P. (1981). *Ação cultural para a liberdade* (5th ed.). Rio de Janeiro: Paz e Terra, Coleção O Mundo Hoje.

Freire, P. (2001). *Política e educação* (5th ed.). São Paulo: Editora Cortez.

Freire, P. (2003). *Pedagogia da esperança: Um encontro com a pedagogia do oprimido* (11th ed.). Rio de Janeiro: Paz e Terra.

Lave, J., & Wenger, E. (2006). *Situated learning legitimate peripheral participation* (15th ed.). New York: Cambridge University Press.

Nonaka, I., & Takeuchi, H. (1995). *The knowledge-creating company: How Japanese companies create the dynamics of innovation*. New York: Oxford University Press.

PUC-SP. (2004). *Projeto aprendizagem: Formas alternativas de atendimento* (Relatório Final). São Paulo: Programa de Pós-Graduação em Educação: Currículo.

Silva, B. D. (2001). *A tecnologia é uma estratégia*. Portugal: Challenges.

Valente, J. A. (2002). A educação à distância possibilitando a formação do professor com base no ciclo da prática pedagógica. In M. C. Moraes, (Ed.), *Educação à distância; fundamentos e práticas* (pp. 27-50). Campinas: Unicamp/NIED.

Valente, J. A. (2005). Pesquisa, comunicação e aprendizagem com o computador: O papel do computador no processo ensino-aprendizagem. In M. E. B. Almeida & J. M. Moran (Eds.), *Integração das tecnologias na educação* (pp. 22-31). Brasília: Ministério da Educação, SEED.

Wenger, E. (1998a). *Communities of practice: Learning, meaning, and identity*. Cambridge, UK: Cambridge University Press.

Wenger, E. (1998b). *Communities of practice: Learning as a social system*. Retrieved from http://www.ewenger.com/pub/pub_systems_thinker_wrd.doc

Wenger, E., McDermott, R., & Snyder, W. M. (2002). *Cultivating communities of practice: A guide to managing knowledge*. Boston: Harvard Business School Press.

ENDNOTE

[1] This was the setup of trainers n Group 1. Groups 2 and 3 were set up differently because PUC-SP Professors started to be the tutors of the groups, and in each group there was one teacher-supervisor who, in most cases, was a member of Group 1; 02 (two) monitor-supervisors of the network and 01 (one) educational assistant-monitor of the Education Technology Regional Center.

Compilation of References

Abowd, G. D., Harvel, L. D., & Brotherton, J. A. (2001). Building a digital library of captured educational experiences. In *Proceedings of the International Conference on Digital Libraries: Research and Practice, 2000, Kyoto* (pp. 467-474). Washington, DC: IEEE.

Acello, R. (2008, October). As worlds collide: ABA groups ponder "real" law rules and applications in virtual environments. *ABA Journal*. Retrieved December 5, 2008, from http://www.abajournal.com/magazine/as_worlds_collide/

Adams, A., & Blandford, A. (2005). Digital libraries' support for the user's 'information journey.' In *Proceedings of the JCDL '05* (pp. 160-169). New York: ACM.

Adelman, C. (1999). *Answers in the tool box: Academic intensity, attendance patterns, and bachelor's degree attainment.* Washington, DC: U.S. Department of Education.

Adelman, C. (2006). *The toolbox revisited: Paths to degree completion from high school through college.* Washington, DC: U.S. Department of Education. Retrieved June 30, 2006, from http://www.ed.gov/rschstat/research/pubs/toolboxrevisit/index.html

AITP. (2009). *Association of Information Technology Professionals (AITP) code of ethics.* Retrieved on August 9, from http://www.aitp.org/organization/about/ethics/ethics.jsp

Allen, I. E., & Seaman, J. (2007). Online nation: Five years of growth in online learning. *Sloan Consortium*. Retrieved January 29, 2008, from http://www.sloan-c.org/publications/survey/pdf/online_nation.pdf

Almeida, M. E. B. (2005). O relacionamento entre parceiros na gestão de projetos de educação a distância: Desafios e perspectivas de uma ação transdisciplinar. In *Proceedings of the II Congresso Mundial de Transdisciplinaridade, Vitória, Brazil.*

Almeida, M. E. B., & Prado, M. E. B. B. (2005). A formação de gestores para a incorporação de tecnologias na escola: Uma experiência de EAD com foco na realidade da escola, em processos interativos e atendimento em larga escala. In *Proceedings of the Congresso ABED, 2005* (pp. 10).

Anagnostopoulos, D., Basmadjian, K. G., & McCrory, R. S. (2005). The decentered teacher and the construction of social space in the virtual classroom. *Teachers College Record, 107*(8), 1699–1729. doi:10.1111/j.1467-9620.2005.00539.x

Anderson, P., Rothbaum, B., & Hodges, L. (2000). Virtual reality: Using the virtual world to improve quality of life in the real world. *Menninger Winter Psychiatry Conference, 65*(1), 78-91.

Andriessen, J., & Schwarz, B. (2009). Argumentative design. In N. Muller Mirza & A.-N. Perret-Clermont (Eds.), *Argumentation and education: Theoretical foundations and practices* (pp. 145-174). New York: Springer.

Angeli, C., Valanides, N., & Bonk, C. (2003). Communication in a Web-based conferencing system: The quality of computer-mediated interactions. *British Journal of Educational Technology, 34*(1), 31–43. doi:10.1111/1467-8535.00302

Annetta, L., Murray, M., Laird, S., Bohr, S., & Park, J. (2008). Investigating student attitudes toward a synchronous, online graduate course in a multi-user virtual learning environment. *Journal of technology and teacher education, 16*(1), 5-34. ACM Council. (2009). *Association for Computing Machinery (ACM) code of ethics and professional conduct.* Retrieved August 9, from http://www.acm.org/about/code-of-ethics

Applegate, J. (2002). Chairs and deans develop strategies to motivate faculty and engage programs. *Spectra, 38*(2), 5.

Arapi, P., Moumoutzis, N., & Christodoulakis, S. (2006). ASIDE: An architecture for supporting interoperability between digital libraries and elearning applications. In *Proceedings of the Sixth International Conference on Advanced Learning Technologies (ICALT '06)*. Washington, DC: IEEE.

Aridor, Y., Carmel, D., Maarek, Y. S., Soffer, A., & Lempel, R. (2002). Knowledge encapsulation for focused search from pervasive devices. *ACM Transactions on Information Systems, 20*(1), 25–46. doi:10.1145/503104.503106

Ashford, E. (2005). The fight over screening students to prevent suicide. *Ed Digest, 71*(1), 52-56. Retrieved February 6, 2009, from http://www.eddigest.com

Astin, A. W. (1984). Student involvement: A developmental theory for higher education. *Journal of College Student Personnel, 25*(3), 297–308.

Astin, A. W. (1993). *What matters in college: Four critical years revisited*. San Francisco: Jossey-Bass.

Baecker, R. M., Fono, D., & Wolf, P. (2007). Toward a video collaboratory. In R. Goldman, R. Pea, B. Barron, & S. J. Denny (Eds). *Video research in the learning sciences* (pp. 462). Mahwah, NJ: Lawrence Erlbaum Associates, Publishers.

Baer, W. (2000). Competition and collaboration in online distance learning. *Information Communication and Society, 3*(4), 457–473. doi:10.1080/13691180010002341

Bailenson, J. N., Beall, A. C., Blascovich, J., Raimundo, M., & Weisbuch, M. (2001). *Intelligent agents who wear your face: Users' reactions to the virtual self*. Paper presented at the Intelligent Virtual Agents: Third International Workshop, Madrid, Spain.

Bailenson, J. N., Blascovich, J., Beall, A. C., & Loomis, J. (2001). Equilibrium theory revisited: Mutual gaze and personal space in virtual environments. *Presence (Cambridge, Mass.), 10*(6), 583–598. doi:10.1162/105474601753272844

Bainbridge, D., Ke, K.-Y., & Witten, I. H. (2006). Document level interoperability for collection creators. In *Proceedings of the JCDL '06* (pp. 105-106). New York: ACM.

Baker, K. S., Gold, A. K., & Sudholt, F. (2003). FLOW: Co-constructing low barrier repository infrastructure in support of heterogeneous knowledge collection(s). In *Proceedings of the 2003 Joint Conference on Digital Libraries* (pp. 397). Washington, DC: IEEE.

Baker, M. J. (2003). Computer-mediated argumentative interactions for the co-elaboration of scientific notions. In J. Andriessen, M.J. Baker, & D. Suthers (Eds.), *Arguing to learn* (pp. 47-78). Dordrecht, The Netherlands: Kluwer Academic Publishers.

Bakhtin, M. M. (1990). *Art and answerability*. Austin, TX: University of Texas Press.

Ball, P. (2004). *Critical mass. How one thing leads to another*. New York: Farrar, Straus and Giroux.

Banathy, B. (1991). *Systems design of education: A journey to create the future*. Englewood Cliffs, NJ: Educational Technology Publications.

Barabási, A.-L. (2002). *Linked. The new science of networks*. Cambridge, MA: Perseus Publishing.

Barak, A. (2007). Emotional support and suicide prevention through the Internet: A field project report. *Computers in Human Behavior, 23*, 971–984. doi:10.1016/j.chb.2005.08.001

Barker, P., VanSchaik, P., & Famakinwa, O. (2007). Building electronic performance support systems for first-year university students. *Innovations in Education and Teaching International, 44*(3), 243–255. doi:10.1080/14703290701486530

Barnett, D. J., Everly, G. S. Jr, Parker, C. L., & Links, J. M. (2005). **Applying** educational gaming to public health workforce emergency preparedness. *American Journal of Preventive Medicine, 28*, 490–495. doi:10.1016/j.amepre.2005.01.001

Bar-Yossef, Z., Keidar, I., & Schonfeld, U. (2007). Do not crawl in the DUST: Different URLs with similar text. In *Proceedings of the WWW 2007 / Track: Data Mining, Mining Textual Data. International World Wide Web Conference Committee (IW3C2)* (pp. 111-120). New York: ACM.

Beatty-Guenter, P. (1994). Sorting, supporting, connecting, and transforming: Retention strategies at community colleges. *Community College Journal of Research and Practice, 18*(2), 113–130. doi:10.1080/1066892940180202

Becker, H. J. (1989). The effects of computer use on children's learning: Limitations of past research and a working model for new research. *Peabody Journal of Education, 64*(1), 81–110.

Bekaert, J., Liu, X., Van de Sompel, H., Lagoze, C., Payette, S., & Warner, S. (2006, June). *Pathways core: A data model for cross-repository services.* In Proceedings of the 6th ACM/IEEE-CS Joint Conference on Digital Libraries (pp. 368-368). New York: ACM.

Bellemain, F., & Capponi, B. (1992). Specificities of the organization of a teaching sequence using the computer. *Educational Studies in Mathematics, 23*(1), 59–97. doi:10.1007/BF00302314

Benoit, P. J., Benoit, W., Milyo, J., & Hansen, G. (2006). *The effects of traditional vs. Web-assisted instruction on student learning and satisfaction.* Columbia, MO: University of Missouri.

Bereiter, C. (2002). *Education and mind in the knowledge age.* Mahwah, NJ: Lawrence Erlbaum Associates.

Bereiter, C., & Scardamalia, M. (1996). Rethinking learning. In D. Olson & N. Torrance (Eds.), *Handbook of education and human development: New models of learning, teaching, and schooling* (pp. 485-516). Cambridge, MA: Basil Blackwell.

Berkun, S. (2007). *The myths of innovation* (1st ed.). Sebastopol, CA: O'Reilly.

Berman, F. (n.d.). One hundred years of data. In *Proceedings of the 2006 International Conference on Digital Government Research* (pp. 3-4). New York: ACM.

Bettinger, E. (2004). Is the finish line in sight? Financial aid's impact on retention and graduation. In C. Hoxby (Ed.), *College choices: The economics of where to go, when to go, and how to pay for it* (pp. 207-233). Chicago: Chicago University Press.

Bettinger, E., & Long, B. T. (2004). *Shape up or ship out: The effect of remediation on underprepared students at four-year colleges* (NBER Working Paper Number 10369). Washington, DC: National Bureau of Economic Research.

Bielaczyc, K. (2007). *Informing design research: Examining the ways that teachers design social infrastructure.* Paper presented at the Building Knowledge Institute, Toronto, Canada.

Bielaczyc, K., & Collins, A. (2005). Fostering knowledge-creating communities. In C. E. Hmelo-Silver, A. M. O'Donnell, & G. Erkens (Eds.), *Collaborative learning, reasoning, and technology.* Mahwah, NJ: L. Erlbaum Associates.

Birnbaum, J. S. (2004). Cybersecurity considerations for digital libraries in an era of pervasive computing. In *Proceedings of the JCDL '04* (pp. 169). New York: ACM.

Blandford, A., Keith, S., Connell, I., & Edwards, H. (2004). Analytical usability evaluation for digital libraries: A case study. In *Proceedings of the 2004 Joint ACM/IEEE Conference on Digital Libraries (JCDL '04)* (pp. 27-36).

Blanton, M. (2008). Online subscriptions with anonymous access. In [New York: ACM.]. *Proceedings of the ASIACCS, 08,* 217–227. doi:10.1145/1368310.1368342

Boase, J. (2008). Personal networks and the personal communication system. *Information Communication and Society, 11*(4), 490–508. doi:10.1080/13691180801999001

Boostrom, R. (2008). The social construction of virtual reality and the stigmatized identity of the newbie. *The journal of virtual worlds research, 1*(2), 2-19.

Borgatti, S. P., Everett, M. G., & Freeman, L. C. (2002). *Ucinet for Windows: Software for social network analysis.* Harvard, MA: Analytic Technologies.

Borko, H. (2004). Professional development and teacher learning: Mapping the terrain. *Educational Researcher, 33*(8), 3–15. doi:10.3102/0013189X033008003

Bostic, J. Q., Rustuccia, C., & Schlozman, S. C. (2001). *The shrink in the classroom: The suicidal student.* Alexandria, VA: Association for Supervision and Curriculum Development.

Botterbusch, H., & Talab, R. (2009). Ethical and legal issues in teaching with Second Life. *TechTrends.*

Bottoni, P., Civica, R., Levialdi, S., Orso, L., Panizzi, E., & Trinchese, R. (2004). MADCOW: A multimedia digital annotation system. In *Proceedings of the AVI '04* (pp. 55-62). New York: ACM.

Boulos, M., Hetherington, L., & Wheeler, S. (2007). Second Life: An overview of the potential of 3-D virtual worlds in medical and health education. *Health Information and Libraries Journal, 24*(4), 233–245. doi:10.1111/j.1471-1842.2007.00733.x

Bound, J., & Turner, S. (2002). Going to war and going to college: Did the G.I. bill increase educational attainment. *Journal of Labor Economics, 20*(4), 780–815. doi:10.1086/342012

Boylan, H. R., Bliss, L. B., & Bonham, B. S. (1997). Program components and their relationship to student performance. *Journal of Developmental Education, 20*(3), 2-8. Braxton, J. (2000). *Reworking the student departure puzzle.* Nashville, TN: Vanderbilt University Press.

Boyle, M., & Greenberg, S. (2005). The language of privacy: Learning from video media space analysis and design. *ACM Transactions on Computer-Human Interaction, 12*(2), 351. doi:10.1145/1067860.1067868

Boyle, T., Bradley, C., Chalk, P., Jones, R., & Pickard, P. (2003). Using blended learning to improve student success rates in learning to program. *Journal of Educational Media, 28*(2/3), 165–178. doi:10.1080/1358165032000153160

Bragg vs. Linden Research Inc. (n.d.). Retrieved April 7, 2009, from http://dockets.justia.com/docket/court-paedce/case_no-e:2006cv04925/case_id- 217858 [subscription required]

Brookfield, S. D., & Preskill, S. (2005). *Discussion as a way of teaching* (2nd ed.). San Francisco, CA: Jossey-Bass.

Brown, A., & Campione, J. (1994). Guided discovery in a community of learners. In K. McGilly (Ed.), *Classroom lessons: Integrating cognitive theory and classroom practice* (pp. 229-270). Cambridge, MA: MIT Press.

Bruer, J. T. (1993). *Schools for thought: A science of learning in the classroom.* Cambridge, MA: MIT Press.

Bruner, J. (1996). *The culture of education.* Cambridge, MA: Harvard College.

Bruner, J. S., Goodenough, J., & Austin, G. (1956). *A study of thinking.* New York: Wiley.

Buchanan, G., & Hinze, A. (2005). A generic alerting service for digital libraries. In *Proceedings of the JCDL '05* (pp. 131-140). New York: ACM.

Buchanan, M. (2002). *Nexus. Small worlds and the ground-breaking science of networks.* New York: W. W. Norton & Company Inc.

Buchs, C., Butera, F., Mugny, G., & Darmon, C. (2004). Conflict elaboration and cognitive outcomes. *Theory into Practice, 43*(1), 23–30.

Bureau of Labor Statistics, U.S. Department of Labor. (2008). *Occupational outlook handbook, 2008-09 edition, speech-language pathologists.* Retrieved November 30, 2008, from http://www.bls.gov/oco/ocos099.htm

Bureau of Labor Statistics, U.S. Department of Labor. (2008). *Occupational outlook handbook, 2008-09 edition, occupational therapists.* Retrieved November 30, 2008, from http://www.bls.gov/oco/ocos078.htm

Bush, A. A., & Tiwana, A. (2005). Designing sticky knowledge networks. *Communications of the ACM, 48*(5), 67–71. doi:10.1145/1060710.1060711

Buty, C., & Plantin, C. (Eds.). (2009). *Argumenter en classe de sciences [Argumentation in science classroom].* Paris: INRP.

Callan, J. Smeaton, Al., Beaulieu, M., Borlund, P., Brusilovsky, P., Chalmers, M., Lynch, C., Riedl, J., Smyth, B., Straccia, U., & Toms, E. (2003, May). *Personalization and recommender systems in digital libraries* (joint NSF-EU DELOS working group report). Retrieved February 6, 2009, from http://dli2.nsf.gov/internationalprojects/working_group_reports/personalisation.html

Calton, J. L., Dickinson, A. R., & Snyder, L. H. (2002). Non-spatial motor-specific activation in posterior parietal cortex. *Nature Neuroscience, 5*(6), 580–588. doi:10.1038/nn0602-862

Calvanese, D., Catarci, T., & Santucci, G. (2000). Building a digital library of newspaper clippings: The LAURIN Project. In *Proceedings of the IEEE Advances in Digital Libraries 2000, ADL 2000* (pp. 15-26). Washington, DC: IEEE.

Capodiferro, L., Neri, A., Nibaldi, M., & Jacovitti, G. (2004). Robust detail recognition and location technique for image retrieval in digital repositories. In *Proceedings of the Eighth International Conference on Information Visualization (IV '04).* Washington, DC: IEEE.

Carnine, D., Kameeniu, E., & Coyle, G. (1984). Utilization of contextual information in determining the meaning of unfamiliar words. *Reading Research Quarterly, 19*(2), 188–204. doi:10.2307/747362

Carron, A. V., Bray, S. R., & Eyes, M. A. (2002). Team cohesion and team success in sport. *Journal of Sports Sciences, 20*(2), 119–126. doi:10.1080/026404102317200828

Carver, C. A., Hill, J. M. D., & Pooch, U. W. (1999). Emerging curriculum issues in digital libraries. In *Proceedings of the 29th ASEE / IEEE Frontiers in Education Conference*. Washington, DC: IEEE.

Castranova, E. (2004). The right to play. *New York Law School Review, 49*. Retrieved from http://ssrn.com/abstract=733486

Castronova, E. (2005). *Synthetic worlds*. Chicago: University of Chicago Press.

Cayley, D. (Producer). (2008, April 30). Simon Schaffer [Episode 1]. *How to think about science*. Podcast retrieved from http://www.cbc.ca/ideas/features/science/index.html

Center for Disease Control and Prevention. (2007). *Prevalence of autism spectrum disorders (ASDs) in multiple areas of the United States, 2000 and 2002* (No. MMWR SS 2007; 56 (SS1)(12)). Atlanta, GA.

Centers for Disease Control and Prevention (CDC). (2008). *Economic consequences of overweight and obesity*. Retrieved March 13, 2008, from http://www.cdc.gov/nccdphp/dnpa/obesity/economic_consequences.htm

Chaplin, C. (Producer). (1936). *Modern times* [Motion picture]. USA: United Artists, MGM Tower.

Charmaz, K. (2006). *Constructing grounded theory: A practical guide through qualitative analysis*. London: Sage Publications.

Chen, C.-C., Wactlar, H. D., Wang, J. Z., & Kiernan, K. (2005). Digital imagery for significant cultural and historical materials: An emerging research field bridging people, culture, and technologies. *International Journal on Digital Libraries, 5*, 275–286. doi:10.1007/s00799-004-0097-5

Chickering, A., & Ehrmann, S. C. (1996). *Implementing the seven principles: Technology as a lever* (AAHE Bulletin). Retrieved May 28, 2008, from http://www.clt.astate.edu/clthome/Implementing%20the%20Seven%20Principles,%20Ehrmann%20and%20Chickering.pdf

Cho, H., & Lee, J. (2008). Collaborative information seeking in intercultural computer-mediated communication groups: Testing the influence of social context using social network analysis. *Communication Research, 35*(4), 548–573. doi:10.1177/0093650208315982

Chou, E. (2002). Redesigning a large and complex website: How to begin, and a method for success. In *Proceedings of the SIGUCCS '02*, Providence, RI (pp. 22-28). New York: ACM.

Christensen, C., Horn, M. B., & Johnson, C. W. (2008). *Disrupting class. How disruptive innovation will change the way the world learns*. New York: McGraw Hill.

Clarkson, E., & Foley, J. D. (2006). Browsing affordance designs for the human-centered computing educational digital library. In *Proceedings of the JCDL '06* (pp. 361). New York: ACM.

Cobb, P., Wood, T., Yackel, E., & McNeal, B. (1992). Characteristics of classroom mathematics traditions: An interactional analysis. *American Educational Research Journal, 29*(3), 573–604.

Cobb, S., Beardon, L., Eastgate, R., Glover, T., Kerr, S., & Neale, H. (2002). Applied virtual environments to support learning of social interaction skills in users with Asperger's Syndrome. *Digital Creativity, 13*(1), 11–22. doi:10.1076/digc.13.1.11.3208

Cohen, J. (1960). A coefficient of agreement for nominal scales. *Educational and Psychological Measurement, 20*, 37–46. doi:10.1177/001316446002000104

Coiro, J. (2003). Reading comprehension on the Internet: Expanding our understanding of reading comprehension to encompass new literacies. *The Reading Teacher, 56*, 458–464.

Cole, M., & Engeström, Y. (1993). A cultural-historical approach to distributed cognition. In G. Salomon (Ed.), *Distributed cognitions: Psychological and educational considerations* (pp. 27-46). Cambridge, UK: Cambridge University Press.

Coleman, A. S., Bartolo, L. M., & Jones, C. (2005). Impact: The last frontier in digital library evaluation. In *Proceedings of the JCDL '05* (pp. 372). New York: ACM.

Committee for Network Science for Future Army Applications. (2005). *Network science*. Washington, DC: The National Academies Press.

Conklin, M. S. (2007). *101 uses for Second Life in the college classroom*. Retrieved February 11, 2009, from http://facstaff.elon.edu/mconklin/pubs/glshandout.pdf

Connor, M., Wright, E., Curry, K., DeVries, L., Zeider, C., Wilmsmeyer, D., & Forman, D. (1996). *Learning: The critical technology*. Retrieved September 25, 2007, from http://learnativity.com/download/Learning_Whitepaper96.pdf

Cooper, B. F., & Garcia-Molina, H. (2005). Ad hoc, self-supervising peer-to-peer search networks. *ACM Transactions on Information Systems*, *23*(2), 169–200. doi:10.1145/1059981.1059983

Corti, K. **(2006).** *Games-based learning: A serious business application.* **PIXELearning** Limited. Retrieved May 2, 2008, from http://www.pixelearning.com/docs/games_basedlearning_pixelearning.pdf

Craik, F. I. M., & Tulving, E. (1975). Depth of processing and the retention of words in episodic memory. *Journal of Experimental Psychology. General*, *104*(3), 268–294. doi:10.1037/0096-3445.104.3.268

Cross, R., Borgatti, S. P., & Parker, A. (2003). Making invisible work visible. In R. L. Cross, A. Parker, & L. Sasson (Eds.), *Networks in the knowledge economy* (pp. 261-282). New York: Oxford University Press.

Curtis, D. D., & Lawson, M. J. (2001). Exploring collaborative online learning. *JALN*, *5*(1), 21–34.

Darian, S. (2008). Preparing for blended e-learning. *Technical Communication*, *55*(3), 285–287.

De Carvalho, M. G., Goncalves, M. A., Laender, A. H. F., & da Silva, A. S. (2006). Learning to deduplicate. In *Proceedings of the JCDL '06* (pp. 41-50). New York: ACM.

Department of Education. The Secretary of Education's Commission on the Future of Higher Education. (2006). *A test of leadership: Charting the future of U. S. higher educa-tion*. Retrieved December 2, 2008, from http://www.ed.gov/about/bdscomm/list/hiedfuture/reports/final-report.pdf

Dickens, W. T., & Flynn, J. R. (2001). Heritability estimates versus large environmental effects: The IQ paradox resolved. *Psychological Review*, *108*(2), 346–369. doi:10.1037/0033-295X.108.2.346

Dickey, M. (2005). Brave new (interactive) worlds: A review of the design affordances and constraints of two 3D virtual worlds as interactive learning environments. *Interactive Learning Environments*, *13*, 121–137. doi:10.1080/10494820500173714

Dickey, M. (2005). Three-dimensional virtual worlds and distance learning: Two case studies of active worlds as a medium for distance education. *British Journal of Educational Technology*, *36*, 439–451. doi:10.1111/j.1467-8535.2005.00477.x

Dickinson, A. R. (2008). Critical review of Prensky, M., "Don't bother me mom – I'm learning !" *Metapsychology Reviews*, *21*(5).

Dickinson, A. R., & Hui, D. (2008, December). *Enhancing school performance in English and mathematics through online educational games*. Paper presented at the 1st international conference on Popular Culture and Education in Asia, Hong Kong.

Dickinson, A. R., & Hui, D. (2008, December). *Role of e-leader in the globalization of a business institution based in Hong Kong*. Paper presented at the first international conference on Globalization: Cultures, Institutions and Socioeconomics, Hong Kong.

Dickinson, A. R., & Hui, D. (2009, June). *Effects of online educational games on students' scholastic achievements*. Paper accepted at the ED-MEDIA 2009 world conference on Educational Multimedia, Hypermedia & Telecommunications, Honolulu, HI.

Dickinson, A. R., & Yung, Y. (2008). Being gifted: Enhancing school performance via online educational games. In *Proceedings of the 10th Asia Pacific Conference on Giftedness*, Singapore.

Donnelly, R., & Fitzmaurice, M. (2005). Collaborative project-based learning and problem-based learning in higher education: A consideration of tutor and student roles in learner-focused strategies. In G. O'Neill, S. Moore, & B. McMullin (Eds.), *Emerging issues in the practice of university learning and teaching*. Dublin, Ireland: AISHE.

Downie, R., & Meadows, J. (1995). Experience with a dissection opt-out scheme in university level biology. *Journal of Biological Education, 29*(3), 187–196.

Dreyfus, T., & Halevi, T. (1990). QuadFun: A case study of pupil computer interaction. *Computers in Mathematics and Science Teaching, 10*(2), 43–48.

Dunn, J.W., & Cowan, W.G. (2005). EVIADA: Ethnomusicological video for instruction and analysis digital archive. *TCDL Bulletin, 2*(1).

Duphorne, P. L., & Gunawardena, C. N. (2005, March). The effect of three computer conferencing designs on critical thinking skills of nursing students. *American Journal of Distance Education, 19*(1), 37–50. doi:10.1207/s15389286ajde1901_4

Duranske, B. (2008). *Virtual law: Navigating the legal landscape of virtual worlds*. Chicago: American Bar Association Publishing.

Dzewaltowski, D. A., Estabrooks, P. A., & Johnston, J. A. (2002). Healthy youth places promoting nutrition and physical activity. *Health Education Research, 17*(5), 41–51. doi:10.1093/her/17.5.541

Edirisingha, P., Salmon, G., & Nie, M. (2008). Modelling of Second Life environments: 3-D multi-user virtual environments for socialisation in distance learning. In *Proceedings of the JISC Programme Project Presentations Association for Learning Technology Conference 2008* (pp. 20-24). Retrieved December 17, 2008, from http://www.jisc.ac.uk/media/documents/publications/altc2008presentationsv2.pdf

Edutopia. (2001). *PBL research summary: Studies validate project based learning*. Retrieved October 19, 2008, from http://www.edutopia.org/project-based-learning-research

Edwards, C., Bresnahan, K., & Edwards, A. (2008). The influence of humorous positive computer-mediated word-of-mouth communication on student motivation and affective learning. *Texas Speech Communication Journal, 33*(1), 1–8.

Elliot, J. (2008). Help-somebody robbed my Second Life avatar! *Journal of virtual worlds research, 1*(1), 1-11.

Ellis, H. D., & Hunt, R. R. (1983). *Fundamentals of human memory and cognition* (3rd ed.). Dubuque, IA: Brown.

Emelianov, M. (2007, December 18). *Metropolitan opera's first simulcast of 2007-2008 breaks attendance records*. Retrieved May 28, 2008, from http://pervegalit.wordpress.com/2007/12/18/metropolitan-operas-first-simulcast-of-2007-08-breaks-attendance-records

Engeström, Y. (1987). *Learning by expanding: An activity-theoretical approach to developmental research*. Helsinki, Finland: Orienta-Konsultit.

Engeström, Y., Miettinen, R., & Punamaki, R. (Eds.). (1999). *Perspectives on activity theory*. Cambridge, UK: Cambridge University Press.

Erduran, S., Osborne, J., & Simon, S. (2005). The role of argument in developing scientific literacy. In K. Boersma, O. de Jong, H. Eijkelhof, & M. Goedhart (Eds.), *Research and the quality of science education* (pp. 381- 394). Dordrecht, The Netherlands: Kluwer Academic Publishers.

Erikson, E. (2008). Hillary is my friend: MySpace and political fandom. *Rocky Mountain Communication Review, 5*(1), 3–16.

Erlich, K., & Chang, K. (2006). Leveraging expertise in global software teams: Going outside the boundaries. In *Proceedings of the IEEE International Conference on Global Software Engineering* (ICGSE '06) (pp. 149-158). Washington, DC: IEEE.

Estabrooks, P. A. (2000). Sustaining exercise participation through group cohesion. *Exercise and Sport Sciences Reviews, 28*(2), 1–5.

Ester, D. (1994). CAI, lecture, and student learning style: The different effects of instructional method. *Journal of Research on Computing in Education, 27*(2), 129–140.

Ethical and legal group. (2007). *Second Life feasibility study: Government, crime and Second Life*. Retrieved April 5, 2009 from http://manfromporlock.wetpaint.com/page/Ethical+and+Legal+Group

EU-US working group on spoken-word audio collections. (n.d.) Retrieved February 6, 2009, from http://www.dli2.

nsf.gov/internationalprojects/working_group_reports/spoken_word.html

Faiola, A., & MacDorman, K. (2008). The influence of holistic and analytic cognitive styles on online information design: Toward a communication theory of cultural cognitive design. *Information Communication and Society, 11*(3), 348–374. doi:10.1080/13691180802025418

Fernández, L., Sánchez, J.A., & García, A. (2000). MiBiblio: Personal spaces in a digital library universe. In *Digital libraries* (pp. 232-233). New York: ACM.

Fetscherin, M., & Lattemann, C. (2007, June). User acceptance of virtual worlds: An exploratory study about Second Life. Retrieved December 7, 2008 from http://www.fetscherin.com/UserAcceptanceVirtualWorlds.htm

Fisher, D. (2006). Helping teenagers get through the worst: SUICIDE. *Education Digest, 72*(2), 9–13.

Fisher, D. (2008). Building community online: A twice-weekly's experience extending its reach with the Hartsville Today citizen-based news site. *Grassroots Editor, 49*(4), 12–18.

Fishman, B. J., Marx, R. W., Best, S., & Tal, R. T. (2003). Linking teacher and student learning to improve professional development in systemic reform. *Teaching and Teacher Education, 19*, 643–658. doi:10.1016/S0742-051X(03)00059-3

Flanagin, A. (2005). IM online: Instant messaging use among college students. *Communication Research Reports, 22*(3), 175–187. doi:10.1080/00036810500206966

Fonte, R. (1997). Structured versus laissez-faire open access: Implementation of a proactive strategy. *New Directions for Community Colleges, 100*, 43–52. doi:10.1002/cc.10004

Foster, N. F., & Gibbons, S. (Eds.). (2007). *Studying students: The undergraduate research project at the University of Rochester.* Association of College and Research Libraries. Retrieved February 12, 2008, from http://www.ala.org/ala/acrl/acrlpubs/downloadables/Foster-Gibbons_cmpd.pdf

Freire, P. (1979). *Conscientização: Teoria e prática da libertação. Uma introdução ao pensamento de Paulo Freire.* São Paulo: Cortez & Moraes.

Freire, P. (1981). *Ação cultural para a liberdade* (5th ed.). Rio de Janeiro: Paz e Terra, Coleção O Mundo Hoje.

Freire, P. (2001). *Política e educação* (5th ed.). São Paulo: Editora Cortez.

Freire, P. (2003). *Pedagogia da esperança: Um encontro com a pedagogia do oprimido* (11th ed.). Rio de Janeiro: Paz e Terra.

Freud, S. (1971). Desire expressed in children's dreams. In A.H. Munsinger (Ed.), *Readings in child development* (pp. 410-412). New York: Holt, Rinehard, and Winston.

Friedkin, N. E. (2004). Social cohesion. *Annual Review of Sociology, 30*, 409–425. doi:10.1146/annurev.soc.30.012703.110625

Friedman, E. (2008, November 21). Florida teen live-streams his suicide online. *ABC News.* Retrieved February 6, 2009, from http://abcnews.go.com/Technology/MindMoodNews/story?id=6306126&page=1

Frommolz, I., & Fuhr, N. (2006). Probabilistic, object-oriented logics for annotation-based retrieval in digital libraries. In *Proceedings of the JCDL '06* (pp. 55-64). New York: ACM.

Gaggioli, A., Gorini, A., & Riva, G. (2007). *Prospects for the use of multiplayer online games in psychological rehabilitation.* Washington, DC: IEEE.

Galloway, A. R., & Thacker, E. (2007). *The exploit: a theory of networks.* Minneapolis, MN: University of Minnesota Press.

Garrison, D. R., Anderson, T., & Archer, W. (2000). Critical inquiry in a text-based environment: Computer conferencing in higher education. *The Internet and Higher Education, 2*(2–3), 87–105. doi:10.1016/S1096-7516(00)00016-6

Garrison, D. R., Anderson, T., & Archer, W. (2003). Critical thinking, cognitive presence, and computer conferencing in distance education. *American Journal of Distance Education, 15*(1), 7–23.

Gartner. (2008). Gartner report: Top ten disruptive technologies 2008-2012. Retrieved May 28, 2008, from http://www.gartner.com/it/page.jsp?id=681107

Gau, S. S.-F., Chen, Y.-Y., Tsai, F.-J., Lee, M.-B., Chiu, Y.-N., Soong, W.-T., & Hwu, H.-G. (2008). Risk factors for suicide in Taiwanese college students. *Journal of American College Health, 57*(2), 135–142. doi:10.3200/JACH.57.2.135-142

Gee, J. P. (2003). *What video games have to teach us about learning and literacy*. New York: Palgrave MacMillan.

Gee, J. P. (2005). *Why video games are good for your soul*. Melbourne, Australia: Common Ground Publishing: The Learner.

George, P. (2002). Student suicide and 9/11. *Education Digest, 77*(9), 12–15.

Gergen, K. (1995). Social construction and the educational process. In L. Steffe & J. Gale (Eds.), *Constructivism in education* (pp. 17-39). Hillsdale, NJ: Erlbaum.

Gibbons, M. M., & Studer, J. R. (2008). Suicide awareness training for faculty and staff: A training model for school counselors. *Professional School Counseling, 11*(4), 272–276.

Gibson, J. (1979). *The ecological approach to visual perception*. Hillsdale, NJ: Lawrence Erlbaum Associates Hawkridge, D. (1977). Communication and education in open learning systems. In D. Lerner & L. Nelson (Eds.), *Communication research: A half-century appraisal* (pp. 70-103). Honolulu, HI: University of Hawai'i Press.

Gillen, J. (2003). *The language of children*. London: Routledge.

Gillman, J. L., Kim, H. S., Alder, S. C., & Durrant, L. H. (2006). Assessing the risk factors for suicidal thoughts at a nontraditional commuter school. *Journal of American College Health, 55*(1), 17–26. doi:10.3200/JACH.55.1.17-26

Glaser, B. G., & Strauss, A. L. (1967). *The discovery of grounded theory: Strategies for qualitative research*. Chicago, IL: Aldine.

Glick, K. L., Wilczek, E., & Dockins, R. (2006). The ingest and maintenance of electronic records: Moving from theory to practice. In *Proceedings of the JCDL '06* (pp. 359).

Gloor, P. A. (2006). *Swarm creativity. Competitive advantage through collaborative innovation networks*. Oxford, UK: Oxford University Press.

Gold, A. K., Baker, K. S., LeMeur, J.-Y., & Baldridge, K. (2002). Building FLOW: Federating libraries on the Web. In *Proceedings of the JCDL '02* (pp. 287-288). New York: ACM.

Golder, C. (1996). *Le développement des discours argumentatifs* [The development of argumentative discourse]. Neuchâtel, Switzerland: Delachaux et Niestlé.

Golder, C., & Coirier, P. (1994). Argumentative text writing: Developmental trends. *Discourse Processes, 18*, 187–210.

Gorton, D., Shen, R., Vemuri, N. S., Fan, W., & Fox, E. A. (2006). ETANA-GIS: GIS for archaeological digital libraries. In *Proceedings of the JCDL '06* (pp. 379). New York: ACM.

Graziano, A. F. (1971). *Drop out survey at the University of Illinois at Urban Champaign* (Report No. HE 004302). Champaign, IL: University of Illinois at Urbana Champaign. (ERIC Document Reproduction Service. No. ED 078750)

Green, M., & Brock, T. (2002). In the mind's eye: Transportation-imagery model of narrative persuasion. In M. Green, J. Strange, & T. Brock (Eds.), *Narrative impact: Social and cognitive foundations* (pp. 315-341). London: Lawrence Erlbaum Associates.

Grieve, C. (1992). Knowledge increment assessed for three methodologies of teaching physiology. *Medical Teacher, 14*, 27–32. doi:10.3109/01421599209044011

Grubb, W. N. (1999). Innovative practices: The pedagogical and institutional challenges. In W. N. Grubb (Ed.), *Honored but invisible: An inside look at teaching in community colleges* (pp. 245-279). New York: Routledge.

Guk, I.-J., & Kellogg, D. (2007). The ZPD and whole class teaching: Teacher-led and student-led interactional mediation of tasks. *Language Teaching Research, 11*(3), 281–299. doi:10.1177/1362168807077561

Gunkel, D., & Hawhee, D. (2008). Virtual reality and the reformatting of ethics. *Journal of Mass Media Ethics, 18*(3/4), 173–194.

Gustafson, D. H., Greist, J. H., Stauss, F. F., Erdman, H., & Laughren, T. (1977). A probabilistic system for identifying suicide attemptors. *Computers and Biomedical Research, an International Journal, 10*, 83–89. doi:10.1016/0010-4809(77)90026-X

Haas, A., Koestner, B., Rosenberg, J., Moore, D., Garlow, S. J., & Sedway, J. (2008). An interactive Web-based method of outreach to college students at risk for suicide. *Journal of American College Health, 57*(1), 15–22. doi:10.3200/JACH.57.1.15-22

Hank, C., Choemprayong, S., & Sheble, L. (2007). Blogger perceptions on digital preservation. In *Proceedings of the JCDL '07* (pp. 477). New York: ACM.

Hansen, C. H., & Hansen, R. D. (1988). Finding the face in the crowd: An anger superiority effect. *Journal of Personality and Social Psychology, 54*, 917–924. doi:10.1037/0022-3514.54.6.917

Hart, L. A., Wood, M. W., & Hart, B. L. (2008). *Why dissection?: Animal use in education.* Westport, CT: Greenwood Press.

Hatala, M., Kalantari, L., Wakkary, R., & Newby, K. (2004). Ontology and rule based retrieval of sound objects in augmented audio reality system for museum visitors. In *Proceedings of the 2004 ACM Symposium on Applied Computing* (pp. 1045-1050). New York: ACM.

Hayes, E. R. (2006). *Situated learning in virtual worlds: The learning ecology of Second Life.* Retrieved February 25, 2009, from http://www.adulterc.org/Proceedings/2006/Proceedings/Hayes.pdf

Heckman, R., & Annabi, H. (2005). A content analytic comparison of learning processes in online and face-to-face case study discussions. *Journal of Computer-Mediated Communication, 10*(2), article 7. Retrieved from http://jcmc.indiana.edu/vol10/issue2/heckman.html

Heller, R. (1990). The role of hypermedia in education: A look at the research issues. *Journal of Research on Computing in Education, 22*(2), 431–441.

Helsel, D. C. (2001). Does your school track the suicidal student? *Clearing House (Menasha, Wis.), 75*(2), 2–95.

Henry, J. Kaiser Family Foundation. (2002, Fall). *Key facts: Children and video games.* Retrieved February 22, 2008, from http://ww.health08.org/entmedia/loader.cfm?url=/commonspot/security/getfile.cfm&PageID=14092

Herrington, J., Reeves, T., & Oliver, R. (2007). Immersive learning technologies: Realism and online authentic learning. *Journal of Computing in Higher Education, 19*(1), 65–84. doi:10.1007/BF03033421

Hewitt, J. (1996). *Progress toward a knowledge-building community.* Unpublished doctoral dissertation, Ontario Institute for Studies in Education of the University of Toronto, Toronto. Holland, J. H. (1998). *Emergence: From chaos to order.* Reading, MA: Helix Books.

Hill, G., Atwater, M., & Wiggins, J. (1995). Attitudes toward science of urban seventh-grade life science students over time, and the relationship to future plans, family, teacher, curriculum, and school. *Urban Education, 30*(1), 71–92. doi:10.1177/0042085995030001006

Hong Kong Digital Entertainment Association or HKDEA. (2009). Hong Kong information and communication technology (ICT) awards ceremony program. *Best Digital Edutainment and Entertainment Awards, 2*, 10.

Hoover, E. (2006). Students: 'Giving them the help that they need': The author of a new book on student suicide says colleges need to think about a lot more than liability. *The Chronicle of Higher Education, •••*, A39–A41.

Horsfield, P. (2002, November). *Continuities and discontinuities in ethical reflections on digital virtual reality.* Paper presented at the Virtual Reality International Conference, University of Illinois at Urbana-Champaign.

Howe, J. (2006). The rise of crowdsourcing. *Wired (San Francisco, Calif.), 14*(6).

Howe, J. (2008). *Crowdsourcing: Why the power of the crowd is driving the future of business.* [Audiobook read by Kirby Heyborne]. New York: Random House Audio.

Hughes, C., Russell, J., & Robbins, T. (1994). Evidence for executive dysfunction in autism. *Neuropsychologia, 32*(4), 477–492. doi:10.1016/0028-3932(94)90092-2

Hui, D. (2006). *Engagement in supporting new teachers: A role for computer-mediated communication in teacher learning within informal professional communities.* Unpublished doctoral dissertation, Washington University in St Louis, Missouri.

Hui, D. (2009). *A dialogic framework for evaluating the effectiveness of teacher engagement within online professional communities.* Manuscript submitted for publication.

Huizina, J. (1998). *Homo ludens: A study of the play element in culture.* New York: Taylor & Francis.

Hüser, C., Reichenberger, K., Rostek, L., & Streitz, N. (1995). Knowledge-based editing and visualization for hypermedia encyclopedias. *Communications of the ACM, 38*(4), 49–51. doi:10.1145/205323.205333

Ignatius, A. (2006, Feb. 20). In search of the real Google. *Time* (Canadian ed.), 20-32.

Il'enkov, E. V. (1977). *Dialectical logic: Essays in its history and theory.* Moscow: Progress.

Inoue, Y. (2007). Concepts, applications, and research of virtual reality learning environments. *International Journal of Social Sciences, 2*(1), 1–7.

Institute of Medicine. (2003). *Health professions education: A bridge to quality.* Washington, DC: National Academies Press.

Intelligent Systems Division. (2008). *The mission. Destination: Mars.* Retrieved May 13, 2008, from http://ti.arc.nasa.gov/destination/mars/our_part.php

Iodannis, J. P. A. (2007). Why most published research findings are false. *PLoS Medicine, 2*(8), 696–701. doi:. doi:10.1371/journal.pmed.0020124

Irwin, C., & Berge, Z. L. (2006). Socialistion in the online classroom. *E-Journal of Instructional Science and Technology, 9*(1). Retrieved December 17, 2008, from http://www.usq.edu.au/electpub/e-jist/docs/vol9_no1/papers/full_papers/irwin_berge.htm

Iverson, L. (2004). Collaboration in digital libraries: A conceptual framework. In *Proceedings of the JCDL '04* (pp. 380). New York: ACM.

Jackiw, N., & Sinclair, N. (2002). Dragon play: Microworld design in a whole new class context. *Journal of Educational Computing Research, 27,* 111–145. doi:10.2190/RYW7-EG6H-QU6V-8REC

Jaeggi, S. M., Buschkuehl, M., Jonides, J., & Perrig, W. J. (2008). Improving fluid intelligence with training on working memory. In *Proceedings of the National Academy of Sciences.* Retrieved February 22, 2008, from www.pnas.org/cgi/doi/10.1073/pnas.08012681056

Janssen, W. C. (2004). Collaborative extensions for the UpLib System. In *Proceedings of the JCDL '04* (pp. 239-240). New York: ACM.

Jaya, R. (2008). Skype voice chat a tool for teaching oral communication. *Language in India, 8*(12), 9.

Jiang, Z., & Potter, W. D. (1994). A computer microworld to introduce students to probability. *Journal of Computers in Mathematics and Science Teaching, 13*(2), 197–222.

Johansson, F. (2006). *The Medici effect. What elephants and epidemics can teach us about innovation.* Boston, MA: Harvard Business School Press.

Johnson, D. W., & Johnson, R. T. (1990). Social skills for successful group work. *Educational Leadership, 47*(4), 29–33.

Johnson, D. W., & Johnson, R. T. (1995). Positive interdependence: Key to effective cooperation. In R. Hertz-Lazarowitz & N. Miller (Eds.), *Interaction in cooperative groups: The theoretical anatomy of group learning* (pp. 174-201). New York: Cambridge University Press.

Johnson, D. W., & Johnson, R. T. (2003). *Learning together and alone: Cooperative, competitive and individualistic learning* (8th ed.). London: Allyn and Bacon.

Johnson, K. (1996). *Language teaching and skill learning.* Cambridge, MA: Blackwell.

Johnson, S. (2001). *Emergence. The connected lives of ants, brains, cities, and software.* Toronto, Canada: Scribner.

Jonassen, D. H., Peck, K. L., & Wilson, B. G. (1999). *Learning with technology: A constructivist perspective.* Upper Saddle River, NJ: Merrill-Prentice Hall.

Jordan, R. (2003). A review of the role of play in theory and practice in autistic spectrum disorders, *Autism: the International Journal of Research and Practice, 7.*

Kadobayashi, R., Lombardi, J., McCahill, M. P., Stearns, H., Tanaka, K., & Kay, A. (2005). Annotation authoring in collaborative 3D virtual environments. In . *Proceedings of the ICAT, 2005,* 255–256. doi:10.1145/1152399.1152452

Kahlenberg, R. D. (2004). *America's untapped resource: Low-income students in higher education.* New York: The Century foundation Press.

Kane, S. (2007, November). Merchants decry copyright chaos. *Reuters.* Retrieved March 30, 2008, from http://secondlife.reuters.com/stories/2007/11/07/merchants-decry-second-life- copyright-chaos/

Kane, T. (1994). College entry by blacks since 1970: The role of college costs, family background, and the returns to education. *The Journal of Political Economy, 10*(5), 878–911. doi:10.1086/261958

Kerbs, R. W. (2005). Social and ethical considerations in virtual worlds. *The Electronic Library, 23*(5), 539–547. doi:10.1108/02640470510631254

Kholief, M., Shen, S., & Maly, K. (2000). Event-based retrieval from digital libraries containing streamed data. In *Proceedings of the International Conference on Information Technology: Coding and Computing* (pp. 234). Washington, DC: IEEE.

Kilgo, J. L., & Bruder, M. B. (1997). Creating new visions in institutions of higher education: Interdisciplinary approaches to personnel preparation in early intervention. In P. J. Winton, J. A. McCollum, & C. Catlett (Eds.), *Reforming personnel preparation in early intervention.* Chapel Hill, NC: SCPP.

Kim, Y.-H., & Kellogg, D. (2007). Rules out of roles: Differences in play language and their developmental significance. *Applied Linguistics, 28*(1), 25–45. doi:10.1093/applin/aml047

King, K. A. (2001). Developing a comprehensive school suicide prevention program. *The Journal of School Health, 71*(4), 132–137.

King, K. A. (2001). Tri-level suicide prevention covers it all. *Journal of School Health* . *Education Digest, 67*(1), 55–61.

Kinzie, M. B., Foss, M. J., & Powers, S. M. (1993). Use of dissection-related courseware by low-ability high school students: A qualitative inquiry. *Educational Technology Research and Development, 41*(3), 87–101. doi:10.1007/BF02297359

Kinzie, M. B., Larsen, V. A., Burch, J. B., & Baker, S. M. (1996). Frog dissection via the World-Wide-Web: Implications for widespread delivery of instruction. *Educational Technology Research and Development, 44*(2), 59–69. doi:10.1007/BF02300541

Kirriemuir, J. (2008). A spring 2008 snapshot of UK higher and further education developments in Second Life. *Eduserv VirtualWorldWatch.* Retrieved December 12, 2008, from http://www.scribd.com/doc/7063700/A-Spring-2008-snapshot-of-UK-Higher-and-Further-Education-Developments-in-Second-Life

Kittross, J., & Gordon, D. (2003). The academy and cyberspace ethics. *Journal of Mass Media Ethics, 18*(3), 286–290. doi:10.1207/S15327728JMME1803&4_9

Kline, A. (1971). A study of the relationship between self directed and teacher directed eighth grade students involved in open ended supplementary ESCP. *Journal of Research in Science Teaching, 8*(3), 263–271. doi:10.1002/tea.3660080310

Knapp, L. G., Kelly-Reid, J. E., & Whitmore, R. W. (2006). *Enrollment in postsecondary institutions, fall 2004: Graduation rates, 1998 & 2001 cohorts; and financial statistics, fiscal year 2004* (NCES 2006-155). Washington, DC: U.S. Department of Education. Retrieved October 1, 2006, from http://nces.ed.gov/pubsearch/pubsinfo.asp?pubid=2006155

Knees, P., Schedl, M., Pohle, T., & Widmer, G. (2006). An innovative three-dimensional user interface for exploring music collections enriched with meta-information from the Web. In [New York: Association for Computing Machinery, Inc.]. *Proceedings of the MM, 06*, 17–24.

Ko, K. H., Maekawa, T., Patrikalakis, N. M., Masuda, H., & Wolter, F.-E. (2003). Shape intrinsic fingerprints for free-form object matching. In [New York: ACM.]. *Proceedings of the SM, 03*, 196–27.

Koballa, T. R. (1993). *Synthesis of science attitude research for elementary grades.* Paper presented at the 1993 annual meeting of the National Association for Research in Science Teaching, Atlanta, GA.

Koballa, T. R., Crawley, F. E., & Shrigley, R. L. (1990). A summary of research in science education- 1988. *Science Education, 74*(3), 252–407. doi:10.1002/sce.3730740304

Kohler Riessman, C. (2008). *Narrative methods for the human sciences.* London: SAGE.

Korwin, A. R., & Jones, R. E. (1990). Do hands-on, technology-based activities enhance learning by reinforcing cognitive knowledge and retention? *Journal of Technology Education, 1*(2), 26–33.

Kozinets, R. V. (1997). I want to believe: A netnography of the X-Philes. *Advances in Consumer Research. Association for Consumer Research (U. S.)*, *25*, 470–475.

Kozinets, R. V. (2002). The field behind the screen: Using netnography for marketing research in online communities. *JMR, Journal of Marketing Research*, *39*(1), 61–72. doi:10.1509/jmkr.39.1.61.18935

Krafft, D. B., Birkland, A., & Cramer, E. J. (2008, June). NCore: Architecture and implementation of a flexible, collaborative digital library. In *Proceedings of the JCDL '08* (pp. 313-322). New York: ACM.

Krebs, V. (2007). *Social network analysis, a brief introduction.* Retrieved August 16, 2007, from http://www.orgnet.com/sna.html

Krowne, A., & Halbert, M. (2005). An initial evaluation of automated organization for digital library browsing. In *Proceedings of the JCDL '05* (pp. 246-255). New York: ACM.

Kuhn, T. (1996). *The structure of scientific revolutions* (3rd ed.). Chicago, IL: University of Chicago Press.

Kumar, A. (2007). Visual understanding environment. In Proceedings of the JCDL '07 (pp. 510). New York: ACM.

Kurlaender, M., & Felts, E. (2008). Bakke beyond college access: Investigating racial/ethnic differences in college completion. In P. Marin & C. Horn (Eds.), *Realizing Bakke's legacy: Affirmative action, equal opportunity, and access to higher education* (pp. 110-144). VA: Stylus Publishers.

Kurzweil, R. (2001). Promise and peril—the deeply intertwined poles of 21st century technology. *Communications of the ACM*, *44*(3), 88–91. doi:10.1145/365181.365215

Kuster, J. (2007). Facilitating group therapy and support meetings. *ASHA Leader*, *12*(7), 30–31.

Kwon, M.-S., & Kellogg, D. (2005). Teacher talk as a game of catch. *Canadian Modern Language Review*, *62*(2), 335–348.

Kwon, O.-R. (2006). *Suggestions for facilitating English education in elementary and middle schools on the basis of the analysis of ten years' elementary English education achievements.* Seoul, Korea: Ministry of Education and Development of Human Recourses.

Kzero Research. (2008). *K Zero Universe chart.* Retrieved December 10, 2008, from http://www.kzero.co.uk/blog/?page_id=2537

LaFromboise, T. (2006). American Indian youth suicide prevention. *Prevention Researcher*, *13*(3), 16–18.

Laird, J. E. (2007). *Using computer games to develop advanced AI.* Retrieved February 22, 2008, from http://ai.eecs.umich.edu/people/laird/papers/Computer01.pdf

Laleuf, J. R., & Spalter, A. M. (2001). A component repository for learning objects: A progress report. In *Proceedings of the JCDL '01* (pp. 33-40). New York: ACM.

Lamb, A. C. (1991). *Emerging technologies and instruction: Hypertext, hypermedia, and interactive multimedia: A selected bibliography.* Englewood Cliffs, NJ: Educational Technology.

Langley, G. R. (1991). Animals in science education: Ethics and alternatives. *Journal of Biological Education*, *25*(4), 274–279.

Lapadat, J. (2002, July). Written interaction: A key component in online learning. *Journal of Computer Mediated Communication*, *7*(4). Retrieved July 12, 2007 from http://jcmc.indiana.edu/vol7/issue4/lapadat.html

Laru, J., & Järvelä, S. (2008). Social patterns in mobile technology mediated collaboration among members of the professional distance education community. *Educational Media International*, *45*(1), 17–32. doi:10.1080/09523980701847131

Lastrowka, G., & Hunter, D. (2004, January). The laws of virtual worlds. *Cal. L. Rev.*, *1*, 49. Retrieved from http://ssrn.com/abstract=402860

Latour, B., & Woolgar, S. (1988). *Laboratory life: The social construction of scientific facts.* London: Sage Publ.

Lave, J., & Wenger, E. (2006). *Situated learning legitimate peripheral participation* (15th ed.). New York: Cambridge University Press.

Lawless, S., Hederman, L., & Wade, V. (2008). Enhancing access to open corpus educational content: Learning in the wild. In [New York; ACM.]. *Proceedings of the HT, 08*, 167–174.

Learning in Informal and Formal Environments (LIFE) Center. (2009). Retrieved January 8, 2009, from http://life-slc.org

Lee, C. (2008, December 13). Web games 'aid learning'. *South China Morning Post, Education Supplement.*

Lee, R. E., & Cubbin, C. (2009). Striding toward social justice: The ecologic milieu of physical activity. *Exercise and Sport Sciences Reviews, 37,* 10–17. doi:10.1097/JES.0b013e318190eb2e

Leonard, W. H. (1989). A comparison of student reactions to biology instruction by interactive videodisc or conventional laboratory. *Journal of Research in Science Teaching, 26*(2), 95–104. doi:10.1002/tea.3660260202

Leong, T. W., Howard, S., & Vetere, F. (2008, Apr.). Choice: Abdicating or exercising. In *CHI 2008 Proceedings – Sound of Music* (pp. 715-724). New York: ACM.

Leontiev, A. N. (1978). *Activity. Consciousness. Personality.* Englewood Cliffs, NJ: Prentice Hall.

Levinsky, A. (2001). Are teen suicide and homicide related? *Education Digest, 66*(8), 49–53.

Lewis, B. (2002). *What went wrong?: Western impact and Middle Eastern response.* New York: Oxford University Press.

Li, K., Liu, H., & Yu, H. (2007). VegaDLib: A service-oriented platform for building digital libraries. In *Proceedings of the The Sixth International Conference on Grid and Cooperative Computing (GCC 2007).* Washington, DC: IEEE.

Linden Labs. (2009). *Second Life economic statistics.* Retrieved February 28, 2009, from http://secondlife.com/statistics/economy-data.php

Loftus, T. (2005). *Virtual world teaches real-world skills.* Retrieved February 27, 2007, from http://www.msnbc.msn.com/id/7012645/

Low, S., Chew Chin, M., & Deurenberg, M. (2009). Review on epidemic of obesity. *Annals of the Academy of Medicine, Singapore, 38,* 57–65.

Ludlow, P., & Wallace, M. (2007). *The Second Life Herald – the virtual tabloid that witnessed the dawn of the metaverse.* Cambridge, MA: MIT Press

Luppicini, R. (2007). Review of computer mediated communication research for education. *Instructional Science, 35*(2), 141–185. doi:10.1007/s11251-006-9001-6

Lynch, C., Parastatidis, S., Jacobs, N., Van de Sompel, H., & Lagoze, C. (2007). The OAI-ORE effort: Progress, challenges, synergies. In *Proceedings of the JCDL '07* (pp. 80). New York: ACM.

Mabrito, M., Dyrud, M., & Worley, R. (2001). Facilitating interactivity in an online business writing course. *Business Communication Quarterly, 64*(3), 81–86. doi:10.1177/108056990106400308

MacCoun, R. J., Keir, E., & Belkin, A. (2006). Does social cohesion determine motivation in combat? *Armed Forces and Society, 32*(4), 646–654. doi:10.1177/0095327X05279181

MacMillan, J., Paley, M. J., Levchuk, Y. N., Entin, E. E., Serfaty, D., & Freeman, J. T. (2002). Designing the best team for the task: Optimal organizational structures for military missions. In M. McNeese, E. Salas, & M. Endsley (Eds.), *New trends in cooperative activities: System dynamics in complex settings.* San Diego, CA: Human Factors and Ergonomics Society Press.

Madrazo, G. (2002). The debate over dissection: Dissecting a classroom dilemma. *Science Educator, 11*(1), 41–45.

Malizia, A. (2004). A cognition-based approach for querying personal digital libraries. In *Proceedings of the 2004 IEEE Symposium on Visual Languages and Human Centric Computing (VLHCC '04).*

Manku, G. S., Jain, A., & Sarma, A. D. (2007). Detecting near-duplicates for Web crawling. In *Proceedings of the WWW 2007/ Track: Data Mining, Similarity Search. The International World Wide Web Conference Committee (IW3C2)* (pp. 141-149). New York: ACM.

Mansfield, R. (2008). *How to do everything with Second Life.* New York: The McGraw-Hill Companies.

Marincioni, F., & Lightsom, F. (2002). Marine realms information bank: A distributed geolibrary for the ocean. In *Proceedings of the JCDL '02* (pp. 399). New York: ACM.

Markscheffel, B., Fischer, D., & Stelzer, D. (2006). A business model-based classification approach for digital libraries. In *Proceedings of the 1st International Confer-*

ence on Digital Information Management (pp. 457-464). Washington, DC: IEEE.

MaryAnnCLT. (2007, August 10). *Educational uses of Second Life* [Video File]. Video posted to http://www.youtube.com/watch?v=qOFU9oUF2HA

Matthews, N. (2008). Conflicting perceptions and complex change: Promoting Web-supported learning in an arts and social sciences faculty. *Learning, Media and Technology, 33*(1), 35–44. doi:10.1080/17439880701868846

Max, M., & Burke, J. (1997). Virtual reality for autism communication and education, with lessons for medical training simulators. *Studies in Health Technology and Informatics, 39*, 46–53.

Mayer, V. J., & Hinton, N. K. (1990). Animals in the classroom: Considering the options. *Science Teacher (Normal, Ill.), 57*(3), 26–31.

Mazer, J., Murphy, R., & Simonds, C. (2007). I'll see you on "Facebook": The effects of computer-mediated teacher self-disclosure on student motivation, affective learning, and classroom climate. *Communication Education, 56*(1), 1–17. doi:10.1080/03634520601009710

McArthur, V. (2008). Real ethics in a virtual world. In *Proceedings of the Conference on Human Factors in Computing (CHI)* (pp. 3315-3320).

McCaffrey, M., & Weston, T. (2005). The climate change collection: A case study on digital library collection review and the integration of research, education and evaluation. In *Proceedings of the International Conference on Digital Libraries. Proceedings of the 5th ACM / IEE-CS Joint Conference on Digital Libraries*, Denver, Colorado (pp. 392).

McConnell, D. (2000). *Implementing computer supported collaborative learning* (2nd ed.). London: Kogan Page.

McConnell, D. (2006). *E-learning groups and communities*. Maidenhead, UK: Open University Press.

McCown, F., Smith, J. A., Nelson, M. L., & Bollen, J. (2006). Lazy preservation: Reconstructing websites by crawling the crawlers. In [ACM.]. *Proceedings of the WIDM, 06*, 67–74.

McGonigle, B. O. (1991). Incremental intelligent systems by design. In J. Arcady-Meyer & S. Wilson (Eds.), *From animals to animals*. Cambridge, MA: MIT Press.

McGonigle, B. O., Chalmers, M., & Dickinson, A. R. (2003). Concurrent disjoint and reciprocal classification by Cebus Apella in seriation tasks: Evidence for hierarchical organization. *Animal Cognition, 6*, 186–197. doi:10.1007/s10071-003-0174-y

McIntyre, S. A., Dennis, S. E., Uijtdehaage, S. H. J., & Candler, C. S. (2004). A digital library for health sciences educators: The Health Education Assets Library (HEAL). In *Proceedings of the JCDL '04* (pp. 387).

McNeill, D. (2005). *Gesture and thought*. Chicago: University of Chicago Press.

Mead, G. H. (1934). *Mind, self, and society*. Chicago: University of Chicago Press.

Mehan, H. (1979). *Learning lessons: Social organization in the classroom*. Cambridge, MA: Harvard University Press.

Mercer, N. (2000). *Words and minds: How we use language to think together*. London: Routledge.

Mercer, N., & Littleton, K. (2007). *Dialogue and the development of children's thinking: A sociocultural approach*. London: Routledge.

Merriam, S. B. (1998). *Qualitative research and case study applications in education* (2nd ed.). San Francisco: Jossey-Bass. Miles, M., & Huberman, M. (1994). *Qualitative data analysis* (2nd ed.). Thousand Oaks, CA: Sage Publications.

Mesch, G. (2006). Online communities. In C. Milofski & R. Cnaan (Eds.), *Handbook in sociology of communities*. New York: Lower Academic/ Plenum Books.

Messick, S. (Ed.). (1976). *Individuality in learning*. San Francisco: Jossey-Bass.

Metz, G. W. (2004). Challenge and changes to Tinto's persistence theory: A historical review. *Journal of College Student Retention Research Theory and Practice, 6*(2), 191. doi:10.2190/M2CC-R7Y1-WY2Q-UPK5

Meyer, K. (2003). Face-to-face versus threaded discussion: The role of time and higher-order thinking. *JALN, 7*(3), 55–65.

Miglietti, C. L., & Strange, C. C. (2002). Learning styles, classroom preferences, teaching styles, and remedial course outcomes for underprepared adults at a two-year college. *Community College Review*, *26*(1), 1–19. doi:10.1177/009155219802600101

Miller, G. A. (2003). The cognitive revolution: A historical perspective. *Trends in Cognitive Sciences*, *7*(3), 141–144. doi:10.1016/S1364-6613(03)00029-9

Miller, V. (2008). New media, networking and phatic culture. *Convergence: The Journal of Research into New Media Technologies*, *14*(4), 387–400. doi:10.1177/1354856508094659

Milsom, A. (2002). Suicide prevention in schools: Court cases and implications for principals. *NASSP Bulletin*, *86*(730), 24–33. doi:10.1177/019263650208663004

Minocha, S., & Roberts, D. (2008). Laying the groundwork for socialisation and knowledge construction within 3D virtual worlds. *Association for Learning Technology Journal*, *16*(3), 181–196.

Minocha, S., & Roberts, D. (2008). Social, usability, and pedagogical factors influencing students' learning experiences with Wikis and blogs. *Pragmatics & Cognition*, *16*(2), 272–306. doi:10.1075/p&c.16.2.05min

Minsky, M. (1988). *Society of mind* (Touchstone ed.). New York: Simon & Schuster Inc.

Mischo, W. H., Habing, T. G., & Cole, T. W. (2003). Integration of simultaneous searching and reference linking across bibliographic resources on the Web. In *Proceedings of the 2nd ACM/IEEE-CS joint conference on digital libraries* (pp. 119-125). Washington, DC: IEEE.

Mitchell, P., Parsons, S., & Leonard, A. (2007). Using virtual environments for teaching social understanding to 6 adolescents with autistic spectrum disorders. *Journal of Autism and Developmental Disorders*, *37*(3), 589–600. doi:10.1007/s10803-006-0189-8

Moro, C., & Rodriguez, C. (2008). Production of signs and meaning-making process in triadic interaction at the prelinguistic level. In E. Abbey & R. Diriwächter (Eds.), *Innovating genesis: Microgenesis and the constructive mind in action* (pp. 207-227). Charlotte, NC: Information Age Publishing.

Morris, C. M., Hembrooke, H., & Rayle, L. (2006). Finding a metaphor for collecting and disseminating distributed NSDL content and communications. In *Proceedings of the JCDL '06* (pp. 354). New York: ACM.

Moss, B. G., & Yeaton, W. H. (2006). Shaping policies related to developmental education: An evaluation using the regression-discontinuity design. *Educational Evaluation and Policy Analysis*, *28*(3), 215–229. doi:10.3102/01623737028003215

Muller Mirza, N. (2005). *Psychologie culturelle d'une formation d'adultes* [Cultural psychology of an adult training]. Paris: L'Harmattan.

Muller Mirza, N., & Perret-Clermont, A.-N. (2008). Dynamiques interactives, apprentissages et médiations: Analyses de constructions de sens autour d'un outil pour argumenter [Interactive dynamics, learning and mediation: Analyses of the construction of meaning around a tool for arguing]. In L. Filliétaz & M.-L. Schubauer-Leoni (Eds.), *Processus interactionnels et situations éducatives* (pp. 231-254). Bruxelles, Belgium: De Boek.

Muller Mirza, N., Perret-Clermont, A.-N., Tartas, V., & Iannaccone, A. (2009). Psychosocial processes in argumentation. In N. Muller Mirza & A.-N. Perret-Clermont (Eds.), *Argumentation and education: Theoretical foundations and practices* (pp. 67-90) New York: Springer.

Mulligan, J., & Petrovsky, B. (2003). *Developing online games: An insider's guide*. Boston: New Riders. Ostrander, M. (2008, March 4). *Interview protocol. Second Life interviews*. Retrieved on December 5, 2008 from http://librariandreamer.wordpress.com/?s=interview+protocol

Muramatsu, B., Giersch, S., McMartin, F., Weimar, S., & Klotz, G. (2004). 'If you build it, will they come?' Lessons learned from the workshop on participant interaction in digital libraries. In *Proceedings of the 2004 Joint ACM / IEEE Conference on Digital Libraries (JCDL '04)* (pp. 396). Washington, DC: IEEE.

Murphy, E. (2003). Moving from theory to practice in the design of Web-based learning from the perspective of constructivism. *The Journal of Interactive Online Learning*, *1*(4). Retrieved October 13, 2008, from http://www.ncolr.org/jiol/issues/PDF/1.4.4.pdf

NASA. (2008, Aprril 23). *Spirit and Opportunity. Mars exploration rovers*. Retrieved May 1, 2008 from http://marsrovers.nasa.gov/home/index.html

National Center for Education Statistics. (2008). *Integrated postsecondary education data system*. Retrieved October 15, 2008, from http://nces.ed.gov/ipeds/

Nelson, M. L., Marchionini, G., Geisler, G., & Yang, M. (2001). A bucket architecture for the Open Video Project. In *Proceedings of the JCDL '01* (pp. 310-311). New York: ACM.

Newton, F. (2008). *Interview*.

Nichols, D. M., Bainbridge, D., Downie, J. S., & Twidale, M. B. (2006). Learning by building digital libraries. In *Proceedings of the JCDL '06* (pp. 185-186). New York: ACM.

Nikolaidou, M., Anagnostopoulos, D., & Hatzopoulos, M. (2003). Using a medical digital library for education purposes. In *Proceedings of the 16th IEEE Symposium on Computer-Based Medical Systems (CBMS '03)*.

Nix, D., & Spiro, R. (Eds.). (1990). *Cognition, education, and multimedia: Exploring ideas in high technology*. Hillsdale, NJ: Lawrence Erlbaum Associates.

Nobis, N. (2002). Animal dissection and evidence-based life-science and health-professions education. *Journal of Applied Animal Welfare Science, 5*(2), 157–161. doi:10.1207/S15327604JAWS0502_06

Nonaka, I., & Takeuchi, H. (1995). *The knowledge-creating company: How Japanese companies create the dynamics of innovation*. New York: Oxford University Press.

Norman, D. (2002). *The design of everyday things*. New York: Basic Books.

O'Sullivan, D., McLoughlin, E., Bertolotto, M., & Wilson, D. C. (2003). Capturing task knowledge for geo-spatial imagery. In [New York: ACM.]. *Proceedings of the K-CAP, 03*, 78–87.

Oblinger, D. (Ed.). (2006). *Learning spaces*. EDUCAUSE. Retrieved May 28, 2008, from http://www.educause.edu/learningspaces

Ogden, C. L., Carroll, M. D., Curtin, L. R., McDowell, M. A., Tabak, C. J., & Flegal, K. M. (2006). Prevalence of overweight and obesity in the United States, 1999-2004. *Journal of the American Medical Association, 295*, 1549–1555. doi:10.1001/jama.295.13.1549

Ogle, R. (2007). *Smart world: Breakthrough creativity and the new science of ideas*. Boston, MA: Harvard Business School Press.

Oravec, J. (2003). Blending by blogging: Weblogs in blended learning initiatives. *Journal of Educational Media, 28*(2/3), 225–233. doi:10.1080/1358165032000165671

Orlans, F. B. (1988). Debating dissection. *Science Teacher (Normal, Ill.), 55*, 36–40.

Orlans, F. B. (1991). Forum: Dissection. The case against. *Science Teacher (Normal, Ill.), 58*(1), 12–15.

Orlans, F. B. (1991). Use of animals in education: Policy and practice in the United States. *Journal of Biological Education, 25*(1), 27–32.

Osborne, J., Erduran, S., & Simon, S. (2004). *Ideas, evidence and argument in science (IDEAS). In-service training pack, resource pack and video*. London: Nuffield Foundation.

Paelke, V., Reimann, C., & Rosenbach, W. (2003). A visualization design repository for mobile devices. In *Proceedings of the 2nd International Conference on Computer Graphics, Virtual Reality, Visualisation and Interaction in Africa* (pp. 57-61). New York: ACM.

Paladino, D., & Minton, C. A. B. (2008). Comprehensive college student suicide assessment: Application of the BASIC ID. *Journal of American College Health, 56*(6), 643–650. doi:10.3200/JACH.56.6.643-650

Palloff, R. M., & Pratt, K. (2001). *Lessons from the cyberspace classroom. The realities of online teaching*. San Francisco: Jossey-Bass.

Palmer, C., Zavalina, O., & Mustafoff, M. (2007, June). Trends in metadata practices: A longitudinal study of collection federation. In *Proceedings of the JCDL '07* (pp. 386-395). New York: ACM.

Panda, S., & Mishra, S. (2007). E-learning in a mega open university: Faculty attitude, barriers and motivators. *Educational Media International, 44*(4), 323–338. doi:10.1080/09523980701680854

Parker, R. (2006). Commuters play large role in flu spread. *FuturePundit.com*. Retrieved from http://www.futurepundit.com/archives/cat_pandemic_isolation.html

Parsad, B., & Lewis, L. (2003). *Remedial education at degree-granting postsecondary institutions in fall 2000* (NCES 2004–010, Table 4). Data from U.S. Department of Education, NCES, Postsecondary Education Quick Information System (PEQIS), *Survey on remedial education in higher education institutions, fall 2000.*

Parsons, S., Leonard, A., & Mitchell, P. (2006). Virtual environments for social skills training: Comments from two adolescents with autistic spectrum disorder. *Computers & Education, 47*(2), 186–206. doi:10.1016/j.compedu.2004.10.003

Pascarella, E. T., & Terenzini, P. T. (1991). *How college affects students.* San Francisco: Jossey-Bass.

Pearlman, B. (2006). *News skills for a new century: Students thrive on cooperation and problem solving. Edutopia.* Retrieved November 10, 2008, from http://www.edutopia.org/new-skills-new-century

Pearson, M., & Lewin, C. (2005). Online education and learner autonomy: Reports from the field. *Learning, Media and Technology, 30*, 259–261.

Pena-Shaff, J., & Nicholls, C. (2004). Analyzing student interactions and meaning construction in Computer Bulletin Board (BBS) discussions. *Computers & Education, 42*, 243–265. doi:10.1016/j.compedu.2003.08.003

Pérez-Quiñones, M. A., Fox, E., Cassel, L., & Fan, W. (2006). Work in progress: Personalizing a course website using the NSDL. 36ᵗʰ ASEE/IEEE Frontiers in Education Conference. San Diego, California. IEEE. M3F-3 to M3F-4.

Perret-Clermont, A.-N. (1980). *Social interaction and cognitive development in children.* London: Academic Press.

Petrides, L. (2002). Web-based technologies for distributed (or distance) learning: Creating learning-centered educational experiences in the higher education classroom. *International Journal of Instructional Media, 29*(1), 69.

Piaget, J. (1959). *The language and thought of the child.* New York: Routledge.

Piaget, J. (2007). *The child's conception of the world.* Lanham, MD: Rowman & Littlefield.

Piaget, J., & Inhelder, B. (1969, 2000). *The psychology of the child.* New York: Basic.

Pind, J., Gunnarsdottir, E. K., & Johannesson, H. S. (2003). Raven's standard progressive matrices: New school age norms and a study of the test's validity. *Personality and Individual Differences, 34*, 375–386. doi:10.1016/S0191-8869(02)00058-2

Piskurich, G. M. (1993). *The ASTD handbook of instructional technology: American society for training and development.* New York: McGraw-Hill.

Police foil teen's suspected Web suicide. (2008, December 2). Retrieved December 2, 2008, from http://www.cbsnews.com/stories/2008/12/02/national/main4642139.shtml?tag=topHome;topStories

Prensky, M. (2006). *Don't bother me mom – I'm learning!* St Paul, MN: Paragon House Publishers.

PUC-SP. (2004). *Projeto aprendizagem: Formas alternativas de atendimento* (Relatório Final). São Paulo: Programa de Pós-Graduação em Educação: Currículo.

Quentin-Baxter, M., & Dewhurst, D. (1992). An interactive computer-based alternative to performing a rat dissection in the classroom. *Journal of Biological Education, 26*(1), 27–33.

Rani, S., Goodkin, J., Cobb, J., Habing, T., & Urban, R. Eke, Jn., & Pearce-Moses, R. (2006). Technical architecture overview: Tools for acquisition, packaging and ingest of Web objects into multiple repositories. In *Proceedings of the JCDL '06* (pp. 360). New York; ACM.

Recker, M., & Palmer, B. (2006). Using resources across educational digital libraries. In *Proceedings of the JCDL '06* (pp. 240-241). New York: ACM.

Reuning, J., & Jones, P. (2005). Osprey: Peer-to-peer enabled content distribution. In *Proceedings of the JCDL '05* (pp. 396). New York: ACM. DELOS / NSF Working Group. (2003). *Reference models for digital libraries: Actors and roles.* Retrieved from http://delos-noe.iei.pi.cnr.it/activities/internationalforum/Joint-WGs/actors/Actors-Roles.pdf

Rinehart, N., Bradshaw, J., Tonge, B., Brereton, A., & Bellgrove, M. (2002). A neurobehavioral examination of individuals with high-functioning autism and Asperger disorder using a fronto-striatal model of dysfunction. *Behavioral and Cognitive Neuroscience Reviews, 1*(2), 164–177.

Risk and Protective Factors. (2008). *Ulifeline.* Retrieved November 14, 2008, from http://www.ulifeline.org/main/page/55/RiskandProtectiveFactors

Robbins, S., & Bell, M. (2008). *Second Life for dummies.* Indianapolis, IN: Wiley Publishing.

Rogers, E. M. (2003). *Diffusion of innovations* (5th ed.). New York: Free Press.

Rogers, S. (2000). Interventions that facilitate socialization in children with autism. *Journal of Autism and Developmental Disorders, 30,* 399–409. doi:10.1023/A:1005543321840

Romme, A. (2003). Learning outcomes of microworlds for management education. *Management Learning, 34*(1), 51–62. doi:10.1177/1350507603034001130

Rosenbaum, J. E., & Person, A. E. (2003). Beyond college for all: Policies and practices to improve transitions into college and jobs. *Professional School Counseling, 6*(4), 252–260.

Rosenberg, M. J. (2001). *Building successful online learning in your organization.* Retrieved September 25, 2007, from http://books.google.com/books?hl=en&lr=&id=hI8643X S3SIC&oi=fnd&pg=PR10&dq=effectiveness+of+online+ learning&ots=mA76zgSdtS&sig=Lql5wAUKPeffeNOsm tLxOebw6SY#PPA44,M1

Roth, M.-W. (1995). *Authentic school science: Knowing and learning in open-inquiry science laboratories.* Dordrecht, The Netherlands: Kluwer Academic Publishing.

Roth, W. (1996). Situating cognition. *Journal of Science Education and Technology, 5*(3), 171–191. doi:10.1007/BF01575302

Roth, W. (2001). Situating cognition. *Journal of the Learning Sciences, 10,* 27–61. doi:10.1207/S15327809JLS10-1-2_4

Rourke, L., & Kanuka, H. (2007). Computer conferencing and distance learning. In H. Bidgoli (Ed.), *The handbook of computer networks, vol. 3* (pp. 831-842). Hoboken, NJ: John Wiley & Sons.

Rovai, A. P. (2007). Facilitating online discussions effectively. *The Internet and Higher Education, 10*(1), 77–88. doi:10.1016/j.iheduc.2006.10.001

Russell, D. (2005). Implementing an innovation cluster in educational settings in order develop constructivist-based learning environments. *Educational Technology and Society, 8*(2).

Russell, S. T., & Marks, S. R. (2006). Preventing suicide risk among sexual minority youth. *Prevention Researcher, 13*(3), 19–20.

Rutter, P. A., & Behrendt, A. E. (2004). Adolescent suicide risk: Four psychosocial factors. *Adolescence, 39*(154), 295–302.

Rutter, P. A., & Estrada, D. (2006). Suicide risk and protective factors: Are there differences among young? *Guidance and Counseling, 21*(2), 89–96.

Sachs, J. (1997, December 11). The IMF is a power unto itself. *Financial Times.*

Salomon, G. (1993). No distribution without individuals' cognition: A dynamic interactional view. In G. Salomon (Ed.), *Distributed cognitions: Psychological and educational considerations.* New York: Cambridge University Press.

Savin-Baden, M. (2008). From cognitive capability to social reform? Shifting perceptions of learning in immersive virtual worlds. *Association for Learning Technology Journal, 16*(3), 151–161.

Sawyer, K. (2007). *Group genius: The creative power of collaboration.* New York: Basic Books.

Scardamalia, C., & Bereiter, M. (2003). Beyond brainstorming: Sustained Creative work with ideas. *Education, 43,* 4–44.

Scardamalia, C., & Bereiter, M. (2003). Knowledge building. In J. W. Guthrie (Ed.), *Encyclopedia of education, second edition* (pp. 1370-1373). New York: Macmillan Reference, USA.

Schroeder, K. (2006). Preventing suicide. *Education News in Brief: The Education Digest, 71*(9), 49–50.

Schroeder, R. (1996). *Possible worlds: The social dynamic of virtual reality technologies.* Boulder, CO: Westview Press.

Schroeder, R. (2007). An overview of ethical and social issues in shared virtual environments. *Futures, 39*(6), 704. Second Life. (2009). *Community standards.* Retrieved March 5, 2009, from http://secondlife.com/corporate/cs.php

Schroeder, R. (2008). Defining virtual worlds and virtual environments. *Journal of Virtual Worlds Research, 1*(1). Retrieved January 5, 2009, from http://journals.tdl.org/jvwr/article/view/294

Schwartz, A. J. (2006). College student suicide in the United States: 1990 – 1991 through 2003 – 2004. *Journal of American College Health, 54*(6), 341–352. doi:10.3200/JACH.54.6.341-352

Schwartz, A. J. (2006). Four eras of study of college student suicide in the United States: 1920 -2004. *Journal of American College Health, 54*(6), 353–366. doi:10.3200/JACH.54.6.353-366

Schwarz, B. (2009). Argumentation and learning. In N. Muller Mirza & A.-N. Perret-Clermont (Eds.), *Argumentation and education. Theoretical foundations and practices* (pp. 91-126). New York: Springer.

Schweizer, K., Paechter, M., & Weidenmann, B. (2003). Blended learning as a strategy to improve collaborative task performance. *Journal of Educational Media, 28*(2/3), 211–224. doi:10.1080/1358165032000165699

Second Life. (2008, April 29). *Second Life economic statistics.* Retrieved April 30, 2008, from http://secondlife.com/whatis/economy_stats.php

Second Life. (2009). *Terms of service.* Retrieved April 7, 2009 from http://secondlife.com/corporate/tos.php

Seifert, T. (1995). *Human learning and motivation: Readings.* St. John's: Memorial University.

Shaffer, D., Squire, K., Halverson, R., & Gee, J. (2005). Video games and the future of learning. *Phi Delta Kappan, 87*(2), 105–111.

Shannon, J., Judson, J., & Nuara, L. (2008). Pirating the metaverse. Second Life as a context for a business/law seminar. *Virtual worlds at Seton Hall.* Retrieved on December 4, 2008, from http://tltc.shu.edu/blogs/projects/virtualworlds/

Shedletsky, L. J., & Aitken, J. E. (2004). *Human communication on the Internet.* Boston: Allyn & Bacon/Longman.

Shin, J.-E., & Kellogg, D. (2007). The novice, the native and the nature of teaching expertise. *International Journal of Applied Linguistics, 17*(2), 159–177. doi:10.1111/j.1473-4192.2007.00144.x

Shutkin, D. (2004). Virtual community and ethical differences in the field of education. *JCT, 20*(4), 91–113.

Silva, B. D. (2001). *A tecnologia é uma estratégia.* Portugal: Challenges.

Silva, E. (2008). Measuring skills for the 21st century. *Education Sector.* Retrieved November 2, 2008, from http://www.newtechfoundation.org/press_research/Measuring-Skills_11-08.pdf

Simske, S., & Lin, X. (2004). Creating digital libraries: Content generation and re-mastering. In *Proceedings of the First International Workshop on Document Image Analysis for Libraries (DIAL '04).* Washington, DC: IEEE.

SimTeach. (2008, December 1). *Universities, colleges & schools* (October 19th, 2007). Retrieved December 7, 2008, from http://simteach.com/wiki/index.php?title=Institutions_and_Organizations_in_SL

SimTeach. (2009). *Institutions and organizations in SL.* Retrieved September, from http://tinyurl.com/2fen2s http://www.simteach.com/wiki/index.php?title=Second_Life:_Educators_Working_with_Teens

Sinatra, G., & Pintrich, R. (2003). The role of intentions in conceptual change learning. In G. Sinatra & R. Pintrich (Eds.), *Intentional conceptual change* (pp. 1-19) Mahwah, NJ: Lawrence Erlbaum Associates.

Sinclair, N., Liljedahl, P., & Zaskis, R. (2006). A coulored window on pre-service teachers' conceptions of random numbers. *International Journal of Computers for Mathematical Learning, 11*(2), 77–203. doi:10.1007/s10758-006-0002-y

Slevin, J. (2008). E-learning and the transformation of social interaction in higher education. *Learning, Media and Technology, 33*(2), 115–126. doi:10.1080/17439880802097659

Smith, B. L., MacGregor, J., Matthews, R. S., & Gabelnick, F. (2004). *Learning communities: Reforming undergraduate education.* CA: Jossey-Bass.

Smith, J. (1997). *Adult learning styles*. Retrieved September 25, 2007, from http://adulted.about.com/cs/learningtheory/a/lrng_patterns.htm

Smith, M. (2005). Eternal bits: How can we preserve digital files and save our collective memory? *IEEE Spectrum*.

Smith, W. (1994). Use of animals and animal organs in schools: Practice and attitudes of teachers. *Journal of Biological Education, 28*(2), 111–118.

Snyder, T. D., Tan, A. G., & Hoffman, C. (2006). Table 181: College enrollment and enrollment rates of recent high school completers, by race/ethnicity: 1960 through 2004. In *Digest of education statistics, 2005*. Washington, DC: U.S. Department of Education, National Center for Education Statistics.

Soergel, D. (2005). Thesauri and ontologies in digital libraries. In *Proceedings of the JCDL '05* (pp. 421). New York; ACM.

Sosnoski, J., Harkin, P., & Carter, B. (2006). *Configuring history: Teaching the Harlem Renaissance through virtual reality cityscapes*. New York: Peter Lang Publishing.

Spence, J. C., & Lee, R. E. (2003). Toward a comprehensive model of physical activity. *Psychology of Sport and Exercise, 4*, 7–24. doi:10.1016/S1469-0292(02)00014-6

Squire, K., & Jenkins, H. (2003). Harnessing the power of games in education. *Insight (American Society of Ophthalmic Registered Nurses), 3*(1), 5–33.

Staggers, J., Garcia, S., & Nagelhout, E. (2008). Teamwork through team building: Face-to-face to online. *Business Communication Quarterly, 71*(4), 472–487. doi:10.1177/1080569908325862

Stanovich, K. E. (2004). *The robot's rebellion. Finding meaning in the age of Darwin*. Chicago: University of Chicago Press.

Sterling-Turner, H., & Jordan, S. (2007). Interventions addressing transition difficulties for individuals with autism. *Psychology in the Schools, 44*(7), 681–690. doi:10.1002/pits.20257

Stern, M. (2008). How locality, frequency of communication and Internet usage affect modes of communication within core social networks. *Information Communication and Society, 11*(5), 591–616. doi:10.1080/13691180802126778

Stichter, J. P., Randolph, J., Gage, N., & Schmidt, C. (2007). A review of recommended practices in effective social competency programs for students with ASD. *Exceptionality, 15*, 219–232.

Stiglitz, J. (2000, April 17). What I learned at the world economic crisis. *New Republic*, 56-60.

Strauss, A., & Corbin, J. (1990). *Basics of qualitative research: Grounded theory procedures and techniques*. Newbury Park, CA: Sage.

Strauss, R. T., & Kinzie, M. B. (1991). Hi-tech alternatives to dissection. *The American Biology Teacher, 53*(3), 154–158.

Strauss, R., & Kinzie, M. B. (1994). Student achievement and attitudes in a pilot study comparing an interactive videodisc simulation to conventional dissection. *The American Biology Teacher, 56*(7), 398–402.

Suicide statistics. (2009). Retrieved February 6, 2009, from http://www.suicide.org/suicide-statistics.html

Suleman, H., Fox, E. A., & Abrams, M. (2000). Building quality into a digital library. In *Proceedings of the 5th ACM Conference on Digital Libraries* (pp. 228-229). New York: ACM.

Sumner, T., & Marlino, M. (2004). Digital libraries and educational practice: A case for new models. In *Proceedings of the JCDL '04* (pp. 170-178). New York: ACM.

Surowiecki, J. (2005). *The wisdom of crowds* (1st Anchor books ed.). New York: Anchor Books.

Surry, D. W. (1997). Diffusion theory and instructional technology. *Instructional Technology Research Online*. Retrieved from http://intro.base.org/docs/diffusion/

Swartout, W., & van Lent, M. (2003). Making a game of system design. *Communications of the ACM, 46*(7), 32–39. doi:10.1145/792704.792727

Talab, R. (2008). Using digital materials in online courses: A cautionary tale of Georgia State University. *TechTrends, 4*(52), 30–35.

Talab, R., & Butler, R. (2007). Shared electronic spaces in the classroom: Copyright, privacy, and guidelines. *Tech-Trends, 1*(51), 12.

Tan, R., & Boon, C. T. N. (2007). e@Leader: Engaging pupils in active learning through a self-paced online edutainment programme. In *Celebrating Learning Through Active Research, NZ CLEAR III*. Singapore: Ministry of Education.

Tarrant, D., Carr, L., & Payne, T. (2008). Releasing the power of digital metadata: Examining large networks of co-related publications. In *Proceedings of the JCDL '08* (pp. 471). New York: ACM.

Taylor, M. (1999). *Imaginary companions and the children who create them*. New York: Oxford University Press.

TechDis. (2005, April). *Guidance on accessibility for JISC exchange for learning and digital libraries in the classroom projects*. Joint Information Systems Committee.

Texas Higher Education Coordinating Board. (2008). *Closing the gaps by 2015: Texas' strategies for improving student participation and success*. Retrieved February 14, 2009, from http://www.thecb.state.tx.us/reports/PDF/1669.PDF

The Alexandria Digital Library Team. (2004). The Alexandria Digital Library and the Alexandria Digital Earth Prototype. In *Proceedings of the JCDL '04* (pp. 410). New York: ACM.

Thomas, R., & Hooper, E. (1991). Simulations: An opportunity we are missing. *Journal of Research on Computing in Education, 23*(4), 497–513.

Tinto, V. (1993). *Leaving college: Rethinking the causes and cures of student attrition*. Chicago: University of Chicago Press.

Tinto, V. (1997). Classrooms and communities: Exploring the educational character of student persistence. *The Journal of Higher Education, 68*(6), 599–623. doi:10.2307/2959965

Tomato. (n.d.) Retrieved August 6, 2008, from http://en.wikipedia.org/wiki/Tomato

Torres, R., McNee, S. M., Abel, M., Konstan, J. A., & Riedl, J. (2004). Enhancing digital libraries with TechLens. In *Proceedings of the JCDL '04* (pp. 228-236). New York: ACM.

Tsai, W.-H., & Wang, H.-M. (2005). On the extraction of vocal-related information to facilitate the management of popular music collections. In Proceedings of the JCDL '05 (pp. 197-206). New York: ACM.

Tsolis, D. K., Tsolis, G. K., Karatzas, E. G., & Papatheodorou, T. S. (2002). Copyright protection and management and a Web based library for digital images of the Hellenic cultural heritage. In *Proceedings of the 2001 Conference on Virtual Reality, Archeology, and Cultural Heritage* (pp. 53-60). New York: ACM.

Tufekci, Z. (2008). Grooming, gossip, Facebook and Myspace. *Information Communication and Society, 11*(4), 544–564. doi:10.1080/13691180801999050

Tungare, M., Yu, X., Cameron, W., Teng, G. F., Pérez-Quiñones, M. A., & Cassel, L. (2007). Towards a syllabus repository for computer science courses. In [New York: ACM.]. *Proceedings of the SIGCSE, 07*, 55–59. doi:10.1145/1227504.1227331

Turner, J., Grube, J., & Meyers, J. (2001). Developing an optimal match with in online communities: An exploration of CMC support communities and traditional support. *The Journal of Communication, 51*(2), 231–251. doi:10.1111/j.1460-2466.2001.tb02879.x

U.S. Department of Health and Human Services, Centers for Disease Control and Prevention. (2008). *Deaths-leading causes*. Retrieved March 13, 2008, from http://www.cdc.gov/nchs/FASTATS/lcod.htm

UNESCO. (2008). *Policy framework. ICT competency standards for teachers*. New York: United Nations Educational, Scientific and Cultural Organization (UNESCO).

United States General Accounting Office. (2003). *College completion: Additional efforts could help education with its completion goals*. Washington, DC: United States General Accounting Office.

University at Buffalo. (2008, February 21). 'V-Frog' virtual-reality frog dissection software offers first true physical simulation. *ScienceDaily*.

University of Houston Office of Institutional Research. (2008). *Statistical handbook 2007-2008*. Retrieved October 12, 2008, from http://www.uh.edu/ir/index.php?id=139

Valente, J. A. (2002). A educação à distância possibilitando a formação do professor com base no ciclo da prática pedagógica. In M. C. Moraes, (Ed.), *Educação à distância; fundamentos e práticas* (pp. 27-50). Campinas: Unicamp/NIED.

Valente, J. A. (2005). Pesquisa, comunicação e aprendizagem com o computador: O papel do computador no processo ensino-aprendizagem. In M. E. B. Almeida & J. M. Moran (Eds.), *Integração das tecnologias na educação* (pp. 22-31). Brasília: Ministério da Educação, SEED.

Van Der Puil, C., Andriessen, J., & Kanselaar, G. (2004). Exploring relational regulation in computer-mediated (collaborative) learning interaction: A developmental perspective. *Cyberpsychology & Behavior, 7*(2), 183–195. doi:10.1089/109493104323024447

Vanhorn, S., Pearson, J., & Child, J. (2008). The online communication course: The challenges. *Qualitative Research Reports in Communication, 9*(1), 29–36. doi:10.1080/17459430802400332

VanLear, C. A., Sheehan, M. A., Withers, L. A., & Walker, R. A. (2005). AA online: The enactment of computer mediated social support. *Western Journal of Communication, 69*(1), 5–26. doi:10.1080/10570310500033941

Vemulapalli, S., Halappanavar, M., & Mukkamala, R. (2002). Security in distributed digital libraries: Issues and challenges. In *Proceedings of the International Conference on Parallel Processing Workshops (ICPPW '02)*. IEEE.

Venezia, A., Callan, P. M., Finney, J. E., Kirst, M. W., & Usdan, M. D. (2005). *The governance divide: A report on a four-state study on improving college readiness and success*. San Jose, CA: The National Center for Public Policy and Higher Education. xxArete2xx. (2007, May 29). *Education in Second Life: Explore the possibilities* [Video File]. Video posted to http://www.youtube.com/watch?v=TMGR9q43dag

Vess, D. L. (2005, October). Asynchronous discussion and communication patterns in online and hybrid history courses. *Communication Education, 54*(4), 355–364. doi:10.1080/03634520500442210

Vosniadou, S. (2002). Mental models in conceptual development [Electronic edition]. In L. Magnani & N. Nersessian (Eds.), *Model-based reasoning: Science, technology, values* (Vol. 2005). New York: Kluwer Academic Press.

Vuorikari, R. (2007). Can social information retrieval enhance the discovery and reuse of digital educational content? In [New York: ACM.]. *Proceedings of the RecSys, 07*, 207–210. doi:10.1145/1297231.1297276

Vygotsky, L. S. (1978). *Mind in society: The development of higher psychological processes*. Cambridge, MA: Harvard University Press.

Vygotsky, L. S. (1987). *Collected works Vol. 1*. New York: Plenum.

Vygotsky, L. S. (1997). *Collected works Vol. 3*. New York: Plenum.

Vygotsky, L. S. (1998). *Collected works Vol. 5*. New York: Plenum.

Waldrop, M. M. (1992). *Complexity. The emerging science at the edge of chaos and order*. New York: Touchstone.

Walsh, D. (2004). *Why do they act that way? A survival guide to the adolescent brain for you and your teen*. New York: Free Press.

Wang, C., Zhang, Y., & Zhang, F. (2007). User modeling for cross system personalization in digital libraries. In *Proceedings of the First IEEE Symposium on Information Technologies and Applications in Education, ISITAE '07* (pp. 238-243). Washington, DC: IEEE.

Wang, J.-H., Teng, J.-W., Cheng, P.-J., Lu, W.-H., & Chien, L.-F. (2004). Translating unknown cross-lingual queries in digital libraries using a Web-based approach. In *Proceedings of the 2004 Joint ACM / IEEE Conference on Digital Libraries (JCDL '04)* (pp. 108-116). New York: ACM.

Wang, Y. D., Phillips-Wren, G., & Forgionne, G. (2005). E-delivery of personalised healthcare information to intermediaries for suicide prevention. *International Journal of Electronic Healthcare, 1*(4), 396–412. doi:10.1504/IJEH.2005.006687

Wang, Z., Walther, J., & Hancock, J. (2009). Social identification and interpersonal communication in computer-mediated communication: What you do versus who you are in virtual groups. *Human Communication Research, 35*(1), 59–85. doi:10.1111/j.1468-2958.2008.01338.x

Warburton, S. (2009). Second Life in higher education: Assessing the potential for and the barriers to deploying virtual worlds in learning and teaching. *British Journal of Educational Technology, 40*(3). doi:10.1111/j.1467-8535.2009.00952.x

Waugh, W. L. Jr, & Streib, G. (2006). Collaboration and leadership for effective emergency management. *Public Administration Review, 66*(Suppl. 1), 131–140. doi:10.1111/j.1540-6210.2006.00673.x

Wenger, E. (1998). *Communities of practice: Learning, meaning, and identity.* Cambridge, UK: Cambridge University Press.

Wenger, E. (1998). *Communities of practice: Learning as a social system.* Retrieved from http://www.ewenger.com/pub/pub_systems_thinker_wrd.doc

Wenger, E., McDermott, R., & Snyder, W. M. (2002). *Cultivating communities of practice: A guide to managing knowledge.* Boston: Harvard Business School Press.

Wertsch, J. (1991). *Voices of the mind. A sociocultural approach to mediated action.* Cambridge, MA: Harvard University Press.

Westerman, D. (2008). How do people really seek information about others?: Information seeking across Internet and traditional communication channels. *Journal of Computer-Mediated Communication, 13*(3), 751–767. doi:10.1111/j.1083-6101.2008.00418.x

Whatley, J., & Bell, F. (2003). Discussion across borders: Benefits for collaborative learning. *Educational Media International, 40*(1/2), 139. doi:10.1080/0952398032000092189

Willenz, P. (2008). *Suicidal thoughts among college students more common than expected.* Retrieved February 6, 2009, from http://www.apa.org/releases/suicideC08.html

Wittengenstein, L. (1958). *Philosophical investigations* (3rd ed.). New York: MacMillan.

Wong, S. C., Crowder, R. M., Wills, G. B., & Shadbolt, N. R. (2006). Knowledge engineering—from front-line support to preliminary design. In . *Proceedings of the DocEng, 06,* 44–52.

Wynstra, S. (1991). A study of high school science anxiety including the development of a science anxiety instrument

(Doctoral Dissertation, Northern Illinois University). *Dissertation Abstracts International, 53-01A,* 0116.

Wynstra, S., & Cummings, C. (1993). High school science anxiety. *Science Teacher (Normal, Ill.), 60*(7), 18–21.

Wynstra, S., & Cummings, C. (1995). High school science anxiety: Easing the common classroom fears. *The Queensland Science Teacher, 21*(4), 5–6.

Xinogalos, S., Satratzemi, M., & Dagdilelis, V. (2006). An introduction to object-oriented programming with a didactic microworld: "objectKarel. *Computers & Education, 47*(2), 148–171. doi:10.1016/j.compedu.2004.09.005

Yang, J., Han, J., Oh, I., & Kwak, M. (2007). Using Wikipedia technology for topic maps design. In . *Proceedings of the ACMSE, 2007,* 106–110.

Yaron, D. J., Davenport, Y. L., Karabinos, M., Leinhardt, G. L., Bartolo, L. M., Portman, J. J., et al. (2008). Cross-disciplinary molecular science education in introductory science courses: An NSDL MatDL collection. In *Proceedings of the JCDL '08* (pp. 70-73).

Ye, J. (2006). Traditional and online support networks in the cross-cultural adaptation of Chinese international students in the United States. *Journal of Computer-Mediated Communication, 11*(3), 863–876. doi:10.1111/j.1083-6101.2006.00039.x

Ye, S., Makedon, F., Steinberg, T., Shen, L., Ford, J., & Wang, Y. (2003). SCENS: A system for the mediated sharing of sensitive data. In [Washington, DC: IEEE.]. *Proceedings of the Joint Conference on Digital Libraries, 2003,* 263–265.

Yee, N., & Bailenson, J. N. (2008). A method for longitudinal behavioral data collection in Second Life. *Presence.* Retrieved February 15, 2009, from http://www.mitpress-journals.org/doi/abs/10.1162/pres.17.6.594

Yin, R. (2003). *Case study research: Design and methods.* Thousand Oaks, CA: Sage Press.

Yung, Y., & Dickinson, A. R. (2008). Being and becoming gifted: Enhancement effects of socio-intellectual study programs. In *Proceedings of the 10th Asia Pacific Conference on Giftedness,* Singapore, (pp. 86).

Zhang, J., Scardamalia, M., & Reeve, R. (2006, April 8). *Designs for collective cognitive responsibility in knowledge building communities.* Paper presented at the American Educational Research Association, San Francisco, CA.

Zhang, M. (2008). Connecting alumni around the world: A study of harmony, memory, and identity online. *China Media Research, 4*(4), 85–91.

Zhao, C., & Kuh, G. D. (2004). Adding value: Learning communities and student engagement. *Research in Higher Education, 45*(2), 115–138. doi:10.1023/B:RIHE.0000015692.88534.de

Zhu, Q., Goncalves, M. A., & Fox, E. A. (2003). 5SGraph Demo: A graphical modeling tool for digital libraries. In *Proceedings of the 2003 Joint Conference on Digital Libraries (JCDL '03).*

Zhuang, Z., Wagle, R., & Giles, C. L. (2005). What's there and what's not? Focused crawling for missing documents in digital libraries. In Proceedings of the JCDL '05 (pp. 301-310). New York: ACM.

Zirkel, P. A. (2006). Student suicide and school liability. *Principal Leadership, 6*(6), 49–53.

Zirkel, P. A. (2006). Student suicide: An update. [from http://www.naesp.org]. *Principal, 85*(5), 10–11. Retrieved February 6, 2009.

About the Contributors

Donna Russell is an Assistant Professor at the University of Missouri-Kansas City and co-owner of Arete' Consulting, LLC. She has a bachelors and masters degree in Education specializing in instructional design. Her PhD is in Educational Psychology with an emphasis on cognition and technology. She is Co-PI on the National Science Foundations grant, Achieving Recruitment, Retention and Outreach With STEM, developing science, technology and engineering programs for urban high school students. She is chair of the Problem-Based Education Special Interest Group committee for the American Education Researchers Association. She has published several articles and book chapters on virtual learning including *Online Professional Development for Educators, A Case Study Analysis using Cultural Historical Activity Theory, Implementing an Innovation Cluster* in *Educational Settings to Develop Constructivist-based Learning Environments, Transformation in an Urban School: Using Systemic Analysis to Understand an Innovative Urban Teacher's Implementation of an Online Problem-Based Unit, Group Collaboration in an Online Problem-based University Course in Creativity and Problem-Based Learning,* and *Understanding the Effectiveness of Collaborative Activity* in *Online Professional Development with Innovative Educators through Inter-Subjectivity* in *Information and Communication Technology for Enhanced Education and Learning: Advanced Applications and Development.*

* * *

Joan E. Aitken (Ed.D., University of Arkansas) is Professor, Communication Arts, Park University, USA 64152. Aitken has taught online or blended courses for four universities and completed online courses at four colleges and universities. Her research interests include human communication on the Internet, communication education, and educational assessment. Aitken can be contacted at joan.aitken@park.edu.

Brent Anders works as an Electronic Media Coordinator for the Office of Mediated Education at Kansas State University. His job duties include: educational media consulting, web accessibility/usability, and videography (directing, capturing, editing and final production). Mr. Anders has a Bachelor's degree in Psychology, human computer interaction focus, and a Master's degree in Education, instructional technology focus. He also serves in the National Guard as a senior instructor for the Basic Non-commissioned Officers Course. Mr. Anders has been in the education field for over 10 years dealing with military training, distance education, educational media and higher education in general.

Ryan Babiuch is an undergraduate student working towards his bachelor's of science in Computer Science and Information Technology with an emphasis in Media Entertainment. His involvement as a member of the iSocial team includes the development of the virtual environment as well the implementation of virtual social orthotics. Ryan has been developing software since before he was in high school. Currently he has eight years of experience programming in C/C++ and four years experience using the Java programming language. He is currently interested in virtual world design, digital art, and software development. Upon graduation, Ryan plans to pursue his master's degree in Educational Technology. After school Ryan plans to pursue a professional career in the entertainment industry.

Hope Roland Botterbusch is a nationally recognized educational copyright specialist with a talent for communicating the fine points that apply to all media. With over 25 years experience in advising educators on the latest copyright information, Ms. Botterbusch has a particular specialty in the Fair Use Guidelines for Educational Uses of Copyrighted Materials. Ms. Botterbusch is past chairman of the Association for Educational Communications and Technology (AECT) Copyright Taskforce, a published author of numerous articles on copyright, author of the Phi Delta Kappa Fastback, *Copyright in the Age of New Technology*, and previous editor of the "Copyright & You" column featured in the education journal, *Tech Trends*. In 1994, Ms. Botterbusch had the distinction of authoring and presenting AECT's position statement at Washington D.C.'s New Media National Conference, resulting in the Fair Use Guidelines for Educational Multimedia introduced to Congress in 1996. She holds an MSLS degree from Wayne State University, MI, a bachelor's degree from Millersville University, Pennsylvania, and is a consultant for sponsored educational projects. Ms. Botterbusch has over 25 years experience in the field of education where she has been a K-12 classroom teacher, school library media specialist, district media curriculum supervisor, educational television station manager, and college & university adjunct instructor and administrator. Ms. Botterbusch is currently the Coordinator of Continuing Education Programs at St. Petersburg College where she works with education and industries to develop continuing education programs and skills assessments for technology-based program for today, tomorrow and beyond.

Patrick J. Connolly has been in the insurance premium auditing industry for 15 years. Connolly is an experienced manager of training, operations and sales for a national service organization providing decision-making tools to insurance, financial and government institutions. Connolly specializes in developing creative learning tools to effectively train dispersed workforces and provide creative business solutions for learning. Connolly works to align business processes with technology to increase employee performance through effective training and reduced cost. Some of the positions that he has held with insurance industry service companies include field auditor, assistant branch manager, operations manager, general manager, and national director of training. Connolly's educational background includes a degree in Theology, a Bachelors in Business Administration and a Masters in Curriculum Design & Instructional Technologies. Connolly has developed virtual learning environments for the insurance industry that have been recognized by the Kansas Insurance Commissioner, have been awarded continuing education credit by American Institute for Commercial Property Casualty Underwriters, and have also been awarded college credit by Colorado Technical University. Connolly also sits on the advisory board of Colorado Technical University and is a representative of the insurance industry for eInstruction.

Anthony R. Dickinson has held the positions of lecturer and professor of Comparative Developmental Psychology (University of Edinburgh, 1990-1999), and Preclinical Neuroscience & Biological psychology (Medical School/Psychology, Washington University in St. Louis, 1999-2006), and is currently President and Research Director of the Academic Research Laboratory of Global Choice Psychometrics, People Impact International, Inc. Research interests and publications have included a wide range of eclectic studies in comparative development cognition, electrophysiology, and pre-clinical neuroscience, based around the core explorations of the evolution and characterization of intelligent systems, in both human and non-human forms.

Margarita Pérez García is a researcher in education science. She has been working in the field of education for 15 years in all levels from primary through secondary to higher education. She has coordinated several projects on digital identity and reputation, user-centric implementation of Europass ePortfolio, social directories, social technologies in education and ePortfolios. She coordinates MU-VEnation: an European programme for training teachers in the use of virtual worlds for education. Her current research interests are the collection and analysis of teaching experiences in virtual worlds through narrative inquiry.

Rebecca Gould is the Director of the Information Technology Assistance Center (iTAC) at Kansas State University which serves as the first point of contact for campus information technology needs. Core functions include the IT help desk; technology training and instructional design; support for technology classrooms/university computing labs, client services and the media development center; and technical support for electronic theses, dissertations and reports. Gould is a professor in the Department of Hospitality Management and Dietetics and publishes on topics related to technology use. For more than 20 years, she has experimented with using technology to improve the teaching and learning environment. She was a co-investigator on the USDA Challenge Grant project, Joint Ventures between Rural Communities and the Classroom, which organized 120 students in two classes to develop web pages and marketing plans for rural communities. Gould served on the Board of Editors for the Journal of the American Dietetic Association and is the editor-in-charge of distance learning for the Journal of Teaching in Travel and Tourism.

Shalin Hai-Jew works as an instructional designer at Kansas State University. She teaches for WashingtonOnline (WAOL). She worked as the instructional designer for the University Life Café project. She writes as Eruditio Loginquitas for the Instructional Design Open Studio (IDOS) blog, which she founded in 2006. She contributes to the E-Learning and Teaching Exchange (ELATE) wiki, which she co-founded in 2009 with Dr. Roger W. McHaney. She has worked on a range of curricular and training builds in biosecurity, leadership, learning, stress management, public health, e-learning, turfgrass management, computer science, rumen metabolism, history, and others. In 2009, she worked as a reviewer for *Educause Quarterly* and the *Journal of Online Learning and Teaching (JOLT)* of MERLOT, by invitation. She has B.A.s in English and psychology, and an M.A. in English from the University of Washington, and an Ed.D., with a focus on Public Administration, from Seattle University (2005), where she was a Morford Scholar. She lived and taught in the People's Republic of China from 1988 – 1990 and 1992 – 1994, the latter two years through the United Nations Volunteer Programme of the UNDP. Her professional interests relate to data repositories and information management, simulations, immersive learning, automated learning, and socio-technical spaces. She is especially interested in creating behavioral change via e-learning.

Kevin Q. Harvey, MA, is Assistant Director of Development for the Center for the Advancement of Distance Education (CADE) located at the University of Illinois at Chicago (UIC), School of Public Health. Kevin has an extensive background in education, training, technology and new media. His experience includes ten years of teaching, seven years in broadcasting, and two years as a user experience analyst and learning architect for an online University. In his studies at UIC College of Communication, Kevin concentrated on the study of mediated communication. He has been working at CADE since 2002 and has been on the game development team since 2005. He manages the Second Life development at CADE and creates comprehensive training opportunities using virtual worlds, including emergency preparedness and response training, violence prevention, counseling scenarios, and business solutions. Kevin is currently doing research on the use of virtual worlds in public health planning. He also speaks regularly at conferences and is the primary workshop developer and facilitator for CADE's Second Life trainings.

Melissa Herzog earned her PhD in Family and Human Development. Currently, she is the Research Specialist for the Behavior and Education Division of the MU Thompson Center where she oversees recruitment and data collection/management for the social competence intervention that serves as the basis for iSocial. She is also an Adjunct Faculty in the Department of Human Development and Family Studies. Dr. Herzog's research has focused on the association between family processes and social development in typically developing children and adolescents, and this interest has now expanded to include youth with ASD. Dr. Herzog has extensive experience in data management and project direction/recruitment in two separate federally funded longitudinal grants (NICHD, DHHS).

Catherine Horn is an assistant professor of educational psychology at the University of Houston. Her work, discussed by national and regional media outlets, cuts across three areas affecting traditionally underserved students: high stakes testing and its impacts at the secondary school level; postsecondary admissions processes - particularly as they consider testing - and the impacts on student body diversity; and developmental testing policies in the post-secondary setting. She received her Ph.D. from Boston College. Most recently, Horn co-edited (with P. Marin) *Realizing* Bakke*'s Legacy: Affirmative Action, Equal Opportunity, and Access to Higher Education* (Stylus Publishers, 2008). She has also co-edited (with P. Gándara and G. Orfield) a special volume of *Educational Policy* (2005) and *Expanding Opportunity in Higher Education* (SUNY Press, 2006) both of which analyze the educational access and equity crisis in California. She is co-editor of *Higher Education and the Color Line* (with G. Orfield and P. Marin, Harvard Education Press, 2005) and Community Colleges and Latino Educational Opportunity (with S. M. Flores and G. Orfield, Jossey Bass, 2006). Horn is the associate editor of the *Review of Higher Education*. Her work has been cited in numerous *amicus curiae* briefs submitted to the U.S. Supreme Court in the *Gratz* and *Grutter* cases and cited in Justice Ginsburg's dissenting opinion.

Diane Hui is a Post-doctoral Fellow and Lecturer in the Faculty of Education, the University of Hong Kong. Diane, a Spencer scholar (USA), received her Ph.D. in Education from Washington University in St Louis, USA. Her research interests include sociocultural and cognitive engagement of teacher and student learning, and the development of an online language diagnostic assessment tool within communities of practice. Her doctoral dissertation examined engagement in supporting new teachers: A role for computer-mediated communication in teacher learning within informal professional communities (2006). She has published articles concerned with intersubjectivity with learning and innovative professional development through technological mediation.

Yongho Kim is a primary school teacher in Seoul, Korea. He has been teaching elementary school students for ten years mostly as a homeroom teacher. He is now getting on with a Ph.D thesis at Korea National University of Education on the relationship between child's foreign language learning and their development. He has published periodically both internationally and domestically. He is interested in philosophy, moral education, socio-cultural theory and play, an interest he shares with his little daughter and his students. He is working on the translation of Vygosky's 'Thought and Language' into Korean in collaboration with Vygotskyan group in Seoul National University of Education. This translation would be the first that triangulates different versions of "Thought and Language" including the original 1934 Russian version.

James Laffey is a Professor in the School of Information Science and Learning Technologies and former researcher and systems developer at Apple Computer, Inc.. Dr. Laffey is internationally recognized as an expert in the area of human-computer interaction (HCI); he currently teaches graduate level courses on development of systems to optimize HCI and learning, including methods to improve the social nature of online communities. He is the principal investigator for a 2 year project funded by AutismSpeaks to advance methods for supporting youth with ASD to learn within 3D VLE. Dr. Laffey also serves as a consultant on information systems issues to the Thompson Center for Autism and Neurodevelopmental Disorders.

Charles S. Layne is a professor and chairperson of the Department of Health and Human Performance at the University of Houston. In addition to his research interests in human movement control, Dr. Layne has extensive experience in the use of web-based technology to promote student learning. He is the recipient of several grants designed to increase the accessibility of web-based learning modules for a diverse student population.

Rebecca E. Lee serves as director of the Texas Obesity Research Center in the Department of Health and Human Performance at the University of Houston, and is an associate professor in the Department and holds a courtesy appointment at the University of Texas School of Public Health. She is an editorial board member of the *International Journal of Women's Health* and the American Journal of Health Promotion. She has authored and co-authored numerous studies in peer-reviewed publications, serves as a charter member on the Community Level Health Promotion Study Section for the Center for Scientific Review at the National Institute of Health, and has received many honors and awards, including the College of Education Research Excellence Award in 2005 and 2008, at the University of Houston, the Award for Outstanding Achievement from the Texas Council on Cardiovascular Disease (CVD) and Stroke, and is a Fellow of the Society of Behavioral Medicine. She is principal investigator for several federally and privately funded research grants including the *International Health Challenge in Second Life*, funded by the USC Annenberg School for Communication.

Christine S. Marszalek, Ed.D., Christine recently retired as Director of Media and Technology within a public school system in the northwest suburbs of Chicago. During that time, she led teams of students and teachers in the formation of several websites, such as "Virtual Renaissance," which appeared on the American Library Association's first "Best Children's Websites," as well as the "Kildeer Countryside Virtual Wetlands Preserve" created in partnership with Brookfield Zoo and the Illinois State Board of Education's Museum in the Classroom state grant. Receiving her doctorate in Instructional Technology from Northern Illinois University in 1998, she has continued working as an adjunct faculty member in the area of educational technology with several universities in the area, as well as helping to develop and facilitate LinC Online, Fermi National Accelerator Laboratory's Leadership Institute integrating Internet instruction and curriculum.

Jacob M. Marszalek, Ph.D., Jacob is an Assistant Professor of Counseling and Educational Psychology in the School of Education at the University of Missouri-Kansas City. He received his Ph.D. in educational psychology from the University of Illinois in 2006. His research interests include (a) applying new quantitative techniques to address research questions in education, program evaluation, testing, and psychology; and (b) examining the construct of flow in computerized learning and assessment environments. Jacob teaches courses in research methodology, statistics and psychological measurement, and has participated in grant projects involving science education.

Brian McFarlin is an Assistant Professor at the University of Houston. Over the past five years he has taught over 2000 undergraduate and graduate students using a variety of blended and e-learning approaches. His dedication to e-learning has resulted in an improvement of his student's learning and content retention, which are chronicled in two recent publications that he had in the Diabetes Educator and Advances in Physiology Education. His dedication to appropriate and effective use of instructional technology has allowed him to become one of the most decorated junior professors at the University of Houston. He is always excited to share his experiences using instructional technology with his peers at the University of Houston and beyond.

Neli Maria Mengalli is a doctoral student in the Graduate Program in Education: Curriculum and professor at the School of Education at the São Paulo Pontifical Catholic University (PUC-SP). She has worked as facilitator in the process of integrating educational technology in training courses to prepare School Managers to be able to use information and communication technology as part of the School Management and Technologies Project. In this project she worked as an educational designer, and developer and administrator of e-learning communities. Her current research projects include development of educational curriculum and design of educational communities of practice (CoP), and the study of collaborative learning environments, interfaces for interaction, and social media.

Nathalie Muller Mirza is associated Professor (Maître assistante) in Social and Cultural Psychology at the University of Lausanne (Switzerland). Her main research foci are on psychosocial processes in learning settings, in and out of school and in multicultural contexts, and on argumentation and its psychological dimensions. Since 2001, she is involved in international projects on argumentation, aiming at developing and analyzing argumentative practices mediated by electronic environments in learning.

Pamela R. Mitchell has over twenty years of research, teaching and collaborative activity in technology applications for individuals with disabilities. Her experiences with interdisciplinary collaboration began during her graduate training, and she has continued a commitment to interdisciplinary process throughout her career. She began development work in Second Life® in 2006 and has utilized the environment to support a blended instruction model in several of her graduate level classes. In addition, she has supervised graduate and undergraduate student research projects in the space, and conducted interprofessional training activities.

Colleen Monahan, DC, MPH, is the Director and founder (since 1998) of the Center for the Advancement of Distance Education (CADE) located at the University of Illinois at Chicago (UIC), School of Public Health. Dr. Monahan is also Adjunct Assistant Professor in the Division of Community Health Sciences. She has pioneered the incorporation of Internet technologies in various areas of public health. She has always been in the forefront of promoting and using technology in the public health arena and making technologies available to those that would not have it otherwise. She co-leads a national training center for public health preparedness. She is currently doing research on the use of virtual worlds in public health planning.

Daniel P. O'Connor is an assistant professor of health and human performance at the University of Houston and the former Director of the Joe W. King Orthopedic Institute in Houston, Texas. His research interests focus on efficacy and effectiveness of medical and health-related interventions, particularly subject-level outcomes and health-related quality of life. He has authored and co-authored many papers in peer-reviewed journals, as well as several chapters in key orthopedic surgery textbooks. He was recently co-awarded the Charles S. Neer, II, MD Award for Outstanding Clinical Science Research by the American Shoulder and Elbow Surgeons. Dr. O'Connor's research has been supported by NASA and various private and public orthopedic surgery foundations. He is a co-investigator for a University of Houston Faculty Development Initiative Program project entitled "Using Digital Communities to Enhance Student Persistence" as well as the International Health Challenge in Second Life, funded by the USC Annenberg School for Communication.

Danielle Oprean holds a BS in digital media with a concentration in 3D visualization as well as an MS in engineering technology with a focus on virtual reality. She has worked on several virtual environments (VE) for competition, freelance work, and educational purposes and, will soon complete a PhD focused on digital media in VE design and development. She has experience in applying web, interface, and 3D environment design to a number of different fields including medical, information & referral, education, and marketing. Her research interests span from entertainment to educational game and VE development to 3D visualization and interface design.

Don Philip holds a BSc, an ArsD (Artist's Diploma) in music, a BEd, and an MA. He worked as a classical musician in the Toronto area for a number of years until synthesizers and budget cutbacks decimated the music industry. Following that, he taught for the Toronto School Board, teaching biology, chemistry, science, math, music, and working in a computer resources lab. Some years ago, he returned to academia, and earned a Masters degree in educational computer applications. Now working on a PhD, he has been privileged to work with the Institute for Knowledge Innovation and Technology (www.ikit.org). Currently, he is teaching in the Department of Chemical and Physical Sciences at the University of Toronto, Mississauge.

Carla Schmidt is a doctoral student in the Department of Special Education at the University of Missouri. She currently holds a Masters of Public Administration and a Masters of Education with a focus in Autism Spectrum Disorders. Her research interest included the use of virtual technologies to teach social skills to individuals with high functioning autism and Asperger's Syndrome as well as providing comprehensive service delivery for families of individuals with autism spectrum disorders. Carla is currently a graduate research assistant at the Thompson Center for Autism and Neurodevelopmental

Disorders where she assists in the delivery of individualized evaluations and intervention services targeting behavioral and communicative deficits. Carla is also a lead implementer of a Cognitive Behavioral Intervention curriculum for individuals with High Functioning Autism.

Matthew Schmidt is a PhD candidate in the School of Information Science and Learning Technologies at the University of Missouri. His current research interests focus on designing and implementing 3D virtual environments for individuals with autism spectrum disorders. He holds a BA and MA in German Language and Literature with an emphasis on Computer-Assisted Language Learning (CALL). He has designed and developed educational technologies and curricula for diverse disciplines including special education, second language acquisition, veterinary medicine, biological anthropology, nuclear engineering, and health physics. Matthew also serves as the project coordinator on a 2 year project funded by AutismSpeaks to advance methods for supporting youth with ASD to learn within 3D VLEs.

Leonard Shedletsky is Professor of Communication at The University of Southern Maine. He is the author of *Meaning and Mind: An Intrapersonal Approach to Human Communication* (1989), *Human Communication on the Internet* (2004, with Joan Aitken), co-editor of *Intrapersonal Communication Processes* (1995), as well as numerous articles and chapters. He wrote the entry, *"Cognition,"* for the *International Encyclopedia of Communication*, 2008. He has been teaching since 1974. He teaches a range of courses in communication with cognition, discourse and meaning as underlying themes. He developed and taught the course "Intergenerational Communication and the Internet," in which college students mentored older adults in Internet use. He was awarded recognition for STELLAR scholarship and teaching, University of Southern Maine (USM) 2003 and 2007. He has received a Center for Technology-Enhanced Learning Development Grant at USM (2007) to develop the course, Research Methods, for online delivery. In 2009 he received a Alfred P. Sloan Foundation grant to expand the online capacity for his department to deliver the major in communication and media studies. His current research interest explores discussion online versus in the classroom. He is trying to find out what facilitates active and high quality discussion in education. His resume is available at: http://www.usm.maine.edu/com/resume.html.

Sameer Siddiqi is a Research Assistant in the Texas Obesity Research Center in the Department of Health and Human Performance at the University of Houston and Mayoral Intern in the City of Houston Mayor's Office of Health and Environmental Policy. He has been actively involved in the *International Health Challenge in Second Life* since its inception, and has significantly contributed to and managed various aspects of its development and ongoing execution. He has co-authored a number of works on Second Life and health interventions in peer-reviewed publications, and has received many honors, including the Barbara Jordan Health Policy Scholars Program Award in 2009.

James J. Sosnoski is the author of *Token Professionals and Master Critic:* and *Modern Skeletons in Postmodern Closets*, as well as various essays on instructional technology, computer-assisted pedagogy, and online collaboration. He has co-edited several issues of *Works and Days* on technology and the forthcoming *Configuring History: Teaching the Harlem Renaissance Through Virtual Reality Cityscapes* (Peter Lang) He is working on a book entitled *Configuring: Learning to Understand Persons Unlike Us*, a study of the role of virtual experiences in bridging gaps in experience that block communication. It also concerns the use of virtual reality as learning tool.

Jordan Stalker received his M.A. in Communication from the University of Illinois at Chicago in 2008. His research focuses on structures and exchanges of knowledge and the formations of disciplines and fields of study. His master's thesis, *Disciplining Communication Studies at the University of Illinois at Chicago, 1973-2007*, examined the decision-making processes – including faculty hiring, course offerings and research agendas – involved in establishing a communication studies program.

Janine Stichter is a Professor of Special Education and the Division Director of the MU Thompson Center for Autism where she developed the social competence intervention that serves as a basis for iSocial. She specializes in conducting direct practice, training professionals and, conducting research on behavioral interventions for youth with ASD. Her research includes the study of social skills assessment and intervention, methodological issues related to intervention and outcome research, and the role of environment on the communication and prosocial behavior of youth with ASD. Dr. Stichter is the principal investigator of a 3-year project funded by the Institute for Education Science to modify the social competence intervention for delivery in school-based settings as another means to increase the reach of this intervention.

Rosemary Talab is Professor and Coordinator of the Educational Computing, Design, and Online Learning graduate online program at Kansas State University. She was rezzed in Second Life June 16, 2008. She is a member of the International Society for Technology in Education and the American Educational Research Association and is a member of their virtual worlds special interest groups. She has graduated 50+ master's students and several doctoral students. She has written two books on technology and copyright law, one currently in the second edition. She has made over 60 presentations at the state, national, and international levels, including keynote addresses, written two books, book chapters, over 30 articles and research papers. She has been chair of the Intellectual Property Committee and IP Column Editor of TechTrends of the Association for Educational Communications and Technology at various times in the last 25 years and is currently the IP Blog editor and a contributing reviewer. She was the first Fulbright Scholar to the Higher Colleges of Technology in Abu Dhabi, the United Arab Emirates, in 2007.

Susan Toth-Cohen, Ph.D., OTR/L (SL: Zsuzsa Tomsen) is Associate Professor in the Department of Occupational Therapy at Thomas Jefferson University in Philadelphia. Dr. Toth-Cohen's research interests include virtual world education, healthy aging, and evidence-based practice. Her publications include peer-reviewed journals such as International Journal of Environmental Research and Public Health, the Health Information and Libraries Journal, and the Scandinavian Journal of Occupational Therapy. Dr. Toth-Cohen has served as guest editor for a special issue of the Journal of Virtual Worlds Research on healthcare and has received funding to develop exhibits on health and wellness in Second Life®.

Elizabeth Unger is currently a professor of Computing and Information Sciences and IT research fellow at Kansas State University. She recently retired from the position of Vice Provost for Academic Services and Technology and Dean of Continuing Education a post that allowed the initiation of classrooms enhanced by information technology and Internet based continuing education. These two initiatives were part of a larger project to improve teaching and learning and to increase access to the university. The university now has 50 technology enhanced classrooms with various environments to meet faculty requirements for learning enhancement and there are over 45 distance degree programs and credit certificates available. Dr. Unger currently is doing research in the "university of the future" and the learning environments that may be present. Her experiences include work on the first non-military network, MERIT, in this country and on the programming of a copy of the Illiac I, the first university owned scientific computer build at the University of Illinois. Work at IBM and as the director of computing centers in universities preceded her doctorate in Computer Science from the University of Kansas.

José Armando Valente is Professor of the Multimedia Department at the Art Institute and Researcher of the Nucleus of Information Technology Applied to Education, (Nied) both at the Universidade Estadual de Campinas (Unicamp), and collaborating Professor in the Graduate Program in Education: Curriculum at the Pontifical Catholic University, (PUC-SP). PhD from the Department of Mechanical Engineering and Division for Study and Research in Education, at MIT, MS in the Interdisciplinary Science and Education Program at MIT, and MS in Computer Science at Unicamp. Currently Professor Valente is participating in the implementation of a new undergraduate course, Medialogy, at the Multimedia Department at Unicamp, and is a member of the Federal Government task force to design the "One Laptop per Student" program in Brazil. Research topics include development of information and communication technology (ICT) based learning environments and training methodology to be utilized in schools and in socio-economical disadvantaged communities, using face-to-face or online approaches, and the study of the potentials of ICT as educational tools.

Steven Warburton is an eLearning manager at King's College London and a Fellow of the Centre for Distance Education at the University of London where he chairs the research strategy group. He moved from his initial research background in the area of neuroscience to one that now encompasses a range of projects in the area of technology-enhanced learning. His fields of expertise include: the impact of digital identities on lifelong learning; the use of social software in distance education; pattern languages for Web 2.0; design for learning in Multi-User Virtual Environments; formative e- Assessment; and support for communities of practice in user innovation and emerging technologies.

Index

Symbols

3D virtual learning environment (3D-VLE) 154
3D-VLE 154, 155, 156, 157, 159, 160, 161, 164, 165, 166, 167

A

Academic domain 268
academic services 46, 47, 48
activity system 213, 214
alienable appropriable dialogue 63
alienable language 63
alienable mediating tools 61
annotation 177, 178, 182, 183, 187, 188
argumentation 95, 96, 97, 98, 99, 100, 101, 102, 103, 104, 105, 106, 107, 108
argumentative debate 95
argumentative map 99, 101, 102, 103, 104
argumentative practices 95, 102, 103, 106
ASD 154, 155, 156, 157, 158, 161, 164, 165, 166, 167, 168
Asperger's Syndrome 157, 167
assessment 214, 215, 216, 217, 218, 219, 222
asynchronous instruction 44
asynchronous learning networks or ALN 252
Autism Spectrum Disorders (ASD) 154
avatar appearance codes 112
avatars 29, 31, 34, 35, 57, 64, 65, 66, 67, 68, 69, 112, 116, 117

B

Bakhtin, Mikhail Mikhailovich 63, 70
bibliometric metadata 177

blended learning 201, 203, 204
blended or hybrid class model 284
boards of education 306
Boards of Education 306, 307
Brainboxes 267, 269, 270, 272
Brainbox knowledge acquisition tool 269
brainstorming 251, 261
bug-level intelligence 285

C

CADE Readiness Training Group 76
The Canyon Crossroads project 72
Center for the Advancement of Distance Education (CADE) 72, 73, 74, 75, 76, 77, 80, 85
CHAT 213, 215
cheat sheets 208
classroom-based tests 278
CLIR (cross-language information retrieval) 176
Cognitive Behavioral Intervention 155
cognitive developmental 263, 264
cognitive learning 264, 266
cognitive neuroscience 266
cognitive revolution 266, 280
cognitive skills 270, 278
collaboration 30, 31, 33, 38, 39, 40, 250, 253
collaborative digital library 181, 189
Collaborative Digital Library 192
collaborative learning 169
collaborative learning environments (CLE) 75
collaborative meaning making 253
Collaborative solutions 196
collaborative virtual environment (CVE) 80, 81, 85, 93, 94

K

knowledge age businesses 293

knowledge-based management
303, 305, 313, 315

knowledge-building 284, 285, 286, 287, 288,
289, 290, 291, 292, 293, 294, 295,
296, 297, 298, 299

Knowledge-building teachers 291

Knowledge Forum™ 286, 287, 292

L

'learning by gaming' system 263, 264

learning center/technology director (LCTD)
122, 123

learning / content management systems (L/
CMSes) 185

learning / course management systems
172, 183

learning environment 42, 43, 44, 45, 48,
49, 50, 53, 56

learning modalities 121

Learning Process Assessments 217

learning styles 121, 125, 126, 128, 133,
134, 135

learning to learn 266, 278

legitimate peripheral participation (LPP) 212

Linden dollars 114, 143, 230, 231

Linden Lab Corporation 113

LinkedIn 288

listservs 194

live-class interactions 284

logical intelligence 270

long-leash control 285

M

machine learning 263, 264

Magic Circle 230

mainstream school student learning 264

Mars Rovers 285

massively multiplayer online games (MMO)
28

mathematics skills 270

mediated learning (ML) 45, 46, 48

memory 268, 270, 274, 280

mental models 287

Metacognitive domain 268

Metadata 174, 192

microworlds 121, 124, 125, 126, 127, 128,
129, 130, 131, 132, 133, 134, 135,
136, 137, 139

Monahan, Colleen 72, 73, 90

multidirectional interaction networks 304

multimedia 123, 124, 125, 128, 135, 138

multi-media format 209

multi-user dungeons (MUD) 28

multi-user virtual environments (MUVEs) 157

multi-user virtual worlds (MUVE)
27, 30, 31, 39

music environment 42, 43

Music Matters project 42, 48

music theory instruction
42, 43, 48, 49, 50, 53, 55

MySpace 32, 140, 288

N

NASA 285, 299

National Anti-Vivisection Society (NAVS) 123

netnography 231, 238

Network 306

network map 288

non-hierarchical groups 291

nonhuman quality of networks 289

normal science 287, 288

O

obesity 110, 111, 112, 113, 114, 116, 118,
119, 120

occupational therapy (OT) 240

on-campus classrooms 197

onground graduate program 194

Online Behavior 154

online café 193

online courses 194, 201, 206, 302

online discussion 249, 250, 251, 252, 253,
254, 255, 256, 257, 258

online discussion group 195

online graduate programs 194

online interactions 284

Online learning 284

online learning environment 284

online program 210, 211, 219, 221, 224,
225, 226